Agrarian Elites and Democracy in Latin America

This groundbreaking book delves into the underexplored realm of agrarian elites and their relationship to democracy in Latin America. With a fresh perspective and new theory, it examines the strategies these elites use to gain an advantage in the democratic system. The book provides a detailed examination of when and how agrarian elites participate in the electoral arena to protect their interests, including a novel nonpartisan electoral strategy. By providing a deeper understanding of how democratic institutions can be used to protect economic interests, this book adds to the ongoing debate on the relationship between economic elites, democracy, and redistribution. *Agrarian Elites and Democracy in Latin America* is a must-read for anyone interested in politics, democracy, inequality, and economic power in the Global South.

Belén Fernández Milmanda is an assistant professor of political science and international studies at Trinity College, USA. Her research explores how economic elites influence policy making in Latin America with a focus on distributive and environmental politics. Her work has appeared in *World Development, Politics and Society,* and the *Oxford Research Encyclopedia of Latin American Politics.*

Agrarian Elites and Democracy in Latin America

BELÉN FERNÁNDEZ MILMANDA
Trinity College

Shaftesbury Road, Cambridge CB2 8EA, United Kingdom

One Liberty Plaza, 20th Floor, New York, NY 10006, USA

477 Williamstown Road, Port Melbourne, VIC 3207, Australia

314–321, 3rd Floor, Plot 3, Splendor Forum, Jasola District Centre,
New Delhi – 110025, India

103 Penang Road, #05–06/07, Visioncrest Commercial, Singapore 238467

Cambridge University Press is part of Cambridge University Press & Assessment,
a department of the University of Cambridge.

We share the University's mission to contribute to society through the pursuit of
education, learning and research at the highest international levels of excellence.

www.cambridge.org
Information on this title: www.cambridge.org/9781009553575

DOI: 10.1017/9781009553551

© Belén Fernández Milmanda 2025

This publication is in copyright. Subject to statutory exception and to the provisions
of relevant collective licensing agreements, no reproduction of any part may take
place without the written permission of Cambridge University Press & Assessment.

When citing this work, please include a reference to the
DOI 10.1017/9781009553551

First published 2025

A catalogue record for this publication is available from the British Library

Library of Congress Cataloging-in-Publication Data
NAMES: Fernández Milmanda, Belén, author.
TITLE: Agrarian elites and democracy in Latin America / Belén Fernández Milmanda.
DESCRIPTION: Cambridge, United Kingdom ; New York, NY : Cambridge
University Press, 2025. | Includes bibliographical references and index.
IDENTIFIERS: LCCN 2024022040 | ISBN 9781009553575 (hardback) |
ISBN 9781009553551 (ebook)
SUBJECTS: LCSH: Elite (Social sciences) – Political activity – Latin America. |
Agriculture and politics – Latin America. | Political participation – Social
aspects – Latin America. | Democracy – Latin America. | Representative
government and representation – Latin America.
CLASSIFICATION: LCC HN110.5.Z9 E444 2025 | DDC 305.5/2098–dc23/
eng/20240904
LC record available at https://lccn.loc.gov/2024022040

ISBN 978-1-009-55357-5 Hardback
ISBN 978-1-009-55356-8 Paperback

Cambridge University Press & Assessment has no responsibility for the persistence
or accuracy of URLs for external or third-party internet websites referred to in this
publication and does not guarantee that any content on such websites is, or will
remain, accurate or appropriate.

To Nano & Lenu

Contents

List of Figures		*page* ix
List of Tables		xi
Acknowledgments		xiii
List of Abbreviations		xv
1	Introduction	1
2	A Theory of Agrarian Elites' Political Participation	22
3	Chile: Agrarian Elites and the Rebuilding of the Partisan Right	65
4	Brazil: Landowners and Their Multiparty Congressional Caucus	108
5	Argentina: The Limits of Nonelectoral Strategies	155
6	Conclusions, Extensions, and Implications	196
Appendix A: List of Interviewees		217
Appendix B: Primary Sources		227
References		229
Index		249

The online appendix can be found here: www.cambridge.org/FernandezMilmanda

Figures

1.1	Total Support Estimate for agriculture as percentage of country GDP: Argentina, Bolivia, Brazil, and Chile, 2000–2020	page 3
1.2	The argument	6
1.3	Evolution of the rural population and croplands: Latin America, 1965–2016	11
2.1	The logic of economic elites' strategic decisions: costs and probability of influence	36
2.2	The argument	42
3.1	Agriculture exports and fruit exports (constant 2003 Chilean pesos): Chile, 1985–2006	85
4.1	Agriculture value added (constant 2010 US$): Brazil, 1965–2017	114
4.2	Cultivated area and rural population: Brazil, 1960–2015	115
4.3	Average number of peasants murdered annually: Brazil, 1970–1988	119
4.4	Number of land occupations per year: Brazil, 1987–2017	132
4.5	Percentage of seats controlled by the president's party versus the Agrarian Caucus: Lower Chamber, 1999–2018	138
4.6	Percentage of money contributed by the largest agribusiness received per party: 2006, 2010, and 2014 congressional elections	142
5.1	Total farmland and area harvested with soybeans: Argentina, 1975–2015	158
5.2	Agricultural value added (constant 2010 US$): Argentina, 1965–2017	159

5.3	Area harvested with soybeans in 2018 and vote for Macri in the general election, 2019	190
5.4	Total corporate contributions by Agro and Alliance: 2019 presidential elections	192

Tables

1.1	Case selection	page 17
2.1	Party-building versus candidate-centered strategies: main characteristics	31
2.2	Agrarian elites' perceived existential threat during the democratic transition	49
2.3	Explanatory factors, observed outcomes, and cases	52
2.4	Electoral rules and agrarian elites' strategies of political influence: predictions and observed outcomes	60
3.1	Expropriated land: Chile, 1965–1973	73
3.2	Unions, strikes, and land occupations in the countryside: Chile, 1963–1973	75
3.3	Number of congressional districts (Lower Chamber) that were split, dominated by the left, and dominated by the right under the binomial system: Chile, 1989–2013	88
3.4	Senate composition: Chile, 1989–2018	88
3.5	Members of Congress who held assets in agriculture by party, alliance, and period as percentage of caucus and in absolute terms: Lower Chamber, 1990–2018	101
3.6	Chile's ministers of agriculture, 1990–2022	103
4.1	Percentage of land held by small and large farms, and land Gini Index: Brazil, 1960–1996	115
4.2	Stance towards land reform by parties in the Constituent Assembly (percentage of legislators)	121
4.3	Number of legislators who were agricultural producers or UDR leaders in the Constituent Assembly by party	128
4.4	Parties with Ruralistas: Lower Chamber, 2015–2019	135

4.5	Presidential legislative coalitions and the Agrarian Caucus: Lower Chamber, 1999–2018	137
4.6	Probability of receiving a contribution from the largest agribusiness by Agrarian Caucus membership: 2006, 2010, and 2014 elections	143
4.7	Forest Code roll-call votes: Lower Chamber, 2011–2012	149
4.8	Party Rice Index and number of members casting a vote; Forest Code votes; Agrarian Caucus versus main parties: Lower Chamber, 2011–2012	150
5.1	Average net prices obtained by agricultural producers compared to international prices and average tax rate on the agricultural sector by administration: Argentina, 1955–1983	166
5.2	Agro-candidates for the Lower Chamber: Argentina, 2009–2013	179

Acknowledgments

The writing of this book has been a long journey through which I have accumulated many debts. First, I would like to thank the members of my Ph.D. dissertation committee – Steve Levitsky, Fran Hagopian, Ben Ross Schneider, and Scott Mainwaring. This project has greatly benefited from their incomparable intellectual rigor, generosity, and kindness. Steve, Ben, and Fran have provided constant guidance and support throughout the years that it took to transform my Ph.D. dissertation into this book. It is hard to convey in words how much I appreciate them. I honestly could not have wished for better mentors.

Generous support from many institutions made this book possible. At Harvard University, the Weatherhead Center for International Studies, the David Rockefeller Center for Latin American Studies, and the Jorge Paulo Lemann fellowship financed my fieldwork. At Trinity College, the Dean's Office and the Political Science Department provided funds that supported the writing and data analysis stages.

The book conference I held at Trinity College on September 2022, generously funded by the Political Science Department and the Dean's Office, was key in the development of this book. During that workshop, Kate Baldwin, Steve Levitsky, Gabriel Ondetti, and Ken Roberts provided invaluable advice on how to strengthen and clarify the book's theoretical contributions. I truly appreciate their willingness to engage with my work. I also want to thank Vicky Murillo, who has been a strong supporter of this project from the beginning and has provided generous feedback and advice through the years. My fellow comparativists at Trinity, Tony Messina and Reo Matsuzaki, have provided crucial intellectual and emotional support since my arrival in Hartford. I feel incredibly lucky to have them as colleagues. I also want to thank our department's administrative assistant, Mary Beth White, for all that she does to support our work. Through the years, I have benefited from the feedback of colleagues on partial drafts of this book presented at several conferences: REPAL (2021, 2023), APSA (2020), and LASA (2022). To all the people that engaged with my work at these instances, thank you.

Portions of Chapters 1, 4, and 6 of this book originally appeared in articles in the *Oxford Research Encyclopedia of Latin American Politics* and *Politics and Society*. I thank the editors for allowing me to include excerpts from those articles here.

This book was possible only because hundreds of strangers agreed to share with me their time and experiences. To all of them my most sincere thank you. In particular, I would like to thank Rodrigo Dolabella, who went above and beyond to help me interview the members of the Bancada Ruralista; João Henrique Hummel, who opened the doors of the Instituto Pensar Agro to me; Felipe and Loreto Cox, who help me contact potential interviewees in Chile; and David Hughes, Florencia Ricchiuti, and the members of Fundación Barbechando in Argentina. I would also like to thank Juan Pablo Luna for receiving me at the Catholic University of Chile while I was conducting fieldwork in the country; and to Rodrigo Zarazaga, Lucas Ronconi, and all the people at the Centro de Investigación y Acción Social in Buenos Aires for providing a warm and cheerful place to write while I was in Argentina.

I thank my editor, Rachel Blaifeder, and Jadyn Fauconier-Herry at Cambridge University Press for their help and encouragement in bringing this book to fruition. I also want to thank Victoria Andersen, my wonderful and hardworking research assistant. In addition, I would like to thank the three anonymous colleagues who reviewed the manuscript for their thoughtful and thorough engagement with it. The book has greatly benefited from their constructive feedback.

I have decided to leave the person I owe the biggest debt to last: Hernán Flom. None of the things I have accomplished since we met would have been possible without his unconditional love and support. He was always there for me to offer constructive feedback and to convince me I could do this, each of the hundred times I doubted myself. Over the past year, he has done significantly more than his fair share of childcare and house chores to allow me to complete this project. In the ultramarathon that has been this book, he was the best trainer, pacer, corunner, and cheerleader that anyone could wish. This book is dedicated to him and our beautiful daughter, Elena, for making my life so much better.

Abbreviations

AACREA	Asociación Argentina de Consorcios Regionales de Experimentación Agrícola (Argentine Association of Regional Consortiums of Agricultural Experimentation)
Aapresid	Asociación Argentina de Productores en Siembra Directa (Argentine Association of No-Till Producers)
ARENA	Aliança Renovadora Nacional (National Renovating Alliance, Brazil)
ARENA	Alianza Republicana Nacionalista (Nationalist Republican Alliance, El Salvador)
CARBAP	Confederación de Asociaciones Rurales de Buenos Aires y La Pampa (Confederation of Rural Associations of Buenos Aires and La Pampa, Argentina)
CC	Coalición Cívica (Civic Coalition, Argentina)
CLPR	closed-list proportional representation
CNA	Confederação da Agricultura e Pecuária do Brasil (National Confederation of Agriculture, Brazil)
CONINAGRO	Confederación Intercooperativa Agropecuaria (Confederation of Agricultural Cooperatives, Argentina)
CORA	Corporación de la Reforma Agraria (Land Reform Corporation, Chile)
CPC	Confederación de la Producción y del Comercio (Confederation of Production and Commerce, Chile)
CPT	Comissão Pastoral da Terra (Pastoral Land Commission, Brazil)
CRA	Confederaciones Rurales Argentinas (Rural Confederations of Argentina)

DEM	Demócratas (Democrats, Brazil)
Embrapa	Empresa Brasileira de Pequisa Agropecuária (Brazilian Agricultural Research Corporation)
FAA	Federación Agraria Argentina (Agrarian Federation of Argentina)
Fedefruta	Federación de Productores de Fruta de Chile (Federation of Fruit Producers, Chile)
FPV	Frente para la Victoria (Front for Victory, Argentina)
INDAP	Instituto de Desarrollo Agropecuario (Agricultural Development Institute, Chile)
IPA	Instituto Pensar Agropecuária (Think Agriculture Institute, Brazil)
ISI	Import Substitution Industrialization
MDB	Movimento Democrático Brasileiro (Brazilian Democratic Movement)
MST	Movimento dos Trabalhadores Rurais Sem Terra (Movement of Landless Rural Workers, Brazil)
OCB	Organização das Cooperativas Brasileiras (Organization of Brazilian Cooperatives)
OLPR	open-list proportional representation
PASO	Primarias Abiertas, Simultaneas y Obligatorias (Simultaneus and Mandatory Open Primaries, Argentina)
PATRI	Patriota (Patriot, Brazil)
PCdoB	Partido Comunista do Brasil (Communist Party of Brazil)
PDC	Partido Demócrata Cristão (Christian Democratic Party, Brazil)
PDC	Partido Demócrata Cristiano (Christian Democratic Party, Chile)
PDS	Partido Democrático Social (Democratic Social Party, Brazil)
PDT	Partido Democrático Trabalhista (Democratic Labor Party, Brazil)
PFL	Partido da Frente Liberal (Party of the Liberal Front, Brazil)
PHS	Partido Humanista da Solidariedade (Humanist Party of Solidarity, Brazil)
PJ	Partido Justicialista (Justicialist Party, Argentina)
PL	Partido Liberal (Liberal Party, Brazil)

PMDB	Partido do Movimento Democratico Brasileiro (Party of the Brazilian Democratic Movement)
PMN	Partido da Mobilização Nacional (Party of National Movilization, Brazil)
PN	Partido Nacional (National Party, Chile)
PNRA	Plano Nacional de Reforma Agrária (National Agrarian Reform Plan, Brazil)
PODE	Podemos (We Can, Brazil)
PP	Partido Progressista (Progressive Party, Brazil)
PPB	Partido Progressista Brasileiro (Brazilian Progressive Party)
PPL	Partido Pátria Livre (Free Motherland Party, Brazil)
PPS	Partido Popular Socialista (Popular Socialist Party, Brazil)
PR	Partido da Republica (Party of the Republic, Brazil)
PR	proportional representation
PRB	Partido Republicano Brasileiro (Brazilian Republican Party)
PRO	Propuesta Republicana (Republican Proposal, Argentina)
PROS	Partido Republicano da Ordem Social (Republican Party of the Social Order, Brazil)
PRP	Partido Republicano Progressista (Progressive Republican Party, Brazil)
PRSD	Partido Radical Socialdemócrata (Socialdemocratic Radical Party, Chile)
PS	Partido Socialista (Socialist Party, Agentina)
PS	Partido Socialista de Chile (Socialist Party of Chile)
PSB	Partido Socialista Brasileiro (Brazilian Socialist Party)
PSC	Partido Social Cristão (Christian Social Party, Brazil)
PSD	Partido Social Democrático (Social Democratic Party, Brazil)
PSDB	Partido da Social Democracia Brasileira (Party of Brazilian Social Democracy)
PSL	Partido Social Liberal (Liberal Social Party, Brazil)
PT	Partido dos Trabalhadores (Workers Party, Brazil)
PTB	Partido Trabalhista Brasileiro (Brazilian Labor Party)
PTdoB	Partido Trabalhista do Brasil (Labor Party of Brazil)
PV	Partido Verde (Green Party, Brazil)

RN	Renovación Nacional (National Renewal, Chile)
SD	Solidariedade (Solidarity, Brazil)
SNA	Sociedad Nacional de Agricultura (National Society of Agriculture, Chile)
SOFO	Sociedad de Fomento Agrícola (Agricultural Development Society, Chile)
SRA	Sociedad Rural Argentina (Argentine Rural Society)
SRB	Sociedade Rural Brasileira (Brazilian Rural Society)
Sunedu	Superintendencia Nacional de Educación Superior Universitaria (National Superintendence of Higher Education, Peru)
TSE	Tribunal Superior Eleitoral (Supreme Electoral Court, Brazil)
UCEDE	Unión del Centro Democrático (Union of the Democratic Center, Argentina)
UCR	Unión Cívica Radical (Radical Civic Union, Argentina)
UDI	Unión Demócrata Independiente (Independent Democratic Union, Chile)
UDR	União Democrática Ruralista (Rural Democratic Union, Brazil)

1

Introduction

In October 2018, five days before the Brazilian presidential election, then candidate Jair Bolsonaro livestreamed a meeting with the leader of the Bancada Ruralista (Rural Bench, Brazil's Agrarian Caucus), Representative Tereza Cristina. In the video, Tereza Cristina expressed the caucus's support for Bolsonaro's candidacy.

The Ruralistas' endorsement was key in signaling Bolsonaro's capacity to govern if elected. At the time, Bolsonaro's party had almost no representation in Congress, while the Agrarian Caucus controlled around a quarter of the Lower Chamber seats, making the Ruralistas' support crucial to advance Bolsonaro's conservative policy agenda. The alliance was sealed when, shortly after winning the presidential run-off, Bolsonaro appointed Tereza Cristina as minister of agriculture. However, the rightwing president has not been the only one to seek the support of the Ruralistas in Congress to guarantee governability. In fact, after defeating Bolsonaro in 2022 to win a third term in office, center-left president Lula da Silva of the Workers Party (PT) also appointed a Ruralista to the ministry of agriculture.[1]

In neighboring Argentina, agrarian elites' political standing could not be more different. Despite the sector's economic importance as the main source of foreign currency for the country, agrarian elites have no meaningful representation in Congress or ties to political parties. Agrarian elites' political weakness manifested itself most clearly in March 2008 when agricultural producers took to the streets to protest a hike in export taxes. After launching a four-month-long production and commercialization stoppage, accompanied by numerous mass protests and roadblocks across

---

[1] Carlos Fávaro, former leader of the soybean growers association.

the country, landowners were able to repeal the most recent increase but not the export tax altogether, which remained at a whopping 35 percent.

Scholars of Latin America have widely studied the role of landed elites as obstacles to democratic consolidation throughout the region's history.[2] However, we know comparatively much less about how landowners have adapted to the new democratic context after the transitions of the mid 1980s. This book addresses this gap in our knowledge by studying the strategies agrarian elites employ to make democracy work to their advantage. As the two opening vignettes illustrate, there is important variation in how agrarian elites organize to influence policymaking. In countries such as Brazil, Chile, and El Salvador, landowners have organized in the electoral arena by building parties, running for office themselves, or supporting likeminded candidates. In other countries, such as Argentina and Bolivia, they have shunned the electoral arena, influencing politics through nonelectoral channels such as lobbying or – when this has failed to block unwanted policies – protests.

Understanding this variation in Latin American agrarian elites' political strategies matters because it affects landowners' ability to influence policy realms of great regional and global significance. In the region with the highest income inequality in the world,[3] and where almost half of the rural population still lives in poverty,[4] agrarian elites have been much more successful in blocking redistributive policies where they have organized in the electoral arena than where they have relied on nonelectoral means of policy influence. Figure 1.1 illustrates the contrasting capacity of governments to redistribute resources away from agricultural producers in four Latin American countries by displaying the evolution of the total support for agriculture as a share of each country's GDP in the last two decades.[5] Positive values indicate net transfers from the rest of society to agriculture. Negative values indicate redistribution from the agricultural sector to the rest of society. As we can see, in the two countries where agrarian elites are organized in the electoral arena (Brazil and Chile), they have been able to secure net transfers towards their sector throughout the period.

---

[2] See, for example, Rueschemeyer et al. (1992), Yashar (1997), Paige (1999), Wood (2000), Mahoney (2002), Baland and Robinson (2008).

[3] Lustig (2015).

[4] According to CEPAL (2018, 13), the rates of poverty and extreme poverty among the rural population in Latin America were 48.6 and 22.5 percent, respectively, in 2016.

[5] IBD-Agrimonitor, Total Support Estimate (TSE). This indicator reflects and includes all effects of public policies that differentially affect the agricultural sector, from support for the sector (for example, subsidies) to penalties (for example, taxes). See: https://agrimonitor.iadb.org.

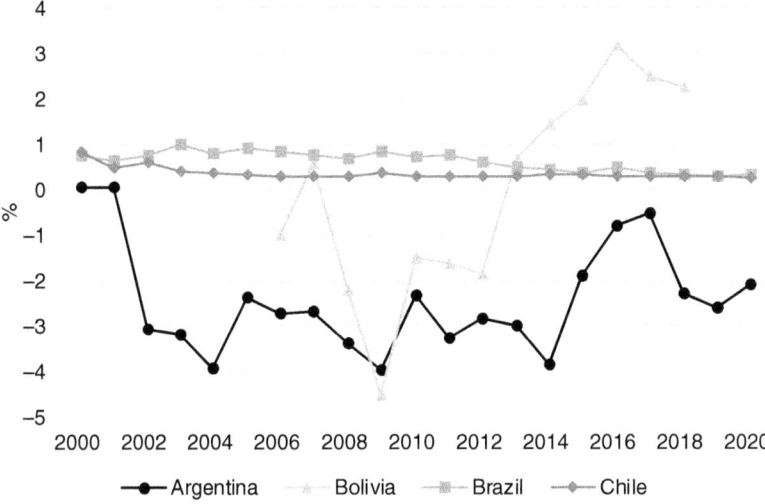

FIGURE 1.1 Total Support Estimate for agriculture as percentage of country GDP: Argentina, Bolivia, Brazil, and Chile, 2000–2020.
Source: Author, based on IDB-Agrimonitor.

In the two countries where agrarian elites lack electoral representation (Argentina and Bolivia), in contrast, governments have extracted resources from them. Nowhere is this difference clearer than when comparing Argentina and Brazil. In Argentina, where agrarian elites have no electoral representation, every government since 2001 has extracted bountiful resources from them, reaching, on average, the equivalent of 3 percent of the country's GDP annually during the administrations of the center-left Frente para la Victoria (Front for Victory, FPV) (2003–2015). In contrast, in Brazil, where agrarian elites are organized in a powerful multiparty congressional caucus, governments have consistently and generously subsidized agribusiness. This includes the leftwing administrations of the PT (2003–2016), which transferred annually, on average, resources equivalent to 0.65 percent of the country's GDP from the rest of society to agriculture. This equals to billions of dollars in subsidies every year to some of the wealthiest people in Brazil, one of the most unequal countries in the world.[6]

Beyond taxes, subsidies, and land reform, agrarian elites' capacity to organize electoral representation has been crucial in shaping another

---

[6] Although this indicator does not differentiate between resources going to small and large producers, research has shown that in Brazil government support for family farmers during the first two Lula administrations (2003–2010) represented only 15 percent of the funds allocated to agribusiness in the same period (Sauer 2019, 112).

policy realm with great redistributive impact: environmental regulations. Environmental policies regulate how producers use natural resources within their properties (e.g., land, water, and forests), as well as the kind of inputs they can employ in their production (e.g., fertilizers, seeds, and pesticides), impacting their profits and constraining their property rights. The literature analysing the relationship between inequality and democracy typically looks at taxes and land reform as the quintessential policy realms of redistributive struggle between governments and agrarian elites. This book also analyses environmental policies as these have become a highly contested issue in the region in the context of the current climate crisis, while land reform has lost relevance in the public agenda, due to urbanization and changes in agricultural production.

Despite their ties to environmental groups and indigenous organizations, leftwing administrations in Latin America have encountered significant obstacles to pass and enforce regulations over the exploitation of natural resources such as forests, minerals, or water.[7] This book explains how agrarian elites have been able to use democratic institutions to block or significantly dilute environmental regulations, a critical issue given Latin America's crucial role in mitigating climate change. For instance, forest protection legislation stalled for years in the countries' legislatures, despite widespread and accelerating deforestation, and passed only after significant accommodations to agribusiness interests.[8]

This book presents a framework to understand the variation in agrarian elites' strategies of political influence. I explain when agrarian elites organize in the electoral arena to protect their interests and how they adjudicate between the different electoral strategies available to them. My work contributes to the ongoing debate on the relationship among economic elites' representation, democracy, and redistribution by specifying the key mechanisms through which agrarian elites can use democratic institutions to protect their economic interests.

1.1 THE ARGUMENT

The main argument of this book is that agrarian elites' strategies of political influence are shaped by two factors: the level of threat they perceive and their level of intra-group fragmentation. The perception

---

[7] See Bebbington and Bury (2013), Svampa (2019), Robins and Fraser (2020), Bratman (2020).
[8] See Fernández Milmanda and Garay (2019, 2020) on Argentina, and Fernández Milmanda (2023) on Brazil.

of an existential threat – defined as a policy that jeopardizes the continuity of agrarian elites' business – is a necessary condition for electoral investment. Land reform, confiscatory taxes, or stringent environmental regulations are examples of existential threats. Nonelectoral strategies, such as lobbying or personal contact with policymakers, are ill-suited to deal with existential threats because they depend on a group's ability to access an administration, but threatening policies are usually implemented by political rivals. By contrast, electoral strategies – such as party-building or sponsoring like-minded candidates – are a more reliable source of influence because they entail electing politicians to key policymaking positions that already share the group's preferences and thus do not need persuading. Therefore, when confronting an existential threat, landed elites will be willing to pay the extra cost of organizing in the electoral arena. Absent this kind of threat, agrarian elites will prefer cheaper, informal means of exerting influence.

The perception of an existential threat at the time of democratic transition, when parties were being (re)built and looking for new constituencies, was particularly crucial for the development of electoral strategies. Organizing in the electoral arena to respond to threats after this foundational moment, when linkages between interest groups and political parties had already consolidated, was harder for groups that had not built these linkages during the transition. Thus, in countries where agrarian elites invested in electoral representation during the democratic transition, they were better positioned to neutralize new threats down the road.

The type of electoral strategy landowners will pursue is conditioned by their degree of intra-group fragmentation. Fragmentation hinders party-building because it increases coordination costs. Agrarian elites may be divided along regional, economic, political, or religious cleavages. When these divisions are significant, all the agreements and negotiations that developing a partisan organization entails – for example, selecting candidates and party leaders, developing a territorial organization, and designing a party platform – will be harder to bring about. For instance, where agrarian elites in different regions of the country have competing economic interests, it will be difficult for them to agree on a national policy platform for their party, while in cases where political divides exist among the rural elites, they may not be able to coordinate a common campaign strategy. Therefore, in cases of high fragmentation, landowners will deploy a nonpartisan, candidate-centered strategy that does not require those kinds of compromises. They will support like-minded candidates individually, across partisan lines. Figure 1.2 summarizes the argument.

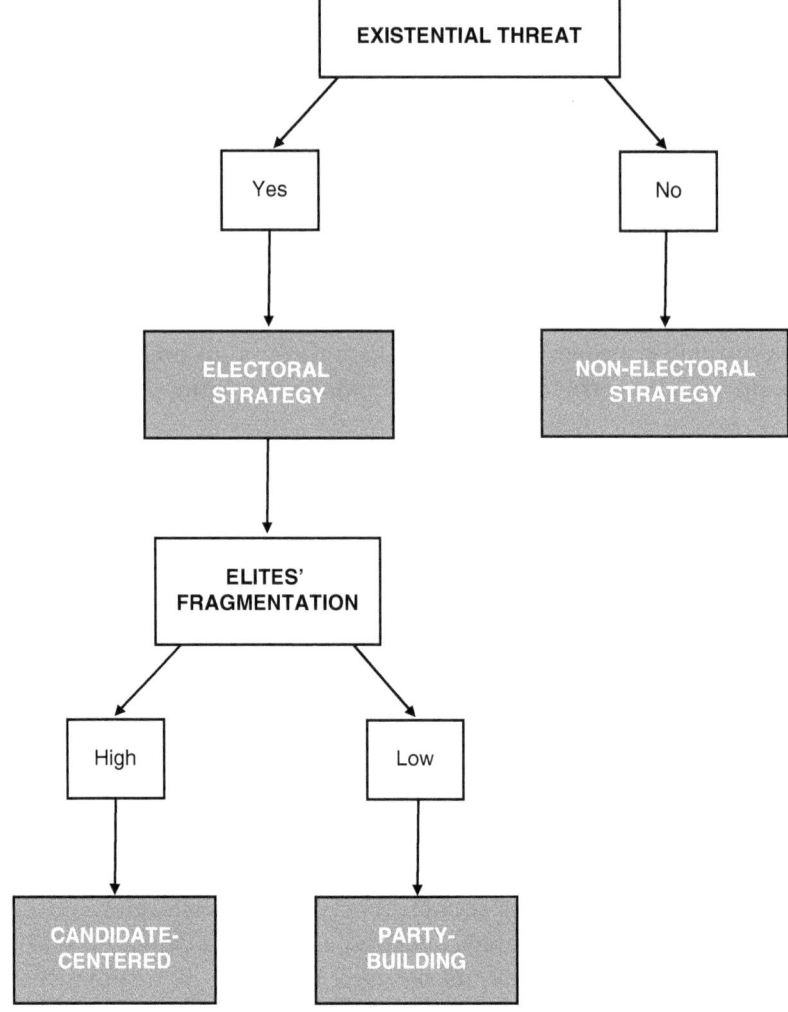

FIGURE 1.2 The argument.

1.2 CONTRIBUTIONS TO THE LITERATURE ON AGRARIAN ELITES AND DEMOCRACY

From the classical works of Gerschenkron (1943) and Moore (1966), who focused on landowners' reliance on labor-repressive institutions, to more recent analyses looking at the relationship between democratization and inequality (Boix 2003; Acemoglu and Robinson 2006; Ansell and Samuels 2010), the consensus has been that agrarian elites' economic interests are incompatible with democracy. Even when scholars disagree on whether democracy will lead to more (Boix 2003; Acemoglu and Robinson 2006) or less (Ansell and Samuels 2014) redistribution from the rich to the poor, they agree on one thing: Agrarian elites will fare better under autocracy, especially in highly unequal societies such as those in Latin America. While Acemoglu and Robinson (2006) and Boix (2003) argue that landowners are easy targets for democratic governments' redistributive ambitions due to the fixed nature of their assets, Ansell and Samuels claim that under autocracy agrarian elites' have greater capacity to restrict labor mobility and influence agrarian policy (Ansell and Samuels 2014, 38). While the causal mechanisms vary, the prediction is the same: "Big landowners oppose democracy of necessity" (Boix 2003, 37) and, therefore, will always be on the side of autocracy (Ansell and Samuels 2014, 12). Considering these theories, it is not surprising that Latin American countries, where land inequality has been extremely high since colonial times, struggled to consolidate democracy before the third wave.

Starting in the 1980s, however, supporting military coups to protect their interests was no longer an option for Latin American agrarian elites. On the one hand, military governments' disastrous management of the economy, combined with their terrible human rights abuses during the dictatorships of the 1970s and 1980s, led economic elites in many countries to question the capacity of the military to govern effectively and protect elites' interests (Bartell and Payne 1995). At the same time, due to changes within the military and in civil–military relations, the armed forces were no longer available as allies for economic elites looking to destabilize democracy (Pion-Berlin 2001). On the other hand, changes in the international community during the 1980s and 1990s increased the costs of coups. The promotion of democracy became a high priority of US foreign policy, and regional organizations such as the Organization of American States (OAS) and the Southern Common Market (MERCOSUR) made democracy a membership requirement (Hagopian and Mainwaring 2005). These domestic and international changes meant that agrarian elites were compelled to look for ways of protecting their interests *within* democracy.

When explaining how agrarian elites may attenuate the distributive effects of democratization, most of the existing literature has emphasized noninstitutional, often violent, mechanisms such as fraud, clientelism, or the use of paramilitaries (Ziblatt 2008; Acemoglu and Robinson 2008).[9]

---

[9] For example, Ziblatt's (2008) analysis of fraud in Germany during the first forty years after the enactment of universal male suffrage finds that in districts with higher land

Much less attention has been paid to *democratic* and institutional channels of elite protection. Following the pioneering work of Albertus and coauthors (Albertus 2015, 2017; Albertus and Gay 2017) and Ziblatt (2017), this book makes an important contribution to the comparative politics literature by studying how landed elites may protect their interests by playing the democratic game.

Albertus and coauthors have shown that landowners can better protect their interests in democracies than in autocracies because democracies offer landowners institutional veto points to block redistribution that are absent in authoritarian regimes (Albertus 2015, 2017; Albertus and Gay 2017). These scholars have focused their attention on explaining how expropriation is easier in autocracies and why, consequently, landowners should support democratization. However, how landowners organize to use the institutional mechanisms of democracy to their advantage or why they sometimes fail to do so remain under-explained. This book addresses precisely these issues by explaining when and how landowners will organize in the electoral arena. Contrary to Albertus (2015, 2017), my research shows that democratization is indeed threatening to landowners. However, contrary to the predictions of *redistributivist* theories of democratization, this perception of threat will not necessarily lead landowners to hamper democracy. Rather, it will motivate them to organize in the electoral arena. This book advances the literature by specifying the various mechanisms through which agrarian elites have been able to protect their interests democratically in contemporary Latin America. Put differently, while the existing literature has focused on understanding why economic elites will concede democracy,[10] this book investigates how they adapt to a democratic regime that they did not choose.

Another important theoretical contribution of this book is to show that economic elites can organize effective electoral representation in the absence of strong conservative parties. The existing comparative politics literature sees conservative parties as the main vehicle for economic elites' electoral representation in democracies. In this vein, scholars of Latin American politics have long emphasized the importance

---

inequality the probability of the landed elite staffing local government positions in order to secure favorable electoral results was higher. In order to preserve their political dominance, landed elites tried to control local bureaucracies by infiltrating their people into key offices such as those of mayor, county commissioner, and election officials.

[10] See Slater and Wong (2013), Albertus and Gay (2017), Albertus and Menaldo (2018), Riedl et al. (2020).

1.2 Contributions to the Literature

of conservative parties for democratic consolidation as economic elites will tolerate democratization only where they believe their interests are well-protected (Di Tella 1971; Gibson 1996; Middlebrook 2000). More recently, Ziblatt (2017) has advanced these ideas by showing how strong conservative parties played a crucial role in helping democracy come about and endure in Western Europe. Where landed elites did not build well-organized mass parties, they feared democracy and tried to undermine it (Ziblatt 2017). At the same time, the literature has also highlighted how difficult and potentially risky party-building is,[11] especially for economic elites who comprise but a small fraction of the electorate.[12] However, as this book shows, the absence of institutionalized, electorally strong conservative parties does not necessarily mean democracy will perish due to the lack of support from the elites. Conservative parties are not the only vehicle for the electoral representation of economic elites in democracies. Rather, economic elites can organize effective electoral representation through nonpartisan means.

This book analyses agrarian elites' choice to build a conservative party in relation to other nonpartisan electoral strategies available to economic elites in democracies. In particular, it discusses a novel strategy by agrarian elites in Brazil: a multiparty congressional caucus. Multiparty caucuses allow interest groups to coordinate legislative work – one of the main functions of political parties in democracy – without necessarily building a centralized electoral machine to select their representatives. This is relevant because party-building has become increasingly harder as political fragmentation, electoral volatility, and the dilution of partisan identities are on the rise across the developing world.[13] In this context, where many parties are little more than the electoral vehicles of ambitious politicians,[14] and candidates' personal characteristics are more reliable indicators of their policy preferences than their partisan affiliation,[15] candidate-centered strategies may become a more effective option for interest group representation than party-building.

---

[11] See Panebianco (1988), Aldrich (1995), Kalyvas (1998), and Levitsky et al. (2016).
[12] See Gibson (1996), Thachil (2014), and Luna and Rovira Kaltwasser (2014).
[13] See, for example, Mainwaring and Zoco (2007), Hicken and Kuhonta (2015), Lupu (2017), and Mainwaring (2018).
[14] See Luna et al. (2021).
[15] See Roberts (2002).

1.3 AGRARIAN ELITES IN CONTEMPORARY LATIN AMERICA: URBANIZATION, THE COMMODITY BOOM, AND THE LEFT TURN

The paradigmatic "undemocratic landowners" that reigned over the Latin American countryside until the last decades of the twentieth century based their power not on the economic importance of agriculture – as most farms were inefficient or outright unproductive – but on the political control of the peasants living on their lands. The Latin American rural landscape, however, has changed dramatically since then. Over the last six decades, a series of structural and political transformations have undermined landowners' old sources of power while increasing their wealth.

Over the last thirty years, agriculture has become one of the pillars of many Latin American countries' economies, with the old unproductive latifundio giving way to highly mechanized farms producing for the international markets. The exhaustion of the import substitution industrialization model (ISI) that ended in the debt crisis of the early 1980s led policymakers to focus on alternative growth models based on the region's comparative advantages. The surge in commodity prices during the boom of the 2000s, which more than doubled in less than a decade,[16] helped consolidate this new development paradigm based on the large-scale production of agricultural commodities for the international markets, China in particular. Between 1980 and 2010 the area occupied by cropland in the region grew by 35 percent (Figure 1.3), turning many Latin American countries into world leaders in the production and export of agricultural commodities. Between 1995 and 2015, the region's share of global agricultural trade rose from 8 to 13 percent (Martel et al. 2015, 1).

However, this prodigious growth in the economic weight of agriculture brought with it the loss of some of the landowners' old sources of political power. The rural population has been in steady decline in the region since the 1960s (Figure 1.3) and the expansion of agriculture did not reverse this trend, as new production techniques required less labor and replaced tenants with seasonal workers (Fearnside 2001; J.T. Roberts and Thanos 2003; Vergara-Camus and Kay 2017a).[17]

---

[16] For instance, the international price of soybeans went from US$212 per metric ton in 2000 to US$523 in 2008; maize prices grew from US$89 per metric ton in 2000 to US$223 in 2008. Source: The World Bank–Commodity Markets. www.worldbank.org/en/research/commodity-markets. Accessed February 5, 2019.

[17] Between 1980 and 2012, agricultural output per worker increased 82 percent in the region (Nin-Pratt et al. 2015, 34).

1.3 Urbanization, the Commodity Boom and the Left Turn

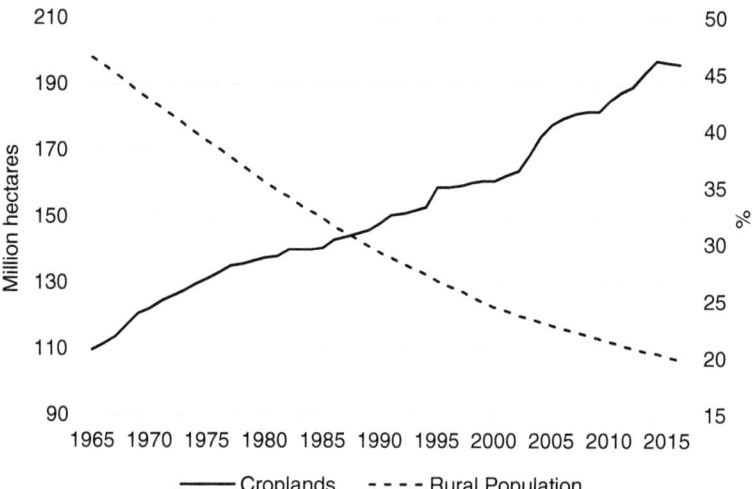

FIGURE 1.3 Evolution of the rural population and croplands: Latin America, 1965–2016.
Source: Author, based on FAOSTAT Land Use domain.

While in the mid-1960s half of the Latin American population was rural, by 2008, in the heyday of the commodity boom, only 22 percent of the region's inhabitants lived in rural areas (Figure 1.3). The decline of the peasant population together with the consolidation of democracy and the expansion of cash transfers to the rural poor undermined the ability of rural elites to mobilize votes through coercion or clientelism,[18] thus leaving landowners without an electoral safeguard against the preferences of the urban majorities. As a consequence, agrarian elites had to find new ways to influence policymaking in the region as they lost their old source of electoral power.

The beginning of the twenty-first century saw another important change in the region, the resurgence of the political left.[19] Many countries elected leftwing presidents who governed until the mid-2010s, when the trend started to reverse. The rise to power of leftwing governments in the region with the highest land inequality in the world (Vollrath 2007) raised alarm among the agrarian elites, especially when in some cases, such as Lula da Silva in Brazil, Evo Morales in Bolivia,

---
[18] See Fried (2012), Weitz-Shapiro (2012), Sugiyama and Hunter (2013), Zucco (2013), Daïeff (2016), De la O (2018).
[19] See Castañeda (2006) and Levitsky and Roberts (2011).

and Fernando Lugo in Paraguay, leftwing presidents had promised to implement land reform during their campaigns and were supported by peasant movements. However, once in power these leftist presidents not only failed to change the unequal structure of land ownership in their countries but also ended up implementing policies that helped the expansion of agribusiness.[20]

There are structural explanations for why the leftwing administrations that governed Latin America during the commodity boom did not challenge agrarian elites' interests. First, the economic transformations described earlier meant that agrarian elites were no longer the backward, inefficient actor that leftist parties impugned in the past. In the Latin America of the commodity boom, agricultural production was an important driver of economic growth and one of the main sources of foreign exchange, which created a tension between leftwing governments' redistributive agenda and their fiscal needs. Second, high levels of urbanization in the region meant there was no longer a large constituency calling for land reform. Consequently, governments prioritized redistributive polices benefiting the urban poor.

Although structural changes may have played a role in explaining why most leftwing administrations in Latin America did not plunder the agricultural sector to finance their redistributive agenda, they cannot explain why agrarian elites' have not been able to block redistributive politics everywhere. A central claim of this book is that agrarian elites' capacity to organize politically to protect their interests is crucial in explaining this variation. As discussed earlier, both Brazil and Argentina, two of the world's biggest exporters of agricultural commodities, were governed by leftist parties with redistributive agendas during the commodity boom of the 2000s. However, while Brazilian agricultural producers managed not only to avoid taxation but also to secure massive subsidies thanks to their representation in Congress, Argentine elites' lack of political connections left them defenseless to fight increasingly high taxation. This quick comparison suggests that even if landowners' structural power has increased throughout the region as agricultural exports have become the pillars of many Latin American economies, agrarian elites' capacity to translate this economic power into political influence has varied. This book proposes a theoretical framework to understand this variation.

---

[20] See, for example, McKay and Colque (2016), Vergara-Camus and Kay (2017b), Robles (2018).

1.4 RESEARCH DESIGN AND CASE SELECTION

The main purpose of this study is to explain the variation in agrarian elites' strategies of political influence across contemporary Latin America. Specifically, this study aims to understand when landowners will invest in electoral representation and why they deploy different electoral strategies. To this end, I compare three country cases since their most recent democratic transitions: Argentina since 1983, Brazil since 1985, and Chile since 1990. Cross-country comparisons are combined with within-case longitudinal analyses of agrarian elites' strategies over the last three decades.[21] A comparative, small-N research design is the best suited for the study of economic elites' strategies as it allows me to focus on the causal mechanisms connecting each explanatory factor to landowners' strategic decisions.[22] Moreover, it is not clear that the research question motivating this book can be adequately addressed through a large-N quantitative analysis since measuring agrarian elites' perceptions and strategic calculations requires access to their thinking. Thus, employing the typical tools of process tracing,[23] I present an in-depth analysis of agrarian elites' incentives to pursue a given strategy of political influence, as well as of how each strategy is deployed and adapted over time.

Following Slater and Ziblatt's (2013) recommendations, I selected cases that both represent the whole range of variation on the dependent variable and maximize control over alternative explanations to generate causal inferences that can extend to a broader set of cases. The three analysed cases are representative of the variation in agrarian elites' strategies of political influence found in the larger case universe.[24] Argentina before 2008 is a case where agrarian elites did not organize in the electoral arena, influencing politics instead through direct contact with public officials and protests. Both Brazil and Chile are cases of electoral participation by agrarian elites but through different channels. In Chile, landowners have built a conservative party to represent their interests. In Brazil, the

---

[21] See Slater and Ziblatt (2013).
[22] See George and Bennett (2005, ch. 10).
[23] On process tracing, see Collier (2011) and Bennett and Checkel (2014).
[24] An important scope condition of the argument is that it applies only to countries where agrarian elites had the economic and/or political means to attempt some kind of political organization at the time of democratic transition. This will leave out countries where extensive and enduring redistributive land reform processes fatally weakened the economic and political power of agrarian elites *before* the democratic transition, as, for instance, in Peru during the 1969–1975 agrarian reform.

electoral strategy has been nonpartisan and candidate-centered. Brazilian agrarian elites have run their congressional candidates in different parties, coordinating their work in a multipartisan caucus.

The country cases were chosen so as to discard alternative explanatory factors while holding certain background conditions constant. In terms of similarities, Argentina, Brazil, and Chile are among the most developed, industrialized, and urbanized countries in Latin America. Moreover, the three countries share a history of military governments that enjoyed the support of agrarian elites in the 1970s, transitions to democracy in the 1980s, and leftwing governments in the 2000s. Similarly, the three countries have presidential systems of government that grant the executive branch considerable legislative power (Mainwaring and Shugart 2003; Samuels and Shugart 2003).

Despite these similarities, the three countries present significant variation in other characteristics, but not in ways that predict the observed outcomes, which allows me to discard these features as alternative explanatory factors. First, the observed variation in agrarian elites' capacity to influence policymaking rules out structural power as an explanation. In capitalist societies, business' structural power emanates from their contribution to a country's economy in terms of employment, investment, value added, or foreign exchange.[25] The three countries are leading exporters of agricultural products, oilseed, and grain in the case of Argentina and Brazil, and fruit in the case of Chile. However, the economic weight of agriculture is quite different for each country. In 2019 agricultural products (foodstuffs, vegetable products, and animal products) comprised 56 percent of total exports in Argentina, 34 percent in Brazil, and 27 percent in Chile.[26] This variation does not, however, map onto the variation in agrarian elites' political influence or capacity to organize in the electoral arena. Argentina, the case where structural accounts of business power would predict that agrarian elites would wield the greatest political influence, is actually where governments have implemented policies most harmful to the interests of producers. Moreover, despite a considerable difference in the importance of agriculture for the economy of their countries, producers have been able to organize in the electoral arena and influence policymaking in both Brazil and Chile. While agrarian elites'

---

[25] On the definition and operationalization of business structural power, see Lindblom (1977), Hacker and Pierson (2002), and Fairfield (2015b).
[26] MIT Observatory of Economic Complexity. See: https://atlas.media.mit.edu (accessed August 8, 2021).

1.4 Research Design and Case Selection

political organization – what the business politics literature calls instrumental power – compensates for their weaker structural power in Chile, it reinforces their economic prominence in Brazil.[27]

The three countries also differ in the degree of institutionalization and fragmentation of their party systems at the time of democratic transition and in their electoral rules. Before the 1973 military coup, Chile had had a stable democracy for forty-one years, while both Argentina and Brazil experienced multiple military coups during that period. Despite this, landowners were able to organize in the electoral arena in both Chile, where a strong democratic tradition existed, and Brazil, where it was much weaker. Party-system fragmentation at the time of transition varies across the three cases but does not correctly predict the observed outcomes. The effective number of parliamentary parties (ENPP) in Chile in 1989,[28] the country where landowners invested in party-building, was considerably higher (4.9) than in Brazil (3.1) in 1985 where agrarian elites chose a multiparty strategy.[29] Despite the common overrepresentation of rural areas (Snyder and Samuels 2004), the three countries have different rules to elect Congress. Argentina and Brazil use proportional representation, but with closed and open lists, respectively. Until 2015, Chile had a unique "binomial" system.[30] Electoral rules cannot be the only factor explaining variation in agrarian elites' strategies of political influence, as landowners organized in the electoral arena in both Brazil and Chile despite very different electoral rules. Moreover, the within-case analysis of Argentina, where agrarian elites changed strategies after the 2008 conflict, highlights the inadequacy of electoral rules as an explanatory factor, given that they remained unchanged through the analysed period.

Brazil and Chile have a history of electoral organization by agrarian elites prior to the last democratic transition that is absent in Argentina. Although this historical antecedent cannot be completely ruled out as a facilitator of landowners' organization in the electoral arena in the first

---

[27] On the relationship between instrumental and structural power, see, for example, Fairfield (2015b) and Young (2015).
[28] The ENPP assesses the fragmentation of a party system through a formula that adjusts the number of parties in congress by their relative strength, measured as the number of seats they hold.
[29] Gallagher (2018).
[30] The electoral system divided the country in two-member congressional districts for both the Senate and the Lower Chamber. Each of the two most-voted lists will get one seat unless the first one doubled the votes of the second one. For more details, see Chapter 3.

two countries, the social, economic, and political transformations the region experienced prior to the third wave limit this factor's explanatory power. First, while the absence of a large peasantry in Argentina has been cited as one of the main causes of the failure to organize partisan representation by the country's landed elites,[31] this difference has become less relevant in explaining agrarian elites' capacity to organize in the electoral arena in the contemporary period due to the erosion of landowners' clientelistic networks elsewhere in Latin America. As the Chilean case suggests, the political control of the rural poor is no longer a necessary condition for agrarian elites' electoral organization. Landowners in this country have obtained electoral representation despite the dismantling of clientelistic networks in the countryside. Second, it is important to remember that in both Brazil and Chile, the military restructured the party system and changed the electoral rules.[32] Therefore, even when agrarian elites had previous experience with electoral involvement, by the time of the transition, the rules and players had changed since their last encounter with democratic competition. Lastly, the fact that Argentine agrarian elites attempted electoral representation after the 2008 conflict indicates that the variable "threat" explains when agrarian elites will organize in the electoral arena better than historical legacies of electoral involvement do. Table 1.1 summarizes the case selection criteria.

My multilevel, longitudinal research design involving cross-country and within-country comparisons across time allows me to discard the influence of alternative explanatory factors that could be driving the observed outcomes. First, I compare the three cases during the democratic transition to show how differences in the level of threat explain agrarian elites' decisions about whether or not to enter the electoral arena. Whereas Brazilian and Chilean landowners feared they could be a target of the new governments' redistributive policies, Argentine producers did not face an equivalent threat and consequently refrained from investing in electoral representation. Second, the within-case analysis of Argentina enables me to show – while controlling for national-level

---

[31] See, for instance, Di Tella (1971), P. Smith (1978), and McGuire (1995).
[32] In Brazil, upon coming to power, the military dictatorship dismantled existing parties and imposed a bipartisan system. Multiparty competition was allowed again during the transition to democracy. In Chile, parties were proscribed during the dictatorship. The military regime designed a party system for the new democracy intended to force parties into two broad coalitions, one on the right and one on the left, discouraging fragmentation. See Valenzuela and Scully (1997), Mainwaring (1999), and Snyder and Samuels (2004).

TABLE 1.1 *Case selection*

	Argentina	Brazil	Chile
Independent Variables			
Perceived threat at the democratic transition	Low	High	High
Agrarian elite fragmentation	High	High	Low
Alternative Explanations			
Agricultural products share of exports (%)[a]	55.7	34.1	26.9
ENPP at the transition[b]	2.7 (1983)	3.1 (1985)	4.9 (1989)
Previous democratic experience	Weak	Weak	Strong
Controls			
World Bank Income Group[c]	Upper-middle-income	Upper-middle-income	High-income
Rural population (%) (1990/2017)[d]	13/8.3	26.1/13.7	16.7/12.5
Overrepresentation of rural districts[e]	Yes	Yes	Yes
Presidential legislative powers[f]	Extensive	Extensive	Extensive
Agrarian elites supported military coups	Yes	Yes	Yes
Outcome			
Agrarian elites' strategy	Nonelectoral (until 2008)	Electoral: candidate-centered	Electoral: party-building

[a] MIT Observatory of Economic Complexity, at: https://atlas.media.mit.edu (accessed August 8, 2021).
[b] Gallagher (2018).
[c] https://datahelpdesk.worldbank.org/knowledgebase/articles/906519-world-bank-country-and-lending-groups (accessed August 8, 2021).
[d] World Bank–World Development Indicators.
[e] Based on Snyder and Samuels (2004).
[f] Based on presidents' formal constitutional powers. In the three countries, presidents have veto, decree, and exclusive introduction powers. See Mainwaring and Shugart (2003) and Samuels and Shugart (2003).

alternative explanations – how variations in level of threat explain changes in agrarian elites' strategies. In that country, landowners entered the electoral arena in the aftermath of the 2008 agrarian conflict, when perceived levels of threat reached existential levels. Third, I compare the two cases of high threat during the transition, Chile and Brazil, to identify the factors that led landowners in these two countries to choose different electoral strategies. In Chile, agrarian elites were politically cohesive, which helped them (re)build a party to protect their interests in the new democracy. In Brazil, in contrast, agrarian elites' political rivalry at the local level hampered the building of a national party to represent agrarian interests. Consequently, Brazilian landowners built their own multiparty congressional caucus instead.

1.5 DATA SOURCES

The main source of data for this study are semi-structured, in-depth interviews with elite informants. In total, I conducted 158 interviews during fieldwork carried out over the course of ten months between 2013 and 2017 in the three countries.[33] Interviewees included leaders from the main national and state-level producers' associations, ministers of agriculture and other high-ranking officials in sectoral agencies, national and state-level legislators with an agricultural background or from districts where agribusiness is an important source of revenue, and party cadres with connections to the sector among other key informants.[34] In addition, in Brazil, I conducted several participatory observations of the work of Bancada Ruralista members in the Agricultural Congressional Committee as well as during private meetings at their headquarters.

I triangulated interview evidence with archival analysis of newspaper articles, business associations' publications, legislative debates, as well as statistical analysis of electoral and campaign contribution records. Through the analysis of historical primary sources,[35] I gained access to what producers' associations were doing and saying at the time of the democratic transition to then compare that information with what my interviewees remembered thirty years later. Statistical analysis of

---

[33] All interviews were conducted by the author in person and audio recorded. Interviews generally lasted around an hour and were conducted in Spanish in Argentina and Chile, and in Portuguese in Brazil.

[34] For a complete list of interviews, see Appendix A.

[35] See Appendix B for a complete list of historical primary sources.

campaign contribution records in Argentina and Brazil allowed me to identify electoral investments by agribusiness.[36] Lastly, secondary sources – historical, anthropological, sociological, and political science studies on agrarian elites by local and foreign scholars in the three countries – were key in operationalizing and measuring the explanatory factor "elite fragmentation" and in checking my assessment of the levels of perceived threat at the democratic transition.

1.6 PLAN OF THE BOOK

This book is organized as follows. The next chapter introduces a new theory to explain the variation in agrarian elites' strategies of political influence. It highlights the role of two independent variables – perception of an existential threat and intragroup fragmentation – to explain when and how agrarian elites will organize in the electoral arena. Chapters 3–5 develop the comparative historical analysis for the cases of Chile, Brazil, and Argentina, respectively.

Chapter 3 analyses a case of party-building by agrarian elites in Chile. It presents evidence of Chilean landowners' financial support of the political right, their identification with rightwing legislators, and the programmatic convergence between agrarian elites' preferences and the policy positions of rightwing parties, Renovación Nacional (National Renewal) in particular. The chapter argues that agrarian elites in Chile decided to invest in an electoral strategy of political influence at the time of the democratic transition because they feared a center-left government would endanger their property rights. It presents evidence of how this perceived threat was founded on landowners' previous experience with democracy during the 1965–1973 period, when their farms were expropriated. The chapter also illustrates how low intragroup fragmentation facilitates party-building. Shared political and economic interests among the Chilean economic elite in general, and agrarian elites in particular, decreased the coordination costs associated with building a party to represent them.

Chapter 4 discusses a novel electoral strategy by which landowners have successfully influenced policymaking in democratic Brazil: a multiparty congressional caucus. It shows how agrarian elites finance the

---

[36] In Chile, identifiable data on corporate contributions were not available for the analysed period. Detail on the campaign contributions data collection and analysis processes is available in Chapter 4 for Brazil and Chapter 5 for Argentina, and in the online appendix.

campaigns, encourage other producers to support, and subsidize the work of like-minded legislators independently of their partisan affiliation, as well as how legislators of agrarian origin collaborate across partisan lines. The chapter argues that Brazil's Agrarian Caucus is the product of agrarian elites' collective efforts to build a channel of electoral representation to protect their interests under democracy in a context of high political fragmentation. The threat of radical land reform during the democratic transition prompted landowners to engage in electoral politics. However, high political fragmentation among the agrarian elite rendered party-building unfeasible. The Brazilian case illustrates the advantages of an electoral, candidate-centered, multipartisan strategy over other strategies available to economic elites in democracies such as lobbying or party-building. First, self-representation has granted Brazilian agrarian elites direct access to key policymaking positions from which they have shaped sectoral policy according to their interests. Second, by being multipartisan, the Agrarian Caucus has multiplied the agenda setting positions it controls in Congress and increased its leverage vis-à-vis the executive.

Chapter 5 analyses the Argentine case, where, until the 2008 conflict, agrarian elites had historically shunned the electoral arena. Prior to 2009, Argentine landowners influenced politics through informal personal contacts with high-ranking government officials and, when lobbying failed, protests. This chapter shows how, in the absence of an existential threat, agricultural producers had no incentive to invest in electoral representation during the democratic transition or in the following elections. This lack of political organization, in turn, left them defenseless against the hostile policies of the center-left Peronist FPV administrations (2003–2015). In 2009, landowners switched strategies and entered the electoral arena to confront the confiscatory policies of the FPV. Given Argentine agrarian elites fragmentation, they deployed a candidate-centered strategy, sponsoring the candidacies of a dozen agricultural producers for Congress under diverse party affiliations. However, institutional features and ideological differences among producers' associations blunted the effectiveness of the strategy and led to its abandonment.

Finally, in Chapter 6 I explore how the arguments developed in this book travel beyond the three analysed cases and discuss their broader implications for the field of comparative politics, in particular for the relationship among economic elites' political representation, democracy, and inequality. First, I test the scope conditions of the argument by analysing agrarian elites' strategies of political influence in a country where democracy is less consolidated: Paraguay during the Lugo administration (2008–2012). Next, I look at party-building by agrarian elites beyond South America, in a different historical context marked by civil war: post-1979 El Salvador. Finally, I extend the argument beyond agrarian elites, focusing on nonpartisan electoral representation by other interest groups in two contemporary cases: for-profit universities in Peru and conservative religious groups in Colombia.

2

A Theory of Agrarian Elites' Political Participation

2.1 INTRODUCTION

Chapter 1 highlighted a puzzling fact: agrarian elites have managed to protect their interests under democracy in contemporary Latin America, even under center-left governments with redistributive ambitions, where they organized in the electoral arena. This chapter develops a theory to explain why agrarian elites have organized electoral representation in some countries but not others as well as the observed variation in the electoral strategies deployed by landowners. The theory emphasizes two causal variables: perception of an existential threat and agrarian elites' fragmentation. The threat that democratic governments may implement redistributive policies that jeopardize the continuity of their business (e.g., land reform) incentivizes agrarian elites to organize in the electoral arena. Absent this existential threat, rural elites will not invest in electoral representation. Levels of fragmentation, in turn, condition the way landowners organize their electoral representation. Where landed elites are a cohesive group, they will engage in party-building. In contrast, where significant cleavages exist among agrarian elites, higher coordination costs will hinder party-building. In these cases, landowners will support like-minded candidates individually, across partisan lines.

This chapter is organized as follows. Section 2.2, defines the actor under study, agrarian elites, and introduces a sectoral approach to the study of agrarian elites' interests. Section 2.3 describes the dependent variable: the strategies of political influence available to agrarian elites in democracies. Section 2.4 discusses the main explanatory factors, existential threat and intragroup fragmentation, as well as the mechanisms through which they shape the outcome of interest. Section 2.5 assesses three main alternative explanations, previous history of electoral organization, electoral rules, and the relevance of congress as a policymaking arena.

2.2 DEFINING AGRARIAN ELITES AND AGRARIAN ELITES' INTERESTS

This book studies agrarian elites collectively as a class whose defining characteristic is the ownership of large landholdings. This includes producers of crops or fruits as well as cattle ranchers. In a region marked by its extreme land inequality, ownership of vast extensions of land gave Latin American agrarian elites not only a prominent place in their countries' economies, but also substantial social and political power until the last decades of the twentieth century. Since most Latin American countries entered global markets as producers of agricultural commodities, landed elites were among the first national economic elites in the region. Moreover, in the countries with large rural populations, before the democratization of the countryside, landowners controlled the votes of peasants living on their lands who relied on agrarian elites for employment, credit, and basic services such as housing and education. Their control of local politics in rural areas granted agrarian elites a prominent role in national politics, and it was common for high-ranking officials to belong or have close ties to the agrarian elites. In turn, their role among the founding economic and political elites in their countries bestowed upon agrarian elites significant and enduring social prestige that persists to this day. Today, large landowners – defined as those with landholdings of at least twice the country average – constitute 9.7 percent of farms in Argentina,[1] 9.1 percent in Brazil,[2] and 7.6 percent in Chile,[3] and control 78 percent, 78.8 percent, and 93 percent of the country's agricultural land, respectively.[4]

I assume members of the agrarian elite – which I indistinctively refer to as agricultural producers or landowners – share some common policy

---

[1] Farms of more than 1,000 hectares (INDEC 2002).
[2] Farms of more than 100 hectares (IBGE 2012).
[3] Farms of 100 basic irrigation hectares or more (ODEPA 2007).
[4] In Argentina the median farm size is between 50 and 100 hectares and the average property size is 588 hectares (INDEC 2002). In Brazil, the median farm size is between 10 and 20 hectares and the average property size is 51.3 hectares (IBGE 2012). In Chile, the median farm size is between 5 and 10 basic irrigation hectares and the average property size is 51 basic irrigation hectares (ODEPA 2007).

preferences. I recognize this is a problematic assumption given that individual producers also have their own particularistic interests and that in terms of policies they will prefer those that favor them over competitors within the sector. Moreover, there is great variation within the agricultural sector across crops in terms of production requirements and characteristics as well as destination markets, which should translate in diverse policy preferences. For instance, those producing for the international market will prefer free trade policies, while those producing for the domestic market may support policies that protect them from international competition. However, since what defines the agrarian elites is their control over large tracts of land, landowners should share common preferences regarding policies that define land ownership and use, such as land reform or environmental regulations.[5] For instance, while ranchers could avoid the effects of price controls on beef by switching to soy-growing, stricter environmental regulations over land clearings will likely affect both activities in similar ways. Fieldwork confirmed the existence of common sectoral interests among agrarian elites. My interviews with leaders of the Agrarian Caucus in Brazil, as well as sectoral business associations in the three countries, revealed they all prioritized working on policies that affect agricultural producers as a whole – regardless of their size and crop – and can therefore draw support across the sector.

Since I am interested in explaining agrarian elites' collective political strategies, my analysis focuses on broad policy areas that affect the sector as a whole – although not necessarily evenly. In addition to the taxation of land and regulations over its ownership and use, in the analysed countries, taxes and restrictions over agricultural exports are examples of such policies with a sector-wide impact.[6] Moreover, because one of the main themes of this book is understanding when agricultural producers will enter the electoral arena to influence policy outcomes, I should focus

---

[5] I am not assuming that agricultural producers will act together all the time, just that to confront certain policies that present a collective threat they might develop a collective strategy. For instance, producers of coffee may act together with producers of corn on issues related to property rights and, at the same time, have different strategies to lobby for crop-specific subsidies.

[6] Most of agricultural production in the analysed countries is for exports. For instance, Argentina exported 84 percent of its soybeans (processed and unprocessed) in 2016 (Bolsa de Comercio de Rosario 2016) and Brazil exported two-thirds of its soybean production in 2020 (Embrapa, "Brazil Is the World's Fourth Largest Grain Producer and Top Beef Exporter, Study Shows," June 1, 2021). In Chile, there are no data at the national level, but an analysis of O'Higgins – the region with the largest area under production – shows that 90 percent of cherries, 89 percent of blueberries, and 83 percent of grapes produced were exported in 2021 (ODEPA 2021).

on policies that can be influenced both through nonelectoral and electoral channels. This is the case of these broad-range regulations which are usually designed and discussed in Congress, as opposed to more particularistic ministerial or agency resolutions which fall outside the realm of electoral politics. In the three countries studied here, important legislation in at least one of these three policy areas (property rights, land use regulations, export taxes) was discussed during the period of analysis, triggering an organized reaction from the sector. I should clarify here that I do not expect these policies to affect every agricultural producer in the same way or to automatically trigger a political reaction from every single one of them. I am only assuming that all producers in the sector will be impacted to some extent and that this will give producers incentives to act collectively. Whether or not they will actually mobilize and with what results are empirical questions.

2.3 AGRARIAN ELITES' STRATEGIES OF POLITICAL INFLUENCE

Political influence is the capacity of a group to bring policy closer to its ideal point. This influence can take different forms such as the promotion of new polices (regulations or legislation) in line with the group's interests, or the modification or veto of policies contrary to its preferences. I assume agricultural producers are rational actors and as such they will prefer policies that protect their property rights and maximize their income. As the empirical chapters will illustrate, the rationality assumption does not, however, preclude actors from making mistakes due to limited information or biased perceptions.[7]

Strategies are paths that actors choose to try to get as close to their policy goals as possible (Frieden 1999, 45). The strategies are conditioned by the environment, other actors and their expected behavior, available information, and power disparities between actors (Frieden 1999, 45). Each strategy yields specific payoffs that are a function of the expected influence to be gained and the costs to be incurred (Kalyvas 1996, 26–27). Agrarian elites will choose strategies they believe maximize their chances of influencing sectoral policy at a lower cost.[8] Strategies of political influence are not mutually exclusive and agrarian elites may combine

---

[7] See, for example, Kahneman et al. (1982), Rasmusen (2007).
[8] As stated before, strategies can be flawed because actors may have incomplete information or biased perceptions.

them in different ways. For instance, in Chile, agrarian elites combine party-building with lobbying. While legislators in the right coalition represent agrarian elites' stances during policy debates in Congress, leaders of producers' associations frequently appear in the media, trying to build public support for those stances. However, because agrarian elites' resources are finite, they cannot pursue all strategies at the same time and hence must choose which ones to prioritize.

2.3.1 Electoral Versus Nonelectoral Strategies

We can divide strategies of political influence available to economic elites in democracies in two broad categories: electoral or nonelectoral, according to the channel through which the interest group tries to secure a policy position from politicians. Under nonelectoral strategies, the group aims at persuading policymakers to support its policy position. Lobbying, bribes, and protests are examples of nonelectoral strategies. With electoral strategies, in contrast, the group attempts to influence policymaking by getting candidates who already share its policy preferences elected. Party-building, running for office, and financing like-minded individual candidates are examples of electoral strategies. Whereas under nonelectoral strategies an interest group will work with whomever is in power, under electoral strategies the group will try to influence electoral outcomes, so that like-minded politician would be elected to key policymaking positions.

2.3.1.1 *Nonelectoral Strategies*

I conceptualize *nonelectoral strategies* as the default option, as business everywhere will try to establish relationships with public officials who have decision power over the policies that affect their assets. When nonelectoral strategies are prevalent, a given interest group channels its demands through direct contact with high-ranking government officials such as the president, governors, ministers, or legislators. In this type of strategy, the group relates to the government, irrespectively of which party controls it, and it may offer campaign contributions, bribes, or technical assistance to policymakers across the partisan spectrum to achieve favorable policy outcomes.[9] Contacts

---

[9] Although professionalized lobbying, campaign contributions, and personal contact with policymakers are theoretically differentiated practices, empirically they tend to go together. Thus, I treat them as equivalent. Moreover, analysts of the US Congress have

2.3 Agrarian Elites' Strategies of Political Influence

between policymakers and businesspeople can be formal (e.g., through participation in consultative councils or official meetings) or informal (e.g., undisclosed private meetings or social events). Moreover, businesspeople may engage with members of the government individually or through their corporatist associations. In Latin America, relations between political and economic elites are mediated frequently by social or family ties. In addition, it is common for governments to recruit top-level officials to staff or hold office in sectoral agencies from the same business sector (Schneider 2010). For instance, in the analysed countries, ministers of agriculture often share a past as leaders of their national agricultural associations. All these facilitate contact between economic elite and policymakers and blur the distinction between formal and informal access.

All else equal, nonelectoral strategies are economic elites preferred channel of political influence given its lower costs compared to other alternatives. Staying out of electoral disputes is not only cheaper in economic but also reputational terms. When possible, business will prefer not to be seen as "meddling with partisan disputes" and instead shape policies behind the scenes. By refraining from partisan politics, business can more easily present their interests as aligned with the common good and reach out to potential allies on both sides of the aisle.[10] By contrast, when openly supporting certain parties or candidates, business risk alienating their political rivals who may retaliate once in power. However, as I will discuss at length in Section 2.3.2.1, nonelectoral strategies are risky and not always available. Channels of access to policymakers may shut down, while politicians' willingness to privilege business interests over those of other groups may vary across policy realms and administrations. When direct contact with policymakers does not work or is not available, groups that have not invested in electoral representation will be defenseless against hostile policies.

When lobbying fails to shape policy, economic elites can engage in contentious politics. Protests are a type of nonelectoral strategy – as they aim at influencing people in office as opposed to shaping electoral outcomes – as well as a symptom of the failure of noncontentious

---

shown that business mostly lobby legislators they have contributed to (Ansolabehere et al. 2003). In most Latin American countries, professionalized lobbying is not regulated by law. Therefore, empirically all contacts between business and politicians – even when they resemble the practices of professionalized lobbyists in Washington – are informal.

[10] See Grzymała-Busse (2015) for a discussion of the advantages and disadvantages of non-partisan versus partisan strategies in the context of state–Church relations.

alternatives. Although contention has been studied mostly as a tool of disadvantaged groups in society, lockouts, commercialization strikes, and demonstrations by businesspeople are common in the developing world (Fairfield 2011). Well-known examples are the protests by Chilean businesspeople against the Socialist government of Salvador Allende that preluded the 1973 military coup and the month-long demonstrations against the Evo Morales administration spearheaded by business organizations in Santa Cruz, Bolivia, in 2008. More recently, business owners around the world demonstrated against Covid lockdowns in places such as South Korea, Ukraine, and Colombia.

The reason why we do not associate protests with economic elites is that contention is the resource of groups that lack other means to influence policy outcomes (Tarrow 1998, 3). Groups with the capacity of influencing policies from within the policymaking process do not need to oppose their implementation. While business are certainly not a resource-poor group in economic terms, they may lack something key to influencing public policy: access to the state. Economic elites will engage in protests only where they are not organized politically and their economic power and social connections are not enough to grant them access to policymaking institutions.[11] For instance, the center-left administration of Cristina Fernández de Kirchner (2007–2015) in Argentina had shut down all channels of access to the state for agrarian elites. Therefore, when this government raised export taxes in 2008, agricultural producers, who could not dissuade policymakers from implementing this policy change, had to launch massive protests to repeal it. As the case of the Argentine 2008 agrarian conflict illustrates, protests are a strategy of last resort. Protests will only take place where economic elites lack institutionalized representation and lobbying has failed.

2.3.1.2 *Electoral Strategies: Parties or Candidates*

Electoral strategies aim at electing into office politicians who share the policy preferences of the group sponsoring them. Electoral strategies can be partisan, where the group identifies with a party program and supports its candidates, or nonpartisan, where the group supports like-minded candidates running under different party labels. What different electoral strategies have in common is that they influence policymaking by shaping electoral outcomes.

---

[11] For a thorough discussion of when business will engage in protests, see Fairfield (2011).

2.3 Agrarian Elites' Strategies of Political Influence

Under *party-building*, a group becomes part of a party's core constituency, providing crucial ideological, economic, and political resources that shape the party's identity (Gibson 1992, 15).[12] Interest groups can affect a party's electoral prospects by financing campaigns and mobilizing voters and activists. Thus, politicians have strong incentives to pay attention to interest groups' preferences when these groups are part of their party's core constituency. Moreover, linkages between parties and interest groups create a bias towards the selection of candidates and leaders who share allied groups' worldviews, further reinforcing the ideological congruence between politicians in the party and its core constituency (Jacobs 2008, 204; Allern and Bale 2012). In this group-centric view, parties will seek office to advance the policy agenda of their core constituency (Bawn et al. 2012, 571). This perspective is compatible with theories of conservative party-building that emphasize the segmented character of these parties' linkages which are programmatic regarding their core constituency (business, upper classes) and clientelistic for other groups in society whose support is needed to win elections (Luna 2014; Thachil 2014).

When the party-building strategy is the prevalent one, agricultural producers will be loyal to an identifiable party independently of whether it is in government or the opposition and channel their policy preferences through it. Producers will contribute systematically more to the campaigns of candidates in that party, independently of the candidate's background or likelihood of winning. Another indicator of partisan linkages is the programmatic convergence between a party's policy position and producers' preferences. For instance, agrarian elites in Chile are a core constituency of the rightwing party Renovación Nacional (RN). Agrarian elites' corporatist connections in rural areas, especially in the south of the country, were key for the foundation of the party during the transition to democracy. Today, landowners identify RN as their party and RN politicians as their representatives. There is close correspondence between the policy demands of producers' associations and the RN agrarian policy platform, and both RN administrations (2010–2014 and 2018–2022) have recruited high-ranking officials in sectoral agencies from the ranks of agrarian elites' associations.

Under *candidate-centered* electoral strategies, the group supports individual candidates whom it identifies as sharing its interests, independently of their partisan affiliation. These candidates may be members of

---

[12] See also Fairfield (2015a).

the group – which can be interpreted as a clear signal that they share the group's policy preferences – or politicians who identify with the group's interests. The key difference between party-building and candidate-centered strategies from the point of view of the interest group is that under candidate-centered strategies, the candidate's partisan affiliation does not signal their policy preferences with regards to the issues the group cares about.

When the candidate-centered strategy is the prevalent one, agricultural producers will not identify with any particular party. Politicians supported by the agrarian elites will get into office under ideologically diverse party labels but, once in office, vote together according to agrarian elites' interests, breaching party discipline if necessary. For instance, Brazil's Agrarian Caucus is composed of legislators from many different parties who are in both the governing coalition and the opposition but vote together on issues related to their sectoral interest, such as deforestation regulations or rural workers' pensions. Moreover, agricultural producers' associations promote and finance the work of legislators tied to the sector, even when that means supporting politicians from multiple parties. Sectoral interests trump partisan identity for both legislators and producers. When the candidate-centered strategy prevails, agricultural producers will systematically contribute more to candidates identified with the sector, independently of their partisan affiliation.

It is important to clarify that the candidate-centered strategy conceptualized here is different from the phenomenon of businesspeople individually deciding to run for office to gain particularistic benefits for their firms, such as the strategy studied by Gehlbach et al. (2010) and Szakonyi (2018, 2020) in post-Soviet Russia. Neutralizing the kind of existential policy threats this book is concerned with requires coordination and cooperation among business elites as it typically entails the concerted work of many legislators. Particularistic strategies cannot protect business elites from redistributive policies. While the average legislator may be capable of securing a firm access to state-subsidized credit or a juicy public works contract, they will not be able to block the passage of land reform by themselves. Businesspeople legislators may use public office to benefit their firm or to hurt competitors (Szakonyi 2020). However, they may also pursue issues that create sector-wide benefits. My theory explains when they will enter the electoral arena to do the later. Table 2.1 compares the two electoral strategies available to economic elites in democracies, party-building and candidate-centered, summarizing their key characteristics.

TABLE 2.1 *Party-building versus candidate-centered strategies: main characteristics*

	Party-building	Candidate-centered
Group collectively identifies with	Party	Individual candidates
Candidates selected by	Party	Interest groups
Campaign contributions from the group	Correlate with partisan identity	Correlate with candidates' background
Legislators' votes determined by	Party affiliation	Interest group affiliation

2.3.2 Comparing Strategies: Costs and Reliability

I argue that agrarian elites will choose strategies of political influence based on their costs and reliability. Costs include monetary expenses, time outlays, coordination efforts, and opportunity costs. Strategies are reliable when they are consistently effective. In other words, reliability has two components, effectiveness and stability. Effectiveness refers to the capacity of securing the preferred policy position from relevant policymakers. Stability means the degree to which a given strategy's effectiveness varies across policies and/or administrations. Stable strategies will have the same probability of success across multiple policy realms and administrations of diverse ideological orientation. Thus, strategies that give agricultural producers a greater chance of getting policymakers to favor their preferences over those of other groups across different issues, arenas, and governments are more reliable.

As developed next, there is a trade-off between strategies' cost, on the one hand, and their reliability, on the other. Strategies that are more reliable are typically costlier than less reliable ones. How much landowners will be willing to invest in influencing a given policy will be determined by the expected negative impact of an unfavorable policy design on sectoral interests. In other words, the greater the threat an unfavorable policy design may present to landowners' interests, the more they will be willing to invest in a strategy that could secure them a favorable policy outcome. For instance, under these assumptions, landowners will be willing to invest more resources in influencing land reform regulations, which could end in the expropriation of their farms, than in influencing regulations on the usage of pesticides, which may increase the costs of production but do not challenge property rights.

2.3.2.1 Nonelectoral versus Electoral Strategies: Reliability

Electoral strategies give economic elites unmediated access to the policymaking process, which makes them more reliable than nonelectoral strategies of political influence. First, electoral strategies are more stable than nonelectoral ones. The effectiveness of nonelectoral strategies, such as lobbying or informal personal contact with policymakers, varies with the capacity of the group to access a given administration, which ultimately depends on that administration's willingness to work with the group. This makes nonelectoral strategies unstable because if an administration comes to power that for ideological reasons, for example, does not want to be associated with the group, the group would be left without means to access the policymaking process.[13] This was the case for agrarian elites in some Latin American countries during the left turn of the 2000s. In Argentina, for example, agrarian elites had enjoyed great access to sectoral agencies during the center-right administration of Carlos Menem (1989–1999), who implemented market-oriented reforms in the country. In contrast, during the administrations of the center-left FPV (2003–2015) officials in the Executive had no ties to the agrarian elite and their ideological views were opposite to those of most agricultural producers' associations. As a consequence, and given their lack of investment in electoral representation, producers were defenseless against the hostile policies implemented by the FPV.[14] Thus, a strategy that had been very effective to influence sectoral policy in previous administrations became useless during the FPV years.

Crucially, by granting economic elites direct access to the policymaking process, electoral strategies attenuate the principal–agent problem inherent to any relationship between policymakers and interest groups. Campaign contributions entail an intertemporal exchange where interest groups give politicians money today in exchange for the promise of future influence. However, politicians – whose ultimate goal is to remain in office – may at times have interests conflicting with those of their contributors while no contemporaneous enforcement mechanism for the contract between them exists. If the politicians do not comply, contributors can only punish them in future

---

[13] Even under corporatist arrangements, where business representation is institutionalized in policymaking bodies (e.g., consultative councils), hostile governments may disempower these bodies or ignore their input. More importantly, such arrangements are rare across the developing world and not relevant in the agricultural sector in any of the three cases analysed here.

[14] See Chapter 5 and Fairfield (2011).

elections (McCarty and Rothenberg 1996). Even then, because of the information asymmetry between policy-demanders and policymakers, it may be difficult for interest groups to evaluate whether or not politicians are advancing their interests, as the success of policy initiatives depends on bargaining processes that are hidden from the public eye and legislators are exposed to competing pressures from different constituencies (McCarty and Rothenberg 1996; Dixit et al. 1997; Hall 1998). Moreover, a given interest group is rarely the only one lobbying on an issue, meaning there is always a chance it will be outbid by another group.[15] In a context where the interests of agrarian elites may clash with those of the median voter (i.e., the urban poor) – for instance, over price controls on staple foods – lobbying might be too expensive or ineffective, as legislators may face pressure from their constituents to vote against landowners' interests.

Culpepper's (2010) analysis of corporate regulation in Europe and Japan exemplifies how electoral strategies are more reliable than nonelectoral ones as their efficacy is less affected by public opinion swings. Culpepper (2010) finds that when the public salience of an issue is high, business influence is lower because lawmakers will be inclined to vote according to their voters' preferences.[16] In cases of high public salience, only legislators from rightwing parties with organic links to business will vote according to business preferences and contrary to public opinion. Therefore, while lobbying may work depending on the public mood regarding the issue, helping elect legislators with a programmatic commitment to business ensures a critical mass of representatives that will consistently vote with business interests.

In sum, economic elites can build a more reliable source of influence by helping elect into office politicians that already share their policy preferences. Electing politicians with the same interests, values and ideologies at the outset reduces the need for persuasion later on (Burden 2007). This is particularly true when the politician is a member of the economic elite. For instance, agrarian elites may safely assume that legislators that

---

[15] Grossman and Helpman (2001) characterize the situation where several interest groups vie to influence the same policy as one of "common agency." Policymakers act as the common agent of the different groups and will decide on a policy outcome that maximizes the contributions they have received from these groups without hurting their constituents. Therefore, policy outcomes are not uniquely determined in such situations.

[16] Similarly, Smith (2000) shows that American business only won legislative battles of high public salience when public opinion aligned with their interests. Looking at the farm lobby, Hansen (1991) found that they obtained better access to Congress at times when farmers were electorally important.

own land – and thus be subjected to expropriation themselves – will have strong "personal" incentives to oppose land reform initiatives.[17] In that fashion, by engaging in self-representation, economic elites can make the principal–agent problem disappear as the principal becomes the agent.[18] Moreover, as the Brazilian case analysed in Chapter 4 shows, the advantages of self-representation are not limited to the voting stage. On the contrary, self-representation is especially important because it opens policymaking instances normally closed to civil society such as congressional committees and other agenda-setting bodies, giving economic elites the capacity to modify, speed up, or kill policy initiatives from within.

For all their advantages, electoral strategies main drawback is their high cost. First and foremost, in order to be effective, electoral strategies require winning elections. This means identifying and capturing an electoral base which, in turn, entails spending great amounts of time and money. Moreover, electoral strategies typically require more intragroup coordination and personal involvement from members of the group than nonelectoral ones. For instance, while lobbying might require some coordination in terms of agreeing on a common message and dividing up tasks (for example, members of a national corporatist association may decide that each will lobby their home state's representatives), building a party also requires recruiting activists and candidates, selecting authorities, building a territorial presence, and campaigning, among other collective and time-consuming activities.

Compounding these costs is the fact that all of this investment in time and money may easily be lost if the supported party or candidate lose the election. Once in place, electoral representation guarantees a more reliable, unmediated source of political influence than nonelectoral strategies. However, building such representation requires making a highly risky investment as the success of electoral strategies depends on electoral results that are always uncertain to some extent.[19] Moreover, building parties that are electorally competitive is particularly hard for

---

[17] Ames' (2001) study of Brazil's 1991–1995 legislature corroborates this expectation. He finds that the strongest predictor of legislators' votes on bills related to agrarian interests, even greater than their constituency's interest (i.e., economic weight of agriculture in their district), was whether they owned land (Ames 2001, 64).

[18] See Szakonyi (2020).

[19] Party system characteristics may affect the level of risk associated with pursuing an electoral strategy. For instance, all else equal, investing in electoral representation should be less risky in proportional representation systems than in majoritarian systems, as in the former the proportion of votes that a party or candidate need to win a seat in Congress is lower than in the latter.

economic elites, since wealthy voters are but a small fraction of the electorate, especially in highly unequal societies (Gibson 1996; Thachil 2014; Luna and Rovira Kaltwasser 2014). In the past, landed elites in Latin America solved this "vote-poor, resource-rich" problem with rural clientelism, mobilizing the votes of the peasants living on their lands in support of conservative parties or candidates. However, urbanization and social policy expansion have limited this option. Some conservative parties in the Global South have circumvented this structural constraint by developing segmented electoral strategies that allow them to represent the interest of economic elites while mobilizing the votes of the poor.[20] Nonetheless, successful cases of party-building by agrarian elites, or economic elites in general, in contemporary Latin America are scant. For instance, a study by Loxton (2021, 16) finds that between 1978 and 2010 as few as sixteen new conservative parties were formed, of which only four were electorally successful.[21]

One of the main questions this book tackles is why economic elites will go beyond the default nonelectoral strategy and invest in costlier strategies that imply playing in the electoral arena. I argue economic elites choose strategies based on the expected negative impact of losing political influence. The higher the expected negative consequences of failing to influence a policy, the more resources economic elites will be willing to spend in neutralizing it. Because nonelectoral strategies are less reliable than electoral ones, they are not suitable for dealing with existential threats. Thus, when influencing politics becomes a matter of survival, economic elites will be willing to pay the extra costs of electoral representation.[22] Figure 2.1 illustrates the logic of economic elites' choice between electoral and nonelectoral strategies. Given two strategies, NE and E, each a different function of costs and probability of influence, landowners will choose one based on how important it is for them to influence a given policy outcome or, put differently, how high the perceived costs of inaction are. Strategy NE (lobbying) has lower

---

[20] See Luna (2014) for the case of UDI in Chile and Thachil (2014) for the case of the BJP in India.
[21] He defines as successful cases of party-building those parties that, at the time of his writing, had won at least 10 percent of the vote in five or more consecutive national legislative elections (Loxton 2021, 15).
[22] Similarly, Kalyvas (1996) argues that interest groups will only engage in party-building when they confront a severe threat and other alternative means of political influence are not available. Looking at the Church, he shows it only mobilized electorally in countries where anticlerical attacks by liberal administrations severely curtailed the Church's power and privileged access to the state.

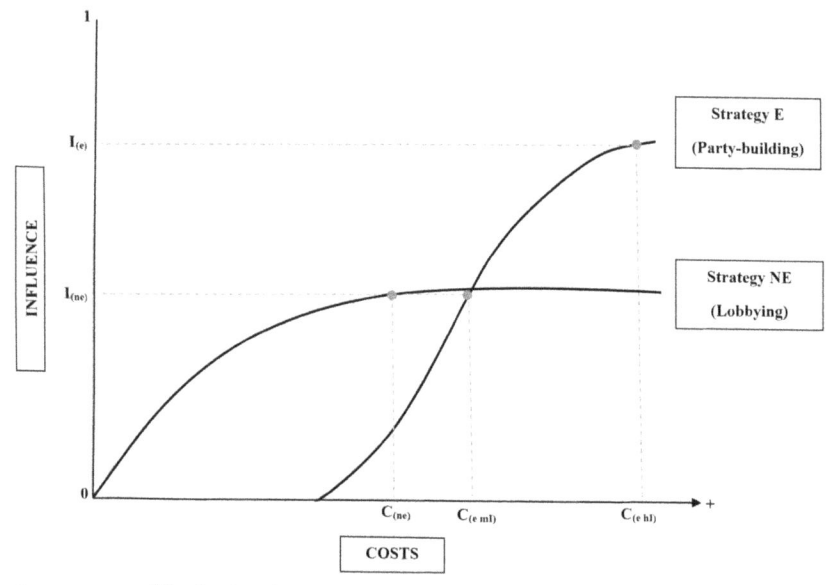

FIGURE 2.1 The logic of economic elites' strategic decisions: costs and probability of influence.

starting costs and can yield a medium probability of influence at lower costs than strategy E (party-building) $\left(C_{(ne)} < C_{(e\,ml)}\right)$. However, after a certain threshold, investing more in NE will not yield higher levels of influence given the principal-agent problem inherent to nonelectoral strategies. Therefore, when stakes are high enough, landowners will be willing to choose strategy E, which can yield higher probabilities of influencing a policy outcome than strategy NE, although at much higher costs. In other words, when failing to influence a policy design presents an existential risk to landowners, they will be willing to pay the extra cost of choosing E, $\left(C_{(e\,hI)} - C_{(ne)}\right)$, given E's higher probability of success $\left(I_{(e)} > I_{(ne)}\right)$.

2.3.2.2 Party-Building Versus Candidate-Centered Strategies: Coordination Costs

Political parties are the most common channel of electoral representation for interest groups in democracies. Parties aggregate demands from social groups and transform them into policy proposals, fulfilling an essential mediating function in modern democracies. In addition, parties solve key collective action and social choice problems for both voters and politicians (Aldrich 1995). They enable legislators to organize their work in Congress, pass bills and avoid endless cycling. Parties not only orient legislators' work, they also help voters decide for whom to vote. Party labels convey information about politicians' stances on issues relevant to citizens. For all these reasons, political scientists cannot conceive of modern democracy without partisan organizations. As Hale (2006) points out, there is a prevalent idea in the literature that because these collective and social choice problems are unavoidable, parties will inevitably form. "Parties, like gases, [expand] to fill an institutional void due to the benefits they bring politicians and voters" (Hale 2006, 8).

In this tradition, the comparative politics literature sees conservative parties as the main instrument of economic elites' protection under democracy. When in power, electorally strong conservative parties guarantee economic elites access to policymakers and the state apparatus (Di Tella 1971; Rueschemeyer et al. 1992). Thus, according to this view, conservative parties are key for democratic consolidation, as economic elites will tolerate democratization only when they believe they have a chance at influencing present or future policies (Middlebrook 2000; Ziblatt 2017). Likewise, economic elites' support and resources are key to the formation and survival of conservative parties (Gibson 1996; Loxton 2021).

This book, however, makes an important contribution to the comparative politics literature by showing that conservative parties are not the only vehicle for the electoral representation of economic elites in democracies. Moreover, I argue that in contexts of high political fragmentation, parties may not be the most effective electoral strategy. Parties require heavy investments in money, time, and labor with highly uncertain payoffs, especially at the outset when electorates have not yet consolidated (Panebianco 1988; Aldrich 1995; Kalyvas 1998; Levitsky et al. 2016). On top of that, party-building entails developing an entire organizational structure as well as power distribution mechanisms, both of which require high levels of coordination among party founders. I argue that these high coordination costs associated with party-building make this strategy unattainable for highly fragmented groups.

For the founding groups, party-building entails a loss in autonomy because it creates a power structure that is parallel and somewhat independent from them (Panebianco 1988; Kalyvas 1996). Creating a party requires the development of a bureaucratic organization with territorial presence across multiple districts, recruiting thousands of activists and candidates, and selecting national, regional, and local leaders. As a result, parties as organizations acquire a life of their own, independent of the groups that built them (Gibson 1996, 19). Party leaders may develop interests in the survival of the organization, which may at points contradict the interests of the group that supports the party.

Like any organization, a party needs a bureaucratic structure. Building the party's institutional structure implies the amalgamation of heterogeneous political groups (Panebianco 1988, 50) who must agree on a power-sharing scheme as they appoint party officials and select party leaders. Moreover, because the main objective of parties is to win elections, party-building entails the development of a territorial organization and a clear party brand. Party founders need to recruit activists and candidates, decide who is going to run for what office in which district, and design a policy platform. All these decisions, like any institution-building process, crystallize power relationships among party founders, distributing resources and incentives. As a consequence, party-building may tilt the balance of power in favor of some faction within the founding group to the detriment of some other faction (Kalyvas 1996).

Divisions within an interest group hinder party-building because they increase the coordination costs associated with it. If strong divides exist within a group, all the agreements and negotiations that developing a partisan organization entails, such as selecting candidates and party leaders or defining a policy platform will be harder to bring about. From the point of view of individual politicians or interest groups who must put their economic or mobilizational resources at the service of building a new independent organization, the coordination costs of party-building are not limited to the expenditure of such resources but also include opportunity costs (i.e., the things they must give up to join the party) (Hicken 2009, 31). For instance, an issue of great importance for an interest group may be neglected in the party agenda if it is of less importance to a more powerful group within the party, or local bosses may have to put their clientelist machines to the service of a state-level politician they would rather not support. These ideological and political compromises will be greater where the interests of those investing in building the party are further apart. By contrast, when individuals or interest groups investing in party-building do not have competing interests among them, their preferences and those of party leaders will coincide more frequently. In this fashion, cohesion among party-builders lowers coordination costs.

Candidate-centered strategies offer an alternative mechanism to obtain direct policy influence for groups with deep internal cleavages that make party-building too onerous. The coordination costs associated with a candidate-centered strategy are lower than those of party-building because the candidate-centered strategy does not require all members of the group to agree, first, on the decision to create a new organization and then, on the characteristics and administration of that organization. Thus, trans-partisan, candidate-centered strategies allow internally divided groups to gain electoral representation without compromising the political autonomy or economic interests of individual members or factions. By backing individual candidates as opposed to a party, different factions within the group can choose the candidate with policy preferences closer to theirs without having to agree on a common platform. Similarly, where members of the group control rival political machines, a candidate-centered strategy allows them to keep their local bulwarks, something that may not be possible under party-building as national and state-level party leaders define campaign strategies.

While the candidate-centered strategy demands less coordination than party-building in the electoral arena, it still necessitates coordination within the legislative arena to enhance individual representatives' effectiveness in influencing legislation. Influencing the treatment of a bill requires the coordinated efforts of multiple legislators. Therefore, the candidate-centered strategy typically leads to the formation of multiparty legislative caucuses. These caucuses consist of informal groups of legislators elected under various party labels and with the support of different political machines who – despite their diverse political origins – represent the same interest group and collaborate to advance this group's policy interests. This second instance of coordination that takes place within the legislative arena is key for the effectiveness of the candidate-centered strategy. Where multiparty caucuses are more institutionalized, having more technical resources and a more permanent structure and membership, their influence over policy will be greater.

Through the formation of multiparty caucuses, the candidate-center strategy presents a channel to organize legislative work alternative to parties. While political scientists see parties as the primary aggregation device organizing work in Congress (Cox and MacCubbins 1993; Cox 1997) without which democracy would be "unworkable" (Aldrich 1995, 3), this book shows that political parties are not the only channel through which interest groups can gain electoral representation and, under certain circumstances, they are not even the most efficient one. Aldrich (1995) and Hale (2006) argue that ambitious politicians will build or join parties when parties are the best means to gain office and realize their policy goals. I argue the same logic extends to the other actor whose support is key for most parties' survival: interest groups. For internally divided groups, the candidate-centered strategy offers a more efficient alternative to fulfil their policy goals, given its lower coordination costs vis-à-vis parties. Like parties, multiparty caucuses coordinate the work of legislators across districts. Unlike parties, however, multiparty caucuses do not require electoral coordination within districts or agreement on a comprehensive policy platform.

Candidate-centered strategies offer a more efficient way of organizing electoral representation where party structures are weak and their policy platforms blurred, which is increasingly the case around the developing world.[23] For instance, in Brazil, issue-specific, multiparty caucuses have become key players in the building of legislative coalitions in the last two decades with the increasing fragmentation of the party system. Similarly, in the 1990s, financial groups in Russia supported candidates from multiple parties in regional legislative elections, in order to maximize their chances of influencing key banking regulations (Hale 2006, 163–64). More recently, religious organizations in Colombia – another country that experienced the collapse of its historic party system – sponsored candidates across the partisan spectrum in the 2022 legislative elections to build a pro-life caucus against the legalization of abortion in the country.[24]

However, candidate-centered strategies may not be feasible everywhere. There are institutional features that facilitate this type of electoral strategy. Multiparty caucuses have higher probability of succeeding in systems with undisciplined, ideologically loose parties, where legislators have autonomy vis-à-vis their party leaders and can stray from party lines without being expelled (Carey and Shugart 1995). The two countries where businesspeople have most clearly invested in individual representatives in Congress, Brazil and Russia,[25] fit this description. In countries with more ideologically cohesive and disciplined parties, in which leaders can punish legislators for defecting, candidate-centered strategies will likely fail because legislators have less autonomy to vote according to the preferences of their financers and against the party line.

---

[23] See, for example, Hicken and Kuhonta (2015), Lupu (2017), Mainwaring (2018), and Luna et al. (2021).

[24] "Se consolida bloque parlamentario provida en Congreso de Colombia," ACI Digital, September 22, 2022.

[25] On Russia, see Hale (2006), Gehlbach et al. (2010), and Szakonyi (2020).

2.4 THE ARGUMENT

This book studies how agrarian elites defend their interests in contemporary Latin American democracies. In particular, it explains when and how landowners will organize in the electoral arena. Agrarian elites will enter the electoral arena when they perceive an existential threat. Due to their lower reliability, nonelectoral strategies will be ill-suited to deal with this kind of threats, as in such a context failing to influence policy means agrarian elites may lose their business. Under these circumstances, agrarian elites will be prompted to organize in the electoral arena with the purpose of electing into office politicians that share their policy preferences. Whether this is accomplished by building a conservative party or by supporting individual candidates across the partisan spectrum will depend on agrarian elites' level of fragmentation. The high coordination costs inherent to party-building will become unsurmountable for deeply divided groups. Where levels of fragmentation are high, agrarian elites will pursue a candidate-centered strategy instead. Figure 2.2 summarizes my argument, illustrating how the two main explanatory factors, existential threat and intragroup fragmentation, interact to produce the three expected outcomes.

The book focuses on the democratic transition as it argues that the strategic choices agrarian elites made then conditioned their future options for political organization. While this is not a "critical junctures" argument in the stricter sense of the term,[26] it borrows from the path dependence framework two key ideas to help flesh out its causal logic.[27] First, I argue that experiences of redistributive conflict in previous democratic periods had long-lasting effects over agrarian elites' strategies of political representation. Where previous attacks on (or attempts at) their property rights existed, they shaped agrarian elites' cognitive frameworks,[28] making the democratic transition appear more threatening to their interests than in places with no history of land conflict. As I will develop in the next section, landed elites' perception of threat at the moment of transition was informed both by contemporary levels of social mobilization around agrarian issues as well as previous episodes of land redistribution. Moreover, previous redistributive conflict not only shaped the kind

---

[26] See Collier and Munck (2022) for the latest discussion on the subject.
[27] See Pierson (2000; 2004) and Thelen (2003).
[28] See Pierson (2000) for a discussion of how cognitive frameworks can act as mechanisms of reproduction in path-dependent political processes. For a recent application of this notion, see Ondetti (2021).

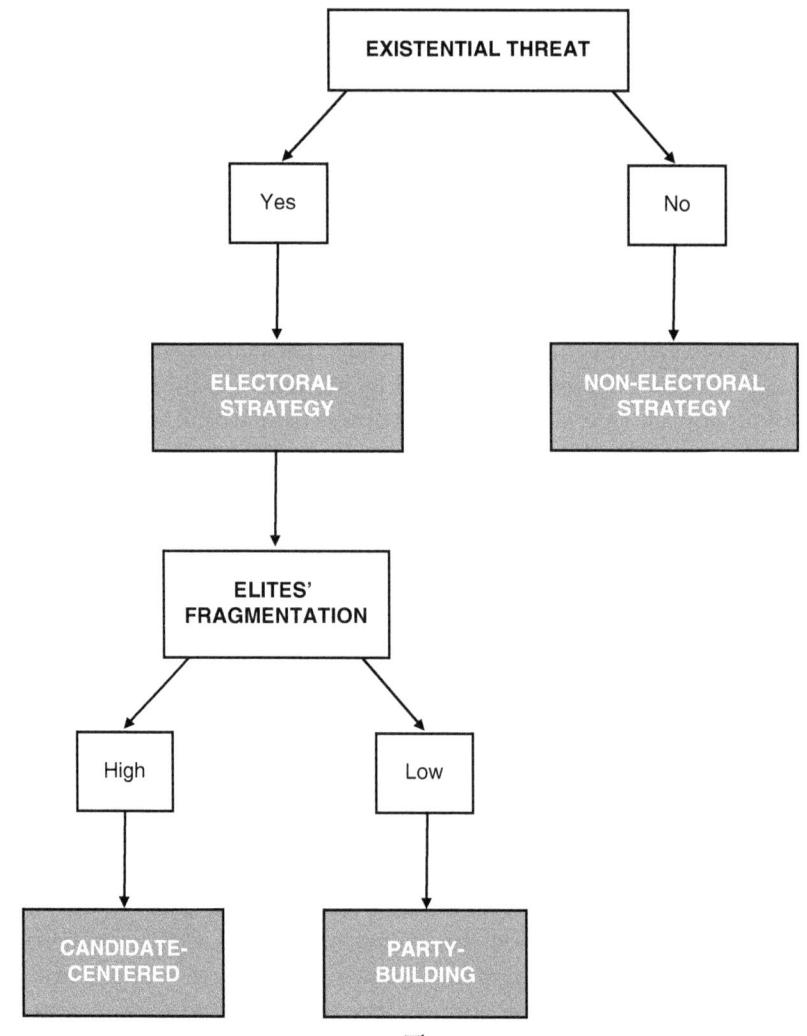

FIGURE 2.2 The argument.

of policies agrarian elites thought they could expect from democratic administrations, but also who they saw as their enemies or allies, conditioning with whom they sought to build political alliances.

The second insight that my theory borrows from the path dependence framework is that the timing of the threat, or *when* in history it happens,[29] is consequential for the success of electoral strategies. Even though in my theory existential threats always act as an incentive for

---

[29] See Pierson (2000).

electoral organization, I argue that whether the existential threat emerged at the democratic transition or appeared afterwards was particularly relevant for agrarian elites' chances at organizing electoral representation. Democratic transitions were moments of exceptional political fluidity that opened the door for the building of linkages between interest groups and parties. After many years of proscription, parties were (re)organizing and new actors entering the political scene. In this context, interest groups could offer parties economic resources (Gibson 1996; Allern and Bale 2012; Luna 2014) as well as the organizational capacity to mobilize voters (Kalyvas 1996; Allern and Bale 2012; Ziblatt 2017). The transitional elections were "founding" events that created new expectations by interest groups about the viability of different political strategies available to them (O'Donnell and Schmitter 1986; Gibson 1996). The linkages that parties and interest groups built in these transitional years set in motion self-reinforcing processes that shaped the structure of their future choices (Panebianco 1988; Kalyvas 1996).[30] The early success of certain strategies incentivized groups to keep investing in them, discouraging the pursuit of alternatives. Partisan linkages became ingrained in groups' identities both for members and nonmembers shaping who they saw (and who saw them) as allies.

I do not claim that interest groups' strategies of political influence are locked in, but I do argue that switching strategies became harder for groups with the passing of time, especially for groups that did not invest in electoral strategies during the transition and attempted to enter the electoral arena later down the path. As the Argentina case demonstrates, groups can switch strategies but organizing electoral representation will be harder after patterns of political competition have consolidated. Because linkages between interest groups and political parties take time to solidify, groups that felt threatened during the transition and hence invested in an electoral strategy at that time had an advantage in influencing policymaking when threats appeared later on. In contrast, groups that had not invested in building such linkages during the transition had a harder time finding political allies to block unwanted policies after this time of exceptional political fluidity had passed and parties had cemented ties with other core constituencies. Similarly, building a new party after the first foundational elections became much harder. Parties that were able to build an electoral base and durable links to certain constituencies early on had a great electoral advantage over newcomers. Once the

---

[30] On self-reinforcing mechanisms, see Pierson (2000).

representation of most social groups had been "claimed" by some party, those trying to enter the electoral arena would be hard-pressed to find the material resources and votes necessary to remain competitive (Gibson 1996). Moreover, there are sunk costs to electoral strategies, which may explain why later down the path interest groups may prefer to continue investing in them even when they are no longer optimal. For instance, investments in party-building, in terms of time, resources, and coordination efforts are much higher at the beginning when the party is starting to compete in the electoral arena than later on when the party structure, label, and electoral base have been consolidated.

2.4.1 Existential Threats and Electoral Investments

I argue that landowners will invest in an electoral strategy when confronted with an existential threat. Existential threats are policy proposals that contest or severely restrict landowners' property rights. Failing to influence such policies will jeopardize agrarian elites' survival as a class. Therefore, when confronted with an existential threat, landowners will look for more reliable, if costlier, sources of political influence. This is not a functional argument. I only argue that a rising threat to the continuity of their business may trigger collective political action by economic elites. High levels of threat to their property rights will increase their incentives to invest in an electoral strategy, but that strategy may not be effective, or the elites may fail to coordinate on an electoral strategy altogether. In other words, I argue that existential threats are *necessary* conditions for electoral organization, but not *sufficient*.[31]

Collective action around polices that constitute an existential threat should be eased by the fact that these policies affect all landowners independently of their size or crop, creating a common interest to stop them. Moreover, landowners are more vulnerable to redistributive threats than other elite groups because their principal asset, land, is immobile and therefore they cannot escape threatening policies, which should lower their threshold for political organization.

That threat will be an incentive for economic elites' political organization is a common assumption in political science literature. For instance, Frieden (1991) argues that Latin American governments' developmental policies during the 1970s and 1980s were shaped by the level of class conflict. In countries where business feared that socialist parties could

---

[31] See Slater (2010, 13).

2.4 The Argument

win office in the future, they united to demand protection for property rights and the creation of a strong, independent private sector. In countries where such a threat was not present, in contrast, each economic sector lobbied for particularistic benefits. Similarly, comparing Latin American countries tax burdens, Ondetti (2021) shows that where economic elites experienced major threats to their property rights, they organized politically to fight state expansion. In contrast, where such a threat did not materialize, economic elites failed to organize effectively to resist state intervention. More generally, classic political science literature has identified this type of existential threat to the economic elite behind the formation of conservative parties (Duverger 1964; Huntington 1968),[32] elites' support of authoritarianism (Linz 1976; Cardoza 1983; O'Donnell 1988), and state building (Slater 2010), among other important outcomes.

But how can we identify what constitutes an existential threat in the eyes of agrarian elites? Measuring threat is not straightforward because threats always have a subjective component. What represents a threat depends on human perception and perceptions are always subject to bias. As empirical studies in cognitive psychology have extensively documented, individual decision-making is plagued with misperceptions, miscalculations, and distortions, especially in contexts of high uncertainty.[33] Another hurdle in measuring existential threat is that human perceptions are not directly observable. As a consequence, we cannot differentiate between *perceived* and *stated* threat. There is no way of objectively knowing if actors that claim to feel threatened actually do; and accepting their statements at face value is obviously problematic since actors may have strategic incentives to exaggerate their claims. For instance, agrarian elites could be agitating the specter of Communism to frighten voters away from leftist candidates, even when they do not believe a leftwing government would implement expropriating policies. At the same time, as Slater (2010, 13) warns us, we should avoid falling into post hoc reasoning by inferring an existential threat actually existed in those cases in which we see a collective response by agrarian elites. What to do then to approximate the actual intensity of the threat perceived by agrarian elites?

My operationalization strategy deals with these obstacles in measuring the variable existential threat in two ways. First, I follow Slater's (2010)

---

[32] For studies focused on Latin America, see Roberts (2014) and Loxton (2021).
[33] For a general discussion of decision under uncertainty and bounded rationality see, for example, Kahneman et al. (1982). For an application of the bounded rationality approach to explain Latin American conservative elites' overestimation of the Communist threat in the 1960s and 1970s, see Weyland (2019).

deductive approach and ask, (1) what kind of policies will threaten the continuity of agrarian elites business, and (2) the presence of which factors will lead agrarian elites to *believe* the implementation of such policies is likely. Second, to deal with the "perceived versus stated threat" problem I look for consistency in agrarian elites' statements across audiences and time. While agrarian elites may had have incentives to exaggerate their perceptions of threat in public statements, this may be less the case in documents destined to internal consumption or in private meetings. Similarly, while agrarian elites may have had political incentives to misrepresent their perceptions of threat during the democratic transition, it is unclear why they would continue to do this two or three decades later and when talking to an academic. The fact that agrarian elites' statements regarding the degree to which a transition to democracy represented a threat to their interests are consistent across the different sources I analyse – contemporary newspapers and internal documents, interviews conducted by me in 2015–2017, and interviews conducted by other scholars at different moments in time – gives me confidence in my scoring of the variable.

I score a case as having an existential threat if at least one of two conditions is met. Either (1) policies that jeopardize the continuity of agrarian elites' interests are being implemented or (2) there are factors that may lead agrarian elites to believe the implementation of such policies is likely. One of those factors is social mobilization around policies that contest landowners' property rights,[34] especially when the social actors demanding those policies have ties to parties in power or with chances of gaining power in the future. Another factor shaping agrarian elites perceptions of threat is past experiences of redistributive conflict under democracy. In the words of Slater (2010, 48), "upper groups' perceptions of *prospective* threat under a future democratic regime are shaped by *retrospective* considerations of how mass politics looked before."[35] Where democratic governments implemented or attempted redistribute land reform, landowners will overestimate the probability that a future democratic government will challenge their property rights.[36] This will

---

[34] In her study of democratic transitions, Bellin (2000) finds that capitalists will fear democratization and oppose it where the poor are organized and mobilized behind a redistributive agenda.
[35] Emphasis in original.
[36] As Weyland (2019, 46–47) argues, the availability heuristic seriously distorts people's probability estimates as experiences with past traumatic events lead to an overestimation of their likelihood of reoccurrence.

be especially true when the parties that may come to power after the democratic transition are the ones that pursued redistribution in the past.

Land redistribution is the greatest threat to agrarian elites because land reform threatens their survival as a class. While urban workers may demand better wages, they do not usually demand expropriation of the factory. Redistributive demands from poor peasants, in contrast, are about agrarian elites' source of income, wealth, social status, and in some cases, political power, making land reform the ultimate threat to landowners' interests. In addition, rural violence (e.g., land occupations) may materialize this threat at the individual level, as producers see that the farm next door is being occupied, increasing individual producers' incentives to invest in an electoral strategy. Aside from land reform, other policies that may present existential threats to landowners as they jeopardize the continuity of their business are: demarcation of indigenous peoples' lands, tax schemes with confiscatory rates, and environmental regulations that severely restrict land or water use. For instance, several South American countries have enacted deforestation regulations that forbid landowners to clear their farms for agriculture in protected areas, encroaching on their property rights (Fernández Milmanda and Garay 2019).

In spite of a common environment of uncertainty, democratic transitions did not present the same level of threat to agrarian elites throughout the region. Everywhere, economic elites were uncertain about the level of access they would enjoy in the new regime and the degree to which new democratic governments would pursue policy agendas in favor of or contrary to their interests. However, how threatening agrarian elites perceived the transition to be varied with their previous experience with democracy, the level of social mobilization around distributive demands, and the policy agenda of the main political parties.

In Brazil and Chile, unlike Argentina, democracy and the threat of land redistribution were linked in producers' experience. In the first two countries, agrarian elites experienced high levels of threat to (and actual attacks on) their property rights during previous democratic regimes. In fact, these threats were among the triggers of the military coups against the governments of Goulart in Brazil (1964) and Allende in Chile (1973). In contrast, in Argentina, previous democratic governments had never challenged agrarian elites' property rights (Lattuada 1988; Hora 2018).

The three countries also differ in the degree of social mobilization around land reform and the redistributive agenda of the main political contenders during the first foundational elections. In Argentina, there was no social demand for land reform and the policy platforms of the main parties did not include any policies that threatened agrarian elites' property rights. As a consequence, producers did not invest in electoral representation during the democratic transition which, in turn, left them defenseless to fight the harmful polices of the Fernández de Kirchner administration (2007–2015). In Brazil, in contrast, there was ample social and political mobilization around land reform. The transitional government of Sarney (1985–1990) started implementing a land reform plan shortly after taking office, and land redistribution figured prominently in the agenda of the 1987–1988 Constituent Assembly. At the same time, landless peasants were mobilizing to demand land redistribution with the support of the Catholic Church. Moreover, the landless peasant movement (MST) had ties to the PT, one of the main contenders in the first democratic presidential elections. In this highly threatening context, Brazilian agrarian elites organized to elect their representatives to the Constituent Assembly. In Chile, like Brazil, agrarian elites felt threatened by the democratic transition. Although there was no comparable social or political mobilization around land reform at the time of the transition, a few years before, the insurrectional massive protests of 1983–1986 had shown profound social discontent with the neoliberal economic model imposed by the dictatorship. The agenda of the center-left Concertación did not include polices that directly threatened the property rights of agrarian elites, but it did contain labor, tax, and environmental reforms to the economic model in which modern agricultural production for export had flourished. Moreover, the coming to power of the Christian Democrats, the party that had implemented land reform and encouraged the unionization of rural workers in the 1960s, made agrarian elites wary of what democracy might bring. The traumatic experience of the land reform of the 1960s and 1970s distorted Chilean agrarian elites' perceptions of the Concertación agenda, making them overestimate the likelihood the new democratic government would pursue redistributive policies. Thus, agrarian elites invested in securing political representation in Congress to block potential policy threats from the center-left. Table 2.2 summarizes the scoring of the cases.

2.4.2 Fragmentation and the Costs of Electoral Strategies

Within the logic of my argument, the variable intragroup fragmentation gains relevance only in cases of high threat. Only when an existential

TABLE 2.2 *Agrarian elites' perceived existential threat during the democratic transition*

	Argentina	Brazil	Chile
Policies jeopardizing the continuity of agrarian elites' business	No	Yes (intense) • Sarney's Land Reform Plan • 1987–1988 Constituent Assembly	Yes (mild) • Tax, labor, and water code reforms
Social mobilization around redistribution	No	Yes • MST with Church support	No
Past experience with redistributive conflict under democracy	No	Yes (mild) • Land reform attempt under Goulart (1964)	Yes (intense) • Redistributive agrarian reform (1965–1973)
Perceived existential threat	No	Yes	Yes

threat exists will the payoffs of investing in an electoral strategy offset its costs. When there is no such threat, agrarian elites will remain outside the electoral arena, independently of their level of fragmentation. In the context of an existential threat, the existence of cleavages among agrarian elites will make it more difficult to organize collective action. As discussed in the previous section, when divisions within the group are entrenched, the coordination costs of party-building will become unsurmountable and members of the group will look for alternative ways of obtaining electoral representation.

Sources of elite fragmentation vary. Cleavages within a group may have regional, ethnic, economic, political, or religious origins. For instance, in his study of conservative party formation in late nineteenth- and early twentieth-century Europe, Ziblatt (2017, 48) finds that traditional elites were able to build parties to represent their interests only where they were not divided along confessional lines. Similarly, Gibson (1996) argues that in the oligarchic period in Latin America (the second half of the nineteenth century and the early twentieth century), conservative parties were formed only in those countries where rural oligarchies had common economic interests across regions. Where this was not the case, regional divisions hindered the development of national conservative parties.

I rely on sociological, historical, and anthropological studies of agrarian elites in the three countries to identify salient cleavages or divisions among landowners that could increase the coordination costs of party-building. Agrarian elites in the three analysed countries were homogeneous along religious and ethnic lines at the time of democratic transition. Therefore, I focus on regional and political differences as potential sources of division within the agrarian elites. Regional differences are relevant when they translate into competing economic interests and, as a result, rival policy preferences.

I employ several indicators of regional and political divisions among the agrarian elites. I measure regional divisions by looking at the heterogeneity of agricultural production across the territory. Where rural elites harvest the same crops for the same markets, I expect them to have compatible economic interests. By contrast, where agrarian elites in one region produce for the domestic market while others export their production, their policy preferences will likely be at odds. The existence of multiple national-level landowners' associations as opposed to a single peak association is another indicator of agrarian elites' economic fragmentation. I assume that multiple associations will not be created to demand the exact same policies. Therefore, where more than one association claims to represent the interests of agricultural producers in a given country, I interpret this as producers having diverse economic interests.

Finally, I define political fragmentation as the degree to which agrarian elites compete with each other for the control of local politics. I measure political fragmentation by considering whether agrarian elites were connected to rival political machines at the time they experienced an existential threat. Although controlling clientelistic machines may give agrarian elites an electoral advantage, where these machines belong to political rivals, it will be costlier to integrate them into the same partisan structure.

In both Argentina and Brazil, agrarian elites were fragmented when their perception of threat rose and they decided to enter the electoral arena, although the sources of that fragmentation were quite different. In Argentina, historic economic cleavages within the agrarian elite translated into heterogeneous policy preferences. Throughout Argentine history, the competing economic interests of rural elites in the prosperous export-oriented Pampas, which favored liberalism, and those of the underdeveloped interior, which depended on state protection to survive, hindered the formation of a national conservative party (Gibson 1996;

Morresi 2015). As a consequence, when an existential threat appeared in 2008, Argentine agrarian elites had no clear partisan allies to turn to. To defend their interests in the electoral arena, landowners developed a candidate-centered strategy, running their candidates under multiple party labels. In Brazil, entrenched political (although not necessarily ideological) divisions at the state and local level existed among the agrarian elite at the time of democratic transition. In rural municipalities, landowners had historically competed among each other for the control of local politics through personal, often family-based clientelistic machines that they connected to different parties or factions within the same party (Gross 1973; Hagopian 1996; Mainwaring 1999; Ames 2001). These political rivalries obstructed the formation of a party to represent agrarian interests during the democratic transition, as rural elites refused to give up their local bulwarks of power.

Chilean economic elites have historically been much more cohesive than their Argentine or Brazilian counterparts (Kurtz 2013). Since the nineteenth century, agricultural interests have been tied to those of other economic sectors such as mining, industry, or commerce as prominent families typically owned assets in all of them (Zeitlin and Ratcliff 1988; Kurtz 2013). Until the first half of the twentieth century, landownership was a gateway to parliamentary politics. Thus, landowners historically were a significant proportion of elite-based parties such as the Conservatives and Liberals (Remmer 1984; Zeitlin and Ratcliff 1988).[37] While the traumatic experience of land reform during the 1960s terminated political linkages between agrarian elites and the Christian Democrats, the process of modernization and liberalization of agriculture during the military dictatorship (1973–1990) reoriented production towards the cultivation of fruit for the international market, homogenizing the political and economic interests of agrarian elites even more. As a consequence, at the time of democratic transition, there were no economic or political cleavages among the Chilean agrarian elites that would preclude party-building. Moreover, agrarian elites shared with other economic sectors a preference for the continuity of the political and economic model installed during the dictatorship. Similarities in the political and economic interests of different sectors of the economic elite lowered the coordination costs of party-building in Chile. Therefore, landowners joined other economic elites and conservative politicians in the foundation of Renovación Nacional (RN).

---

[37] In 1966, Liberals and Conservatives merged, creating the National Party (PN).

TABLE 2.3 *Explanatory factors, observed outcomes, and cases*

		Existential Threat	
		Yes	No
Fragmentation	Low	Electoral: Party-building *Chile*	Nonelectoral
	High	Electoral: Candidate-centered *Brazil Argentina (2009–2013)*	Nonelectoral *Argentina (pre-2008)*

Table 2.3 shows the values that both independent variables, existential threat and fragmentation, and the dependent variable, strategy of political influence, take in each of the analysed cases.

One might question whether previous threats explain the level of intragroup fragmentation. According to this logic, existential threats should help overcome intragroup divisions as they create incentives to act collectively against a common enemy, and the greater the threat, the greater the incentives to unify. Following this line of argument, groups appear unified today because they faced a threat in the past. However, the empirical evidence gathered for this study indicates that although threat and fragmentation interact to determine agrarian elites' strategies of political influence, the intensity of the threat does not explain the level of fragmentation. The existence of cleavages is independent of threat, and affects how interest groups react to threatening events. Cleavages determine how difficult it would be for the group to organize collective action to confront threatening policies. For instance, in both of the cases analysed here where agrarian elites pursued electoral strategies, Brazil and Chile, high levels of threat triggered electoral investments. However, the seriousness of the threat does not correlate with the type of electoral strategy pursued. During the democratic transition, threats to agrarian elites' interests were higher in Brazil than in Chile, but party-building was only possible in the latter. In Brazil, the actual implementation of a land reform by the transitional government of Sarney (1985–1990) and a Constitutional Assembly where land reform was one of the main subjects to be discussed were not enough for agrarian elites to overcome their political divisions and engage in party-building. By contrast, Chilean agrarian elites contributed to the organization of a party during the democratic transition, even when the immediacy of the threat they perceived was lower than in Brazil. In Chile, party-building was facilitated by the lack of divisions among the agrarian elites, not by a higher level of threat.

2.5 ALTERNATIVE EXPLANATIONS

There are three main competing explanatory variables for agrarian elites' strategies of political influence: previous history of electoral organization, electoral rules, and the relevance of Congress as a policymaking arena. In this section, I discuss why neither of these factors can adequately explain the observed variation in (1) when agrarian elites will decide to enter the electoral arena to protect their interests, or (2) the type of electoral strategy agrarian elites deployed in each case.

2.5.1 Previous History of Electoral Organization

A competing explanation for why agrarian elites pursued an electoral strategy in Brazil and Chile but not in Argentina during the democratic transition is their previous history of electoral organization. Before the democratic transitions of the third wave, Brazilian and Chilean agrarian elites had been active in electoral competition while the Argentines had remained aloof from partisan politics. This historic difference cannot be completely discarded as a critical antecedent of agrarian elites' pursue of an electoral strategy in Brazil and Chile during the democratic transition.[38] However, the social, economic, and political transformations that the region experienced in the second half of the twentieth century limit this historical factor's capacity to explain the observed variation in agrarian elites' strategies of political influence in the democracies of the third wave. Scholars studying conservative party-building in Latin America before the third wave have highlighted the absence of a large peasantry in Argentina as one of the main causes of the failure to organize partisan representation by the country's landed elites.[39] While landlords elsewhere in Latin America (including Brazil and Chile) controlled through coercion and clientelism the votes of the peasants living on their domains, the Argentine lacked this source of electoral power. However, by the time the three analysed countries transitioned to democracy, urbanization and

---

[38] Slater and Simmons (2010, 891) define critical antecedents as factors that condition actors' strategic choices and behavior, predisposing (but not predestining) cases down a certain causal path.
[39] See, for instance, Di Tella (1971), P. Smith (1978), and McGuire (1995).

the organization of rural workers by the left had significantly erode or extinguished this electoral advantage that Brazilians and Chileans used to have vis-á-vis Argentines.

Nowhere in Latin America is the contrast between pre- and post-transition landowners' electoral power clearer than in Chile. The political changes in the countryside triggered by the reforms of the late 1950s and mid 1960s dismantled conservatives' old source of political power: the control of the votes of the peasants through the *inquilinaje* system.[40] The introduction of the secret ballot in 1958 and the legalization of rural unions in 1967 undermined landowners' political control of the countryside to the advantage of leftwing parties (Scully 1992). By the time the Partido Nacional (PN) dissolved itself to integrate into the military administration after the 1973 coup, the rural clientelistic networks that conservatives used to control had already been pulled to pieces. Therefore, when the partisan right started to reorganize in the late 1980s, their old source of electoral power was no longer available. Thus, even when Chilean agrarian elites had previous experience organizing electoral representation, the causal mechanisms through which this experience could have helped party-building during the democratic transition are not clear. On the one hand, previous links between agrarian elites and the old PN facilitated their integration into its successor, RN, and helped this party build a presence in rural areas. On the other, the whole social, political, and economic order under which agrarian elites had mobilized votes for the right had completely broken down more than two decades ago. Therefore, even when the party-building strategy was not new, its bases of sustentation had to be. In fact, one of Chile's main rightwing parties, the UDI, was built from scratch and in open opposition to the old right (Loxton 2021). UDI brought new people into politics and developed a novel electoral strategy that combined the support of the economic elite with the mobilization of the urban poor (Luna 2014).

In Brazil, there was continuity in the sources of agrarian elites' electoral power pre- and post-transition. Rural clientelistic networks were active throughout the dictatorship as the military allowed for controlled electoral competition between two official parties. These networks were key in the development of Brazilian landowners' candidate-centered strategy. In fact, as we will see in Chapter 4, it was the fragmented character of these networks that prevented party-building by agrarian elites

---

[40] For a discussion of *inquilinaje*, see Chapter 3.

in Brazil. However, while these preexisting rural clientelistic networks undoubtedly helped agrarian elites organize electoral representation and get their people first in the 1987–1988 Constituent Assembly and then into Congress, it is important to highlight that the strategy of organizing a multiparty caucus to represent their class interests was new. Agrarian elites in Brazil had historically been involved in politics due to the overlap between economic and political elites in the country. However, it was the land reform threat that pushed rural elites to organize politically around their landowning identity. While landowners were not new to politics, the political mobilization of their corporatist associations as well as the number of landowners elected during and after the democratic transition were unprecedented.[41] The organizing efforts of producers' associations and cooperatives were key to elect agrarian representatives in regions where clientelist networks were weaker such as the south or the center-west. Moreover, while rural clientelist networks, especially in the northeast, were fundamental to the electoral success of the rightwing PFL/DEM (Power 2000; Paiva 2002), as we will see in Chapter 4, agrarian elites did not channel their electoral representation only or mainly through this party. More importantly, while these clientelist networks were eroded by urbanization and the expansion of social policy in the decades following the democratic transition (Fried 2012; Montero 2012; Zucco 2013; Sugiyama and Hunter 2013; Daïeff 2016), the Agrarian Caucus kept growing in strength and size.

It is also important to remember that both in Brazil and Chile the military dissolved existing political parties and changed the electoral rules.[42] Therefore, even when agrarian elites may had had previous experience in electoral involvement, the rules and players had changed since their last encounter with democratic competition. This added to the fact that their old sources of electoral power had disappeared or started to erode limit how much this previous experience could had facilitated agrarian elites' electoral organization in Brazil and Chile during the last democratic transition. Finally, the fact that Argentine agrarian elites attempted electoral representation after the 2008 conflict indicates that while previous experience with electoral organization may help, it is not a necessary condition for the development of electoral strategies.

---

[41] The average number of landowners per legislature was 41 between 1967 and 1983 (with a maximum of 48 in 1967–1971) (Fleischer 1980, 175) and 111 between 1999 and 2019 (author's calculations, see Chapter 4).

[42] See Valenzuela and Scully (1997), Mainwaring (1999), and Snyder and Samuels (2004).

Argentina within-case variation demonstrates that previous experience with electoral politics cannot explain when agrarian elites will pursue an electoral strategy versus a nonelectoral one. The variable perception of threat better explains the timing of electoral organization.

2.5.2 Electoral Rules

The literature on how electoral rules affect politicians' and voters' incentives is vast. Since Duverger's (1964) seminal work, political scientists have extensively explored how electoral rules determine the number of parties in a party system by shaping how politicians campaign, what type of electoral alliances they pursue, and how voters decide whom to vote for.[43] However, the effects of electoral rules on the outcome of interest of this book – that is to say, how interest groups organize to influence policymaking – has been much less explored.[44]

Interest groups' decisions on how to organize political representation are in part determined by the structure of the party system and the availability of potential political allies. However, party system fragmentation does not automatically predict a given group's electoral strategies. Thus, the question of how economic elites organize to influence policymaking is analytically different from that of how many conservative parties there are in a party system. For instance, in the case of landowners, in a system where conservatives are fragmented in many parties, agrarian elites could choose to support any number of those conservative parties (all, one, none); or in systems with only one conservative party, landowners may try to secure influence in every administration by supporting both sides, conservatives and nonconservatives. The research question this book aims at answering is how agrarian elites organize their support of parties or candidates in a given system, not what explains that party system configuration.

Interest groups' decisions on how to organize their political representation, although not the main factor explaining party-system fragmentation, do have an impact on the supply side of party systems. Economic elites are core constituencies of conservative parties. Therefore, the existence of such parties is a product of elite groups' decisions to create and/or support them.

---

[43] See, for example, Taagepera and Shugart (1991), Carey and Shugart (1995), Cox (1997), Amorim Neto and Cox (1997), and Lijphart (1999).

[44] Exceptions are Freytes' (2015) work on agrarian elites in Argentina and Brazil, and Farrer's (2018) analysis of environmental groups in developed countries.

2.5 Alternative Explanations

This book claims that the existence of a conservative party (or parties) in a system is partially endogenous to economic (agrarian) elites' decision to invest in their formation. As developed in Section 2.3.2, elites' level of fragmentation conditions these decisions. Thus, it is not the case that agrarian elites will support a conservative party where a strong conservative party exists and that they would deploy another strategy where there is no such party. Rather, agrarian elites' strategic choice to support the building of a conservative party (or parties) contributes to the existence of such a party in the first place. This is more so during democratic transitions when parties are being formed and interest groups have greater chances to integrate with parties and shape their agendas and the selection of their candidates. One of the questions this book aims at answering is when agrarian elites will choose to support the creation of such parties.

According to the existing literature, there are three main ways in which electoral rules may shape landowners' political strategies. First, by influencing the chances of both agrarian parties and/or candidates of winning a seat through the overrepresentation of rural areas, or by allowing candidates to target exclusively rural constituencies. Second, by conditioning how parties structure themselves to compete in elections, making them more or less open to outsider candidates. Third, by affecting the levels of internal party discipline and party system fragmentation, shaping coalitional dynamics within legislatures, and conditioning the leverage small parties and individual legislators can have vis-à-vis the executive. I discuss each of these mechanisms next.

Electoral rules are constant at the country level and did not change in the studied countries during the period of analysis. Thus, if electoral rules were the main factor explaining agrarian elites' strategic choices, we should see landowners in a country pursuing the same strategy of political influence as other interest groups, and we would not observe agrarian elites deploying the same strategy across countries with different electoral rules. In addition, agrarian elites' strategies should not change during the period under analysis. Evidence from the analysed cases, however, reveals both that agrarian elites pursued similar strategies of political influence in countries with very different electoral rules, and that the strategies landowners deployed during the democratic transition were different from what other interest groups were doing in the same countries at that time. Moreover, in the Argentine case, agrarian elites changed strategies even when electoral rules did not change.

According to institutional explanations, electoral rules should predict where agrarian elites enter the electoral arena because agrarian candidates or agrarian parties' chances of winning a seat are shaped by district boundaries, district magnitude, and apportionment rules. Variation in these factors, however, fails to correctly predict observed differences in agrarian elites' strategies in Argentina, Brazil, and Chile. First, although authoritarian governments in the three analysed countries modified apportionment rules just before the transition to increase the representation of rural conservative districts in future elections (Snyder and Samuels 2004), agrarian elites did not enter the electoral arena in all three countries during the transition. Second, both Argentina and Brazil have systems that combine proportional representation with high magnitude districts. The literature argues such electoral systems lower the threshold for smaller groups to access the political system, as they reduce the psychological incentives for strategic voting (Amorim Neto and Cox 1997; Cox 1997). However, agrarian elites have successfully organized in the electoral arena only in Brazil. Agrarian elites' levels of perceived threat do a better job at predicting when landowners will enter the electoral arena in each of the analysed cases.

Electoral rules also fail to predict differences in the type of electoral strategy pursued by agrarian elites. Both Brazil's system of open-list proportional representation (OLPR) combined with high district magnitude and Chile's binomial system[45] created incentives for candidate-centered politics (Carey and Shugart 1995). Apportionment rules under the binomial system, where a list will only win both seats if it more than doubles the votes received by the second most-voted list, usually resulted in the election of one candidate from each of the two most-voted lists. Therefore, competition in Chilean legislative elections in the period under analysis was more intense between running mates than between candidates across lists. However, agrarian elites pursued a candidate-centered strategy only in Brazil while building a party in Chile. Even when the binomial system virtually guaranteed a seat for the right in each district, creating a huge incentive for conservative political elites in Chile to build a party, electoral rules per se cannot explain why agrarian elites supported that party instead of hedging their bets. Differences in agrarian elites' levels of political fragmentation do a better job at predicting these outcomes.

Differences between the incentives created by Argentina's closed-list proportional representation system (CLPR) and Brazil's OLPR have been proposed as the cause of Argentine producers' failure to organize

---

[45] The binominal system, changed in 2015, was in place throughout the period of analysis of this book.

in the electoral arena (Freytes 2015). According to this approach, OLPR in Brazil favors weak, ideologically loose parties and candidate-centered elections (Carey and Shugart 1995), which, in turn, facilitates interest groups infiltrating party lists (Ames 2001). In Argentina, in contrast, CLPR gives party leaders great control over nominations, making it harder for interest groups to win a place in the ballot. The problem with this account is that even when electoral rules make Brazilian parties easier to infiltrate than Argentine parties, it cannot explain why other interest groups have not followed agricultural producers' candidate-centered strategy in Brazil. The writing of a new constitution during the democratic transition was of great importance for many interest groups. However, while agrarian elites invested in a multiparty caucus to advance their interests in the 1987–1988 Constituent Assembly, industrialists invested in a nonelectoral strategy, creating two new lobbying associations, PNBE (National Thinking of the Business Bases) and UBE (Brazilian Union of Entrepreneurs).[46] Labor, on the other hand, channelized its representation through a new party, the Workers Party (PT), founded a few years earlier during the democratic transition. In the same vein, accounts based on electoral rules neither can explain why other interest groups, such as labor unions, have been successful in penetrating party structures in Argentina while agrarian elites have failed. Lastly, if landowners in Argentina had only considered the incentives created by electoral rules, they would have entered the electoral arena through party-building, as PR in combination with high district magnitude increases the electoral chances of small new parties while closed lists make existing parties harder to infiltrate. However, when the level of threat rose after the 2008 conflict, agrarian elites (unsuccessfully) deployed the candidate-centered strategy given their high political fragmentation. Table 2.4 summarizes predictions derived from electoral rules and observed outcomes with regards to agrarian elites' decisions to enter the electoral arena and which type of electoral strategy to pursue.

Electoral rules, like any institution, reflect the preferences of those who design them (North 1990, 16). Therefore, the historic overlap between agrarian elites and political elites in Latin America raises the question about the endogeneity of electoral rules with respect to agrarian elites' political interests, which I claim are shaped by their degree of intragroup fragmentation. This dynamic is clearer in the case of Brazil. As Mainwaring (1999, 38–39) has eloquently argued, the weakness of

---

[46] See Dreifuss (1989) and Schneider (1997; 2004).

TABLE 2.4 *Electoral rules and agrarian elites' strategies of political influence: predictions and observed outcomes*

	Argentina	Brazil	Chile[47]
Incentives to enter the electoral arena	Yes • Overrepresentation of rural districts • PR and high M lower thresholds to enter the electoral system	Yes • Overrepresentation of rural districts. • PR and high M lower thresholds to enter the electoral system.	Yes • Overrepresentation of rural districts • Binomial guarantees the right electoral success
Entered the electoral arena during the democratic transition?	No	Yes	Yes
Incentives for a candidate-centered versus partisan electoral strategy	Partisan • CLPR makes infiltrating existing parties harder • CLPR and high M create incentives to campaign on a partisan platform • PR and high M increase the electoral chances of small new parties	Mixed • OLPR makes infiltrating existing parties easier. • OLPR and high M create incentives to cultivate a personal reputation. • PR and high M increase the electoral chances of small new parties.	Candidate-centered • M=2 creates incentives to cultivate a personal reputation. • Binomial "rule to double" exacerbates competition between running mates.
Electoral strategy deployed	Candidate-centered (2009–2013)	Candidate-centered	Partisan

[47] Predictions are based on the binomial system in place until 2015.

Brazilian parties is explained by the desire of political elites and their economic allies to maintain a political system in which parties are not major actors. In that fashion, the OLPR system institutionalized traditional political elites' preferences for parties with loose structures that would allow them to attend to local interests with limited interference from national party leaders (Mainwaring 1999, 75). As will be analysed in more detail in Chapter 4, agrarian elites in Brazil were still a relevant political actor in rural municipalities during and after the democratic transition, competing among themselves for the control of local politics through rival clientelistic networks (Hagopian 1996, 19). Because these political divisions predate the consolidation of the post-1979 multiparty system, they cannot be explained by electoral rules. Even when the military dictatorship imposed a bipartisan system (1965–1979) agrarian elites were still divided among different factions of the pro-government ARENA (Jenks 1979; Kinzo 1988; Power 2000, Grinberg 2009). Moreover, political elites' (among them agrarian elites') preference for a fragmented party system where they could maintain control over their electoral bulwarks and preserve their local political autonomy explains why attempts during the 1987–1988 Constituent Assembly to replace OLPR with a German-style mixed-district system, as well as proposals to increase party leaders' control over legislators, failed (Mainwaring 1999, 258; Power, 2000; Ames 2001, 30). Summing up, because electoral rules crystalize the preferences of political elites and their economic allies, they cannot satisfactorily explain agrarian elites' political fragmentation, as they are partially endogenous to it.

2.5.3 The Relevance of Congress As a Policymaking Arena

Differences in the relevance of Congress as a policymaking arena are another alternative explanation for the variation in agricultural producers' strategies of political influence. Investing in an electoral strategy would only make sense where legislatures are a relevant arena for policy debate and design. In contrast, where most policies are decided by the executive, interest groups should focus on lobbying relevant agencies. In the three analysed countries, presidents have similarly extensive formal legislative powers (Mainwaring and Shugart 2003; Samuels and Shugart 2003). In Argentina, Brazil and Chile, presidents can veto bills passed by Congress and they can introduce new legislation through decree (avoiding legislative debate). In addition, presidents in Brazil and Chile have exclusive powers to introduce legislation in certain areas. All these give presidents in the three countries great control over the policy agenda. However, this has not discouraged agrarian elites in Brazil and Chile from investing in electoral representation. Moreover, even when agrarian elites in Brazil have penetrated sectoral agencies; for example, the Ministry of Agriculture, they have continued to invest in building representation in Congress (see Chapter 4).

The formal legislative powers of the executive are not, however, the only factor shaping the relevance of Congress as a policymaking arena. As developed by Mainwaring and Shugart (2003), the partisan powers of the president, defined as the share of seats in Congress held by the president's party and the president's ability to manage their own party, also shape presidents' control over the policy agenda. On this, the three analysed countries differ. Argentine presidents have stronger partisan powers than Brazilian or Chilean presidents. Between their respective democratic transitions and 2022, in both Brazil and Chile, the party of the president has almost never held a majority in both chambers,[48] while in Argentina presidents have held a legislative majority in both chambers 60 percent of the time.[49] In countries where the partisan powers of the president are lower, individual legislators' leverage vis-à-vis the executive is higher. Legislators can use this leverage to obtain policy favors from the executive. In this context, becoming a legislator has potentially high rates of return for businesses whose profitability depends in part on government regulations, increasing their incentives to enter the electoral arena (Schneider 2013, 144). Freytes (2015) argues that differences in coalitional dynamics within Congress due to high party-system fragmentation in Brazil and low fragmentation in Argentina explain why landowners have been able to successfully organize a congressional caucus in Brazil but not in Argentina.

I argue that even when the leverage that individual legislators have vis-à-vis the executive may affect the effectiveness of candidate-centered strategies, this does not determine the decision of interest groups to invest in an electoral strategy. For instance, Brazil's high party-system fragmentation requires presidents to build oversized and ideologically disconnected multipartisan legislative coalitions in order to govern (Power 2010). This indeed increases individual legislators bargaining power, augmenting the relevance of Congress as a policymaking arena. However, it also raises the incentives of interest groups to elect representatives to Congress *as*

---

[48] In Brazil, no president has held a majority in both chambers since 1990. In Chile, the second Bachelet administration (2014–2018) was the exception.

[49] Argentine presidents did not hold a majority in both chambers in 1984–1989, 1998–1999, 2000–2001, 2010–2011, and 2016–2019.

well as to lobby legislators. In fact, if we look at how different interest groups in Brazil have organized to influence policymaking in the legislative arena we will see that while agrarian elites have invested in electing their own legislators to build a multiparty caucus, industrialists have preferred to lobby legislators (Diniz and Boschi 2004; Mancuso 2004). Put differently, the relevance of Congress as a policymaking arena will increase interest groups' incentives to influence the legislative branch but it will not determine how they organize to exert that influence. Similarly, in Argentina, coalitional dynamics would indicate that in order to make a difference in Congress an interest group needs to engage in party-building – that is to say, develop organic ties with a major party the way unions did with Peronism. However, this is not what agrarian elites did when they entered the electoral arena in 2009, deploying a candidate-centered nonpartisan strategy instead.

Despite their limited capacity to explain agrarian elites' strategic choices, institutional factors do play a role in shaping feedback effects and reinforcing mechanisms behind the continuity of strategies of political influence down the path. As the case of Brazil shows (see Chapter 4), rising party-system fragmentation in the past decades has augmented the power of multiparty caucuses in the Brazilian Congress which, in turn, has increased agrarian elites' incentives to keep investing in a candidate-centered strategy. High fragmentation has made building legislative coalitions vital for Brazilian presidents, increasing small parties' expectations of extracting concessions from the executive, which, in turn, has encouraged further party-system fragmentation. In contrast, in Argentina, legislators' dependence on party-leaders limited the *agrodiputados'* capacity to advance sectoral interests after their election in 2009,[50] while low party fragmentation diluted individual legislators' leverage vis-à-vis the executive. As a consequence of these institutional limitations, the *agrodiputados* failed to deliver the expected policy changes, leading producers to abandon the strategy in the subsequent elections.

2.6 CONCLUSION

This chapter presented a theory to explain agrarian elites' strategies of political influence. I argue that agrarian elites' choice to enter the electoral arena is conditioned by the policy threats they face. When agrarian

---

[50] *Agrodiputados* is how the group of representatives elected to the Argentine Congress in 2009 that were agricultural producers and participated in the 2008 protests is popularly known.

elites are confronted with an existential threat – a policy that jeopardizes the continuity of their business – their incentives to enter the electoral arena to protect themselves will rise. Absent this kind of threat, agrarian elites will prefer nonelectoral strategies of political influence which, although less likely to secure policy influence, are much cheaper than electoral ones. The type of electoral strategy agrarian elites will pursue, in turn, is shaped by their level of fragmentation. Internal cleavages within the agrarian elites, which can have diverse origins, will increase the coordination costs of party-building, rendering the strategy unviable. Under conditions of high fragmentation, agrarian elites will invest in a candidate-centered electoral strategy, which requires less coordination among different factions within the group in terms of developing a territorial structure or deciding on candidatures, and allows them to preserve their local political autonomy.

I argue that the strategic choices agrarian elites made at the democratic transition are especially consequential for their political organization later on. Democratic transitions were times of exceptional political fluidity that opened up the electoral arena to interest groups. After the first few elections, existing linkages between parties and core constituencies consolidated, making it harder to build new ones. Thus, in the countries where agrarian elites organized in the electoral arena to respond to an existential threat during the democratic transition, they were better positioned to fight threatening policies from center-left governments later on.

3

Chile

Agrarian Elites and the Rebuilding of the Partisan Right

3.1 INTRODUCTION

Before the last democratic transition, Chilean agrarian elites were the epitome of the undemocratic landowner often referenced in the comparative politics literature. However, starting in 1958, the political changes that culminated in one of the most redistributive land reforms in the history of Latin America destroyed the source of Chilean landowners' political power: the control over the votes of the peasants living in their latifundia. The loss of their old source of power, however, does not seem to have crippled agrarian elites' capacity to defend their interests in the new democracy. In the thirty-two years that have passed since the last democratic transition and 2022 – twenty-four of them under a center-left administration – agrarian elites have been able to veto or crucially modify changes to the labor, tax, and environmental legislation left in place by the Pinochet dictatorship (1973–1990) that threatened their interests.

This chapter shows how agrarian elites have protected their interests in democratic Chile by becoming a core constituency of the rightwing parties, in particular Renovación Nacional (RN). Core constituencies support a party by contributing financial, ideological, political, and/or human resources (Gibson 1992; Fairfield 2015a). Moreover, a party's policy positions should reflect the preferences of its core constituencies. The chapter presents evidence of landowners' financial support of the partisan right, of their identification with the legislators of the right, and of the programmatic convergence between agrarian elites' preferences and the policy positions of RN and the Unión Demócrata Independiente (UDI).

This chapter argues that agrarian elites in Chile decided to invest in an electoral strategy of political influence at the time of the democratic transition because they feared a center-left government would endanger their property rights. It presents evidence of how this perceived threat was founded on the landowners' previous experience with democracy during the 1965–1973 period, when their farms were expropriated. As developed in Chapter 2, the perception of an existential threat incentivized agrarian elites to invest in an electoral strategy since nonelectoral strategies appeared unreliable in the environment of high uncertainty that surrounded the democratic transition. Agrarian elites doubted the Concertación's willingness to continue with the neoliberal model installed by the authoritarian regime. In addition, they feared that lobbying strategies would be ineffective to influence the policy agenda of the center-left as previous Christian Democratic and Socialist governments had cut off landowners' informal access to the state. Thus, anticipating a Concertación victory in the presidential elections after Pinochet's defeat in the 1988 referendum, Chilean agrarian elites joined conservative politicians in the (re)building of the partisan right to secure representation of their interests in Congress.

The low fragmentation of the economic elite decreased coordination costs and facilitated the building of a party to represent conservative interests in Chile. Also, the electoral system designed by the dictatorship for the new democracy augmented the chances of the right while punishing fragmentation. Chilean economic elites have historically been highly cohesive, sharing strong social and family ties as well as economic interests. The structural transformation of Chile during the military government (1973–1990) further reinforced this cohesion by giving economic elites a common policy agenda: the continuation of the free-market economy model into the democratic era. Moreover, unlike Brazil where landowners controlled rival political machines in rural areas, in Chile landowners lacked competing prior political investments and therefore had nothing to lose in joining a new partisan structure. The binomial electoral system guaranteed the partisan right a strong representation in Congress but only if they competed in a unified front.[1] This, in turn, increased economic elites' incentives to support a single party that could function as a veto player against the reformist agenda of the Concertación.

---

[1] Because of its seat-allocation rule, the electoral system designed by the military made it very hard for the most-voted list to gain both seats at play in a district, splitting most districts between the left and right. See Section 3.2.2 for more details.

3.2 Agriculture and Politics: Historical Background

The rest of the chapter is organized as follows. Section 3.2 reviews the role of landowners as political actors in Chile before the last democratic transition. Section 3.3 develops the argument. First, it shows how the memory of land reform during the governments of Frei Montalva (1964–1970) and Allende (1970–1973) made elites overestimate the threat posed by a potential victory by the Concertación, leading them to organize in the electoral arena. Then, it shows how agrarian elites' low fragmentation, both in terms of economic and political interests, as well as the incentives created by the new electoral system designed during the military regime, facilitated building a conservative party. Section 3.4 presents evidence of landowners' investment in the partisan right in terms of ideological, financial, and human resources. Section 3.5 analyses the case of Aylwin's tax reform to show how the partisan strategy of political influence works as well as to illustrate its policy implications.

3.2 AGRICULTURE AND POLITICS IN CHILE: HISTORICAL BACKGROUND

3.2.1 Agrarian Elites' Corporatist Organizations

The National Society of Agriculture (SNA) is the main and oldest organization of agricultural producers in Chile. It was the first business association to be founded in the country, in 1838, and represents medium and large producers across Chile. However, the interests of large producers in the fertile Central Valley have historically been hegemonic within the SNA. The SNA is a federation grouping both individual producers as well as regional and crop-specific associations.

The Federation of Fruit Producers (Fedefruta) is the other main agriculture corporatist association in contemporary Chile. It was founded by fruit producers in 1985 to advance their specific policy demands. The Federation groups individual producers as well as regional associations and today represents around 24,000 producers across the country.[2] Fedefruta is affiliated with the SNA and there is much overlap among their leadership. With the exception of exchange rate polices,[3] the two

---

[2] Author's interview with Juan Carlos Sepúlveda, CEO of FEDEDRUTA. Santiago, September 26, 2016.
[3] Producers in Fedefruta unanimously support a weak Chilean peso that will make their products more competitive in the international market, while some in SNA producing exclusively for the domestic market (ranchers and grain producers) prefer a strong Chilean peso.

associations share the same policy preferences (i.e., a flexible labor market, free trade, and minimum state intervention in the economy) and frequently work together on policy proposals.

3.2.2 Agrarian Elites Before 1965: Legislative Power in a Restricted Democracy

Before the 1973 coup, Chile stood out among Latin American countries for its political stability. While most countries in the region suffered recurrent military interventions throughout the twentieth century, Chile sustained a democratic regime between 1932 and 1973. The secret of Chilean political stability lay, however, in the limited character of its democracy which did not reach the countryside (Wright 1981; Silva 1987; Correa 2005).

Until the mid 1960s, Chilean landowners enjoyed extended access to the policymaking process through their representatives in Congress and through informal relations with high-ranking government officials. Landowners were well represented in the Chilean Congress thanks to their capacity to control the votes of the rural poor living on their lands through the *inquilinaje* system.[4] Until the 1960s, rural workers were the largest category within the labor force. According to Wright (1981, 53), landowners had direct control over an agricultural labor force of some 40,000 workers and exercised considerable influence over some 150,000 small holders who looked to them for credit and seasonal employment. In a context of restricted democracy where less than 10 percent of the population participated in elections (Bethell 1993, 93),[5] the votes of the rural poor controlled by landowners amounted to a significant share of the electorate. In fact, Baland and Robinson's (2008) analysis of the 1957 parliamentary election shows that the proportion of *inquilinos* in a municipality was highly correlated with the share of votes for rightwing parties. Even when most peasants were illiterate and therefore could not vote according to the electoral law, in practice, landlords deployed

---

[4] *Inquilinaje* was a rural labor system inherited from the colonial period in which peasants were allowed to live on their patron's land in exchange for their labor. All members of the family had to work for the patron. Landowners controlled the rule of law and the police within their latifundia.

[5] Until the expansion of the electorate in 1952, the exclusion of women and illiterates (approximately 25 percent of the population) reduced the electorate to some 20 percent of the population. Among those eligible to vote, fewer than half usually registered (Bethell 1993, 93).

3.2 Agriculture and Politics: Historical Background

several gimmicks to circumvent this restriction (Valenzuela 1977, 207).[6] Until 1958, when a reform of the voting system put an end to fraudulent practices in the countryside, control over the peasant vote in addition to the overrepresentation of rural districts in Congress gave landowners disproportionate political power in relation to their economic weight. Moreover, agrarian elites were directly represented in Congress, as many politicians in the parties of the right and center were landowners themselves (Remmer 1984; Zeitlin and Ratcliff 1988). Their political strength, in turn, gave agrarian elites the ability to neutralize any policy attempting to modify property or power relations in rural areas. As Wright (1981, 80) puts it, through their representatives in Congress and their contacts in the executive, landowners made sure that reformist policies towards the countryside "contained a maximum of good intentions and a minimum of teeth." Thus, while economic elites in other Latin American countries had to summon the military each time democratic governments threatened their interests, Chilean agrarian elites did not need to: they had Congress.

Chilean landowners' capacity to influence policymaking was, however, tied to the electoral success of the partisan right. Consequently, Chilean elites' commitment to democracy started to fade with the landslide victory of the Christian Democrats in 1965, who swept the right out of Congress, leaving the agrarian elites without partisan representation (Wright 1981; Correa 2005). In what was the worst performance of the partisan right in Chilean history until then, Conservative and Liberals elected only 9 out of 147 deputies to the Lower Chamber, losing 36 seats. Only one of the deputies elected in 1965 was a member of SNA (Carrière 1980, 65), down from 11 members of Congress during 1961–1965 and 15 in 1958–1961. Their legislative majority allowed Christian Democrats to advance two policies that the landed elites had fought off for decades: unionization of rural workers and land reform, both sanctioned in 1967.

In addition to losing effective representation in Congress, the agrarian elites also saw their informal access to the executive cut off with the triumph of the Christian Democrats and the Socialists in the presidential elections of 1964 and 1970 respectively. Until then, the SNA had had close ties, by virtue of family and class, with cabinet members – who were often SNA members themselves – in all administrations (Carrière 1980). Moreover, it was frequently the case that the ministry

---

[6] In her vivid portrait of Chilean elites, Stabili (2003) reports testimonies of these practices in the countryside.

of agriculture was a former leader of the SNA.[7] By contrast, no cabinet members in the Frei Montalva (1964–1970) or Allende (1970–1973) governments were members of SNA, and the association's ties to officials in these administrations were very tenuous (Carrière 1980, 60). This, added to the loss of their representation in Congress, seriously diminished the landowners' capacity to influence Christian Democrat policies towards the sector, namely land reform and rural labor regulations. When Salvador Allende's government accelerated and radicalized the implementation of these reforms, the agrarian elites lost all interest in the continuity of democracy. They mobilized to destabilize Allende's government and wholeheartedly supported Pinochet's September 1973 military coup.

3.3 LANDOWNERS INVEST IN A PARTY: EXISTENTIAL THREATS AND ELITE COHESION

The main argument of this book is that agrarian elites will enter the electoral arena when facing an existential threat and that the type of electoral strategy they will pursue will be conditioned by their level of fragmentation. In this section, first, I present evidence of how fear that a government of the center-left Concertación would implement policies that jeopardized the continuity of their business prompted Chilean agrarian elites to organize in the electoral arena during the democratic transition. Then, I show how cohesion within the agrarian elite lowered the costs of party-building in Chile. Lastly, I describe how agrarian elites in Chile supported the (re)building of the partisan right during the democratic transition.

3.3.1 High Perceived Threat during the Democratic Transition: The Trauma of Land Reform

Agrarian elites in Chile decided to enter the electoral arena during the democratic transition because they felt threatened by the prospects of a new center-left administration. Landowners' perception of threat rose when the military government announced a plebiscite on the authoritarian regime for October 1988. A government defeat in the plebiscite would lead to free and competitive elections being held, opening up the

---

[7] Between the creation of the ministry in 1924 and 1940, SNA directors occupied the office 35 percent of the time (Wright 1981, 90).

3.3 Landowners Invest in a Party

possibility of a victory by the center-left. Based on their previous experience during the governments of Frei Montalva and Allende, who implemented land reform through expropriation, landowners in Chile feared that a new administration by the Christian Democrats and Socialists would similarly advance policies against their interests. As argued in Chapter 2, due to their lower reliability, nonelectoral strategies of political influence were not suitable in this context where failing to influence policymaking could have deleterious consequences for agrarian elites. Moreover, agrarian elites had reasons to believe the chances of influencing the Concertación's policy agenda through lobbying were slim. In the past, agrarian elites' attempts to influence the policy agenda of Christian Democrats and Socialists through lobbying had failed. Likewise, during the democratic transition, agrarian elites' ties to politicians in the Concertación were weak. In this unfavorable context, landowners needed a strategy that – unlike lobbying, which entails persuading legislators who may or may not be sympathetic to agrarian interests – could secure the election of like-minded policymakers.

In retrospect, observers may find it difficult to believe that there was an existential threat to agrarian elites in Chile in the late 1980s and early 1990s and dismiss landowners' statements to that effect as mere overreaction or political posturing. After all, in the three decades since the democratic transition, the country has held fast to neoliberalism and the multiple Concertación administrations, even those led by Socialists, have been highly responsive to business interests. Indeed, scholars studying the Chilean democratic transition have highlighted the power of the military to shape its terms (Haggard and Kaufman 1995), especially the institutional safeguards the military built into the 1980 constitution to avoid drastic policy swings (Garretón 2003). Moreover, the popularity of the authoritarian regime and its neoliberal economic model among the business community at the time of the democratic transition, led Concertación leaders to emphasize their attachment to the market economy during the 1989 campaign in the hope of winning entrepreneurs' trust (Haggard and Kaufman 1995).

While there is no denying of those facts, I would like to bring the readers' attention to two issues. First, it is not a problem for my theory if agrarian elites overestimated the threat that the transition to democracy posed to their interests, as my operationalization of existential threat includes a subjective dimension. What matters for my argument is that agrarian elites *believed* Concertación governments could implement policies that jeopardize the continuity of their business. The evidence gathered from multiple sources for this study shows they did. This belief was based on their traumatic memories of the land reform years – which had been revived by the insurrectional protests of the mid 1980s – as well as on the actual policy agenda of the center-left. Second, and relatedly, the fact that Concertación administrations did not implement policies that seriously challenged business interests does not mean they did not intend to. As we will see, the policy agenda of the center-left included modifications to the framework of low taxation and lax labor and environmental regulations in which agricultural producers in Chile were thriving. That these modifications failed to pass should not be interpreted as evidence that the agrarian elites had nothing to fear during the democratic transition but, on the contrary, as an outcome of landowners' political organization which was sparked precisely by fear of the Concertación's agenda.

Archival and interview evidence gathered for this study shows that, despite the reassurance of a military-sanctioned constitution and the efforts of the leaders of the Concertación to appear business-friendly, Chilean agrarian elites still felt deeply threatened by the democratic transition. This perception of threat was rooted in the traumatic experience of the 1965–1973 land reform. The memory of the radical land reform process shaped agrarian elites' perceptions towards the parties of the Concertación in particular and the distributive dangers of democracy in general. In consonance with previous studies of Chilean business elites during the transition years,[8] I found that since the political parties making up the Concertación were the same parties that had implemented land reform in the previous democratic period, agrarian elites believed that their property rights would be in danger if these parties came back to power.

The Chilean case highlights the subjective dimension of the explanatory factor threat. In the Brazilian case analysed in Chapter 4, agrarian elites' investment in an electoral strategy was triggered by the *actual* implementation of expropriating policies. In Chile, in contrast, agrarian elites' past experience with democracy biased their calculations, making them overestimate the likelihood that a center-left administration would attack their property rights. Fear that the parties that had implemented land reform in the past could advance similar redistributive policies in the new democratic era pushed agrarian elites to invest in parliamentary representation even when the actual policy agenda of the Concertación did not include confiscatory policies.[9]

---

[8] See, for example, Frieden (1991), Bartell (1995), and Rehren (1995).
[9] See Aylwin (1988).

3.3.1.1 *Land Reform in Chile, 1965–1973*

The Chilean land reform of 1965–1973 stands out among others in the region for two reasons. First, unlike other redistributive land reforms advanced by Communist revolutionary regimes (e.g., Cuba 1959–1964) or military dictatorships (e.g., Peru 1969–1975), the Chilean land reform was implemented by democratically elected governments. Moreover, in the case of Frei Montalva's, it was not a far-left government that advanced land reform, but a center-left administration that had counted with the electoral support of the right.[10] Second, its extent and redistributive character set the Chilean land reform apart from other similar experiences in Latin America. The land reform implemented by the Frei Montalva and Allende administrations was the most radical ever executed by a democratic government in the history of the region. In less than ten years, all large estates in the country, productive or unproductive, were eliminated. Between 1965 and 1973, nearly 67 percent of the country's agricultural land was expropriated (Garrido et al. 1988, 175), amounting to 10 million hectares (Table 3.1). In contrast to other initiatives in the region where state-owned land was distributed or where landowners subject to expropriation were compensated,[11]

TABLE 3.1 *Expropriated land: Chile, 1965–1973*

Year	Number of farms	Total area (ha)
1965	99	539,723
1966	265	525,171
1967	217	284,889
1968	223	655,867
1969	314	868,848
1970	297	1,218,349
1971	1,374	2,028,599
1972	2,189	3,099,246
1973	831	835,208
Total	5,809	10,055,900

Source: Garrido et al. (1988, 174).

[10] In the 1964 elections, Conservatives and Liberals supported Frei Montalva in the hope of avoiding a Socialist victory.
[11] For instance, during the land reform process in Colombia in the 1960s, half of the lands affected were public, and private owners were compensated at market value, 10 percent in cash and the rest in bonds (Lynch 1993; Lapp 2004). Similarly, in Brazil, only one-third of the land distributed through land reform between 1985 and 2005 came from the expropriation of private holdings; the rest was public land owned by

Chilean landowners saw their lands expropriated without any monetary compensation,[12] divided and given to their former workers.

The process of land reform formally started in 1962 during the Alessandri administration (1958–1964) when, in line with the recommendations of the Alliance for Progress, a law authorizing the expropriation of unproductive farms was promulgated and an agency charged with implementing land reform (the Land Reform Corporation, CORA in Spanish) as well as another providing technical assistance to small peasants (Agricultural Development Institute, INDAP in Spanish) were created. At the time, land reform was seen as a modernizing tool that would both increase the low productivity of the Chilean agricultural sector – which had not produced enough food to feed the country's growing population since the 1940s,[13] as well as prevent the radicalization of the peasantry by improving their extremely poor living conditions (Correa 2005). Diminishing land inequality in the country was not, however, among President Alessandri's priorities. The extent of the land reform during his administration was very limited, gaining it the epithet of "the flowerpot reform."[14] Only 358,000 hectares were expropriated, with no real impact on the country's land tenure structure. By 1965, latifundia in the Central Valley – the most fertile land in the country – still occupied more than half (55.3 percent) of arable land while small holdings, which made up 82 percent of the farms, occupied only 9.7 percent of the land (Bethell 1993, 152). Nevertheless, the institutions created by Alessandri, CORA, and INDAP would play crucial roles in the expansion of land reform during the Frei Montalva and Allende administrations.

It was during the Christian Democrats' administration that the process of land reform started to take shape. Frei Montalva promulgated a new land reform law in 1967 and a constitutional amendment facilitating expropriation. After this amendment, the Constitution no longer guaranteed the inviolability of private property and compensation in

---

federal or state governments (Ondetti 2008, 229). Moreover, most expropriated private holdings in Brazil were underutilized lands located far from economic centers, which in many cases their owners were happy to sell given the government's generous compensation (Pereira 2003).

[12] However, landowners were allowed to keep 80 irrigation hectares of their former holdings, equivalent to a mid size farm.

[13] While between 1935 and 1939, agriculture had an annual commercial surplus of US$11.8 million, the sector's annual commercial deficit was US$67.8 million between 1953 and 1957 (Correa 2005, 236). By 1965, the cost of food imports was equivalent to 22.2 percent of the value of nonagricultural exports (Bethell 1993, 137).

[14] "*Reforma del macetero*" in Spanish.

cash to owners of expropriated estates was abolished (Garrido et al., 1988, 131). As a consequence, land reform accelerated considerably and during Frei Montalva's administration, around 3.6 million hectares were expropriated, amounting to 15.1 percent of the country's total area.

Another crucial step in transforming power relations in the countryside was the promulgation of the peasant unionization law in 1967. This law allowed for the organization of rural workers, something the landowners had fought for decades. Thanks to this change in legislation, and the organizational efforts of Christian Democrats and the left who competed to win the electoral support of the peasantry (Scully 1992), rural unions grew from 32 in 1965 to over 400 in 1969, with more than 100,000 peasants unionized (Table 3.2). Numerous rural cooperatives and peasant committees were also created. By 1970, 18 percent of rural workers were unionized (Valenzuela 1978, 30), an impressive number taking into account that five years before that percentage was practically zero. The unionization law empowered peasants who had endured poor living conditions and repression for decades. Unionized workers started organizing strikes demanding better wages and working conditions, as well as land occupations to pressure the government to speed up land reform. The number of strikes skyrocketed from only 13 in 1963 to almost 700 in 1967 (Table 3.2). Land occupations also multiplied towards the end of the Frei Montalva administration.

TABLE 3.2 *Unions, strikes, and land occupations in the countryside: Chile, 1963–1973*

Year	Number of unions	Unionized peasants	Strikes	Land occupations
1963	22	1,500	13	0
1964	24	1,658	45	0
1965	32	2,118	142	13
1966	201	10,417	586	18
1967	211	42,474	693	9
1968	371	78,419	648	26
1969	421	104,666	1,127	148
1970	510	114,112	1,580	456
1971	632	127,782	1,054	1,278
1972	709	136,527	796	307[a]
1973	870	229,836	316[b]	n.a.

[a] Up to March 1972.
[b] Up to September 1973.
Source: Author, based on Valenzuela (1978) and Garrido et al. (1988, 106).

The land reform and peasant unionization laws implemented by the Christian Democrats disrupted the power relations that had held sway over rural life until then. Together with their lands, agrarian elites also lost the capacity to control the peasants working for them. The Christian Democrats took from agrarian elites not only their source of income but also their base of political power and social status. As a consequence, conservatives felt betrayed by Frei Montalva whom they had supported in the 1964 election to prevent an Allende victory. The fact that the center-left was implementing the very same policies agrarian elites had dreaded from a Socialist government engendered a profound mistrust towards the Christian Democrats that would persist into the post-Pinochet era.

Under the legal framework passed by the Christian Democrats, Socialist Salvador Allende accelerated and radicalized the land reform process. In his first year in office, Allende seized over 1,300 farms, 300 more than the total number expropriated during the Frei Montalva administration (Valenzuela 1978, 53) (Table 3.1). In just three years, his government expropriated 6.6 million hectares, virtually all remaining large estates, in a context of increasing violence. Peasant unionization continued and accelerated during the government of Allende while rural unrest escalated to unprecedented proportions. By 1973, peasant unions had grown to 870, with some 230,000 members (Table 3.2). In the first year of Allende's government the number of occupied farms increased threefold, reaching a record high of 1,278 (Table 3.2).

The radicalization of the land reform process and growing unrest in the countryside, added to the fact that landed elites had no access to the Allende administration, led agrarian elites to pursue nondemocratic means to protect their interests. Through their corporatist association, SNA, landowners played a leading role in business' destabilization efforts against the government of the Unidad Popular. Landowners actively participated in the business lockouts organized against Allende in 1972 and 1973. Moreover, through their radio station, which had a vast audience in rural areas across the country, SNA leaders encouraged the military to intervene and put an end to Allende's socialist experiment (Silva 1992).

Soon after assuming office, the military government implemented a series of counter-reform measures dismantling both land reform and the unionization of rural workers. Of the land expropriated during the land reform process, 35 percent was returned to its former owners.

Another 16 percent was auctioned off, while 34 percent was distributed to peasants.[15] However, due to lack of access to credit and technical assistance, around 60 percent of these peasants ended up selling their plots of land to larger producers (Bethell 1993, 184), which favored a re-concentration of landownership in the countryside. At the same time that the land reform was being dismantled, the military intervened rural unions. Persecuted, union leaders were also forbidden from owning land reform parcels. Peasant unionization dropped drastically from 38.1 percent in 1971 to 7.1 percent in 1985. Similarly, the number of strikes plummeted from a record of 1,054 in 1971 to only 1 in 1985, and even after the return to democracy, there were only 9 strikes in 1992 (Kurtz 1999, 285). Due to the rural unions being quashed, which curtailed the peasants' capacity to bargain collectively or to ensure even the most basic labor rights, and the disciplining effects of growing unemployment,[16] Chilean landowners were able to benefit from a cheap, docile labor force.

The process of democratization of the Chilean countryside that started with the electoral reforms of 1958 and abruptly ended with the military dictatorship of Pinochet, restructured agrarian elites' political allegiances and crucially shaped their stance toward democracy. The electoral reform of 1958 freed peasants from the landlords' political control,[17] creating a new constituency that the center-left and left were eager to mobilize (Scully 1992). Electoral competition for the peasant vote and the unionization of rural workers made possible by the Christian Democrat's law of 1967, empowered the peasantry to demand land and better living conditions which, in turn, pressured the government into accelerating the land reform process. As a consequence, in the landowners' experience, democratic competition was inextricably

---

[15] The rest of the expropriated land was transferred to the state (land reform records retrieved from: www.indap.gob.cl/reforma-agraria (accessed April 6, 2019)).
[16] Unemployment grew from 5.7 percent in 1970 to 16.5 percent in 1975 and to more than 30 percent in 1982 (Bethell 1993, 186).
[17] Until 1958, each party printed their own ballots separately. Thus, each landlord could just give his *inquilinos* the ballot of the candidate he favored and take them to the polling place. Baland and Robinson (2008) found that after the introduction of the Australian ballot system, the electoral advantage of the right decreased in localities with more pervasive patron–client relations. Relatedly, Baland and Robinson (2012) show that this change in the voting system led to a fall of about 26 percent in land prices in the areas where these patron–client relationships were predominant, suggesting the political value of those holdings decreased as well.

associated with the kind of social mobilization that could push even center-left governments to implement radical redistributive policies. By contrast, Pinochet's authoritarian regime had restored their property rights and the balance of power in the countryside. Thus, from the perspective of Chilean agrarian elites, there was much to lose with democratization, even under a moderate administration.

3.3.1.2 *The Land Reform Trauma and the Decision to Invest in Electoral Representation*

As can be inferred from the description in the previous subsection, the land reform was a very traumatic event for agrarian elites in Chile and one that, as I learned from my fieldwork in the country in 2016, continued to inform their political views fifty years later. Six out of the thirteen leaders of producers' associations and two out of the five legislators who are also farm producers whom I interviewed brought up the subject of the land reform of the 1960s and 1970s without prompting. As a former president of Fedefruta put it, "the land reform is a thorn that every agricultural producer carries inside themselves and our skins are really thin, anything related to it immediately hurts."[18] Along the same lines, Luis Mayol, minister of agriculture under Sebastián Piñera and former SNA president told me, "What the land reform does is to remind everybody in the [agricultural] sector that these things do happen, that they may happen."[19] These views were shared by many of my interviewees. Five of the thirteen leaders of producers' associations and two of the five producers-legislators whom I interviewed referred to the land reform as a "traumatic event." Another example of how the land reform is still vividly remembered today by Chilean landowners as a tragedy is the full-page letter that the SNA published in the Sunday edition of *El Mercurio* – the largest and oldest newspaper in the country – in July 2017, on the fiftieth anniversary of the land reform, lamenting the government celebration of the event. In the letter, the SNA president described the land reform as "one of the most traumatic events in Chilean history, causing death, destruction and scarcity" and "the first step leading to the breakdown of the rule of law and, eventually, democracy in Chile."[20] Seeing the distress with which agrarian elites remember the land reform fifty years later, even after four

---

[18] Author's interview with Juan Carolus Brown, Santiago, October 4, 2016.
[19] Author's interview, Santiago, October 20, 2016.
[20] See "La SNA ante la celebración de la Reforma Agraria," *El Mercurio*, July 30, 2017.

Concertación administrations that had been very respectful of property rights, it should not be surprising that landowners at the time felt threatened by the democratic transition and a prospective electoral victory by the center-left.

My analysis of the editorials of *El Campesino* – the SNA magazine – and the speeches of SNA leaders at their members' annual assemblies in the 1987–1989 period reveals the landowners' anxiety with respect to the security of their property rights in a future democracy. SNA leaders were particularly concerned about a democratic government ceding to social pressure for redistribution. Thus, they believed that in order to preserve their property rights, they needed to convince Chilean society of the valuable contributions that agriculture made to the country's economy. SNA leaders urged its members to show society that the abusive, unproductive landowner was a myth of the past. Producers should showcase their modern farms and improve their workers' conditions as much as possible. The reasoning was that democratic governments would have no incentives to implement land reform if there was no social demand for it.[21] In addition, in late 1987, the SNA started pressuring the military government to repeal the land reform decrees that were still formally in place from the last democratic period, so that an eventual center-left government would not have the legal tools to expropriate their lands. To the landowners' relief, the military government did so before the 1988 plebiscite.

Agricultural elites were especially suspicious of the Christian Democrats' presidential candidate, and later president, Patricio Aylwin because of his participation in the design of the land reform during Frei Montalva's government.[22] Bill 17,280 – known as "Aylwin's Law" – was introduced by the then senator to facilitate the expropriation of farms for the land reform. This law authorized CORA to take immediate possession of the expropriated estates, reducing the owners' possibility of appealing in the courts. These key modifications under the Aylwin Law allowed for an acceleration of the land reform process, first under Frei Montalva and then Allende (Garrido et al. 1988, 126).

Public opinion data from the period around the plebiscite confirm that a significant proportion of businesspeople feared their property rights would not be protected in the new democracy. A survey of small and

---

[21] *El Campesino* 118, no. 11 (November 1987), 27–31; 119, no. 11 (November 1988), 38–41; 120, no. 11 (November 1989), 28.

[22] Author's interview with Mayol. See also Rehren (1995).

medium entrepreneurs in Santiago conducted by the Centro de Estudios Políticos y Sociales (CEP), one of Chile's most prestigious think tanks, in September 1987 showed that 42.8 percent of respondents believed it was likely that a land reform would be implemented while 47.5 percent said that private firms will be nationalized if the parties opposing Pinochet won the 1989 elections.[23]

Other scholars studying Chilean conservative business and political elites during the democratic transition similarly highlight how the traumatic experiences of the 1960s and 1970s shaped these elites' distrustful views of the Concertación. For instance, Bartell's (1995, 64–67) interviews with Chilean economic elites in 1987 and 1988 – right before the plebiscite that kicked off the democratic transition – revealed that a significant proportion of businesspeople felt anxious about the extent to which center-left politicians would preserve their property rights and implement market friendly policies. Similarly to what I observed thirty years later, his interviewees frequently cited collective memories of land reform during the governments of Frei Montalva and Allende as a source of their mistrust (Bartell 1995, 65). Likewise, in his analysis of Chilean business associations during the democratic transition, Rehren (1995, 19–20) notes that the SNA mounted the strongest opposition to the Concertación during the plebiscite and how its rejection of Aylwin was based on the land reform experience during the Christian Democrat administration of 1964–1970. In the same vein, Weyland (2019, 127) recalls how a leader of the right began an interview he conducted in 2007 about the democratic transition by producing the "Resolution of Chillán," a 1967 document where the Socialist Party had committed to armed struggle.

Agrarian elites' perception of threat was not only based on the distant memory of the land reform, but also on the more recent massive, insurrectional protests of 1983–1986. As a reaction to the economic debacle of 1982,[24] mass protests erupted across the country, almost paralyzing the nation (Garretón 1987). Protests were spearheaded first by labor unions and then by shantytown dwellers (*pobladores*). Led by the Communists, *pobladores* organized in self-defense groups carried out violent street demonstrations (Oxhorn 1995). This was part of the

---

[23] "Estudio Social y de Opinión Pública entre Pequeños y Medianos Empresarios de Santiago. Septiembre 1987," CEP, Documento de Trabajo N 95, available at: www.cepchile.cl/cep/site/docs/20160304/20160304092757/cuestionario_ddeto95.pdf (accessed, April 9, 2019).

[24] Chile's GDP dropped 14 percent while unemployment skyrocketed to around 24 percent of the workforce (Weyland 2014, 196).

3.3 Landowners Invest in a Party 81

Communist's Party strategy of "popular rebellion" that included from nonviolent tactics, such as protests, to bombings and guerrilla warfare and aimed at generating a state of ungovernability that would force a democratic transition (Roberts 1998; Weyland 2014). However, this strategy had the opposite effect, galvanizing business and conservative elites' support for the military (Frieden 1991; Weyland 2014). The spectacle of hundreds of thousands of Chileans fighting the authoritarian regime on the streets reminded business elites of the dangers of democracy. If civil society had mobilized so strongly under the dictatorship, despite the regime's crude repression, then who knew what could happen under conditions more auspicious to social mobilization.[25]

More importantly, in addition to the uncertainty surrounding the new democratic government's commitment to the protection of their property rights, agrarian elites had tangible reasons to fear a center-left administration since the Concertación's policy agenda included a series of reforms that could affect the viability of the neoliberal model in the countryside. During the dictatorship, modern agricultural producers had thrived in a context of very lax labor and environmental regulations and low taxation. In its 1989 government program, the Concertación stated its intentions to both change the labor law, empowering unions, and make the country's tax scheme more progressive by, among other things, eliminating tax cuts benefiting business (Marcel 1997; Rehren 1995).

A Concertación victory could mean the empowerment of unions, more stringent labor and environmental regulations, and an increased tax burden on business,[26] resulting in the alteration of power relations in the countryside and in a reduction on the agrarian elites' profit margins. Based on the center-left coalition's program and their previous experiences with those parties, agrarian elites expected the Concertación governments to advance policies with an "antibusiness bias" and were skeptical, at least at first, of the center-left commitment to maintaining the free market economic model.[27] As one of them put it, "regarding labor regulations, for

---

[25] As Sergio Molina explained to Jeff Frieden in an interview in 1985, business will not support the democratic opposition to the regime, even after all the Christian Democrats' reassurances about their commitment to private property, because "businessmen worry about the social demands that would arise from civil society with democracy" (Frieden 1991, 174).

[26] See "Compromiso Económico y Social por el No," in Aylwin (1988).

[27] Author's interviews with Juan Andrés Fontaine, minister for the economy during the first Piñera administration, Santiago, October 12, 2016; Ricardo Ariztía de Castro, SNA and CPC president, Santiago, November 15, 2016; Gastón Caminondo, president

instance, agricultural producers naturally do not expect center-left governments to do much except making your life harder."[28]

Given these high stakes as well as their previous experience with Christian Democrat and Socialist administrations cutting off their channels of informal access, agrarian elites decided to invest in an electoral strategy of political influence for the new democratic era. As argued in Chapter 2, in these threatening circumstances, nonelectoral strategies were inadequate given their lower reliability. In their view, failing to influence the policy agenda of the new democratic government could have serious consequences for agrarian elites who believed that the center-left would pursue policies that in the best-case scenario would reduce their profits and, in the worst, expropriate their assets. In this context, agrarian elites could not rely on their capacity to persuade Concertación politicians, they needed to elect legislators that already shared their commitment to a market economy, flexible labor markets, and minimum state intervention. If future Concertación administrations showed the same unwillingness to take agrarian elites' interests into account as center-left governments had in the past, a strong right caucus in Congress would protect landowners. As stated in the Chilean business 1988 annual meeting: "If the parties related to the [military] regime won half of Congress, they would be an equilibrium factor, even if the new president were adverse. From this position of strength, [rightwing parties] would be able to defend the bases of the economic policy or any other principle of the free society."[29]

3.3.2 Lowering the Costs of Party-Building: Elite Cohesion and the Electoral Incentives to Unify

The perception of an existential threat during the democratic transition led agrarian elites in Chile to invest in electoral representation. Chilean landowners joined other economic elites in the (re)building of the partisan right in the hope that through an equilibrium between the left and the right in Congress they would be able to block or blunt the Concertación's reformist agenda.[30] As discussed in Chapter 2, party-building is an

---

of the Southern Agriculture Association (SOFO), Temuco, November 10, 2016; and José Antonio Galilea, Piñera minister of agriculture and RN legislator (1990–2006), Temuco, November 10, 2016.

[28] Author's interview with Galilea.
[29] ENADE '88. *Encuentro Anual de la Empresa* (cited in Rehren (1995, 39)).
[30] Author's interview with Fontaine, Caminondo, Galilea, Mayol, and Jorge Prado, Pinochet minister of agriculture (1982–1988) and SNA president during the transition (1989–1993), Santiago, November 8, 2016.

arduous undertaking that requires substantial investments in time and money and high coordination among founding groups. Why were Chilean conservatives successful where so many were not?[31] I argue two factors helped agrarian elites in Chile to channel the representation of their interests through a conservative party. First, low levels of fragmentation within the Chilean agrarian elite (and the economic elite in general) reduced the inherently high coordination costs of party-building. The Chilean economic elite (among them the agrarian elite) was socially and ideologically homogenous and shared one main political goal during the democratic transition: ensuring the continuity of Pinochet's neoliberal model. Relatedly, unlike Brazil, where at the time of democratic transition agrarian elites were invested in rival local political machines, in Chile rural clientelistic machines had been destroyed by the structural and political changes of the 1960s and 1970s, while the remaining partisan structures of the right had unified in the PN before the military coup. Second, a new electoral system designed to boost the chances of the right also decreased the costs of building a conservative party by lowering electoral uncertainty and creating incentives to unify.

3.3.2.1 A Cohesive Elite

Chilean economic elites have historically been very cohesive, with the same family-owned conglomerates holding assets in very diverse sectors of the economy (Schneider 2004; Correa 2005; Fairfield 2015a). The close-knit character of Chilean economic and political elites led David Rothkopf to describe Chile in his 2009 book on the global elite as "not so much a country as a country club" (Rothkopf 2009, 56). Going back to the nineteenth century, linkages among the dominant sectors of the Chilean economy were already extensive. Acquisition of landed estates was a common means for the nouveaux rich to gain social status commensurate with their wealth, as well as access to political office (A. Bauer 2008). At the same time, landowners used their estates as collateral to diversify their portfolio and invest in other sectors such as mining, industry, or commerce. Intermarriage between members of the colonial landholding aristocracy and the descendants of nineteenth-century immigrants who had made their money in mining and commerce was also frequent (Wright 1981; Bauer 2008). These dense interlinkages between different economic sectors created a unified elite with similar economic

---

[31] See Levitsky et al. (2016) on the general challenges of party-building in Latin America, and Loxton (2021) on conservative party-building in particular.

and political interests and a common vision for the country (Correa 2005; Kurtz 2013). This unity was further reinforced by the national character of the elite. Most economic activities were concentrated in the central region of the country, around Santiago. And even those families whose wealth came from enterprises in the interior chose the capital as their place of residence. Consequently, no regional cleavages, like those that precluded the formation of a strong partisan right in other Latin American countries,[32] arose in Chile.

The structural transformation of Chile during the military government (1973–1990) further reinforced this cohesion by giving economic elites a common policy agenda: the continuation of the free-market economy model into the democratic era. In the countryside, the liberal economic model implemented by the military government triggered a profound transformation that can be described as one of selective modernization. The military government drastically reduced tariffs, eliminated nontariff barriers, liberalized trade flows, and increased the exchange rate to favor a reorientation of the Chilean economy towards the export of products in which the country had a comparative advantage. While those producers who were able to modernize their farms and survive the opening of the markets by switching to nontraditional crops like fruits or nuts saw their profits increase handsomely, a significant proportion of producers of traditional crops and small producers without the necessary capital to modernize went broke.[33] In addition to these macroeconomic measures, the military government implemented more specific policies to stimulated nontraditional agricultural exports, such as tax reductions and subsidized credit after the economic crisis of the early 1980s (Barham et al. 1992, 63).

As a consequence of this selective modernization, agricultural production greatly expanded and the country went from being a net importer to a net exporter of food. Between 1977 and 1992, agriculture GDP grew 105 percent (INE 2007, 17).[34] At the same time, agricultural production switched from products for the domestic market, such as beef and grain, to the cultivation of nontraditional crops for the external market, especially fruit. Between 1976 and 1997, the area cultivated with fruit increased by 161.5 percent, while the area cultivated with

---

[32] See Gibson (1996).
[33] Fruit production requires higher initial capital investments than traditional crops and has a much longer gestation period. Thus, many producers could not afford the transition from traditional to nontraditional crops.
[34] Includes silviculture.

3.3 Landowners Invest in a Party

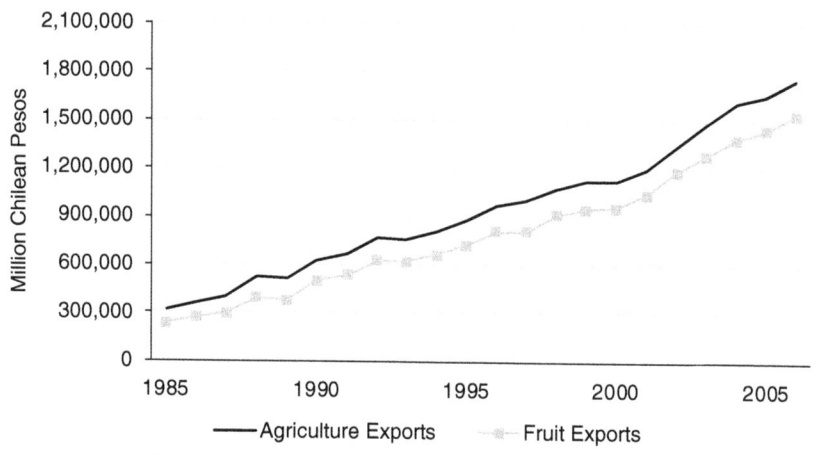

FIGURE 3.1 Agriculture exports and fruit exports (constant 2003 Chilean pesos): Chile, 1985–2006.
Source: Author, based on INE (2007).[35]

cereals decreased 23.2 percent (INE 2007, 37). Driven by the spectacular expansion of fruit, agricultural exports have been increasing uninterruptedly since the mid 1980s (Figure 3.1). Today, fruits are the country's main non-mineral export, representing 8.9 percent of total exports value.[36]

The profound transformation of the countryside that began with the land reform process (1965–1973) and continued during the military government (1973–1989) resulted in the consolidation of a new modern agrarian elite with even more unified economic and political interests than before. The old unproductive latifundio disappeared, never to return. It was replaced by modern efficient capitalist farms producing for the external market. These highly mechanized production systems that employ mostly seasonal labor today control the great majority of land in the Central Valley and neighbouring regions.[37] This new class of agricultural elite shares with the rest of Chilean business a strong preference for an open market economy, international integration, and labor market flexibility.

---

[35] Includes silviculture.
[36] Source: The Observatory of Economic Complexity, 2020 data, available at: https://oec.world/ (accessed, June 10, 2022).
[37] While farms of 100 hectares or more represent only 4.2 percent of units producing fruit, they control 42.8 percent of the land under fruit production in the country (ODEPA 2021, data for 2019–2021).

A clear indicator of Chilean economic elites' cohesion is the existence of a business peak association in the country, the Confederation of Production and Commerce (CPC) representing agriculture, commerce, mining, industry, construction, and finance. Nothing like this exists in Argentina or Brazil, where not only business representation is sectoral, but there are also multiple associations representing the same sectors. In both countries – and in striking contrast to Chile where the SNA represents all agricultural producers in the country – multiple associations claim the representation of agrarian interests at the national level.

Chilean agrarian elites not only had homogeneous economic interests at the time of the transition, but they also enjoyed political cohesion. Until the mid 1960s, the Chilean right had been divided between two parties, Conservatives and Liberals. This division had originated around disputes over the relationship between the Church and the state but did not reflect further ideological differences or socioeconomic cleavages. Leaders in both parties belonged to the same social circles, owned assets in the same multiple sectors of the economy and were related to each other through family ties (Zeitlin and Ratcliff 1988; Correa 2005). Landowners, in particular, were well represented in both parties and guaranteed significant electoral support to rightwing candidates through the clientelistic machines built upon their *fundos* (Wright 1981; Remmer 1984). In 1966, the two parties unified to better confront the policy agenda of the Frei Montalva administration, creating the PN. The PN mounted a fierce opposition in Congress to Frei Montalva's and Allende's policies of land reform and peasant unionization (Arellano 2009). Soon after Pinochet's military coup, PN leaders dissolved the party to join the authoritarian government (Valenzuela and Scully 1997; Pollack 1999).

Unlike their counterparts in Brazil who at the time of democratic transition were politically fragmented, controlling rival clientelistic machines, in Chile agrarian elites had no competing previous political investments. Structural and political changes during the 1960s and 1970s severely crippled agrarian elites' clientelistic machines. First, the introduction of the Australian ballot in 1958 restricted the landowners' capacity to monitor who their clients voted for (Loveman 1976; Bauer 1995; Baland and Robinson 2008). Later, the processes of land reform and unionization in the countryside in the mid 1960s and early 1970s ended the peasants' economic and political dependence on their former bosses.

Although losing their clientelistic machines was without a doubt disadvantageous to agrarian elites electorally, it helped them coalesce in a single partisan organization. When the defeat of the military regime in the 1988 plebiscite launched the process of democratic transition, agrarian elites no longer controlled rural politics. Moreover, what remained of their former partisan structures had already been unified through the creation of the PN. As landowners were not competing among themselves for the control of local politics, there were less opportunity costs for them in coordinating an electoral strategy. As we will see in Chapter 4, party-building was not an attractive option for agrarian elites in Brazil because it would have meant ceding control of their electoral bulwarks. In contrast, Chilean landowners had nothing to lose from coordinating local electoral representation, as their political strongholds had long been gone.

3.3.2.2 *A New Electoral System Designed to Boost the Right*

Besides the existence of a broad base of common political and economic interests within the economic elites, conservative party-building in Chile was further facilitated by the electoral rules engineered by the military. After Pinochet's defeat in the plebiscite, government officials designed a new electoral system with the objective of preventing the formation of an overwhelming leftist majority in Congress (Navia 2002; Zucco 2007). Under the binominal system – in place between 1989 and 2015 – the country was divided into districts with a magnitude of two both for the Senate and the Lower Chamber, and each party or coalition of parties was allowed to run a maximum of two candidates per district. What was crucial for the electoral chances of the right was the seat allocation rule, which made it extremely difficult for a single list to obtain both of the two seats at stake in a single district. To win both seats, the most voted list needed to double the votes of the second-placed list. As a result, at least one seat was virtually guaranteed for the right in each district, even in leftist strongholds. As Table 3.3 shows, in every election under the binomial system, the overwhelming majority of districts elected a deputy from each party. The maximum number of districts the left was able to double were 11 out of 60 in the 1989 and 1993 elections. To boost the electoral chances of the right even more, Lower Chamber districts were redrawn based on the 1988 referendum results to overrepresent rural areas, where support for the continuity of Pinochet had been greater (Siavelis 2002; Rojas and Navia 2005; Kurtz 2006). Until the constitutional reform of 2005, the strength of the right in Congress was further increased by the presence of nine designated senators and Pinochet himself who as a former president could sit in it for life. As Table 3.4 shows, the nonelected senators prevented the Concertación from having

TABLE 3.3 *Number of congressional districts (Lower Chamber) that were split, dominated by the left, and dominated by the right under the binomial system: Chile, 1989–2013*

Election year	Split	Left doubled	Right doubled	Total
1989	49	11	0	60
1993	48	11	1	60
1997	51	9	0	60
2001	55	4	1	60
2005	53	6	1	60
2009	59	0	1	60
2013	49	10	1	60

Source: Author's calculations based on Siavelis (2002) and Servel.[38]

TABLE 3.4 *Senate composition: Chile, 1989–2018*

Legislative period	Center-left coalition	Right coalition	Independents	Nonelected	Total
1990–1994	22	16	0	9	47
1994–1998	21	17	0	9	47
1998–2002	20	18	0	11	49
2002–2006	20	18	0	10	48
2006–2010	20	17	1	–	38
2010–2014	19	17	2	–	38
2014–2018	21	15	2	–	38

Source: Author's calculations based on Servel.[39]

a majority in the Senate necessary to pass major policy reforms. This only changed during the second Bachelet administration (2014–2018).

The binomial system lowered the costs of party-building for economic elites in Chile in two ways. First, by virtually guaranteeing conservative economic and political elites the success of their party-building efforts, the binomial system significantly reduced the uncertainty inherent in any electoral enterprise. Second, apportionment rules augmented the costs of a fragmented representation. The binomial system made it much easier for the right to win a seat in each district but only if they presented a unified list. Dividing the conservative vote among more than one list would

[38] Chilean Electoral Service, available at: www.servel.cl/elecciones-parlamentarias-resultados-eleccion-de-diputados/ (accessed April 2019).
[39] Available at: www.servel.cl/elecciones-de-senadores-1989-al-2013-por-circunscripcion-electoral/ (accessed April 2019).

likely result in the election of two nonconservative candidates. Thus, if conservative forces did not unify, they would lose the chance of being a counterbalancing power in Congress. This created strong incentives for conservatives to coordinate their electoral offer.

Although electoral rules cannot be discarded as an explanatory factor of the success of conservative Chilean elites in party-building, they cannot explain by themselves why agrarian elites decided to join this enterprise. On the one hand, even when electoral rules in Chile decreased the costs of party-building for the right, this does not explain the agrarian elites' decision to make this, if now cheaper, still substantial investment. If anything, political institutions, by favoring a balance of power between the parties of the center-left and the right in Congress should have soothed agrarian elites' fears of democracy, lowering their incentives to enter the electoral arena. The qualitative evidence analysed in this chapter, however, indicates that Chilean agrarian elites felt highly threatened during the democratic transition and that this perception of threat led them to make the initial investment in electoral representation.

On the other hand, electoral rules cannot fully account for why the Chilean agrarian elites chose to support one party instead of hedging their bets. At the same time that it decreased the costs of party-building for the right, the binomial system also created incentives for candidate-centered politics.[40] As shown in Table 3.3, apportionment rules under the binomial system usually resulted in the election of one candidate from each of the two most-voted lists. Therefore, competition in Chilean legislative elections was more intense among running mates than between candidates across lists. Given that agrarian elites knew the right's chances of controlling the presidency were very low, they could have invested in a candidate-centered strategy to secure the election of like-minded candidates in rural districts under both coalitions, trying to infiltrate the parties closer to the center in the Concertación. No feature of the Chilean electoral system precluded landowners from doing this; their distrust of the Christian Democrats did.

The ties between conservative economic and political elites in Chile and their connections to the military regime raise the question of whether the military-designed electoral rules can be treated as exogenous to the political interests of the economic elite and to their level of fragmentation. The electoral rules for the new democracy were designed by the civilians

---

[40] Carey and Shugart (1995) argue that proportional representation systems in combination with low district magnitude create incentives for candidates to cultivate a personal vote instead of a partisan one.

within the military regime (Siavelis 1997; Pastor 2004) and therefore cannot be considered as exogenous to the interests of the conservative political elites. The main architects of the new system – Jaime Guzmán and Sergio Fernández – belonged to the Movimiento Gremial[41] and had closer ties to the new economic elite that had surge under the military than to the agrarian elite. However, because of the high ideological coherence within the economic elites, it can be argued that the political interests of those designing the electoral rules were not significantly different from those of the agrarian elite. Moreover, it is hard to imagine that the architects of the new electoral system would have chosen the binomial system if they believed the conservative political and economic elite could not hold together an electoral alliance without fragmenting into many different political factions. In the past, fragmentation had been a characteristic more of the parties on the left than of those on the right. The ideological distance between Christian Democrats, Socialists, and Communists was greater than which existed within the regime, between *gremialistas*, old conservatives, and the Chicago Boys. Therefore, in the eyes of the designers of the new electoral system, it was far more likely that the imposition of the binomial system would result in the electoral weakening of the left than that of the right. The right's chances of maintaining a unified front were higher given its lower levels of previous fragmentation, and that explains, in part, why the conservative political elites chose the binomial electoral system.

3.3.3 Agrarian Elites in Action: The "Yes" Campaign and the (Re)building of the Partisan Right

When the military government announced a plebiscite in 1988 to decide whether or not Pinochet should continue in power for another eight years, agrarian elites organized to support the "Yes" alternative. With some notable exceptions,[42] the business community in general was behind the continuity of Pinochet in power – which they saw as the only guarantee the economic model would not be changed – but the SNA was the most

---

[41] The Movimiento Gremial was a conservative political group born in the late 1960s at the prestigious Catholic University of Chile in reaction to the (leftist) radicalization of the student body. The Gremialistas were at the forefront of the struggle against the Allende government and among the staunchest supporters of Pinochet's regime. During the dictatorship, Gremialistas integrated into the state, at all levels of government. Jaime Guzmán, the founder of the movement, was one of Pinochet's closest advisers. Gremialistas formed their own political party, the UDI, in 1983 to guarantee the continuity of the dictatorship political and economic model into an eventual democratic regime (Loxton 2021, 62–69).
[42] Such as Sebastián Piñera.

militant of the employers' associations (Rehren 1995, 19). SNA leaders played a leading role in the organization of the *comités cívicos* (civic committees), a broad coalition of businesspeople and citizens groups campaigning for the "Yes" side (Silva 1998). At the time, the SNA was also deeply involved in the organization of the campaign "Empresarios por el Desarrollo" (Entrepreneurs for Development), an initiative of the peak association of Chilean business, the CPC, which aimed to raise public awareness on the benefits of private entrepreneurship for Chilean society as a whole and the importance of preserving the market economy model. "Empresarios por el Desarrollo" was launched just before the October 1988 plebiscite, and its activities intensified after the defeat of the military government and consequent onset of the democratic transition. The SNA was key to the organization of the campaign, especially in the interior of the country where its networks were stronger (Rehren 1995, 20). For instance, the SNA disseminated the following message by the president of the CPC, Manuel Feilú, about the 1988 referendum, not only through its magazine but also its national radio station, *Radio Agricultura*, which has a large audience in rural areas throughout the country:

When Chileans find themselves at the crossroads of having to decide *whether or not we want to go back to the dark past* or project ourselves freely into the future, we the businessmen have something to say and we should do so loud and clear, so the community understands that the way to move forward is intimately linked to the free market economy.

And then, paraphrasing John F. Kennedy, he added:

[D]o not ask what the government will do for you, but *what can you do to have a government that will support private initiative*.[43]

In April 1989, the SNA elected a new president to lead the agrarian elites' defense of the military legacy in the countryside during the transition to democracy: Jorge Prado. Prado had until recently been Pinochet's minister of agriculture and he was one of the architects of the sector's modernization in the 1980s. In another clear sign of where their loyalties stood, less than two months before the presidential election, in October 1989, the SNA paid homage to Pinochet by giving him a gold medal in recognition of all his work in benefit of the sector.[44] On that occasion, Pinochet delivered a speech reminding agricultural producers that the politicians now in the Concertación were the same ones that in the

---

[43] *El Campesino* 119, no. 5 (June 1988), 6, emphasis added.
[44] An unprecedented recognition.

1960s and 1970s had expropriated their lands and destroyed agricultural production. He remarked, "Whatever the outcome of the next electoral contest, agriculture will always be subject to the threat of those who, following doctrinal and ideological postulates, consider armed struggle as a method of political action."[45]

After Pinochet's defeat in the 1988 referendum, it was clear to agrarian elites in Chile that the next democratic government was going to be from the center-left but the results of the plebiscite also showed that the authoritarian government still enjoyed the support of a considerable share of the population – 44 percent of voters chose the "Yes" alternative – especially in rural areas. For example, in Maule, the most rural region of the country, with 40.2 percent of its population living in rural areas, and one of the main producers of fruit, support for the "Yes" alternative was 48.3 percent. La Araucania, the region with the third largest rural population (38.7 percent) and the country's main producer of grain and meat, was also the region where the "Yes" alternative had the most votes, 54 percent, and one of the only two regions where "Yes" won. The other region was Los Lagos, the second most rural region of the country (38.9 percent rural population, 50.1 percent of votes for the "Yes" alternative). Rightwing politicians, who supported the continuation of the dictatorship economic model, could capitalize on this popular support for Pinochet to build a strong representation in Congress. To do this, they depended on the help of economic elites who were equally invested in the continuation of the market economy.

Reactivating their partisan linkages was easy for agricultural elites given the close, intimate nature of the Chilean upper classes and the considerable overlap between the economic and political elite. The SNA as a business association had to remain officially neutral during the election, which nonetheless did not stop its leaders from advising producers to give their support to candidates sharing SNA's principles who, needless to say, belonged to the right. One month before the election, in the general assembly of members, the SNA president and former minister of agriculture of the military government Jorge Prado said: "I call upon each one of you to take a stand in these forty days up to the election, to work in your communities, but fervently, for those men who defend our principles, those of the Sociedad Nacional de Agricultura, to defend the rights to freedom, private property and private entrepreneurship."[46]

[45] *El Campesino* 120, no. 11 (November 1989), 24.
[46] Ibid., 32.

Candidates' personal links to agricultural producers facilitated fundraising efforts, as producers were happy to help the campaigns of friends and relatives. Among the parties of the right, agricultural producers, especially in the south of the country, had closer links to RN politicians, many of whom came from the old PN (Pollack 1999; Navia and Godoy 2014). Agrarian elites supported the reorganization of the partisan right during the democratic transition both economically and logistically.[47] As Jorge Prado explained to me:

Business associations were like the backbone for the organization of the right ... between the referendum and the [presidential] election ... it was a very messy time politically [for the right] and it happened that Aylwin won by a large margin. And then, business associations, since parties were disorganized after seventeen years without functioning, business associations were the ones that helped to re-structure the center-right.

Why did you say that business associations were the backbone of the center-right? What did they do to reorganize it?

... business associations are very powerful in the interior and through many personal friendships at the local level, firms were a major source of support ... more businesspeople than firms, especially agricultural producers, for the reconstruction of the partisan right during the first years of democracy [...].

Did businesspeople think "we are going to help to have representation in Congress"?

Sure, because it was an *insurance policy against the government*. The government may promise many great things, but it was much more reassuring to have a majority in Congress.[48]

3.4 AGRARIAN ELITES AS A CORE CONSTITUENCY OF THE PARTISAN RIGHT

After the military defeat in the 1988 plebiscite, economic elites, landowners among them, aided conservative politicians in the building of a new conservative party, Renovación Nacional (RN). RN brought together various rightwing political and economic groups, which included elements of the old and new right. The old right was represented by former members of the PN, while young Pinochetista activists – known as *gremialistas* – who had founded their own party, the UDI in 1983, represented the new right. Family and professional ties connected *gremialistas* to the

---

[47] Author's interviews with Ariztía de Castro, Caminondo, Galilea, Mayol, and Prado.
[48] Author's interview, emphasis added.

diversified business conglomerates that had grown under the military regime (Pollack 1999). Agrarian elites, in contrast, had closer connections to former PN members. Soon after the foundation of RN, due to internal disputes, UDI members split to form their own party. Agrarian elites' allegiances at the time, however, remained with RN due to their previous linkages with its leaders.

Agrarian elites' networks helped cement electoral support for RN in the countryside. UDI, in contrast, was essentially an urban party. UDI leaders were mostly former student activists from the Catholic University who had held local office during the military regime and, as a consequence, the party's networks in the countryside were scant. In contrast, the RN structure in rural areas was much more extensive thanks to networks headed by agrarian elites that were inherited from the old Partido Nacional (Pollack 1999; Barozet and Aubry 2005; Rosenblatt 2018, 106). For instance, in the 1989 elections, the UDI did not run candidates for the Senate in any of the three most important agricultural regions, O'Higgins, Maule, or La Araucania, while the RN ran candidates in all three and elected two senators. For the Lower Chamber, the RN ran eighteen candidates in the three regions and elected nine, while the UDI ran only four candidates, in O'Higgins and Maule, and elected two, showing the importance of RN rural networks in these foundational elections.

In this section, I present evidence of party-building by agrarian elites in Chile since the last democratic transition. As defined in Chapter 2, interest groups engage in party-building when they become a core constituency of a party. Core constituencies contribute to a party with financial, ideological, political, and/or human resources. Moreover, a party's policy positions should reflect the preferences of its core constituencies (Gibson 1996; Fairfield 2015a). Here, I show Chilean landowners' ideological identification with the legislators of the right and their financial support for the parties in the rightwing alliance. I also reveal a systematic difference in terms of recruitment of agrarian elites between the parties in the right and center-left coalitions.

3.4.1 Ideological Identification between Agrarian Elites and the Partisan Right

My interviews with leaders of agricultural producers' associations in Chile revealed a degree of ideological identification between agrarian elites and the partisan right that I did not observe in either of the other two countries under study. Leaders from producers' associations frequently referred to Concertación politicians as "the other side" and to legislators from UDI and RN as "our members of Congress." At no time did leaders of producers' associations in Argentina or Brazil ever identify a party as "our party." The contrast with Brazil illustrates well the difference between party-building and a nonpartisan, candidate-centered electoral strategy. Although in Brazil leaders of producers' associations frequently talked of the Agrarian Caucus as "our caucus," because legislators from the Agrarian Caucus belong to many different parties, this pronouncement never carried a partisan connotation. When leaders from producers' associations in Chile talked about "our caucus," on the other hand, it was clear they were referring to the rightwing coalition. Twelve out of the twenty leaders of producers' associations and politicians connected to the sector whom I interviewed said that there is an ideological affinity between agrarian elites and the partisan right. In their view, legislators from RN and UDI value private entrepreneurship and share their same commitment to the market economy model and the protection of property rights, ideals they do not perceive in the parties of the left. For instance, when I asked him if agricultural producers in his region supported the center-right, a large fruit producer and leader of SNA responded without hesitation and evoking the memory of Allende's land reform:

A hundred percent yes. The agricultural sector is not even on the center-right, it is on the right. You should not forget that in '73 the sector was expropriated by the left. That's there, it's not recent, but it's there. Many people from my dad's or my grandparents' generation had their farms expropriated. Obviously, that shocks you. So yes, the sector is completely biased towards the right.[49]

Given the high affinity between agrarian elites' and rightwing legislators' policy preferences, the former see their capacity to influence policymaking as tied to the electoral success of the later and the existence of partisan equilibrium in Congress. The presence of like-minded lawmakers can only be effective when there is equilibrium between the two ideological blocks in Congress and the left needs the votes of the right to pass its legislative initiatives.[50] Partisan balance opens a bargaining arena for legislators in the rightwing coalition and, consequently, agricultural producers can use their partisan ties to work together with friendly

---

[49] Author's interview with Ricardo Ariztía Tagle, SNA director, Santiago, October 26, 2016.
[50] Author's interviews with Ariztía de Castro, Crespo, Prado, and José Miguel Stegmeier, president of the Agriculture Society of the Biobío Region, Santiago, October 24, 2016.

lawmakers in modifying bills that interest them. As the leader of the Biobío producers' association explained to me, "*our* parliamentary block used to be enough to veto those important laws (we opposed). Smaller things passed, things that were not that important to us. However, major things never passed because we were in equilibrium."[51]

The Water Code reform approved in March 2022, which was being heatedly debated at the time of my fieldwork in Chile (September-November 2016), is a clear example of the ideological affinity between rightwing legislators and landowners, as well as of what losing the equilibrium between left and rightwing forces in Congress could entail for agrarian elites. The military-sanctioned 1981 Water Code effectively created private property rights over water by separating the property of land from the water resources in it and allowing for the free transaction of water rights. Under this legislation, the state granted water usage rights to those who requested them for free and in perpetuity without any restrictions in the exploitation or commercialization of those rights. This framework had been key to the spectacular expansion of export-oriented agriculture (fruit production, in particular) in Chile during the 1980s and 1990s by granting landowners permanent water rights at no cost that were constitutionally protected and constituted untaxed valuable capital assets (Bauer 1998; Budds 2013). However, critics of the 1981 Water Code argued that it jeopardized Chilean society, by privatizing a public good of vital importance and facilitating speculation and hoarding (Dourojeanni and Jouravlev 1999). With almost a million hectares under irrigation, agricultural producers are the largest consumers of water, owning 73 percent of the consumptive water rights in the country[52] and have been the staunchest opponents of any modifications to the 1981 Water Code.

Changing the Water Code has been a policy ambition of the center-left since the democratic transition. In 1992, President Aylwin sent to Congress the first attempt at modifying water property rights but the reform went nowhere due to strong opposition from the agrarian elites and their representatives in Congress (Bauer 1998, 68–70). It was only under President Lagos in 2005 that a reform to the Water Code finally passed. However, this bill only imposed fines on water rights holders that were not consuming them without touching property rights.

---

[51] Author's interview with Stegmeier, emphasis added.
[52] Available at: www.odepa.gob.cl/sustentabilidad/agricultura-sustentable/agua (accessed, June 13, 2022).

In 2014, during the second Bachelet administration and after gaining a majority in the Senate breaking the partisan equilibrium that had prevailed until then, the center-left governing coalition made a new attempt at changing the property regime over water rights. Bachelet's bill stipulated that new water usage rights would be granted to producers in thirty-year concessions instead of indefinitely and that they could be revoked if not used. In addition, the bill prioritized human consumption over other usages and augmented the monitoring capabilities of the state.

Agricultural producers used their connections to rightwing legislators as well as their influence in the media to mount a fierce opposition to the reform.[53] In the interviews I conducted in late 2016, leaders from producers' associations, legislators from UDI and RN, and legislative advisers from rightwing think tanks all gave me the same explanation for what was wrong with the proposed Water Code reform: it constituted an expropriation of producers' water rights and was, therefore, unconstitutional. In their view, the reform created "legal uncertainty" which disincentivized investments, therefore aggravating the water scarcity problem.[54] Agricultural producers' associations and rightwing think tanks made these same arguments in Congress hearings and media appearances, which rightwing legislators repeated time and again during the legislative debate.[55]

The Lower Chamber passed the bill in November 2016. The votes followed partisan lines, with no legislator in the rightwing coalition voting in favor[56] and no center-left legislator voting against. In the Senate, pressure from agrarian elites and their political and economic allies prevented the bill for moving forward, even after the government dropped some of the bill's most controversial provisions.[57] During the 2017 presidential race, rightwing candidate Piñera campaigned on protecting producers' water rights[58] and during his administration reformist efforts stalled.

---

[53] See also Madariaga et al. (2021).
[54] See Appendix A for a complete list of interviewees.
[55] "Historia de la Ley 21,435," Biblioteca del Congreso Nacional de Chile.
[56] Two UDI and one RN legislators abstained.
[57] Together with agricultural producers, mining and hydroelectric power firms lobbied Congress and the Executive against the reform ("El exitoso lobby que tumbó artículos clave de la Reforma al Código de Aguas," *CIPER Chile*, May 26, 2017).
[58] Reestablishing water rights was the first on his list of, "Proposals to improve the quality of life of our people and our countryside." Sebastián Piñera, "Propuestas para mejorar la calidad de vida de nuestra gente y nuestro campo," September 12, 2017.

It was only after the end of the binomial system and the political upheaval that brought leftist Gabriel Boric to the presidency that a comprehensive reform to the 1981 Water Code could be passed in March 2022. The reformed code grants new water usage rights to producers in thirty-year concessions that can be revoked if not used within five years. More importantly, the law establishes water as a public national good and declares access to water a human right of essential and inalienable character.[59] However, because the bill was the product of years of bargaining and multiple compromises between the center-left and the right, it applies exclusively to water rights granted after its passage, which constitute only around 10 percent of all water rights in the country.[60] Therefore, thanks to the work of rightwing legislators, agrarian elites were able to severely limit the impact the reform would have on their assets.

3.4.2 Agrarian Elites' Financial Support of the Partisan Right

Systematic data on campaign financing in Chile are scant. Data on campaign financing of elections previous to 2003 are not available, restricting our ability to study business donations to parties during the transition and the foundational elections following it. Moreover, until 2016, contributions by firms were allowed but Chilean legislation protected the confidentiality of large political donations, by firms or individuals, preventing analysts from identifying relationships between specific donors and candidates or parties.[61] Despite these limitations, there is some evidence that businesspeople in Chile, and agrarian elites in particular, systematically contribute more to the campaigns of the candidates in the rightwing alliance.

Previous analyses have argued that candidates of the rightwing coalition in Chile systematically receive more campaign contributions from big business than do those in the center-left coalition (Pollack 1999; Luna 2014; Fairfield 2015a; Giraudy 2015). As a way around the confidentiality issue of campaign contributions data in Chile, Luna (2014, 211) analysed the amounts of confidential contributions a party receives. Because the

---

[59] "Tras más de una década en tramitación, Senado aprueba de forma unánime Reforma al Código de Aguas y es despachada a ley," *La Tercera*, January 12, 2022.
[60] Tamayo and Carmona (2019, 147).
[61] Until 2016, large campaign contributions were confidential. In 2016, a new law regulating campaign finance was promulgated. The new law ended the confidentiality of large contributions but it also forbade contributions from firms and restricted the amount individuals can contribute.

largest contributions fall into this category,[62] it can be assumed they came from business, which are usually wealthier than other interest groups. Following this logic, Giraudy (2015) and Fairfield (2015a) show that candidates in the rightwing coalition systematically received more confidential contributions than those in the center-left during the 2005 and 2009 elections. In the 2005 election, candidates of the rightwing Alianza received US$1,451,878 more in confidential contributions than those of the Concertación. In 2009, the difference was US$ 2,836,853 (Giraudy 2015, 95). UDI candidates captured more confidential contributions than candidates of any other party. Compared to their coalition partners from the RN, they received three times more confidential contributions in 2005 and 1.2 more in 2009 (Giraudy 2015, 87).[63] In 2013, UDI and RN were again the parties with the largest confidential contributions but the difference between them had grown even larger. In that election, the UDI received 5.3 times as much as the RN.[64] Data on campaign financing leaked during corruption investigations supports the claim that Chilean economic elites favor the right in their campaign donations, especially the UDI. For instance, documents uncovered during the so-called "Pentagate" in 2014[65] showed that firms associated with the group – one of the largest in Chile with holdings in finance, insurance, real estate, and agriculture among other sectors – had made contributions both via the legal system and illegally to seven candidates in the 2013 presidential and legislative elections. Five of those candidates were UDI, one RN and one center-left.[66] Summing up, existing analyses show that the Chilean business community as a whole supports the right more than the center-left. Limitation in quantitative data availability, however, prevent us from knowing if that is also the case for agrarian elites in particular.

---

[62] Until 2016, Chilean legislation distinguished between anonymous contributions (less than US$800) and confidential contributions (*aportes reservados*) (between US$800 and US$22,500). In both cases, the identity of the donor was not publicly known. The difference was that contributions of less than US$800 could be made anonymously, while in confidential contributions the identity of the donor was concealed from the recipient and general public but known by the electoral agency.
[63] Contributions to candidates for Congress and Regional Councils.
[64] Ibid.
[65] The criminal investigation against the Chilean holding Penta is one of the biggest corruption scandals in the country's recent history. Several firm executives were convicted of tax fraud. The investigation revealed they had issued fake invoices to conceal campaign contributions to, mainly, rightwing politicians. See "Caso Penta: La caja negra de las platas políticas que sacude a la UDI," CIPER Chile, May 1, 2015.
[66] "La lista de donaciones a campañas del ex ejecutivo de Penta," CIPER Chile, October 8, 2014.

My interviews indicate that agricultural producers systematically contribute more to candidates of the right than the center-left. Interviewees reported that agricultural producers contribute to rightwing candidates much more often than they do to leftwing candidates. Seven out of the thirteen leaders of producers' associations I interviewed explicitly said agricultural producers only support the campaigns of the right while none of them indicated that agrarian elites contribute financially to the center-left or hedge their bets.[67] For instance, when I asked him whether agricultural producers hedged their bets or only contributed to rightwing candidates, an SNA leader and large fruit exporter answered:

Definitely, if you can donate some money, in a high proportion, I would say 90 percent, maybe even 100 percent [of agricultural producers], will always support the candidates of the right. Here, *we do not have the concept of other sectors that support candidates across the ideological spectrum*. That does not exist. It would never cross your mind to support someone *from the other side*, zero.[68]

Similarly, in the words of the leader of the Biobío producers' association, "agricultural producers are much franker from that point of view [campaign contributions]. In general, producer policy is to give to the center-right and not to both sides."[69] In contrast, a Christian Democrat legislator from a rural district who works with small producers and peasants told me, "it is impossible that big producers will help me, because I work with peasants' unions ... it is impossible that the big ones will help you when, for them, you are more part of the problem than the solution."[70]

3.4.3 Landowners within the Rightwing Parties

Agrarian elites' ties to the rightwing parties are also evident when comparing the recruitment patterns of the center-left and right alliances both for elected and nonelected offices. Table 3.5 shows representatives with assets in agriculture by party and alliance as a proportion of the party/alliance caucus and in absolute numbers. Since the democratic transition until 2018, on average 12 percent of the representatives in

---

[67] Although some of the producers and politicians I interviewed also stated that contributions by agricultural producers to the right are usually rather small compared to those of big business groups and that contributions are frequently motivated by family ties and friendship and not just ideological affinity.
[68] Author's interview with Ariztia Tagle, emphasis added.
[69] Author's interview with Stegmeier.
[70] Author's interview with Alejandra Sepúlveda Orbens, O'Higgins legislator (Independent former PDC), Valparaíso, November 9, 2016.

TABLE 3.5 *Members of Congress who held assets in agriculture by party, alliance, and period as percentage of caucus and in absolute terms: Lower Chamber, 1990–2018*[71]

	1990–1994		1994–1998		1998–2002		2002–2006		2006–2010		2010–2014		2014–2018	
	%	no.	%	no.	%	no.	%	no.	%	no.	%	no.	%	no.
Right	29.2	14	24	12	25.5	12	21.1	12	16.7	9	10.3	6	22.4	11
RN	37.9	11	31	9	43.5	10	50	9	31.6	6	16.7	3	21	4
UDI	27.3	3	20	3	11.8	2	9.7	3	9.1	3	8.1	3	20.7	6
Center-left	2.8	2	4	3	8.6	6	4.8	3	3.7	2	7	4	10.4	7
Total Lower Chamber	13.3	16	12.5	15	14.2	18	12.5	15	9.2	11	9.2	10	15	18

Source: Author's calculations based on Avendaño and Escudero (2016), Congreso Nacional de Chile and Servel.

the Lower Chamber have held assets in agriculture. On average, almost 75 percent of agricultural producers in Congress have been in the rightwing alliance. Agrarian elites represent a much larger proportion of the rightwing caucus than of the center-left alliance (21 versus 6 percent on average, respectively). In my interviews, four leaders of producers' associations revealed that they had been offered to run for Congress, always by rightwing parties.[72] Until 2010, RN was the party with the greatest concentration of agricultural producers, which is not surprising given the party inherited the old PN rural networks while its coalitional partner, UDI, was born as an urban party.

If a considerable number of Chilean legislators of different party affiliations are agricultural producers, then why do I argue that the landowners' strategy in Chile has been party-building instead of candidate-centered, as in Brazil? I do so because agrarian elites' representation in the Chilean Congress has a partisan bias. Unlike in Brazil, where landowners infiltrate the ranks of multiple parties across the ideological spectrum, in Chile the overwhelming majority of landowner legislators belong to rightwing parties with a clear preference for RN until the mid 2000. While members of the Brazilian Bancada Ruralista organize their work in Congress around their sectoral identity, Chilean legislators who are

---

[71] Representatives who own land or shares in a firm in the agricultural sector according to their declaration of assets available at: www.declaracionjurada.cl/pubsistema/patrimonio.web.publico/pu/index.html?sid=716 (last accessed April 23, 2023).

[72] Author's interviews with Ariztía de Castro, Caminondo, Stegmeier, and María Inés Figari, president of the Northern Agriculture Association, Santiago, October 18, 2016.

landowners do not work as a sectoral caucus. Their legislative behavior, like that of any other Chilean member of Congress, is dictated by their partisan identity. As the leader from the Biobío producers' association eloquently explained to me when talking about the behavior of a center-left representative from his region who is an agricultural producer:

> One of the legislators from our region who was president of the Agriculture Committee for many years, Mr. José Perez [PRSD, Biobío], look, there in the region he said exactly what we [the producers] said, bla, bla, bla, that he would defend our rights. Then, when he had to vote here, in Santiago, this is the button he should be pushing according to his discourse, he pushed the other which was the instruction of his party or the government. Legislators in general, 90 percent of the time, vote according to the order given by the government or their party. [...] This guy dresses like a rancher, he owns a horse, a farm ... we are friends, but I told him "Look Don José, we can only be friends, I will never vote for you in any election because you always vote against us in Congress." He answered, "Well, there you have to vote with your party."[73]

Similarly, another sectoral leader expressed their frustrations at trying to build a representation in Congress that would cut across partisan alignments:

> There is a quote and quote agrarian caucus but, as I told you, when it is time to vote, if the party orders are to vote "white" and the agrarian caucus determined that the correct thing was [to vote] "black," [legislators] will vote "white."[74]

Given the close-knit character of the Chilean political and economic elite and the high diversification of the latter's portfolio, it is not surprising to find that a handful of center-left legislators in Chile own assets in agriculture. However, these center-left legislators do not identify as representatives of the sector. Agricultural producers who want to work for the sector in Chile run in rightwing parties with which they have ideological affinity. The Lower Chamber roll call on the modification of the Water Code in late 2016 clearly illustrates this assessment. Legislators voted according to partisan lines, not their economic interests. Every legislator with ties to agriculture in the center-left voted in favor of the bill modifying the 1981 Water Code, which was forcefully opposed by the SNA and local producers' associations. In contrast, rightwing legislators followed their parties' position, which coincided with agrarian elites' interest and opposed the bill, irrespectively or their personal ties to the sector.[75]

---

[73] Author's interview with Stegmeier.
[74] Author's interview with Jorge Gúzman, president of the Sugar Beet Growers Association, Temuco, November 11, 2016.
[75] "Historia de la Ley N 21,434," Biblioteca Nacional del Congreso de Chile.

TABLE 3.6 *Chile's ministers of agriculture, 1990–2022*

Minister	Period and administration	Profession	Party	Producers' association leader?
Juan Agustín Figueroa	1990–1994 (Aylwin–Concertación)	Lawyer–businessman	PRSD	No
Emiliano Ortega	1994–1996 (Frei Ruiz-Tagle–Concertación)	Agronomist–civil servant	PDC	No
Carlos Mladinic	1996–1999 (Frei Ruiz-Tagle–Concertación)	Economist–CEO	PDC	No
Ángel Sartori	1999–2000 (Frei Ruiz-Tagle–Concertación)	Veterinarian–civil servant	PDC	No
Jaime Campos	200–2006 (Lagos–Concertación)	Lawyer–politician	PRSD	No
Álvaro Rojas	2006–2008 (Bachelet–Concertación)	Veterinarian–academic	PDC	No
Marigen Hornkohl	2008–2010 (Bachelet–Concertación)	Social worker–politician	PDC	No
José Antonio Galilea	2010–2011 (Piñera–Coalición por el Cambio)	Agricultural producer–politician	RN	No
Luis Mayol	2011–2014 (Piñera–Coalición por el Cambio)	Lawyer–businessman	RN	Yes (SNA)
Carlos Furche	2014–2018 (Bachelet–Nueva Mayoría)	Agronomist–civil servant	PS	No
Antonio Walker	2018–2021 (Piñera–Chile Vamos)	Agricultural producer	Independent	Yes (Fedefruta and SNA)
María Emilia Undurraga	2021–2022 (Piñera–Chile Vamos)	Agricultural producer–civil servant	Evópoli	No

There is also a systematic difference between the center-left administrations and the governments of the rightwing alliance in terms of recruitment to high-ranking executive positions in sectoral agencies. Concertación ministers are usually civil servants with a long career in sectoral agencies while the right recruits their agricultural ministers from the private sector. While none of the eight ministers of agriculture in the five center-left governments had a past as a leader of one of the sectoral associations, two of the four ministers of agriculture during the rightwing administrations did (Table 3.6). Also, leaders from producers' associations frequently serve as technical consultants to RN and UDI politicians. For instance, five of the SNA leaders I interviewed reported having worked in the presidential campaign of a rightwing candidate.[76]

3.5 AGRARIAN ELITES' FIRST POLICY FIGHT IN DEMOCRACY: AYLWIN'S TAX REFORM

In this section, I analyse the design and passage of the Concertación first fiscal reform, sent to Congress shortly after the democratic transition, to show the policy implications of agrarian elites' effective electoral representation. This case clearly illustrates that agrarian elites were a core constituency of the main rightwing party at the time, RN, and how that allowed them to introduce key modification to the bill blunting its economic impact on producers.

One of the first policy initiatives that the Aylwin administration sent to Congress was an ambitious fiscal reform. The Concertación had campaigned on the promise of expanding social spending to address the country's pressing issues of poverty and inequality. In order to do this, in April 1990, Aylwin sent a bill to Congress modifying the tax system with two main goals: increasing the state's fiscal resources and dampening the highly regressive character of the prevailing system. Among the many modifications that the bill introduced to the existing system, one was of special interest to agricultural producers: the abolition of levies on estimated income for the agriculture, mining, and transportation sectors in favor of taxes on actual earnings. The government believed the "estimated income" system allowed producers to underreport their actual earnings and that the proposed change would reduce tax evasion. Agricultural producers opposed the change, arguing the new system was too complicated to implement and that because it established

---

[76] Author's interviews with Ariztía de Castro, Ariztía Tagle, Crespo, Mayol, and Prado.

3.5 The First Fight in Democracy: Aylwin's Tax Reform

an earnings threshold over which producers should pay taxes under the "actual earnings" system, it created inequalities among tax-paying producers. In reality, the proposed threshold was quite high and the new system would have affected only the largest producers, fewer than 5 percent of the total (Marcel 1997).

The SNA took the lead in organizing agrarian elites' opposition to the tax reform. The association developed an extensive lobbying campaign targeting both the executive branch and Congress. SNA leaders met with President Aylwin as well as with Finance Minister Alejandro Foxley and the minister of agriculture. In Congress, the SNA testified against the reform in committee hearings in both chambers.[77] However, the capacity of agrarian elites to influence the legislative debate lay not only, or mainly, in the effectiveness of these pleas but in the seats controlled by the right, especially by the RN. Thanks to their political connections, agrarian elites were, according to a close colleague of Minister Foxley during the design of the tax reform of 1990, the only business sector that was able to substantively influence the design of the reform (Marcel 1997, 69).

The tax reform bill was negotiated, both before its submission and later in Congress, between the government and a handful of senators from the main opposition party, RN. Senator Sergio Romero Pizarro (RN) who was an agricultural producer himself and who had very close ties to the SNA after serving on its council for more than twenty years (1968–1989)[78] was one of the legislators most involved in these discussions (Marcel 1997, 55; Romero Pizarro 2015). RN coalition partner UDI refused to take part in the discussion of the reform and opted instead to oppose it outright. As a consequence, RN represented the sole voice of agrarian elites during the legislative debate.

The importance of agricultural producers as a core constituency of RN is shown in the fact that one of the main changes to the draft bill that the party negotiated with the executive was related to the implementation of the new "actual earnings" tax system for agriculture. UDI legislators opposed the bill altogether arguing that an increase in taxation could never fulfill the government's goal of reducing poverty in the country because it would hurt investment. RN legislators, in contrast,

---

[77] *El Campesino* 121, no. 4 (April 1990); 121, no. 5 (May 1990).
[78] Sergio Romero Pizarro held various leadership positions in the SNA. He was secretary-general (1968–1976), council member (1980–1990), and vice president (1987–1989). In addition, he was secretary of agriculture under Pinochet (1986) and vice president of the CPC during the transition (1989).

took part in the negotiation of the tax reform in an effort to move towards the center and to show the party's commitment to democracy (Pollack 1999). However, they made sure supporting the reform would not hurt the interests of their core constituency, objecting to the change in the system taxing agriculture specifically. All RN legislators who spoke in the Lower Chamber and the Senate during the bill's debate referred explicitly to agriculture and the negative effects a change in the taxing system would have on the sector. To give a sense of how important agricultural producers were as a RN constituency, neither of the other two sectors affected by the same change to the tax system, mining and transportation, were ever mentioned in the legislators' speeches against the proposed switch to the "actual earnings" calculation.[79] The arguments RN legislators presented during the bill's treatment were very similar to those stated in a report prepared by the SNA that the association had delivered to the finance minister and published in its magazine *El Campesino*.[80]

The SNA's two-pronged strategy of lobbying the executive and working in Congress through RN legislators was quite successful. In response to SNA demands, two key modifications were introduced to the executive's original bill. First, the (already quite high) threshold for paying taxes under the old "estimated income" system was raised by 33.3 percent. As a result, agriculture ended up being the sector with the highest threshold. After this change, only the largest 2.6 percent of all agricultural producers, or about 1,520 people, would have to pay taxes according to the new system. The other key modification was that contrary to the government's intentions to make the change retroactive to January 1, 1990, application of the new system was postponed until the following fiscal year.[81] In spite of these victories, the SNA continued to lobby against the reform, petitioning the executive to suppress the modification and go back to the old system. This did not happen. However, Congress twice voted to postpone implementation of the new "actual earnings" system while several modifications were introduced to make it less complex. As a result, a simplified version of the new tax system for agriculture was first applied during the fiscal year 1994, four years after the promulgation of the law (Marcel 1997).

---

[79] *Historia de la Ley* 18,985, Biblioteca del Congreso Nacional de Chile.
[80] *El Campesino* 121, no. 4 (April 1990); 121, no. 5 (May 1990); *Historia de la Ley* 18,985.
[81] *Historia de la Ley* 18,985. For a detailed analysis of the negotiations against Aylwin's tax reform, see Pizarro (1995) and Marcel (1997).

3.6 CONCLUSION

This chapter analyses a case of party-building by agrarian elites. Since the last democratic transition, Chilean landowners have invested financial, ideological and human resources in supporting first the RN and later, with the electoral growth of UDI, both parties in the rightwing coalition. The chapter presents evidence of the landowners' financial support of the partisan right, of their identification with the legislators of the right, and of the programmatic convergence between the agrarian elites' preferences and the policy positions of RN and UDI. As developed in Chapter 2, agrarian elites entered the electoral arena during the democratic transition because they perceived an existential threat. Cohesion within the Chilean agrarian elite (and the economic elites in general) facilitated party-building by lowering its coordination costs.

The Chilean case highlights the subjective dimension of the explanatory factor perception of threat. The chapter shows how agrarian elites' perception of an existential threat during the transition created incentives for them to organize in the electoral arena. This perception was based not only, or mainly, on the policy agenda of the center-left but on agrarian elites' previous experience with democracy where governments of the center-left and left implemented an extensive land reform. It presents evidence of how the memory of this traumatic event shaped agrarian elites' perceptions towards the parties of the *Concertación* in particular and the distributive dangers of democracy in general, leading them to believe they needed to organize in the electoral arena to protect their interests in the new democracy. In addition, agrarian elites feared that lobbying strategies would be ineffective to influence the policy agenda of the center-left as previous Christian Democratic and Socialist governments had cut off landowners' informal access to the state. Agrarian elites believed a strong rightwing legislative front could serve as a check on the center-left-controlled executive. As the cases of the Aylwin tax reform and the Water Code reform analysed here show, through partisan representation in Congress, agrarian elites have indeed been able to veto or crucially modify unwanted policies towards the sector.

4

Brazil

Landowners and Their Multiparty Congressional Caucus

4.1 INTRODUCTION

Despite its massive revenues and unlike in neighboring Argentina, the Brazilian agricultural sector has not been a target of the redistributive ambitions of leftwing governments. Quite the contrary, during the fourteen years of Workers Party (PT) administrations (2003–2016), the agricultural sector was the recipient of handsome state transfers in the form of subsidies and debt rollovers, averaging 0.65 percent of the country's GDP annually.[1] While the PT significantly increased the resources destined to small farmers and the rural poor, these paled in comparison to the funds allocated to agribusiness. For instance, between 2002 and 2011, funds for family farmers amounted only to 15 percent of the resources allocated to agribusiness in the same period (Sauer 2019, 112). In 2021, agribusiness represented 43 percent of Brazil's total exports (Barros and Silva 2022), and the country leads the international markets of soybean, corn, and sugarcane, among other commodities. That agricultural exports have not only been spared from taxation in the country with the highest tax burden in Latin America (Ondetti 2021) but subsidized during a period of soaring international prices and leftwing administrations, speaks volumes about the political clout of agrarian elites in Brazil.

This chapter shows how agrarian elites have adapted to democracy in Brazil, organizing in the electoral arena to protect their interests

---

[1] IBD-Agrimonitor, Total Support Estimate. This indicator reflects and includes all effects of public policies that differentially affect the agricultural sector, from support for the sector (e.g., subsidies) to penalties (e.g., taxes). See: https://agrimonitor.iadb.org (last accessed July 16, 2022).

through a nonpartisan, candidate-centered strategy. Brazilian landowners have formed their own multiparty congressional caucus, the Frente Parlamentar da Agropecuária (popularly known as the Bancada Ruralista). With size, voting discipline, and technical resources superior to those of most Brazilian parties, in the last two decades the support of the Agrarian Caucus has become crucial for the realization of the legislative agenda of right and leftwing presidents alike, granting agrarian elites great political leverage. Since its formation during the Constituent Assembly of 1987–1988, the Agrarian Caucus has secured an important and growing share of congressional seats, equivalent to between 14 and 23 percent of the Lower Chamber. During 2015–2019, the Agrarian Caucus had 119 members, 1.7 times the size of the largest party in the Lower Chamber.[2] Members of the Agrarian Caucus come from every region of the country and from parties across the ideological spectrum. The Agrarian Caucus is the most institutionalized caucus in the Brazilian Congress (Cascione and Araújo 2019). Ruralistas meet every week outside of Congress, at the caucus headquarters. The caucus has a permanent staff and a clear internal structure which facilitates legislators' coordination. Other large, well-known caucuses, such as the Evangelicals (known as the Bancada da Bíblia), lack this support structure and, consequently, have been less successful in bridging internal differences to advance their preferred policies.[3]

While industry caucuses are common in parliaments around the world, what sets the Brazilian Agrarian Caucus apart is that its legislators belong to the economic sector they represent. While members of the Rural Caucus in the USA represent districts where agriculture is a main economic activity, they are not farmers themselves. In contrast, most members of the Agrarian Caucus in Brazil are agricultural producers. During the 2015–2019 period, 95 percent of Ruralistas were agricultural producers themselves or came from a landowning family. Frequently, legislators in the Agrarian Caucus start their political careers as leaders of

---

[2] In the Brazilian Congress, caucuses or parliamentary fronts must register their members and authorities and these membership lists are publicly available (see Appendix B). Frequently, legislators will sign their belonging to a caucus to support its creation but without any real involvement in it. Therefore, I count as members of the Agrarian Caucus those legislators whom, in addition to being formally registered in the Frente Parlamentar da Agropecuária (FPA) also: (a) disclosed having been members of the caucus, agricultural producers, or leaders of agricultural associations on their Lower Chamber's official website or on their personal websites, (b) hold a leadership position in the FPA or the Instituto Pensar Agropecuária (IPA), or (c) participate actively within the FPA.

[3] See Freston (2001), Cascione and Araújo (2019), and Barbalho and Barboza (2020).

local producers' associations. This was the case for at least 44 percent of Agrarian Caucus leaders and 19 percent of all Ruralistas in 2015–2019.[4] In that fashion, while close collaboration between caucuses and interest groups sharing a policy interest is common,[5] agrarian elites in Brazil have gone one step further, blurring the insider–outsider dynamic that characterizes these relationships. Producers' associations and agribusiness firms in Brazil not only lobby the Agrarian Caucus: their leaders are part of it.

This chapter explains why agricultural producers in Brazil decided to invest in this form of nonpartisan electoral representation. Like in Chile, the perception of an existential threat during the democratic transition pushed Brazilian landowners to enter the electoral arena. The writing of a new constitution in an environment of unprecedented social mobilization and political support for land redistribution led agrarian elites to believe their property rights were in jeopardy. As argued in Chapter 2, nonelectoral strategies were not suitable in this setting. In a context where social and political support for land reform was widespread and most parties did not have a unified stance towards the issue, lobbying was unreliable. Through an electoral strategy, in contrast, agrarian elites could ensure redistributive land reform will not advance in the Constituent Assembly by electing legislators that would oppose it out of principle or self-interest.

Why did Brazilian agrarian elites not build a party to represent their interests in the Constituent Assembly? Agrarian elites' high political fragmentation impeded party-building. Unlike agrarian elites in Chile who had congruent economic and political interests and common ties to the same political machine during the democratic transition, in Brazil landowners had competing political interests. In rural municipalities, agrarian elites controlled rival clientelistic political machines connected to different parties or factions at the state and national level. For agrarian elites, coordinating in building a party to represent their interests in Congress would have meant losing control over their political bulwarks. As argued in Chapter 2, these high coordination costs hindered party-building in Brazil. For a fragmented agrarian elite, a candidate-centered strategy was more suitable because it allowed them to influence policymaking at the national level while retaining political autonomy at the local level.

The success of the Agrarian Caucus in advancing Brazilian agrarian elites' interests illustrates the advantages of a candidate-centered electoral

---

[4] As disclosed on the Lower Chamber official website or on legislators' personal websites.
[5] See Hammond (2001), Heaney (2010), and Ringe and Victor (2013).

strategy compared to other strategies available to economic elites in democracy (e.g., lobbying or party-building) theorized in Chapter 2: self-representation and multipartisanship. Self-representation has granted Brazilian agrarian elites direct access to the policymaking process. Unlike other stakeholders, agrarian elites do not need to persuade legislators to help their cause, as they are the ones drafting the bills and sitting on the committees that decide which ones make it to the floor. In turn, having members in many parties has increased the number of these agenda-setting positions landowners can control in the Brazilian Congress as well as guaranteed their presence in the legislative coalition of right and left-wing presidents alike. This chapter shows how both advantages were crucial for two of the most important legislative victories by Brazilian landowners: the 1988 Constitution article on land reform and the New Forest Code of 2012.

The rest of the chapter is organized as follows. Section 4.2 provides a historical background on Brazilian agriculture and landowners' corporatist organizations. Section 4.3 demonstrates how my theory's two independent variables – perception of an existential threat and intragroup fragmentation – shaped Brazilian agrarian elites' decision to pursue a candidate-centered electoral strategy during the democratic transition. Section 4.4 explains the continuity of the candidate-centered strategy into the contemporary period. Section 4.5 presents empirical evidence on how agrarian elites finance legislative campaigns, mobilize voters, and subsidize the legislative work of politicians from their ranks, independently of their partisan affiliation. Section 4.6 illustrates how the Agrarian Caucus works by analysing the passage of a bill highly relevant to agrarian elites' interests, the New Forest Code.

4.2 AGRICULTURE AND POLITICS IN BRAZIL: HISTORICAL BACKGROUND

4.2.1 The Conservative Modernization of the Countryside (1965–2002)

The military government that ruled Brazil between 1964 and 1985 implemented an ambitious development plan centered on industrialization. However, the military also believed that in order for the industrialization plan to succeed, the Brazilian countryside needed to modernize. Increasing agricultural productivity was key to feeding industrial workers and generating the foreign exchange earnings needed to import supplies for the developing industries. To that end, the military implemented a series of policies during the 1960s and 1970s that resulted in an unequal modernization of the countryside. While export-producing sectors expanded spectacularly, incorporating new production technologies, producers for the domestic market, mostly small and medium-sized farmers, stagnated. Between 1965 and 1977, agricultural production for export grew substantially at an average annual rate of 22 percent (Baer 2014, 281). Soybean expansion was particularly impressive: between 1970 and 1989, the area under cultivation grew by 767.8 percent, while its production increased by 1231.1 percent (Baer 2014, 289).

Three policies implemented by the military were key for the impressive expansion of agriculture in the 1960s and 1970s. The first was the creation of the Brazilian Agricultural Research Corporation (Empresa Brasileira de Pesquisa Agropecuária – Embrapa in Portuguese), a state agency dedicated to developing human capital and technology in the sector. The second was a policy of highly subsidized credit – with interest rates substantially below the rate of inflation – benefiting mostly large export-oriented producers. From 1975 to 1982, the annual subsidy through credit to the agricultural sector averaged 14.7 percent of the value of agricultural production (Helfand 1999, 7). However, only 11 percent of these loans were allocated to small producers (Baer 2014, 298). Moreover, while export-oriented producers benefited from subsidized credit, producers for the domestic market were hurt by price controls. Subsidies to credit were discontinued in the mid 1980s when the fiscal crisis made them unsustainable. The third policy was a program of colonization of the Amazon and the center-west savannah as a substitute for land reform. Through infrastructure development and credit, the government incentivized settlements in frontier areas. Embrapa's development of new crop varieties suitable for arid soils was key to the expansion of agriculture in these new colonized areas. As a result, the northern and center-west regions of the country combined experienced a 47.3 percent increase in the amount of cultivated land during the 1970s (Ondetti 2008, 63).

The modernization of agriculture also had a political purpose: to halt rural unrest. Besides repressing peasants' organizations, the military established a new legal framework for land reform, the Land Statute (*Estatuto da Terra*) in 1964. The Land Statute laid the bases for a land reform that would, if implemented, have resulted in a substantive redistribution of rural land, fulfilling property's social welfare purpose sanctioned in the 1946 Brazilian Constitution.[6] At the same time, the military regime approved a constitutional amendment allowing the state to compensate expropriated landowners with state bonds rather than cash, which made land reform implementation much more feasible by greatly reducing its fiscal cost (Ondetti 2016). Despite this propitious legal framework, land reform did not advance during the dictatorship, due to ample resistance from the landed elites whose political support the military needed. However, the Land Statute provided the legal basis for an extensive program of land redistribution that could be implemented under more favorable political circumstances.

In the early 1990s, the end of ISI policies that had discriminated against agriculture for many decades gave new impulse to export-oriented producers. The Collor administration (1990–1992) launched a broad program of economic liberalization and deregulation that the Cardoso administration (1995–2002) continued and deepened. The role of the state in agricultural markets was substantially reduced. Restrictions on exports, taxes, and price controls were eliminated as well as tariff and nontariff protections for agricultural products. From the early 1990s on, Brazilian agriculture was increasingly exposed to international competition, which forced producers to modernize. Agribusiness growth continued and accelerated in the 2000s, driven by the increase in international commodity prices.

As a result of all these changes, Brazilian agriculture was radically transformed. It was no longer the backward, unproductive, state-dependent sector of the early 1960s. By the end of the 1990s, agribusiness was one of the most dynamic and modern sectors of the Brazilian economy. Between 1990 and 2017, agriculture's value added tripled (Figure 4.1). By 2003, Brazil was the world's second largest producer of soybeans, the third largest producer of corn, and the largest producer of coffee, sugar, alcohol, and fruit juice. Brazil's share of world agricultural exports grew from 2.34 percent in 1990 to 3.34 percent in 2002 (Baer 2014, 302).

However, the modernization of the countryside and the expansion of export-oriented agriculture had negative impacts on the peasantry. The abundance of cheap credit facilitated the mechanization of production, which, in turn, together with the growth of less labor-intensive commercial crops, led to the expulsion of permanent resident laborers from large latifundia. Between 1985 and 1996, employment in agriculture decreased

---

[6] Art. 147 of the 1946 Constitution established that "the use of property should be conditioned upon social welfare," subordinating private property rights to social interests.

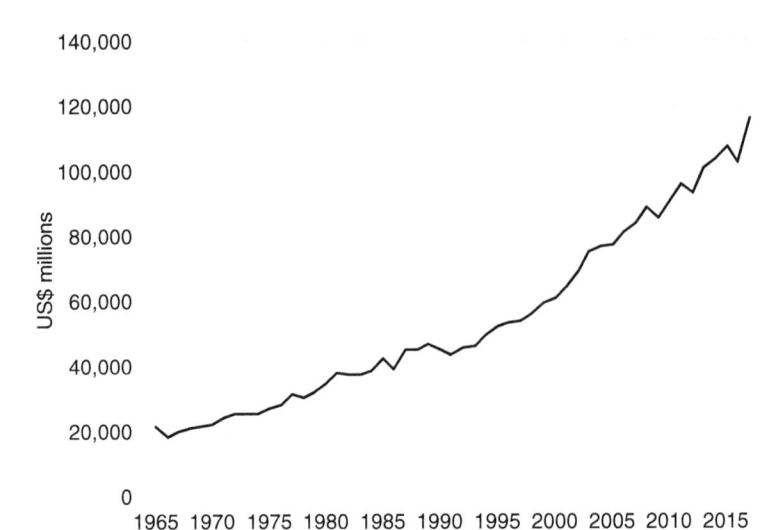

FIGURE 4.1 Agriculture value added (constant 2010 US$): Brazil, 1965–2017. Source: World Bank.[7]

by 23 percent while total agricultural output rose by 30 percent (Baer 2014, 303). In addition, the rise of land prices undermined small producers' access to farmland, while rural wages continued to be much lower than urban ones. In 1988, the average per capita income of a rural household was only 31 percent of the average per capita income of an urban household, up from 26 percent in 1970 (Baer 2014, 298). As a consequence, even when rural poverty had fallen from 69.6 percent in 1970 to 42 percent in 1980, it rose again during the 1980s, remaining at very high levels, with 52.1 percent of rural households living below the poverty line in 1988 (Cavalcanti and Villela 1991, 49).[8]

Land inequality, historically very high, also worsened as a result of the modernization process. Between 1960 and 1996, the share of agricultural land in farms with 100 hectares or less shrunk from 23 percent to 19.9 percent. At the same time, the percentage of agricultural land in farms with 1,000 hectares or more grew from 43.5 to 45.1 (Table 4.1). As a consequence of these changes, millions of people emigrated from the countryside to the peripheries of the main urban areas. The share of the country's rural population decreased from 49 percent in 1965, to

---

[7] See: https://data.worldbank.org/indicator/NV.AGR.TOTL.ZS (accessed April 2019). Includes forestry and fishing.
[8] Poverty line established at a quarter of the minimum wage per capita.

4.2 *Agriculture and Politics: Historical Background*

TABLE 4.1 *Percentage of land held by small and large farms, and land Gini Index: Brazil, 1960–1996*

	<100 ha	> 1,000 ha	Gini Index
1960	23	43.5	84.2
1975	21.3	42.9	85.5
1985	21.2	43.7	85.8
1995/6	19.9	45.1	85.7

Source: Author's calculations based on IBGE Agrarian Census.

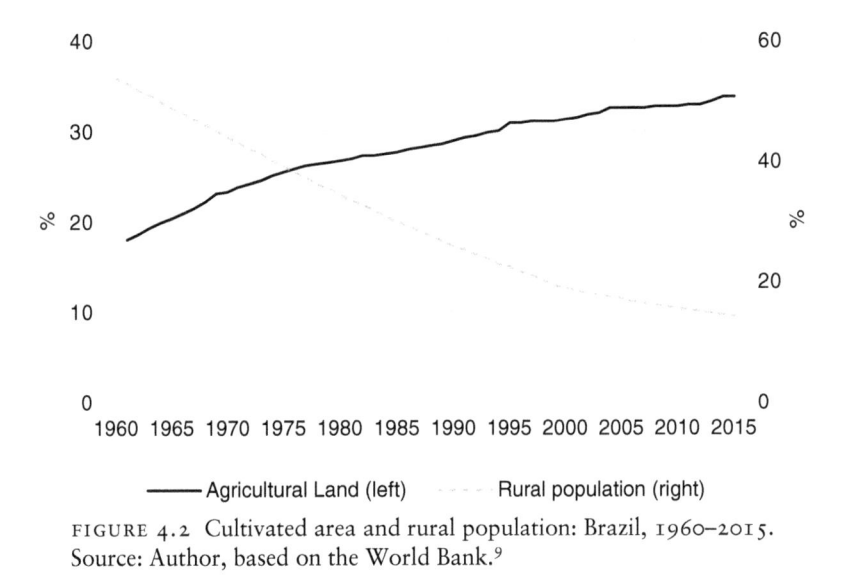

FIGURE 4.2 Cultivated area and rural population: Brazil, 1960–2015. Source: Author, based on the World Bank.[9]

30 percent in 1985, and further to 22.4 percent in 1995 (Figure 4.2). At the same time, the area under cultivation expanded from 20.4 percent of the country's total area in 1965 to 27.6 percent in 1985, and to 32.6 percent in 2005 (Figure 4.2).

4.2.2 Agrarian Elites and Politics Before the Third Wave

Throughout Brazilian history, land ownership has been a source of political power. During the Old Republic (1889–1930), Brazilian local politics

---

[9] See: https://data.worldbank.org/indicator/SP.RUR.TOTL.ZS (accessed April 2019).

was dominated by *coronéis*.[10] *Coronéis* were local bosses who delivered the votes of their clients to state-level and national-level politicians who, in exchange, gave the *coronéis* liberty to rule their bailiwicks as they pleased. At the local level, the *coronéis* controlled access to jobs in the public administration, as well as the provision of welfare and justice. In this fashion, the *coronéis* were intermediaries linking voters to parties and to the state. *Coronéis* were usually landlords who mobilized the votes of the peasants living on their lands. Although most peasants were illiterate and therefore could not vote, fraud was a recurrent practice (Love 1970, 10).

The emergence of urban workers as a relevant political actor and the secular drop in rural population undermined the bases of *coronelismo*, and by the 1960s the system had collapsed in most states. However, patron–client relations continued to dominate politics in the interior of the country. When the rural electorate shrunk, local bosses used the control of employment in the public sector to capture the urban vote (Hagopian 1996). During the military regime, rural bosses continued using their clientelistic machines to secure support for the official party. As a consequence, at the time of the democratic transition, most parties were little more than the patronage machines of regional oligarchies (Hagopian 1990). In rural areas, landed elites controlled these machines.

4.2.3 Agrarian Elites' Corporatist Organizations

Symptomatic of their political fragmentation, agrarian elites in Brazil are organized in multiple corporatist associations. Parallel to the official corporatist structure are many non-state-sanctioned organizations, which can be both sector-wide and product specific. Four of these associations played an important role in the political organization of agrarian elites during the democratic transition.

The first is the National Confederation of Agriculture (CNA), founded in 1951. The CNA belongs to the official corporatist structure and, until 2017, received compulsory contributions from every agricultural producer in the country.[11] Agricultural producers are organized at the local level in associations that form state-level federations and these federations make up the CNA. In 2021, the CNA claimed to represent five

---

[10] The description of *coronelismo* in this paragraph is based on Leal (1948).
[11] The labor reform of July 2017 (Law 13,467/2017) made contributions to all corporatist associations (business and labor) voluntary.

million rural producers organized into 2,000 local rural associations and twenty-seven state federations.[12]

The second association, also part of the state-sanctioned corporatist structure, is the Organization of Brazilian Cooperatives (OCB) founded in 1969. Cooperatives are also organized in state-level federations that form the OCB. Within the OCB, agricultural cooperatives are strong actors, especially in the south of the country where cooperatives are an important source of employment and state GDP. In 2017, the OCB claimed to represent a million producers, organized in some 1,500 agricultural cooperatives.[13]

The third association is the Brazilian Rural Society (SRB). The SRB is not part of the corporatist structure that until 2017 benefited from producers' compulsory contributions. Founded in 1919, the SRB is the oldest of the four associations described here. The association represents mostly producers in the state of São Paulo. Although not a strong actor today, the SRB was very active politically during the democratic transition and participated in the founding of the Agrarian Caucus.

Lastly, the Rural Democratic Union (UDR) was a non-state-sanctioned association of mostly large ranchers from the states of Goiás, Paraná, and São Paulo, that emerged in 1985 as a reaction against President Sarney's land reform plan. Of the producers' associations, the UDR was the most radical and militant opponent of land reform, frequently recurring to violent means. The UDR expanded throughout the country very quickly and was very active during the democratic transition, especially in the 1987–1988 Constituent Assembly. However, after landowners managed to kill the prospects of redistributive land reform in the Constituent Assembly, the association was officially dismantled in 1993 amidst internal disputes.

4.3 THE BIRTH OF THE AGRARIAN CAUCUS: EXISTENTIAL THREATS AND POLITICAL FRAGMENTATION DURING THE DEMOCRATIC TRANSITION

This section presents evidence on how the perception of an existential threat as well as their political fragmentation explain why Brazilian agrarian elites decided to form a multiparty caucus during the democratic transition. The threat of a radical redistribution of land prompted

---

[12] See: www.cnabrasil.org.br/cna/quem-somos-cna (accessed, August 12, 2021).
[13] Author's interview with Fabiola Motta, OCB director of government relations, Brasília, March 27, 2017.

agrarian elites in Brazil to organize in the electoral arena but political divisions between them hampered party-building. Agrarian elites were invested in rival political machines that competed for power at the state and local level. Given the high coordination costs that cohabitating in a single national partisan structure would have entailed, Brazilian agrarian elites deployed instead a candidate-centered electoral strategy.

4.3.1 The Threat of Land Reform and the Need for Electoral Representation

Agrarian elites had several reasons to feel threatened during Brazil's democratic transition. First, the status quo regarding land reform was unfavorable to landowners' interests because under the Land Statute and the 1946 constitution, property rights were subordinated to the "social interest."[14] Accordingly, the state could expropriate holdings that were not fulfilling "their social welfare function" and compensate owners with state bonds.[15] In 1985, only 14 percent of farmland was under production (Baer 2014, 289), which meant that the great majority of large farms were subject to expropriation under the prevailing legal framework. During the military regime, it was never in the government's interest to implement the Land Statute, so landowners were safe. However, it was unclear what a new democratic government would do, especially given that social mobilization demanding land reform was mounting.

Social and political support for land reform ran high in Brazil during the democratic transition. Land inequality was very high and poverty in rural areas was pervasive. In 1985, fewer than 1 percent of landowners owned 44 percent of Brazilian land while 53 percent of farms occupied less than 3 percent of the land and 2.6 million rural workers lacked land or land titles (Lapp 2004, 120). At the time, the poverty rate among agricultural workers was 72.7 percent (Ondetti 2008, 64).

Growing unrest in the countryside accompanied the process of political opening since the late 1970s. In 1975, a group of progressive priests and nuns created the Pastoral Land Commission (Comissão Pastoral da Terra – CPT in Portuguese) with the explicit goal of helping peasants to organize politically. Building on these initial organizational efforts, the powerful Movimento dos Trabalhadores Rurais Sem Terra (MST) was formed in the early 1980s.[16]

---

[14] See Section 2.1.
[15] Unlike compensations in cash, bonds entailed a deferred payment and their future value was uncertain.
[16] On the MST history since its formation until the early 2000s, see Ondetti (2008).

4.3 The Birth of the Agrarian Caucus

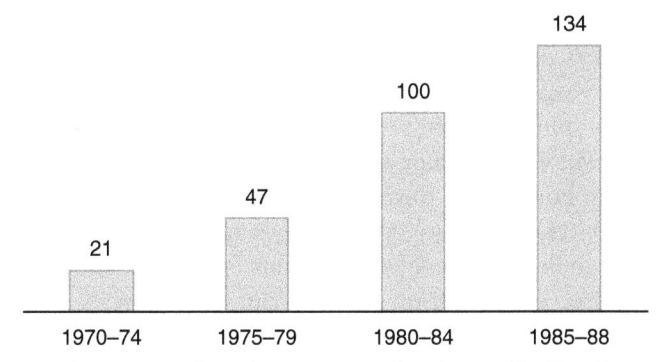

```
                                                    134
                                        100
                              47
                  21
              ┌──────┐    ┌──────┐   ┌──────┐   ┌──────┐
              1970–74    1975–79    1980–84    1985–88
```

FIGURE 4.3 Average number of peasants murdered annually: Brazil, 1970–1988. Source: Author, based on CPT and Ondetti (2008, 87).

The grassroots organizational work of the CPT in the countryside was key to the emergence of the MST, helping to turn isolated outbursts of local protest into a large and sustained social movement (Ondetti 2008). Moreover, the Catholic Church's support of the land reform struggle increased the movement's social legitimacy. Rural conflict multiplied across the country in the early years of the democratic regime. Between 1985 and 1988, the CPT recorded more than 700 conflicts per year.[17] These conflicts were both defensive attempts by squatters or resident farmworkers to avoid expulsion by landowners or speculators as well as offensive initiatives meant to pressure the authorities for land reform. Landowners met organization by the peasants with outright violence. Murders in the countryside related to rural conflict increased greatly. Between 1970 and 1988, the average number of peasants murdered annually multiplied sixfold (Figure 4.3).

The alliance of opposition parties that came to power in 1985 had committed to land reform, as many of its members saw land inequality as the root of other social inequalities in Brazil. Many Brazilian politicians at the time considered the high concentration of land ownership in the countryside and the allocation of the best land for producing export commodities as the key causes of growing poverty on the outskirts of the main urban areas (Martínez-Lara 1996, 41). As a presidential candidate, Tancredo Neves of the PMDB had promised a broad-ranging land reform program through the implementation and enforcement of the Land Statute, and after his election, he appointed a long-time supporter of the

---

[17] Conflicts related to land, rural labor, and agrarian policy.

cause, Nelson Ribeiro, to the key position of minister of land reform. After Tancredo's death, President Sarney – who had been a member of the pro-military party for his entire career until his defection to the opposition in 1984 – put Tancredo's reform plans in motion. In a gesture that shocked agrarian elites, Sarney unveiled his National Agrarian Reform Plan (PNRA in Portuguese) during a national meeting of rural workers in March 1985 (Helfand 1999, 31). Sarney's ambitious PNRA promised to resettle 1.4 million landless families in his five-year presidential term. However, intense pressure from agrarian elites led Sarney's administration first to delay the implementation of the PNRA and then to significantly limit its scope. Conceding to landed elites, the PNRA ultimately specified that productive lands, even latifundia, were not subject to expropriation and that expropriation was a solution of last resort where agreement was not possible (Baltar 1990).

The writing of a new constitution, however, opened a new window of opportunity for pro-land reform interests to advance their cause. Land reform figured prominently in the agenda of the 1987–1988 Constituent Assembly. For Brazilian landowners, two issues to be defined in the new constitution were central. First, agrarian elites, along with the rest of the business community, wanted to redefine private property to decouple it from its "social welfare purpose," a proviso that allowed unproductive land to be expropriated. Second, producers wanted a constitutional article on land reform to state explicitly that productive farms could not be expropriated, regardless of their size (Dreifuss 1989, 53).

The problem for landowners was that given the consensus on the necessity of land reform that existed among the main political actors, including many rightwing politicians, potential allies were very hard to identify on a partisan basis. The enfranchisement of illiterates – disproportionately the rural poor – moreover, added a new dimension of concern for agrarian elites who feared that politicians trying to win over those new votes in national and state-level elections might be tempted to support land redistribution (Lapp 2004). Illiterates represented around 25 percent of the Brazilian population at the time, or more than 18 million people.[18] A survey of legislators conducted during the Constituent Assembly showed that only 4 percent of legislators fully rejected the idea of a land reform, while most (66 percent) supported restricting redistribution to

---

[18] According to Brazil's Institute of Statistics, IBGE. See: https://seriesestatisticas.ibge.gov.br/ (accessed July 3, 2019).

4.3 The Birth of the Agrarian Caucus

TABLE 4.2 *Stance towards land reform by parties in the Constituent Assembly (percentage of legislators)*

Party	Total rejection	Limited to nonproductive holdings	Radical
PMDB	3	62	35
PFL	7	83	10
PDS	10	90	–
PDT	4	46	50
PTB	6	94	–
PT/PC/PSB	–	4	96
PL/PDC	–	100	–
Total	4	66	30

Source: Author, based on Martínez-Lara (1996, 74).

nonproductive farms (Table 4.2).[19] This was the case also of the great majority of legislators in parties of the right. Support for land reform restricted to nonproductive land ran as high as 90 percent among PDS representatives and 80 percent within the PFL. Crucially, 35 percent of PMDB legislators, the largest party in the Constituent Assembly with 53 percent of the seats, supported a radical redistribution of land (i.e., including productive landholdings) that would "change the structure of landholdings in the country and correct social injustice" (Martins Rodrigues 1987, cited in Martínez-Lara 1996, 74).[20]

As argued in Chapter 2, nonelectoral strategies of political influence were not suitable in this scenario where failing to influence policymaking could have been very costly for agrarian elites. Lobbying was too risky in a context where legislators' electoral incentives to support land reform were strong. Agrarian elites needed to secure the presence of legislators in the Constituent Assembly who would oppose land reform out

---

[19] Although the survey was conducted among legislators elected to the Constituent Assembly and therefore postdates the 1986 elections, the results are still representative of the uncertainty producers faced at the time because they show that even after producers had secured the election of a significant number of like-minded politicians, the great majority of the Assembly still supported land reform.

[20] The question was: With regards to land reform, with which of the following sentences do you agree the most? (a) Instead of land reform entailing the distribution of land, the government should stimulate and protect farmers and rural producers; (b) A land reform is necessary but the distribution of land should be limited to nonproductive properties; (c) A radical land reform is necessary in order to change the structure or rural landowning in Brazil and to correct social injustice. (Lapp 2004, n. 52.)

of principle (or self-interest) without ceding to electoral incentives or popular pressure. As the president of the SRB during the Constituent Assembly told me in an interview, the safest way of doing this was to help politicians among their ranks get elected to Congress:

We might have been the only business sector [...] that truly understood what the Constituent Assembly was about. Other sectors or social groups [...] did not have a notion of what the Constituent Assembly meant at the time. [...] *The thing is that we were a target, we felt that all we had, all that agricultural producers had built in the last two or three generations, was in jeopardy.* We felt it all could disappear. In a situation like that you are much more willing to build a resistance, a political movement to prevent that from happening. [...] I believe that was what mobilized our base, producers in the interior [...] because *it was all or nothing.* [...] I believe that is why we organized, we recognized the gravity of the situation and *that is why we mobilized before the elections to elect a big enough group of legislators that could defend our interests in Brasília.*[21]

As the previous quote illustrates, the threat of a radical land reform was decisive for rural producers' electoral mobilization. Like Teles de Menezes highlights in his testimony, in that regard Brazilian landed elites were different from other business elites that did not perceive such an existential threat and, hence, did not see the need to organize in the electoral arena. Thus, even when electoral rules in Brazil may facilitate party infiltration by interest groups, they do not explain why certain groups decided to organize in the electoral arena during the democratic transition while others did not. Perceived levels of threat explain this variation better.

4.3.2 Brazilian Elites' Political Fragmentation and the High Cost of Party-Building

Why did actors with the political, economic, and organizational resources to build a national political party decided instead for a candidate-centered strategy? Consider the options faced by UDR founder and current Governor of Goiás Ronaldo Caiado. Born to a family of large agricultural producers and one of the most important political dynasties of the state of Goiás,[22] Caiado had the political connections and economic resources to build a political party and run for Congress in 1986.

---

[21] Author's interview with Flávio Teles de Menezes, São Paulo, May 9, 2017, emphasis added.
[22] The political roots of the Caiado family go back to 1860, with the governor's great-great-grandfather being the first to occupy public office (Gonçalves Costa 2012, 112).

Instead, he used his resources to connect with other influential producers throughout the country and build the UDR. But rather than registering the UDR as a political party, Caiado used the UDR's national structure – which at the time was more extensive than many parties – as well as producer federations and cooperatives to identify, finance, and mobilize votes for like-minded candidates running under diverse party labels.[23]

I argue that Brazilian agrarian elites could not engage in party-building because they were politically fragmented at the local level. By political fragmentation I mean that agrarian elites controlled rival political machines that competed for local power. Brazilian politics at the time of the democratic transition was regional, personalistic and clientelist (Hagopian 1996; Mainwaring 1999). Political elites competed with each other for the control of local politics through clientelistic networks that were most often family-based (Hagopian 1996, 19). Thus, partisan divides at the time reflected personal or family rivalries more than ideological divisions (Mainwaring, Meneguello, and Power 2000). In rural areas, local bosses were frequently large landowners.

As argued in Chapter 2, this political fragmentation increased the coordination costs of party-building for Brazilian landowners. For agrarian elites whose power was based on local clientelistic political machines, party-building would have meant surrendering their local sources of power. For instance, building a national party would have entailed coordinating among local bosses on candidacies for local and state-level offices, putting their clientelistic networks at the service of former political rivals. By contrast, agrarian elites and their political allies at the state level were interested in a coordination strategy that would allow them to elect enough representatives to block radical land reform attempts, yet at the same time preserve their autonomy to compete in local politics.[24] Through a candidate-centered strategy, local elites could keep their partisan structures for themselves, choose their favorite candidates, and mobilize their clientelist networks to get these candidates elected. By building a multiparty caucus, agrarian elites across districts could coordinate to influence national-level policies without having to coordinate with rival political elites in their state or municipality.

---

[23] Author's interviews with Caiado, Brasília, March 22, 2017, Roberto Rodrigues, São Paulo, May 5, 2017, and Teles de Menezes, São Paulo, May 9, 2017, presidents of UDR, OCB and SRB, respectively, at the time of the Constituent Assembly.
[24] On Brazilian political elites' preference for personalistic, local electoral channels, and how this has negatively affected party-system institutionalization in the country, see Mainwaring (1999).

Agrarian elites' political fragmentation cannot be a product of electoral rules as it predates the current post-1979 system. Agrarian elites' political fragmentation has been a constant across Brazil's changing electoral rules and party systems. Brazil has today the most fragmented party system in the world (Zucco and Power 2021), but this has not been always the case. Political factionalism, however, has always been high among rural elites. Landowners belonged to rival factions even under the bipartisan system imposed by the military government between 1965 and 1979. During this period, the military forced conservative political elites into one official party, ARENA. Nonetheless, it was a common practice for agrarian elites to infiltrate the ranks of both the government and the opposition party to maximize their political influence. For instance, in 1979, 14.3 percent of ARENA senators and 12 percent of MDB senators were landowners (Fleischer 1988, 124–29). More importantly, competition among factions, particularly within ARENA, was so fierce that the military government – attending to a demand by local politicians and against its own will – had to modify electoral rules to allow parties to run multiple candidates for first-past-the-post elections (mayors and senators) (Jenks 1979; Kinzo 1988; Power 2000; Grinberg 2009). Like a multiparty caucus, the *sublegendas* system, in place between 1966 and 1979, was a way of accommodating various groups within a national-level organization (ARENA) while allowing politicians to maintain their rivalries at the state and local level (Power 2000). As an ARENA legislator at the time explained: "The reconciliation of electoral and partisan interests of the remnants of previously adversarial organizations was the *most difficult problem faced by the [military] government*. How to put them together in the same boat, and particularly, how to *choose from among them the candidates* for the next legislative elections?"[25]

Gross's (1973) study of factionalism in local politics in rural Brazil describes a scene common in the Northeast before the democratic transition that offers a clear illustration of the concept of political fragmentation utilized here and how it may hinder party-building. In Victoria, a rural town in the state of Bahia, two political dynasties, both with ties to agriculture, had competed for local power for decades. Electoral competition in the town centered around two ARENA factions, one supported by the Rocha family, who were ranchers, and the other supported by

---

[25] Mem de Sá cited in Kinzo (1988, 18), emphasis added.

the Morais family, who cultivated sisal. When the military government pressured ARENA to field just one candidate for mayor in 1972, the excluded faction ordered its clientele to leave their ballots blank. Out of a total of 3,000 ballots cast in that election, 1,000 were blank (Gross 1973, 138).

Factional divides among the agrarian elite continued into the transition to democracy. Describing political alignments during the 1986 elections in the Northeast, Lapp (2004, 140) notes that in Rio Grande do Norte, four political families controlled six parties, meaning that in some cases the same family owned more than one party. In the same vein, Lula da Silva, then a young candidate to the governorship of São Paulo, said in 1982, "PDS and PMDB are flour from the same sack [...]. This is even more visible when we go to the interior of São Paulo and see the landowner candidate from the PDS running against the landowner candidate from the PMDB."[26]

4.3.3 The Candidate-Centered Strategy in Action

As the theory introduced in Chapter 2 predicts, the threat of a new legal framework allowing for a radical redistribution of land prompted agrarian elites in Brazil to organize in the electoral arena. Because landowners were connected to fragmented local political machines, party-building was not feasible. Instead, agrarian elites pursued a nonpartisan, candidate-centered electoral strategy. Agricultural producers had two assets to help bring their people into politics, their corporatist organizations and their ties to local political machines. This section first describes how agricultural producers used those resources to elect candidates from their ranks to the 1987–1988 Constituent Assembly. Then, it shows how agrarian elites organized within and outside of the Assembly to stop redistributive land reform.

4.3.3.1 Producers' Associations and the Mobilization of the Rural Vote during the 1986 Elections

Landowners activated their local political networks with the objective of electing a sufficient number of legislators to block land reform in the Constituent Assembly. Producer federations, local UDR branches, and agricultural cooperatives across the country began to identify, finance, and mobilize votes for candidates sharing their policy preferences,

---
[26] Cited in Lapp (2004, 139).

effectively becoming, as UDR national leader Ronaldo Caiado put it, political brokers for these candidates.[27]

Among landowners' organizations, UDR was the most active in the implementation of the candidate-centered electoral strategy and its nation-wide structure was key to its success. After its foundation in 1985, the UDR quickly expanded across Brazil; by the end of 1986, it already had fifty-five local offices in fourteen states and approximately 50,000 members.[28] Analysing the 254 newspaper articles that mentioned UDR between 1986 and 1990 in the archives of the Brazilian Congress Library,[29] I found a geographical correlation between the location of UDR local offices and the areas where rural conflict was most intense at the time, which suggests a connection between landowners' perception of threat and their incentives for political organization.[30] UDR local leaders frequently stated Sarney's land reform plan and MST land occupations as the main reason for landowners' political mobilization and commented on the difficulty of organizing UDR branches where rural conflict was low.

Given the high political fragmentation of agrarian elites, the founders of UDR resisted the idea of turning their association into a political party. My analysis of newspaper articles shows that UDR leaders believed that turning their corporatist association into a partisan one would limit its capacity to represent agrarian elites' interests. UDR leaders frequently stated that it was not possible for UDR to become a party or to integrate into an existing one because agricultural producers had multiple different political affiliations. Therefore, becoming partisan would divide agrarian producers and weaken their political influence. UDR leaders insisted the organization remained a "supra-partisan" one. In their view, by

---

[27] The Brazilian expression is *"cabos eleitorais,"* brokers who mobilize support for a given politician at the local level, organizing rallies, distributing goods, and mobilizing voters on election day. "UDR leiloa mil cabeças de gado e arrecada fundos para campanha," *Folha de São Paulo*, September 26, 1986.

[28] "UDR vai apoiar 40 candidatos à Constituinte," *Folha de São Paulo*, September 25, 1986;"UDR revelará nomes de todos os candidatos que apóia", *Jornal do Brasil*, November 1, 1986.

[29] This archive reviews seven national newspapers: *Folha de São Paulo, O Estado de São Paulo, Jornal do Brasil, Jornal da Tarde, Jornal de Brasília, Correio Brasiliense,* and *O Globo*. Articles are organized in folders by theme and chronologically.

[30] For instance, the largest and more active UDR local offices were in the region of Pontal do Paranapanema in the interior of the state of São Paulo, Eastern Mato Grosso, West Goiás, and the so-called region of bico do papagaio at the confluence between Northern Tocantins, Southeast Pará, and Southwest Maranhão, all zones with high levels of rural conflict at the time. "O trator da direita," *Veja*, June 18, 1986.

4.3 The Birth of the Agrarian Caucus

supporting multiple parties, agrarian elites could increase the number of candidates they could help elect to Congress, state, and local-level offices.

During the 1986 electoral campaign, the UDR organized several cattle auctions to raise funds for approximately forty candidates from multiple parties, including the PMDB, PTB, PFL, PDS, PDC, and PL.[31] These auctions were major political events whose purpose was not only to raise funds but also to introduce candidates to potential voters (Payne 2000). In addition, the UDR printed a list of all the candidates it supported and distributed it among its members.[32] In an interview, UDR founder Ronaldo Caiado explained to me the kind of work that the UDR and other producers' associations did to get like-minded candidates into the Constituent Assembly, highlighting the local character of the endeavor:

> Each local leader from the associations identified a representative, a candidate in that region and he would campaign for that person in his municipality. He [the local leader] had the responsibility to use his time and prestige to defend that candidate and win votes for him.
>
> *How did you know whom to support?*
>
> It was a *local decision*, there is no way to decide that from Brasília [...]. We talked to the person; "look, we are going to support you, so you are our representative for federal legislator," something like that. It could be a member of the local producers' union, or the federation, or a cooperative, sometimes it will be a local politician that identified himself with the sector.[33]

The candidate-centered strategy was not partisan. Associations supported the campaigns of like-minded candidates belonging to many different parties. This included right-of-center parties, but also numerous candidates in the, at the time, center-left PMDB. What was relevant for agrarian elites when choosing whom to support was not their partisan affiliation but their identification with sectoral interests. The statements of two UDR leaders to the press at that time illustrate the nonpartisan character of agrarian elites' electoral strategy:

> We are going to ask our affiliates to give financial support to the *candidates chosen by our class* [...]. We *support no party* [...]. We *support candidates* because we need representatives inside Congress to turn to *when our class is in trouble*.[34]

---

[31] "A UDR quer eleger 51% dos constituintes," *Jornal da Tarde*, June 19, 1986; "UDR vai apoiar 40 candidatos à Constituinte," *Folha de São Paulo*, September 25, 1986; "UDR leiloa mil cabeças de gado e arrecada fundos para campanha," *Folha de São Paulo*, September 26, 1986; *Correio Braziliense*, March 3, 1988.

[32] "UDR revelará nomes de todos os candidatos que apóia," *Jornal do Brasil*, November 1, 1986.

[33] Author's interview, emphasis added.

[34] Roosevelt dos Santos, *Folha de São Paulo*, September 25, 1986, emphasis added.

If someone identifies with our ideas, we invest in those people, we make candidates out of them, we win elections and we build our political base. *Partisan identities are not relevant.*[36]

The work of the sectoral associations in the 1986 campaign paid off and agricultural producers ended up being the best self-represented interest group in the Constituent Assembly. The number of landowners in Congress more than doubled with respect to the previous legislative period. At ninety-one legislators, agricultural producers made up 16 percent of the members of the Constituent Assembly. In contrast, rural workers, the main constituency for land reform, had no direct representation (Fleischer 1988, 32–33). All major parties had agricultural producers in their ranks, except, unsurprisingly, those on the extreme left, but most of the producers were in PMDB and PFL, the largest parties in the Assembly. Many of these legislators were leaders of producers' associations. The UDR alone elected twenty-four legislators from its ranks in six different parties.[37] As Table 4.3 shows, these landowner legislators were not only in right-of-center parties but, in fact, the majority of them were in the center-left, in the PMDB and PDT. The offensive against land reform within the Constituent Assembly was led by Allyson Paulinelli, a PFL legislator from Minas Gerais and president of the CNA;

TABLE 4.3 *Number of legislators who were agricultural producers or UDR leaders in the Constituent Assembly by party*[35]

	Total legislators	Agricultural producers	UDR local leaders
PMDB	298	54	6
PFL	133	18	11
PDS	38	6	2
PDT	26	3	–
PTB	19	5	2
PL	7	1	1
PDC	6	4	2
Total	527	91	24

Source: Author's calculations based on Fleischer (1988) and *Correio Braziliense*, March 3, 1988.

[35] Table 4.3 only displays parties with landowners in their ranks. In total, there were 559 legislators in the Assembly from thirteen different parties.
[36] Ronaldo Caiado, *Jornal do Brasil*, April 27, 1988, emphasis added.
[37] "Na aliança com Centrão, a força na Constituinte," *Correio Braziliense*, March 3, 1988.

Roberto Cardoso Alves, a PMDB legislator from São Paulo and leader of the SRB; and Arnaldo Rosa Prata, a PMDB legislator from Minas Gerais and leader of the ranchers' association. The fact that two of the main advocates for the agrarian elites' agenda in the Constituent Assembly were in a party – the center-left PMDB – whose leadership supported the expropriation of productive latifundia is indicative of landowners' multiple and flexible partisan loyalties.

Agrarian elites' choice for a candidate-centered, multipartisan strategy did not respond to a lack of viable conservative partisan options. Even though most Brazilian parties are today catchall parties, since the democratic transition and until the early 2000s, a rightwing party, the Partido da Frente Liberal (PFL)[38] was the second-largest in Congress and held important cabinet positions in every government (Power 2000; Power and Rodrigues-Silveira 2019). Moreover, the PFL is the only Brazilian party that has consistently remained on the right of the partisan spectrum since its foundation (Zucco and Power 2021, 484). However, despite the PFL being a viable authoritarian successor party with a clear programmatic commitment to private property and free enterprise (Power 2000, 80–81; 2018), it did not enjoy the undivided support of the Brazilian agrarian elites in the way the RN did in Chile during the democratic transition. As Table 4.3 shows, in the 1986 elections, agrarian elites run their candidates in parties across the ideological spectrum, including the PFL but also its main center-left rival, the PMDB, and other center-right regional parties like the PL, PDC, and PTB. Even when agrarian elites had a nation-wide structure and the potential political allies to build a strong rightwing party, their political fragmentation at the local level impeded party-building. Instead, they pursued an electoral strategy that would give them the autonomy to integrate their local clientelistic machines to different parties according to regional political dynamics.

4.3.3.2 *The Fight against Land Reform in the Constituent Assembly*
The strong presence of agrarian elites in the Constituent Assembly was not, however, enough to guarantee them veto power over land reform attempts. The reporter of the Land Reform Subcommittee, the legislator in charge of drafting the constitutional chapter on land reform, was not sympathetic to producers' interests. Oswaldo Lima Filho of the

---

[38] In 2007, the PFL changed its name to Democratas (DEM) and in 2021 to União Brasil.

PMDB, who had been minister of agriculture under the leftwing administration of Goulart (1961–1964), drafted a bill that established payment of expropriated property in bonds according to the value declared for taxes,[39] immediate possession of targeted land by the state, and a fixed limit on the number of hectares that could be owned by any one person. Moreover, the draft proposed more stringent criteria to establish if a farm was fulfilling land's social welfare purpose, effectively making a larger number of properties susceptible of expropriation.

Agrarian elites developed a two-pronged strategy to defeat this unfavorable draft. First, they worked with their own legislators to draft and push forward an alternative proposal for the new constitutional section on land reform and agricultural policy. Second, producers organized an extensive lobbying campaign to pressure undecided legislators and even those not sympathetic to their position from within and outside of Congress. The UDR and the associations in the Frente Ampla de Agropecuária (under the leadership of CNA, OCB and SRB) coordinated numerous demonstrations,[40] mobilizing thousands of producers when crucial votes were scheduled (Payne 2000). As rural workers associations, leftist parties and the Church were mobilizing to pressure legislators into supporting land reform, the UDR mobilized producers across the country to counterbalance this pressure from the left. Producers wanted to show legislators that those voting in favor of landowners' interests could count on their support in their home districts.[41] With municipal elections approaching in 1988, the UDR and other rural organizations mobilized local politicians to pressure their federal legislators, highlighting the connection between legislators' vote on the land reform chapter and the performance of their local allies in the upcoming elections (Dreifuss 1989).

The Brazilian agrarian elites' strategy to block radical land reform from both within and outside the Constituent Assembly worked. Lima Filho's draft was replaced by one introduced by a member of the agrarian elite, Rosa Prata, the PMDB representative from Minas Gerais who was also the leader of the ranchers' association. Crucially, landowners' representatives introduced a new article stating that productive farms could

---

[39] Significantly lower than their market value.
[40] The *Frente Ampla* was born as an organization to coordinate the work of the many producers' associations that were lobbying the Assembly (approximately forty between agriculture federations and crop-specific organizations). It excluded the UDR, whose radical methods the other associations did not officially approve.
[41] *Jornal do Brasil*, April 27, 1988; *Jornal da Tarde*, September 7,1988.

not be expropriated. The fact that this provision was in clear contradiction with the social function of property also sanctioned by the 1988 Constitution demonstrates agrarian elites effectiveness in protecting their interests. While the article on the social function of property in the Constitution states that large properties can be expropriated if not efficiently exploited or in infringement of labor and environmental laws, the agrarian reform article introduced by the agrarian elites protects productive properties from expropriation, regardless of their size or compliance with labor and environmental regulations (Ondetti 2016, 31). Therefore, compared to the status quo under the military-sanctioned Land Statute, the new democratic constitution made expropriation of land by the state more difficult. Moreover, key issues regarding land reform were not specified in the new constitution and were left to be regulated by ordinary legislation, which delayed implementation. The new constitution did not define what "productive" property was nor the actual procedure to be followed during expropriations (*rito sumário*). Since Congress passed legislation defining these procedures only in 1993, the failure to establish them during the Constituent Assembly effectively resulted in a five-year moratorium on the land reform process (Lapp 2004, 152).

The success of agrarian elites in the Constituent Assembly is even more evident when compared to the performance of other business sectors that did not organize in the electoral arena. Unlike the agrarian elites, these economic sectors did not have their own representatives and hence were unable to stop unfriendly bills from within the Constituent Assembly. Among the most notorious business legislative defeats were the restrictions on foreign capital in the health and mining sectors and the nationalization of telecoms (Dreifuss 1989, 244–47; Schneider 1997). As Ronaldo Caiado eloquently put it when asked if agricultural producers had won in the Constituent Assembly because of their economic resources: "We [agricultural producers] won because we were mobilized and organized, not because of our money. If money made any difference, then bankers and multinationals would not have lost a single vote in the Constituent Assembly."[42] Paradoxically, the fact that agrarian elites confronted a higher threat than other business sectors during the democratic transition, prompted them to organize in the electoral arena and, consequently, left them better prepared to fend off legislation harmful to their interests in the new democracy.

---

[42] "A UDR vem aí com toda a forca," *Jornal da Tarde*, October 16, 1988.

4.4 THE AGRARIAN CAUCUS IN THE CONTEMPORARY PERIOD

More than three decades after the threat of expropriation was defeated in the Constituent Assembly, why would Brazilian landowners continue to invest in the Agrarian Caucus? This section studies the causes of the continuity of the candidate-centered strategy into the contemporary period. I argue that agrarian elites have had two incentives to remain organized in a multiparty caucus. First, continuously high levels of threat during the first two decades after the democratic transition prompted agrarian elites to keep investing in electoral representation. Second, the advantages that the internal rules of the Brazilian Lower Chamber as well as growing party system fragmentation created for multipartisan caucuses reinforced the choice of a candidate-centered strategy.

4.4.1 The Continuity of the Land Reform Threat

Notwithstanding the success of landed elites in shaping the new constitutional article on land reform according to their interests, the threat on their property rights did not disappear with the end of the Constituent Assembly. First, Congress had still to define the criteria by which farms could be subject to expropriation (i.e., what constituted "productive exploitation") as well as the expropriation procedure per se. These were make-or-break issues for the implementation of a redistributive land reform. Second, rural unrest and social mobilization to demand land reform continued to grow along with the rise of the MST during the first decade after the democratic transition. As Figure 4.4 shows, the number

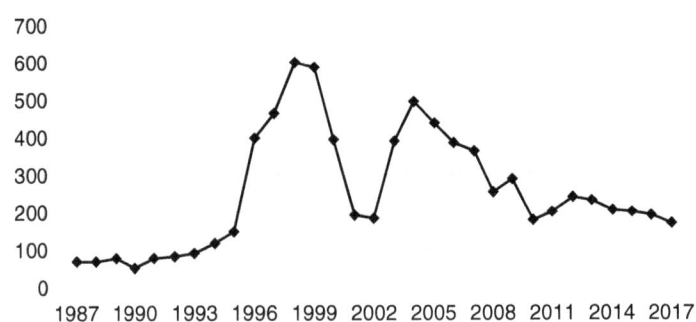

FIGURE 4.4 Number of land occupations per year: Brazil, 1987–2017.
Source: Author, based on CPT.

4.4 The Agrarian Caucus in the Contemporary Period

of land occupations continued to rise, spiking in 1996–1998 and remaining at very high levels during the next decade. Third, in this environment of intense political mobilization and widespread social support for it, there was an acceleration of the land reform process during the Fernando H. Cardoso administrations (1995–2002). The center-right president settled more landless peasants than all of his predecessors combined, redistributing 5.6 percent of the country's total farmland (Ondetti 2007, 20). Moreover, 46.5 percent of the land redistributed by Cardoso was acquired through expropriation (Esquerdo and Bergamasco 2013, 565).[43]

Compounding agrarian elites' perceptions of threat was the fact that in every presidential election between 1989 and 2002, one of the two main contenders was Lula da Silva of the leftwing PT, a party with organic links to the MST and a programmatic commitment to land reform.[44] A survey of agricultural producers across Brazil conducted by the CNA right after Lula's victory in December 2002 shows the overwhelming majority of them felt threatened by the prospects of a PT administration. While 79 percent of surveyed producers manifested feeling uneasy about the new government, 80 percent of them said they believed the number of land occupations would grow as a consequence of the PT victory.[45] In fact, after a few years of relative calm, rural unrest spiked again following the election of Lula (Figure 4.4) as the MST mobilized to pressure the new leftwing president into fulfilling his campaign promises on land reform (Ondetti 2008). Therefore, continuing high levels of threat during the first two decades of democracy gave rural producers every incentive to remain in Congress. By the time the threat started to recede, after Lula's administration had made it clear it would not implement a redistributive land reform, the Agrarian Caucus had had enough time to consolidate as a highly effective representative of agrarian interests in Congress. The Agrarian Caucus' past legislative victories together with its growing bargaining power within Congress created new incentives for agrarian elites to continue investing in this strategy to represent their interests in other policy areas beyond land reform, such as environmental regulations.

---

[43] Although, as critics of the process have pointed out, most expropriated private holdings were underutilized lands located far from markets which their owners were frequently happy to cede, given the government's generous compensation (Pereira 2003; Robles and Veltmeyer 2015).

[44] On how the candidacy of Lula made business and conservative elites felt threatened, see Weyland (1996).

[45] "CNA alerta sobre pessimismo de produtores." *Estado de São Pablo*, December 12, 2002.

4.4.2 The Advantages of Multipartisanship

Since its beginnings, during the Constituent Assembly of 1987–1988, Brazilian agrarian elites' strategy of legislative infiltration has been multipartisan. Agrarian Caucus members have always come from multiple parties, both in the governing and opposition legislative coalition, ranging from eight different parties represented in the 1995–1999 period to seventeen during the 2015–2019 period.[46]

The multiparty character of the Agrarian Caucus has proven to be a formidable advantage in the Brazilian context where high party fragmentation and the internal rules of Congress confer great power on party leaders.[47] This, in turn, has created new incentives for landowners to remain politically fragmented, as having people in more parties increases their influence within Congress, reinforcing the choice of a candidate-centered strategy. Having legislators in multiple parties gives agrarian elites two advantages. First, it multiplies the agenda setting positions they control in Congress. Second, it guarantees their presence in the legislative coalition of left or right wing presidents alike, increasing their bargaining power vis-à-vis the executive.

4.4.2.1 *Control of Agenda-Setting Positions*

Parliaments are typically organized along partisan lines and the Brazilian Congress is no exception. Leadership and agenda-setting positions as well as committee composition are distributed according to partisan affiliations, giving party leaders great power (Amorim Neto et al. 2003, 557; Figueiredo and Limongi 2007). Therefore, investing in a multiparty strategy gives a group the opportunity to occupy more positions of power in Congress than if it were organized in a single party. For instance, in the Brazilian Congress, the College of Leaders (Colégio de Líderes in Portuguese), composed of leaders of parties with at least 1 percent of seats plus a legislator representing the government, decides the legislative agenda (Amorim Neto, et al. 2003, 557; Figueiredo and Limongi 2007). While a party can have only one representative on the College, the most important decision-making body of the Lower Chamber,[48] a multiparty caucus could potentially have as many representatives as the number of different parties in which it has members. As the minimum party size

---

[46] INESC (2007) and author's calculations.
[47] Partisan affiliations are so determinant for the internal organization of Congress that Power (2010, 28) talks of a "rules-induced partyarchy" in the Brazilian Lower House.
[48] Amorim Neto et al. (2003, 558).

4.4 *The Agrarian Caucus in the Contemporary Period*

TABLE 4.4 *Parties with Ruralistas: Lower Chamber, 2015–2019*

Party	Ruralistas (no.)	Ruralistas (as % of party)	Party president is a Ruralista?
(P)MDB	25	49	Yes
PP	13	26.5	Yes
PSDB	12	24.5	No
PR	11	27.5	Yes
PSD	11	28.9	Yes
PSB	10	38.5	Yes
DEM	8	18.6	Yes
PDT	6	31.6	Yes
PTB	6	37.5	Yes
SD	6	54.5	Yes
PHS	3	75	Yes[49]
PRB	3	14.3	Yes
PPS	1	12.5	No
PSC	1	11	No
PSL	1	12.5	No
PODE	1	20	No
PV	1	33.3	No
Lower Chamber	119	29.3	

Source: Author's calculations.[50]

required to occupy a seat in the College is very low – five party members – interest groups within Congress have an incentive to organize in many small parties rather than in one large one.

Prominent members of the Agrarian Caucus typically occupy leadership positions in their parties. Between 1999 and 2006, on average 25 percent of Agrarian Caucus members were party leaders (president or vice president) (Paulet Piedra 2013, 75). In the 2015–2019 period, 40 percent of Ruralistas occupied a leadership position in their party and, more importantly, ten were presidents of parties with at least 1 percent of the Chamber seats, meaning that Ruralistas at the time controlled ten out of twenty-two seats on the College of Leaders (Table 4.4). Crucially, the (P)MDB and the PP, two of the largest parties in Congress, have been under the leadership of a Ruralista almost every year since 1999.[51]

---

[49] Less than 1 percent of the Chamber seats. No representation in the College of Leaders.
[50] For the sake of conserving space, this table only displays parties that had Ruralistas in the 2015–2019 legislature.
[51] Paulet Piedra (2013) and author's calculations.

Controlling the leaderships of multiple parties in Congress gives Ruralistas a privileged position to influence the passage and design of bills affecting their interests. As the case of the New Forest Code analysed below shows, the Agrarian Caucus has been able to influence the legislative agenda, choose friendly reporters for relevant bills,[52] secure Ruralista presence on the committees most important to them (e.g., Agriculture and Environment), and make sure bills affecting agrarian interests are sent to Ruralista-controlled committees. Between 1995 and 2022, in all but three years, a member of the Agrarian Caucus has presided over the Agriculture Committee.[53] Holding the committee presidency is critical because presidents control the agenda and advance or stall discussion on bills according to their interests. Looking at bills sent to the Agriculture Committee in 1996 and 2003, two years when land reform was a major political issue, Paulet Piedra finds that while 92 percent of those bills that had a pro-rich distributive effect were approved, 96 percent of those hurting the interest of landowners were rejected and thus never debated on the floor (Paulet Piedra 2013, 47).

4.4.2.2 Increased Bargaining Power

In fragmented party systems, investing in a multiparty strategy may increase an interest group's bargaining power vis-à-vis the executive, as presidents typically rely on legislators outside their party to pass legislation. When a group controls seats in many different parties, it becomes an attractive potential ally for executives who lack a legislative majority. Extremely high fragmentation in the Brazilian Congress diminishes the legislative power of the president at the same time that it increases the relevance of Congress as a bargaining arena. This is particularly true of the Lower Chamber where fragmentation is higher than in the Senate and the larger numbers needed to pass legislation mean presidents need to build ideologically disconnected multipartisan coalitions to advance their policy agenda (Power 2010). Passing ordinary legislation in the Lower Chamber requires at least 129 votes, while constitutional amendments need 308. Extreme fragmentation means presidents will never be close to those numbers by relying only on their co-partisans. Between 1990 and 2019, the party of the president has never controlled more than 99 out of 513 seats in the Lower Chamber, while the Agrarian Caucus has controlled between 73 and 119 (Table 4.5).

---

[52] *Relator* in Portuguese, the reporter is a member of the committee charged with evaluating a given bill and recommending its approval or rejection to the floor.

[53] Paulet Piedra (2013) and author's calculations.

TABLE 4.5 *Presidential legislative coalitions and the Agrarian Caucus: Lower Chamber, 1999–2018*

President	Presidents' party share (no.)	Coalition share (no.)	AC share (no.)	AC as % of presidential coalition (no.)
Fernando H. Cardoso II (1999–2002)	PSDB 19.3% (99)	PSDB, PMDB, PTB, PFL, PPB, PPS 79.1% (406)	17.3% (89)	21.2% (86)
Lula da Silva I (2003–2006)	PT 17.7% (91)	PT, PL, PMDB,[a] PSB, PDT,[b] PTB, PC do B, PP,[c] PPS,[b] PV[b] 66.67% (342)	14.2% (73)	15.2% (52)
Lula da Silva II (2007–2010)	PT 15.6% (80)	PT, PMDB, PP, PR, PSB, PDT, PTB, PCdoB, PV, PRB 70.2% (360)	22.6% (116)	18.9% (68)
Dilma Rousseff I (2011–2014)	PT 17.1% (88)	PT, PMDB, PP, PR, PTB, PDT, PSC, PSB, PCdoB, PRB, PMN, PTdoB 67.4% (380)	22.8% (117)	21.6% (82)
Dilma Rousseff II (2015–August 2016)	PT 13.6% (70)	PT, PMDB,[d] PP, PR, PDT, PSD, PRB, PROS, PCdoB 59.3% (304)	23.2% (119)	22.7% (69)
Michel Temer (August 2016–2018)	PMDB 12.7% (65)	PMDB, PSDB, PP, PR, PSD, DEM, PRB, PTB, SD, PSC, PPS, PROS, AVANTE, PATRI, LIVRES, PRP 68.4% (351)	23.2% (119)	27.9% (98)

[a] Joins in 2004.
[b] Leaves in 2005.
[c] Joins in 2005.
[d] Leaves in 2016.

Source: Author's calculations based on Vigna (2001), Figueiredo and Limongi (2007), INESC (2007), DIAP (2010), and Paulet Piedra (2013).

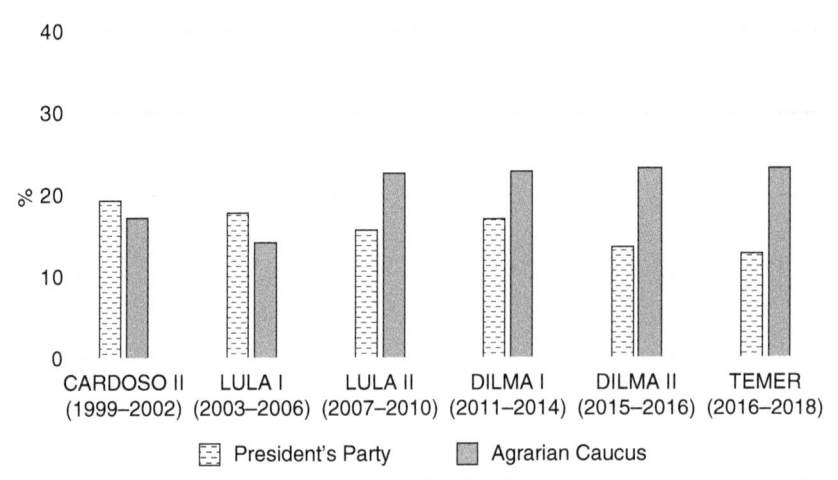

138 *Brazil: Landowners & Their Multiparty Congressional Caucus*

FIGURE 4.5 Percentage of seats controlled by the president's party versus the Agrarian Caucus: Lower Chamber, 1999–2018.
Source: Author's calculations.

Its sheer size has made the Agrarian Caucus an appealing partner for presidents looking to expand their legislative coalition (Figure 4.5), giving the caucus substantial leverage over the executive. As Table 4.5 shows, Ruralistas comprised between 15.2 and 27.9 percent of the governing coalition of all presidents from the second administration of Fernando Henrique Cardoso (FHC) (1999–2002) up to the presidency of Michel Temer (2016–2018). Its weight has been equally important in governments on the center-left and center-right. The power of the Agrarian Caucus in the Lower Chamber has been further increased by the fact that many party leaders are Ruralistas. This means that the Agrarian Caucus controls not only the votes of its members but also, potentially, the votes of legislators in the parties led by a Ruralista.[54] Controlling the leadership of the (P)MDB has been especially important in this regard for the Agrarian Caucus, as this party has been a key player in every government coalition since 1995.

In exchange for their support for the president's legislative agenda, Ruralistas have obtained key cabinet positions in every government, right or left. Despite the party's organic ties to the landless peasant movement and the opposition of environmentalists among its ranks, seven out of

---

[54] In certain decisions, such as to request an urgent consideration or a roll call, the signature of the party president automatically represents the will of all members of their party (Amorim Neto et al. 2003, 558).

the nine ministers of agriculture during the PT administrations were affiliated with the Agrarian Caucus.[55] For instance, Lula's first minister of agriculture was Roberto Rodrigues (2003–2006), one of the founders of the Agrarian Caucus, who as president of the OCB led the legislative opposition to land reform during the Constituent Assembly. Similarly, President Rousseff appointed Kátia Abreu (2015–2016), a former president of CNA and one of the historic leaders of the Ruralistas. And, upon his return to power in 2023, Lula appointed former leader of the soybean producers, Carlos Fávaro. On this, they were no different from rightwing President Bolsonaro (2019–2022), who appointed Tereza Cristina, at the time the president of the Agrarian Caucus, as minister of agriculture in 2019. Crucially, by controlling the Ministry of Agriculture, Ruralistas have been able to veto updates to the land productivity index, which determines if farms can be legally expropriated, thus protecting most of their unproductive holdings (Sauer and Mészáros 2017, 403). Similarly, ministers from the Agrarian Caucus' ranks have shaped governmental priorities when it comes to funding agricultural development. Even when resources destined to family farming quadrupled during the Lula administrations, they still only represented 15 percent of the funds allocated to agribusiness in the same period (Sauer 2019, 112).

4.5 AGRARIAN ELITES' INVESTMENT IN THE AGRARIAN CAUCUS

This book argues that Brazilian landowners' success in influencing policymaking is in part explained by their deployment of a nonpartisan, candidate-centered strategy (the Agrarian Caucus) that allows them to maximize their power within Congress. This section analyses several quantitative and qualitative data sources to test some important observable implications of this claim. It presents evidence on (1) agrarian elites' investment in the Agrarian Caucus, (2) the advantages of such strategy in furthering landowners' interests in Congress, and (3) Ruralistas' loyalty to the caucus over their parties. It shows how Brazilian landowners, individually and through their corporatist associations, contribute financial and logistical resources to help elect pro-agribusiness candidates independently of their partisan affiliation. Once elected, agrarian elites

---

[55] Roberto Rodrigues (2003–2006), Reinhold Stephanes (2007–2010), Wagner Rossi (2010–2011), Antônio Andrade (2013–2014), Neri Geller (2014), Kátia Abreu (2014–2016), and Carlos Fávaro (2023–).

subsidize the work of Ruralistas in Congress, ensuring these legislators coordinate their efforts to advance sectoral interests.

4.5.1 Getting Ruralistas into Congress: An Analysis of Agribusiness Campaign Contributions

To test whether agrarian elites contribute more to the campaigns of candidates that are landowners or members of the Agrarian Caucus, independently of their partisan affiliation, I built an original firm-level dataset of the campaign contributions by the fifty-three largest agribusiness firms in Brazil for the 2006, 2010, and 2014 legislative elections.[56] These are the last three elections for which corporate contributions were allowed before the Brazilian Supreme Court banned them in 2015. I recorded whether these contributions went to landowning candidates and members of the Agrarian Caucus. Data on campaign contributions come from Brazil's Supreme Electoral Court (TSE in Portuguese).[57] Data on Agrarian Caucus membership comes from Congress's own records, *Transparência Brasil*[58] and INESC (2007). Data on land ownership comes from candidates' asset declarations, available on the UOL notícias website.[59]

To the best of my knowledge, this is the first analysis that looks at agribusiness contributions from the perspective of donors as opposed to recipients, allowing me to make inferences about the type of candidates that agribusiness prefers. If the theory developed in Chapter 2 is correct and the Agrarian Caucus is the result of a candidate-centered strategy by agrarian elites looking to elect representatives of their sector across the partisan spectrum, then the data should show that: (1) contributions are concentrated on a few candidates, (2) contributions are dispersed across

---

[56] Firms were identified from the annual rankings of two specialized magazines, *Exame* (2012, 2013, 2014) and *Valor Economico* (2013, 2014). I selected the firms that appeared more than once among the fifty largest in terms of sales. Of the fifty-three identified firms, twenty-eight made at least one campaign contribution in one of the analysed elections. The list includes private firms in the sugar cane, meatpacking, grain processing, seed, and agrochemical sectors as well as producers' cooperatives in the coffee, sugar cane, and orange juice sectors. For a complete list of firms, see the online appendix.

[57] I searched the TSE database for contributions using each firm's name and fiscal identification number.

[58] See: www.transparencia.org.br/ (last accessed July, 20, 2018).

[59] See: https://noticias.uol.com.br/politica/politicos-brasil/resultado.htm (last accessed July, 20, 2018). Candidates who declare owning a rural property aside from their family home that exceeded one *modulo fiscal*, cattle, or shares at an agribusiness firm were coded as "landowners."

the partisan spectrum, (3) agribusiness contribute more to landowning candidates, and (4) Agrarian Caucus members systematically receive more campaign contributions than nonmembers.

As expected, contributions are concentrated on a relatively few candidates, despite the high number of candidates competing in each election in Brazil. For example, in the legislative elections of 2010, there were 4,904 candidates for the Lower Chamber in all Brazil.[60] However, contributions from the analysed firms went to only 70 of these candidates. Across the three elections, the largest firms in agribusiness supported 119 candidates for Congress. Of these, 55 percent were landowners, while 79 percent of the money went to candidates who owned land. The concentration of contributions on a few landowner congressional candidates indicates that agribusiness recognize certain types of candidates as better representatives of their interests.

This is not fully explained by incumbency or the candidate's perceived electoral chances.[61] Even when two-thirds of the candidates receiving contributions won, there were 1,539 winning candidates in the analysed elections and the largest agribusiness firms contributed to only 82 (5 percent) of them. Incumbency could be another reason why these candidates are being selected by agribusiness. Incumbent candidates are usually better known and have higher chances of winning, although both assumptions are less true for Brazil than for other places such as the USA.[62] Taking into account that out of the 584 members of the Brazilian Congress, around 70–80 percent run for re-election (Samuels 2003, 37), the number of incumbents financed by large agribusiness is relatively low, fifty-eight across the three analysed elections, which indicates that they do not finance any incumbent but only those identified with the sector.

Evidence from my interviews with members of the Agrarian Caucus and leaders from producers' associations supports both claims that producers coordinate among themselves which politicians to support, and that they prefer candidates from their own ranks. For instance, the president of the national soybean association explained,

---

[60] TSE, *Estatísticas de Candidaturas* Available at: www.tse.jus.br/eleicoes/estatisticas (last accessed July, 20, 2018).
[61] Because my dataset is limited to those candidates who received a campaign contribution from agribusiness, I cannot statistically test the relationship between receiving a contribution and incumbency or winning as I do not have data on how these variables are distributed among candidates who did not receive a contribution.
[62] See Samuels (2003) and Klašnja and Titiunik (2017).

142 *Brazil: Landowners & Their Multiparty Congressional Caucus*

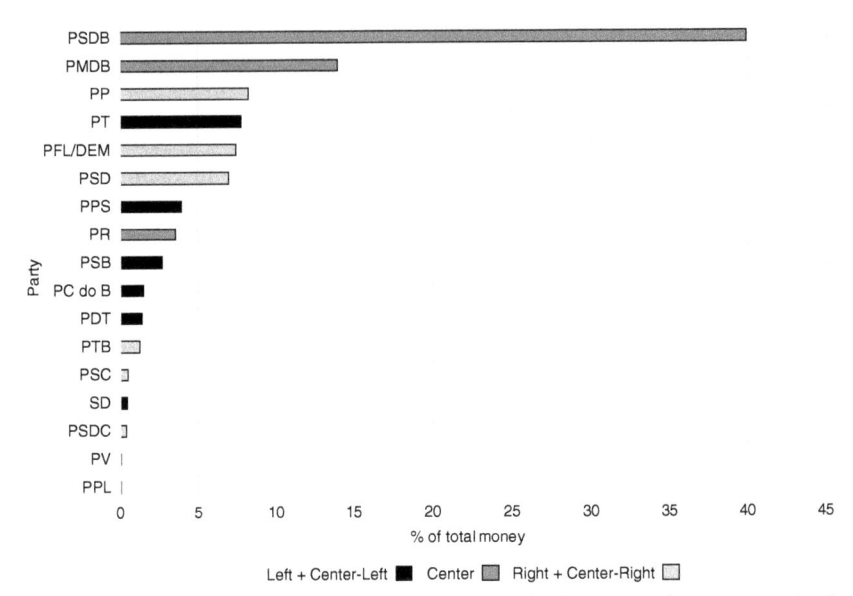

FIGURE 4.6 Percentage of money contributed by the largest agribusiness received per party: 2006, 2010, and 2014 congressional elections.
Source: Author's calculations based on TSE data.

I live in East Mato Grosso, if Carlos Fávaro [former president of the Soybean Producers' Association and vice-governor of the state at the time] decided to run for Congress ... I will support him, tell producers [in the area] to vote for him. *We cannot risk electing a lawyer, a doctor, or an engineer*, we need people directly related to the sector.[63]

Moreover, eight out of the twelve Agrarian Caucus members I interviewed when asked why they decided to run for office, stated that producers' associations encouraged them.

Figure 4.6 shows that, consistent with the expectations from my argument, contributions are dispersed across the partisan spectrum. Candidates for Congress from a total of seventeen different parties from different ideological orientation received money from the firms under study. It is important to highlight that this is not only explained by the high fragmentation of the Brazilian right. If that were the case, we would see contributions going only to candidates running on conservative party tickets. Even when right-of-center parties received a larger share than those to the left-of-center (25 versus 18 percent), the majority of

---

[63] Author's interview with Marcos Da Rosa, Brasília, March 29, 2017, emphasis added.

4.5 Agrarian Elites' Investment in the Agrarian Caucus

the contributed money (57 percent) went to center parties. Notably, the share of the contributions going to the leftwing PT is similar to that of the rightwing PP and PFL/DEM. Thus, the evidence presented in Figure 4.6 supports my theory prediction that partisan affiliation is not a determinant criterion for Brazilian agribusiness when selecting candidates to support.

Looking at campaign contributions from the point of view of donor firms as opposed to members of Congress has the advantage that we can analyse data for both winning and losing candidates. However, we are missing the subset of all candidates that did not receive a contribution from these firms which prevents a statistical analysis of these data.[64] To avoid this potential bias, I now focus on the subset of winning candidates and compare contributions to members and nonmembers of the Agrarian Caucus.

As expected, membership in the Agrarian Caucus strongly predicts the probability of receiving a contribution from agribusiness. For the subset of winning candidates, the correlation between being a Ruralista and receiving a contribution from the largest firms in agribusiness is statistically significant for all three elections ($p < 0.001$).[65] Table 4.6 reports the results of an independent t-test for each legislative election. Ruralistas had statistically significant ($p < 0.01$) higher probabilities of receiving a

TABLE 4.6 *Probability of receiving a contribution from the largest agribusiness by Agrarian Caucus membership: 2006, 2010, and 2014 elections*

	Probability of receiving a contribution	
	Ruralista	Non-Ruralista
2006	8%	0.5%
	$t = 2.9$ df = 120 $p = 0.005$	
2010	27%	5%
	$t = 5.3$ df = 132 $p = 0.000$	
2014	15%	3%
	$t = 2.7$ df = 186 $p = 0.007$	

Source: Authors' calculations based on TSE.

---

[64] Since I do not know how land ownership is distributed among non-receiving candidates, the results of a statistical analysis could be biased and difficult to interpret.
[65] 2006 $r = 0.21$, 2010 $r = 0.32$, 2016 $r = 0.22$.

contribution from the analysed firms in all the elections under study. For instance, in the 2010 election, legislators in the Agrarian Caucus had a 27 percent probability of receiving a contribution from an agribusiness firm, while for those that did not belong to the Agrarian Caucus the probability was much lower, 5 percent.[66]

These findings are supported by qualitative evidence from my interviews with members of the Agrarian Caucus and leaders of producers' associations. Of the twenty-six politicians associated with agriculture whom I interviewed, fourteen said they received campaign donations from agribusiness. Moreover, four out of the eleven association leaders who were asked what producers do to help candidates connected to the sector get elected mentioned donating money to campaigns. The interviews also revealed that producers support the candidacies of politicians close to the sector by organizing meetings, publicizing their legislative work in favor of agriculture, and mobilizing voters. In some cases, this support is more significant than what Ruralistas receive from their own parties. For instance, an Agrarian Caucus leader explained, "I survive in politics more thanks to rural producers than because of my party; my party does not give me as much support as cooperatives and producers do."[67] Fifteen out of the twenty-six politicians whom I interviewed from the sector stated they received this type of support from local producers' associations, cooperatives or individual producers in their districts. Nine out of the eleven association leaders who were asked about how they might help candidates confirmed this. Here again, partisanship was not mentioned as a determining factor. All the leaders from producers' associations who were asked the question said that they supported politicians who work for the sector independently of their party.[68] These words of the then president of the CNA are illustrative of how producers' associations work for the candidacies of politicians they identify as friendly to the sector independently of partisan affiliation:

I'm from the state of Bahia, we have a newsletter we send to all the local associations. Last election I wrote: 'These are the legislators who, *independent of their party, are committed to our class.*' [...] the decision to vote for that legislator, from PMDB, PR, PPB, belongs to each producer. [...] *We had a broad variety and one from the PT was even elected.*[69]

---

[66] The results are similar for differences in amount of money received, except for the year 2006 when the results are not statistically significant ($p = 0.2$).
[67] Author's interview with Valdir Colatto, Brasília, August 5, 2015.
[68] Although some of them recognized that it is less likely that some parties on the extreme left, such as PC do B, will have legislators willing to work with them.
[69] Author's interview with João Martins Jr, Brasília, July 24, 2015, emphasis added.

4.5.2 Coordinating Ruralista's Work in Congress: The Instituto Pensar Agro

Producers' support of Ruralista legislators does not end when they win their election. On the contrary, producers' associations work side by side with members of the Agrarian Caucus writing legislation and devising strategies to get it passed. The peak association Instituto Pensar Agropecuária (IPA) provides the space for Ruralista legislators from multiple parties and producers' associations from different sectors to develop and coordinate their legislative goals and strategies. The IPA was created in 2011 by the initiative of producers' associations from the frontier state of Mato Grosso,[70] one of the deforestation hotspots in the country, to coordinate the work of the Agrarian Caucus and producers' associations during the debate on the new Forest Code (see Section 4.6). At the IPA, legislators meet with their core constituency, receive technical assistance in analysing and drafting bills and exchange ideas with their colleagues.

The IPA is a vehicle for agribusiness to subsidize the work of the Agrarian Caucus in Congress. Brazilian law forbids corporations and interest groups, but not NGOs, from financing individual legislators or parliamentary groups' legislative work. Thus, associations contribute to IPA so that the Instituto can provide the space, infrastructure, and technical assistance for the Agrarian Caucus to operate. The IPA rents the house where Ruralista's weekly meetings take place – the same building where the soybean growers' association has its Brasília headquarters – and pays the salary of the consultants who draft the bills legislators in the Agrarian Caucus will later promote. In 2022, forty-two associations from every region of the country contribute to the IPA, representing products as varied as soybeans, cotton, corn, sugarcane, coffee, beef, poultry, pork, timber, agrochemicals, vegetable oil, and seeds.[71] The IPA is also supported by the producers' federations of the states of Mato Grosso, Paraná, and São Paulo, and the OCB.[72]

---

[70] On the organizational strength of Mato Grosso associations, see Richardson (2012)
[71] According to the site *De Olho Nos Ruralistas*, each member organization pays a monthly fee of approximately US$5,000 to IPA. "Multinacionais são financiadoras ocultas da Frente Parlamentar da Agropecuária," May 21, 2019, available at: https://deolhonosruralistas.com.br/2019/05/21/multinacionais-sao-financiadoras-ocultas-da-frente-parlamentar-da-agropecuaria/ (accessed July 28, 2020).
[72] Author's interviews with Fábio Meirelles Filho, president of IPA (2016–2018), Brasília, July 4, 2017, and João Henrique Hummel, IPA executive director, Brasília, July 28, 2015 and March 14, 2017.

The IPA has been crucial for the institutionalization of the Agrarian Caucus, setting it apart from other caucuses in the Brazilian Congress. The IPA and the Agrarian Caucus have a clear division of labor structure organized in thematic commissions which facilitates coordination among the different interests represented by the caucus. When a bill affecting the sector is introduced in Congress, IPA consultants analyse it and send their report to the contributing sectoral associations for them to take a position. Those with a stake in the issue report back to IPA consultants who, if there is consensus, present the associations' position to Ruralista legislators at their weekly meeting. In addition, associations' leaders and technical staff meet regularly at the IPA ,where they exchange views on sectoral issues. In that fashion, as one Agrarian Caucus member and founder of the Brazilian Association of Cotton Growers put it, the IPA provides the space and technical assistance for Ruralista legislators to "align their thinking to, then, be able to discuss bills and vote on them."[73] When the members of the Agrarian Caucus reach an agreement, with the help of IPA staff, they devise a strategy and divide tasks among legislators to guarantee that the caucus position will be well defended in Congress. Ruralistas coordinate to make sure they are represented on all the congressional committees that will analyse the bill, and they have the responsibility of persuading their parties to vote with the Agrarian Caucus.

By providing the arena and technical resources to settle differences in policy preferences among the agrarian elites' many political and corporatist representatives, the IPA has helped consolidate Ruralistas power in Congress. The Agrarian Caucus only pursues issues for which there is consensus among its members and the different interests they represent. Divisive issues that could end in legislative defeats, and hence, weaken the caucus, are avoided. A clear example of this is the 2015 Cultivar Law which sought to regulate the use of genetically modified seeds.[74] The bill, which proposed that farmers pay royalties for using leftover seeds from one harvest to the next, pitted two contributing members of IPA: producers versus biotechnology multinationals. Therefore, the bill did not enjoy the full support of the Agrarian Caucus and never made it out of committee. Similarly, the Agrarian Caucus only engages with bills that affect the whole agricultural sector such as those related to rural workers, environmental regulation, or land issues. More narrow issues, such as a

---

[73] Author's interview with Adilton Sachetti, Brasília, March 16, 2017.
[74] PL 827/2015 de Proteção de Cultivares.

subsidy to a particular crop, are delegated to crop-specific associations and the legislators closely connected to them.

4.6 THE AGRARIAN CAUCUS IN ACTION: SHAPING THE NEW FOREST CODE

The New Forest Code (Law 12,651) – signed into law by President Rousseff in May 2012 – was one of the bills most relevant to landowners' interests discussed in the Brazilian Congress since the approval of the new Constitution in 1988. Crucial to agribusiness' interests, the New Forest Code regulates land use and land clearings in privately owned plots, requires landowners to replant areas deforested within protected areas and establishes penalties for noncompliers. Although the new law is closer to agrarian elites' interests than the previous code, the debate in Congress was long and contentious as Ruralista interests met with strong opposition from environmental groups.

The passage of the New Forest Code clearly illustrates the advantages of electoral strategies that rely on self-representation and multipartisanship theorized in Chapter 2. First, landowners had an advantage over other stakeholders in shaping the contents of the New Forest Code because self-representation granted them direct access to the drafting of the bill. In the twelve years that the reform was in discussion, several alternatives were proposed but the one that finally made it to the floor was authored by the then president of the Agrarian Caucus, Valdir Colatto, who before becoming a federal legislator was the leader of a producers' association in the state of Santa Catarina. In that fashion, while other stakeholders (e.g., environmental NGOs, peasants, indigenous peoples) had to lobby members of Congress from the outside, agricultural producers influenced the writing of the bill directly, through their legislators.

Multipartisanship gave landowners another key advantage during the passage of the New Forest Code because it allowed them to increase the number of sympathetic legislators they could place in positions crucial to the approval of the bill in the Lower Chamber. As shown in Table 4.4, many Ruralista leaders are also the leaders of their parties. Party leaders assign legislators to congressional committees. Ruralistas used their leadership positions to choose sympathetic legislators within their parties to the Special Committee that analysed the bill. As a result, 63 percent of the members of the Committee belonged to the Agrarian Caucus (Pereira 2013, 68). Ruralistas not only secured a majority within the committee, but also its president, Moacir Micheletto a historic leader of the Agrarian Caucus and a sympathetic reporter. Thus, through the work of the Special Committee, the Agrarian Caucus was able to shape the bill before it reached the floor for its final vote.

We have seen how by being one of the largest multiparty groups in Congress, the Agrarian Caucus makes up a significant proportion of the president's legislative coalition. The passage of the New Forest Code is a clear example of how the Ruralistas can use their leverage vis-à-vis the executive to advance their policy interests. There were five roll-call votes on the New Forest Code bill in the Brazilian Lower Chamber between May 2011 and April 2012 (Table 4.7). Their analysis shows not only how the Agrarian Caucus can force the government to support its legislative initiatives in exchange for Ruralista support of governmental priorities but, more importantly, how the Agrarian Caucus can maintain discipline when confronting the government and get Ruralista legislators in the governing coalition to vote against the president.

As shown in Table 4.7, Ruralistas won all the roll call votes on the Forest Code, even when confronting the government. Of particular interest are the votes on Amendment 164 in May 2011 and the Senate version in April 2012. On both occasions, the Agrarian Caucus broke its agreement with the executive and was able to win the vote because Ruralistas in the governing coalition voted with the caucus and against the government. In May 2011, the Agrarian Caucus and the government reached a compromise to move the bill forward. Ruralistas agreed to withdraw Amendment 164 from the reporters' version of the bill in exchange for the government support of the rest of the project (Vigna 2012; Pereira 2013). Authored by a member of the Agrarian Caucus, Amendment 164 included an amnesty to illegal deforestation that had occurred before 2008, allowing economic activities in cleared areas to continue without penalty and was thus vehemently opposed by environmentalists in the governing coalition (Pereira 2013). The government held its end of the bargain and the bill (without Amendment 164) passed handsomely. However, seeing they may have the votes to reintroduce the amendment, the Ruralistas forced a vote on it during the same session (Vigna 2012; Pereira 2013). This was a huge defeat for the executive as the Agrarian Caucus was able to break the governing legislative coalition compelling Ruralistas in it to vote with the caucus. Of the sixty-nine members of the Agrarian Caucus in the government's legislative coalition that voted that day, sixty (87%) voted with their fellow Ruralistas and against the government. Crucially, the leader of the government's largest coalitional partner – the PMDB – a Ruralista, ordered its legislators to vote against the government. As Table 4.8 shows, almost every PMDB legislator followed the party whip. At the time, the PMDB represented a fifth of the government legislative coalition.

TABLE 4.7 *Forest Code roll-call votes: Lower Chamber, 2011–2012*

Date	Vote description	Government position	Ruralista position	Yes	No	Result
05/03/2011	Req.7573/2010. Urgency requirement to vote on the bill	Yes	Yes	399	18	Approved
05/24/2011	AMD. 186. Bill proposed by the reporter of the Special Committee (without AMD. 164)	Yes	Yes	410	63	Approved
05/24/2011	AMD. 164. Amendment to the reporter's bill proposed by Ruralistas guaranteeing amnesty to deforesters	No	Yes	273	182	Approved
04/25/2012	Senate version. Vote to keep the version of the bill passed in the Senate against a new bill, closer to the Ruralista interests	Yes	No	184	274	Rejected
04/25/2012	Art. 62. Proposal by the PT to reintroduce regulations on land use near riverbanks.	Yes	No	184	228	Rejected

Note: Greyed rows represent votes on which the government and Ruralistas were at odds.
Source: Author, based on Lower Chamber records.

TABLE 4.8 *Party Rice Index and number of members casting a vote; Forest Code votes; Agrarian Caucus versus main parties: Lower Chamber, 2011–2012*

	AC	DEM	PDT	PMDB	PP	PR	PSB	PSD	PSDB	PTB	PT
Req. 7573/2010	1 (94)	1 (36)	0.82 (22)	1 (63)	1 (33)	1 (31)	0.83 (24)	–	0.95 (43)	1 (15)	1 (77)
AMD. 186	1 (106)	1 (38)	0.55 (27)	1 (74)	1 (39)	0.88 (33)	0.8 (30)	–	0.92 (49)	1 (21)	0.12 (80)
AMD. 164	0.8 (101)	0.89 (37)	0.33 (27)	0.97 (73)	0.35 (34)	0 (32)	0.52 (29)	–	0.84 (49)	0.5 (20)	0.97 (79)
Senate Version	0.94 (101)	0.85 (26)	0.42 (24)	0.92 (74)	0.54 (35)	0.85 (26)	0.28 (25)	0.63 (43)	0.08 (48)	0.87 (15)	0.97 (79)
Art. 62	0.88 (86)	0.78 (18)	0 (24)	0.94 (64)	0.36 (28)	0.79 (29)	0.63 (27)	0.66 (41)	0.08 (39)	0.86 (14)	0.94 (71)
Average	0.92	0.9	0.42	0.96	0.65	0.7	0.61	0.64	0.57	0.85	0.8

Source: Author, based on Lower Chamber records.

4.6 The Agrarian Caucus and the New Forest Code

The vote in April 2012 – to choose between the Senate version of the bill or a new one closer to Ruralista interests – represented another devastating defeat for the government. Analysts called it "the most important legislative rebellion in Brazil in nearly a decade" (Gatto and Power 2016, 58) The Senate, where the Agrarian Caucus is not as well-organized as in the Chamber, made important pro-environmental modifications to the bill that overturned some of the changes introduced by the Ruralistas with amendment 164.[75] In response, the Agrarian Caucus proposed a new version of the bill that reversed these unwanted modifications. Lacking the votes to approve the Senate version, the government ordered its legislators to block the discussion of the bill. However, in April 2012, the executive needed the support of the Agrarian Caucus to pass the World Cup law, a legislative priority of the Rousseff administration. In exchange, the government agreed to allow the vote on the Senate version of the Forest Code reform as long as the Ruralistas withdrew their version (Vigna 2012; Pereira 2013). Once again, the Agrarian Caucus betrayed the government and ordered its legislators to vote against the Senate version. Almost every Ruralista in the president's legislative coalition, 97 percent of them, obeyed the caucus whip. The Senate bill was defeated and, therefore, the new bill incorporating all Ruralistas' modifications was passed (Vigna 2012; Pereira 2013).[76]

The bargaining power of the Agrarian Caucus resides in controlling multiple votes across partisan lines, but this can only be effective if Ruralistas are willing to disobey their party leaders' recommendations and vote with the Agrarian Caucus, or if Ruralista leaders can get the rest of their party to vote with them. To see if the Agrarian Caucus was able to maintain cohesion during the Forest Code debate, I calculated the Rice Index for the five roll-call votes (Table 4.8). The Rice Index measures the degree to which members of a party vote together.[77] It ranges from 1 (all members vote together) to 0 (half the members vote one way and half the other). As we can see in Table 4.8, on average Ruralistas

---

[75] The Senate version established more stringent regulations on land use near riverbanks and took out the amnesty to deforesters. Moreover, the Senate gave back to the federal government important competencies – such as the capacity to define which illegally deforested areas should be restored and which economic activities could be allowed in protected areas – that the Ruralistas had delegated in state governments where agrarian interests are politically stronger.

[76] After Congress passed the bill, President Rousseff vetoed some of the most controversial changes made by the Ruralistas.

[77] $AI_i = \dfrac{|Y_i - N_i|}{Y_i + N_i}$

voted on the New Forest Code more cohesively than most parties, except for, surprisingly, the PMDB, a party that usually exhibits lower levels of cohesion.[78] We should remember that the PMDB president at the time was a Ruralista who worked actively to get his party behind the caucus' position on the matter.[79] Moreover, on this issue of great relevance to agricultural producers, the Agrarian Caucus had higher levels of cohesion than parties that are usually more cohesive, such as the PSDB, PTB, and even the PT, which has historically exhibited higher levels of discipline than any other Brazilian party.[80] The data show that most parties were divided on this environmental issue, with some legislators privileging environmental concerns while other prioritizing economic growth. In contrast, the Agrarian Caucus was able to maintain a unified position across votes. Notably, during the vote on the reporter's bill (Amendment 186), while the government had negotiated with the Agrarian Caucus supporting it, almost half of the PT legislators – who were hoping for a more protectionist draft – disobeyed the executive and voted against.

Interview evidence supports the claim that the Agrarian Caucus is more influential than parties in directing members' votes. Of the 12 leaders of the Agrarian Caucus whom I interviewed, when asked with whom they vote on issues related to the sector – their party or the caucus – ten of them stated that they vote with the latter. Tellingly, the ones who did not say they vote with the Agrarian Caucus said they vote according to their personal convictions or their constituency's interests, but none of them said they would follow the party whip if it opposed the Agrarian Caucus. Moreover, six Agrarian Caucus members said that when there is dissent, they usually try to persuade their party to vote with the caucus. In this sense, the Agrarian Caucus does not replace partisan organizations but works through them, colonizing partisan spaces of power to extend its influence within Congress. The testimony of one of the more active members of the Agrarian Caucus and the sponsor of the New Forest Code Law is illustrative of this relationship between the caucus and political parties:

When the issue is in the interest of agriculture, *we follow the Agrarian Caucus, independent of our party*. When the issue is not related to agriculture, if we still have an interest, we take a position as a caucus and if the caucus has no interest,

---

[78] The average Rice Index for the PMDB between 1988 and 2006 was 0.72 (Figueiredo and Limongi 2007, 170).

[79] Author's interview with legislative consultant Rodrigo Dolabella, Brasilia, July 22, 2015.

[80] Between 1988 and 2006, the average Rice Index values for the PSDB, PDT, and PT were 0.78, 0.85, and 0.97, respectively (Figueiredo and Limongi 2007, 170).

we follow our party. However, in the cases when our party has a position different from the Agrarian Caucus, we try to persuade the party to vote with us [...]. The truth is that when the Agrarian Caucus takes a position, in order to know if the bill is going to pass, people count the votes in the caucus, everybody wants to know how the Agrarian Caucus is going to vote, that's the position that matters, because today, *the caucus is bigger than the parties*.[81]

4.7 CONCLUSION

This chapter analyses a novel electoral strategy by which landowners have successfully influenced policymaking in democratic Brazil: a multiparty congressional caucus. It demonstrates that Brazil's Agrarian Caucus is the result of agrarian elites' collective efforts to build a channel of electoral representation to protect their interests under democracy in a context of high political fragmentation. As the theory developed in Chapter 2 predicted, the threat of radical land reform during the democratic transition prompted landowners to engage in electoral politics. However, high political fragmentation among the agrarian elite rendered party-building unfeasible. Brazilian agrarian elites thus designed an alternative coordination device that enabled them to influence federal policy and at the same time preserve their local autonomy.

By analysing the work of the Agrarian Caucus in Congress, the chapter shows the advantages of an electoral, candidate-centered, multipartisan strategy over other strategies available to economic elites in democracies such as lobbying or party-building. First, self-representation has granted Brazilian agrarian elites direct access to key policymaking positions from which they have shaped sectoral policy according to their interests. Second, by being multipartisan, the Agrarian Caucus has multiplied the agenda setting positions it controls in Congress and increased its leverage vis-à-vis the executive. Thanks to their power in the Lower Chamber, Ruralistas have obtained important policy concessions and cabinet positions from governments of every ideological orientation.

The study of the Agrarian Caucus makes and important contribution to the comparative politics literature by showing that conservative parties are not the only vehicle for the electoral representation of economic elites in democracies. Brazilian landowners have organized in the electoral arena through a different channel, showing that economic elites can have stakes in democratic continuity even in systems where conservative

---

[81] Author's interview with Colatto, emphasis added.

parties are weak and fragmented. Multiparty caucuses allow interest groups to coordinate legislative work – one of the main functions of political parties in democracy – without necessarily building a centralized electoral machine to select their representatives. This is relevant because party-building has become increasingly harder as political fragmentation, electoral volatility, and the dilution of partisan identities are on the rise across the developing world. In this context where many parties are little more than the electoral vehicles of ambitious politicians and candidates' personal characteristics are more reliable indicators of their policy preferences than their partisan affiliation, candidate-centered strategies may become a more effective option for interest group representation than party-building.

5

Argentina

The Limits of Nonelectoral Strategies

5.1 INTRODUCTION

More than a decade ago, in March 2008, Argentine agricultural producers stunned observers by launching a four-month-long production and commercialization stoppage, accompanied by numerous mass protests and roadblocks across the country. Analysts wondered why one of the wealthiest groups in the country was taking to the streets in protest, borrowing a strategy typical of dispossessed groups. These "protests of abundance," as President Cristina Fernández de Kirchner (2007–2015) called them, were not, however, new to the agrarian elites' repertoire. Throughout history, Argentine agricultural producers had frequently organized protests against unwanted policies, although never before with that intensity or scale. The farm lockouts of 2008 – triggered by an increase in export taxes crowning a series of policies and regulations that encroached producers' profits – were a clear symptom of agrarian elites' inability to influence sectoral policymaking. In fact, while most left-turn governments in Latin America subsidized agribusiness, agricultural exports in Argentina were heavily taxed, transferring on average each year the equivalent of 2.5 percent of the country's GDP from agricultural producers to the rest of society.[1]

This chapter shows how Argentine agrarian elites' lack of electoral investments previous to 2008 left them vulnerable to hostile policies.

---

[1] Yearly average for the 2007–2016 period. IBD-Agrimonitor, Total Support Estimate. This indicator reflects and includes all effects of public policies that differentially affect the agricultural sector, from support for the sector (for example, subsidies) to penalties (for example, taxes). Available at: https://agrimonitor.iadb.org (last accessed July 16, 2022).

Since the last democratic transition, Argentine landowners' preferred strategy of political influence had been a combination of informal access to high-ranking executive officials and, when this was not enough to deter policies contrary to agrarian interests, protests. However, this nonelectoral strategy proved to be ineffective to influence policymaking during the administrations of the center-left Frente para la Victoria (FPV) (2003–2015). As developed in Chapter 2, the success of nonelectoral strategies ultimately depends on the capacity of an interest group to access the state. Because agrarian elites had no ties to public officials in the FPV administration and policymakers held ideological views opposite to theirs, informal channels of policy influence were closed to the agrarian elites, leaving them with no means to block unwanted policies.

I argue that Argentine agrarian elites did not invest in an electoral strategy prior to 2008 because they did not experience an existential threat. I present evidence on how, unlike their peers in Brazil and Chile, landowners in Argentina did not fear that the democratic governments elected after the transition would implement policies jeopardizing the continuity of their business. I also show how landowners decided to enter the electoral arena when this perception changed, with the rise of an existential threat in the form of confiscatory taxes.

Due to high levels of intragroup fragmentation, agrarian elites in Argentina opted for a candidate-centered electoral strategy in 2009. Regional and economic cleavages have historically divided rural producers in Argentina between those in the prosperous export-oriented Pampas, who favored liberalism, and those in the underdeveloped interior, who depended on state protection to survive. As a consequence of these competing economic interests within the rural elites, no formal linkages between parties and agricultural producers as a class have ever been built. Thus, when agrarian elites felt threatened during the 2008 conflict, they had no clear partisan allies to turn to, and because linkages between interest groups and parties cannot be built overnight, individual producers run under the labels of the different parties they felt closer to. After the failure of the candidate-centered strategy and with the consolidation of a viable center-right electoral alternative, part of the Argentine agrarian elite has engaged in party-building. While economic cleavages within Argentine agricultural producers continue to undermine the kind of sector-wide party-building effort that we saw in Chile during the democratic transition, producers for export in the Pampas have lent electoral, financial, and personnel support to the center-right alliance spearheaded by Propuesta Republicana (Republican Proposal, PRO).

The rest of the chapter is organized as follows. Section 5.2 provides a historical background on Argentine agriculture and landowners' corporatist organizations. Sections 5.3 and 5.4 develop the argument. Section 5.3 shows how the lack of an existential threat explains why agrarian elites in Argentina remained outside the electoral arena until 2008, preferring to influence policy through informal nonelectoral channels. Section 5.4 shows how a rise in the perception of threat triggered by a confiscatory tax scheme led agrarian elites to organize in the electoral arena in 2009 and how their high fragmentation led landowners to pursue a candidate-centered electoral strategy. Section 5.5 explains why the candidate-centered strategy failed in Argentina. It analyses how backbenchers' dependence on party leaders as well as ideological differences between producers' associations hindered the formation of a multiparty caucus *à la* Brazil in the Argentine Congress. Lastly, Section 5.6 analyses the extent to which agrarian elites have built partisan linkages to the PRO and the center-right alliance led by it.

5.2 AGRICULTURE AND POLITICS IN ARGENTINA: HISTORICAL BACKGROUND

5.2.1 Agriculture and the Argentine Economy

From the beginning of the Argentine Republic until the 1930s, agriculture was the driving force of Argentine capitalism and land ownership was the main source of economic wealth and social prestige. At the beginning of the twentieth century, Argentina was a leading exporter of agricultural commodities, contributing one fifth of the world's total wheat exports and three-fifths of world exports of beef (Hora 2012, 154). Between the 1930s and 1980s, however, the implementation of ISI policies shifted the center of the Argentine economy from agriculture to the industrial sector. Nonetheless, agricultural exports continued to be the main source of foreign currency for the country and thus the main source of financing for the industrialization process. ISI policies hurt agriculture by maintaining an appreciated currency and establishing trade barriers and price controls. Consequently, economic growth in the sector, which until the 1930s had been the most dynamic of the Argentine economy, deaccelerated. From the 1940s until the onset of the commodity boom in the 2000s, the cultivated area in the country remained constant (Figure 5.1). However, the land tenure structure changed significantly during the second half of the

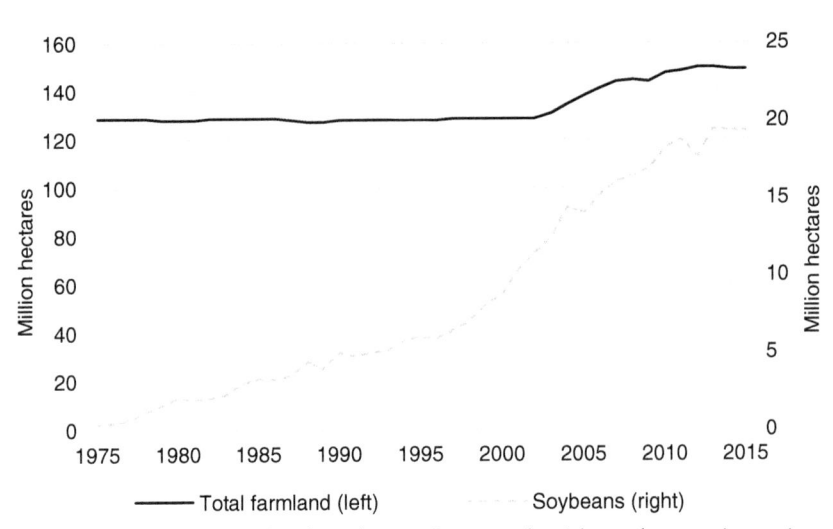

FIGURE 5.1 Total farmland and area harvested with soybeans: Argentina, 1975–2015.
Source: Author, based on FAOSTAT.

twentieth century. The Peronist agrarian policies of the 1940s and 1950s made it easier for former sharecroppers to buy land,[2] while hereditary partitions put an end to many large latifundia (Hora 2010). Because of these changes, the rural middle class expanded during those decades. Between the agrarian censuses of 1947 and 1969, the area harvested by tenants was reduced by 50 percent. Consequently, by 1969, producers who owned their farm harvested 73 percent of the agricultural land in the Pampas region, the richest farmland in the country (Hora 2002, 331).[3]

Beginning in the 1990s, a series of policy and technological changes gave new dynamism to Argentine agriculture. The administration of Carlos Menem (1989–1999) put an end to ISI by liberalizing trade and minimizing state intervention in the economy. The government also abolished export taxes. Overvaluation of the peso resulting from the currency peg in place throughout the decade had mixed consequences for agricultural producers. Although it hurt the competitiveness of

---

[2] Formalizing a 1943 decree, the tenancy law enacted in 1948 during the first Perón administration (1946–1952) froze rent values and forbade peasant eviction for five years. Subsequent governments kept extending these measures until 1968 (Barsky and Gelman 2009).

[3] Buenos Aires province, west of La Pampa, south of Córdoba, Santa Fe, and Entre Ríos.

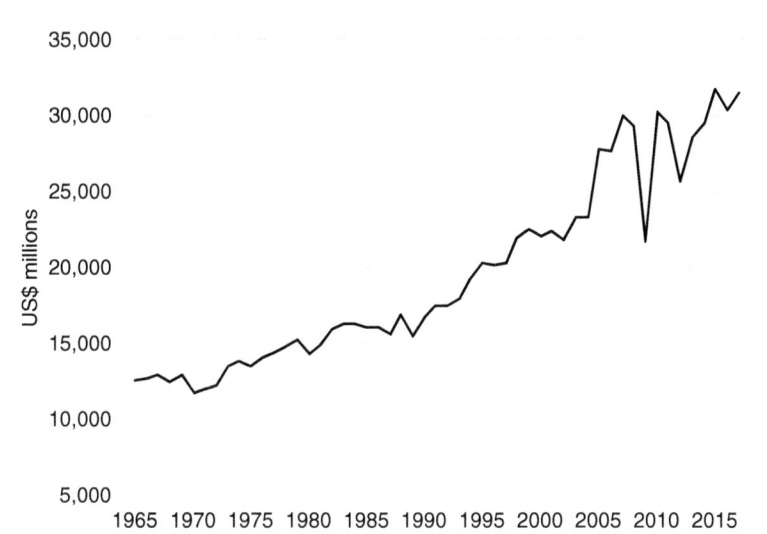

5.2 Agriculture and Politics: Historical Background

FIGURE 5.2 Agricultural value added (constant 2010 US$): Argentina, 1965–2017. Source: Author, based on the World Bank.[4]

agricultural products in the international market, it also allowed for the incorporation of new technologies and mechanization of production by lowering the prices of imported supplies such as machines and fertilizers. The introduction of genetically modified seeds in the mid 1990s gave agriculture a new impulse, lowering production costs, increasing yields, and allowing for the incorporation of new lands that until then had been unsuitable for crops. As a consequence of all these changes, the agricultural sector's value added accelerated its growth (Figure 5.2) and farmland area started to expand for the first time in many decades (Figure 5.1). This expansion was explained mainly by the growth of soybean cultivation. Until the mid 2000s, the area planted with soybeans had grown, replacing other activities such as ranching and cereal crops without a change in total farmland, but skyrocketing international prices during the commodity boom of the 2000s fueled the expansion of the agricultural frontier (Figure 5.1). Modern agricultural production, which until then had been concentrated in the fertile Pampas region, now expanded into the backward provinces of the interior, creating new common interests between producers across the country.

---

[4] Includes forestry and fishing.

5.2.2 Agrarian Elites' Corporatist Associations

The Argentine Rural Society (SRA), founded in 1886, is the oldest of the country's producers' associations and was for several decades the sector's only representative. Originally, the SRA represented the interests of the large ranchers in the province of Buenos Aires. Until the first decades of the twentieth century, being a member of the SRA was a clear sign of economic wealth and social prominence (Imaz 1959; Palomino 1988). Historically, the SRA has been an advocate of economic liberalism, opposing state intervention in the economy and barriers to free trade (Palomino 1988). According to estimates by its leaders, the association had around 3,000 members in 2018.[5] In contrast to the other sectoral national-level associations, the SRA is not a federation and, consequently, lacks territorial organization outside the city of Buenos Aires where it is headquartered.

The Rural Confederations of Argentina (CRA) was founded in 1943 by medium-sized producers who did not feel represented by the large-rancher-dominated SRA. Like the SRA, the CRA has also advocated for economic liberalism and minimal state intervention in the sector. However, unlike the SRA, the CRA is a confederation with a nationwide organization. Historically, the CRA has maintained a more militant style than the SRA and has been much more prone to organizing protests and lockouts, frequently in collaboration with organizations representing smaller producers. Today, thirteen provincial federations, comprising 310 local rural unions, make up the CRA. In 2008, the confederation claimed to have 110,000 members.[6] Within CRA provincial federations, the largest and more politically active at the national level is the Confederation of Rural Associations of Buenos Aires and La Pampa (CARBAP). CARBAP is also the staunchest advocate of liberalism and antistatism within the CRA (Palomino 1987).

The Confederation of Agricultural Cooperatives (CONINAGRO) was founded in 1958. In 2008, the confederation comprised about 500 agroindustrial cooperatives from all over the country producing a variety of

---

[5] "Carlos Vila Moret: 'Queremos sembrar el ruralismo en la mente joven,'" and "Marcos Pereda: 'Tenemos un proyecto para una universidad agroindustrial,'" *La Nación*, September 17, 2018.

[6] "Quién es quién en el sector agropecuario," *La Nación*, March 30, 2008. Palomino (1988, 79) estimates CRA had some 100,000 members in the 1980s. Richardson (2012, 45) estimates CRA's true membership in 2008 was much lower than what they claimed, around 60,000.

5.2 Agriculture and Politics: Historical Background

goods such as oilseeds, grains, tea, cotton, dairy products, and wine.[7] Most of the cooperatives in CONINAGRO are small and medium-sized, but some of the largest cooperatives in the country are also affiliated with it. Moreover, CONINAGRO represents all cooperatives in the sector, from producers to suppliers and traders. Because of the heterogeneous interests it represents, the association frequently lacks a clear stance on government policies towards the sector.

The Agrarian Federation of Argentina (FAA) was founded in 1912 when immigrant sharecroppers in the province of Santa Fe confronted landowners over high rents and unfavorable contracts.[8] It represents small and medium-sized agricultural producers (both tenants and landowners) organized in local associations across the country. In 2008, the federation claimed to represent 100,000 producers.[9] Unlike the SRA or the CRA, it does not have a liberal discourse and has historical links to leftwing parties. The FAA has historically advocated for state intervention in the sector and differentiated polices towards tenants and smallholders (Lissin 2010). The changes in agricultural production associated with the expansion of genetically modified soybeans impacted the FAA, bringing to the fore a new type of member with interests closer to those of large producers. While many small producers went bankrupt during the 1990s, others were able to capitalize and expand their business. This change in the profile of the average *federado* created common grounds for joint actions between the FAA and the large producers' associations – especially CRA – starting in the late 1990s (Hora 2010; Lissin 2010). While the other three producers' associations have their headquarters in the city of Buenos Aires, FAA's headquarters are in Rosario, Santa Fe.

Amidst the 2008 conflict, two new "technical" (as opposed to corporatist) associations, the Argentine Association of Regional Consortiums of Agricultural Experimentation (AACREA) and the Argentine Association of No-Till Producers (Aapresid), gained prominence. Members of these organizations are typically large and medium-sized producers in the more developed Pampas region. Founded in 1957, AACREA groups local clusters of producers that meet periodically

---

[7] "Quién es quién en el sector agropecuario," *La Nación*, March 30, 2008.
[8] In 1914, about 58 percent of farms in the Pampas were cultivated by sharecroppers, of whom 78 percent were foreigners (Manzetti 1992, 594).
[9] "Quién es quién en el sector agropecuario," *La Nación*, March 30, 2008. Richardson (2012, 45) estimates that in 2008, the FAA had 5,000 direct members plus between 60,000 and 70,000 indirect members in affiliated cooperatives.

to exchange technological and managerial knowledge (Gras 2012b). In 2019, there were 218 CREA groups in the country, most of them in the Pampas region, grouping some 1,900 agricultural producers.[10] Aapresid was created in 1989 with the specific purpose of promoting the implementation of no-till techniques. It is headquartered in the city of Rosario, the epicenter of the soybean boom of the 2000s. In 2006, the association had some 2,000 members, who manage highly technologized firms, epitomizing the modern Argentine agricultural producer (Hernandez 2007, 336). During the 2008 lockouts, both associations played a key role in framing a discourse about sectoral grievances and the contribution of agriculture to the Argentine economy, which producers used to gain social support (Richardson 2012).

All in all, the existence of six associations that claim to represent Argentine producers is an indicator of the high degree of fragmentation of the agricultural sector in the country. Unlike in Chile where a single organization, the SNA, represents agrarian elites' unified economic and political views, in Argentina there are many associations with different, sometimes opposing, policy preferences. As it will be developed in Section 5.4, as a consequence of this heterogeneity in interests, throughout Argentine history there has not been any single party with which agrarian elites identify. Members of the SRA, who embrace economic liberalism, have mostly identified with liberal Buenos Aires-based parties;[11] while the other associations, which represent a more heterogeneous group of agricultural producers comprising protected activities in the interior, harbor among their ranks – in addition to liberals – Peronists, Radicals, and in the case of FAA, even Socialists.

5.2.3 Agrarian Elites and Politics before the Third Wave

Unlike landlords in Brazil and Chile until the mid twentieth century, landowners in Argentina have never been local political bosses. Historically, agricultural production in Argentina (mainly cattle and grains) has not been labor intensive (Remmer 1984).[12] Therefore, Argentine landowners could not count on the control of the peasantry's vote as a source of political power. Compared to other Latin American societies, Argentina

---

[10] Richardson (2012, 45); see: www.crea.org.ar/regiones-y-grupos-crea/ (accessed, April 2019).
[11] Such as UCEDE, Acción por la República, Recrear, or the PRO.
[12] With the important exception of some labor-intensive crops outside the Pampas such as sugarcane.

urbanized very early. In the province of Buenos Aires there were already more workers employed in manufacturing by 1914 than in crop agriculture and ranching combined (Hora 2002, 195). Moreover, unlike the Chilean Central Valley and the Brazilian Northeast, in the Argentine Pampas access to land was not restricted to large landowners. Alongside the latifundia existed a rural middle class of medium-sized producers who were economically and politically independent from the local agrarian elites (Hora 2002; 2018; Losada 2009). Moreover, Argentine landowners were residents of the city of Buenos Aires, with little interest in the politics of the towns where their *estancias* (ranches) were located (Hora 2002; Losada 2009). Because of these structural differences, large landowners in the Pampas did not control local political machines and had no partisan linkages.

Their lack of control over local political machines did not, however, mean that agrarian elites in Argentina had no political influence. Argentine landowners' political power came from the centrality of agriculture to the country's economy. Their privileged position in society guaranteed landowners access, through family and social ties, to high-ranking government officials and party leaders. Historically, landed elites looked at partisan structures with distrust and preferred to influence politics though nonelectoral channels such as direct access to the state (Losada 2009). Throughout the twentieth century, this strategy was quite successful, since most ministers of agriculture and many other officials in top positions in the economic bureaucracy belonged to the agrarian elite (Schneider 2004, 184). Members of the SRA enjoyed prominent representation in every administration between 1910 and 1943, whether Conservative or Radical. Five presidents and thirty-nine out of ninety-three cabinet members appointed during that period were members of the SRA. Representation in the Ministry of Agriculture was especially strong. Out of fourteen appointees to the post of minister, twelve belonged to the SRA (P. Smith 1969, 48). This continued to be the case even during the first two Perón administrations (1946–1955) when two out of three ministers of agriculture were members of the SRA (Palomino 1988, 72). After 1955, however, access to the executive became highly contingent on the ideological orientation of the government and its ties to the agricultural sector. For instance, whereas the military government of the Revolución Argentina (1966–1973) appointed thirty members of the SRA to cabinet positions, the Peronist government that followed (1973–1976) did not appoint any (Palomino 1988, 75). The fact that agrarian elites' capacity to influence policymaking was so dependent on the government's willingness to grant the sector access to the state left them defenseless against hostile administrations. As we will see, this problem became particularly acute during the administrations of the center-left FPV (2003–2015).

5.3 NO THREAT, NO ELECTORAL ORGANIZATION: AGRARIAN ELITES AND POLITICS BEFORE 2008

One of the main arguments of this book is that agrarian elites will enter the electoral arena when they perceive an existential threat, which I define as policies jeopardizing the continuity of their business. Absent this kind of threat, landowners would prefer nonelectoral strategies of political influence (e.g., lobbying) because of their lower costs. The Argentine case before the 2008 agrarian lockouts is a clear example of this proposition. From the democratic transition until the beginning of the Cristina Fernández de Kirchner first administration (2007–2011), Argentine agrarian elites influenced politics through informal contacts with high-ranking government officials in the executive and, when lobbying did not work, protests. This section shows how absent any serious threat to their property rights and enjoying extensive access to administrations of every political sign, Argentine landowners remained aloof from electoral politics. This, in part, explains why agrarian elites did not join the party-building efforts of conservative politicians who during the 1980s and early 1990s were trying to establish the Unión del Centro Democrático (UCEDE) as the electoral vehicle of the Argentine right.

5.3.1 A Nonthreatening Transition to Democracy

Unlike their counterparts in Brazil and Chile, Argentine agrarian elites had no reason to feel threatened by the democratic transition. In contrast to Brazil, land reform was not part of the political debate in Argentina (Hora 2018, 186). No social actor was mobilized around the demand of land reform and neither of the two major parties were proposing any policies that could entail a threat to agrarian elites' property rights. In fact, the policy platform presented by both the Radical and Peronist parties for the transitional elections abandoned past promises to distribute land to small farmers – which, as we shall see, were merely rhetorical and never seriously considered – and focused on the technical modernization of the countryside (Lattuada 1986; Nun and Lattuada 1991). Although both parties continued to propose export taxes and a tax on idle land, rates were moderate and similar to those already in place. All in all, in the midst of a serious economic crisis, the policies that agrarian elites could expect from the next democratic government, whether it was Radical or Peronist, were not very different from those being implemented by the authoritarian government at the time.

In contrast to Chile, where the agrarian elites had been the victims of an extensive radical redistribution of land under democracy, in Argentina, past democratic administrations had never seriously threatened landowners' property rights. While the nation's economic policy since the 1930s had typically shown a bias against the agricultural sector and the Peronist Party had maintained an antagonistic rhetoric towards agrarian elites, land reform had never been on the political agenda in Argentina. No matter which party or military faction was in power, Argentine agrarian elites had always been successful in protecting their property rights and keeping land reform off the table. Lattuada's (1988) thorough analysis of agricultural policy in the country between 1946 and 1983 shows that proposals that threatened landed elites' property rights were systematically ignored by the Argentine Congress regardless of which party was in government. Proposals for unproductive land expropriation presented by Peronist (PJ) legislators during Juan Perón's second term (1949–1955) never made it onto the congressional agenda despite the PJ's absolute majority in both chambers.[13] Similarly, during the administration of Arturo Frondizi (1959–1961), the president blocked the implementation of provincial land reform laws and vetoed bills that improved the working conditions of rural workers and sharecroppers, even when they had been introduced by legislators of his own party – the Unión Cívica Radical Intransigente (UCRI), a developmentalist faction within the UCR. During the third Peronist administration (1973–1976), which in ideological terms was probably the most hostile towards agrarian elites of any administration in the history of the country, Congress also blocked a bill that proposed the expropriation (with compensation) of unexploited lands, while a tax on idle land that Congress passed in 1973 was never implemented by the executive (Lattuada 1986).

---

[13] As Vazelesk Ribeiro's (2008) analysis of Perón's agrarian policy highlights, the goal of such policies was never to redistribute land but to avoid unrest in rural areas. Peronists believed that if they improved the living and working conditions of peasants, they would prevent Communism from taking hold in the countryside.

TABLE 5.1 *Average net prices obtained by agricultural producers compared to international prices and average tax rate on the agricultural sector by administration: Argentina, 1955–1983*

	Prices obtained by producers relative to international prices (=100)[b]	Taxes on the sector (as % of sector GDP)
Perón II (PJ) (1952–1955)[a]	47	n/d
Revolución Libertadora (1955–1958)	69	n/d
Frondizi (UCRI)[c] (1958–1962)	84	10
Guido (UCRI) (1962–1963)	82	6
Illia (UCRP)[c] (1963–1966)	88	6
Revolución Argentina (1966–1973)	93	12
Perón III (PJ) (1973–1976)	57	14
Proceso de Reorganización Nacional (1976–1983)	68	14

[a] Data from 1955.
[b] Actual price paid to producers for their exported products after discounting export taxes and unfavorable exchange controls, as percentage of international prices.
[c] UCRI and UCRP (Unión Cívica Radical del Pueblo), were UCR factions.
Authoritarian administrations are shaded.
Source: Lattuada (1988, 108).

At the moment of democratic transition, the clear-cut contrast in policy towards the sector that existed between democratic and authoritarian administrations in Brazil and Chile was absent in Argentina. In the first two countries, democratic governments had empowered rural workers and threatened (Brazil) or attacked (Chile) landowners' property rights while authoritarian regimes had repressed peasants' organizations and restored private property. In Argentina, all governments had respected landowners' property while, as Table 5.1 shows, taxes on exports as well as manipulations of the exchange rate that reduced agricultural producers' earnings were policies common to both military and civilian administrations of different partisan affiliation (Lattuada 1988; Manzetti 1992). For instance, the tax rate paid by the sector was the same during the third Peronist administration (1973–1976) as it was during the military government that deposed it (1976–1983). Even when the net prices obtained by producers (i.e., discounting what the state appropriated via export taxes and exchange controls) were at their lowest during the Peronist administrations, agricultural producers' situation was not unambiguously better during authoritarian

5.3 Agrarian Elites and Politics Before 2008

administrations that under democratic ones. In fact, prices received during the democratic Radical administrations were on average significantly better than the average during authoritarian governments (84.7 versus 76.7 percent of international prices). Therefore, even when agrarian elites' profits had been slimmer during the Peronist administrations, no democratic government, Peronist or Radical, had pursued the kind of policies that constitute an existential threat (e.g., land reform) and could elicit electoral organization.

My analysis of internal documents of agricultural producers' associations[14] and their leaders' statements to the press during 1982 and 1983 reveals that producers did not feel threatened by the upcoming democratic transition. Given the military's failure to tackle accelerating inflation and a growing fiscal deficit, leaders of producers' associations welcomed a change in regime, hoping democracy would breathe new air into the Argentine economy and offer a more stable environment in which to conduct their business. For instance, the president of the Buenos Aires Grain Exchange in a message to its members expressed optimism that the transition to democracy would "open an opportunity for the country for institutionalization (...) [which is] fundamental to overcome the crisis, achieving the needed equilibrium and stability."[15] References to the democratic transition and the 1983 presidential elections are scarce in the analysed documents. In fact, agricultural producers did not seem to care much about which party would win. Their main concern at the time was, as the previous quote illustrates, institutional stability. As the then president of the SRA put it, "we do not care about who is in government. We just want them to last."[16] In terms of policies, agrarian elites at the time were hopeful the new democratic administration would take measures to improve the prices producers received for selling their goods in the international market, that is to say, eliminate export taxes and liberalize the exchange rate. In clear contrast to what I found in Brazil and Chile, landowners never expressed any concerns over the security of their property rights. Moreover, commenting on the proposals of the presidential candidates, a SRA editorial highlighted how both parties had refrained from "traditional demagogic promises of massive transfers of resources from the agricultural sector to other sectors."[17]

---

[14] *Anales* (SRA magazine) and the annual report of the Buenos Aires Grain Exchange.
[15] Bolsa de Cereales de Buenos Aires (1983, 21).
[16] "Commodities and Agriculture: Noah's Ark Symbolism of the Post-Malvinas Era," *Financial Times*, September 7, 1983.
[17] *Anales* 117, no. 6 (June 1983).

Summing up, agrarian elites in Argentina did not dread democracy. With a history of both democratic and authoritarian governments having implemented export taxes and exchange rates unfavorable to the sector while, at the same time, respecting property rights, and in a context of economic crisis, agrarian elites were hopeful the democratic transition will bring the political and economic stability that had eluded the country for so long. Moreover, agrarian elites had no reason to believe the democratic transition would restrict their easy access to government officials. In the past, agrarian elites' informal access to high-ranking officials in the executive branch had allowed them to keep proposals targeted at changing the land tenure structure of the country off the table under both Radical and Peronist administrations. Thus, in the absence of an existential threat, landowners had no incentives to enter the electoral arena as the potential gains in policy influence derived from investing in electoral representation were not high enough to offset the costs of organizing.

5.3.2 The UCEDE, a Lost Opportunity for Party-Building?

Why did agrarian elites in Argentina not support the building of UCEDE, a liberal party whose policy platform coincided with their historical demands?[18] Following Gibson (1996), I argue that agrarian elites had no incentives to engage in party-building during the founding years of the UCEDE (mid 1980s–early 1990s) as they were able to block policy threats through nonelectoral strategies, combining access to high-ranking government officials with protests. Absent an existential threat, the eventual costs of losing some minor policy battles continued to be lower than those associated with coordinating electoral representation.

During the first years after the democratic transition, a window of opportunity opened for UCEDE leaders to court agrarian elites. President Alfonsín (1983–1989) was at first antagonistic to agrarian interests. He increased the export taxes that the military government had reinstated in 1982, imposed price controls on agricultural products, and established exchange controls that discriminated against the agricultural sector, further diminishing producers' income in a context of declining international prices. In addition, in the years 1984–1986, Alfonsín's administration worked on a draft bill to tax idle land, which the CRA and SRA fiercely opposed because they considered it a violation of their property

---

[18] On UCEDE, see Gibson (1996) and Loxton (2021).

5.3 Agrarian Elites and Politics Before 2008

rights (Nun and Lattuada 1991). Moreover, representatives from the agricultural sector were excluded from government-business consultation arrangements (Gibson 1996, 162), closing an important avenue of access to the executive. As a reaction to these hostile policies, producers' associations launched a series of lockouts and demonstrations across the country throughout 1986, some of them jointly (Acuña 1995).

UCEDE leaders were eager to capitalize on the sector's confrontation with the government. In the hope of gaining the support of the sector for the 1987 legislative elections, the UCEDE publicly backed agricultural producers and demanded the end of policies that transferred resources from agriculture to other less competitive sectors, such as export taxes, differentiated exchange rates, and price controls (Nun and Lattuada 1991, 121; Gibson 1996, 163; Fair 2017, 11). However, the party's efforts to attract agricultural elites bore little fruit when the government, pressured to reduce social unrest before the elections, moved quickly to deescalate the conflict. Not only did Alfonsín give in to producers' main demands, cutting export taxes, granting debt rollovers, and killing the idle land tax bill, but he also reestablished landowners' access to the policymaking process. He formed an agricultural policy consulting body with representatives of the producer associations and appointed a new secretary of agriculture from the SRA ranks (Nun and Lattuada 1991; Acuña 1995). Once again, agrarian elites' nonelectoral strategies had proved effective in neutralizing threatening policies, thereby eliminating landowners' incentives to invest in electoral representation.

The Peronist administration of Carlos Menem (1989–1999) further reinforced Argentine agrarian elites' incentives to continue investing in nonelectoral strategies of political influence. First, Menem's policy agenda of liberalization and privatization fulfilled many of agrarian elites' historical demands (Lattuada 2006). The government abolished export taxes in 1991 and deregulated agricultural markets in 1992. Moreover, the establishment by law of a currency peg between the peso and the dollar in 1991 eliminated the possibility of discussing the exchange rate. Second, agrarian elites, especially SRA members, enjoyed ready access to state officials during Menem's administration. The president frequently consulted with SRA leaders about agricultural policy and appointments to sectoral agencies.[19] Ideological affinities between government officials

---

[19] Author's interview with Alchouron, SRA president (1984–1990), Buenos Aires, July 8 and 17, 2014.

and SRA leaders were high,[20] as the association's enthusiastic public support for Menem's neoliberal agenda shows. Tellingly, during the SRA annual exhibition in 1991, SRA president Eduardo de Zavalía told Menem he could count on agricultural producers as "the most loyal soldiers" in his struggle to liberalize the Argentine economy.[21]

Enjoying direct access to policy makers and in the absence of policy threats, agrarian elites had no incentives to invest in electoral representation, leaving UCEDE without a crucial resource for the survival of conservative parties, the support of business elites.[22] The words of a sectoral leader who was a UCEDE provincial legislator in the 1990s are illustrative of how agrarian elites at the time valued informal access to government officials over the construction of partisan linkages: "When they [the associations' leaders] had an issue, instead of talking to me [a legislator from the sector], they preferred talking directly to the provincial government because they had direct access to the executive."[23]

5.4 LANDOWNERS ENTER THE ELECTORAL ARENA: THE *AGRODIPUTADOS* (2009–2013)

If Menem's neoliberal policy agenda had led agrarian elites to believe that Peronists were no longer hostile to their interests, the administrations of the FPV (2003–2015), especially from 2006 on, showed them that had been a hasty judgement. Néstor Kirchner and his wife and successor Cristina Fernández implemented a series of policies that were so increasingly threatening to the sector that agricultural producers launched the largest protest in their history. But agrarian elites did not only deploy their traditional nonelectoral strategies. Facing a government that had cut off all channels of informal access to state officials, for the first time since the democratic transition, agricultural producers also decided to organize in the electoral arena. The emergence of an existential threat in the form of a confiscatory tax increased the costs for Argentine producers of failing to influence policymaking to the point that they surpassed the coordination costs of organizing electoral representation. Due to historic economic cleavages among the agrarian elites

---

[20] Author's interviews with specialized journalist and SRA leader, Not for Attribution, Buenos Aires, 2014. See also Lattuada (2006).
[21] *Anales* 124, no. 7/9 (July/September 1991), 16.
[22] On conservative party-building, see Loxton (2021).
[23] Author's interview with Horacio Salaverry, president of CARBAP, Buenos Aires, June 11, 2014.

and the lack of organic linkages to any party, landowners deployed a nonpartisan strategy of electoral participation, running their candidates under multiple party labels.

5.4.1 The 2008 Agrarian Conflict and the Decision to Enter the Electoral Arena

Argentine agrarian elites entered the electoral arena in the aftermath of the 2008 lockouts. This conflict had showed Argentine landowners the Achilles' heel of their nonelectoral strategy of political influence: lobbying only works when government officials are willing to meet with you. Without access to policymakers, nonelectoral strategies are useless. Hence their unreliability. Facing an administration that increased their taxes to confiscatory levels and imposed onerous regulations on them, jeopardizing the continuity of their business, landowners realized they needed a more reliable source of political influence. Failing to influence policy outcomes had become too costly. In order to ensure public officials will take their policy preferences into account, agrarian elites needed to elect politicians from their ranks. As a provincial legislator from the sector explained: "Politicians are the only ones with the capacity to change reality. You, as a leader of a producers' association, may rant and rave, organize protests, talk to the media, whatever you want ... but the one making the decision is the politician."[24]

The 2008 protests were triggered by a new system for calculating export taxes that producers deemed confiscatory. Implemented in March 2008, it established rates that varied according to fluctuations in international prices. With international commodity prices soaring, the change represented an increase in the tax rate on soybeans from 35 percent to 44 percent. After Menem abolished export taxes in 1991, they were reinstated by President Eduardo Duhalde (2001–2003) during the economic meltdown of 2001. At the time, agrarian elites agreed to the tax because they saw it as a necessary tool to help the country recover from one of the worst economic and political crises in its history. Moreover, the tax was not onerous for producers who, in a context of increasing international commodity prices, had greatly benefited from the 400 percent depreciation of the peso and the conversion to pesos of their dollar-denominated debts. Initially, the tax rate was established at 5 percent, but it was soon increased to 10 and then 20 percent. Néstor

---

[24] Author's interview with María del Huerto Ratto, Buenos Aires, August 13, 2014.

Kirchner continued this policy, raising the tax rate twice in 2007 until it reached 35 percent for soybeans.

Three features of the new tax scheme implemented in March 2008 led producers to interpret it as a threat to the continuity of their business and help explain why this particular tax increase provoked an unprecedented reaction from them. First, the variable tax rate – which could reach values as high as 95 percent if international prices rose over US$600/ton[25] – was particularly outrageous to producers because it meant farm profits would increase much more slowly than international prices, frustrating producers' expectations of future earnings in a context where international prices were forecast to keep rising (Fairfield 2011). At the same time, the minimum tax rate was quite high, meaning that even if international prices fell drastically, producers would continue to pay onerous taxes.[26] Lastly, the timing of the tax increase contributed to the producers' outcry. The new tax rate was announced just days before the harvest, which for producers seemed as though the state was stealing their hard-earned profits. A producer participating in one of the roadblocks in the province of Buenos Aires explained why he was protesting in this way, "profit margins are not great, and producers are certain that their harvest is being confiscated."[27] Moreover, the tax hike was worst for soybeans which affected not only large producers in the Pampas, but also small and medium farmers throughout the country, creating common cause across the sector.[28]

Other policies contributed as well to agricultural producers' view of FPV policies as confiscatory. Starting in Néstor Kirchner's administration (2003–2007), the government intervened in grain and beef markets with the objective of controlling domestic inflation. Price controls on beef started in 2005. In 2006, the government prohibited beef exports for four months to force a drop in domestic prices. Quotas for wheat and beef exports were established in 2007. A registry of exports was also created which restricted the ability of producers and exporters to decide when to sell and when to cash in their sales (Barsky and

---

[25] In 2008, when the new tax scheme was implemented, the international price of soybeans was around US$523/ton.
[26] The tax rate for soybeans if international prices dropped to US$100/ton – an extremely low price – would be 23.5 percent.
[27] "El grito del campo," *La Nación*, March 29, 2008.
[28] In 2008, soy products accounted for half of the country's total export value. The area harvested with soybeans totaled more than 18 million hectares in 13 different provinces, while 82 percent of soybean producers were harvesting plots of land of 250 hectares or less (Barsky and Dávila 2008, 65).

5.4 Landowners Enter the Electoral Arena 173

Dávila 2008). In this context of rising taxation and state intervention in agricultural markets, producers saw Fernández de Kirchner's agrarian policy as an existential threat. As a former leader of CARBAP explained when I asked him why producers decided to participate in politics in 2008 but not before, given that sectoral policies had also been unfavorable during the previous administrations of Alfonsín and Menem, "it is one thing to confront a bad policy and a very different one to feel attacked, to feel they are coming for you."[29]

If market liberalization in the 1990s had left agricultural producers' organizations without an agenda for petitioning the state, the Kirchners' interventions gave it back to them. The problem was that, unlike in the past, government officials were now unwilling to listen to the agricultural sector. Agrarian elites had no social or family ties to high-ranking politicians in the executive branch who, as the leftwing Peronists that they were, regarded agricultural producers as oligarchic rentiers that did not need the help of the state. Consequently, nonelectoral strategies of political influence became ineffective and agricultural producers were left helpless before a government threatening the continuity of their business.[30]

The Kirchners' increasingly hostile policy agenda triggered a strong reaction among producers who started to demand action from their leaders. As a consequence, the four national associations put their historical differences aside and began to coordinate collective action. Their first joint action was a nine-day stoppage of cattle sales in November 2006 to protest the government's interventions in the beef markets (Lissin 2010, 73).[31] After that, producers associations organized several demonstrations and market stoppages. However, the events of 2008 were unprecedented in their extent and intensity. The four associations coordinated a four-month-long commercialization strike[32] that was accompanied by hundreds of road blockages across the countryside. Moreover, to the surprise of the government, producers gained the support of the urban middle classes, who joined them in massive demonstrations in the cities of Buenos Aires and Rosario (Hora 2010; Fairfield 2011).[33]

---

[29] Author's interview with Jorge Srodek, Buenos Aires, June 12, 2017.
[30] Especially in a context where, unlike in the past, the military option was off the table.
[31] Organized by the CRA and FAA and supported by the SRA.
[32] During the strike, producers halted the sale and delivery of agricultural products, especially meat and grains, to domestic and export markets (Fairfield 2011, 441).
[33] In the demonstration that took place in Rosario in May 2008, 200,000 people participated (Hora 2010, 92). For an explanation of why the protestors gained widespread urban support, see Hora (2010).

As a consequence of producers' mass mobilization and its widespread urban support, the government was ultimately forced to repeal the tax increase in July 2008 after the new tax scheme bill was defeated in Congress. At first, the new tax was enacted by decree. However, as a way of deescalating the conflict with producers and giving more legitimacy to the tax, the president sent a bill to Congress ratifying the new tax scheme in June 2008. The government expected the bill to pass easily, given that the party of the president, the FPV, controlled the majority of seats in both chambers and that the producers had no partisan allies. Yet, despite their lack of political connections, producers were able to narrowly defeat the bill by organizing a pervasive lobby, pressuring legislators both in Congress and in their home districts. Key to this was a split within the governing coalition created by the conflict, between legislators representing districts where agriculture is one of the main economic activities and those where it is marginal. Groups of producers visited legislators' offices every day to talk about the negative impact of the tax on their home districts. At the same time, producers' organizations pitched a tent in front of Congress with giant screens to follow the legislative debate. In the interior of the country, local associations mobilized to pressure their representatives to reject the bill. As a result, twenty-eight deputies in the governing coalition broke ranks and opposed the bill. Thirteen of them represented core agricultural provinces and five represented provinces to which the agrarian frontier had recently expanded. Nevertheless, the bill passed by a slim margin.[34] On July 15, 2008, the day before the Senate was scheduled to vote on the bill ratifying the new tax scheme, 237,000 people participated in a rally organized by agricultural producers' associations in the city of Buenos Aires.[35] In the Senate, pressure from the producers provoked a tie when ten senators in the governing coalition voted against the bill. Four of them represented core agricultural districts while another four were from provinces where agriculture had recently expanded. The bill was eventually defeated when the vice resident of the country voted against it to break the tie.

The agrarian elites' victory was, however, a pyrrhic one. After mounting such a tremendous mobilization effort, the agricultural producers were able to repeal the last tax rate increase, but not to eliminate export taxes altogether. In fact, the export tax rate continued

---

[34] The votes were: 129 votes in favor, 122 against, and 2 abstentions.
[35] "Contundente acto del agro en Palermo," *La Nacion*, July 16, 2008.

to be around 35 percent until the end of the Fernández de Kirchner administration in 2015. Moreover, after the conflict, the government increased price controls and export quotas for beef and other agricultural products. Thus, it became evident to landowners that nonelectoral strategies were ineffective to confront a hostile administration unwilling to concede the group access to the state. In this context, leaders of producers' associations started to entertain the idea of participating in electoral politics.

5.4.2 Elite Fragmentation and Lack of Partisan Linkages

Why did agrarian elites enter the electoral arena through a candidate-centered strategy in Argentina where electoral rules discourage party infiltration by interest groups?[36] Why did agrarian elites not build organic linkages to a party instead? I argue that agrarian elites in Argentina pursued a candidate-centered electoral strategy due to their high fragmentation. Regional and economic cleavages have historically divided rural producers in Argentina between the Pampas and the interior. As a consequence, agrarian elites hold competing policy preferences, which has prevented them from building organic sector-wide linkages to a party, even after the consolidation of the center-right PRO as a viable alternative. In this section, I review the historical sources of agrarian elites' divisions.

Throughout Argentine history, economic and political elites have been divided by regional cleavages (Kurtz 2013). The competing interests of regional elites in the prosperous Pampas – who controlled the best land in the country as well as international trade – and those of the underdeveloped interior hindered the formation of a national conservative party (Gibson 1996, 41–44). As a consequence, the right in Argentina has historically been divided between the conservatives in the interior (also known as federalists) and the liberals in Buenos Aires. The federalists were a heterogeneous group of provincial elites with ties to the old conservative National Autonomist Party but without a coherent ideology or common economic interest beyond the defense of protectionism to guarantee the survival of regional industries. Through the control of clientelistic machines in their provinces, federalists were able to build successful electoral alliances with different nonconservative national parties

---

[36] See Chapter 2, Section 2.5.2 for a discussion on how electoral rules affect interest groups' linkages to parties and their ability to influence the policy agenda.

throughout the twentieth century (Morresi 2015). Liberals represented the interests of the Buenos Aires oligarchy, that is to say, agro-exporters and financial capital. Consequently, they were against protectionism and were fervent supporters of free trade. Unlike the federalists, they were electorally weak and influenced politics through informal channels such as personal relationships with high-ranking government officials, who were frequently recruited from their ranks, and leaders of the main parties (Morresi 2015).

Agrarian elites, as members of the economic and political elite, have also been fragmented around this regional cleavage. As a symptom of agrarian elites' profound divisions, four national-level associations claim producers' representation, with frequent factional disputes within these corporatist organizations. Historically, landowners in the fertile Pampas have been highly competitive producers of beef and cereals for the international market and have therefore favored liberalism. Represented mainly by the SRA and CARBAP, landowners of the Pampas have been politically closer to liberal conservatives – who themselves have not constituted a party but built relationships with liberal factions within the main parties.[37] Unlike agrarian elites elsewhere in Latin America before the third wave transitions, landowners in the Pampas lacked clientelistic networks over which to build partisan representation, as cattle ranching and cereal production are not labor-intensive activities. As a consequence, they preferred to influence politics through informal social and family relations with politicians or through the appointment of people from their ranks to government agencies related to the agricultural sector. Far away from ports and working less fertile lands, agrarian elites in the interior have historically been more dependent on state protection for the viability of their business than those in the Pampas. Therefore, they have not embraced liberalism and instead have demanded state intervention to protect regional products such as sugarcane and cotton in the north and fruit in the center-west and south. Throughout the twentieth century, unlike landowners in the Pampas, some regional oligarchies such as, for example, sugarcane producers in the province of Tucumán who controlled the votes of sugar mill workers and small producers, dominated extensive clientelistic machines that guaranteed them a prominent role in provincial politics (Losada 2009). Thus, in some provinces of the interior, agrarian elites were part of conservative provincial parties that frequently allied with Peronists and Radicals at the national level (Gibson 1997).

[37] See Gibson (1996) and Morresi (2015).

5.4 Landowners Enter the Electoral Arena

Because of these regional and economic cleavages, no organic linkages between parties and agrarian elites as a group were ever built in Argentina. Associations have been closer to some parties than to others according to their ideological orientation, for example, the SRA and CARBAP to liberal Buenos Aires-based parties and the FAA to popular and leftwing parties, but the sector as a class at no point invested in party-building efforts.[38] Prior to 2009, the few landowners that pursued political careers under various party labels did so out of personal ambition and not as part of a collective strategy of representation.[39] Argentine agrarian elites were historically suspicious of party structures, which they saw as machines oriented toward winning the votes of the urban majority, and therefore insensitive to agrarian interests (Lattuada 1992). Thus, when agrarian elites felt threatened in 2008, they had no political allies to turn to. In need of electoral representation, and given the long-time horizons of party-building, agrarian elites developed a candidate-centered strategy, supporting individual candidates under multiple party labels.

It is important to clarify that the source of agrarian elites' political fragmentation is different in Argentina than in Brazil with significant consequences for their electoral representation. In Argentina, economic cleavages within the agrarian elites translate into competing policy preferences that have historically hindered the formation of a conservative party to represent their interests. In Brazil, political division among landowners do not originate in economic cleavages but in factional disputes for the control of local politics. As a consequence, political divisions among the Brazilian agrarian elite are not ideological and landowners in different parties have common policy preferences which facilitates their joint action in Congress. In Argentina, political divisions among agricultural producers are ideological which hinders any type of collective electoral representation, partisan or multipartisan.

---

[38] Exceptions to this are two failed party-building attempts by agrarian elites in the province of Buenos Aires, one at the end of the nineteenth century, the Unión Provincial and the other at the beginning of the twentieth century, Defensa Rural. See Hora (2002; 2009).

[39] The best known examples are Jorge Aguado, president of the CRA (1978–1981), who served as congressman for the province of Buenos Aires (1989–1993) in the rightwing UCEDE; Guillermo Alchouron, president of the SRA (1984–1990), who served as congressman for the City of Buenos Aires (1999–2007) in the rightwing Acción por la Republica; and Humberto Volando, president of the FAA (1971–1996), who served as congressman for Córdoba (1997–2001) for the center-left FREPASO.

5.4.3 The *Agrodiputados* (2009–2013)

Agrarian elites entered the electoral arena in 2009 to defend themselves from an increasingly hostile administration that was implementing policies that threatened their businesses at the same time that it had cut off their access to the state. Because agrarian elites had no party to represent their interests and these linkages could not be built overnight, individual agricultural producers ran for office under diverse party labels. As shown in Table 5.2, between 2009 and 2013, twenty-eight candidates from the sector ran for a lower chamber seat under twelve different party labels across the ideological spectrum, from the Socialist Party to the center-right PRO.[40]

In the aftermath of the 2008 protests, producers saw in the 2009 legislative election an opportunity to build a space of direct representation within Congress. What better example of this strategy than the Brazilian Agrarian Caucus? (See Chapter 4.) So, the Buenos Aires Grain Exchange and the Rosario Stock Exchange sent a delegation of consultants to Brasília to study the Bancada Ruralista with the intention of replicating it in Argentina (Bolsa de Cereales de Buenos Aires and Bolsa de Comercio de Rosario 2009).[41] After learning about the Brazilian Agrarian Caucus's great effectiveness in defending agribusiness interests, some leaders from producers' associations started to talk with party leaders about the possibility of placing people from their ranks on their respective parties' ballots. It is worth mentioning that consultants also studied the case of the Country/National Party in Australia – founded at the end of the nineteenth century by farmers and very influential in the 1920s – but given the high political fragmentation of the sector in Argentina, this option was quickly discarded.[42]

Because agrarian elites as a group had no previous links with any party, individual agricultural producers who had political ambitions joined the party they felt closer to ideologically or the party that offered them the highest position on the ballot. Some of the producers' associations scouted their membership for potential candidates to run for a range of offices at the local, provincial and national level. They drew

---

[40] I classified as agro-candidates those candidates who had held office in a sectoral association or declared agricultural production as one of their economic activities, even if not the main one.

[41] Author's interviews with Juan Cruz Jaime and Adolfo Castro Almeyra, consultants who travelled to Brasília, Buenos Aires, June 14 and 17, 2014; and Mario Acoroni, executive director of the Rosario Stock Exchange, Rosario, June 24, 2014.

[42] Author's interview with Jaime.

TABLE 5.2 *Agro-candidates for the Lower Chamber: Argentina, 2009–2013*

Candidate	Province	Year	Elected?	Party	Association
Pablo Orsolini	Chaco	2009	Yes	UCR	FAA
Ulises Forte	La Pampa	2009	Yes	UCR	FAA
Ricardo Buryaile	Formosa	2009	Yes	UCR	CRA
Atilio Benedetti	Entre Ríos	2009	Yes	UCR	–
Hilma Ré	Entre Ríos	2009	Yes	CC	SRA
Jorge Chemes	Entre Ríos	2009	Yes	UCR	CRA
Lucio Aspiazu	Corrientes	2009	Yes	UCR	CRA
Laura Fernández Cagnone	Buenos Aires	2009	No	CC	–
Pedro Vigneau	Buenos Aires	2009	No	CC	–
Gumersindo Alonso	Córdoba	2009	Yes	PJ[a]	CRA
Estela Garnero	Córdoba	2009	Yes	PJ	FAA
Daniel Vázquez	Río Negro	2009	No	CC	FAA
Juan Casañas	Tucumán	2009	Yes	UCR	–
Clara Raspo	Córdoba	2009	No	UCR	CRA
Alfredo Olmedo	Salta	2009	Yes	PJ	–
Mario Llambías	Buenos Aires	2011	No	CC	CRA
Guillermo Bernaudo	Entre Ríos	2011	No	UPT[b]	AACREA
Marcos Giraudo	Córdoba	2011	No	UCR	CONINAGRO
Myriam Marto	Tucumán	2011	No	UCR	–
Omar Barchetta	Santa Fe	2011	Yes	PS	FAA
Ana Galmarini	Santa Fe	2011	No	Sur[c]	FAA
Soledad Diez de Tejada	Santa Fe	2011	No	PJ	SRA
Juan Ruiz Orrico	Entre Ríos	2011	No	PJ	SRA
Ricardo Buryaile	Formosa	2013	Yes (R)	UCR	CRA
Juan Casañas	Tucumán	2013	Yes (R)	UCR	FAA
Hilma Ré	Entre Ríos	2013	No	CC	SRA
Néstor Roulet	Córdoba	2013	No	PRO	CRA
Soledad Diez de Tejada	Santa Fe	2013	No	PJ	SRA
Alberto Colombres Garmendia	Tucumán	2013	No	PRO	–
Paul Bleckwedel	Tucumán	2013	No	PRO	–
Jorge Solmi	Buenos Aires	2013	No	PJ	FAA
Gilberto Alegre	Buenos Aires	2013	Yes	PJ	–

Winning candidates are shaded.
[a] Includes six different non-Kirchnerista factions within Peronism.
[b] Unión por Todos. Small center-right party that existed between 2003 and 2018 mainly in Buenos Aires.
[c] Proyecto Sur. Small center-left party with a nationalist and environmentalist orientation.
Source: Author, based on "Agro diputados," *La Nación*, May 23, 2009; "El campo buscará llegar al poder en cuatro provincias," *La Nación*, June 28, 2011; "Tras el cierre de listas: el campo prevé menos bancas," *La Nación*, June 29, 2013.

up lists and presented them to the different parties.[43] As a leader of the SRA explained, "we made lists of people [who wanted to participate in politics], their location and 'political instincts.' Then we talked to party leaders [and said], 'look, this is so-and-so, he has a calling for politics, he identifies with your party, consider him.'"[44] Because individual producers had different partisan identities, it was not a viable option to try to coordinate all agricultural candidacies under the same party label.[45] As the president of the SRA at the time commented, "there is no way we will build our own party, but we support the participation of producers in the different parties they have an affinity with, because we are pluralists. What matters is that we participate in the public sector from the inside, in whatever space is possible."[46]

Party leaders from the opposition were eager to attract leaders from producers' associations to their list of candidates for Congress in 2009. The defeat of the export tax bill in Congress had been a major political setback for the Kirchners. Massive rallies in support of agricultural producers in the cities of Rosario and Buenos Aires during the 2008 conflict had showed that producers' associations at the time had a mobilization capacity greater than that of any party in the opposition. During the four-month-long conflict, leaders from producers' associations enjoyed a lot of airtime in the mass media and, as a consequence, became well-known figures among the urban middle classes who saw them as the standard-bearers of the anti-Kirchner backlash (Richardson 2012). All this made leaders from producers' associations attractive potential candidates for the parties in the opposition (Del Cogliano 2016). In fact, as every leader from the sector I interviewed recognized, all opposition parties except those on the extreme left were trying to recruit someone from the agricultural sector in 2009. The producers who had led the 2008 protests were approached by the UCR, the Coalición Cívica (CC), PRO, and the non-Kirchnerist PJ.[47] As my interviewees put it, everybody wanted a "beret" on their ballot.[48]

---

[43] Author's interviews with leaders of the SRA, FAA, and CARBAP, Not for Attribution, 2014 and 2017.
[44] Author's interview with leader of the SRA, Not for Attribution, 2014.
[45] Similarly, large producers interviewed by Gras (2012a) in the months following the 2008 conflict discarded party-building and said that the sector should work to elect politicians who think like them in different parties.
[46] Hugo Biolcati, "El campo busca ampliar su participación en las elecciones legislativas del año próximo," *La Nación*, December 30, 2008.
[47] Author's interviews with leaders of the SRA, CRA, and FAA, Not for Attribution, 2014.
[48] The hat typically worn by farmers in Argentina.

5.4 Landowners Enter the Electoral Arena

The conjunction of politicians' interest in recruiting leaders from the agricultural sector with agrarian elites' need to find a new channel of political influence resulted in the congressional candidacies of fifteen people from the sector (Table 5.2). Leaders from producers' associations, some more actively than others, bargained with party leaders to secure good positions on the ballot for their members.[49] Given Argentina's CLPR system, the higher on the list a candidate is placed, the greater their chances of being elected. The CRA, the association with the widest network across the country, was also the one that ran the most candidates, five. The FAA ran four and the SRA only one. The rest were independent producers (Table 5.2). Some associations provided logistical support for the campaigns of agro-candidates. Leaders from the associations accompanied candidates on their campaign tours across their provinces and helped with fundraising efforts. Out of the seventeen leaders of producers' associations whom I asked about campaign financing – ten of whom had run for office themselves at some point – nine said that agricultural producers contributed to the campaigns of candidates from the sector.

Of the fifteen candidates the sector ran under different party labels in 2009, eleven were elected, representing eight different provinces (Table 5.2). These were provinces with a strong agricultural tradition such as Entre Ríos and Córdoba as well as provinces to which the agricultural frontier had expanded recently, such as Formosa, Chaco, and Salta. Most elected *agrodiputados* ran on the ballot of the Acuerdo Cívico y Social, an electoral alliance between the UCR, the CC, the Socialist Party, and independent agricultural producers. The UCR elected seven *agrodiputados*, various factions of the non-Kirchnerista PJ elected three and the CC one (Table 5.2).

The extent of agricultural producers' newfound interest in electoral politics did not end with congressional elections. A study of all the agro-candidates in the 2009 elections found 262 producers run in fifteen different provinces for national, provincial and municipal office (Del Cogliano 2016). For instance, in the province of Buenos Aires, forty agricultural producers ran for municipal council seats on the ticket of an electoral alliance between the non-Kirchnerista PJ and the center-right PRO.[50] In the province of Santa Fe, ninety members of the FAA ran for different provincial and local offices under multiple party labels.[51]

---

[49] Author's interviews with leaders of SRA, CARBAP, and FAA, Not for Attribution, 2014.
[50] "Agro diputados," *La Nación*, May 23, 2009.
[51] Ibid.

According to the AACREA 2014 census, 8.5 percent of its members reported having held public office at some point during the five years previous to the survey, most of them at the municipal level (CREA 2014). Moreover, the CRA and SRA, together with other civil organizations, created an NGO dedicated to training thousands of election monitors across the country to prevent electoral fraud.[52] Producers believed that deploying election monitors in the FPV-controlled Greater Buenos Aires, where almost a third of the country's voters live, was crucial for the opposition to have a fair chance of winning the election. In my survey of members of the think tank Barbechando,[53] 30 percent of the respondents reported serving as monitors in the 2009 election, and 50 percent in the 2015 presidential election when the center-right candidate Mauricio Macri defeated the Kirchnerist Daniel Scioli.[54] Serving as monitors was the electoral activity most frequently cited by respondents.

5.5 DISADVANTAGES OF A CANDIDATE-CENTERED STRATEGY WITHIN THE ARGENTINE PARTY SYSTEM

In 2009, eleven *agrodiputados* were elected to Congress with a mandate to change the export tax regime. However, unlike their Brazilian counterparts who, as we saw in Chapter 4, have successfully defended agrarian interests in Congress since the democratic transition, Argentine *agrodiputados* were unable to advance their sectoral interests. Why did *agrodiputados* fail to represent agrarian interests in Congress? Although the *agrodiputados* were only 4 percent of the Argentine Lower Chamber in the period from 2009 to 2013, their presence was not insignificant. At that time, if the eleven *agrodiputados* had worked together, they would have been the fourth largest party in the Lower Chamber. Moreover, between 2009 and 2011, the governing FPV did not hold a majority in the Lower Chamber, controlling only 34 percent of the seats,[55] which

---

[52] *Fiscales* in Spanish. Because Argentine elections use paper ballots printed separately for each party, parties need monitors at the polls to make sure nobody steals their ballots or miscounts their votes. The name of the organization, which was still active at the time of this writing (August 2023), is *Ser Fiscal*.
[53] For a description of this survey, see Appendix B.
[54] Barbechando is a think tank that focuses on Congress founded by agricultural producers after the 2008 conflict. Members of Barbechando are more interested in politics than the average producer; therefore, it is reasonable to believe that the percentage of producers that served as monitors in the total universe is much lower.
[55] A low proportion by Argentine Congress standards. Since the democratic transition, Argentine presidents have held a legislative majority in the Lower Chamber during twenty-four out of the thirty-nine years.

5.5 Disadvantages of a Candidate-Centered Strategy 183

increased the leverage of opposition legislators. But the Argentine *agrodiputados* did not work as a unified group, which diluted their bargaining power and undermined their capacity to advance legislation of interest to the sector. This was true even when one of the *agrodiputados* was the president of the Lower Chamber's Agriculture Committee.[56] Institutional factors as well as economic cleavages within the agrarian elite explain why the *agrodiputados* failed to work as a unified multiparty caucus in the Argentine Congress.

As previous work has highlighted, institutional differences between Argentina and Brazil help explain why Argentine *agrodiputados* failed to advance agrarian interests in Congress (Freytes 2015). In Argentina, individual legislators' bargaining power vis-à-vis their party leaders is much lower than in Brazil. CLRP in Argentina gives party leaders control over the political future of backbenchers. Legislative candidacies are decided behind closed doors, through bargaining among provincial party bosses, usually governors, who control extensive political and economic resources at the district level (De Luca et al., 2002; Jones 2008). Thus, to keep their seats or advance their political careers, legislators must be loyal to their provincial bosses, voting according to their instructions. At the same time, in Argentina most governors depend on fiscal resources held by the national executive and use the votes of their legislators in Congress as a bargaining chip in negotiations with the president (Tommasi et al. 2001). Therefore, legislators' dependence on their provincial bosses hinders the formation of multiparty coalitions in Argentina as party leaders can easily punish members that do not toe the party line.[57]

The aforementioned institutional differences make it more difficult for legislators outside the governing party to advance their policy preferences in Argentina than in Brazil. As developed in Chapter 4, due to high fragmentation within the Lower Chamber, Brazilian presidents need the support of legislators from many different parties to govern, which gives multiparty groupings such as the Bancada Ruralista great bargaining power. In Argentina, by contrast, since the democratic transition, presidents have controlled their own legislative majorities most of the time, without needing the support of legislators outside their party. Even in 2009–2011 when the governing FPV did not control a majority of the

---

[56] Ricardo Buryaile (UCR-Formosa) in 2009–2011.
[57] This was in fact the case of the eighteen FPV legislators who voted against the export tax in 2008 as none of them was reelected under that party label (Murillo and Pinto 2022, 575).

seats in the Lower Chamber, it was still the largest caucus which, added to its high cohesion, allowed it to block the opposition's legislative initiatives, including those of the *agrodiputados* (Freytes 2015). This means that even if legislators in different parties could break party discipline and work together, they would have a hard time gaining the support of a legislative majority to advance their projects. A congress dominated by the party of the president discourages the formation of multiparty groupings in Argentina (Freytes 2015).

Without disputing the value of institutional features in explaining the success of a multipartisan strategy in Brazil and its failure in Argentina, my perspective highlights the role of Argentine agrarian elites' economic cleavages in accounting for these diverging outcomes. The candidate-centered strategy was ill-suited for the Argentine Congress given the incentives created by electoral rules and coalitional dynamics. However, the *agrodiputados* were unable to advance sectoral interests in Congress not because their joint proposals failed to gain support from other legislators but because there were no joint proposals to speak of in the first place. Differences in policy preferences among the producers' associations due to economic cleavages within the Argentine agrarian elite help explain the *agrodiputados* failure to work together. As we saw in Chapter 4, the success of Bancada Ruralista members in influencing legislation is not only explained by their capacity to break party ranks and vote according to the caucus' interests, but also by their ability to persuade members of their parties to vote with them. Ruralistas can do this because their policy positions are backed by the main sectoral associations in Brazil who are united in their policy preferences. In contrast, due to differences in policy preferences among Argentine producers' associations, the *agrodiputados* lacked such outside unified support. This greatly diminished *agrodiputados* bargaining power in Congress and within their parties. For instance, during the *agrodiputados* tenure, producers' associations were not even able to jointly sponsor a single bill regarding the sector main grievance, export taxes. While representatives from the CRA and SRA wanted to eliminate export taxes altogether, those from the FAA favored establishing a progressive tax rate that would exempt small and medium producers.[58] Discrepancies in policy preferences between the representatives coming from different producers'

---

[58] Author's interviews with *agrodiputados* Ricardo Buryaile, Buenos Aires, June 19, 2014; Juan Casañas, Buenos Aires, August 6, 2014; Jorge Chemes, Buenos Aires, August 13, 2014; and Omar Barchetta, August 6, 2014.

associations also hindered the *agrodiputados'* chances of influencing the debate over bills of interest to the sector sponsored by legislators in the governing party. A clear example was Law 26,737 regulating the sale of farmland to foreign citizens. A former president of the SRA explained the differences among *agrodiputados* in this way, "While La Rural supports total freedom, Federación Agraria, by contrast, considers that anything larger than 500 hectares is a latifundio."[59] Moreover, the associations' failure to mobilize jointly in support of the different bills their legislators introduced undermined *agrodiputados'* capacity to gain support within their parties. Party leaders, seeing the proposals had no unified sectoral backing, did not take *agrodiputados'* bills seriously.[60]

Due to its ineffectiveness, the *agrodiputados* 2009 strategy was short-lived. In the following congressional election in 2011, eight candidates from the sector ran but mostly in low ballot positions. Consequently, only one was elected. In 2013, nine ran and three were elected, including two of the three *agrodiputados* running for reelection (Table 5.2). That only three out of the eleven *agrodiputados* elected in 2009 ran for reelection in 2013 shows that agrarian elites lost interest in continuing this electoral strategy. In fact, only a handful of representatives from the sector ran in the following 2015 legislative elections.

5.6 AGRICULTURAL PRODUCERS AND THE PRO: AN OPPORTUNITY FOR PARTY-BUILDING?

In November 2015, for the first time in Argentina's democratic history, a conservative coalition, Cambiemos, spearheaded by Mauricio Macri's PRO won the presidency. Even when agricultural producers had not been involved in the foundation of the party or had supported it in its beginnings,[61] the emergence of the PRO as an electorally viable center-right party at the national level presented Argentine agrarian elites with an unprecedented opportunity for party-building. On the one hand, the PRO's economic platform envisioned greater integration into the international market through the promotion of agroindustry exports, giving agriculture a central role as one of the pillars of the country's economy. On the other hand, the PRO was, at the time, a City of Buenos Aires-based party with a weak presence in the rest of

---

[59] Author's interview, Not for Attribution, 2014.
[60] Author's interview with Casañas.
[61] On the PRO's origins, see Vommaro and Morresi (2015).

the country (Vommaro 2019; 2021), which made agricultural producers potential allies to help expand the reach of the party in rural areas.

The years under FPV rule had taught agricultural producers about the unreliability of nonelectoral strategies to protect their interests, while the *agrodiputados* experience had showed them the unsuitability of nonpartisan strategies within the Argentine political system. The consolidation of the PRO as a center-right electoral alternative re-opened the door for a partisan strategy of electoral representation that had been closed since the dismantling of UCEDE in the early 1990s. Have Argentine agrarian elites seized this opportunity to build partisan representation? Even when economic cleavages within agricultural producers continue to hinder the coordination of the sector's electoral representation through a single party, my analysis reveals that ideological, electoral, personnel, and financial linkages are being built between the PRO and producers for the international market.

Ideological affinity between the PRO and the agricultural associations, especially the more liberal ones (i.e., SRA, CARBAP, and AACREA) is strong. President Mauricio Macri's (2015–2019) campaign proposals for the agricultural sector as well as his policies while in office responded to agricultural producers' long-held demands: reduction or elimination of export taxes on agricultural products, elimination of price controls on domestic products, and the lifting of export restrictions. This was no coincidence as the PRO's agrarian policy platform had been developed with the help of members of these more liberal associations who first joined the party's think tank, Fundación Pensar, in the years previous to Macri's election,[62] and then filled his administration. During his first week on the job, President Macri lifted export restrictions and eliminated or reduced export taxes. In a clear signal to the sector, Macri announced these policies from a cornfield in the agrarian town of Pergamino, one of the epicenters of the 2008 lockouts, surrounded by his agriculture cabinet – which was packed with former leaders of the producers' associations.

Macri's administration (re)opened formal and informal channels of access to the state for agrarian elites after more than a decade of

---

[62] Author's interviews with José de Anchorena, director of government planification, Fundación Pensar, Buenos Aires, August 2, 2017; Ricardo Negri, coordinator of Fundación Pensar Agroindustry Roundtable, member of AACREA, Buenos Aires, June 13, 2017; Guillermo Bernaudo, member of Fundación Pensar Agroindustry Roundtable, member of AACREA, Buenos Aires, June 12, 2017; and Jorge Srodek, member of Fundación Pensar Agroindustry Roundtable, former CARBAP vice president, Buenos Aires, June 12, 2017.

political isolation. In sharp contrast with the previous FPV administrations, Macri recruited most of the sectoral agencies' high-ranking officials from the ranks of producers' associations, AACREA and CRA especially. The agrarian leaders that had worked in Fundación Pensar writing the party's agricultural policy platform filled the ranks of the Ministry of Agriculture at the federal level and in the province of Buenos Aires.[63] According to Mangonnet et al. (2018, 18), twelve out of the twenty-nine high-ranking initial appointees to the Ministry of Agroindustry, including the minister, came from the associations' ranks. My analysis shows similar patterns for the other sectoral agencies such as the National Agricultural Technology Institute and the National Food Safety and Quality Service. Producers' infiltration of sectoral agencies was so pervasive that, on the day the new appointees to the Ministry of Agriculture were sworn in, Secretary Néstor Roulet – himself a former leader of CRA – joked that the Ministry resembled "an assembly of agricultural producers."[64]

Agrarian elites' penetration of the Macri administration and the PRO's technical teams, however, has not been replicated at the party level. Agrarian elites have not integrated into the partisan structure of the PRO. Despite the ideological affinities between the PRO and the more liberal producers' associations such as the SRA, CARBAP, or AACREA and the party's need to expand in the interior of the country, very few producers ran for office on the PRO ticket in the elections between 2015 and 2021, and they did it in similar proportions that under other party labels. For instance, in all the gubernatorial elections of 2015, 2017, and 2019, only three producers ran, one in the PRO, one in the UCR, and one in a PJ faction, but none won. In legislative elections, producers' participation has been higher but still not very significant within the PRO or in general. In 2017, eight producers were elected to Congress, three in the PRO, two in the PJ, one in the UCR and one Socialist.[65] In 2019, three producers entered Congress, two in the PRO and one in the UCR. In the 2021 legislative elections, the participation of the sector increased. Around twenty-five agro-candidates ran for Congress under multiple party labels – including provincial parties, Peronism and Socialism – with the great majority of them in Juntos por el Cambio.[66]

---

[63] Cambiemos also won the governorship of the Buenos Aires Province in 2015.
[64] "Buryaile llamó al diálogo y dijo que se 'terminó' el conflicto con el campo," *La Nación*, December 12, 2015.
[65] Barbechando (2017)
[66] "El campo y las elecciones: los 29 precandidatos a legisladores nacionales que provienen del sector agropecuario," *Infobae*, August 1, 2021.

However, most of them ran in lower places in the ballots and only six entered Congress, five of them in Juntos por el Cambio (three in the UCR and two in the PRO).[67] Moreover, unlike in 2009, producers' associations do not appear to have played a role in the placement of agro-candidates in the elections since 2015, as most of the candidates are not affiliated with any, suggesting that those producers that run for office did so out of personal ambition and not as part of a coordinated sectoral strategy of representation.

An in-depth analysis of why agrarian elites have supplied the PRO with technical cadre but not electoral candidates is beyond the scope of this book. The fieldwork I conducted in 2017 revealed that PRO leaders were not interested in agricultural producers as a group that could supply candidates or mobilize votes in the interior of the country. Institutional, structural, and political factors may explain why PRO leaders are uninterested in agrarian elites as a source of political resources. First, as Freytes (2015) has argued, CLPR in combination with the geographical concentration of agricultural producers in electoral districts that also host large urban and industrial areas makes rural candidates unattractive to party leaders. Under CLPR, party leaders need to place on top of their ballots candidates that can draw the most votes which, in highly urbanized districts, are concentrated in large cities. However, these institutional and structural factors alone cannot explain why we do not see more candidates from the sector running on lower (but still electable) places in urbanized districts or on top of the ballots in less industrialized provinces. One potential explanation could be the low embeddedness of producers' associations in local politics. In order to be attractive to party leaders, producers need to show they are well-known figures in their communities with connections to local political organizations. It is not clear the extent to which agrarian elites have, after the 2008 conflict, abandoned their historical refrainment from politics and built links to other social and political organizations in the communities where they produce. Moreover, even if Argentine producers' associations were capable of mobilizing votes in agricultural districts, the PRO is not the type of party that recruits candidates through interest groups. Those studying the party since its beginnings have highlighted the centralized character of candidate selection in the PRO (Vommaro 2019). Relatedly, while the "machine parties" of the past relied on interest

---

[67] "Quiénes son los 8 legisladores ligados al campo que ingresaron al Congreso," *Clarín*, November 15, 2021.

5.6 Agricultural Producers and the PRO

groups to mobilize electoral appeal, the PRO was born in a different political era where mass-based organization, strong local branches, and extensive grassroots participation are no longer needed to reach voters. They have been replaced by media and social networks (Roberts 2002). In this type of parties, candidacies are decided by media strategies based on polling and focus group research (Conaghan 2000) rather than through linkages to groups. As a PRO politician put it when I asked him if the PRO had thought of agrarian producers as a potential source of candidates in the interior:

That is not how our political operators think. Our political operators look for popularity. If the person comes from the agricultural sector, fine; if he is the shopkeeper from the corner, fine; and if he is a famous actor, it is also fine [...]. PRO's political logic is different, it's more Facebook and less interest groups.[68]

Despite the lack of agro-candidates in the center-right alliance ballots, there is a clear geographical correlation between votes for Cambiemos/Juntos por el Cambio (the electoral alliance between the PRO, the UCR, and the CC) and agricultural production for export. As Figure 5.3 shows, outside of the city of Buenos Aires, support for the center-right alliance has been stronger in the Pampas region, the agricultural core of the country, indicating that voters in areas economically dependent on agriculture identify more with Juntos por el Cambio than with other electoral alternatives. I found strong and statistically significant correlations between percentage of votes for Macri and several different agricultural production indicators at the department level for both the primary and general 2019 presidential elections.[69] Similarly, analysing the first round of the 2015 election, Mangonnet et al. (2018, 13) found that area harvested with soybeans is a strong predictor of vote for Macri at the department level. The 2008 conflict and the hostility of the FPV administrations towards the sector seem to have galvanized support for the PRO in agricultural areas, as the authors also found

---

[68] Author's interview with Miguel Braun, secretary of commerce, executive director of Fundación Pensar, Buenos Aires, August 18, 2017.

[69] For the primary, the correlation coefficients with votes for Macri were: 0.45 for total hectares harvested in 2018; 0.36 for area harvested with soybeans in 2018; 0.3 for area harvested with corn in 2018; and 0.37 for heads of cattle. For the general elections, the correlation coefficients with votes for Macri were: 0.44 for total hectares harvested in 2018; 0.36 for area harvested with soybeans in 201; 0.31 for area harvested with corn in 2018;, and 0.34 for heads of cattle. All correlation coefficients were significant at the 99.999 percent level and became stronger when I excluded from my calculations the City of Buenos Aires (a district with strong support for Juntos por el Cambio but no agricultural production). See the online Appendix for data sources.

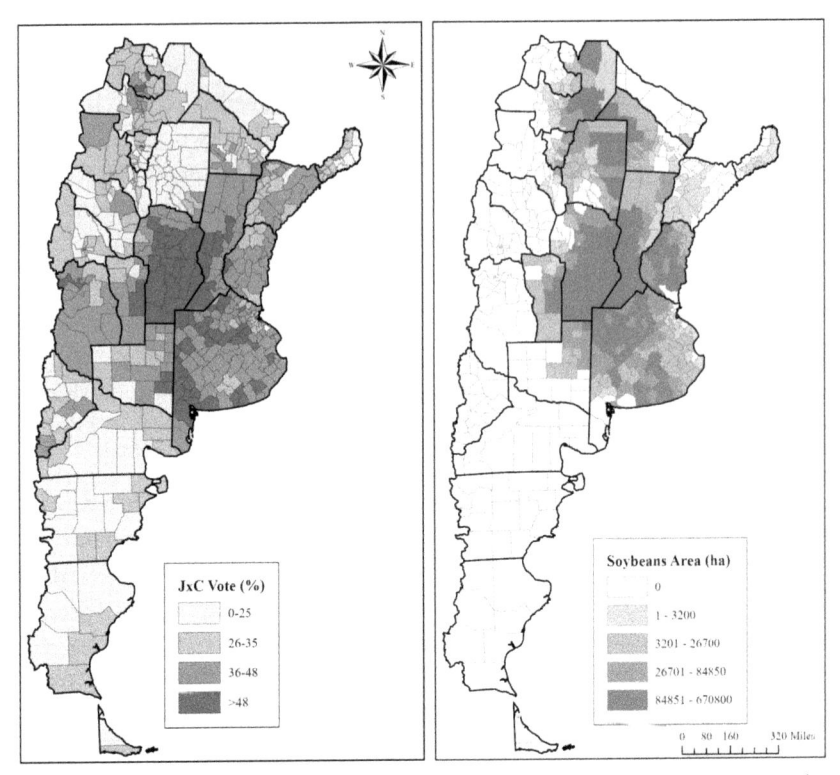

190 *Argentina: The Limits of Nonelectoral Strategies*

FIGURE 5.3 Area harvested with soybeans in 2018 and vote for Macri in the general election, 2019.
Source: Author, based on Cámara Nacional Electoral and Subsecretaría de Agricultura.

a correlation between the number of producers' lockouts in 2008 and vote for Macri (Mangonnet et al., 2018, 13). Survey data confirms the affinity of agricultural producers with the center-right alliance. In a poll of agricultural producers conducted by the consulting firm Amplificagro in July 2021,[70] Juntos por el Cambio was the party or political faction better evaluated in terms of its representation of agricultural interests, with 25 percent of respondents saying it represented the sector very well or well and 50 percent moderately well.[71] Similarly, in my survey of

---

[70] "El Sector Agropecuario y el contexto político-electoral. Julio 2021," *Amplificagro*, available at: https://agrolink.com.ar/wp-content/uploads/2021/07/Informe-AMPLIFICAGRO-Julio-2021.pdf (accessed, June 2022).
[71] As a reference, only 1 percent said the governing Peronist Frente de Todos represented the sector very well or well.

members of Barbechando conducted in 2017,⁷² 82.6 percent of respondents, when asked which party they considered closer to the sector, said the PRO while the rest picked the PRO's coalition partners, Coalición Cívica (13%) or UCR (4.3%).

Agricultural producers are among the main financers of Cambiemos/Juntos por el Cambio. My analysis of campaign contributions data reveals that firms and businesspeople in agriculture or related activities contribute a significant share of the campaign funds declared by Cambiemos/Juntos por el Cambio and that most of the funds contributed by firms or businesspeople in the sector go to the center-right alliance.⁷³ In Argentina, campaign contributions by both firms and persons are allowed with amount limitations.⁷⁴ Before 2019, campaign contributions by firms were illegal, so only data on persons' donations for the 2015 and 2017 national elections are available.⁷⁵ Because I am interested in campaign donations by business elites, when analysing persons' contributions, I exclude from my analysis contributions made by politicians or public officials. I also limit my analysis to relatively large contributions.⁷⁶

Across all the elections analysed, the center-right alliance Cambiemos/Juntos por el Cambio received a greater proportion of contributions by firms or private entrepreneurs than the center-left FPV/Frente de Todos.

---

⁷² See Appendix B for details.

⁷³ Data on campaign contributions in Argentina are self-reported by parties and donors. They are compiled by the Cámara Nacional Electoral and are publicly available at: www.electoral.gob.ar/financiamiento/. See the online Appendix for details on the data collection and analysis process.

⁷⁴ Argentina has a mixed system of campaign financing, with both a public and a private component. Public funding is allocated to all political parties through a common pool, with 50 percent of funds divided equally among parties and the rest divided according to each party's vote share in the previous election. There are limits to how much parties can spend per electoral cycle and to private contributions. These limits are adjusted every electoral cycle. Parties can receive from private contributors up to the difference between what they received in public funding and what the cap for that electoral cycle is. Individual contributions (by persons or firms) cannot exceed 2 percent of the total private amount allowed for that electoral cycle.

⁷⁵ Data are available since 2011. However, records for the 2011 and 2013 elections are grossly incomplete.

⁷⁶ Contributions equal or larger than AR$50,000 (US$5,429) in 2015; larger than AR$50,000 (US$2,924) in 2017; equal or larger than AR$50,000 (US$980) for the presidential and AR$100,000 (US$1,961) for the legislative elections in 2019; and equal or larger than AR$ 150,000 (US$1,550) in 2021. The underlining assumption is that business elites have more economic resources available for campaign financing than the average citizen. An exploratory analysis of the data supported this assumption, showing that businesspeople campaign contributions are in fact concentrated in the higher end of the distribution while most small contributions were made by members of each party's organization.

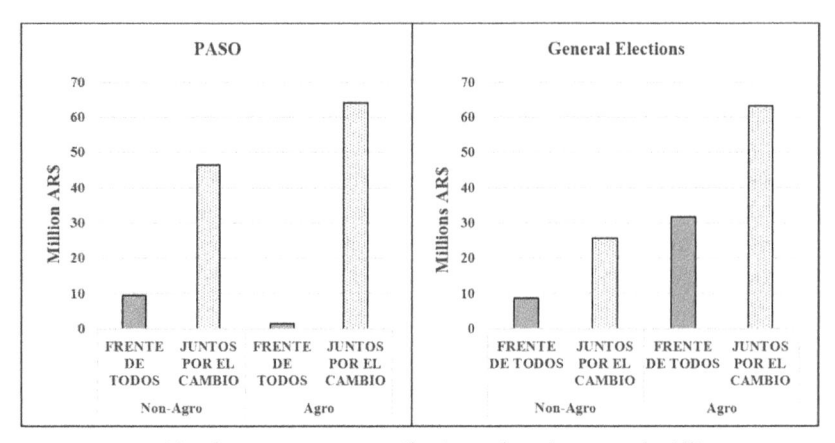

FIGURE 5.4 Total corporate contributions by Agro and Alliance: 2019 presidential elections.
Note: Agro includes: agriculture, agribusiness, meatpacking, rural real estate, grain broker, livestock broker, forestry, and manufacturing related to agriculture (ex: fertilizers, agro machinery).
Source: Author, based on Cámara Nacional Electoral.

My analysis of the corporate donations to the 2019 presidential elections reveals a strong preference for Macri within firms in general and those related to the sector (agriculture, agribusiness, food, and meatpacking) in particular. As Figure 5.4 shows, the Juntos por el Cambio alliance reported corporate contributions much larger than those reported by the Peronist alliance Frente de Todos, AR$110.45 million versus AR$10.9 million (US$1.94 million versus US$191,228) for the primary election (PASO)[77] and AR$88.9 million versus AR$40.4 million (US$1.53 million versus US$693,920) for the general election. For the PASO, firms related to agriculture represented a much larger share of the total contributions for Macri than for Alberto Fernández, 58 versus 13 percent. The difference is also stark in absolute terms. Firms related to agriculture contributed AR$64 million to Macri and only AR$1.46 million to Fernández (US$1.1 million versus US$25,729). After the PASO resulted

---

[77] Argentina's primary elections, known by the acronym PASO (Primarias Abiertas, Simultáneas y Obligatorias), follow an open, simultaneous, and mandatory format. These elections determine each party's candidate for the upcoming general election, as well as which parties will qualify for the general election (those surpassing the 1.5 percent threshold of valid votes). Parties have the option to nominate a single pre-candidate or multiple pre-candidates, while voters are permitted to select just one candidate per position. Due to the common practice of parties fielding only one candidate – seen in both JxC and Frente de Todos in 2019 – the PASO essentially serve as a very accurate poll of the general election.

in Macri's defeat, some big firms in agribusiness decided to hedge their bets and contribute to Fernández's campaign as well. However, the amount of money contributed to Macri's campaign by firms related to agriculture still doubled Fernández's (Figure 5.4). This is a clear indicator of the sector's strong preference for Macri as, after the PASO results, his defeat was all but certain. Looking at specific activities, agricultural producers and the meatpacking industry feature among the main financers of Macri's campaign, together representing 40 percent of total contributions received for the PASO and 57.4 percent for the general election. Tellingly, firms in both activities reported no contributions to the Fernández's campaign. Contributions by individual entrepreneurs in agriculture or related activities show a similar strong preference for the center-right alliance. Focusing on large contributions for the presidential campaign, I found that 89 percent of the money contributed by individuals in activities related to agriculture went to the Cambiemos alliance in 2015, and 85 percent to the Juntos por el Cambio alliance in 2019.[78]

Summing up, my analysis shows that ideological, financial, electoral and personnel linkages have been built between the center-right coalition spearheaded by the PRO and producers for export in the core agricultural region of the country. However, historical economic cleavages within the agrarian elite continue to undermine party-building. Agricultural producers as a class have not mobilized politically in support of the PRO and its coalitional partners. Producers' electoral support at the individual level for the center-right alliance has not translated into collective endorsement by the sectoral associations. While leaders of the SRA urged producers to vote for Macri in 2015 and 2019 and were highly supportive of the Cambiemos administration,[79] the rest of the associations did not publicly support any candidate and maintained a more critical stance during the center-right government.

5.7 CONCLUSION

This chapter presents a case of nonelectoral strategies of political influence by agrarian elites and the limitations of such strategies. Until 2008, Argentine landowners influenced politics through informal

---

[78] I also analysed large contributions to the 2017, 2019, and 2021 legislative campaigns and found a similar strong preference for Cambiemos/Juntos por el Cambio.
[79] "Luis Etchevehere renovó sus críticas contra el Gobierno y llamó a usar el voto como 'un arma cargada de futuro,'" *La Nación*, August 1, 2015; "Elecciones. El pedido de la Rural: 'Distingamos quién hizo y quién promete,'" *La Nación*, September 28, 2019.

personal contact with high-ranking government officials and, when lobbying failed, through protests. In the absence of an existential threat, agricultural producers had no incentives to invest in electoral representation. In 2008, agricultural producers switched strategies and entered the electoral arena to confront a hostile administration that was implementing policies that jeopardized the continuity of their business. In the aftermath of the 2008 conflict, producers deployed a candidate-centered strategy. However, institutional features that lower the autonomy and bargaining power of individual legislators, as well as the difference in policy preferences among the producers' associations prevented the *agrodiputados* from constituting a unified front, leading to the abandonment of the strategy. Later on, with the consolidation of the PRO as a viable electoral alternative and the continuity of hostile polices, exports-oriented producers have become a core constituency of the center-right alliance, providing electoral, financial, and ideological support.

The case of Argentina illustrates two important theoretical contributions of this book. First, it shows that an existential threat is a necessary condition for electoral investments by agrarian elites as well as the unsuitability of both nonelectoral strategies and structural power to deal with such threats. Argentine agricultural producers had endured unfavorable policies for decades. However, it was only after an existential threat appeared in the form of confiscatory taxes in 2008 that they invested in electoral representation, first through a candidate-center strategy and later through party-building. As argued in Chapter 2, policies that jeopardized the continuity of agrarian elites' business raised the costs of failing to influence policymaking for agrarian elites to the point that they outbalanced the coordination costs of electoral participation. To confront this existential threat, lobbying and protesting were not enough. Nonelectoral strategies were unsuitable for fighting such an existential threat because they depended on agrarian elites' capacity to access the state, which had been severely curtailed by the election of a center-left administration to which landowners had no social, professional or family ties. Thus, the case of Argentine agrarian elites during the FPV administration illustrates the unreliability of nonelectoral strategies, especially as they can become useless when interest groups need them the most, to fight the policies of a hostile government.

Second, the comparison between the Argentine and Chilean cases calls our attention to the crucial role that support from business plays in the success of conservative party-building and to how existential threats incentivize that support. While certainly not the only factor explaining why the UCEDE dissolved after a few elections while the RN and UDI consolidated, the support in the form of financial, organizational, and human resources that the Chilean partisan right received from business, including agrarian elites, during the first foundational elections was crucial for their success (Pollack 1999; Luna 2014; Loxton 2021). By contrast, the lack of support from the groups whose interests it aspired to represent ultimately led to the UCEDE's dissolution (Gibson 1996; Loxton 2021). After decades of hostile administrations and the consolidation of the PRO as a viable electoral alternative, agrarian elites in the Pampas seem to have abandoned their historical refrainment from politics to become a core constituency of the party. The extent to which this relationship will consolidate, helping the party in future electoral cycles is an open question.

6

Conclusions, Extensions, and Implications

6.1 RECAPITULATION

This book tackles an important question for the future of democracy in Latin America: how agrarian elites protect their interests through electoral participation. In the 2000s, Latin American agrarian elites' wealth increased greatly thanks to the commodity boom at the same time that leftwing governments with a redistributive agenda came to power. Contrary to what one may have expected, however, these leftwing governments, with few notable exceptions, did not tax the agrarian elites to redistribute to the urban poor. That agrarian elites have been able to protect their interests through democratic means in the most unequal region in the world is particularly remarkable considering that urbanization and social policy expansion have severely diminished landowners' ability to secure electoral representation through mobilization of the rural poor. This book analyses the different strategies through which agrarian elites may protect their interests in this new context of augmented economic power but diminished electoral strength. It shows that landowners have been more successful in influencing policy outcomes where they organized in the electoral arena than where they invested in nonelectoral strategies. Moreover, this book demonstrates that agrarian elites can still organize in the electoral arena even where conservative parties are weak by deploying a nonpartisan, candidate-centered strategy. By studying how agrarian elites organize in the electoral arena to block redistributive policies, this book helps us understand why democracy may perpetuate, instead of reduce, inequality. In Latin America, four decades of democracy have accomplished little in terms of diminishing extremely high levels of inequality, even after many years of leftist dominance.

6.1 Recapitulation

The main argument of this book is that agrarian elites' strategies of political influence are shaped by two factors: the perception of an existential threat and their level of intragroup fragmentation. The cases analysed here show that the perception of an existential threat – defined as a policy that jeopardizes the continuity of agrarian elites' business – is a necessary condition for electoral investment. Absent this threat, rural elites will not organize in the electoral arena. Existential threats such as land reform, confiscatory taxes, or stringent environmental regulations facilitate collective action because they affect all landowners, irrespective of their size and type of production. Put simply, common threats create unified interests.

As the case of Argentina shows, nonelectoral strategies, such as lobbying or personal ties to policymakers, are ill suited to deal with existential threats because they depend on a group's ability to access an administration, but threatening policies are usually implemented by political rivals. By contrast, electoral strategies – such as party-building or sponsoring like-minded candidates – are more reliable because they entail electing politicians who share the group's preferences to key policymaking positions. Therefore, electoral strategies are more apt to confront existential threats than nonelectoral ones. In Brazil, legislators in the Agrarian Caucus, who are agricultural producers themselves and/or elected with agrarian elites' support, have been instrumental in blocking land reform and watering down environmental regulations.

As the analysed cases show, the perception of an existential threat at the time of democratic transition when parties were being (re)built and looking for new constituencies was particularly crucial for the development of electoral strategies. Organizing in the electoral arena to respond to threats after this foundational moment, when linkages between interest groups and political parties had already consolidated, was harder for groups that had not built these linkages during the transition. Thus, in countries where agrarian elites invested in electoral representation during the democratic transition, they were better positioned to neutralize new threats down the road. In Brazil and Chile, the perception that democratic governments could implement redistributive policies jeopardizing the continuity of their business gave agrarian elites the incentives to organize in the electoral arena during the democratic transition. In Brazil, agrarian elites built a multiparty caucus to block land reform in the 1987–1988 Constituent Assembly. This Agrarian Caucus was later instrumental in protecting agrarian interests during the leftwing administrations of the PT in the 2000s. In Chile, agrarian elites joined other economic elites in rebuilding the partisan right because they feared a new government by the center-left would relaunch the confiscatory and antibusiness policies they had implemented in the 1960s and 1970s. Even when this existential threat did not materialize, a strong representation of the right in Congress has been key to tempering the redistributivist ambitions of the center-left Concertación, protecting economic elites' interests when designing tax, labor, and environmental policies. In Argentina, by contrast, agrarian elites did not enter the electoral arena during the democratic transition because they did not perceive democratic governments to threaten their interests. This lack of electoral representation, however, left them defenseless against the confiscatory policies of the Kirchners in the 2000s. Without a party or individual legislators to represent their interests in Congress, agrarian elites in Argentina were left with no channels to influence policymaking when politicians to whom they had no informal ties came to power.

The comparison of agrarian elites' strategies of political influence across the analysed cases reveals that the degree of intragroup fragmentation conditions the type of electoral strategy landowners will pursue. Fragmentation increases the coordination costs of party-building. When strong divides exist within a group, all the agreements and negotiations that developing a partisan organization entails – for example, selecting candidates and party leaders, developing a territorial organization and designing a party platform – will be harder to bring about. Where landed elites are a cohesive group, they will engage in party-building. This was the case of agrarian elites in Chile during the transition, as they shared economic and political interests. In contrast, where significant cleavages exist among agrarian elites, higher coordination costs will hinder party-building. For instance, agreeing on a policy platform or developing a partisan structure will be harder for agrarian elites that have diverse economic preferences or are already invested in rival political machines. Where threatened agrarian elites cannot come together under the same political organization, they will support like-minded candidates individually, across partisan lines. This is the case of Brazil where agrarian elites were invested in rival political machines at the local level at the time of the democratic transition and therefore party-building entailed very high opportunity costs for them. Because landowners, who were local political bosses, did not want to sacrifice their political bulwarks on the altar of party-building, they designed an alternative coordination device that enabled them to influence federal policy and at the same time preserve their local political autonomy: a multiparty congressional caucus.

In the rest of this concluding chapter, I explore how the arguments developed in this book travel beyond the three analysed cases and discuss their broader implications for the field of comparative politics, in particular for the relationship among economic elites' political representation, democracy, and inequality.

6.2 SCOPE AND EXTENSIONS

How far can these theoretical claims reasonably travel? Under what conditions will landowners respond to existential threats with electoral organization instead of by trying to destabilize democracy? Under what conditions are candidate-centered strategies a viable substitute for party-building? Do the same factors that shape agrarian elites' strategic choices explain how other interest groups organize to influence policymaking? This section deals with these questions, extending the book's arguments beyond Argentina, Brazil, and Chile. First, I test the scope conditions of the argument by analysing agrarian elites' strategies of political influence in a country where democracy is less consolidated: Paraguay during the Lugo administration (2008–2012). Next, I look at party-building by agrarian elites beyond South America, in a different historical context marked by civil war: post 1979 El Salvador. Finally, I extend the argument beyond agrarian elites, focusing on nonpartisan electoral representation by other interest groups in two contemporary cases: for-profit universities in Peru and conservative religious groups in Colombia.

6.2.1 Testing the Scope of the Argument: Paraguay under Lugo

This book proposes a theory about how agrarian elites organize to protect their interests in democracy. Therefore, the argument presented here only applies to political systems where the interruption of democracy is not a viable option. The role of agrarian elites as obstacles to democratic consolidation has been widely studied by the comparative politics literature. Scholars have analysed how in Latin America as well as in the developed world, landed elites have responded to redistributive threats by supporting the interruption of democracy or by engaging in undemocratic practices such as electoral fraud or outright violence against the rural poor.[1] One of the starting premises of this book is that after the transitions of the third wave, these undemocratic practices were no

---
[1] For a review of these studies, see Chapter 1.

longer an option for agrarian elites in most of Latin America. The reasons why this was the case, which are varied and include domestic as well as international factors,[2] exceed the scope of this investigation. Among them, an issue worth exploring in future research is how the structural transformations of the sector in the past decades have affected agrarian elites' political preferences. The classic studies of the undemocratic preferences of landowners emphasized the labor-repressive character of agricultural production.[3] However, as we have seen in the cases analysed here, contemporary agrarian elites are modern capitalists controlling efficient, capital-intensive, highly mechanized farms. For landowners who do not depend on servile labor relations or on the state-backed coercion of peasants to make profits, democracy should be less threatening.

I expect that where the interruption of democracy is still an option for dealing with existential threats, agrarian elites' calculations about whether or not to invest in electoral representation would be different from those where democracy is the only game in town. As we have discussed, electoral representation, especially party-building, is expensive, time-consuming, and requires high levels of coordination. More importantly, electoral investments are high-risk, as they depend on electoral results that agrarian elites do not control, especially in contexts where fraudulent and clientelistic practices are not prevalent. Thus, where undemocratic practices are still a viable option for protecting elites' interests, threatened landowners may prefer to undermine democracy rather than to risk electoral defeat.

The impeachment of President Fernando Lugo (2008–2012) in Paraguay offers an interesting case for evaluating how agrarian elites may react to existential threats where democracy is not fully consolidated. Even when Lugo's impeachment was far from resembling the military coups with which agrarian elites had neutralized redistributive threats in the past, the serious irregularities committed during the process led many analysts to question its constitutionality.[4] It was an episode of land conflict that precipitated Lugo's impeachment when a violent clash between land squatters and the police ended in seventeen deaths (Pérez-Liñán 2014). Paraguay is the country with the highest

---

[2] See, for example, Hagopian and Mainwaring (2005) for a general picture and Bartell and Payne (1995) specifically on the attitudes of businesspeople.
[3] See, for example, Moore (1966) and Rueschemeyer et al. (1992).
[4] Lugo was removed from office on vague charges of malperformance with no evidence presented against him. His impeachment took place in less than 48 hours, leaving no time for the president to mount a defense.

land inequality in the world.[5] Lugo came to power with the support of the peasant movement and promising land reform. However, during his administration, no advances were made on this front, while the expansion of the agrarian frontier fueled conflict between peasants and large producers (Abente-Brun 2012). Through their representatives in Congress, especially in the opposition Colorado Party and in the state bureaucracy, large landowners were able to block attempts by the Lugo administration at redistribution (Guereña and Rojas Villagra 2016; Ezquerro-Cañete and Fogel 2017).[6] Despite this, landowners still considered Lugo a menace to their interests given his leniency towards land occupations and his strict enforcement of environmental regulations (Guereña and Rojas Villagra 2016). Therefore, when the opportunity to replace the president presented itself, landowners supported his impeachment through their congressional representatives and corporatist associations. Following Lugo's ouster, the country elected as president Horacio Cartes of the Colorado Party, one of the largest ranchers in Paraguay. During the Cartes administration (2013–2018), leadership positions in key agricultural agencies were filled with individuals recruited from landowners' corporatist associations, while the government relaxed environmental regulations, intensified repression against peasants and implemented a tax reform that benefited large exporters to the detriment of consumers and small producers (Turner 2014; Guereña and Rojas Villagra 2016). Summing up, as the case of Paraguay illustrates, where democracy has not yet fully consolidated, agrarian elites may resort to regime destabilization to protect their interests. In that country, agrarian elites have influenced policymaking through both party-building and undemocratic practices.

6.2.2 Party-Building in Post-1979 El Salvador

Like RN in Chile, the rightwing Nationalist Republican Alliance (ARENA) in El Salvador is a clear case of party-building by agrarian elites. The case of ARENA shows how agrarian elites who had historically influenced politics through informal nondemocratic means were able to adapt their strategies to a new political context, investing in the

---

[5] Latifundia (more than 10,000 hectares) which are only 0.2 percent of the farms, control 40 percent of the land in the country. At the other extreme, smallholders (less than 5 hectares) constitute 40 percent of the farms but control less than 1 percent of the land (Guereña and Rojas Villagra 2016, 14).

[6] For instance, Lugo attempts to tax agricultural exports were quashed by Congress.

formation of a conservative party to protect their interests during the democratic transition and in the new democracy.

As in the three cases analysed in detail in this book, agrarian elites in El Salvador entered the electoral arena in reaction to an existential threat. During the 1980s, Salvadoran landowners faced a double menace, both from insurgent groups in the countryside and from the state (Johnson 1993; Zamora 1998). The reformist military that took power in 1979 believed that the precarious situation of the peasantry was a major source of discontent fueling the armed conflict between the government and guerrilla groups in the countryside (Loxton 2021). Consequently, the military, in alliance with the Christian Democrats and with the crucial support of the United States, started a series of reforms to undermine the social bases of the insurgency (Johnson 1993; Wood 2000). However, these reforms included policies that also threatened the economic sources of the agrarian elites' political power: land reform and the nationalization of the export and financial sectors.

Agrarian elites' traditional nonelectoral tools for dealing with such redistributive threats were neither available nor sufficient in the new context.[7] First, unlike in the past, agrarian elites had no ties to the reformist military that ruled the country between 1979 and 1982. The new government had completely shut down informal and corporatist channels, leaving landowners without access to the executive for the first time in Salvadoran history (Johnson 1993). Second, outright violence and electoral fraud were no longer options for dealing with peasant demands due to a change in the United States' stance regarding democracy in the region. The Carter administration made it clear to Salvadoran elites that they would not tolerate another coup in the country, tying military aid – which was critical for combatting insurgency – to the holding of free and fair elections (Brockett 1998; Loxton 2021). Thus, unable to continue defending their interests through the state, agrarian elites in El Salvador decided to create their own party, ARENA, to secure political influence in the nascent democracy.

As in Chile, high political cohesion among the agrarian elites facilitated conservative party-building in El Salvador. In contrast to the rural clientelistic machines in Brazil, which were controlled by political rivals, in El Salvador, the clientelistic networks that served as the

---

[7] Agrarian elites' strategy for dealing with this new context was two-pronged. Electoral investment was combined with the organization and financing of death squads responsible for the assassination of thousands of political activists and peasants (Wood 2001; Loxton 2021).

base for ARENA's expansion in the countryside belonged to the same political machine before they joined ARENA, that of the Party of the National Concertation. Moreover, the fact that agrarian elites in El Salvador pursued party-building in an electoral system that, unlike Chile's, does not discourage political fragmentation,[8] renders support for this book's argument that the level of agrarian elites' internal fragmentation explains their electoral strategies of political influence better than electoral rules.

Agrarian elites' financial support and organizational resources were key to ARENA's formation and initial electoral success. Many of the founding leaders of ARENA were landowners and no other party had as many agrarian elites in its ranks (Zamora 1998, 50). These connections allowed the party to secure electoral strongholds in the countryside through clientelistic networks built upon former rural paramilitary organizations (Wood 2001; Loxton 2021). In addition, landlords in the coffee industry garnered support for the party through tight social control over their workers. The few existing studies of business political investments in El Salvador find that the most important business conglomerates in the country have financed mostly ARENA politicians (Koivumaeki 2010; Canales 2021, 182; Cárdenas and Robles-Rivera 2021, 101). These are large family business groups with highly diversified assets that include investments in the agribusiness and agro-export sectors.

Until the collapse of El Salvador's party system in 2021, ARENA politicians protected the interests of the agrarian elite through administrations of varied ideological orientation thanks to their strong presence in Congress and the state bureaucracy. ARENA legislators were key to undermining the land reform process initiated during the democratic transition and to blocking any further reform attempts. During the Constituent Assembly of 1982–1983, ARENA secured protection from expropriation for most coffee, sugar, and cotton farms targeted by the 1980 land reform law (Brockett 1998).[9] In subsequent Christian Democratic governments, ARENA politicians controlled the Ministry

---

[8] Until 2012, El Salvador elected its unicameral legislature through CLPR in multimember districts, ranging from three to twenty-four seats. Since 2012, legislators have been elected through OLPR. High-magnitude proportional systems increase the electoral chances of small and new parties.

[9] Under the land reform law, individuals could own up to 100 hectares. The 1983 constitution raised this threshold to 245 hectares and prohibited expropriation for two years.

of Agriculture and land reform institutions, blunting the law's implementation (Wood 2001, 872). Agrarian interests were further advanced during the ARENA administrations (1989–2009). Soon after taking office, ARENA's first president, Alfredo Cristiani (1989–1994) – himself a member of the agrarian elite – reprivatized the financial and export sectors, reduced export taxes, and deregulated food and agricultural markets. Armando Calderon Sol (1994–1999) continued and deepened the privatization process. Many landowning families took the opportunity created by the privatizations to diversify their assets (Velásquez Carrillo 2020; Canales 2021). During the leftwing administrations of the former guerrilla Farabundo Martí National Liberation Front (2009–2019), the government increased regulations over the economy to enhance competition and consumer protection, as well as the state participation in certain sectors such as energy or communications (Canales 2021). However, ARENA was still the largest party in Congress during the center-left administrations and agrarian interests were not challenged.[10]

The ascent to the presidency of populist leader Nayib Bukele in 2019 and the electoral collapse of ARENA in 2021[11] have left Salvadoran economic elites without electoral representation. While it is too soon to see how economic elites will adapt to this new scenario, it is important to point out that Bukele has not moved away from the neoliberal economic model consolidated during the two decades of ARENA administrations, and ARENA legislators supported the president' cuts to social programs in 2020.

6.2.3 Conservative Interests and Nonpartisan Electoral Representation in Peru and Colombia

While no other case of multipartisan organization in Congress has reached the level of institutionalization of the Brazilian Agrarian Caucus – which is almost forty years old and supported by an interest group with extensive economic and logistical resources – nonpartisan groupings that defend particular interests within Congress are common around the world. Here, I analyse two of them: the caucus of for-profit

---

[10] With the exception of a significant increase in the minimum wage of agricultural workers from US$118 to US$224 (Cárdenas and Robles-Rivera 2021, 108).
[11] While until then the party had been the largest in El Salvador's Congress, in the legislative elections of 2021, ARENA got only 12.18 percent of the vote, securing fourteen out of eighty-four seats. The newly formed party of the president gained fifty-six seats.

private universities in Peru[12] and the Pro-Life Caucus in Colombia. Even when these are smaller groupings that lack the formalized, permanent structure of the Bancada Ruralista, these caucuses similarly exemplify a model of corporatist electoral representation where interest groups help politicians get elected to Congress because of their affiliation with that group and independently of their partisan identity. Once in office, these legislators are expected to prioritize their sponsoring group's legislative agenda.

Together with the case of the Brazilian Agrarian Caucus, the Peruvian caucus of for-profit universities and the Colombian Pro-Life Caucus illustrate how nonpartisan groupings can become better strategies of electoral representation for corporatist interests in contexts of weak parties and highly fragmented legislatures. Given Latin America's high, and increasing, levels of electoral volatility, party-system fragmentation and dilution of partisan brands, candidate-centered strategies offer interest groups a more stable avenue to secure policy influence. In a volatile electoral landscape, where parties can quickly lose popular support, ambitious politicians frequently switch labels in order to survive their parties' debacle. In this context, betting on candidates across the partisan spectrum allows interest groups to have a more continuous representation in Congress that is not tied to the electoral fortunes of specific parties.

6.2.3.1 *The Caucus of for-Profit Universities in Peru*

For-profit universities in Peru are a multimillion-dollar business. Since neoliberal reforms allowed for the foundation of for-profit universities in 1996, these private enterprises have mushroomed across the country (Dargent and Camacho 2023). In 2021, for-profit universities matriculated more students than nonprofit private or public universities, around half the country's student body (Salto and Levy 2021). Concerns with the poor quality of the educational services of these for-profit institutions – in particular to low-income students, who constitute a significant share of their student body – sparkled regulatory efforts from several governments since 2012.

In 2014, the administration of the center-left president Ollanta Humala (2011–2016) sanctioned the New Law of Higher Education (Law 30,220) that increased regulation over the sector. One of the most

---

[12] This caucus is informally known as Bancada Telesup, in reference to the most egregious case of a for-profit university whose license was revoked for not meeting the most basic quality standards. I thank Eduardo Dargent and Paula Muñoz for suggesting this case to me and for their help in finding bibliographical references on it.

resisted features of the reform was the creation of an independent oversight body, the Sunedu – Spanish acronym for National Superintendence of Higher Education, charged with monitoring the quality of the academic offer and granting licenses for universities to function. According to the new law, the Sunedu would evaluate every university in the country, public and private, on a set of basic quality conditions, to decide if they could continue operating or should close.

Peru's New Law of Higher Education is a clear case of what I define as an existential threat, since its passage jeopardized the continuity of an entire economic sector, that of poor-quality for-profit universities. In fact, for-profit universities were the main "casualty" of the creation of Sunedu. At the time of writing, of the 145 universities existing in the country in 2015, the Sunedu had revoked the license to 50, 3 public and 47 private of which 33 were for-profit entities.[13]

The threat of regulation that could significantly reduce their profits and even terminate their business prompted the electoral involvement of businesspeople in the education sector. Owners of for-profit universities in Peru have used their educational institutions to sponsor their political careers as well as those of their family members, employees and alumni (Barrenechea 2014). In the Peruvian context of extreme party system deinstitutionalization and where the barriers to forming new electoral vehicles are very low (Levitsky 2018), lucrative educational institutions have functioned as party substitutes.[14] Universities have contributed valuable political resources to the proselytizing efforts of their owners and the candidates associated with them, such as a recognizable brand, a source of jobs and other clientelistic opportunities (like scholarships), as well as logistical resources like staff and facilities (e.g., printing presses) (Barrenechea 2014).[15] However, the electoral mobilization of businesspeople in higher education has not been circumscribed to their own personalistic electoral vehicles. Politicians with ties to for-profit universities have also run for Congress under a multitude of other electoral labels, including *fujimorismo* and other smaller rightwing parties.

---

[13] See: www.sunedu.gob.pe/lista-de-universidades-denegadas/ (accessed November 27, 2023).

[14] On party substitutes, see Hale (2006). The paradigmatic case is Alianza Para el Progreso, founded by the owner of three for-profit universities, politician César Acuña (see Barrenechea 2014). Another case is Podemos Perú, founded by José Luna Galvez, owner of Telesup, one of the first for-profit universities to have their license revoked.

[15] Similarly to the phenomenon described by Barndt (2016) in other Latin American countries, where businesspeople have used their corporations to propel their political careers.

6.2 Scope and Extensions

That businesspeople in higher education have opted for a nonpartisan electoral strategy in Peru, a country where traditional party structures have basically disappeared,[16] is hardly surprising. However, the case is intriguing because it illustrates a key theoretical contribution of this book: economic elites do not need parties to obtain electoral representation and coordinate to protect their interests in Congress. Like agribusiness in Brazil used their economic resources and corporatists organizations to build multipartisan representation in Congress to block or dilute land reform initiatives, businesspeople in higher education in Peru have used their corporations to sponsor legislators to, first, try to block state regulation over the sector and, when this failed, weaken it (Brou 2020; Vergara and Augusto 2022:257). As Bancada Ruralista members do in Brazil, legislators in the caucus of for-profit universities have strategically sought to control congressional committees of high relevance to the sector, like, in this case, education (Chaccha 2018; Hidalgo 2023).

Legislators with ties to private universities and that had received campaign contributions from these institutions worked together in Congress to block the passage of the New Law of Higher Education (Chaccha 2018; Brou 2020; Hidalgo 2023:13). Despite the joint opposition of the caucus of for-profit universities, the parties controlled by university owners, and *fujimorismo*, the bill passed after two years of congressional debate in June 2014. After the reform was passed, owners of private universities ran for Congress or financed the candidacies of politicians with ties to these institutions (employees and alumni) with the mandate of introducing reforms to the new law that would blunt its effects.[17] From the Congressional Educational Committee, these legislators initiated congressional investigations of Sunedu's procedures and sponsored several bills that undermined its independence. In the context of the progressive deterioration of party organizations, increased party system fragmentation, and empowerment of Congress vis-à-vis the executive that has characterized Peruvian politics in the last few years,[18] the caucus of for-profit universities was finally able to claim victory over Sunedu. In July 2022, after overriding a presidential veto, Congress sanctioned a law weakening the oversight body. The new law changed the composition of the

---

[16] See Levitsky (2018).
[17] "16 congresistas están vinculados a universidades," Serperuano.com, November 25, 2016. "Las veces que el Congreso intentó bajarse la reforma universitaria," *La República*, June 8, 2020.
[18] See Dargent and Rousseau (2022) and Vergara and Augusto (2021).

Board of Directors to include members designated by the universities, the same institutions Sunedu is supposed to control, and circumscribed the oversighting role of the agency. Similar to the case of agribusiness in Brazil, a strategy of self-representation and multipartisan legislative collaboration has allowed a sector of Peruvian business to overcome their political fragmentation and economic rivalries and fight legislation threatening the continuity of their business. Sunedu's defeat clearly illustrates how the effectiveness of nonpartisan candidate-centered strategies increases where parties are weak but Congress is strong.

6.2.3.2 The Pro-Life Caucus in Colombia
Religious groups around the world, with varying degrees of success, have mobilized in the electoral arena as a reaction to the expansion of women's and LGBTQ rights in the last few decades. Policies like same-sex marriage and adoption, the legalization of abortion, and the legal recognition of nonbinary gender identification, challenged core traditional ideals of family and gender roles constituting what I define as an existential threat in the eyes of conservative religious groups. In Latin America, Evangelicals, sometimes in alliance with conservative Catholics, have been at the forefront of this conservative backlash, promoting electoral participation with the purpose of blocking socially progressive legislation (Pérez Guadalupe and Grundberger 2018; Boas 2023). Given the doctrinal cleavages that separate Catholics from Evangelicals and Evangelicals among themselves, it is hardly surprising that these religious groups have opted for candidate-centered strategies that transcend partisan alignments rather than party-building to defend their interests in Congress.

Colombia offers an interesting case to study how conservative religious groups, Evangelicals in particular, have reacted to recent existential threats by pursuing a nonpartisan candidate-centered strategy. Starting in 2011, a series of decisions by the Constitutional Court,[19] together with the increasing political mobilization around the decriminalization of abortion challenged traditional conceptions of family as well as gender roles and hierarchies in Colombian society. Religious groups saw these policy changes as an existential threat to their core values, allowed, in part, by their lack of electoral representation (Boas 2023).

---

[19] Including the legalization of same-sex marriage, allowing transgender people to change their gender designation on their identity cards and granting same-sex couples the right to adopt children.

Consequently, several new religious parties emerged and Evangelical candidacies increased to an all-time high in the 2018 elections (Ortega 2018, Velasco Montoya 2018). Aside from their own personalistic parties, religious leaders run under multiple party labels, including traditional rightwing parties such as the Conservative Party and the Uribista Democratic Center (Ortega 2018). Although Evangelical candidates have not being as electorally successful in Colombia as in other Latin American countries like, for instance, Brazil,[20] in the last few years, they have tried to increase their leverage in Congress by joining forces with conservative Catholics and creating a multipartisan pro-life caucus.

In 2020, around twenty legislators (Representatives and Senators) from five different parties including Christian parties such as Fair and Free Colombia and traditional rightwing ones created the Pro-Life Caucus.[21] Two policy threats were key for the agglutination of conservative religious interests in the Colombian Congress: the decriminalization of abortion and assisted suicide. The Pro-Life caucus was very active in mobilizing public opinion against the decriminalization of abortion by the Constitutional Court, arguing the matter should be decided by the legislative branch. Moreover, legislators in the Pro-Life Caucus presented several projects to protect life since the moment of conception that never made it to the floor. After the Constitutional Court decriminalized abortion up to twenty-four weeks of pregnancy in February 2022, the Pro-Life Caucus together with religious grassroots organizations sponsored a, ultimately unsuccessful, referendum campaign on abortion. In this context of high political mobilization around sexual politics, after the legislative elections of March 2022, the Pro-Life Caucus expanded to around fifty members from seven different parties that, in addition to Christian and rightwing parties, also included some on the center-left, like Green Alliance and the Liberal Party.[22]

It is too soon to tell if the Colombian Pro-Life Caucus will evolve into a multipartisan grouping that is as institutionalized and strong as the Brazilian Bancada Ruralista. So far, the Pro-Life Caucus has failed in its attempts to block progressives' policy advances or promote conservative legislation. Nonetheless, the fact that conservative religious groups in Colombia have reacted to the threat posed by the rise of sexual politics

---

[20] See, for example, Pérez Guadalupe and Grundberger (2018) and Boas (2023).
[21] "Estrategias camufladas para frenar el avance del derecho al aborto en Colombia," *El Diario*, November 16, 2021.
[22] "Se consolida bloque parlamentario provida en Congreso de Colombia," *ACI Digital*, September 22, 2022.

by promoting candidates that are coreligionist but belong to political parties of diverse ideological orientation highlights the applicability of the arguments developed in this book beyond agrarian elites. In particular, it exemplifies how nonpartisan electoral strategies can offer interest groups a channel of representation where political fragmentation and electoral volatility dilute the effectiveness of parties.

6.3 IMPLICATIONS

6.3.1 Economic Elites, Conservative Parties, and Democracy

This book makes two important contributions to the literature on party-building. First, it highlights the role of economic elites for the success of conservative party-building as well as how existential threats are crucial in persuading economic elites into making such investment in party organization. Second, it shows that conservative parties are not the only channel for the electoral representation of elite interests in democracy. These findings are relevant for the prospects of democracy in the developing world given the centrality of economic elites' representation for the stability of democratic regimes.

In this study, I look at conservative parties as the result of a strategic decision made by economic elites. In contrast to most analyses of political investment by business, which look at conservative parties as organizations that exist separately from economic elites' decision to support them, this book treats party-building as endogenous to business' strategic decisions. Strong conservative parties exist where economic elites decided to support them during their formative years. As Kalyvas (1996, 14) observes, mainstream structuralist accounts of party-building "'blackbox' the process of party formation, ignore its micro-foundations, lose track of agency, and do not specify how and by whom parties are formed." I follow non-structuralist accounts in treating party formation as the conscious, strategic decision of political actors (Van Cott 2005). While these accounts have examined the role of political elites in party-building, I underscore the contribution economic elites may make to party formation. Scholars studying conservative parties agree that support from economic elites is crucial for parties to survive in their formative years,[23] but very few studies analyse the motivations of economic elites to support party-building. This

---

[23] See, for example, Gibson (1996), Luna (2014), and Loxton (2021).

study analyses agrarian elites' choice to build a party in relation to other nonpartisan electoral strategies available to economic elites in democracies. It looks at both why landowners will decide to organize in the electoral arena and when this organization will take a partisan form. As the cases analysed in this book show, landowners will invest in electoral representation only when they perceive an existential threat. However, as the comparison between the Chilean and Brazilian cases reveals, party building will be feasible only when no cleavages exist within the agrarian elite.[24]

The representation of economic elites' interests is crucial for the consolidation of democracy. As scholars of Latin America have long argued, economic elites will tolerate democratization only when they believe they have a chance at influencing present or future policies.[25] The literature has deemed conservative parties a necessary condition for democratic consolidation because, when in power, electorally strong conservative parties guarantee economic elites access to policymakers and the state apparatus (Di Tella 1971; Middlebrook 2000; Ziblatt 2017). However, as I argue in Chapter 2, party-building is an expensive and potentially risky investment, especially for economic elites who are but a small fraction of the electorate. Unsurprisingly, since the democratic transition, very few conservative party-building attempts have been successful in Latin America.[26] Nevertheless, democracy has consolidated throughout the region, which indicates that economic elites have found alternative channels to obtain political representation. This book analyses one of those alternative channels: the formation of multiparty congressional caucuses.

Aldrich (1995) famously answered the question "Why parties?" by arguing that political parties perform two crucial tasks in democracy: helping candidates and voters coordinate in the electoral arena and aggregating legislators' work in Congress. While previous literature has studied how other institutions such as business groups or civil society organizations can substitute parties in the electoral arena, providing candidates with the economic, logistical, or symbolic resources they need to get elected (Hale 2006), this book shows that there are substitutes for parties in the

---

[24] Similarly, in his analysis of Europe's first wave of democratization, Ziblatt (2017) argues that the formation of strong conservative parties was feasible only in countries where the landed elites were not divided along confessional lines.
[25] See Di Tella (1971), Rueschemeyer et al. (1992), Gibson (1996), Middlebrook (2000), and Loxton (2021).
[26] See Loxton (2021).

legislative arena as well. As the case of the Brazilian Bancada Ruralista shows, multipartisan caucuses can replace parties in fragmented legislatures by helping legislators from different parties, but with common policy interests, coordinate their work and pass legislation.

This book's finding that economic elites can gain electoral representation in the absence of strong conservative parties helps explain why democracy has consolidated in Latin America beyond what the literature emphasizing the importance of conservative parties would predict. Moreover, it suggests brighter prospects for democratic continuity in the contemporary period where party-building has become increasingly harder due to rising party system fragmentation, electoral volatility and the dilution of partisan identities among the electorate throughout the region.[27] In this context where many parties are little more than the electoral vehicles of ambitious politicians,[28] and candidates' personal characteristics are more reliable indicators of their policy preferences than their partisan affiliation,[29] candidate-centered strategies may become a more effective option for interest group representation than party-building.

However, candidate-centered strategies may not be feasible everywhere or for every interest group. On the one hand, as the contrast between the Brazilian and Argentine cases analysed here shows, there are institutional features that facilitate this type of electoral strategy. Multiparty caucuses have higher probability of succeeding in systems with undisciplined, ideologically loose parties, where legislators have autonomy vis-à-vis their party leaders and can stray from party lines without being expelled (Carey and Shugart 1995). The two countries where businesspeople have most clearly invested in individual representatives in Congress, Brazil and Russia,[30] fit this description. As the unsuccessful experience of the *agrodiputados* in Argentina illustrates, in countries with more ideologically cohesive and disciplined parties, in which leaders can punish backbenchers for defecting, legislators have less autonomy to form multiparty caucuses. On the other hand, not all interest groups are as well suited as landowners to claim loyalty from legislators. Members of the Agrarian Caucus in Brazil vote to defend and advance agricultural interests because agrarian elites finance their

---

[27] See, for example, Mainwaring and Zoco (2007), Lupu (2017), and Mainwaring (2018).
[28] See Luna et al. (2021).
[29] See Roberts (2002).
[30] On Russia, see Hale (2006), Gehlbach et al. (2010), and Szakonyi (2020).

campaigns, mobilize voters to support them, and subsidize their legislative work. However, not many interest groups have both economic and mobilizational resources as extensive as those of the agrarian elites, which raises questions about which interests can gain electoral representation in a context where parties are increasingly weaker and about what that may mean for the future of democracy. The fact that not all social groups are equally suited to claim loyalty from their legislators may reinforce the elite-biased character of political institutions. Moreover, direct representation of privileged groups in Congress is at odds with the redistributive expectations often associated with democracy and may result in socially harmful policy outcomes. For instance, Brazilian agrarian elites have used their strength in Congress to secure laxer environmental regulations and massive transfers from consumers towards agribusiness, while businesspeople in the higher education sector in Peru, through their representatives in Congress, have weakened legislation aiming at improving the quality of private universities that serve low-income students.

6.3.2 Democracy and Redistribution

This book challenges a well-established theory in comparative politics by showing that landowners can protect themselves from redistribution in urban democracies. In Latin America, democracy has coexisted with extremely high rate of land inequality during the last four decades. After the transitions of the third wave, agrarian elites who had historically protected their interests by undermining democracy accepted it, for the most part, as the only game in town and developed different strategies to influence policymaking through democratic means.

Understanding the factors that shape agrarian elites' capacity to organize electoral representation is key for the study of contemporary Latin American politics because, as the empirical chapters in this book show, this has important consequences for redistributive outcomes, from old issues such as land reform or taxation to new ones like environmental regulations. During the 2000s, many leftwing parties with ambitious redistributive agendas came to power across the region. To varying degrees these governments succeeded in implementing these agendas, expanding social services to the poor and improving workers' income. However, they also faced challenges when trying to increase taxes on economic elites, distribute land or strengthen environmental regulations. Previous literature has extensively studied the relationship between these leftwing governments and their core constituencies such as social movements, indigenous groups, or unions, and how these have shaped their policy agendas. The question of how administrations have dealt with economic elites during Latin America's left turn has, however, been much less explored, offering a fertile avenue for future research. This book addresses this gap in the literature by showing how agrarian elites have been able to condition the policy agenda of leftwing administrations where they are organized in the electoral arena. In Argentina, agrarian elites' lack of electoral representation limited their capacity to block increasing taxation and regulations over agricultural markets during the FPV administrations (2003–2015). In both Brazil and Chile, in contrast, agrarian elites were able to crucially shape the policy agenda of the PT (2003–2016) and the Concertación/Nueva Mayoría (1990–2010 and 2014–2018) respectively through their representatives in Congress. In Brazil, a powerful multiparty caucus was able to not only block redistributive land reform but also shape environmental regulations as well as direct sizable resources toward the sector. As a result, leftwing governments ended up increasing subsidies to agribusiness during a commodity boom in one of the most unequal countries in the world. Even when the PT greatly expanded support for small farmers, these resources paled in comparison to those directed to agribusiness. Similarly, Chilean agrarian elites were able to block or crucially shape tax and environmental policies during the center-left governments of the Concertación/Nueva Mayoría.

It is also remarkable that agrarian elites have been able to successfully organize in the electoral arena in contemporary Latin America where urbanization has shrunk their traditional electoral base, the rural poor. Before the third wave, landowners tolerated restricted democracy as long as they could control the votes of the rural poor living on their lands. In contemporary Latin America, however, agrarian elites have supported the continuity of democracy even when they have lost this electoral advantage. Despite the sharp decrease in rural population, agrarian elites have been able to secure electoral representation in some countries such as Brazil, Chile, and El Salvador. The case of Brazil is particularly interesting because in that country, agrarian elites have deployed an electoral strategy of direct representation. Landowners themselves run for office, campaigning as agricultural producers. Contemporary Brazil is a highly urbanized country, with only 12 percent of its population living in rural areas.[31] This means that most legislators, including those in the

---

[31] See: https://data.worldbank.org/indicator/SP.RUR.TOTL.ZS (accessed June 8, 2024).

6.3 Implications

Agrarian Caucus, depend on urban votes to get elected. Future scholarship should study why the urban poor vote for rural elites. Investigating how agrarian elites mobilize the vote of non-elite urban groups is crucial for understanding how agrarian elites can protect themselves from redistribution in contemporary democracies.

The question of how minorities may protect their rights from the will of the majority is as old as the idea of democracy itself. The thesis that landowners will prefer autocracy to democracy because under the latter they cannot protect their wealth from majoritarian redistributive demands has recently been challenged by studies that show how democracies better protect economic elites' interests through institutional veto points which can be used to block redistribution (Albertus 2015; 2017). This book goes one step further by explaining when and how agrarian elites will organize in the electoral arena to take advantage of those veto points. Contrary to Albertus (2015), this book shows that democratization is indeed threatening to landowners. However, unlike what *redistributivist* theories of democratization predict,[32] this perception of threat will not necessarily lead landowners to hamper democracy. This book shows that in Latin America during the third wave, agrarian elites responded to redistributive threats by investing in electoral representation. I specify the mechanisms through which agrarian elites were able to block redistribution democratically. As the analysed cases demonstrate, where the transition to democracy was threatening to agrarian elites, they invested in electoral representation. This electoral investment, in turn, helped democratic consolidation as it lowered the costs of tolerating democracy for agrarian elites. Where agrarian elites had the opportunity to influence policy outcomes, their incentives to undermine democracy were lower. However, at the same time, as the empirical chapters illustrate, agrarian elites' representation is inimical to democracies' equalitarian aspirations. By protecting the interests of wealthy elites, democracies have frustrated the redistributive expectations of the same dispossessed groups that the process of democratization incorporated into the political arena. This creates a new challenge for democracy itself as the alienation of these groups may constitute breeding grounds for undemocratic movements. Future scholarship should investigate how the capacity of agrarian elites to protect their interests under democracy and the resulting redistributive consequences affect the prospects for democratic continuity in Latin America and beyond.

---

[32] See Boix (2003), Acemoglu and Robinson (2006), and Ansell and Samuels (2010).

Appendix A

List of Interviewees

1 ARGENTINA

Leaders of Producers' Associations

Mario Acoroni, executive director of the Rosario Stock Exchange (1977–). Rosario, June 24, 2014.
Guillermo Alchouron, SRA president (1984–1990) and director (1969–1996), legislator for Buenos Aires City (1999–2007) (Acción por la República). Buenos Aires, July 8 and 17, 2014.
Mariano Andrade, SRA director in the province of Córdoba since the 1990s. Buenos Aires, July 24, 2014.
Luis Arias, president of the Sunflower Association (Asagir) (2013–2015). Buenos Aires, June 16, 2014.
Alejandro Blacker, president of AACREA. Buenos Aires, July 23, 2014.
Carlos Borla, vice president of the Buenos Aires Grain Stock. Buenos Aires, July 7, 2014 and June 8, 2017.
Dardo Chiesa, president of CRA (2015–2019), president of CARBAP (1998–2002). Buenos Aires, August 10, 2017.
Julio Curras, vice president of FAA. Rosario, June 23, 2014.
Gabriel De Raedemaeker, president of the Confederation of Rural Associations of the Third Region (CARTEZ) (2016–). Buenos Aires, June 28, 2017.
Raúl Dientre, leader of the Grain Stockpilers Federation. Buenos Aires, July 7, 2014.
Martín Fraguío, executive director of the Argentine Corn Association (Maizar). Buenos Aires, July 7, 2014.
Abel Guerrieri, secretary of the SRA. Buenos Aires, June 5, 2014.
David Hughes, president of the Argentine Wheat Association (Argentrigo) (2007–2011) (2015–), founder of Barbechando. Buenos Aires, December 27, 2013 and July 6, 2017.
Carlos Iannizzotto, president CONINAGRO (2016–2021). Buenos Aires, August 3, 2018.

Santiago Labourt, president of Argentrigo (2011–2013). Buenos Aires, June 5, 2014.

Mario Llambías, president of CRA (2005–2009), CARBAP president (1994–1998 and 2002–2005) and director (1979–1999). Buenos Aires, August 13, 2014.

Luciano Miguens, SRA president (2002–3008) and director since 1979. Buenos Aires, July 18, 2014.

Arturo Navarro, president of CRA (1989–1993) and CARBAP (1986–1989). Buenos Aires, June 8, 2017.

Daniel Pelegrina, vice president of the SRA (2012–2017). Buenos Aires, June 13 and 19, 2014 and August 7, 2017.

Hugo Rossi, president of the Rural Society of Guardia del Monte, Buenos Aires; member of GAPU–Agro (UCR). Buenos Aires, July 16, 2014.

Rodolfo Rossi, president and founder of the Argentine Soybean Association (ACSOJA) (2004–2009 and 2014–2018). Rosario, June 24, 2014.

Horacio Salaverry, president of CARBAP (2012–2016), Buenos Aires provincial legislator (1991–1995 and 1999–2003) (UCEDE). Buenos Aires, June 11, 2014.

Luis María San Román, vice president of the Rural Society of Rosario (2011–2015) and vice president of the Confederation of Rural Associations of Santa Fe (CARSFE). Rosario, June 23, 2014.

Gustavo Sutter Schneider. President of the Rural Society of Rosario (2013–2015). Rosario, June 23, 2014.

Carlos Vaquer, SRA secretary, AACREA president (1999–2001). Buenos Aires, June 10, 2014.

Pedro Vigneau, president (2016–2018) and vice president of Aapresid (2014–2016). Buenos Aires, June 16, 2014 and June 12, 2017.

Raúl Vitores, president of the Rural Society of San Pedro (2002–). Buenos Aires, July 24, 2014.

Agro-politicians

Gilberto Alegre, legislator for Buenos Aires (2013–2017) (Frente Renovador), president of the Lower Chamber Agriculture Committee (2015–2017), mayor of Gral. Villegas (1989–2013). Buenos Aires, June 22, 2017.

Alfredo de Angelis, senator for Entre Ríos (2013–) (PRO), leader of the FAA. Buenos Aires, June 26, 2014.

Omar Barchetta, legislator for Santa Fe (2011–2015) (Socialist Party), vice president of FAA (2009–2011). Buenos Aires, August 6, 2014.

Ricardo Buryaile, legislator for Formosa (2009–2015) (UCR), CRA vice president (2007–2009). Buenos Aires, June 19, 2014.

Juan Francisco Casañas, legislator for Tucumán (2009–2015) (UCR), member of AACREA and FAA. Buenos Aires, August 6, 2014.

Jorge Chemes, legislator for Entre Ríos (2009–2013) (UCR), president of the Federation of Rural Societies of Entre Ríos (FARER) (2007–2009 and 2013–2015). Buenos Aires, August 13, 2014.

María del Huerto Ratto, Buenos Aires provincial legislator (2013–2017) (Frente Renovador), Pergamino councilwoman (2011–2013). Buenos Aires, August 13, 2014.

Appendix A: List of Interviewees

Jorge Solmi, Buenos Aires provincial legislator (2009–2013) (Unión PRO), director of the FAA (2007–2015). Buenos Aires, August 7, 2014.

Pablo Torello, legislator for Buenos Aires (2015–) (PRO), member of the Agriculture Committee. Buenos Aires, July 6, 2017.

High-Ranking Government Officials

Guillermo Bernaudo, chief of staff, Ministry of Agroindustry (2015–2017); member of the Agroindustry Roundtable, Fundación Pensar (PRO); member of AACREA. Buenos Aires, June 12, 2017.

Mariano Bosch, vice president of INTA (2015–2019), member of AACREA. Buenos Aires, August 1, 2017.

Miguel Braun, secretary of commerce (2015–2019), executive director of Fundación Pensar (PRO). Buenos Aires, August 18, 2017.

Ricardo Negri, secretary of agriculture (2015–2017), research coordinator of AACREA until 2015, coordinator of the Agroindustry Roundtable, Fundación Pensar (PRO). Buenos Aires, June 13, 2017.

Néstor Roulet, secretary of value added, Ministry of Agroindustry (2015–2017); vice president of CRA (2008–2009), president (2003–2005) and vice president (2005–2009) of CARTEZ. Buenos Aires, June 26, 2017.

Leonardo Sarquis, minister of agroindustry, Buenos Aires Province (2015–); Monsanto CEO (2005–2007). La Plata, June 21, 2017.

Jorge Srodek. Chief of staff, ministry of agroindustry, Buenos Aires Province (2015–); Buenos Aires provincial legislator (2009–2013) (Unión PRO), vice president of CARBAP. Buenos Aires, June 12, 2017.

Specialized Journalists

Mercedes Colombres, consultant for some of the agrodiputados (2009–2013). Buenos Aires, August 7, 2014.

Juan Cruz Jaime, travelled to Brasília to study the Bancada Ruralista. Buenos Aires, June 18, 2014.

Others

Adolfo Castro Almeyra, political consultant for the Buenos Aires Grain Exchange and Coordinator of the SRA leadership seminar. Travelled to Brasília to study the Bancada Ruralista. Buenos Aires, December 18, 2013, June 17, 2014, and June 5, 2017.

José Francisco de Anchorena, director of government planification, Fundación Pensar (PRO), Buenos Aires, August 2, 2017.

Barbechando Member no. 1. Buenos Aires, December 18 and 27, 2013.

Barbechando Member no. 2. Buenos Aires, December 18 and 27, 2013.

Barbechando Member no. 3. Buenos Aires, December 18, 2013 and June 19, 2017.

Barbechando Member no. 4. Buenos Aires, December 18, 2013 and June 19, 2017.
Barbechando Member no. 5. Buenos Aires, December 18, 2013.
Barbechando Member no. 6. Buenos Aires, June 19, 2017.
Gerardo Bongiovanni, president of Fundación Libertad. Buenos Aires, August 1, 2017.
Silvina Campos Cartes, director of institutional relations, CONINAGRO. Buenos Aires, June 28, 2017.
Gustavo Grobocopatel, Los Grobo CEO. Cambridge, MA, November 23, 2013.
Martin Maquieyra, legislator for La Pampa (2013–) (PRO), secretary of the Agriculture Committee (2015–2017). Buenos Aires, June 21, 2017.
David Miazzo, research coordinator of the Fundación Agropecuaria para el Desarrollo de Argentina (FADA) (2012–). Buenos Aires, August 7, 2017.
Pedro Nazar, president of Fundación Barbechando (2015–3017), AACREA member. Buenos Aires, July 26, 2017.
Not for Attribution, producer in Santa Fe province. Participated of the 2008 protests. Member of the PJ in the province. They have run for several local offices. Rosario, June 24, 2014.
Not for Attribution, president of the Rural Society of Rosario Young Ateneo. Rosario, June 25, 2014.
Not for Attribution, CRESUD. Buenos Aires, July 23, 2014.
Diego Ramírez, CEO of RIA (Reporte Institucional Agropecuario) Consulting. Buenos Aires, July 26, 2017.
Florencia Richiutti, executive director of Fundación Barbechando. Buenos Aires, June 19, 2017.
Cornelia Schmidt-Liermann, legislator for the City of Buenos Aires (2011–) (PRO), member of the Agroindustry Roundatable, Fundación Pensar. Buenos Aires, June 22, 2017.
Fernando Santillán, advisor, secretary of commerce (2015–2019); member of Fundación Pensar (PRO). Buenos Aires, August 18, 2017.

2 BRAZIL

Bancada Ruralista Members

Ana Amelia, senator for Rio Grande do Sul (2011–2019) (PP), vice president of FPA. Brasília, August 10, 2015.
Ronaldo Caiado, senator for Goiás (2015–2019) (DEM), DEM leader in the Senate, founder of UDR. Brasília, March 22, 2017.
Júlio Cesar de Carvalho Lima. Legislator for Piauí (1995–) (PSD). Brasília, April 4, 2017.
Valdir Colatto, legislator for Santa Catarina (1987–) (PMDB). Brasília, August 6, 2015.
Tereza Cristina, legislator for Mato Grosso do Sul (2015–) (PSB), vice president of FPA (2017–2018), PSB leader in the Lower Chamber. Brasília, April 5, 2017.

Cesar Hallum, legislator for Tocantins (2011–2022) (PRB). Brasília, April 6, 2017.
Luiz Carlos Heinze, legislator for Rio Grande do Sul (1999–2019) (PPB). Brasília, April 4, 2017.
João Henrique Hummel, executive director of the FPA since its foundation. Brasília, July 28, 2015 and March 14, 2017.
Nilson Leitão, legislator for Mato Grosso (2011–) (PSDB), president of FPA (2017–2018). Brasília, April 11, 2017.
Nelson Marquezelli, legislator for São Paulo (1999–2019) (PTB). Brasília, March 30, 2017.
Evair de Melo, legislator for Espírito Santo (2015–) (PV). Brasília, March 23, 2017.
Waldemir Moka, senator for Mato Grosso do Sul (2011–) (PMDB). Brasília, August 6, 2015.
Marcos Montes, legislator for Minas Gerais (2011–2019) (PSD), president of FPA (2015–2016). Brasília, August 4, 2015.
Alceu Moreira, legislator for Rio Grande do Sul (2011–) (PMDB). Brasília, August 6, 2015.
Luiz Nishimori, legislator for Paraná (2011–) (PR). Brasília, March 21, 2017.
Luis Gonzaga Patriota, legislator for Pernambuco (1987–) (PSB). Brasília, March 13, 2017.
Adilton Sachetti, legislator for Mato Grosso (2015–) (PSB), founder of AMPA. Brasília, March 16, 2017.
Zé Silva, legislator for Minas Gerais (2011–) (SD). Brasília, March 22, 2017.
Reinhold Stephanes, legislator for Paraná (1979–2019) (PSD), minister of agriculture (2007–2010). Brasília, March 30, 2017.

State Legislators

Anibelli Neto, Paraná state legislator (2010–) (PMDB), leader of the Parliamentary front for Subsistence Agriculture. Curitiba, April 18, 2017.
Evandro Araujo, Paraná state legislator (2014–) (PSC). Curitiba, April 17, 2017.
Pedro Lupion, Paraná state legislator (2010–2019) (DEM), president of the Agriculture Committee. Curitiba, April 17, 2017.
Saturnino Masson, Mato Grosso state legislator (2015–2018) (PSDB). Cuiabá, August 12, 2015.
José Antônio Gonçalves Viana, Mato Grosso state legislator (2010–) (PDT). Cuiabá, August 11, 2015.

Leaders of Producers' Associations

Carlos Albuquerque, director of the Federation of Agricultural Producers of Paraná (FAEP). Curitiba, April 19, 2017.
Frederico Azevedo e Silva, director of institutional relations, Soybean Producers Association of Mato Grosso (APROSOJA–MT). Cuiabá, August 13, 2015.

Mario Antonio Pereira Borba, vice president of the CNA. Brasília, July 24, 2015.

Pedro de Camargo Neto, president of the SRB (1990–1992), secretary of production and trade of the ministry of agriculture (2000–2002). São Paulo, April 25, 2017.

Daniel Kluppel Carrara, executive secretary SENAR/CNA (National System of Agricultural Education). Brasília, July 24, 2015.

Luiz Carlos Corrêa Carvalho, president of the Agribusiness Brazilian Association (ABAG). São Paulo, May 5, 2017.

Fábio Meirelles Filho, president of IPA (2016–2018), director of the CNA. Brasília, April 4, 2017.

Fabiola Motta, director of institutional relations of the OCB. Brasília, March 27, 2017.

José Roberto Ricken, president of the Association of Cooperatives of Paraná (OCEPAR). Curitiba, April 17, 2017.

Roberto Rodrigues, president of the OCB (1985–1991), president of SRB (1991–1993), minister of agriculture (2003–2006), founder of ABAG. São Paulo, May 5, 2017.

Fabricio Rosa, executive director of the Soybean Producers Association (APROSOJA–Brasil). Brasília, March 29, 2017.

Marcos da Rosa, president of APROSOJA–Brasil (2016–2018). Brasília, March 29, 2017.

João Martins da Silva Júnior, CNA president (2015–). Brasília, July 24, 2015.

Muni Lourenco Silva Júnior, president SENAR/CNA. Brasília, July 24, 2015.

Flavio Páscoa Teles de Menezes, president of the SRB (1984–1990). São Paulo, May 9, 2017.

Décio Tocantins, executive director of the Cotton Growers Association of Mato Grosso (AMPA). Cuiabá, August 13, 2015.

Francisco Turra, president of the Brazilian Association of Animal Protein (ABPA) (2014–). São Paulo, April 26, 2017.

Marcelo Wayland Barbosa Vieira, president of the SRB (2017–). São Paulo, May 3, 2017.

Legislative Consultants

Ana, legislative consultant for the landless movement (MST) in the Senate. Brasília, April 7, 2017.

José Cordeiro de Araújo, legislative consultant of the Brazilian Congress (1991–2010), specialist in agriculture. Brasília, March 29, 2017.

Rodrigo Hermeto Corrêa Dolabella, legislative consultant of the Brazilian Congress since 2003, specialist in agriculture. Brasília, July 22, 2015 and March 8, 2017.

Luis Antonio Guerra Conceicão Silva, legislative consultant of the Brazilian Congress, specialist in agrarian politics. Brasília, July 22, 2015.

Nelson Fraga, legislative consultant of the CNA in the Senate since the 1990s. Brasília, August 6, 2015.

Suely Vaz Guimaraes de Araujo, legislative consultant of the Brazilian Congress (1991–2016), specialist in environmental law. Brasília, July 21, 2015.
Not for attribution, legislative Consultant for the CNA, specialist in labor law. Brasília, July 24, 2015.

Others

Leonardo Minaré Brauna, technical consultant of APROSOJA-Brasil. Brasília, August 7, 2015.
Gustavo Carneiro, technical coordinator of IPA. Brasília, March 14, 2017.
Coaraci Nogueira de Castilho, chief of staff, ministry of agriculture. Brasília, April 12, 2017.
Antonio Costa, director of FIESP (Industry Federation of São Paulo) agribusiness department (Deagro). São Paulo, May 8, 2017.
Neri Geller, secretary of agricultural policy (2016–2019), minister of agriculture (2014–2015). Brasília, March 21, 2017.
Carlos Fávaro, vice governor of Mato Grosso (2015–2018) (PP), president of APROSOJA-MT (2010–2014). Cuiabá, August 12, 2015.
Antonio Carlos Teixeira, press secretary of Senator Waldemir Moka. Brasília, August 6, 2015.
Nilto Tatto, legislator for São Paulo (2015–) (PT). Brasília, April 6, 2017.
Gerson Teixeira, advisor to the PT caucus on agrarian policy since 1992, president of the Brazilian Association for Agrarian Reform (ABRA) (2012 – and in the 1990s). Brasília, March 8 and 9, 2017.
Nilton Tubino, advisor to the PT caucus on agrarian policy since 2003. Brasília, April 12, 2017.

3 CHILE

Leaders of Producers' Associations

Ricardo Ariztía de Castro, CPC president (2002–2004), SNA president (1997–2000), Fedefruta president (1989). Santiago, November 15, 2016.
Ricardo Ariztía Tagle, director of the SNA since 2011. Santiago, October 26, 2016.
Patricio Crespo, president of the SNA (2012–2016). Santiago, October 26, 2016.
Gastón Caminondo, SOFO president (2005–2015), president of the Agriculture Consortium of the South (CAS) (2012–2014). Temuco, November 10, 2016.
Juan Carolus Brown, president of Fedefruta (2014–2016). Santiago, October 4, 2016.
María Inés Figari, president of the North Agriculture Society (SAN) (2015–), director of the SNA and Fedefruta. Santiago, October 18, 2016.
Jorge Guzmán, president of the Sugar Beet Growers Association since 1990. Temuco, November 11, 2016.

Andreas Kobrich, secretary of SOFO since 2010. Temuco, November 10, 2016.
Juan Carlos Sepúlveda Meyer, CEO of Fedefruta. Santiago, September 26, 2016
José Miguel Stegmeier, president of the Agriculture Society of the Bio Bio Region (Socabio) since 1982, president of CAS (2014–2016). Santiago, October 24, 2016.

High-Ranking Government Officials

Juan Andrés Fontaine, ministry of economy (2010–2011), member of Libertad y Desarrollo council. Santiago, October 12, 2016.
José Antonio Galilea, ministry of agriculture (2010–2011), legislator (RN–La Araucanía) (1990–2006). Temuco, November 10, 2016.
Luis Mayol, ministry of agriculture (2011–2014), president of the SNA (2009–2011). Founder of RN. Santiago, October 20, 2016.
Jorge Prado, ministry of agriculture (1982–1988), president of the SNA (1989–1993). Santiago, November 8, 2016.

National Legislators

Ramón Barros Montero, legislator (O'Higgins – UDI) (2002–2022). Valparaíso, October 5, 2016.
René Manuel García, legislator (La Araucanía – RN) (1990–2022). Valparaíso, October 6, 2016.
Alejandro García-Huidobro, senator (O'Higgins – UDI) (2011–2022), legislator (Rancagua– Union of the Progressive Center–Center/UDI) (1994–2011), vice president of the Agricultural Producers Confederation (1988–1993). Valparaíso, October 5, 2016.
Sergio Romero Pizarro, senator (Valparaíso – RN) (1990–2010). Secretary general (1968–1976), council member (1980–1990), and vice president of the SNA (1987–1989). Secretary of agriculture under Pinochet (1986), vice president of the CPC (1989). Santiago, November 16, 2016.
Alejandra Sepúlveda Orbenes, legislator (O'Higgins – Independent, former Christian Democrat) (2002–). Valparaíso, November 9, 2016.
Ignacio Urrutia Bonilla, legislator (Maule – UDI) (2002–2022). Valparaíso, October 5, 2016.

Others

René Araneda, councilman of Temuco (UDI) (2012–2018), regional secretary of agriculture (2010–2012), secretary of SOFO (1990–2010). Temuco, November 11, 2016.
Erika Farías, legislative consultant, Fundación Jaime Guzman. Santiago, October 19, 2016.

Appendix A: List of Interviewees

Susana Jimenez, public policy coordinator, Libertad y Desarrollo. Santiago, November 3, 2016.

Miguel Mellado, president of the Regional Council of La Araucanía (RN) (2013–2016), governor of Cautín Province (2010–2013). Temuco, November 10, 2016.

Teodoro Rivas Sius, deputy director of ODEPA (Office of Studies and Agricultural Policy – Ministry of Agriculture) (2014–2018). Santiago, October 27, 2016.

Appendix B

Primary Sources

1 NEWSPAPER ARTICLES

Argentina

I browsed the internet for newspaper articles mentioning agricultural producers between 1982 and 2022 using the search engine Google, and I searched the *La Nación* digital archive which contains articles published since 1994.

Brazil

I reviewed every newspaper article under the labels "agrarian reform," "Confederação da Agricultura e Pecuária (CNA)," and "União Democrática Ruralista (UDR)" between 1980 and 2017 in the archives of the library of the Brazilian Congress. This archive reviews seven national newspapers: *Folha de São Paulo, O Estado de São Paulo, Jornal do Brasil, Jornal da Tarde, Jornal de Brasilia, Correio Brasiliense,* and *O Globo*. Articles are organized in folders by theme and chronologically.

2 PUBLICATIONS BY PRODUCERS' ASSOCIATIONS

Argentina

Anales, magazine published by the SRA, 1983–1994.
Annual reports of the Buenos Aires Grain Exchange, 1982–1990.

Chile

El Campesino, monthly magazine published by the SNA, 1987–2016.

3 CONGRESSIONAL RECORDS

Brazil

Voting records: Bills, congressional trajectories and treatment, including committees and floor roll-call votes are available at: www.camara.leg.br/busca–portal/proposicoes/pesquisa–simplificada.

Legislators' personal information: Including profession, caucus and committee membership, and previous civil society/political leadership positions was retrieved from: www.camara.leg.br/deputados/quem–sao.

Congressional caucus composition: Caucuses' composition since 2006 is available at: www.camara.leg.br/internet/deputado/frentes.asp

Chile

Voting records: Bills, congressional trajectories and treatment, including committees and floor roll-call votes are available at: www.bcn.cl/historiadelaley.

Legislators' personal information: Including profession and previous civil society/political leadership positions was retrieved from: www.bcn.cl/historiapolitica/resenas_parlamentarias.

4 BARBECHANDO SURVEY

I ran a small web survey of producers in Argentina with the help of a local NGO called Barbechando in October–November 2017. Barbechando is a civil society organization funded by producers in the aftermath of the 2008 conflict to monitor and lobby Congress. Members of this association are more politically involved than the median Argentine producer. I administered the web survey using Barbechando's donor database. Of the fifty-two donors, twenty-three responded to the survey, a response rate of 44 percent, which is very high for elite surveys. Questions in the survey were modeled after the interview questionnaire applied to other producers individually, so that the answers could be comparable.

References

Abente-Brun, Diego. 2012. "Paraguay: Crecimento Económico, Conflicto Social e Incertidumbre Política." *Revista de Ciencia Política* 32 (1): 229–44.
Acemoglu, Daron, and James A. Robinson. 2006. *Economic Origins of Dictatorship and Democracy*. Cambridge; New York: Cambridge University Press.
  2008. "Persistence of Power, Elites, and Institutions." *American Economic Review* 98 (1): 267–93.
Acuña, Carlos. 1995. "Business Interests, Dictatorship, and Democracy in Argentina." In *Business and Democracy in Latin America*, edited by Ernest J. Bartell and Leigh A. Payne, 3–48. Pitt Latin American Series. Pittsburgh, PA: University of Pittsburgh Press.
Albertus, Michael. 2015. *Autocracy and Redistribution: The Politics of Land Reform*. Cambridge Studies in Comparative Politics. New York: Cambridge University Press.
  2017. "Landowners and Democracy." *World Politics* 69 (02): 233–76.
Albertus, Michael, and Victor Gay. 2017. "Unlikely Democrats: Economic Elite Uncertainty under Dictatorship and Support for Democratization." *American Journal of Political Science* 61 (3): 624–41.
Albertus, Michael, and Victor Menaldo. 2018. *Authoritarianism and the Elite Origins of Democracy*. Cambridge: Cambridge University Press.
Aldrich, John Herbert. 1995. *Why Parties? The Origin and Transformation of Political Parties in America*. American Politics and Political Economy Series. Chicago: University of Chicago Press.
Allern, Elin H., and Tim Bale. 2012. "Political Parties and Interest Groups: Disentangling Complex Relationships." *Party Politics* 18 (1): 7–25.
Ames, Barry. 2001. *The Deadlock of Democracy in Brazil*. Interests, Identities, and Institutions in Comparative Politics. Ann Arbor: University of Michigan Press.
Amorim Neto, Octavio, and Gary W. Cox. 1997. "Electoral Institutions, Cleavage Structures, and the Number of Parties." *American Journal of Political Science* 41 (1): 149–74.

Amorim Neto, Octavio, Gary W. Cox, and Mathew D. McCubbins. 2003. "Agenda Power in Brazil's Câmara Dos Deputados, 1989–98." *World Politics* 55 (4): 550–78.
Ansell, Ben, and David Samuels. 2010. "Inequality and Democratization: A Contractarian Approach." *Comparative Political Studies* 43 (12): 1543–74.
  2014. *Inequality and Democratization: An Elite-Competition Approach*. New York: Cambridge University Press.
Ansolabehere, Stephen, John M. de Figueiredo, and James M. Snyder. 2003. "Why Is There So Little Money in U.S. Politics?" *Journal of Economic Perspectives* 17 (1): 105–30.
Arellano, Juan Carlos. 2009. "El Partido Nacional en Chile: Su Rol en el Conflicto Político (1966–1973)." *Atenea (Concepción)* 1 (499): 157–74.
Avendaño, Octavio, and María Cristina Escudero. 2016. "Elitismo y Poder Gremial en la Sociedad Nacional de Agricultura (SNA)." *Revista CS* 20 (December): 37.
Aylwin Azócar, Patricio. 1988. *Un Desafío Colectivo*. Santiago de Chile: Editorial Planeta.
Baer, Werner. 2014. *The Brazilian Economy: Growth and Development*. 7th ed. Boulder, CO: Lynne Rienner Publishers.
Baland, Jean-Marie, and James A. Robinson. 2008. "Land and Power: Theory and Evidence from Chile." *American Economic Review* 98 (5): 1737–65.
  2012. "The Political Value of Land: Political Reform and Land Prices in Chile." *American Journal of Political Science* 56 (3): 601–19.
Baltar, Ronaldo. 1990. "Os Empresarios Rurais e a Reforma Agraria no Governo de Transição (1985–1988)." M.A. Dissertation, Campinas: Universidade Estadual de Campinas.
Barbalho, Alexandre, and Giulano Barboza. 2020. "Bancada Evangélica: Uma Elite Parlamentar?" *Revista do Instituto de Políticas Públicas de Marília* 6 (1): 131–46.
Barbechando. 2017. *Mapa Político de Actores. El Campo en el Congreso*. Buenos Aires.
Barham, Bradford, Mary Clark, Elizabeth Katz, and Rachel Schurman. 1992. "Nontraditional Agricultural Exports in Latin America." *Latin American Research Review* 27 (2): 43–82.
Barndt, William T. 2016. "The Organizational Foundations of Corporation-Based Parties." In *Challenges of Party-Building in Latin America*, edited by Brandon Van Dyck, James Loxton, Jorge I. Domínguez, and Steven Levitsky, 356–80. Cambridge: Cambridge University Press.
Barozet, Emmanuelle, and Marcel Aubry. 2005. "De las Reformas Internas a la Candidatura Presidencial Autónoma: Los Nuevos Caminos Institucionales de Renovación Nacional." *Política* 45: 165–96.
Barrenechea Carpio, Rodrigo. 2014. *Becas, Bases y Votos: Alianza Para el Progreso y La Política Subnacional en el Perú*. Serie Colección Mínima 69. Lima: IEP Instituto de Estudios Peruanos.
Barros, Sergio, and Vandoir Silva. 2022. "Brazilian Economic and Agricultural Overview." BR2022-0011. United States Department of Agriculture – Foreign Agricultural Service.

Barsky, Osvaldo, and Mabel Dávila. 2008. *La Rebelión del Campo. Historia del Conflicto Agrario Argentino*. Buenos Aires: Sudamericana.
Barsky, Osvaldo, and Jorge Gelman, eds. 2009. *Historia del Agro Argentino: Desde la Conquista hasta Comienzos del Siglo XXI*. Colección Historia Argentina. Buenos Aires: Ed. Sudamericana.
Bartell, Ernest J. 1995. "Perceptions by Business Leaders and the Transition to Democracy in Chile." In *Business and Democracy in Latin America*, edited by Ernest J. Bartell and Leigh A. Payne, 49–104. Pittsburgh, PA: University of Pittsburgh Press.
Bartell, Ernest J., and Leigh A. Payne, eds. 1995. *Business and Democracy in Latin America*. Pitt Latin American Series. Pittsburgh, PA: University of Pittsburgh Press.
Bauer, Arnold J. 1995. "Landlord and Campesino in the Chilean Road to Democracy." In *Agrarian Structure & Political Power: Landlord & Peasant in the Making of Latin America*, edited by Evelyne Huber and Frank Safford, 21–38. Pitt Latin American Series. Pittsburgh, PA: University of Pittsburgh Press.
  2008. *Chilean Rural Society from the Spanish Conquest to 1930*. Cambridge and New York: Cambridge University Press.
Bauer, Carl J. 1998. *Against the Current: Privatization, Water Markets, and the State in Chile*. Boston, MA: Springer US.
Bawn, Kathleen, Martin Cohen, David Karol, Seth Masket, Hans Noel, and John Zaller. 2012. "A Theory of Political Parties: Groups, Policy Demands and Nominations in American Politics." *Perspectives on Politics* 10 (03): 571–97.
Bebbington, Anthony, and Jeffrey Bury. 2013. *Subterranean Struggles: New Dynamics of Mining, Oil, and Gas in Latin America*. Austin: University of Texas Press.
Bellin, Eva Rana. 2000. "Contingent Democrats: Industrialists, Labor, and Democratization in Late-Developing Countries." *World Politics* 52 (2): 175–205.
Bennett, Andrew, and Jeffrey T. Checkel. 2014. *Process Tracing: From Metaphor to Analytic Tool*. Cambridge: Cambridge University Press.
Bethell, Leslie, ed. 1993. *Chile since Independence*. Cambridge and New York: Cambridge University Press.
Boas, Taylor C. 2023. *Evangelicals and Electoral Politics in Latin America: A Kingdom of This World*. Cambridge Studies in Social Theory, Religion and Politics. Cambridge: Cambridge University Press.
Boix, Carles. 2003. *Democracy and Redistribution*. Cambridge Studies in Comparative Politics. Cambridge and New York: Cambridge University Press.
Bolsa de Cerales de Buenos Aires. 1983. "*Memoria e Informe. Ejercicio 1982.*" Buenos Aires: Bolsa de Cereales de Buenos Aires.
Bolsa de Cereales de Buenos Aires, and Bolsa de Comercio de Rosario. 2009. *La Interacción Público-Privada*. Estudio de Caso: La Bancada Ruralista de Brasil.
Bolsa de Comercio de Rosario. 2016. "Informativo Semanal."
Bratman, Eve. 2020. "Sustainable Development Reconsidered: The Left Turn's Legacies in the Amazon." In *Legacies of the Left Turn in Latin America*,

edited by Manuel Balán and François Montambeault, 280–309. Notre Dame, IN: Notre Dame University Press.

Brockett, Charles D. 1998. *Land, Power, and Poverty: Agrarian Transformation and Political Conflict in Central America*. 2nd ed. Thematic Studies in Latin America. Boulder, CO: Westview Press.

Brou, Penélope. 2020. "Aportes Dudosos e Influencia Parlamentaria en Partidos Porosos: El Caso de Fuerza Popular y Algunos Grupos de Interés (2016–2018)." B.A. Thesis, Lima: Pontificia Universidad Católica del Perú.

Budds, Jessica. 2013. "Water, Power, and the Production of Neoliberalism in Chile, 1973–2005." *Environment and Planning D: Society and Space* 31 (2): 301–18.

Burden, Barry C. 2007. *Personal Roots of Representation*. Princeton, NJ: Princeton University Press.

Canales, Lissette Cristalina. 2021. "Grupos Empresariales Familiares: Cambios Económicos y Políticos en El Salvador." *Tiempo y Economía* 8 (2): 162–89.

Cárdenas, Julián, and Francisco Robles-Rivera. 2021. "Corporate Networks and Business Influence in Panama, Costa Rica, and El Salvador." *Colombia Internacional*, 107: 87–112.

Cardoza, Anthony L. 1983. *Agrarian Elites and Italian Fascism: The Province of Bologna, 1901–1926*. Princeton, NJ: Princeton University Press.

Carey, John M, and Matthew Soberg Shugart. 1995. "Incentives to Cultivate a Personal Vote: A Rank Ordering of Electoral Formulas." *Electoral Studies* 14 (4): 417–39.

Carrière, Jean. 1980. *Landowners and Politics in Chile: A Study of the "Sociedad Nacional de Agricultura", 1932–1970*. Amsterdam: CEDLA/FORIS Publications.

Cascione, Silvio, and Suely Mara Vaz Guimarães de Araújo. 2019. "Obstáculos para Protagonismo das Frentes Parlamentares em Coalizões Presidenciais no Brasil." *Revista de Sociologia e Política* 27 (72): 1–23.

Castañeda, Jorge. 2006. "Latin America's Left Turn." *Foreign Affairs* 85 (3): 28–43.

Cavalcanti de Albuquerque, Roberto, and Renato Villela. 1991. "A Situação Social no Brasil: Um Balanço de Duas Décadas." In *A Questão Social no Brasil*, edited by João Paulo Dos Reis Velloso, 23–104. São Paulo: Livraria Nobel.

CEPAL, Comisión Económica para América Latina y el Caribe. 2018. "*Panorama Social de América Latina, 2017*." (LC/PUB.2018/1-P). Santiago. https://repositorio.cepal.org/bitstream/handle/11362/42716/7/S1800002_es.pdf.

Chaccha, Hilda. 2018. "El Poder de las Coaliciones en la Arena de las Políticas Públicas: Caso Ley Universitaria." B.A. Thesis, Lima: Pontificia Universidad Católica del Perú.

Collier, David. 2011. "Understanding Process Tracing." *PS: Political Science & Politics* 44 (4): 823–30.

Collier, David, and Gerardo L. Munck, eds. 2022. *Critical Junctures and Historical Legacies: Insights and Methods for Comparative Social Science*. Lanham, MD: Rowman & Littlefield.

Conaghan, Catherine. 2000. "The Irrelevant Right: Alberto Fujimori and the New Politics of Pragmatic Peru." In *Conservative Parties, the Right, and*

Democracy in Latin America, edited by Kevin J. Middlebrook, 255–84. Baltimore, MD: Johns Hopkins University Press.

Correa, Sofía. 2005. *Con las Riendas del Poder*. Santiago: Sudamericana.

Cox, Gary W. 1997. *Making Votes Count: Strategic Coordination in the World's Electoral Systems*. Political Economy of Institutions and Decisions. Cambridge and New York: Cambridge University Press.

Cox, Gary W., and Matthew D. MacCubbins. 1993. *Legislative Leviathan: Party Government in the House*. California Series on Social Choice and Political Economy. Berkeley: University of California Press.

CREA (Consorcios Regionales de Experimentación Agrícola). 2014. "Censo 2014." Buenos Aires: Movimiento CREA.

Culpepper, Pepper D. 2010. *Quiet Politics and Business Power: Corporate Control in Europe and Japan*. Cambridge Studies in Comparative Politics. Cambridge: Cambridge University Press.

Daïeff, Lorenzo. 2016. "Social Policies for Social Polities: How Conditional Cash Transfers Are Undermining Traditional Patrons in Northeast Brazil." *Revue Interventions Économiques. Papers in Political Economy*, no. 56 (November).

Dargent, Eduardo, and Gabriela Camacho. 2023. "Two Roads of Neoliberal Reform in Higher Education." In *State and Nation Making in Latin America and Spain: The Neoliberal State and Beyond*, edited by Miguel A. Centeno and Agustin E. Ferraro, 213–44. Cambridge: Cambridge University Press.

Dargent, Eduardo, and Stéphanie Rousseau. 2022. "Choque de Poderes y Degradación Institucional: Cambio de Sistema sin Cambio de Reglas en el Perú (2016–2022)." *Política y Gobierno* 29 (2): 1–28.

De La O, Ana Lorena. 2018. *Crafting Policies to End Poverty in Latin America: The Quiet Transformation*. New York: Cambridge University Press.

De Luca, Miguel, Mark P. Jones, and María Inés Tula. 2002. "Back Rooms or Ballot Boxes?: Candidate Nomination in Argentina." *Comparative Political Studies* 35 (4): 413–36.

Del Cogliano, Natalia. 2016. "Después del Conflicto con el Campo en 2008, ¿Los Partidos Abrieron sus Listas a los Dirigentes Agropecuarios? Un Estudio sobre la Coordinación Electoral de Elites Partidarias y Agropecuarias en Argentina." *Desarrollo Económico* 56 (218): 101–30.

Di Tella, Torcuato. 1971. "La Búsqueda de la Fórmula Política Argentina." *Desarrollo Económico* 11 (42/44): 317–25.

DIAP. 2010. "Radiografia do Novo Congresso. Legislatura 2011–2015." *Estudos Políticos*. Brasília: DIAP-Departamento Intersindical de Assessoria Parlamentar.

Diniz, Eli, and Renato Raul Boschi. 2004. *Empresários, Interesses e Mercado: Dilemas do Desenvolvimento no Brasil*. Humanitas 110. Belo Horizonte: Rio de Janeiro: Editora UFMG; IUPERJ.

Dixit, Avinash, Gene M. Grossman, and Elhanan Helpman. 1997. "Common Agency and Coordination: General Theory and Application to Government Policy Making." *Journal of Political Economy* 105 (4): 752–69.

Dourojeanni, Axel, and Andrei Jouravlev. 1999. "*El Código de Aguas de Chile: Entre la Ideología y la Realidad.*" Santiago de Chile: CEPAL.

Dreifuss, René Armand. 1989. *O Jogo da Direita*. Petrópolis: Vozes.

Duverger, Maurice. 1964. *Political Parties. Their Organization and Activity in the Modern State*. New York: John Wiley & Sons, Inc.
Esquerdo, Vanilde, and Sonia Bergamasco. 2013. "Balanço sobre a Reforma Agrária Brasileira nas Duas Últimas Décadas." *Interciencia* 38 (8): 563–69.
Ezquerro-Cañete, Arturo, and Ramón Fogel. 2017. "A Coup Foretold: Fernando Lugo and the Lost Promise of Land reform in Paraguay." *Journal of Agrarian Change* 17 (2): 279–95.
Fair, Hernán. 2017. "Las Principales Entidades Agropecuarias de la Argentina en la Etapa Previa al Orden Neoliberal. Posicionamientos Políticos, Disputas en Torno al Modelo Económico y Social y Eficacia Interpelativa." *Mundo Agrario* 18 (37): 1–22.
Fairfield, Tasha. 2011. "Business Power and Protest: Argentina's Agricultural Producers Protest in Comparative Context." *Studies in Comparative International Development* 46 (4): 424–53.
  2015a. *Private Wealth and Public Revenue in Latin America: Business Power and Tax Politics*. New York: Cambridge University Press.
  2015b. "Structural Power in Comparative Political Economy: Perspectives from Policy Formulation in Latin America." *Business and Politics* 17 (03): 411–41.
Farrer, Benjamin. 2018. *Organizing for Policy Influence: Comparing Parties, Interest Groups, and Direct Action*. New York: Routledge.
Fearnside, Philip M. 2001. "Soybean Cultivation as a Threat to the Environment in Brazil." *Environmental Conservation* 28 (1): 23–38.
Fernández Milmanda, Belén. 2023. "Harvesting Influence: Agrarian Elites and Democracy in Brazil." *Politics & Society* 51 (1), 135–61.
Fernández Milmanda, Belén, and Candelaria Garay. 2019. "Subnational Variation in Forest Protection in the Argentine Chaco." *World Development* 118 (June): 79–90.
  2020. "The Multilevel Politics of Enforcement: Environmental Institutions in Argentina." *Politics & Society* 48 (1): 3–26.
Figueiredo, Argelina, and Fernando Limongi. 2007. "Instituições Políticas e Governabilidade: Desempenho do Governo e Apoio Legislativo na Democracia Brasileira." In *A Democracia Brasileira: Balanço e Perspectivas para o Século 21*, edited by Carlos Ranulfo Melo and Manuel Alcántara Saez, 147–98. Belo Horizonte: Editora UFMG.
Fleischer, David. 1980. "A Evolução do Bipartidismo Brasileiro 1966–1979." *Revista Brasileira de Estudios Politicos* 51 (2): 155–85.
  1988. "Perfil Sócio-Econômico e Político da Constituinte." O Processo Constituinte 1987–1988. Documentação Fotográfica [Sobre] a Nova Constituição.
Freston, Paul. 2001. *Evangelicals and Politics in Asia, Africa, and Latin America*. Cambridge and New York: Cambridge University Press.
Freytes, Carlos. 2015. "The Cerrado Is Not the Pampas: Explaining Tax and Regulatory Policies on Agricultural Exports in Argentina and Brazil (2003–2013)." Ph.D. Dissertation, Evanston, IL: Northwestern University.
Fried, Brian J. 2012. "Distributive Politics and Conditional Cash Transfers: The Case of Brazil's Bolsa Família." *World Development* 40 (5): 1042–53.

Frieden, Jeffry. 1991. *Debt, Development, and Democracy: Modern Political Economy and Latin America, 1965–1985*. Princeton, NJ: Princeton University Press.
    1999. "Actors and Preferences in International Relations." In *Strategic Choice and International Relations*, edited by David A. Lake and Robert Powell, 39–76. Princeton, NJ: Princeton University Press.
Gallagher, Michael. 2018. "Election Indices Dataset." 2018. www.tcd.ie/Political_Science/people/michael_gallagher/ElSystems/index.php.
Garretón, Manuel A. 1987. *Reconstruir la Política: Transición y Consolidación Democrática en Chile*. Santiago de Chile: Editorial Andante.
    2003. *Incomplete Democracy: Political Democratization in Chile and Latin America*. Latin America in Translation / En Traducción / Em Tradução. Chapel Hill, NC: University of North Carolina Press.
Garrido, José, Cristian Guerrero, and María Soledad Valdés. 1988. *Historia de la Reforma Agraria en Chile*. Santiago de Chile: Editorial Universitaria.
Gatto, Malu A. C., and Timothy J. Power. 2016. "Postmaterialism and Political Elites: The Value Priorities of Brazilian Federal Legislators." *Journal of Politics in Latin America* 8 (1): 33–68.
Gehlbach, Scott, Konstantin Sonin, and Ekaterina Zhuravskaya. 2010. "Businessman Candidates." *American Journal of Political Science* 54 (3): 718–36.
George, Alexander L., and Andrew Bennett. 2005. *Case Studies and Theory Development in the Social Sciences*. BCSIA Studies in International Security. Cambridge, MA: MIT Press.
Gerschenkron, Alexander. 1943. *Bread and Democracy in Germany*. Cornell Paperbacks. Ithaca, NY: Cornell University Press.
Gibson, Edward L. 1992. "Conservative Electoral Movements and Democratic Politics: Core Constituencies, Coalition Building, and the Latin American Electoral Right." In *The Right and Democracy in Latin America*, edited by Douglas Chalmers, Maria do Carmo Campello de Sousa, and Atilio Borón, 13–42. New York: Praeger.
    1996. *Class and Conservative Parties: Argentina in Comparative Perspective*. Baltimore, MD: Johns Hopkins University Press.
    1997. "The Populist Road to Market Reform: Policy and Electoral Coalitions in Mexico and Argentina." *World Politics* 49 (3): 339–70.
Giraudy, María Eugenia. 2015. "Conservative Popular Appeals: The Electoral Strategies of Latin America's Right Parties." Ph.D. Dissertation, Berkeley, CA: University of California.
Gonçalves Costa, Sandra. 2012. "A Questão Agrária no Brazil e a Bancada Ruralista no Congresso Nacional." M.A. Dissertation, São Paulo: Universidade de São Paulo.
Gras, Carla. 2012a. "Elites Rurales Contemporáneas: Cambio Tecnológico, Liderazgo Empresarial y Acción Política en la Argentina Sojera." In *Democracia y Reconfiguraciones Contemporáneas del Derecho en América Latina*, 342–68. Madrid: Editorial Biblioteca Iberoamericana Vervuert.
    2012b. "Empresarios Rurales y Acción Política en Argentina." *Estudios Sociológicos* 30 (89): 459–87.

Grinberg, Lucia. 2009. *Partido Político ou Bode Expiatório: Um Estudo sobre a Aliança Renovadora Nacional, ARENA (1965–1979)*. Rio de Janeiro: FAPERJ: Mauad X.

Gross, Daniel R. 1973. "Factionalism and Local Level Politics in Rural Brazil." *Journal of Anthropological Research* 29 (2): 123–44.

Grossman, Gene M., and Elhanan Helpman. 2001. *Special Interest Politics*. Cambridge, MA: MIT Press.

Grzymała-Busse, Anna Maria. 2015. *Nations under God: How Churches Use Moral Authority to Influence Policy*. Princeton, NJ: Princeton University Press.

Güereña, Arantxa, and Luis Rojas Villagra. 2016. "*Ivy Jára. Los Dueños de la Tierra En Paraguay*." Asunción: Oxfam.

Hacker, Jacob, and Paul Pierson. 2002. "Business Power and Social Policy: Employers and the Formation of the American Welfare State." *Politics & Society* 30 (2): 277–325.

Haggard, Stephan, and Robert R. Kaufman. 1995. *The Political Economy of Democratic Transitions*. Princeton, NJ: Princeton University Press.

Hagopian, Frances. 1990. "Democracy by Undemocratic Means?: Elites, Political Pacts, and Regime Transition in Brazil." *Comparative Political Studies* 23 (2): 147–70.

  1996. *Traditional Politics and Regime Change in Brazil*. Cambridge Studies in Comparative Politics. Cambridge and New York: Cambridge University Press.

Hagopian, Frances, and Scott Mainwaring. 2005. *The Third Wave of Democratization in Latin America: Advances and Setbacks*. Cambridge: Cambridge University Press.

Hale, Henry E. 2006. *Why Not Parties in Russia? Democracy, Federalism, and the State*. Cambridge and New York: Cambridge University Press.

Hall, Richard L. 1998. *Participation in Congress*. London: Yale University Press.

Hammond, Susan Webb. 2001. *Congressional Caucuses in National Policy Making*. Baltimore, MD: Johns Hopkins University Press.

Hansen, John Mark. 1991. *Gaining Access: Congress and the Farm Lobby, 1919–1981: American Politics and Political Economy Series*. Chicago, IL: University of Chicago Press.

Heaney, Michael T. 2010. "Linking Political Parties and Interest Groups." In *The Oxford Handbook of American Political Parties and Interest Groups*, edited by Sandy Maisel, Jeffrey Berry, and George Edwards III, 568–88. Oxford: Oxford University Press.

Helfand, Steven M. 1999. "The Political Economy of Agricultural Policy in Brazil: Decision Making and Influence from 1964 to 1992." *Latin American Research Review* 34 (2): 3–41.

Hernandez, Valeria A. 2007. "El Fenómeno Económico y Cultural del Boom de la Soja y el Empresariado Innovador." *Desarrollo Económico* 47 (187): 331–65.

Hicken, Allen. 2009. *Building Party Systems in Developing Democracies*. Cambridge and New York: Cambridge University Press.

Hicken, Allen, and Erik Martinez Kuhonta, eds. 2015. *Party System Institutionalization in Asia: Democracies, Autocracies, and the Shadows of the Past*. New York: Cambridge University Press.

Hidalgo, Martin. 2023. *¿Cuándo Se Jodió el Congreso?* Lima: Planeta.
Hora, Roy. 2002. *Los Terratenientes de la Pampa Argentina: Una Historia Social y Política, 1860–1945.* 1. ed. Argentina. Colección Historia y Política 3. Buenos Aires: Siglo Veintiuno de Argentina Editores.
   2009. *Los Estancieros Contra el Estado: La Liga Agraria y la Formación del Ruralismo Político en la Argentina.* Historia y Cultura. Buenos Aires: Siglo Veintiuno Editores.
   2010. "La Crisis del Campo del Otoño de 2008." *Desarrollo Económico* 50 (197): 81–111.
   2012. "La Evolución del Sector Agroexportador Argentino en el Largo Plazo, 1880–2010." *Historia Agraria* 58 (December): 145–81.
   2018. *¿Cómo Pensaron el Campo los Argentinos?* Buenos Aires: Siglo Veintiuno Editores.
Huntington, Samuel P. 1968. *Political Order in Changing Societies.* New Heaven, CT, and London: Yale University Press.
IBGE (Instituto Brasileiro de Geografia e Estatística). 2012. "Censo Agropecuário 2006. Brasil, Grandes Regiões e Unidades da Federação. Segunda Apuração." Rio de Janeiro, RJ.
Imaz, Jose Luis De. 1959. *La Clase Alta de Buenos Aires.* Buenos Aires: Universidad de Buenos Aires.
INDEC (Instituto Nacional de Estadísticas y Censos). 2002. "Censo Nacional Agropecuario." Available at: https://sitioanterior.indec.gob.ar/cna_index.asp.
INE (Instituto Nacional de Estadísticas). 2007. "Cambios Estructurales en la Agricultura Chilena. Análisis Intercensal, 1976-1997-2007." Instituto Nacional de Estadísticas.
INESC. 2007. "Bancada Ruralista: O Maior Grupo de Interesse no Congresso Nacional." 12. Year VII. Instituto de Estudos Socioeconômicos.
Jacobs, Alan M. 2008. "The Politics of When: Redistribution, Investment and Policy Making for the Long Term." *British Journal of Political Science* 38 (2): 193–220.
Jenks, Margaret. 1979. "Political Parties in Authoritarian Brazil." Ph.D. Dissertation, Durham, SC: Duke University.
Johnson, Kenneth. 1993. "Between Revolution and Democracy: Business Elites and the State in El Salvador during the 1980s." Ph.D. Dissertation, New Orleans, LA: Tulane University.
Jones, Mark P. 2008. "The Recruitment and Selection of Legislative Candidates in Argentina." In *Pathways to Power. Political Recruitment and Candidate Selection in Latin America*, edited by Peter M. Siavelis and Scott Morgenstern, 41–75. University Park: Pennsylvania State University Press.
Kahneman, Daniel, Paul Slovic, and Amos Tversky, eds. 1982. *Judgment under Uncertainty: Heuristics and Biases.* Cambridge and New York: Cambridge University Press.
Kalyvas, Stathis N. 1996. *The Rise of Christian Democracy in Europe.* The Wilder House Series in Politics, History, and Culture. Ithaca, NY: Cornell University Press.
   1998. "From Pulpit to Party: Party Formation and the Christian Democratic Phenomenon." *Comparative Politics* 30 (3): 293.

Kinzo, Maria D'Alva G. 1988. *Legal Opposition Politics under Authoritarian Rule in Brazil: The Case of the MDB, 1966–79*. St Antony's / Macmillan Series. Houndmills: Macmillan in association with St Antony's College, Oxford.

Klašnja, Marko, and Rocío Titiunik. 2017. "The Incumbency Curse: Weak Parties, Term Limits, and Unfulfilled Accountability." *American Political Science Review* 111 (01): 129–48.

Koivumaeki, Ritta-Ilona. 2010. "Business, Economic Experts, and Conservative Party Building in Latin America: The Case of El Salvador." *Journal of Politics in Latin America* 2 (1): 79–106.

Kurtz, Marcus J. 1999. "Free Markets and Democratic Consolidation in Chile: The National Politics of Rural Transformation." *Politics & Society* 27 (2): 275–301.

  2006. *Free Market Democracy and the Chilean and Mexican Countryside*. Cambridge: Cambridge University Press.

  2013. *Latin American State Building in Comparative Perspective: Social Foundations of Institutional Order*. New York: Cambridge University Press.

Lapp, Nancy D. 2004. *Landing Votes*. New York: Palgrave Macmillan US.

Lattuada, Mario J. 1986. *La Política Agraria Peronista (1943–1983)/2*. Buenos Aires: Centro Editor de América Latina.

  1988. *Política Agraria y Partidos Políticos (1946–1983)*. Biblioteca Política Argentina 233. Buenos Aires: Centro Editor de América Latina.

  1992. "Notas sobre Corporaciones Agropecuarias y Estado." *Estudios Sociales* 2: 123–48.

  2006. *Acción Colectiva y Corporaciones Agrarias en la Argentina: Transformaciones Institucionales a Fines Del Siglo XX*. Colección Convergencia. Bernal, Buenos Aires: Universidad Nacional de Quilmes Editorial.

Leal, Victor Nunes. 1948. *Coronelismo, Enxada e Voto. O Município e o Regimen Representativo no Brasil*. Rio de Janeiro: Companhia Das Letras.

Levitsky, Steven. 2018. "Peru: The Institutionalization of Politics without Parties." In *Party Systems in Latin America: Institutionalization, Decay, and Collapse*, edited by Scott Mainwaring, 1st ed., 326–55. Cambridge: Cambridge University Press.

Levitsky, Steven, James Loxton, and Brandon Van Dyck. 2016. "Introduction: Challenges of Party-Building in Latin America." In *Challenges of Party-Building in Latin America*, edited by Steven Levitsky, James Loxton, Brandon Van Dyck, and Jorge Dominguez, 1–35. New York: Cambridge University Press.

Levitsky, Steven, and Kenneth M. Roberts, eds. 2011. *The Resurgence of the Latin American Left*. Baltimore, MD: Johns Hopkins University Press.

Lijphart, Arend. 1999. *Patterns of Democracy: Government Forms and Performance in Thirty-Six Countries*. New Haven: Yale University Press.

Lindblom, Charles Edward. 1977. *Politics and Markets: The World's Political Economic Systems*. New York: Basic Books.

Linz, Juan. 1976. "Some Notes towards a Comparative Study of Fascism in Sociological Historical Perspective." In *Fascism: A Reader's Guide*, edited by Walter Laqueur, 3: 121. Berkeley and Los Angeles: University of California Press.

Lissin, Lautaro. 2010. *Federación Agraria Hoy: El Campo Argentino en Discusión*. Claves Para Todos. Buenos Aires: Capital Intelectual.

Losada, Leandro. 2009. *Historia de las Elites en la Argentina: Desde la Conquista hasta el Surgimiento del Peronismo*. Colección Historia Argentina. Buenos Aires: Editorial Sudamericana.

Love, Joseph L. 1970. "Political Participation in Brazil, 1881–1969." *Luso-Brazilian Review* 7 (2): 3–24.

Loveman, Brian. 1976. *Struggle in the Countryside; Politics and Rural Labor in Chile, 1919–1973*. International Development Research Center. Studies in Development, No. 10. Bloomington: Indiana University Press.

Loxton, James. 2021. *Conservative Party-Building in Latin America: Authoritarian Inheritance and Counterrevolutionary Struggle*. New York: Oxford University Press.

Luna, Juan Pablo. 2014. *Segmented Representation: Political Party Strategies in Unequal Democracies*. 1st ed. Oxford Studies in Democratization. Oxford: Oxford University Press.

Luna, Juan Pablo, and Cristóbal Rovira Kaltwasser, eds. 2014. *The Resilience of the Latin American Right*. Baltimore, MD: Johns Hopkins University Press.

Luna, Juan Pablo, Rafael Piñeiro Rodríguez, Fernando Rosenblatt, and Gabriel Vommaro, eds. 2021. *Diminished Parties: Democratic Representation in Contemporary Latin America*. Cambridge: Cambridge University Press.

Lupu, Noam. 2017. *Party Brands in Crisis: Partisanship, Brand Dilution, and the Breakdown of Political Parties in Latin America*. New York: Cambridge University Press.

Lustig, Nora. 2015. "Most Unequal on Earth." *Finance and Development* 52 (3): 14–16.

Lynch, Edward A. 1993. *Latin America's Christian Democratic Parties: A Political Economy*. Westport, CT: Praeger.

Madariaga, Aldo, Antoine Maillet, and Joaquín Rozas. 2021. "Multilevel Business Power in Environmental Politics: The Avocado Boom and Water Scarcity in Chile." *Environmental Politics* 30 (7): 1174–95.

Mahoney, James. 2002. *Legacies of Liberalism: Path Dependence and Political Regimes in Central America*. Baltimore, MD: Johns Hopkins University Press.

Mainwaring, Scott. 1999. *Rethinking Party Systems in the Third Wave of Democratization: The Case of Brazil*. Stanford, CA: Stanford University Press.

ed. 2018. *Party Systems in Latin America: Institutionalization, Decay, and Collapse*. New York: Cambridge University Press.

Mainwaring, Scott, and Matthew Soberg Shugart, eds. 2003. *Presidentialism and Democracy in Latin America*. Cambridge Studies in Comparative Politics. Cambridge: Cambridge University Press.

Mainwaring, Scott, and Edurne Zoco. 2007. "Political Sequences and the Stabilization of Interparty Competition: Electoral Volatility in Old and New Democracies." *Party Politics* 13 (2): 155–78.

Mainwaring, Scott, Rachel Meneguello, and Timothy J. Power. 2000. "Conservative Parties, Democracy, and Economic Reform in Contemporary Brazil." In *Conservative Parties, the Right, and Democracy in Latin*

America, edited by Kevin J. Middlebrook, 164–222. Baltimore, MD: Johns Hopkins University Press.

Mancuso, Wagner Pralon. 2004. "The Industrial Lobby in Congress: Business Leaders and Politics in Contemporary Brazil." *Dados* 47 (3): 505–47.

Mangonnet, Jorge, María Victoria Murillo, and Julia María Rubio. 2018. "Local Economic Voting and the Agricultural Boom in Argentina, 2007–2015." *Latin American Politics and Society*, May, 1–27.

Manzetti, Luigi. 1992. "The Evolution of Agricultural Interest Groups in Argentina." *Journal of Latin American Studies* 24 (3): 585–616.

Marcel, Mario. 1997. "Políticas Públicas en Democracia: El Caso de la Reforma Tributaria de 1990 en Chile." *Colección de Estudios CIEPLAN* 45 (June): 33–83.

Martínez-Lara, Javier. 1996. *Building Democracy in Brazil: The Politics of Constitutional Change, 1985–95*. Basingstoke: Macmillan.

McCarty, Nolan, and Lawrence S. Rothenberg. 1996. "Commitment and the Campaign Contribution Contract." *American Journal of Political Science* 40 (3): 872.

McGuire, James. 1995. "Political Parties and Democracy in Argentina." In *Building Democratic Institutions*, edited by Scott Mainwaring and Timothy R. Scully, 200–46. Stanford, CA: Stanford University Press.

McKay, Ben, and Gonzalo Colque. 2016. "Bolivia's Soy Complex: The Development of 'Productive Exclusion.'" *The Journal of Peasant Studies* 43 (2): 583–610.

Middlebrook, Kevin J. 2000. "Introduction: Conservative Parties, Elite Representation, and Democracy in Latin America." In *Conservative Parties, the Right, and Democracy in Latin America*, edited by Kevin J. Middlebrook, 1–50. Baltimore, MD: Johns Hopkins University Press.

Montero, Alfred P. 2012. "A Reversal of Political Fortune: The Transitional Dynamics of Conservative Rule in the Brazilian Northeast." *Latin American Politics and Society* 54 (1): 1–36.

Moore, Barrington. 1966. *Social Origins of Dictatorship and Democracy: Lord and Peasant in the Making of the Modern World*. Boston, MA: Beacon Press.

Morresi, Sergio. 2015. "'Acá Somos Todos Democráticos' El PRO y las Relaciones entre la Derecha y la Democracia en Argentina." In *"Hagamos Equipo": PRO y la Construcción de la Nueva Derecha en Argentina*, edited by Gabriel Vommaro and Sergio Morresi, 163–202. Los Polvorines: Universidad Nacional de General Sarmiento.

Murillo, María Victoria, and Pablo M. Pinto. 2022. "Heeding to the Losers: Legislators' Trade-Policy Preferences and Legislative Behavior." *Legislative Studies Quarterly* 47 (3): 539–603.

Navia, Patricio. 2002. "You Select the Rules of the Game and Lose? Advantages and Constraints When Choosing Electoral Rules: The Case of Chile." Ph.D. Dissertation, New York: New York University.

Navia, Patricio, and Ricardo Godoy. 2014. "The Alianza's Quest to Win Power Democratically." In *Democratic Chile: The Politics and Policies of a Historic Coalition, 1990–2010*, edited by Kirsten Sehnbruch and Peter Siavelis, 43–68. Boulder, CO: Lynne Rienner Publishers, Inc.

Nin-Pratt, Alejandro, César Falconi, Carlos E. Ludeña and Pedro Martel. 2015. "Productivity and the performance of agriculture in Latin America and the Caribbean: from the lost decade to the commodity boom." Inter-American Development Bank Working Paper No. 608 (IDB-WP-608), Washington DC.

North, Douglass C. 1990. *Institutions, Institutional Change, and Economic Performance. The Political Economy of Institutions and Decisions.* Cambridge and New York: Cambridge University Press.

Nun, José, and Mario J. Lattuada. 1991. *El Gobierno de Alfonsín y las Corporaciones Agrarias.* Colección "Sentido Común y Política." Buenos Aires: Manantial.

ODEPA, (Oficina de Estudios y Políticas Agrarias). 2007. "Nuevo Escáner al Campo Chileno: VII Censo Nacional Agropecuario y Forestal 2007." INE-Odepa. Available at: https://hdl.handle.net/20.500.12650/3206.

2021. "Catastro Frutícola. Principales Resultados. Región de O'Higgins."

O'Donnell, Guillermo A. 1988. *Bureaucratic Authoritarianism: Argentina, 1966–1973, in Comparative Perspective.* Berkeley: University of California Press.

O'Donnell, Guillermo A., and Philippe C. Schmitter. 1986. *Transitions from Authoritarian Rule: Tentative Conclusions about Uncertain Democracies.* Baltimore, MD: Johns Hopkins University Press.

Ondetti, Gabriel A. 2007. "An Ambivalent Legacy: Cardoso and Land Reform." *Latin American Perspectives* 34 (5): 9–25.

2008. *Land, Protest, and Politics: The Landless Movement and the Struggle for Land reform in Brazil.* University Park: Pennsylvania State University Press.

2016. "The Social Function of Property, Land Rights and Social Welfare in Brazil." *Land Use Policy* 50 (January): 29–37.

2021. *Property Threats and the Politics of Anti-statism the Historical Roots of Contemporary Tax Systems in Latin America.* New York: Cambridge University Press.

Ortega, Bibiana. 2018. "Political Participation of Evangelicals in Colombia 1990–2017." *Politics and Religion Journal* 12 (1): 17–54.

Oxhorn, Philip. 1995. *Organizing Civil Society: The Popular Sectors and the Struggle for Democracy in Chile.* University Park : Pennsylvania State University Press.

Paige, Jeffery M. 1999. *Coffee and Power: Revolution and the Rise of Democracy in Central America.* Cambridge, MA: Harvard University Press.

Paiva, Denise Ferreira. 2002. *PFL x PMDB: Marchas e Contramarchas (1982–2000).* Goiania: Editora Alternativa.

Palomino, Mirta L. de. 1987. "Las Organizaciones Empresarias Ante el Gobierno Constitucional. Las Entidades Agropecuarias." In *Ensayos sobre la Transición Democrática en la Argentina,* edited by José Nun and Juan Carlos Portantiero, 195–224. Buenos Aires: Puntosur Editores.

1988. *Tradición y Poder: La Sociedad Rural Argentina, 1955–1983.* Buenos Aires: CISEA: Grupo Editor Latinoamericano.

Panebianco, Angelo. 1988. *Political Parties: Organization and Power.* Cambridge Studies in Modern Political Economies. Cambridge and New York: Cambridge University Press.

Pastor, Daniel. 2004. "Origins of the Chilean Binominal Election System." *Revista de Ciencia Política* 24: 38–57.

Paulet Piedra, Nicole. 2013. "Legislative Hurdles to Land Reform: The Role of the Bancada Ruralista in the Brazilian Chamber of Deputies, 1995–2006." Senior Thesis, Cambridge, MA.: Harvard University.

Payne, Leigh A. 2000. *Uncivil Movements: The Armed Right Wing and Democracy in Latin America*. Baltimore, MD: Johns Hopkins University Press.

Pereira, Amanda Maria Campanini. 2013. "A Lógica da Ação na Reforma do Código Florestal." M.A. Dissertation, São Paulo: Universidade de São Paulo.

Pereira, Anthony. 2003. "Brazil's Land reform: Democratic Innovation or Oligarchic Exclusion Redux?" *Latin American Politics and Society* 45 (2): 41–65.

Pérez Guadalupe, José Luis, and Sebastian Grundberger, eds. 2018. *Evangélicos y Poder en América Latina*. Lima: Konrad Adenauer Stiftung / Instituto de Estudios Social Cristianos.

Pérez-Liñán, Aníbal. 2014. "A Two-Level Theory of Presidential Instability." *Latin American Politics and Society* 56 (01): 34–54.

Pierson, Paul. 2000. "Increasing Returns, Path Dependence, and the Study of Politics." *American Political Science Review* 94 (02): 251–67.

   2004. *Politics in Time: History, Institutions, and Social Analysis*. Princeton, NJ: Princeton University Press.

Pion-Berlin, David, ed. 2001. *Civil-Military Relations in Latin America: New Analytical Perspectives*. Chapel Hill: University of North Carolina Press.

Pizarro, Crisóstomo. 1995. "La Primera Reforma Tributaria durante el Gobierno de Transición: Concertación y Debate." In *Políticas Económicas y Sociales en el Chile Democrático*, edited by Joaquín Vial, Dagmar Raczynski, and Crisóstomo Pizarro, 93–128. Santiago de Chile: CIEPLAN – UNICEF.

Pollack, Marcelo. 1999. *The New Right in Chile 1973–97*. St Antony's Series. Basingstoke: Macmillan.

Power, Timothy J. 2000. *The Political Right in Postauthoritarian Brazil: Elites, Institutions, and Democratization*. University Park: Pennsylvania State University Press.

   2010. "Optimism, Pessimism, and Coalitional Presidentialism: Debating the Institutional Design of Brazilian Democracy." *Bulletin of Latin American Research* 29 (1): 18–33.

   2018. "The Contrasting Trajectories of Brazil's Two Authoritarian Successor Parties." In *Life After Dictatorship: Authoritarian Successor Parties Worldwide*, edited by James Loxton and Scott Mainwaring, 229–53. New York: Cambridge University Press.

Power, Timothy J., and Rodrigo Rodrigues-Silveira. 2019. "The Political Right and Party Politics." In *Routledge Handbook of Brazilian Politics*, edited by Barry Ames, 251–68. New York: Routledge.

Rasmusen, Eric. 2007. *Games and Information: An Introduction to Game Theory*. 4th ed. Malden, MA, and Oxford: Blackwell Publishing.

Rehren, Alfredo. 1995. "Empresarios, Transición y Consolidación Democrática en Chile." *Revista Chilena de Ciencia Política* 17 (1/2): 5–61.

Remmer, Karen L. 1984. *Party Competition in Argentina and Chile: Political Recruitment and Public Policy, 1890–1930*. Lincoln: University of Nebraska Press.

Ribeiro, Vanderlei Vazelesk. 2008. *Cuestiones Agrarias en el Varguismo y el Peronismo: Una Mirada Histórica*. Colección Convergencia. Entre Memoria y Sociedad. Bernal, Buenos Aires: Universidad Nacional de Quilmes Editorial.

Richardson, Neal. 2012. "The Politics of Abundance: Export Agriculture and Redistributive Conflict in South America." Ph.D. Dissertation, Berkeley, CA: University of California, Berkeley.

Riedl, Rachel Beatty, Dan Slater, Joseph Wong, and Daniel Ziblatt. 2020. "Authoritarian-Led Democratization." *Annual Review of Political Science* 23 (1): 315–32.

Ringe, Nils, and Jennifer Nicoll Victor. 2013. *Bridging the Information Gap: Legislative Member Organizations as Social Networks in the United States and the European Union*. Ann Arbor: University of Michigan Press.

Roberts, J. Timmons, and Nikki Demetria Thanos. 2003. *Trouble in Paradise: Globalization and Environmental Crises in Latin America*. New York: Routledge.

Roberts, Kenneth. 1998. *Deepening Democracy? The Modern Left and Social Movements in Chile and Peru*. Stanford, CA: Stanford University Press.

  2002. "Party–Society Linkages and Democratic Representation in Latin America." *Canadian Journal of Latin American and Caribbean Studies* 27 (53): 9–34.

  2014. "Democracy, Free Markets and the Rightist Dilemma in Latin America." In *The Resilience of the Latin American Right*, edited by Juan Pablo Luna and Cristóbal Rovira Kaltwasser, 25–47. Baltimore, MD: Johns Hopkins University Press.

Robins, Nicholas A., and Barbara J. Fraser. 2020. *Landscapes of Inequity: Environmental Justice in the Andes-Amazon Region*. Lincoln, NE: University of Nebraska Press.

Robles, Wilder. 2018. "Revisiting Land reform in Brazil, 1985–2016." *Journal of Developing Societies* 34 (1): 1–34.

Robles, Wilder, and Henry Veltmeyer. 2015. *The Politics of Land Reform in Brazil*. New York: Palgrave Macmillan US.

Rojas, Priscilla, and Patricio Navia. 2005. "Representación y Tamaño de los Distritos Electorales en Chile, 1988–2002." *Revista de Ciencia Política* 25 (2): 91–116.

Romero Pizarro, Sergio. 2015. *Una Mirada a Chile: Al Rescate de los Valores Republicanos*. Santiago de Chile: Aguilar Chilena de Ediciones.

Rosenblatt, Fernando. 2018. *Party Vibrancy and Democracy in Latin America*. New York: Oxford University Press.

Rothkopf, David J. 2009. *Superclass: The Global Power Elite and the World They Are Making*. New York: Farrar, Straus and Giroux.

Rueschemeyer, Dietrich, Evelyne Huber, and John D. Stephens. 1992. *Capitalist Development and Democracy*. Chicago, IL: University of Chicago Press.

Salto, Dante, and Daniel Levy. 2021. "La Educación Superior con Fines de Lucro en América Latina: ¿Excepción o Precursora?" *International Higher Education* 108: 34–36.
Samuels, David. 2003. *Ambition, Federalism, and Legislative Politics in Brazil.* Cambridge: Cambridge University Press.
Samuels, David and Matthew Soberg Shugart. 2003. "Presidentialism, Elections and Representation." *Journal of Theoretical Politics* 15 (1): 33–60.
Sauer, Sérgio. 2019. "Rural Brazil during the Lula Administrations: Agreements with Agribusiness and Disputes in Agrarian Policies." *Latin American Perspectives* 46 (4): 103–21.
Sauer, Sérgio, and George Mészáros. 2017. "The Political Economy of Land Struggle in Brazil under Workers' Party Governments." *Journal of Agrarian Change* 17 (2): 397–414.
Schneider, Ben Ross. 1997. "Organized Business Politics in Democratic Brazil." *Journal of Interamerican Studies and World Affairs* 39 (4): 95–127.
  2004. *Business Politics and the State in Twentieth-Century Latin America.* Cambridge; New York: Cambridge University Press.
  2010. "Business Politics in Latin America: Patterns of Fragmentation and Centralization." In *The Oxford Handbook of Business and Government*, edited by David Coen, Wyn Grant, and Graham Wilson, 307–29. Oxford: Oxford University Press.
  2013. *Hierarchical Capitalism in Latin America: Business, Labor, and the Challenges of Equitable Development.* Cambridge: Cambridge University Press.
Scully, Timothy. 1992. *Rethinking the Center: Party Politics in Nineteenth- and Twentieth-Century Chile.* Stanford, CA: Stanford University Press.
Siavelis, Peter. 1997. "Continuity and Change in the Chilean Party System: On the Transformational Effects of Electoral Reform." *Comparative Political Studies* 30 (6): 651–74.
  2002. "The Hidden Logic of Candidate Selection for Chilean Parliamentary Elections." *Comparative Politics* 34 (4): 419.
Silva, Eduardo. 1998. "Organized Business, Neoliberal Economic Restructuring, and Democratization in Chile." In *Organized Business, Economic Change, and Democracy in Latin America*, edited by Francisco Durand and Eduardo Silva, 217–52. Coral Gables, FL: North-South Center Press.
Silva, Patricio. 1987. *Estado, Neoliberalismo y Política Agraria en Chile 1973–1981.* Amsterdam: CEDLA / FORIS Publications.
  1992. "Landowners and the State: From Confrontation to Cooperation?" In *Development and Social Change in the Chilean Countryside: From the Pre-Land Reform Period to the Democratic Transition*, edited by Cristóbal Kay and Patricio Silva, 275–88. Amsterdam: CEDLA.
Slater, Dan. 2010. *Ordering Power: Contentious Politics and Authoritarian Leviathans in Southeast Asia.* Cambridge Studies in Comparative Politics. Cambridge: Cambridge University Press.
Slater, Dan, and Erica Simmons. 2010. "Informative Regress: Critical Antecedents in Comparative Politics." *Comparative Political Studies* 43 (7): 886–917.
Slater, Dan, and Joseph Wong. 2013. "The Strength to Concede: Ruling Parties and Democratization in Developmental Asia." *Perspectives on Politics* 11 (3): 717–33.

Slater, Dan, and Daniel Ziblatt. 2013. "The Enduring Indispensability of the Controlled Comparison." *Comparative Political Studies* 46 (10): 1301–27.

Smith, Mark A. 2000. *American Business and Political Power: Public Opinion, Elections, and Democracy*. Studies in Communication, Media, and Public Opinion. Chicago, IL: University of Chicago Press.

Smith, Peter. 1969. *Politics and Beef in Argentina. Patterns of Conflict and Change*. New York: Columbia University Press.

    1978. "The Breakdown of Democracy in Argentina." In *The Breakdown of Democratic Regimes: Latin America*, 3–27. Baltimore, MD: Johns Hopkins University Press.

Snyder, Richard, and David Samuels. 2004. "Legislative Malapportionment in Latin America." In *Federalism and Democracy*, edited by Edward L. Gibson, 131–72. Baltimore, MD: Johns Hopkins University Press.

Stabili, María Rosaria. 2003. *El Sentimiento Aristocrático: Elites Chilenas frente al Espejo (1860–1960)*. Santiago de Chile: Ed. Andrés Bello.

Sugiyama, Natasha Borges, and Wendy Hunter. 2013. "Whither Clientelism?: Good Governance and Brazil's Bolsa Família Program." *Comparative Politics* 46 (1): 43–62.

Svampa, Maristella. 2019. *Neo-extractivism in Latin America: Socio-environmental Conflicts, the Territorial Turn, and New Political Narratives*. Cambridge Elements. Elements in Politics and Society in Latin America. Cambridge: Cambridge University Press.

Szakonyi, David. 2018. "Businesspeople in Elected Office: Identifying Private Benefits from Firm-Level Returns." *American Political Science Review* 112 (02): 322–38.

    2020. *Politics for Profit: Business, Elections, and Policymaking in Russia*. New York: Cambridge University Press.

Taagepera, Rein, and Matthew Soberg Shugart. 1991. *Seats and Votes: The Effects and Determinants of Electoral Systems*. New Haven, CT: Yale University Press.

Tamayo Grez, Tania, and Alejandra Carmona López. 2019. *El Negocio del Agua: Cómo Chile se Convirtió en Tierra Seca*. Santiago de Chile: B.

Tarrow, Sidney G. 1998. *Power in Movement: Social Movements and Contentious Politics*. 2nd ed. Cambridge Studies in Comparative Politics. Cambridge and New York: Cambridge University Press.

Thachil, Tariq. 2014. *Elite Parties, Poor Voters: How Social Services Win Votes in India*. Cambridge: Cambridge University Press.

Thelen, Kathleen. 2003. "How Institutions Evolve." In *Comparative Historical Analysis in the Social Sciences*, edited by Dietrich Rueschemeyer and James Mahoney, 208–40. Cambridge Studies in Comparative Politics. Cambridge: Cambridge University Press.

Tommasi, Mariano, Sebastián Saiegh, Pablo Sanguinetti, Ernesto Stein, and Mauricio Cárdenas. 2001. "Fiscal Federalism in Argentina: Policies, Politics, and Institutional Reform [with Comments]." *Economía* 1 (2): 157–211.

Turner, Brian. 2014. "Paraguay: La Vuelta del Partido Colorado al Poder." *Revista de Ciencia Política* 34 (1): 249–66.

Valenzuela, Arturo. 1977. *Political Brokers in Chile: Local Government in a Centralized Polity*. Durham, NC: Duke University Press.

1978. *Chile. The Breakdown of Democratic Regimes*. Baltimore, MD: Johns Hopkins University Press.

Valenzuela, J. Samuel, and Timothy R. Scully. 1997. "Electoral Choices and the Party System in Chile: Continuities and Changes at the Recovery of Democracy." *Comparative Politics* 29 (4): 511.

Van Cott, Donna Lee. 2005. *From Movements to Parties in Latin America the Evolution of Ethnic Politics*. Cambridge: Cambridge University Press.

Velasco Montoya, Juan David. 2018. "Colombia: De Minorías Dispersas a Aliados Estratégicos." In *Evangélicos y Poder en América Latina*, edited by José Luis Pérez Guadalupe and Sebastian Grundberger, 221–45. Lima: Konrad Adenauer Stiftung/ Instituto de Estudios Social Cristianos.

Velásquez Carrillo Carlos. 2020. "La Reconsolidación del Régimen Oligárquico en El Salvador: Los Ejes de la Transformación Neoliberal." In *Concentración Económica y Poder Político en América Latina*, edited by Liisa North, Blanca Rubio, Alberto Acosta, and Carlos Pástor, 180–215. CLACSO.

Vergara, Alberto, and María Claudia Augusto. 2021. "Fujimorismo and the Limits of Democratic Representation in Peru, 2006–2020." In *Diminished Parties: Democratic Representation in Contemporary Latin America*, edited by Juan Pablo Luna, Rafael Piñeiro Rodríguez, Fernando Rosenblatt, and Gabriel Vommaro, 236–63. Cambridge University Press.

Vergara-Camus, Leandro, and Cristóbal Kay. 2017a. "Agribusiness, Peasants, Leftwing Governments, and the State in Latin America: An Overview and Theoretical Reflections." *Journal of Agrarian Change* 17 (2): 239–57.

2017b. "The Agrarian Political Economy of Leftwing Governments in Latin America: Agribusiness, Peasants, and the Limits of Neo-Developmentalism." *Journal of Agrarian Change* 17 (2): 415–37.

Vigna, Edélcio. 2001. "Bancada Ruralista: Um Grupo de Interesse." *Argumento* 8 (December): 1–52.

2012. "Análise das Negociações entre a Bancada Ruralista e o Governo Federal nas Votações do Código Florestal." INESC.

Vollrath, Dietrich. 2007. "Land Distribution and International Agricultural Productivity." *American Journal of Agricultural Economics* 89 (1): 202–16.

Vommaro, Gabriel. 2019. "De la Construcción Partidaria al Gobierno: PRO-Cambiemos y los Límites del 'Giro a la Derecha' en Argentina." *Colombia Internacional* 99: 91–120.

2021. "Horizontal Coordination and Vertical Aggregation Mechanisms of the PRO in Argentina and Its Subnational Variations." In *Diminished Parties: Democratic Representation in Contemporary Latin America*, edited by Juan Pablo Luna, Rafael Piñeiro Rodríguez, Fernando Rosenblatt, and Gabriel Vommaro, 1st ed., 48–69. New York: Cambridge University Press.

Vommaro, Gabriel, and Sergio Morresi, eds. 2015. *"Hagamos Equipo": PRO y la Construcción de la Nueva Derecha en Argentina*. Colección Política, Políticas y Sociedad. Los Polvorines: Ediciones UNGS, Universidad Nacional de General Sarmiento.

Weitz-Shapiro, Rebecca. 2012. "What Wins Votes: Why Some Politicians Opt Out of Clientelism." *American Journal of Political Science* 56 (3): 568–83.

Weyland, Kurt Gerhard. 1996. *Democracy without Equity: Failures of Reform in Brazil*. Pitt Latin American Series. Pittsburgh, PA: University of Pittsburgh Press.
  2014. *Making Waves: Democratic Contention in Europe and Latin America since the Revolutions of 1848*. Cambridge and New York: Cambridge University Press.
  2019. *Revolution and Reaction: The Diffusion of Authoritarianism in Latin America*. Cambridge and New York: Cambridge University Press.
Wood, Elisabeth Jean. 2000. *Forging Democracy from Below: Insurgent Transitions in South Africa and El Salvador*. Cambridge Studies in Comparative Politics. Cambridge: Cambridge University Press.
  2001. "An Insurgent Path to Democracy: Popular Mobilization, Economic Interests, and Regime Transition in South Africa and El Salvador." *Comparative Political Studies* 34 (8): 862–88.
Wright, Thomas C. 1981. *Landowners and Reform in Chile: The Sociedad Nacional de Agricultura 1919–1940*. Chicago: University of Illinois Press.
Yashar, Deborah J. 1997. *Demanding Democracy: Reform and Reaction in Costa Rica and Guatemala, 1870s–1950s*. Stanford, CA: Stanford University Press.
Young, Kevin. 2015. "Not by Structure Alone: Power, Prominence, and Agency in American Finance." *Business and Politics* 17 (3): 443–72.
Zamora, Rubén. 1998. *El Salvador, Heridas que No Cierran: Los Partidos Políticos en la Post-Guerra*. San Salvador: FLACSO.
Zeitlin, Maurice, and Richard Earl Ratcliff. 1988. *Landlords & Capitalists: The Dominant Class of Chile*. Princeton, NJ: Princeton University Press.
Ziblatt, Daniel. 2008. "Does Landholding Inequality Block Democratization?: A Test of the 'Bread and Democracy' Thesis and the Case of Prussia." *World Politics* 60 (04): 610–41.
  2017. *Conservative Parties and the Birth of Democracy*. Cambridge Studies in Comparative Politics. Cambridge: Cambridge University Press.
Zucco, Cesar. 2007. "Where's the Bias? A Reassessment of the Chilean Electoral System." *Electoral Studies* 26 (2): 303–14.
  2013. "When Payouts Pay Off: Conditional Cash Transfers and Voting Behavior in Brazil 2002–10." *American Journal of Political Science* 57 (4): 810–22.
Zucco, Cesar, and Timothy J. Power. 2021. "Fragmentation Without Cleavages? Endogenous Fractionalization in the Brazilian Party System." *Comparative Politics* 53 (3): 477–500.

Index

AACREA. *See* Argentine Association of Regional Consortiums of Agricultural Experimentation (AACREA)
Aapresid, 161–62
Abreu, Kátia, 139
Agrarian Caucus, Bancada Ruralista, in Brazil, 1, 95, 108–11, 117–53, 178, 183–85
  agribusiness campaign contributions, 140–44
  analysis of, 153–54
  candidate-centered strategy for, 125–31
    in 1986 election, 125–29
    producers' association and, 125–29
    UDR leaders and, 125–29
  in Constituent Assembly, 135–36
    agenda-setting positions in, 134–36
    bargaining power within 136–39
    land reform threats and, 121–22
    multipartisanship advantages in, 134–39
  contemporary analysis of, 132–39
  of land reform threats, 132–33
  electoral representation and, 118–22
  elites' investment in, 139–47
  Frente Ampla de Agropecuária, 130
  Instituto Pensar Agropecuária, 145–47
  land reform threats, 118–22
    Constituent Assembly response to, 121–22
    contemporary analysis of, 132–33
    political fights against, 129–31
    Movimento Sem Terra and, 118–19

  New Forest Code and, 147–53
    multipartisanship and, 147–48
    roll-call votes for, 149
    Senate amendments to, 151
  party-building and, 122–25
  political fragmentation and, 122–25
  presidential legislative coalitions and, 137
agrarian elites. *See also* electoral strategies, for agrarian elites; political participation, of agrarian elites; *specific countries; specific topics*
  under Allende, 27–28, 70
  in autocracies, 7
  commodity boom and, 10–12
  conceptual approach to, 4–5, 6, 196–99
  democracy and, 211
  in El Salvador, 2, 201–4
  left turn and, 10–12
  literature on, 6–9
  methodological approach to, 13–21
    case selection in, 17
    cross-country comparisons in, 13–18
    data sources in, 18–19
    research design in, 13–18
  in Paraguay, 199–201
  Pinochet support by, 70
  political role of, 2–4
    electoral strategies, 5
    loss of political power, 10–11
    nonelectoral strategies, 5
    redistributive land reform as influence on, 13
  urbanization and, 10–12

Index

Agrarian Federation of Argentina (FAA), 161
agricultural exports. *See* exports, agricultural
agricultural industry, agriculture and, in Latin America. *See also* exports, agricultural; *specific countries*
  evolution of, 11
  mechanization of, 10
  modernization of, 84–85
  peasant unionization law, 75–76, 77
agrodiputados, in Argentina, 63, 170–82
  Barbechando think tank, 182
  candidate-centered strategies for, 182–85
  as political candidates, 178–82
  political capacity of, 63
Alessandri Rodríguez, Jorge Eduardo, 74
Alfonsín, Raúl, 168–69
Allende, Salvador, 27–28, 47, 70
  land reform under, 70–71, 73–74, 76–77, 86, 95
ARENA. *See* Nationalist Republican Alliance (ARENA)
Argentina
  agrarian elites in, 1–2
    before 2008, 164–70
    during 2008 elections, 171–75
    after third wave of democracy, 162–64
    analysis of, 193–95
    campaign financing by, 191–93
    corporatist associations for, 160–62, 187–88
    cross-country comparisons for, 13–18
    electoral organization by, 164–70
    electoral participation of, 171–75
    executive power and, 62
    under Kirchner, C., administration, 171–75
    lack of partisan linkages for, 175–77
    landholdings of, 23
    party-building by, 177, 185–93
    political fragmentation of, 175–77
    relevance of Congress as policymaking arena for, 61–63
    Republican Proposal party and, 185–93
    Unión del Centro Democrático and, 168–70
  agricultural industry in
    economic impact of, 157–59
    exports for, 24, 157–59
    historical background for, 157–64
    during Kirchner, C., administration, 171–75
    liberalization of, 32, 158–59, 173
    Peronist policies, 157–58, 163–64, 165, 166–67
    pricing rates for, 166
    Rural Confederations of Argentina, 160
    soybean products, 158, 172, 190
    tax rates/schemes for, 166, 172
    under tenancy laws, 158
    Total Support Estimate for, 155
    value of, 159
  agrodiputados, 170–82
    Barbechando think tank, 182
    candidate-centered strategies for, 182–85
    as political candidates, 178–82
    political capacity of, 63
  electoral organization in, 53–56
    for primary elections, 192
  electoral rules in, 57–61
    closed-list proportional representation system, 58–59
  Frente para la Victoria in, 3, 156, 163–64
  land reform threats in, 47–48, 164–65, 166–67
  military regimes in, 163–64
  party system in
    candidate-centered strategy in, 182–85
    fragmentation of, 15
    institutionalization of, 15
    party-building in, 168–70
    by agrarian elites, 177, 185–93
    political history of, 157–64
  transition to democracy in, 164–70
    land reform as part of, 164–65
    as nonthreatening, 164–68
Argentine Association of Regional Consortiums of Agricultural Experimentation (AACREA), 161–62
Argentine Rural Society (SRA), 160
autocratic regimes, agrarian elites in, 7
Aylwin, Patricio
  Concertación agenda under, 104–5
  tax reform policies under, 104–6

Bancada Ruralista. *See* Agrarian Caucus, Bancada Ruralista, in Brazil
Bancada Telesup, caucus of for-profit universities, 204–8

Barbechando think tank, 182
binomial electoral rules, 15
Bolivia
  agrarian elites in, 2
  left turn in, 11–12
Bolsonaro, Jair, 139
Bancada Ruralista and, 1
Boric, Gabriel, 98
bounded rationality, 45
Brazil. *See also* Agrarian Caucus, Bancada Ruralista, in Brazil; Bancada Ruralista; Constituent Assembly, in Brazil
  agrarian elites in, 2, 3
    analysis of, 153–54
    clientelism and, 54–55, 123
    corporatist organizations and, 116–17
    cross-country comparisons for, 13–18
    electoral organization by, 15–16
    executive power and, 62
    existential threats for, 117–53
    government support for, 3
    landholdings of, 23
    party-building by, 54–55, 122–25
    political fragmentation of, 122–25
    relevance of Congress as policymaking arena for, 61–63
  agricultural industry in
    Brazilian Agricultural Research Corporation, 112
    under Cardoso, 113
    under Collor de Mello, 113
    conservative modernization of, 111–15
    exports, 24, 108, 112
    historical background for, 111–17
    land Gini Index, 115
    subsidies for, 12
    value of (from 1965–2017), 114
  annual GDP in, total support estimate for agriculture, 3
  Brazilian Union of Entrepreneurs, 59
  clientelism in, 51, 54–55, 123
  coronelismo in, 115–16
  Cultivar Law, 146–47
  electoral organization in, 53–56
    fragmentation of, 15
    institutionalization of, 15
  electoral representation in, 118–22
  electoral rules in, 57–61
    open-list proportional representation, 58–59
  land redistribution threats in, 47–48
  land reform in, 52–53, 73–74
    colonization of Amazon and, 112
    in Constituent Assembly, 130–31
    land occupations per year (1987–2017), 132, 133
    under Land Statute, 112–13, 118, 119–20, 131
    as political threat, 54–55, 118–22
  landless peasant movement in, 48
  left turn in, 11–12
  lobbying associations in, 59
  military regimes in
    dissolution of party system in, 55–56
    expansion of agricultural industry under, 112
  New Forest Code, 111, 147–53
    multipartisanship and, 147–48
    roll-call votes for, 149
    Rousseff and, 147
    Senate amendments to, 151
  Partido da Frente Liberal in, 129
  party system in, 16
  party-building in, 122–25
  political history for, 111–17
    before third wave of democracy, 115–16
  Rural Democratic Union in, 117, 125–29
  Workers Party, 1, 3, 108
Brazilian Agricultural Research Corporation, 112
Brazilian Rural Society (SRB), 117
Brazilian Union of Entrepreneurs (UBE), 59
Bukele, Nayib, 204

Calderon Sol, Armando, 204
Cambiemos/Juntos por el Cambio, in Argentina, 191–93
campaign financing
  in Argentina, 191–93
  Bancada Ruralista and, 140–44
  in Chile
    for New Left, 100
    for rightwing parties, 98–100
candidate-centered electoral strategies
  for Agrarian Caucus, 125–31
    in 1986 election, 125–29
    producers' association and, 125–29
    UDR leaders and, 125–29
  for agrarian elites, 29–30, 31, 36–40

candidate-centered electoral (cont.)
  for *agrodiputados*, 182–85
  in Chile, 89
CARBAP. *See* Confederation of Rural Associations of Buenos Aires and La Pampa (CARBAP)
Cardoso, Fernando Henrique, 113, 133, 137, 138
Cartes, Horacio, 201
caucus of for-profit universities. *See* Bancada Telesup
Chile
  agrarian elites in, 2
    before 1965, 68–70
    analysis of, 107
    cohesion of, 83–87
    corporatist organizations, 67–68
    cross-country comparisons for, 13–18
    electoral organization by, 15–16
    executive power and, 62
    existential threats for, 70–82
    financial support of rightwing parties, 98–100
    ideological identification for, 94–98
    inquilinaje system and, 54, 68–69, 77
    landholdings of, 23
    as partisan right constituency, 93–104
    party-building costs for, 82–90
    relevance of Congress as policymaking arena for, 61–63
    in restricted democracy, 68–70
    tax reform and, 104–6
  agricultural industry in
    exports, 24, 84–85
    history of, 67–70
    imports in, 84–85
    modernization of, 84–85
    under Pinochet, 91–92
  annual GDP in, total support estimate for agriculture, 3
  Christian Democrats in, 51, 69–70, 74–75
    land reform and, 74–75, 76–77, 81
  Concertación agenda in, 48, 66, 70
    under Aylwin, 104–5
    land reform, 71–72, 78–80, 81–82
    party-building and, 82–83
  electoral organization in, 53–56
  electoral rules in, 15, 57–61, 89
    binomial system, 15, 58, 89
    candidate-centered incentives, 89
  Entrepreneurs for Development initiative, 91
  existential threats for agrarian elites, 70–82
    during democratic transition, 70–82
    land reform as, 70–82
  gremialistas in, 93–94
  land redistribution threats in, 47–48
  land reform in
    from 1965–1973, 73–78
    under Alessandri Rodríguez, 74
    under Allende, 70–71, 73–74, 76–77, 86, 95
    Christian Democrats and, 74–75, 76–77, 81
    in Concertación agenda, 71–72, 78–80, 81–82
    as existential threat to agrarian elites, 70–82
    expropriated land, 73, 76
    under Frei Montalva, 70–71, 73–74, 75–76, 86
    land occupations, 75–76
    under peasant unionization law, 75–76, 77
    as trauma, 78–82
    union strikes as result of, 75–76
  military regimes in
    dissolution of party system in, 55–56, 87–90
    electoral system designed by, 66
    structural transformation under, 84
  ministers of agriculture (from 1990–2022), 47–48
  New Left in, 72
    financial support for, 100
    Water Code reform and, 96–97
  Partido Nacional, 94
  partisan right in
    agrarian elites as core constituency of, 93–104
    financial support of, 98–100
    ideological identification with, 94–98
    landowners within, 100–4
    party system and, 29, 87–90
    party-building for, 86–93
    Water Code reform and, 96–97
  party system in, 16
    architects of, 90
    fragmentation of, 15
    institutionalization of, 15

military regimes' dissolution of,
    55–56, 87–90
  party-building and, 29, 87–90
  rightwing parties and, 87–90
  Senate composition, 88
  party-building in
    clientelism and, 83, 86–87
    Concertación agenda and, 82–83
    costs of, 82–90
    for partisan right, 86–93
    party system and, 29, 87–90
    under Pinochet, 87–90
    "YES" campaign and, 90–93
  political history for, 67–70
  protests in, 27–28
  Renovación Nacional, 29, 54, 65,
    93–95, 105–6
  Unidad Popular, 76
  Unión Demócrata Independiente, 65, 99
Christian Democrats, 51, 69–70. *See also*
    Frei Montalva, Eduardo
  in Chile, 51
  land reform and, 74–75, 76–77, 81
class conflict, agrarian elites' response to,
    44–45
clientelism, 7–8
  in Argentina, 176
  in Brazil, 51, 54–55, 123
  in Chile, 83, 86–87
  in El Salvador, 202–3
  in Peru, 206
  voter mobilization and, 11
closed-list proportional representation
    system (CLPR), 58–59
CNA. *See* National Confederation of
    Agriculture (CNA)
Collor de Mello, Fernando, 113
Colombia
  collapse of party system in, 40
  conservative political interests in, 204–8
  land reform process in, 73–74
  nonpartisan electoral representation in,
    204–8
  Pro-Life Caucus in, 208–10
commodity boom
  agrarian elites and, 10–12
  international price increases and, 10
Concertación agenda, in Chile, 48, 66, 70
  under Aylwin, 104–5
  land reform, 71–72, 78–80, 81–82
  party-building and, 82–83

Confederation of Agricultural
    Cooperatives (CONINAGRO),
    160–61
Confederation of Production and
    Commerce (CPC), 86
Confederation of Rural Associations
    of Buenos Aires and La Pampa
    (CARBAP), 160–61
CONINAGRO. *See* Confederation
    of Agricultural Cooperatives
    (CONINAGRO)
conservative parties, democracy and,
    210–13
Constituent Assembly, in Brazil, 109–10
  agenda-setting positions in, 134–36
  Bancada Ruralista, 135–36
  bargaining power within, 136–39
  fight against land reform in, 130–31
  land reform threats and, 121–22
  multipartisanship advantages in, 134–39
coronelismo, in Brazil, 115–16
corporatist organizations. *See also specific
    organizations*
  in Argentina, 160–62, 187–88
  in Brazil, 116–17
  in Chile, 67–68
  in Paraguay, 201
CPC. *See* Confederation of Production and
    Commerce (CPC)
CRA. *See* Rural Confederations of
    Argentina (CRA)
Cristiani, Alfredo, 204
Cristina, Tereza, 1, 139
Cultivar Law, Brazil (2015), 146–47

democratic regimes, democracy and. *See
    also specific topics*
  agrarian elites' interest in, 211
  conservative parties and, 210–13
  destabilization of, 7
  redistribution theories for, 8, 213–15
  restricted, 68–70
  third wave of
    in Argentina, 162–64
    in Brazil, 115–16
  Duhalde, Eduardo, 171–72

economic elites. *See* agrarian elites
El Salvador
  agrarian elites in, 2, 201–4
  clientelism in, 202–3

El Salvador (cont.)
  Farabundo Martí National Liberation Front, 204
  land reform in, 203–4
  Nationalist Republican Alliance in, 201–4
  party system in, 203
    collapse of, 203–4
    party-building in, 201–4
electoral fraud, 7–8
electoral investments, 44–48
electoral rules
  in Argentina, 57–61
    closed-list proportional representation system, 58–59
  in Brazil, 57–61
    open-list proportional representation, 58–59
  in Chile, 15, 57–61, 89
    binomial system, 15, 58, 89
    candidate-centered incentives, 89
    political participation of agrarian elites influenced by, 56–61
    political strategies and, 57
electoral strategies, for agrarian elites, 5, 26–30
  candidate-centered, 29–30, 31, 36–40
  costs of, 34–40, 48–53
  fragmentation of, 48–53
  party-building as, 29, 36–40
  reliability of, 32–36
Entrepreneurs for Development initiative, 91
existential threats, for agrarian elites, 44–48, 49
  bounded rationality and, 45
  in Brazil, 117–53
  in Chile, 70–82
    during democratic transition, 70–82
    land reform as, 70–82
  deductive approach to, 45–46
  fragmentation and, 52
  land redistribution as, 47–48
exports, agricultural
  from Argentina, 24, 157–59
  from Brazil, 24, 108, 112
  from Chile, 24, 84–85
expropriated land, in Chile, 73, 76

FAA. *See* Agrarian Federation of Argentina (FAA)
Farabundo Martí National Liberation Front (FMLN), 204

Federation of Fruit Producers (Fedefruta), 67–68
Fernández, Alberto, 192–93
Fernández, Sergio, 90
FMLN. *See* Farabundo Martí National Liberation Front (FMLN)
FPV. *See* Frente para la Victoria (FPV)
fraud. *See* electoral fraud
Frei Montalva, Eduardo, 70
  land reform under, 70–71, 73–74, 75–76, 86
Frente para la Victoria (FPV), 3, 156, 163–64

Goulart, João, 47, 129–30
gremialistas, 93–94
Guzmán, Jaime, 90

Humala, Ollanta, 205–6

import substitution industrialization model (ISI), 10
inquilinaje system, in Chile, 54, 68–69, 77
Instituto Pensar Agropecuária (IPA), 145–47
IPA. *See* Instituto Pensar Agropecuária (IPA)
ISI. *See* import substitution industrialization model (ISI)

Kirchner, Cristina Fernández de, 48, 155, 164, 170–71
  agrarian elites' electoral participation under, 171–75
Kirchner, Néstor, 170–71, 172–73

land Gini Index, 115
land occupations, in Chile, 75–76
land reform. *See also* Chile
  Agrarian Caucus and, 118–22
    Constituent Assembly response to, 121–22
  contemporary analysis of, 132–33
  political fights against, 129–31
  in Argentina, 164–65, 166–67
  in Brazil, 52–53, 73–74
    colonization of Amazon and, 112
    in Constituent Assembly, 130–31
    land occupations per year (1987–2017), 132, 133
    under Land Statute, 112–13, 118, 119–20, 131

as political threat, 54–55, 118–22
in Colombia, 73–74
in El Salvador, 203–4
in Peru, 13
redistributive processes for, 13
Land Statute, Brazil (1964), 112–13, 118, 119–20, 131
landless peasant movement (Movimento Sem Terra, MST), 48
left turn, in Latin America. *See also* democratic regimes, democracy and; Lugo, Fernando; Lula da Silva, Luiz Inácio (Lula); Morales, Evo; *specific countries*
agrarian elites and, 10–12
evolution of, 11–12
lobbying, lobbyists and
in Brazil, 59
farm lobby, 33
political participation of agrarian elites through, 26–27
Lugo, Fernando, 11–12, 200–1
Lula da Silva, Luiz Inácio (Lula), 1, 3, 11–12, 137, 138–39

Macri, Mauricio, 182, 192–93
Republican Proposal party (PRO), 185–93
Menem, Carlos, 32, 158–59, 169–70
military regimes
in Argentina, 163–64
in Brazil
dissolution of party system in, 55–56
expansion of agricultural industry under, 112
in Chile
dissolution of party system in, 55–56, 87–90
electoral system designed by, 66
ministers of agriculture, in Chile (from 1990–2022), 47–48
Morales, Evo, 11–12, 27–28
Movimento Sem Terra. *See* landless peasant movement (Movimento Sem Terra, MST)
MST. *See* landless peasant movement (Movimento Sem Terra, MST)

National Agrarian Reform Plan (PNRA), 119–20
National Confederation of Agriculture (CNA), 116–17

National Society of Agriculture (SNA), 67–68, 69–70, 90–93, 105–6
National Thinking of the Business Bases (PNBE), 59
Nationalist Republican Alliance (ARENA), 201–4
Neves, Tancredo, 119–20
New Forest Code, Brazil (2012), 111
multipartisanship and, 147–48
roll-call votes for, 149
Rousseff and, 147
Senate amendments to, 151
New Law of Higher Education, Peru, 205–6, 207
New Left, in Chile, 72
financial support for, 100
Water Code reform and, 96–97
nonelectoral strategies, for agrarian elites, 26–30
through protests, 27–28
reliability of, 32–36

OCB. *See* Organization of Brazilian Cooperatives (OCB)
oligarchies, oligarchic systems and, in Latin America, 49
open-list proportional representation (OLPR), 58
Organization of Brazilian Cooperatives (OCB), 117

Paraguay
agrarian elites in, 199–201
corporatist associations in, 201
left turn in, 11–12
paramilitary forces, use of, 7–8. *See also* military regimes
Partido da Frente Liberal (PFL), 129
Partido Nacional, 94
partisan right, in Latin America. *See* Chile; *specific parties*
party systems. *See also* Chile
in Argentina
candidate-centered strategy in, 182–85
fragmentation of, 15
institutionalization of, 15
in Brazil, 16
ENPP and, 15
fragmentation of, 15
institutionalization of, 15

party systems (cont.)
  in Colombia, 40
  in El Salvador, 203
    collapse of, 203–4
party-building. *See also* party systems;
    specific countries
  Agrarian Caucus and, 122–25
  in Argentina, 168–70
  by agrarian elites, 177, 185–93
  in Brazil, 54–55, 122–25
  in Chile
    clientelism and, 83, 86–87
    Concertación agenda and, 82–83
    costs of, 82–90
    for partisan right, 86–93
    party system and, 29, 87–90
    under Pinochet, 87–90
    "YES" campaign and, 90–93
  in El Salvador, 201–4
  as electoral strategy, 29, 36–40
Pastoral Land Commission, in Brazil, 118–19
path-dependent framework, for political participation argument, 41, 42–43
peasant unionization law, in Chile, 75–76, 77
Peron, Juan
  agricultural policies under, 157–58, 163–64, 165, 166–67
  tenancy laws under, 158
Peru
  agrarian reform in, 13
  caucus of for-profit universities, Bancada Telesup in, 204–8
  clientelism in, 206
  conservative political interests in, 204–8
  New Law of Higher Education, 205–6, 207
  nonpartisan electoral representation in, 204–8
PFL. *See* Partido da Frente Liberal (PFL)
Pinochet, Augusto
  agrarian elites' support for, 70
  agricultural industry under, 91–92
  gremialistas and, 93–94
  party-building under, 87–90
PNBE. *See* National Thinking of the Business Bases (PNBE)
PNRA. *See* National Agrarian Reform Plan (PNRA)
political participation, of agrarian elites
  alternative explanations for, 53–63

electoral rules and, 56–61
executive power and, 62
history of electoral organization, 53–56
relevance of Congress as policymaking arena, 61–63
argument for, 41–53
  existential threats in, 44–48
  path-dependent framework in, 41, 42–43
bounded rationality and, 45
class conflict as factor in, 44–45
conceptual approach to, 22–23, 45
control of local politics, 23
definition of, 23–25
electoral investments and, 44–48
electoral rules and, 56–61
  political strategies influenced by, 57
electoral strategies in, 26–30
  candidate-centered, 29–30, 31, 36–40
  common agency conflicts, 32–33
  costs of, 34–40, 48–53
  fragmentation of, 48–53
  party-building, 29, 36–40
  reliability of, 32–36
existential threats as factor for, 44–48, 49
  bounded rationality and, 45
  deductive approach to, 45–46
  fragmentation and, 52
  land redistribution as, 47–48
  landholdings as influence on, 23
nonelectoral strategies in, 26–30
  through protests, 27–28
  reliability of, 32–36
special interest groups and, 43–44, 56–57
strategies of political influence, 25–40
  comparisons between, 31–40
  decision-making for, 25–26
  flawed, 25
  professional lobbying, 26–27
Prado, Jorge, 91, 93
PRO. *See* Republican Proposal party (PRO)
Pro-Life Caucus, in Colombia, 208–10
PT. *See* Workers Party (PT)

redistribution theories
  for democratic regimes, 8, 213–15
  land reform in, 13

Renovación Nacional (RN), 29, 54, 65, 93–95, 105–6
Republican Proposal party (PRO), 185–93
restricted democracies, in Chile, 68–70
RN. *See* Renovación Nacional (RN)
Rodrigues, Roberto, 123, 139
Ronaldo Caiado, Goiás, 122–23, 125–26, 131
Rousseff, Dilma, 137, 139
  New Forest Code and, 147
Rural Confederations of Argentina (CRA), 160
Rural Democratic Union (UDR), 117, 125–29

Sarney, Josê, 48, 52–53, 119–20
SNA. *See* National Society of Agriculture (SNA)
SRA. *See* Argentine Rural Society (SRA)
SRB. *See* Brazilian Rural Society (SRB)

tax reform policies
  in Argentina, 166, 172
  in Chile, 104–6

Temer, Michel, 137, 138
tenancy laws, in Argentina, 158

UBE. *See* Brazilian Union of Entrepreneurs (UBE)
UCEDE. *See* Unión del Centro Democrático (UCEDE)
UDI. *See* Unión Demócrata Independiente (UDI)
UDR. *See* Rural Democratic Union (UDR)
Unidad Popular, 76
Unión del Centro Democrático (UCEDE), 168–70
Unión Demócrata Independiente (UDI), 65, 99
urbanization, agrarian elites and, 10–12

voter mobilization, clientelism and, 11

Water Code reform, in Chile, 96–97
Workers Party (PT), 1

"YES" campaign, in Chile, 90–93

Milton Keynes UK
Ingram Content Group UK Ltd.
UKHW050955011124
2511UKWH00005B/17

מסורה

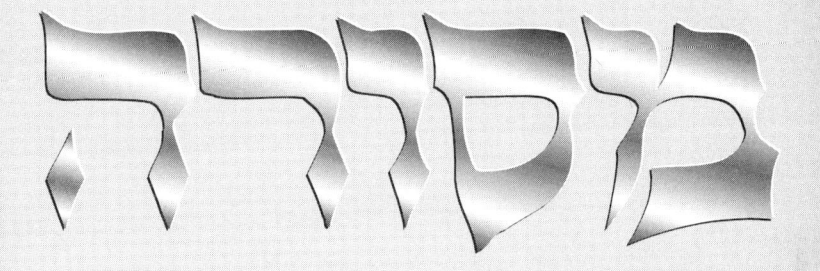

ArtScroll Mesorah Series®

Rabbi Nosson Scherman / Rabbi Meir Zlotowitz
General Editors

Table

by
Rabbi Raphael Pelcovitz

Published by
Mesorah Publications, ltd

Talk

Shabbos and Yom Tov Divrei Torah

FIRST EDITION
First Impression ... April 1999

Published and Distributed by
MESORAH PUBLICATIONS, LTD.
4401 Second Avenue / Brooklyn, N.Y 11232

Distributed in Europe by
J. LEHMANN HEBREW BOOKSELLERS
20 Cambridge Terrace
Gateshead, Tyne and Wear
England NE8 1RP

Distributed in Israel by
SIFRIATI / A. GITLER
10 Hashomer Street
Bnei Brak 51361

Distributed in Australia and New Zealand by
GOLDS BOOK & GIFT SHOP
36 William Street
Balaclava 3183, Vic., Australia

Distributed in South Africa by
KOLLEL BOOKSHOP
Shop 8A Norwood Hypermarket
Norwood 2196, Johannesburg, South Africa

THE ARTSCROLL SERIES®
TABLE TALK
© Copyright 1999, by MESORAH PUBLICATIONS, Ltd.
4401 Second Avenue / Brooklyn, N.Y. 11232 / (718) 921-9000

ALL RIGHTS RESERVED
*The text, prefatory and associated textual contents and introductions
— including the typographic layout, cover artwork and ornamental graphics —
have been designed, edited and revised as to content, form and style.*

No part of this book may be reproduced
IN ANY FORM, PHOTOCOPING, OR COMPUTER RETRIEVAL SYSTEMS
— even for personal use without written permission from
the copyright holder, Mesorah Publications Ltd.
*except by a reviewer who wishes to quote brief passages
in connection with a review written for inclusion in magazines or newspapers.*

THE RIGHTS OF THE COPYRIGHT HOLDER WILL BE STRICTLY ENFORCED.

ISBN:
1-57819-283-8 (hard cover)
1-57819-284-6 (paperback)

Typography by CompuScribe at ArtScroll Studios, Ltd.
Printed in the United States of America by Noble Book Press Corp.
Bound by Sefercraft, Quality Bookbinders, Ltd., Brooklyn N.Y. 11232

Table of Contents

Preface — ix
Acknowledgments — xiii

SEFER BEREISHIS

Bereishis / בראשית — *Education, Growth and Maturity* — 2
Noach / נח — *Reordering Our Priorities* — 5
Lech Lecha / לך לך — *Possession and Ownership —
　Are They the Same?* — 8
Vayeira / וירא — *Man's Potential for Good or Evil* — 11
Chayei Sarah / חיי שרה — *Nature vs. Nurture* — 14
Toldos / תולדות — *Appearance and Reality* — 17
Vayeitzei / ויצא — *It's All Relative* — 21
　When a Pupil Becomes a Participant — 22
Vayishlach / וישלח — *What's in a Name?* — 24
Vayeishev / וישב — *Heeding the Heavenly Voice* — 27
Mikeitz / מקץ — *Self-worth* — 30
Vayigash / ויגש — *Day of Judgment, Day of Admonition* — 33
　Dignity and Self-Respect — 34
Vayechi / ויחי — *Jewish Unity: Ethnicity and Faith* — 37

SEFER SHEMOS

Shemos / שמות — *Not to Lose Sight of the Tree for the Forest* — 40
　No Excuses, Please! — 41
Va'eira / וארא — *For Your Own Good* — 44
Bo / בא — *The Light That Shines in the Darkness* — 47
　Second, but Not Last or Final — 48
Beshalach / בשלח — *Message in a Jar* — 51
　Hearing and Reading — 53
Yisro / יתרו — *United We Stand* — 55
Mishpatim / משפטים — *A Unique Derech Eretz* — 58
　From Revelation to Legislation — 60
Terumah / תרומה – *Gateway to Heaven* — 61

The Cherubim: Face-to-Face or Face-Off	62
Tetzaveh / תצוה – *The Art of Communication*	64
Ki Sisa / כי תשא – *Human Standard*	67
Vayakhel / ויקהל – *Style or Substance?*	70
Pikudei / פקודי – *Accounting and Accountability*	73

SEFER VAYIKRA

Vayikra / ויקרא – *Listening, Hearing and Understanding*	76
Tzav / צו – *Consecrating One's Ear, Hand and Foot*	79
Shemini / שמיני – *Instruction or Admonition —*	
Which Is More Effective?	82
Tazria / תזריע – *Transforming the "Nega" into "Oneg"*	85
Metzora / מצורע – *Who Shall Live and Who Shall Die?*	88
Acharei / אחרי – *Environmental Pollution and Education*	90
Kedoshim / קדשים – *How to Understand the Word* כָּמוֹךָ	93
Emor / אמור – *The Ordeal of the Ordinary*	96
Behar / בהר – *Putting First Things First*	99
Which Direction Are You Facing?	100
Bechukosai / בחקתי – *Lessening Links —*	
Diminishing Merits	102

SEFER BAMIDBAR

Bamidbar / במדבר – *To Count and Be Counted*	106
Nasso / נשא – *To Be Blessed and to Be a Blessing*	109
Coexistence and Peace — שְׁלֵמוּת וְשָׁלוֹם	111
Beha'aloscha / בהעלותך – *What Do You Miss?*	113
Shelach / שלח – *Logical Is Not Always Reasonable*	116
Squandered Opportunity	117
Korach / קרח – *Not to Capture but to Captivate*	120
Chukas / חקת – *Excess Causes Affluenza*	123
Balak / בלק – *Israel's Vulnerability*	126
Pinchas / פנחס – *The Secret Is Timing*	129
Mattos / מטות – *When* שֶׁפַע *(Abundance)*	
Becomes פֶּשַׁע *(Iniquity)*	132
Masei / מסעי – *Travel Broadens Horizons*	135

SEFER DEVARIM

Devarim / דברים – *A Balanced Judgment*	140

A Light Unto the Nations	141
The Hidden Seeds of Redemption	142
Va'eschanan / ואתנן – A Beneficial Decree	145
Seize the Moment	147
Eikev / עקב – Use It or Lose It	149
Avinu Malkeinu — Our Father, Our King	150
Man's Creative Spirit	151
Re'eh / ראה – Berachah, the Enabler	153
Shoftim / שופטים – A Clever or a Wise Person?	156
The Other Man	158
The Public and Private Persona	160
Ki Seitzei / כי תצא – Chodesh or Yerach?	163
A True Measure of Faith	164
False Economy	165
Ki Savo / כי תבוא – A Basketful of Blessings	167
Evoking the Divine Voice	168
The Mezuzah at the Gateway to Eretz Yisrael	169
Nitzavim / נצבים – Action Inspires and Motivates	171
Means and Ends — Cause and Effect	172
Choosing Our Destiny — Is It Ours To Choose?	173
Vayeilech / וילך – A National Affirmation	175
Haazinu / האזינו – How to Give Mussar	178
An Eternal Link	179
A Void or a Blemish?	181
Vezos Haberachah / וזאת הברכה – Fire and Water — Coexistence	183
Linking the Conclusion to the Beginning	184

YOMIM TOVIM

Rosh Hashanah / ראש השנה — The Inner Voice	188
Yom Kippur / יום כיפור — Appreciation, Priorities and Values	191
Succos / סוכות — Illusory or Real Security	194
Chanukah / חנוכה — Sanctity of Time, Place and Klal Yisrael	197
Why "Mehadrin"?	199
Purim / פורים — The Correct Response	201
Pesach / פסח — The Profound Lesson of Rabbi Gamliel	204
Shavuos / שבועות — The Power of Renewal	207

Preface

YEARS AGO, THE SERMON, OR *DERASHAH,* WAS VERY POPULAR AND served as the focal point of the Shabbos morning services. People might be late for *Shacharis,* or even miss some of the Torah reading, but they usually came in time to listen to the Rabbi's sermon. In that era, books on sermons were quite plentiful, and Rabbis who had served in the rabbinate for many years, and had perfected the art of the sermon, would gather together their best efforts and put them in book form for the benefit of their younger colleagues, and even for their contemporaries.

In recent years the role of the sermon has suffered. Indeed, in the more Torah-oriented and *frumer minyanim,* the sermon is omitted or treated with a certain degree of disdain. The reason for this can more readily be explained by sociologists and psychiatrists than by an old-time Rabbi, but it is the reality of the moment. Truth be told, publishers are not interested in accepting books on sermons for they would but gather dust on the shelves of bookstores. On the other hand, in this generation there are, thank G-d, many more *bnei Torah* who are anxious to give a *dvar Torah* or, as it is called, a "*vort,*" at the Shabbos table. This is most commendable and certainly serves as an educational tool for the entire family.

Many of these *bnei Torah,* however, are too occupied with their profession or occupation to delve into the *Parashah* of the week and find a meaningful thought to share at the Shabbos table, at a *simchah seudah,* or whenever family and friends gather and socialize on a Shabbos or Yom Tov. The purpose of this *sefer* is to allow the reader to thumb through the book and glance at some *divrei Torah* based on the *Parashah* of the week, thereby contributing to his peace of mind on *erev* Shabbos, and on Shabbos and Yom Tov as well.

The various chapters in this *sefer* are drawn from many decades of experience in delivering *divrei Torah* in informal as well as formal settings, at the Shabbos table or at various *simchah seudos.* As such, they are not sermons in the classical, traditional sense, but, as the title of the book implies, they are "Table Talk." Unlike various *likkutim* which are on the market, consisting of a variety of Torah thoughts gathered from *talmidei chachamim* and *darshanim* where the source of each *dvar Torah* is given, I have decided not to cite the source and the origin of each Torah thought. They are culled from a variety of sources, and the author makes no claim to originality. I have, however, developed these thoughts and added a נפך משלי, a spark of my own, and in a number of cases the thoughts are original.

I have taken the liberty of bypassing the Talmudic dictum which cautions us to attribute *divrei Torah* to the original author, for I have found that many of the *Rishonim* took the liberty of publishing the thoughts of their contemporaries, and of previous generations, without attribution. This was fully accepted in Torah circles from the 12th through the 15th centuries. The Sforno does so constantly without explaining or justifying his practice, but the Chizkuni (Chizkiyah ben Menachem), who lived in the mid-13th century, does explain, in the introduction to his commentary, why he does not attribute much of his commentary to those whom he is quoting. He gives four reasons: First, because he does not wish to equate a lesser Torah teacher with a greater one; second, because he is concerned that the reader will not accept the interpretation of a lesser-known commentator, thereby embarrassing him; and third, because it is difficult to determine with exactitude the original source of all *divrei Torah.* This third reason is echoed by the *Rambam* in his writings as well. These words of the Chizkuni encouraged me to present many of these *divrei Torah* without attribution. The fourth reason he gives is, in my opinion, the strongest. He cites the *pasuk* in *Koheles*: דִּבְרֵי חֲכָמִים ... בַּעֲלֵי אֲסֻפּוֹת נִתְּנוּ מֵרֹעֶה אֶחָד, "The words of the wise ... the sayings of the masters of collections, coming from one Shepherd" (*Koheles* 12:11). In the final analysis, in the view of many *Rishonim* all words and wisdom of Torah are true, meaningful and authoritative, regardless of who said them, as long as the source and origin emanates from Hashem, the רֹעֶה אֶחָד.

Let the reader study each *dvar Torah* and attempt to understand it in the proper spirit, judging its value by its own inherent wisdom and the truth of Torah. In other words, *what* is being said, not *who* said it, should be the final arbiter. Hopefully, these *divrei Torah* will enrich the Shabbos and Yom Tov table, as well as stimulate the mind of the reader, encouraging him or her to add original thoughts and interpretations, for the Torah is a never-ending well of inspiration and instruction.

Raphael Pelcovitz
Nissan 5759

Acknowledgments

To write and publish a book requires not only the creative labor of the author, but the assistance and cooperation of many others as well. Thoughts and ideas must be formulated and written, or dictated to a competent stenographer. How fortunate I am to have access to the talents of a gifted secretary, Frieda Lapides, with whom I have worked for the past number of years. Her skill, competence, patience and spirit of cooperation have facilitated the completion of this *sefer,* and I am deeply grateful to her, not only for her excellence of execution, but for her helpful recommendations as well.

My daughter, Ethel Gottlieb, shared her valuable time with me and contributed her incomparable talent as an editor to this project. Her careful reading of the manuscript, helpful suggestions and creative titling of many chapters is greatly appreciated.

My beloved wife, Shirley, encouraged me to publish these *divrei Torah* for the Shabbos table. The custom in her family, over the years, has been for someone at the table to say a *dvar Torah* on the *Sedrah,* and hopefully this work will stimulate others to do so as well, each week at their Shabbos *seudah.* She also gave of her time and talent to read, correct, edit and title a number of these essays. I appreciate her assistance and sage counsel over the years. She is my true *ezer* and has enriched my life these past years.

I wish to express my heartfelt thanks to Rabbi Nosson Scherman and Rabbi Meir Zlotowitz, the general editors of ArtScroll, for their friendship and *chizuk* during the years of our fruitful relationship, and for being so responsive when I suggested this project to them. May they continue to disseminate Torah to *Klal Yisrael* for many years to come.

R.P.

Sefer Bereishis

PARASHAS BEREISHIS

Education, Growth and Maturity

AFTER THE TORAH RELATES THE MAJESTIC STORY OF CREATION and introduces us to Adam, Chavah and the serpent, and after man has been driven from Gan Eden, we are presented with a simple yet most puzzling and profound verse. In Chapter 5, verse 1, we read: זֶה סֵפֶר תּוֹלְדֹת אָדָם, "This is the account of the descendants of Adam." Commenting on this verse, an obscure Midrash states: ל׳א לְאָדָם אֲנִי נוֹתֵן הַתּוֹרָה כִּי לְבָנָיו, "I will not give the Torah to Adam, but to his children." The Midrash is apparently interpreting the word סֵפֶר (book) in this verse as referring to the Sefer Torah, and the word תּוֹלְדֹת as meaning the offspring of Adam, as opposed to Adam himself. In other words, we are being given an answer to a question which has bothered many commentators: Why was the Torah not given immediately to Adam when he was created, since the Torah is the ultimate book of instruction meant to guide man in how he should live and conduct himself? The Midrash seems to be saying that the giving of the Torah had to be postponed for a while and given only to the descendants of Adam, to future generations.

Our Sages pose a most interesting question regarding the creation of man, as well as the creation of all living creatures. They ask: At what stage of development was Adam created — as an infant, a child, an adolescent, or a young adult? They answer that the creation of all living creatures, including man, was בְּקוֹמָתָן לְדַעְתָּן וּלְצִבְיוֹנָן, "with full stature, full capacity and full beauty" (*Rosh Hashanah* 11a). In other words, they were all finished products, which makes sense logically, for they had to be self-sufficient since there were no others to care for them and meet their needs. However, there is a much deeper thought hidden in this statement of our Sages, for we are being taught that, psychologically, for man to fulfill the charge given to him from the beginning of Creation, לְעָבְדָהּ וּלְשָׁמְרָהּ, "to work it and preserve it" (2:15), he required a vision of the end product to motivate him to labor and sacrifice in order to develop and nurture the growth of all creation. Since the dawn of Creation, man needed an image of the finished product from the very outset, a model, as it were, to inspire him. What motivates us always is the potential; our imagination is inspired by the knowledge of what the end product will be. That is why, at Creation, man could not be an infant or a child, but had to be complete, for how else would one know the full capacity and full beauty of a human being or, for that matter, of any living creature?

A writer once wrote that all education requires a constant vision of greatness, in order to spur us on and motivate us to reach noble goals. Obviously, the potential of every human being is realized only through the process of growth, development and maturation. Torah is taught to a child at a very early age, and we continue to educate our children for many years, in order to create the finished product. Even after we are adults, we continue to study Torah for we realize that our "full stature and full capacity" has not been reached, and we must ever strive to actualize our potential — the potential of man who is created in the image of G-d.

Torah was given to us for this reason, and that is why there is no greater *mitzvah* than to learn and teach Torah, be it for ourselves or to our children. True, those who come to Judaism later on in life can still master the Torah and live according to its teachings, but we appreciate how difficult it is for the *baal teshuvah* to change and reorder the values and priorities of his life.

This is what the Midrash is teaching us. Since Adam was created as a young adult, the Sefer Torah could not be given to him for he lacked one of the most essential elements, namely a period of childhood and growth. The Torah, the Book of Torah, had to be reserved for, and given to, the descendants of man, to those who could be taught and trained from childhood to understand the teachings of the Almighty as revealed in the Torah. Without *chin-*

uch, "education," the Sefer Torah would be of minimal value. Hence, זֶה סֵפֶר תּוֹלְדֹת אָדָם, this Book was meant for the descendants of man, not for Adam, for they, unlike him, will go through the stages of infancy, childhood and adolescence before they mature into adults. Adam, who was created as an adult, lacked this experience of gradual growth.

This may well explain why Cain called his son חֲנוֹךְ, for it would always remind him that his child needed חִינוּךְ, *chinuch*, "education." But even that is insufficient, so Cain built a city and named the city חֲנוֹךְ as well, for it is not enough to educate your child; there must also be an environment and society in which he can live, one which appreciates and values what education teaches.

The lesson taught at the dawn of Creation in our *Sedrah* is one that we must learn and also teach to subsequent generations.

PARASHAS NOACH

Reordering Our Priorities

WHEN THE ALMIGHTY TELLS NOACH THAT HE INTENDS TO BRING a deluge, a *mabul,* on the face of the earth, there are a number of verses where the Torah mentions the various creatures that are to be brought into the Ark to ensure the perpetuation of all species. The order in which these animals, birds and creeping things are listed is very intriguing. The first verse is the general commandment, given by Hashem to Noach, in Chapter 6, verse 20. When G-d tells Noach that he is to bring these various living creatures into the Ark, the verse states: "From each bird according to its kind, and from each animal according to its kind, and from each thing that creeps on the ground, etc." In the next chapter, Chapter 7, verse 14, where the Torah speaks of the entrance of Noach, his family and all these living creatures into the Ark, the order changes. "They and every beast after its kind, every animal after its kind, every creeping thing ... and every bird after its kind." Here the birds are mentioned last, rather than first. In Chapter 8, where we are told of the exit from the Ark, verse 17 reads: "Every living being that is with you of all flesh, of birds, of animals, etc." Here, again, birds are mentioned first!

It is important for us to understand this change in sequence. The birds, who are mentioned first at the beginning of the *Sedrah,* are relegated to last place when everyone enters the Ark, and then, once again, given preeminence upon leaving the Ark. The *baalei mussar,* the great Jewish ethical teachers, saw in this unusual order a lesson in establishing a scale of priorities.

If the yardstick used is one of might and power, then beasts and animals are much stronger and more powerful than the bird kingdom. Logically, they should be mentioned before the birds when the Torah speaks of the importance of the survival of all species during the deluge. However, one must be mindful of the fact that birds possess an attribute which beasts and animals do not: It is their ability to fly! Their wings are a gift, and even a power, which other creatures do not possess. Indeed, this may be alluded to in one of the verses quoted above (7:14), where the Torah uses the expression: כֹּל צִפּוֹר כָּל כָּנָף, "every bird of any kind of wing." However, this superiority of birds, who were given wings with which to fly and soar, was true only as long as they were free to do so. Once they were confined to the Ark and their wings were of no use to them, they are indeed relegated to last place. When the general command was given by G-d to gather all the creatures and preserve them, at that time the birds were able to fly, as was the case when permission was granted to Noach and all the creatures to leave the Ark. This explains why, before and after the deluge, birds are mentioned first, whereas during their confinement in the Ark they are mentioned last. When they were free to fly, they were first, but when confined to the Ark and unable to fly, they were listed last.

The *baalei mussar* applied this explanation to the world at large, to humanity in general and to the people of Israel in particular. The Torah characterizes us as the מְעַט מִכָּל הָעַמִּים, "the least of all the nations" (*Devarim* 7:7). Our superiority does not lie in our numbers, nor in our might and power, for most nations of the world outnumber us and are much more powerful than we are. What, then, is our special significance and the reason for our being chosen as the *am hanivchar*? It is our superior intellectual powers and, above all, our spirituality. These, in turn, are derived from our Torah, which is akin to the wings of *Klal Yisrael,* permitting us to soar heavenward and transcend all material circumstances and physical shortcomings.

But when our wings are clipped and we are unable or unwilling to use the special gift and power of Torah, we are relegated to an inferior position in the registry of the nations. How tragic therefore is when we ourselves no longer develop our ability to fly and to soar with these special wings of Torah.

The sequence and order of the *pesukim* in the story of the *mabul* teach us a lesson for all time regarding the secret strength of Israel, which is summarized by the prophet Zechariah when he says: לֹא בְחַיִל וְלֹא בְכֹחַ כִּי אִם בְּרוּחִי אָמַר ה׳, "Not with might and not with power, but with My Spirit, said Hashem" (*Zechariah* 4:6). This is a lesson which, if learned and practiced, guarantees our ability to survive every deluge which may threaten us throughout our difficult, but glorious, history.

PARASHAS LECH LECHA

Possession and Ownership — Are They the Same?

AFTER LOT PARTS FROM AVRAHAM, G-D APPEARS TO AVRAHAM and tells him: שָׂא נָא עֵינֶיךָ וּרְאֵה . . . כִּי אֶת כָּל הָאָרֶץ אֲשֶׁר אַתָּה רֹאֶה לְךָ אֶתְּנֶנָּה וּלְזַרְעֲךָ עַד עוֹלָם, "Raise your eyes and see . . . for all the Land that you see, to you will I give it and to your descendants forever" (13:14-15). It is interesting to note, however, that after Avraham is told to look and see the entire Land which is promised to him and his children, he is then told to perform an act of *kinyan*, "acquisition," by traversing the length and breadth of the Land: קוּם הִתְהַלֵּךְ בָּאָרֶץ . . . כִּי לְךָ אֶתְּנֶנָּה, "Arise, walk about the Land . . . for to you I will give it" (13:17). In this verse, the key phrase זַרְעֲךָ, "your descendants," is omitted! The reason for this omission can be understood if one differentiates between *vision* and *acquisition*. The vision of Eretz Yisrael belongs to every generation. We know from history that even those who are far removed from Torah observance, and to a certain degree even from Jewish identification, somehow always retain a certain attachment to the Land of Israel. The vision does not dim, and whether they pray three times a day, asking the Almighty for their return to Zion, or not, they are almost instinctively aware of the unique character of Eretz Yisrael, as a מוֹרָשָׁה.

The Torah uses this phrase — מוֹרָשָׁה, an inheritance or heritage — in regard to the Land of Israel and regarding the Torah itself. תּוֹרָה צִוָּה לָנוּ מֹשֶׁה, מוֹרָשָׁה קְהִלַּת יַעֲקֹב, "The Torah Moshe taught us is the heritage of the Congregation of Yaakov" (*Devarim* 33:4).

8 / Table Talk

Both the Torah and the Land of Israel are an integral part of our heritage and our national destiny. This explains why the expression זַרְעֶךָ, "your descendants," is used in conjunction with the "vision" of Eretz Yisrael, for the children of Avraham will never lose sight of that vision.

However, when Avraham is told to "walk about the Land" — which is as an act of acquisition, of *kinyan,* for by so doing he takes possession of the Land — the phrase זַרְעֶךָ, "your descendants," is omitted. This indicates that insofar as the actual possession of the Land is concerned, there will be many interruptions during the course of time when Avraham's descendants will not possess the Land. Even after Jews will be permitted to repossess the Land, only a relative few will take advantage of that opportunity; hence the word זַרְעֶךָ is not used.

There is also an additional dimension regarding ownership and possession, which is especially true of the Jewish people's relationship to Eretz Yisrael. That added dimension is the necessity of appreciating the value of an item, and certainly of a land, on the part of those who wish to take possession of it. Ownership cannot be established through possession alone, if one is not aware and cognizant of the true value of an item. There is a fascinating case brought by the *Hagahos Ashri,* the annotated commentary to the Rosh in *Bava Metzia.* A *she'eilah* (question) was once brought to Rabbi Elazar of Metz. A Jew had purchased a sheet of tin from a non-Jew and subsequently sold it to his neighbor. The new purchaser, upon scraping off some of the tin, discovered silver underneath. Apparently, a layer of tin had been used as a veneer to conceal the precious silver. The question presented to Rabbi Elazar was whether the purchaser was obligated to pay the seller the difference between the price of silver and that of tin. The *psak* (decision) given was that the seller was not entitled to any additional money from the purchaser, since the seller himself never knew that the item was silver, nor did he have any intent to acquire silver in the initial transaction when he purchased it from the non-Jew! This *psak* was quoted by a great teacher of *mussar* to prove that acquisition and ownership must be accompanied by knowledge and appreciation of the value of an item. Only then is true ownership established.

How true this is of the Land of Israel and our relationship to it. Not everyone who lives in the Land becomes a true possessor of it. There must be an understanding and appreciation of its holiness and historic significance in order for one to become an "owner" of the Land. This explains why the word זַרְעֲךָ is not used when the Torah speaks of taking possession of the Land, for not every descendant of Avraham has that sense of appreciation — as indeed we see today.

We can now understand another teaching of our Sages regarding a Jew's attachment to, and appreciation of, the Land of Israel. We are taught that Yosef merited to have his *aron* (coffin) transported from Egypt to Eretz Yisrael, whereas Moshe was not granted entry to the Land, nor even the privilege to be buried there. Our Sages explain the reason for this: יוֹסֵף הוֹדָה בְּאַרְצוֹ, "Yosef acknowledged his Land," while Moshe "denied his Land," כָּפַר בְּאַרְצוֹ. This refers to the fact that Yosef told his captors and the authorities that he was taken from the Land of Israel and brought to Egypt. He did not deny his origins. Moshe, on the other hand, when he rescued the daughters of Yisro and overheard them telling their father that an Egyptian man saved them, did not refute their assumption!

The question, however, is asked: Did not each of these great men merely acknowledge the truth? Yosef was indeed taken from the Land of Israel, where he lived the early years of his life, while Moshe was born in Egypt and never set foot on the soil of Israel! The answer given is that, from the moment in history when G-d promised the Land of Israel to Avraham and his descendants, every Jew should feel that this Land is his, for it is the Land which was given to his forefathers. The attachment of every Jew to Eretz Yisrael is supposed to be so deep and profound that whenever he is identified, it must be not only as a member of his people, but also as a son and daughter of the Land of Israel. That is why Yosef is praised for his readiness to acknowledge his identity, while Moshe is criticized. The *Bris HaAretz,* "the Covenant of the Land," which is taught to us in this week's *Sedrah,* is a Covenant which spans the ages, from the time of Avraham to this very day.

PARASHAS VAYEIRA

Man's Potential for Good or Evil

ACCORDING TO OUR TRADITION, ANGELS WHO ARE CALLED *malachim,* "messengers," are sent by G-d to perform a specific mission. Indeed, we are taught that an angel cannot perform more than one mission at a time. It is for this reason that the angels who came to the house of Avraham after he fulfilled the commandment of the Almighty and circumcised himself were each given a specific task and mission to fulfill. Rashi tells us that one came to heal Avraham, while the second came to inform Sarah that she would have a child. The third one was sent to destroy the wicked city of Sodom. The question, however, presents itself: Why did this third angel come to the house of Avraham at all, since his mission and purpose was totally unrelated to the house of Avraham?

There are two answers given to resolve this difficulty. According to the first, when G-d decided at the time of Creation to create Adam, the angels in Heaven were divided into two camps: those who were in favor of creating a human race, and those who were opposed. חֶסֶד אוֹמֵר יִיבָּרֵא שֶׁהוּא גוֹמֵל חֲסָדִים, וֶאֱמֶת אוֹמֵר אַל יִיבָּרֵא שֶׁכֻּלוֹ שְׁקָרִים. צֶדֶק אוֹמֵר יִיבָּרֵא שֶׁהוּא עוֹשֶׂה צְדָקוֹת, שָׁלוֹם אוֹמֵר אַל יִיבָּרֵא דְּכוּלֵיהּ קְטָטָה. The Heavenly forces in favor of creating man argued that man possesses many virtues, including those of kindness and compassion, as well as righteousness. The opposing camp argued that human beings are dishonest, and are creatures of contention, incapable of living peacefully with one another (*Bereishis Rabbah* 8).

When the city of Sodom was built and eventually evolved into a place of evil and wickedness, where strangers who wandered into town were treated with callousness and cruelty, the Heavenly forces who had been opposed to the creation of man were able to point to this evil community as proof of the correctness of their stance. Since G-d had decided, in spite of their opposition, to create man, He was, as it were, on the defensive because of the actions and behavior of the inhabitants of Sodom.

When He reluctantly came to the decision that Sodom had to be destroyed, and sent the third angel to implement this decision, the Almighty wanted to demonstrate to this angel, and through him to the Heavenly forces, that Sodom should not be considered as a model of humankind. He therefore commanded the angel of destruction to first visit the house of Avraham, for there the angel would observe that man *is* capable of kindness and generosity, and this would justify G-d's decision to create man. Lest the Heavenly forces believe that mankind is represented by evil Sodom, it was important to hold Avraham up as a model of the nobility that man *can* achieve. It is for this reason that the angel, charged with the destruction of Sodom, made this detour on his way to fulfill his mission.

A second answer is given, alluded to in a brief commentary by the Sforno. Commenting on the verse: וַיִּפְנוּ מִשָּׁם הָאֲנָשִׁים, "and the men turned from there" (18:22), the Sforno comments: "They turned from the house of kindness" and proceeded to Sodom. According to the Sforno, the Torah is contrasting the house of Avraham, which was characterized by kindness, with the city of Sodom, a place steeped in cruelty and wickedness.

According to some Bible commentators, the final decision of the Heavenly Court was reached at that moment, in the house of Avraham. It was this contrast between the house of kindness and the wickedness of Sodom which sealed the fate of that city. Since the minimum number of judges on a court is three, this explains, according to these commentators, why it was necessary for the third angel to accompany his colleagues. This also explains the commentary of Rashi on the verse: וְהוּא יֹשֵׁב פֶּתַח הָאֹהֶל, "while he was sitting at the entrance of the tent" (18:1).

When the *Shechinah* appeared, Avraham wanted to stand up, but G-d said to him: You sit and I will stand, to symbolize for all time that whenever a Jewish court sits in judgment, the Almighty will be present, as it is written: אֱלֹקִים נִצָּב בַּעֲדַת קֵל, "G-d stands in the Divine assembly" (*Tehillim* 82:1). This proves that there was a trial going on at that time, and a verdict was being reached based upon the comparison between the house of Avraham and the city of Sodom.

This may well explain why Avraham became so agitated when G-d revealed to him His intent to destroy Sodom, and also clarifies why Avraham interceded so passionately on behalf of the city. He attempted to change G-d's decree because he felt responsible for the destruction of Sodom since he had inadvertently sealed their fate!

Be it the first answer or the second, the presence of the third angel in Avraham's house is now understandable. It was important for the angels in Heaven to know the potential for *chesed* that human beings possess, thereby justifying G-d's creation of man; and it is also important for us to appreciate the need for due process of law before a decision to punish a community is reached.

PARASHAS CHAYEI SARAH

Nature vs. Nurture

WHEN AVRAHAM FEELS THAT HIS SON YITZCHAK IS READY TO make a *shidduch,* he entrusts this delicate task to his servant Eliezer, ordering him to return to his land of origin in Aram Naharaim, there to find a fitting match for his son. He also adjures him not to take a wife for his son from the daughters of the Canaanites.

Considering that both the Canaanites and the family of Avraham, who still lived in Aram Naharaim were idol worshipers, what difference would it make whether the bride chosen for Yitzchak came from that country or from a place closer to home, the land of Canaan? The answer given is that there was a fundamental difference in the *character* of the Canaanites, as opposed to that of the inhabitants of Aram Naharaim. True, they were both idol worshipers, but that was a flaw in their religious beliefs. Their character traits, however, were radically different from one another.

The *baalei mussar* differentiate between what is known as *dei'os* and what is called *middos.* The term *dei'os* refers to the faith and religious practice of an individual or a community, whereas the term *middos* is applied to the collective character of a people or the behavior pattern of an individual. There is a fundamental difference between the two, for one is ingrained in the nature of a person and is very difficult to change, whereas the other is acquired and can be changed. The *sifrei mussar* teach that שְׁלֵמוּת בְּמִדּוֹת, "perfection in one's behavior pattern," can outweigh the flaws and defects which may be found in one's *dei'os,* a person's theology and religious behavior.

Avraham knew that the people of Aram Naharaim in general, and his family in particular, possessed good *middos,* whereas the inhabitants of Canaan had corrupt *middos.* It is for this reason that he made Eliezer swear he would not take a bride for Yitzchak from the Canaanites, for their character traits were almost impossible to change. True, the Canaanites and his compatriots from Aram Naharaim were both idol worshipers, but Avraham was convinced that a young lady brought from his hometown and exposed to the environment of his house could, through education and example, be weaned away from idolatry and taught to embrace the true faith.

This concept is also reflected in *Parashas Vayeira,* where we read of Avraham's and Sarah's experience in the land of the Philistines. When Avimelech chastised Avraham for claiming that Sarah was his sister and not his wife, thereby causing Avimelech to take her into his palace and subsequently be punished, Avimelech seemed to be justified in scolding Avraham for this deception. Avraham answered in his own defense: "Because I said there is no fear of G-d in this place, and they will slay me because of my wife." Rashi comments that the reason Avraham was convinced that the people of Gerar were not G-d fearing is because when Avraham and Sarah arrived there, the question asked of them was the identity of this beautiful woman, and not, "Do you have a place to stay or food to eat?" Rashi explains that since the inhabitants were not concerned for the welfare of strangers, but only interested in the relationship of Avraham and Sarah, that was proof that אֵין יִרְאַת אֱלֹקִים בַּמָּקוֹם הַזֶּה, "There is no fear of G-d in this place" (20:11). From this we see that a lack of *chesed,* which is a serious character flaw, is an indication of a lack of *yiras Shamayim.* This shortcoming in *middos* is an index to a shortcoming in *dei'os.*

This concept will also explain why Eliezer used, as a test of Rivkah's character, her willingness to perform an act of *chesed.* If she passed that test, a test in *middos,* then there was nothing to fear regarding her *dei'os,* for that was an area which could be corrected and changed.

Yitzchak is characterized as a *yirei Shamayim,* and a proper *shidduch* for him must perforce be a young lady who is also G-d fearing. But the only way one can determine this *middah* is to see whether there is perfection in her *middos.* Just as the shortcoming of the people in Gerar, insofar as their lack of *chesed* was concerned, indicated a lack of *yiras Shamayim,* so the converse was true. Rivkah's manifestation of *chesed* revealed an inherent piety which she possessed, and indicated that she was a good match for Yitzchak.

This lesson of the preeminence of *middos* over *dei'os,* and the link between the two, is one that the Torah is teaching us in a most subtle manner through these two episodes — the sojourn of Avraham and Sarah among the Philistines, and the guidelines given by Avraham to Eliezer when he charged him to find a *shidduch* for his son.

PARASHAS TOLDOS

Appearance and Reality

IN THIS WEEK'S *SEDRAH*, WE READ OF THE BIRTH OF YAAKOV AND Esav, the twin sons of Yitzchak and Rivkah. The Torah tells us that Yitzchak loved Esav, whereas Rivkah loved Yaakov. In itself this is not unusual; however, there is a subtle difference in the words used by the Torah to describe the love of Yitzchak and Rivkah for their children. When the Torah tells us that Yitzchak loved his son Esav, the expression used is וַיֶּאֱהַב (past tense), whereas regarding Rivkah's feelings for Yaakov, the choice of words is וְרִבְקָה אֹהֶבֶת אֶת יַעֲקֹב (present tense) (25:28). This difference indicates that Yitzchak's love for Esav was conditional. It could be characterized, in the words of our Sages, as אַהֲבָה שֶׁהִיא תְלוּיָה בְדָבָר (*Avos* 5:19), a love which emanated from specific motivations, as the Torah itself states: כִּי צַיִד בְּפִיו, "for game was in his mouth" (25:28), meaning that Esav provided his father with meat prepared from animals caught by him in the field. Rivkah's love for Yaakov, on the other hand, was pure and altruistic. This explains why, in her case, the word אֹהֶבֶת is used — in the present tense — implying a constant and ongoing unconditional love.

Many of the commentators, however, give a different explanation. They point out that Yitzchak was incapable of recognizing the *rama'us*, "deception," of Esav, whereas Rivkah saw it very clearly and therefore favored Yaakov, who represented the epitome of truth. They explain that Yitzchak was incapable of recognizing dishonesty and deception, for he had grown up in the home of Avraham and Sarah, protected from the outside world, and exposed exclusively to honesty and decency. Rivkah, on the other hand, had grown up in a home with her brother Lavan who was the personification of a *ramai*. With her training and background, she was able to recognize her son Esav's serious shortcomings, and therefore rejected him, while embracing her son Yaakov.

In conjunction with this, we should point out that the Mishnah in *Avos* (4:1), which states: אֵיזֶהוּ חָכָם? הַלּוֹמֵד מִכָּל אָדָם, "Who is a wise man? He who learns from *everyone*," is interpreted as meaning that by exposure to different elements in society, one's ability to judge people is developed and sharpened, and he is able to discern who is wicked. Such a person becomes wiser for he learns about the unpleasant realities of life from his own experiences with a variety of people. In other words, he "learns" from his dealings with "everyone."

Yitzchak was not granted this opportunity. The one person from whom he could have learned about the seamier side of life would have been Yishmael, but he was driven out of the house by his father Avraham, at the behest of Sarah! Indeed there are those who interpret the verse in *Parashas Vayeira* regarding that episode in a most interesting manner. When Avraham reluctantly went along with the demand of his wife Sarah and sent away his son Yishmael, the Torah states: וַיֵּרַע הַדָּבָר מְאֹד בְּעֵינֵי אַבְרָהָם עַל אוֹדֹת בְּנוֹ, "The matter greatly distressed Avraham regarding his son" (21:11). Note that it does not say "regarding Hagar," nor does it specify his son Yishmael. Some commentators therefore interpret the verse in a unique fashion as meaning that Avraham was distressed not only by his need to banish Yishmael from his household, but also "regarding his son" Yitzchak, who would now be deprived of the experience of being exposed to his brother Yishmael, whose presence would add an important dimension to Yitzchak's understanding of the unpleasant challenges that life has in store. Had Yishmael not been sent away, it is very possible that Yitzchak would also have been able to detect the deceptive character of Esav.

This naivete of Yitzchak is reflected as well in a most interesting Midrash which depicts a conversation between Yitzchak and Moshe. According to this Midrash, Yitzchak said to Moshe, "When I was on the altar, about to be sacrificed by my father, the heavens opened up and I saw the face of the *Shechinah*." What Yitzchak was saying is that Moshe, who spent 40 days and 40 nights in Heaven receiving the Torah, should not feel overly proud, for Yitzchak had already been granted the privilege of seeing the Divine Presence well before Moshe our teacher was invited to spend time with the Almighty and the angels. Moshe, however, responded, "Indeed, you did see the face of the *Shechinah,* but your eyes became dim, whereas I spoke with G-d, face-to-face, and my eyes never became dim."

The Midrash is giving us a deeper insight into the reason for Yitzchak's eyes being affected in his old age, as compared to Moshe, of whom the Torah testifies that on the day of his death at the age of 120, he could see as clearly as he did in his younger days. The Torah is not only speaking of the physical condition of the eyes of Yitzchak and Moshe, but is alluding to their ability to see and perceive the reality and truth of situations presented to them. We know that Yitzchak was blind to the evil of his son Esav and incapable of detecting his deceptive character. Moshe, on the other hand, was confronted throughout his life by many challenges on the part of wicked people such as Dasan and Aviram, and Korach. But he was always able to detect their motivations, protect himself from their machinations and counter their attempts to undermine his authority and leadership. It is this which Moshe alludes to when he said to Yitzchak, "You saw the *Shechinah* and became so spiritualized that you were blinded to the evil around you, whereas I spoke with the Almighty, face-to-face, but was able to retain my ability to see and properly evaluate the realities of life." Perhaps this is what our Sages mean when they tell us that Moshe, who was called *ish Elokim,* was indeed part man and part Divine creature. His *ish* aspect was not affected by his *Elokim* character, and he was ever able to balance the two.

We should hasten to add that although Yitzchak was unable to see the evil side of his son Esav, nonetheless his behavior toward him, according to our Sages, granted Yitzchak the right to challenge G-d when He wanted to punish His children. Yitzchak was able to argue that he also had a wicked son, but was forbearing and forgiving, and therefore he urged the Almighty to do likewise. Perhaps the reason for this can be understood from another verse which reads: וַיָּרַח אֶת רֵיחַ בְּגָדָיו, "and he smelled the aroma of his garments" (27:27), whereupon he remarks: רָאֵה רֵיחַ בְּנִי כְּרֵיחַ שָׂדֶה אֲשֶׁר בֵּרְכוֹ ה׳, "Behold, the aroma of my son is like the aroma of a field which G-d has blessed" (ibid.). Our Sages play on the word בְּגָדָיו and read it as בּוֹגְדָיו, "his traitors." They comment that even the worst among us, who are seemingly devoid of any virtues, are nonetheless מְלֵאִים מִצְווֹת כְּרִמּוֹן, "filled with *mitzvos* as a pomegranate is filled with seeds."

Does it not seem from this that our Sages are also being overly tolerant and naive? A great Torah teacher, however, explains this statement. He points out that the reason Yitzchak compared the aroma of his son to that of a *field* was to teach the following lesson: The *halachah* is that one cannot overcharge another for the sale of land, for even if it does not produce now, in the future it can produce a bountiful harvest. So too, every Jewish person, though he may seem to be a בּוֹגֵד, "traitor," or an אִישׁ רֵיק, "empty" person, nonetheless, he himself, or future generations coming from him, may very well bring forth Jewish fruits and be productive Jewishly. This may well explain Yitzchak's tolerant conduct with his son Esav, and hopefully will serve as a guide for Yitzchak's children in every generation.

PARASHAS VAYEITZEI

It's All Relative

WHEN YAAKOV REACHED HIS DESTINATION AFTER FLEEING FROM his brother Esav, he met Rachel at the well where the shepherds had gathered to water their flocks. The Torah tells us that Yaakov introduced himself by telling Rachel: כִּי אֲחִי אָבִיהָ הוּא וְכִי בֶן רִבְקָה הוּא, "that he was her father's relative and that he was Rivkah's son" (29:12).

Rashi explains that the word אֲחִי does not mean that Yaakov was her father's brother, since he was his nephew, but the word אָח in the Hebrew language can mean a relative. Rashi, however, also explains the choice of the word אָח Midrashically. He states that Yaakov was implying that if Lavan would conduct himself *b'rama'us*, "deceitfully," then Yaakov was prepared to do likewise. But if Lavan would conduct himself with honesty, then Yaakov would also do so. This explains why he identified himself in this dual fashion: "I am your father's brother, and I am the son of Rivkah," the first identification meaning, "I am on guard against your father's well-known character and personality of deceit and falsehood which I am prepared to combat." The second identification means, "I am also a son of Rivkah the righteous one, and if you will act in a proper and fitting manner, I will reciprocate."

The Midrash adds to this interpretation by quoting a verse in *Sefer Shmuel:* עִם נָבָר תִּתָּבָר וְעִם עִקֵּשׁ תִּתַּפָּל, "With the pure be pure, and with the perverse be subtle" (*II Shmuel* 22:27). To understand this Midrashic interpretation, one must appreciate that the term אָח is a generic one describing the relationship of two individuals who are like siblings. It implies that there is an equality, a parallel and a balance between the two of them. Not so the term בֶּן, "son," which describes one who is formed and shaped by his parents, and is an heir, acquiring character traits as well as training from parents. A great teacher of *mussar* explained that when Yaakov used the expression, "I am your father's brother," he wanted Rachel to convey to her father not only that he was prepared to match her father's *rama'us,* as *Rashi* explains, but that he would do so correspondingly, no more and no less. On the other hand, if Lavan would conduct himself as a good uncle should, with honesty and consideration, then Yaakov would not only match his kindness, but would do so with the same generosity that his mother Rivkah demonstrated when she responded to the request of Eliezer by giving water not only to him but to his animals as well. This explains why Yaakov used both terms, אָח and בֵּן.

The second interpretation quoted by Rashi is from the Talmud in *Megillah*. In the Midrash, however, the expression used is even more explicit: אִם לְרַמָּאוּת אֲחִי אָבִיהָ וְאִם לְצֶדֶק בֶּן רִבְקָה, "If deceit is the game, then I am the same; if righteousness, then I am as decent as my mother Rivkah." We are being taught an important *hashkafah* by Yaakov. Righteousness demands that our response not be a calculated one, and it should not just mirror the action of another. Rather, it should be an expression of our own character and our own attribute of *chesed.* On the other hand, when our response is dictated by another whose behavior may be harmful and damaging to us, we must be extremely careful to calibrate that response and utilize our *rama'us* in the exact same measure, not one iota more.

Yaakov who is characterized as an אִישׁ אֱמֶת, "man of truth," is capable of acting in this manner. Others must examine their motivation and their actions very carefully before they can determine whether to behave as a brother of Lavan or a son of Rivkah.

When a Pupil Becomes a Participant

AT THE END OF OUR *SEDRAH,* AFTER YAAKOV AND LAVAN HAVE declared a truce, the Torah tells us that Yaakov took a stone and raised it up as a monument. He then proceeded to build a mound, a *gal,* and "they ate there on the mound." In order to build this mound, Yaakov needed help, and the Torah tells us: וַיֹּאמֶר יַעֲקֹב לְאֶחָיו לִקְטוּ אֲבָנִים, "And Yaakov said to his brethren, 'Gather stones' " (31:46). Rashi comments that the term אֶחָיו in this verse means בָּנָיו, "his sons," who were like brothers to him in the sense that they were prepared to stand by him and assist him whenever he was confronted with *tzarah v'milchamah,* "trouble and battle." As we know, a *talmid*, "student," is also referred to as a בֵּן. The Talmud (*Berachos* 64a) interprets the phrase בָּנַיִךְ, "your sons," as implying בּוֹנַיִךְ, "your builders." When Yaakov asked for assistance and help in gathering the stones, the Torah chooses to use the term אֶחָיו, "brethren," rather than בָּנָיו, "his sons." What is the reason for this choice of terminology?

A great Jewish teacher explained that the relationship between a father and a son, as well as the relationship between a teacher and a student, is not a static one, but dynamic and evolving. At the beginning a child or a student is the recipient, but he evolves and eventually becomes a participant. In Hebrew we would describe the son or the student in the early stages as being a *mekabel,* "recipient," but with the passage of time he becomes a *mishtatef,* "one who participates and even becomes a partner." That is why our Sages, when they speak of *talmidim*, say that from a בֵּן one becomes a בּוֹנֶה, for he is a co-builder.

When Yaakov asked his sons to help him gather the stones to build a mound, he was casting them in the role of אַחִים rather than בָּנִים. At this stage in their lives, as they were leaving the house of Lavan and preparing to return to the Land of Israel to build the House of Jacob, Yaakov chose to call them אַחִים rather than בָּנִים, for they had reached a new level of responsibility.

This great teacher cautioned his colleagues to be extremely sensitive to the needs of their students and to appreciate and recognize the process of growth which takes place in the relationship of a student to a teacher and of a child to a parent. Only if one appreciates one's passage from being a *mekabel,* "recipient," to becoming a *mishtatef,* "partner and participant," will the relationship between father and son, teacher and *talmid*, be a productive and meaningful one.

PARASHAS VAYISHLACH

What's in a Name?

ACCORDING TO JEWISH TRADITION, WHEN AN ANGEL IS BESTED by a human being, he gives a gift to the person who has vanquished him. One of the examples of a human being battling and overcoming an angel is found in this week's *Sedrah*.

We are told that after Yaakov sent his family ahead, he was confronted by a mysterious adversary who wrestled with him the entire night. Our Sages tell us that this mysterious stranger was the heavenly representative of Esav. The confrontation between this angel and Yaakov was on two levels, one theological and philosophical, the other physical. In both areas, this confrontation is a metaphor for the eternal conflict between Israel and the nations of the world. Even in this first encounter, there was no clear victor; rather there was a negative kind of victory which the Torah summarizes in the expression: וַיַּרְא כִּי לֹא יָכֹל לוֹ, "And he perceived that he could not overcome him" (32:26). In other words, the angel could not prevail, but by the same token, Yaakov could not overcome him either. The result of this historic encounter was inconclusive, as it continues to be throughout history, and so it shall be until the end of time when, as the prophet teaches us, Israel will prevail.

However, in spite of this stalemate, when Yaakov asked the angel to bless him, the angel was forced to do so. The blessing he gave Yaakov was a change of name. וַיֹּאמֶר לֹא יַעֲקֹב יֵאָמֵר עוֹד שִׁמְךָ כִּי אִם יִשְׂרָאֵל, "No longer will it be said that your name is Yaakov, but Yisrael" (32:29).

Superficially, this would mean that the angel who represented Esav reluctantly acknowledged that our forefather's name will no longer be Yaakov, which implies deceit, but Yisrael, which denotes superiority. As the verse states: כִּי שָׂרִיתָ עִם אֱלֹקִים וְעִם אֲנָשִׁים וַתּוּכָל, "for you have striven with the Divine and with man and have overcome" (ibid.). However, there is a different interpretation given to this exchange between Yaakov and the angel. As mentioned, when man overcomes an angel, the angel gives him a gift. This gift must be one that contains the power and potency to counteract and vanquish that angel! What the angel was revealing to Yaakov was the secret of Israel's survival when attacked by the forces of Esav. He was teaching him that as long as he would conduct himself as a Yaakov, which comes from the word עָקֵב, "heel", as long as he is submissive and overly humble when confronted and challenged by Esav, he will be defeated. It is only when he becomes Yisrael that he is able to be victorious over Esav. This may well be the meaning of the verse: כִּי יַעֲקֹב בָּחַר לוֹ יָ-הּ יִשְׂרָאֵל לִסְגֻלָּתוֹ, "For G-d has chosen Yaakov for His own, Yisrael as His treasure" (*Tehillim* 135:4). We are told that in our relationship with the Almighty we must be humble and submissive, as reflected in the name Yaakov, but in our relationship with the nations of the world we must be prepared to assert ourselves and act with justified superiority, as reflected in the name Yisrael.

A similar explanation can be given to the statement of our Sages in *Shabbos* 89a. When Moshe ascended to Heaven, he was challenged by the angels who argued that man was unworthy to receive the Torah. After Moshe refuted them, all the angels, including the Angel of Death, gave him a *berachah* and a gift. The gift he received from the Angel of Death was the secret of the *ketores,* "incense," which had the power to check a plague. Indeed, when a plague was visited upon the Children of Israel as a Divine punishment in the aftermath of Korach's rebellion, Moshe instructed Aharon to circulate among the people with the *ketores,* which had the power to combat death, as the Angel of Death himself had taught Moshe. Here again, we see that the gift given to one who has vanquished an angel is the secret of how to overcome the potency and power of that very angel!

It is interesting to note that when the Almighty confirmed Yaakov's change of name, He used a different phraseology than that of the angel who first changed Yaakov's name. Whereas שָׂרוּ

שֶׁל עֵשָׂו, "the Heavenly representative of Esav," stated: לֹא יַעֲקֹב יֵאָמֵר עוֹד שִׁמְךָ, eliminating the name Yaakov completely and substituting it with the new name Yisrael, G-d, on the other hand, says: שִׁמְךָ יַעֲקֹב . . . כִּי אִם יִשְׂרָאֵל יִהְיֶה שְׁמֶךָ, "Your name is Yaakov . . . but your name will be Yisrael" (35:10), reaffirming the original name of Yaakov before He concurs with the angel and agrees that Yisrael will be his name. This is interpreted as meaning that both names are to be used.

The explanation for this double usage is as follows: Whereas in our relationship with Esav our stance and position vis-a-vis the forces who would destroy us must be that of a Yisrael, yet in relationship to Hashem we must ever retain the character of Yaakov, who is the servant of G-d, submissive and accepting. We were chosen because of our Yaakov character — "for G-d has chosen Yaakov." We are G-d's treasure because we attained the status of יִשְׂרָאֵל סְגֻלָּתוֹ, "Yisrael, His beloved treasure."

PARASHAS VAYEISHEV

Heeding the Heavenly Voice

THE ENMITY BETWEEN THE BROTHERS AND YOSEF REACHES ITS climax in the episode which we read at the beginning of this week's *Sedrah,* when Yosef, at the behest of his father, goes to see his brothers who are tending the sheep. We are told that when the brothers saw him approaching, they conspired against him to kill him. They were not only determined to kill Yosef, but they also mockingly said: וְנִרְאֶה מַה יִּהְיוּ חֲלֹמֹתָיו, "then we shall see what will become of his dreams" (37:20). Rashi comments that this phrase was said, not by the brothers, but by רוּחַ הַקֹּדֶשׁ, "the Holy Spirit." Rashi explains that when they said, "Let us kill him," the conclusion of that verse, "then we shall see what will become of his dreams," should be interpreted as follows: G-d said to them, "We will see whose plan will be fulfilled, yours or Mine." According to Rashi's commentary, the Almighty proclaimed from Heaven that their plot would never succeed, for it was destined and ordained that Yosef would become the leader of his brothers and play a historic role in the unfolding of the destiny of the Children of Yaakov.

The very next *pasuk* begins with the words: וַיִּשְׁמַע רְאוּבֵן וַיַּצִּלֵהוּ מִיָּדָם, "And Reuven heard and rescued him from their hands" (37:21). The difficulty with this phraseology lies in the fact that the *pasuk* does not tell us specifically what Reuven heard. If it means that he was aware of his brothers' nefarious plan, the verse should have been more specific. Indeed, it is for this reason that some of the commentators submit that when the verse tells us that Reuven "heard," it is referring to that voice from Heaven. In other words, he was sensitive to G-d's reaction to his brothers' plot to kill Yosef, and when he realized that the Almighty intended to prevent this murder, for He had other plans for Yosef, Reuven was determined to rescue him from the hands of his brothers.

There are a number of latter-day Bible commentators who see in this episode a lesson for all time. Very often there are evil plans and plots, devised by men who mislead those who are deaf to the Heavenly voice, which proclaims its opposition to these wicked plans. The problem is that very few people can hear that voice, which includes the still, quiet voice of one's own conscience. However, when one *does* hear that voice while others do not, he must realize that it is because he has been chosen to take action and do whatever can be done to help implement the will of Heaven.

The Talmud, in *Taanis* 21a, records a most interesting story involving two great Talmudic scholars, Rabbi Yochanan and Ilfa. Due to economic circumstances, they decided to leave the Beis Medrash and go out into the world to seek their fortune. At the conclusion of the first day of their journey, they sat down to rest and eat at the foot of an unstable wall. Two angels who were perched on top of the wall had a discussion. One said to the other, "Behold these two young scholars who have left the walls of the Beis Medrash and the occupation of Torah. They are not worthy to be protected, and I suggest that we throw this wall down on top of them." The second angel disagreed, saying, "But one of them is destined to be a great man and head the yeshivah." Rabbi Yochanan heard this discussion and turned to Ilfa, asking him whether he had heard anything. Ilfa responded in the negative, whereupon Rabbi Yochanan said to himself: Since I heard and Ilfa did not, then I am the one who has been chosen, and therefore I must return to the yeshivah. He did so and eventually became the Rosh Yeshivah.

This story illustrates most emphatically that when a person is sensitive to the desire and will of Heaven, he hears; and when he hears, he must accept the challenge! Why is it, then, that certain people choose a way of life which is more spiritual and demanding than others, and why do some people assume communal responsibility while others do not? It is because they have heard the *bas kol* which others have not.

When Yeshayahu was first called upon to assume the role of

prophet, the verse reads: וָאֶשְׁמַע אֶת קוֹל ה׳ אֹמֵר אֶת מִי אֶשְׁלַח ... וָאֹמַר הִנְנִי שְׁלָחֵנִי, "And I heard the voice of Hashem saying: 'Whom shall I send . . .' and I said, 'Here I am, send me' " (*Yeshayahu* 6:8). Here again, when G-d is seeking someone whom He can designate as His prophet, He is depicted as saying, "Whom shall I send?" But were there any who heard that question of Hashem? Apparently not. Yeshayahu however said: וָאֶשְׁמַע, "I heard." And that is why he was chosen. A person who is sensitive and "hears" while others only listen, who "sees" while others look, is the one who must assume responsibility and and accept burdens and oligations — precisely because he hears.

Reuven was one, Yeshayahu was another, and Rabbi Yochanan realized, when he heard the dialogue of the angels and Ilfa did not, that the message was meant for him. This is a great lesson for all of us for all time: to be sensitive to the call from on High, and to respond.

PARASHAS MIKEITZ

Self-worth

THIS WEEK'S *SEDRAH, MIKEITZ,* CONTINUES THE STORY OF YOSEF which began in the previous one, *Vayeishev.* At the beginning of this week's *Sedrah,* Yosef is released from prison by Pharaoh, who is desperate to find someone who can interpret his dreams. At the recommendation of the *sar hamashkim* (the wine steward), Yosef is released from the dungeon to interpret the king's dreams, and consequently becomes the viceroy of Egypt.

The Torah tells us that Yosef was "rushed from the dungeon; he shaved and changed his clothes" before he came to Pharaoh. Rashi comments: מִפְּנֵי כְּבוֹד הַמַּלְכוּת, "in deference to the honor and dignity of the king" (41:14). One of the great *baalei mussar* speculates that Yosef was actually reluctant to groom himself before he came to Pharaoh, especially to trim his hair! Yosef was aware that his troubles in the house of Potiphar began when, as our Rabbis tell us, he was מְסַלְסֵל בִּשְׂעָרוֹ, which means he was overly concerned with his physical appearance and paid special attention to his hair. Realizing the source of his sin, which led to his downfall, he was not interested in improving his appearance, especially by grooming his hair. This was Yosef's initial reaction when he was told that he had been summoned to appear before the king. Upon further consideration, he changed his mind and permitted his hair to be cut as a courtesy to the king. However, a great ethical teacher suggests that the dignity and honor of Pharaoh would not have been sufficient reason for Yosef to change his mind. He therefore suggests that the phrase כְּבוֹד הַמַּלְכוּת does not refer to the Egyptian king, but to the מַלְכוּת of his father Yaakov!

In the Land of Canaan, Yaakov was considered a royal personage, and was so treated by his family. His children were concerned for the dignity of their father and the need to conduct themselves in a manner which would bring honor to him and to the family. It is this כְּבוֹד הַמַּלְכוּת, "honor of kingship," which Rashi is referring to, for Yosef realized that when he would appear in the royal court and ultimately tell Pharaoh his family background, it was vital for him not to appear in a disheveled state, but in a dignified manner which would reflect honor on his father and his family. In other words, the phrase כְּבוֹד הַמַּלְכוּת refers to Yaakov and not to Pharaoh.

That Yosef was constantly aware of his connection to his father, and sensitive to the teachings of Yaakov, can also be seen in last week's *Parashah,* when the wife of his master attempted to seduce him and he resisted. Rashi, in his commentary on that episode, quotes from the Talmud in *Sotah,* where our Sages tell us that when Yosef's resolve began to weaken, he saw דְּמוּת דְּיוּקְנוֹ שֶׁל אָבִיו, "the image of his father." Our Rabbis are teaching us that even when he was not in his father's house, he was constantly aware of his father's presence and values. It is interesting to note that when the Torah uses the phrase וַיְמָאֵן (39:8), which means that he adamantly refused to acquiesce to the request of his master's wife, the cantillation (טַעַם הַמִּקְרָא) is a שַׁלְשֶׁלֶת, "chain." This subtly teaches us that there was a chain which linked Yosef to his father at all times, and it was this link which gave him the strength to retain his identity and integrity, be it in his moral behavior or pride in his family.

Yosef was not alone in manifesting this characteristic of self-respect. We see in our *Parashah* that his brothers acted the same way when challenged by Egyptian authority. When the brothers were brought to the viceroy, whom they did not recognize as their brother Yosef, and accused of being spies, they refuted the charge and stated: כֻּלָּנוּ בְּנֵי אִישׁ אֶחָד נָחְנוּ כֵּנִים אֲנַחְנוּ, "All of us, sons of one man are we; we are truthful people" (42:11).

Rabbi Samson Raphael Hirsch explains the strange variation of the word "we," נָחְנוּ, which is first spelled without the *aleph*, followed immediately with אֲנַחְנוּ using the letter *aleph*. The word נָחְנוּ, where the *aleph* is omitted, denotes a diminishment of one's self, whereas the word אֲנַחְנוּ implies a sense of self-worth. Rabbi Hirsch explains that in this dialogue between the brothers and the viceroy, two areas were under discussion. Initially, they introduce and identify themselves as brothers and as "sons of one man." Here, Rabbi Hirsch submits, they are describing their social condition and therefore modestly use the term נָחְנוּ. However, when their character and honesty is questioned, they assert their dignity with pride. It is then that the נָחְנוּ becomes אֲנַחְנוּ. As Rabbi Hirsch puts it, the brothers stated: We are realists and prepared to be humble, and even submissive, in the presence of one who wields power and whose favor we court. However, we cannot meekly and quietly accept any unjust accusation which questions our integrity. When that happens, the sons of Yaakov firmly state כֵּנִים אֲנַחְנוּ, "We are truthful men!"

A sense of self-worth has ever been the hallmark of the Children of Israel, especially when their honesty and integrity is questioned. So it was when the sons of Yaakov first came to Egypt, and this sense of self-pride, which Yosef demonstrated even as a slave and prisoner, paved the way for his family as they prepared to go into *galus Mitzraim.* And it was this spirit which ensured their survival in the first exile, as it has in every subsequent *galus.*

PARASHAS VAYIGASH

Day of Judgment, Day of Admonition

IN THIS WEEK'S *SEDRAH,* YOSEF REVEALS HIMSELF TO HIS BROTHERS. Our Sages depict this moving episode as one which represents the paradigm of the ultimate Divine revelation of Hashem to humanity. The Midrash states, in the name of Abba Kohen Bardela, "Woe unto us from the Day of Judgment, woe unto us from the Day of Admonition." He considers the words spoken by Yosef to his brothers — when he finally tells them who he is — as representing a Day of Judgment and also a Day of Admonition. As he says, "If Yosef, who was the youngest of the brothers, struck such fear and confusion in the hearts of his brothers when he revealed himself, so that they were unable to respond to him, how much more so will this be true when the Almighty confronts every person on the great Day of Judgment and chastises each one: לְפִי מַה שֶׁהוּא, "According to 'who he is' " (*Bereishis Rabbah* 93).

This great Sage is making a number of salient points. The revelation of Yosef consists of two simple words: אֲנִי יוֹסֵף, "I am Yosef" (45:3), and when G-d will reveal Himself to mankind, He will also use but two words: אֲנִי ה', "I am Hashem." These two succinct words, אֲנִי יוֹסֵף, and similarly, אֲנִי ה', have the power and impact to pierce the armor of man's self-assurance and dispel his doubts, while answering all his questions without the necessity to elaborate further. There is no longer room left to debate. The brothers were firmly convinced of their evaluation of Yosef, self-righteous in their anger towards him, as well as their moral superiority over this harsh ruler. Yet, all these feelings are dispelled once he says, "I am [your brother] Yosef." And so it will be when G-d simply states: אֲנִי ה׳, "I am Hashem," thereby diffusing all of man's anger and dispelling all his doubts, so that we are able to recognize G-d and to appreciate how correct His justice and His Divine decisions are.

Yosef does not accuse his brothers of wrongdoing nor does he belabor their sins against him. He merely states the fact that he is their brother Yosef, whom they sold into captivity, and he allows them to become their own accusers and their own judges. And so it will be on the great *Yom HaDin,* "the great Day of Judgment," when we will realize that so much of our life has been built on false premises, just as the anger of the brothers was built on their false premises. So many of our problems are the consequence of our mistakes and illusions, as was also the case with the brothers and Yosef. It is not difficult for us to relate to this truism when we read the story of Yosef and his brothers, nor will it be difficult for man to grasp the infinite righteousness of Hashem, once he is brought to this realization through the words אֲנִי ה׳. So many of our mistaken and false assumptions will be clarified when we merit to hear those words and clearly see the righteousness and logic of the Almighty.

Another result of Yosef's revelation was that, by identifying himself, he created a moment of self-recognition on the part of his brothers, and there is nothing more frightening for man than such a moment. This is the meaning of the expression לְפִי מַה שֶׁהוּא, when man is forced to recognize *who he is*.

Small wonder that this great Sage refers to the dramatic event which we read in this week's *Sedrah* as both יוֹם הַדִּין, "the Day of Judgment," and יוֹם הַתּוֹכָחָה, "the Day of Admonition."

Dignity and Self-respect

AFTER YOSEF REVEALS HIS IDENTITY TO HIS BROTHERS, HE URGES them to return home and bring their father and families to Egypt, where they will be able to live in safety and security. Many

Bible commentators teach us that Yaakov was most reluctant to accept this invitation, fearing that his family would find the Egyptian environment too overpowering and tempting, thereby resulting in their acculturation and assimilation. The Almighty reassures Yaakov and tells him to accept his son's invitation to join him in Egypt, promising that He will accompany Yaakov to Egypt and be with him, as the verse states: אָנֹכִי אֵרֵד עִמְּךָ, "I will descend with you" (46:4). Our Sages tell us that this promise was one that the Almighty kept not only in Egypt, but in every exile of the Jewish people, for the *Shechinah* accompanies the Jewish people in every *galus*.

Yaakov was concerned not only about the negative influence Egypt would have upon his family, but he also realized that this was the beginning of a long, difficult exile experience for the Children of Israel. Indeed, our Sages tell us that originally the decree was that Yaakov was destined to leave the Land of Canaan and be brought to Egypt "in iron chains and fetters."

However, this decree was changed due to the great merit of Yaakov, and, as a result, he came down in the royal wagon that his son Yosef sent for him. A great Torah teacher asked a most logical and cogent question regarding this *maamar Chazal:* At what price did Yaakov come down to Egypt in such style? Was it worth the 22 years of anguish he endured when he and his son Yosef were separated, and the departure of the *Ruach HaKodesh,* "the Divine Spirit," from him? And was it worthwhile for Yosef to be sold as a slave and spend all those years in a dungeon so that his father could come to Egypt in these royal wagons? Wasn't this much too high a price to pay for a journey of approximately 10 days from the Land of Canaan to Egypt in style?

To be sure, it was not the comfort and luxury afforded Yaakov that was of such importance. Rather, there was a more profound reason for Yaakov and his children to come down to Egypt in this manner. It was destined that the Children of Israel be enslaved in that land, and it is only natural for a slave people to feel inferior to their masters and develop a strong tendency to become assimilated into their culture and become so submissive that their greatest desire is to imitate their masters and accept their culture. If Yaakov and his children would have gone into *galus* in chains, they would have come to Egypt, from the very beginning, with a slave mentality, which would have shaped their attitude and made them prone to adopt the culture of the "master race." However, by coming down in royal style, their self-respect and dignity was left intact, and they were able to retain their sense of self-worth all the years they were destined to spend in Egypt, even though they were in bondage! It was for this preservation of dignity and spirit of freedom, which they brought from Canaan to Egypt, that the price paid was worthwhile. Parenthetically, we must note that even with these safeguards, only one fifth of the Israelites merited to be freed from Egypt and come to Sinai, ultimately becoming the nucleus of the Jewish nation.

Indeed, we are taught that the reason it was destined that Yosef precede his family was to allow them, in the initial stage, to establish their own "homeland" in the land of Goshen, which gave them the opportunity and strength of character to retain their identity, even after they were enslaved. The *agalos* (wagons) which Yosef sent to his father are not to be viewed merely as vehicles for the journey, but as a key to the ability of his family to remain intact as a proud, self-respecting people.

PARASHAS VAYECHI

Jewish Unity: Ethnicity and Faith

THERE IS A *PASUK* IN THIS WEEK'S *SEDRAH* WHICH REQUIRES EXplanation and clarification. We know that the name Yaakov was given to our father Yaakov at birth, but the name Yisrael was added later, first by the angel who fought with him, and then confirmed by the Almighty Himself. We are taught that the name Yaakov reflects a lesser status than the name Yisrael. Therefore, whenever these two names appear in the same *pasuk*, clarification is in order.

In our *Parashah*, the *pasuk* reads: הִקָּבְצוּ וְשִׁמְעוּ בְּנֵי יַעֲקֹב וְשִׁמְעוּ אֶל יִשְׂרָאֵל אֲבִיכֶם, "Gather yourselves and listen, sons of Yaakov, and listen to Yisrael your father" (49:2). Here is an example of both names being used in the same verse. We must also attempt to understand why the word וְשִׁמְעוּ ("and listen") is repeated twice.

Yaakov was the father of 12 sons who ultimately became the 12 Tribes of Israel. Their relationship to each other functioned on two levels. They were brothers with familial ties which later became the ethnic factor that united them and gave them their national identity. In this sense, they were similar to all people who began as family units, evolved into tribal groupings, and then became an identifiable people and nation. These ties and national identity are referred to by the name Yaakov, and create a sense of עֲרֵבוּת, of mutual responsibility, as we find in the expression כָּל יִשְׂרָאֵל עֲרֵבִים זֶה בָּזֶה, "All Israel is responsible for one another" (*Shevuos* 39a).

However, this is not the major cement which holds us together, for with the passage of time and our dispersion among the nations of the world, were it not for a second factor, we would probably have disappeared as a people long ago. This second factor is that we are all members of a faith community, sharing beliefs and practices which link us together and, in some mystical manner, transform us into one נֶפֶשׁ, one people with a collective soul.

In last week's *Sedrah*, *Vayigash*, the Torah uses the expression נֶפֶשׁ when it tells us that 70 souls of the House of Yaakov came to Egypt; כָּל הַנֶּפֶשׁ לְבֵית יַעֲקֹב is the expression used (46:27). Rashi comments on that verse, in the name of our Rabbis, that Esav had six offspring, and the Torah calls them נַפְשׁוֹת בֵּיתוֹ, "members of his household," using the plural נְפָשׁוֹת, whereas Yaakov came to Egypt with 70 offspring, and they are referred to as נֶפֶשׁ in the singular! The reason for this difference is that the children of Esav served different gods, while the children of Yaakov served only One G-d. Hence, Esav's descendants were separate, but we are united by our faith.

If the ethnic identity of the 12 tribes, as the children of Yaakov, created a sense of עַרְבוּת, their religious beliefs created one נֶפֶשׁ. In the spiritual realm, they are בְּנֵי יִשְׂרָאֵל, rather than בְּנֵי יַעֲקֹב. It is for this reason that the word וְשִׁמְעוּ, "and listen," is repeated twice in the same verse. The first וְשִׁמְעוּ is meant to appeal to their sense of brotherhood and their nationalistic feelings. The second one, however, refers to their spiritual beliefs and values, urging them to listen to their innermost, soulful longings and commitments. To this very day, if we listen carefully and hear that קוֹל דְּמָמָה דַקָּה, that quiet, soft and most meaningful voice, then we will realize that we are בְּנֵי יִשְׂרָאֵל, not only בְּנֵי יַעֲקֹב.

Jewish unity becomes a reality only when the spiritual component is added to the national, ethnic one. Both are imperatives which cannot be ignored. However, it is vital for us to appreciate that common memories and shared experiences of life are not sufficient to guarantee our unity, as we see from history and the reality which confronts us both in Israel and in the Diaspora. Ultimately, it is not as בְּנֵי יַעֲקֹב that we ensure our continuity as a people, but as בְּנֵי יִשְׂרָאֵל that we secure our role as the עַם הַנֶּצַח, "the eternal people."

Sefer Shemos

PARASHAS SHEMOS

Not to Lose Sight of the Tree for the Forest

THE TORAH TEACHES US: וַיִּגְדַּל מֹשֶׁה וַיֵּצֵא אֶל אֶחָיו וַיַּרְא בְּסִבְלֹתָם, "Moshe grew up and went out to his brethren and observed their burdens" (2:11). The Torah then proceeds to tell us that Moshe saw an Egyptian man striking a Hebrew man of his brethren, whereupon Moshe struck down the Egyptian. The Torah adds that before he did so, וַיִּפֶן כֹּה וָכֹה וַיַּרְא כִּי אֵין אִישׁ, "He turned this way and that, and saw that there was no man" (2:12).

In this brief episode, the Torah teaches us a number of important lessons. We know from the subsequent episode related in our *Parashah* that there was strife and dissension and a lack of unity among the Jewish people at that time. Our Sages also tell us that the commitment of the Jewish people to the teachings of the Patriarchs had dramatically eroded, and their merits were few. Yet, when Moshe went out to his brothers, he did not observe or see their shortcomings and faults, but as the Torah tells us: וַיַּרְא בְּסִבְלֹתָם, "he saw their burdens" (2:11), which is indeed the true measure of maturity. The Torah subtly refers to this maturing of Moshe with the word וַיִּגְדַּל. However, it was not only with a sense of empathy for his brothers that Moshe manifested his maturity and understanding of their lot. His sense of responsibility was revealed as well in his swift response to the Egyptian man's beating of his fellow Hebrew. When the Torah states that he looked around and saw that אֵין אִישׁ, that there were no others able or willing to help, he fulfilled what was later to become a dictum of

40 / Table Talk

our Rabbis: בִּמְקוֹם שֶׁאֵין אֲנָשִׁים הִשְׁתַּדֵּל לִהְיוֹת אִישׁ, "Where there is no man, try to be a man" (*Avos* 2:6).

We should also note that even though the Torah tells us that Moshe immediately observed the general condition of the Children of Israel in Egypt, a people enslaved and persecuted, still he was not blinded to the plight of the individual. He did not allow the overall situation of the *klal* to obscure the *prat,* the pain and the need of the individual. וַיַּרְא אִישׁ מִצְרִי מַכֶּה אִישׁ עִבְרִי, "And he saw an Egyptian was beating a Hebrew man" (2:11) — a single oppressor and a single victim.

There is a saying that the smaller the focus of attention, the harder the task. It is easier to be a civic leader than a good husband and father; easier to be a patriot than a decent, honest citizen; and easier to be a humanitarian than to help a neighbor or a single person. The greatness of Moshe was that even as he saw the burdens of his brethren in general, he was still able to focus on the trouble besetting one individual Jew.

The Torah, in these brief verses, teaches us the following vital lessons: first, the importance of seeing the problems, not the faults of a community; second, to assume responsibility and not be deterred by the apathy of others; and third, not to allow one's involvement with the community at large to blind one to the plight of the individual.

No Excuses, Please!

THERE IS A TENDENCY ON THE PART OF MANY, WHEN ASKED TO participate in a project that is meant to strengthen Jewish education or Jewish institutions in general, to say that the place involved is not conducive to *kedushah* (sanctity). Many times an attempt to establish a *shul* or a yeshivah has been stymied by people who take this negative attitude and use it as a convenient excuse to do nothing.

Similarly, there are those who will use a different rationalization for their unwillingness to respond to these challenges; they claim that it is the wrong *time* for such a project, in addition to being the wrong *place*. And some people of ability and means, when invited to assume a leadership role in the Jewish community, will say that they are the wrong *person.* The common denominator of these three excuses is precisely that — they are excuses. They are excuses for inaction and a lack of responsiveness due to lethargy and laziness, rather than legitimate reasons.

If we look carefully at this week's *Sedrah,* we see a strong refutation of the first excuse. When G-d spoke to Moshe from the burning bush, in the wilderness of Chorev, and the angel of Hashem cautioned Moshe not to come closer and to remove his shoes, the reason given is: כִּי הַמָּקוֹם אֲשֶׁר אַתָּה עוֹמֵד עָלָיו אַדְמַת קֹדֶשׁ הוּא, "for the place upon which you stand is holy ground" (3:5). This is the simple *pshat*, but the *pasuk* can be interpreted in a different manner as well. The Torah is teaching us that wherever a person stands, that place is holy ground, and the word of Hashem can come to him even in the wilderness. Let him not say that this place is the wrong place, for the first encounter of Moshe with Hashem occurred in the most unlikely place and under the most unexpected circumstances. The place where he was tending Yisro's flocks had no inherent holiness, and the burning bush was not a sacred one. Still, it was there that G-d first appeared and spoke to Moshe, challenging him to assume leadership, and charging him to return to Egypt and bring the Children of Israel out of bondage.

Many centuries later, Hillel taught us: אִם אֵין אֲנִי לִי מִי לִי, "If I am not for myself, then who will be for me?" as well as teaching every man to say to himself: אִם לֹא עַכְשָׁו אֵימָתַי, "If not now, then when?" (*Avos* 1:14). The episode at the burning bush mirrors these two admonitions of the great Hillel. When Moshe was chosen by Hashem to be the leader of His people and the Almighty's emissary, his immediate response was: מִי אָנֹכִי, "Who am I" (3:11), that I should be the one to lead the Jews? He protested: וְלֹא יִשְׁמְעוּ בְּקֹלִי, "They will not listen to my voice" (4:1). However, Hashem reassured him that they would heed his voice, and by reading the phraseology of G-d's assurance carefully, we can understand what Hashem was saying. In Chapter 3, verse 18, G-d said: וְשָׁמְעוּ לְקֹלֶךָ, "They will heed your voice," whereas when Moshe protested, he said: וְלֹא יִשְׁמְעוּ בְּקֹלִי, "They will not heed my voice." In one case, the letter *lamed* is the prefix, whereas, in the second case, the letter *beis* is used. The difference is a fundamental one. בְּקוֹל means the substance of what is being said, the words and the message, to which the Children of Israel were not prepared to listen. The phrase לְקֹלֶךָ refers to the voice itself; i.e., they will hear *how* you speak, and not only what you say. The tone of the voice, its sincerity, warmth and feeling of concern is what people will respond to.

We are being taught that when a person feels that he is the wrong person for the job, he can derive courage and inspiration from the ultimate willingness of Moshe to accept the role of leadership given to him, despite the fact that he was a *kevad peh* (a man of halting speech). There is an additional lesson here: One's sincerity and deep belief in his message can overcome his impediments and shortcomings.

As for timing, our Rabbis teach us that Moshe was deeply concerned that the time for redemption had not yet arrived. He was aware of the tradition transmitted from the time of Avraham that the Jews were destined to be in bondage 400 years, and they had been in Egypt only 210 years! But the Torah teaches us that when the time of *geulah* arrives, that moment must be grasped, and "If not now, then when?"

These are the lessons being taught to us by the dialogue between the Almighty and Moshe. There is no such thing as the wrong place, the wrong time and the wrong person — when destiny and Hashem call. Any *makom* can be transformed into holy ground; when Heaven determines that the moment of *geulah* has arrived, then "If not now, when?" And when a person is asked to assume responsibility, he must respond, "If not I, then who?"

PARASHAS VA'EIRA

For Your Own Good

WHEN MOSHE, AT THE BEHEST OF THE ALMIGHTY, TOLD THE Children of Israel the good news that Hashem was preparing to take them out of the land of Egypt and bring them to the Promised Land, they refused to listen to him מִקֹּצֶר רוּחַ וּמֵעֲבֹדָה קָשָׁה, "because of shortness of breath and hard work" (6:9). The phrase קֹצֶר רוּחַ is also translated as meaning "insufficiency of spirit," with the word רוּחַ being used in the spiritual sense, referring to belief. The Torah, then, is telling us that the Children of Israel refused to listen to Moshe for two reasons: They were impatient because of the unusual hard labor, and, in addition, their faith was weakened due to fatigue and exhaustion.

However, if this is the interpretation of the verse, it is difficult to understand Moshe's subsequent argument when he said to the Almighty, "Behold, the Children of Israel did not listen to me, so how will Pharaoh listen to me?" (6:12). If this is meant to be a *kal vachomer* (an inference from minor to major), it would be a very weak argument, since Pharaoh, unlike the Jews, was not impatient from hard labor, nor did he exhibit a deficiency of spirit due to physical exhaustion.

We can, however, interpret this phrase of וְלֹא שָׁמְעוּ, "they did not listen," not as a refusal to listen to Moshe's transmission of G-d's message to them, but rather as a refusal to listen to his argument. Moshe attempted to explain why his mission had resulted in such cruel and unbearable consequences, where the people were no longer given straw for their production of bricks, while the quota was to remain the same. It was this unusual punishment and the increased pain and suffering imposed on them which the Children of Israel found so difficult to comprehend. They could not understand why Moshe's mission should have resulted in added affliction rather than a lessening of their suffering.

Moshe attempted to explain to them that there were two reasons for this. The original Heavenly decree had been that they would be enslaved and afflicted for 400 years. Now, they were told that their sentence was being reduced by 190 years and the *geulah* was at hand. The only way this could happen, Moshe argued, was by intensifying the degree of their labor, accelerating the work and the affliction, thereby compressing it into a shorter time period. This intensification was such that the equivalent of 400 years of עֲבוֹדָה (labor) and עִנּוּי (affliction) were compressed into 210 years! This is one reason, Moshe told the Jews, for the worsening of their lot. It was for their benefit that it was happening! It was the argument contained in the phrase עֲבֹדָה קָשָׁה, but it was an argument to which they refused to listen.

The second reason for their deteriorating situation is found in the phrase קֹצֶר רוּחַ, their erosion of faith. The Bible commentators point out that after 200 years of dwelling in Egypt, many of the Children of Israel had forgotten their history and abandoned the faith of their fathers. Their very identity was in danger of being eroded, and if they were to remain in Egypt the full 400 years, there would be no Jews left to redeem. It is this which Moshe was explaining to his people in the brief phrase קֹצֶר רוּחַ. Although the 400 years were far from complete, the redemption had to be hastened lest the people be lost completely.

However, they refused to accept this argument just as they had refused to accept the argument of עֲבֹדָה קָשָׁה, even though it was for their benefit. Moshe, therefore, correctly argued that if the Children of Israel refused to listen, how much more so will Pharaoh refuse, since sending out the Israelites would be to his detriment and cause him great economic loss! This is indeed a good *kal vachomer*.

The last *pasuk* in the previous *Parashah* (6:1) can now also be more clearly understood. There it is written that Hashem said to Moshe: עַתָּה תִרְאֶה אֲשֶׁר אֶעֱשֶׂה לְפַרְעֹה, "Now you will see what I shall do to Pharaoh." Our Rabbis interpret this to mean that G-d reproached Moshe for complaining and told him that he would merit to see the punishment of Pharaoh, but not what would happen to the 31 kings in the Land of Canaan when the Jews conquered the Land.

The Chafetz Chaim asks: Was it right for Hashem to respond to Moshe's anguished cry — "Why have You done this to Your people?" — which came from a broken heart and sincere concern for his people, by telling him that he would not live to bring his beloved people into the Promised Land? He therefore submits that this declaration of Hashem to Moshe, עַתָּה תִרְאֶה, should be understood not as a statement of admonishment, but rather as a statement of consolation. Instead of emphasizing the word עַתָּה, "now," — implying that only now will he see the punishment of Pharaoh and the redemption of the Jews but not later — we should emphasize the word תִרְאֶה, you will be granted the opportunity to witness the Exodus and see the fruits of your labor. What G-d was saying is similar to what we have said regarding Moshe's attempt to explain and justify the intensification of the people's labor, thereby comforting them. By the intensification of their suffering, the redemption was being hastened. And this is the same argument which G-d presented to Moshe. You ask why I have done evil to the people and why I have sent you. The reason is to accelerate and hasten the redemptive process so that *you* can also see what will happen to Pharaoh, and how the Jews will be brought forth from Egypt. If the redemption had to wait another 190 years, you would not be alive at that time, and would not be able to witness the great *geulah*. G-d was comforting Moshe and saying to him עַתָּה תִרְאֶה, now that the labor has been intensified and the redemption process accelerated, you will merit to see all this. The Chafetz Chaim points out that in Jewish history events that may seem to be tragic and destructive are ultimately seen and appreciated as being positive.

The last *pasuk* in *Parashas Shemos* and the verse quoted above from our *Parashah* now correspond. G-d's words of comfort to Moshe, עַתָּה תִרְאֶה, are echoed by him in his words to the Children of Israel. Unfortunately, they were not able to appreciate them, and it is very possible that Moshe, as well, did not appreciate what G-d was saying to him at the moment of his anguish. However, with the passage of time, man realizes that the actions of the Almighty are just and merciful, as we see both from G-d's response to Moshe's complaint in last week's *Sedrah* and from Moshe's explanation to his people in this week's *Parashah*.

PARASHAS BO

The Light That Shines in the Darkness

THE NINTH PLAGUE, חֹשֶׁךְ (DARKNESS), IS DESCRIBED IN THIS week's *Sedrah*. The *pasuk* reads: לֹא רָאוּ אִישׁ אֶת אָחִיו וְלֹא קָמוּ אִישׁ מִתַּחְתָּיו, "No man could see his brother, nor could anyone rise from his place" (10:23).

Rashi explains that the darkness was not only the absence of light, but it also had substance. As he puts it, "If one was sitting, he could not rise; and if he was standing, he could not sit." It is for this reason that the expression used in the Torah is חֹשֶׁךְ אֲפֵלָה, "a thick darkness" (10:22). However, homiletically speaking, this verse can be interpreted in a most instructive manner, carrying with it a great moral lesson. Human nature is such that even when people are in need of assistance and help, there is often a lack of action on the part of many who are capable of helping, simply because they are not paying attention. There are times when we are unaware of another's need either because we are not looking, or because we shut our eyes to the reality of an unpleasant situation. When that happens, nothing is done to alleviate the suffering of others, nor is any attempt made to be of assistance.

It is this which the Torah is alluding to when the verse states, "No man could see his brother," and therefore "[no one] could rise from his place." One has to be able to observe and see what is happening around him if he is to be spurred into action. If לֹא רָאוּ occurs, if one is not cognizant of his brother's need, then you can rest assured that לֹא קָמוּ will follow, and no one will rise from his place to help.

The latter part of this *pasuk* reads: וּלְכָל בְּנֵי יִשְׂרָאֵל הָיָה אוֹר בְּמוֹשְׁבֹתָם, "But for all the Children of Israel there was light in their dwellings." A famous *maggid* once interpreted this phrase as follows. A person who possesses talents and intellectual gifts may be unappreciated and unrecognized due to particular circumstances. He may reside in a community where people are desensitized to intellectual or artistic pursuits and, as a result, cannot appreciate the accomplishments and contributions he makes to society. It is not enough for a person to be blessed with certain abilities. He must also be fortunate to live at a time and in a place where these talents are recognized and appreciated by others. In other words, *setting* is very important. For example, a beautiful, flawless diamond may not be fully appreciated unless it is placed in a proper setting. Over the years, Jews have been oppressed and discriminated against, isolated from the world around them and ostracized by society, and thereby denied the ability to shine. Indeed, in free countries we see how Jews have filled important roles in many areas, be it medicine, law or the arts, because they found themselves in the proper setting.

It is to this which the Torah is alluding when it states that "for all the Children of Israel there was light," depending upon מוֹשְׁבֹתָם, "their dwelling place," which may well mean their setting. If it is proper and correct, then the thick darkness cannot obscure their talents. Rather, their natural, inherent light shines through, and their brilliance is recognized and appreciated, just as a beautiful diamond is admired, provided it is set properly.

Second, but not Last or Final

IN THIS PARASHAH, THE TORAH TEACHES US THE RITUAL OF THE FIRST *korban pesach* (paschal lamb), which the Almighty commanded the Jews to bring as an offering in Egypt. They were told to take the blood of the lamb and smear it on the two doorposts of their respective houses. The Torah proceeds to explain the reason for this ritual: וְהָיָה הַדָּם לָכֶם לְאֹת עַל הַבָּתִּים, "The blood shall be a sign for you upon the houses where you are" (12:13).

A most interesting variation of this verse is given by one of the outstanding latter-day Bible commentators, who links it with an episode recorded in *Parashas Shemos* (4:3-9). There we read how G-d first appeared to Moshe in the burning bush and gave him the mission of returning to Egypt and speaking to the Jews in G-d's name. When Moshe expressed his misgivings as to whether the Jews would believe him, the Almighty gave him three signs, which the Torah refers to as אותות. The first was the transformation of his stick into a serpent; the second was the placing of his hand in his bosom and its becoming leprous, and then its being healed by returning to his bosom; and the third sign was the changing of water into blood. It is important to note that the Torah calls the second of the three signs הָאֹת הָאַחֲרוֹן, "the last sign" (4:8). We see from here that even though a third sign was given subsequently, the second sign is referred to as אַחֲרוֹן.

Based upon this, there is a story told of a churchman who once confronted a great *talmid chacham* and challenged him to explain a *pasuk* in *Tanach*. The *Navi* states: גָּדוֹל יִהְיֶה כְּבוֹד הַבַּיִת הַזֶּה הָאַחֲרוֹן מִן הָרִאשׁוֹן, "The glory of this latter Temple will be greater than that of the former" (*Chaggai* 2:9). The verse refers to the second Temple as אַחֲרוֹן, the last one! Does this not prove, the cleric said, that there will not be a third Temple, as your tradition teaches? The first and second Temples were both destroyed, and then Jews were dispersed among the nations. How then can you believe that they will return some day to the Land and rebuild the Holy Temple?

The Sage explained to him that the Hebrew word אַחֲרוֹן (last) does not mean that there is nothing following it, and he proved his point from the verses we have quoted from *Parashas Shemos* regarding the three signs given to Moshe. He buttressed his argument by pointing to the verse quoted above (4:8), where the second sign is called אַחֲרוֹן, yet is followed by another sign — "And the blood shall be for you a sign upon the houses" (12:13). The Torah is referring to the sign of the blood given to Moshe when G-d first spoke to him, and states that it will be a sign עַל הַבָּתִּים, "upon the houses," alluding to the Holy Temples, which are called "houses." The fact that the second sign is called אַחֲרוֹן and yet is followed with the third sign of blood is an indication that when the prophet speaks of the second *Beis HaMikdash* and refers to it as אַחֲרוֹן, it can still be followed with a third one! In this brilliant manner, the Sage was able to counter the argument of the churchman who questioned the possibility of the Jews returning to their Land and there rebuilding the *Beis HaMikdash*.

PARASHAS BESHALACH

Message in a Jar

IN THIS WEEK'S *SEDRAH*, THE STORY OF THE MANNA IS RELATED. The food provided by the Almighty to the Jewish people in the wilderness was called manna, and the Torah describes in great detail the appearance of this food, the quantity apportioned to each family, how it was gathered, and the unique relationship between Shabbos and this Heavenly food. The description of the manna is found not only in this *Sedrah,* but also in the Book of *Bamidbar* (11:7), where certain additional details are given.

In our *Parashah,* it is interesting to note that when this phenomenon is first introduced (16:4) the verses relate how the manna appeared on the surface of the wilderness, to the amazement of the Children of Israel, who were commanded by Moshe to gather a specific amount in accordance with their daily requirements. They were prohibited from leaving over any of the manna from day to day except on the sixth day when they gathered a double portion of it in preparation for Shabbos.

A close study of the verses in this chapter shows that, after introducing the subject of the manna, its actual description is not given until the conclusion of the chapter. Then we are told, in verse 31: "It was like coriander seed, it was white, and it tasted like a cake fried in honey." The question arises as to why the Torah does not give us this description among the details at the very beginning of the chapter, when we are introduced to this great miracle.

One of the great Bible commentators of recent years, Rabbi Yehoshua Leib Diskin, asks why it was necessary to describe the appearance and shape of the manna, both here and in *Sefer Bamidbar*. He explains that the reason can be found in Moshe's directive to Aharon (verse 33) that he should take a jar, put manna into it, and set it aside for safekeeping for all generations. Rashi comments, regarding this directive, that in the days of the prophet Yirmiyahu, when he admonished the Jewish people for neglecting the study of Torah, they responded that they could not abandon their work and occupy themselves with Torah, for then they would have no source of livelihood. Yirmiyahu countered their argument by taking out the צִנְצֶנֶת הַמָּן, "the jar of manna," and saying to them, "Behold and observe this container of manna, for this is how your forefathers were sustained during their journey in the wilderness." He continued: הַרְבֵּה שְׁלוּחִים יֵשׁ לַמָּקוֹם לְהָכִין מָזוֹן לִירֵאָיו, "G-d has many ways of providing food for those who fear Him."

We see from this episode that the container of manna served to remind the Jews of the great miracle which occurred and to reassure them that they would have food, just as their forefathers did in the wilderness, providing they would keep the faith and place their reliance on Hashem. However, the question is: How could the Jews be sure that this was indeed a sample of the manna, and that the contents of this jar were authentic? The answer must be because it fit perfectly the description given in the Torah of the appearance of the manna, which was like coriander seeds that are normally black, but these were white and shiny like crystal beads! The uniqueness of its appearance substantiated and authenticated the contents of the jar as being a sample of the miraculous Heavenly food which sustained our forefathers in the wilderness. It is for this reason that the description of the manna is not given at the beginning of the chapter, but at the end. The Torah wanted to link this description to the verse which speaks of the צִנְצֶנֶת הַמָּן that was set aside as a testimony of G-d's concern for His people and His readiness to feed them. This willingness was one which would repeat itself in all times, especially for those who are prepared to dedicate themselves to the study of the Almighty's Torah.

Hearing and Reading

AT THE VERY END OF THIS WEEK'S *SEDRAH*, THE STORY OF Amalek's attack against the Children of Israel when they left Egypt is recorded. We are taught that Moshe appointed Yehoshua to lead the counterattack against Amalek, and the Torah tells us that he was successful in weakening Amalek and its people with the sword. After this victory, Hashem said to Moshe: כְּתֹב זֹאת זִכָּרוֹן בַּסֵּפֶר וְשִׂים בְּאָזְנֵי יְהוֹשֻׁעַ כִּי מָחֹה אֶמְחֶה אֶת זֵכֶר עֲמָלֵק, "Write this as a remembrance in the Book, and recite it in the ears of Yehoshua that I shall surely erase the memory of Amalek from under the heavens" (17:14).

It is important to understand why G-d's promise to erase the memory of Amalek had to first be written in a book, and then recited in the ears of Yehoshua.

The *baalei mussar,* the great ethical teachers of Torah, often write that there is a difference between hearing an evil tiding directly from Hashem or a prophet, as compared to reading it. The former is far more difficult to accept. They prove this thesis from the fact that when Hashem spoke to Moshe the very first time, He told Moshe to tell the Jewish people that His name was אֶהְיֶה, which literally means, "I will be." Our Sages explain this as meaning that the Almighty told Moshe to reassure the Jews that He will be with them in future exiles as He is with them in Egypt. To which Moshe responded: It is sufficient to confront troubles and persecutions when they actually happen, and it is better not to speak of them in advance. The question, however, is asked: Is not the expression אֶהְיֶה אֲשֶׁר אֶהְיֶה written in the Torah, and so the Jews would know that the *galus* of Mitzraim was not destined to be the last one? That is why it was necessary for G-d to reassure them that He would be with them in future times of need. Note, however, that this phrase is *written*, but was not said by Moshe to them, and therefore it was easier for the people to accept it. Thus we see that Moshe was correct in arguing with the Almighty that

דַּיִּ לְצָרָה בְּשַׁעֲתָהּ, and his argument indeed prevailed.

The same is true with Amalek, who represent the eternal enemy of the Jewish people. When G-d said: אֶמְחֶה, "*I* will erase the remembrance of Amalek," that would conceivably cause the Jewish people great anguish and concern, for it would mean that Israel on their own would not be worthy or able to vanquish Amalek. Therefore Hashem said: כְּתֹב זֹאת, precisely this promise of אֶמְחֶה should be written, and not said, for it would be difficult and traumatic for the Jewish people to hear it at this early period of their history as a people. The only one who was strong enough to hear it was Yehoshua, and that is why the verse states, "Write this as a remembrance in the Book," but as far as saying it, "Recite it (only) in the ears of Yehoshua!"

PARASHAS YISRO

United We Stand

WHEN THE JEWS WERE APPROACHED BY MOSHE TO ACCEPT THE Torah, we are told: וַיַּעֲנוּ כָל הָעָם יַחְדָּו וַיֹּאמְרוּ כֹּל אֲשֶׁר דִּבֶּר ה׳ נַעֲשֶׂה, "And the entire people answered in unison saying, 'Everything that Hashem has spoken we will do' " (19:8). The phraseology is a bit perplexing and seemingly redundant. Once we are told וַיַּעֲנוּ, why is it necessary to add the phrase וַיֹּאמְרוּ? And if it is כָל הָעָם, "the entire people," why the word יַחְדָּו, "together"?

The answer is given that initially Moshe spoke to the elders of the people, the זִקְנֵי הָעָם, and this seemed, to the masses, exclusionary. They felt that it implied the Torah was meant only for the elite, who possessed special intellectual and spiritual qualities, and that the superior character of Torah was such that it could not be shared with the common folk. Yet, they wanted very much to be included, even though they were not on the same level as the זִקְנֵי הָעָם, "the elders of the people." In order to qualify, they decided that their only hope was in expressing their willingness to accept the Torah, which would then be given to them as well, based upon their unified expression of acquiescence and the strength that would come from such unity and unanimity. A number of Torah commentators, especially *maggidim,* have explained this matter by means of a *mashal* (parable): A group of small businessmen went to a fair in the company of some moguls to participate in an auction of merchandise. Both the small and the big businessmen desperately needed this merchandise. Realizing that individually they could not possibly outbid these wealthy merchants, the small businessmen decided to form a cooperative and buy the merchandise together. By pooling their resources, they would be able to match the bids of their wealthy, powerful colleagues. This *mashal* is used to explain the verse quoted above. After Moshe came and spoke to the elders of Israel, the simple Jews first had to negotiate with one another, and that is the meaning of וַיַּעֲנוּ, implying a dialogue among a number of people, asking and answering, discussing and negotiating. They then decided that they would do things together, and that is the significance of the word יַחְדָּו. As a united group, וַיֹּאמְרוּ, they said to Moshe, "All that Hashem has spoken, we will do."

This idea helps to explain the meaning of the words of the *zemiros* which we sing at the Shabbos table: וּבָאוּ כֻלָּם בִּבְרִית יַחַד, נַעֲשֶׂה וְנִשְׁמָע אָמְרוּ כְּאֶחָד... בָּרוּךְ הַנּוֹתֵן לַיָּעֵף כֹּחַ, "And they came together in one covenant. We will do and we will listen, they responded as one . . . Blessed is He Who grants strength to the weary."

These lyrics are very strange, for in the midst of singing the praises of Shabbos, we introduce the idea of unifying and coming together to accept the Torah, after which we thank G-d for giving strength to the weak. However, with the explanation offered above we see that there is indeed a link between the acceptance of the commandment of Shabbos by the masses and our expression of gratitude to the Almighty for giving strength to weaker Jews. What we are stating is that we never would have been deemed worthy to receive the Torah for we are not among the elite of the elders of Israel. Therefore it was necessary that we join together and pool our resources. By doing so, every Jew was able to receive the Torah, regardless of his intellectual gifts and spiritual level. That is how G-d became the G-d of *all* Israel, regardless of class or status. In this manner, strength was indeed given to the weaker Jews — i.e., those weaker in intelligence, piety and wisdom — through the coming together of all Jews at the time when the Torah was given. And since Shabbos is the force which unites the Jewish people and gives them the strength needed for their survival, we say these words in the *zemiros* of Shabbos. In this manner, we remind ourselves each week that we were able to enter the covenant with G-d only because we said נַעֲשֶׂה וְנִשְׁמָע, as one, thereby drawing strength from one another.

The Brisker Rav adds an additional dimension to this concept. He explains why it was so important to put the נַעֲשֶׂה before the נִשְׁמָע, the readiness to "do" before the commitment to "listen." He explains that listening to and understanding Torah is varied. It is different with each person, for understanding is not uniform. However, the action, the doing, is the same for everyone. Hence, נַעֲשֶׂה had to precede נִשְׁמָע for only by accepting the discipline of observance and performance could the concept of אִישׁ אֶחָד, "as one man," and עַם אֶחָד, "one people," become a reality. This is the meaning of the words: וּבָאוּ כֻלָּם בִּבְרִית יַחַד, נַעֲשֶׂה וְנִשְׁמָע אָמְרוּ כְּאֶחָד, "And they entered the covenant as one," because they grasped this concept of giving precedence to the action over the listening. We celebrate this concept every Shabbos by singing this beautiful song at the Shabbos table.

PARASHAS MISHPATIM

A Unique Derech Eretz

THE FIRST LAW MENTIONED IN THIS WEEK'S *PARASHAH* IS THAT OF an *eved Ivri,* a Hebrew slave. The Torah teaches us that if one has been sold as a slave by the court because of his inability to pay for something he has stolen, or if he is so pressed financially that he sells himself, he serves his master for a period of six years, after which he is set free. The Torah also speaks of an *amah Ivriyah*, a Jewish bondwoman who is sold by her father to a master. In this latter case, a unique *mitzvah* is given called *yi'ud*, which means that she is designated for the master or his son as a wife.

Our Sages teach us that הַקּוֹנֶה עֶבֶד עִבְרִי כְּקוֹנֶה אָדוֹן לְעַצְמוֹ, "He who acquires a Hebrew slave, it is as though he has acquired a master for himself." Our Sages make this statement because the law is very strict governing the behavior of a master toward his Jewish slave. He is taught to be so considerate of his *eved* that if there is but one bed in the house, it is the slave who will sleep in the bed, while the master must sleep on the floor! The Jewish bondwoman who is betrothed to her master or his son by means of the purchase price, which is treated as "betrothal money," must be treated no differently than any other wife, and is entitled to all the rights and privileges of a Jewish wife.

Based upon these laws, a great *mussar* teacher interpreted the Mishnah in *Avos* (3:21): אִם אֵין תּוֹרָה אֵין דֶּרֶךְ אֶרֶץ, "If there is no Torah, there is no ethical path in life," in the following manner: Normally, we consider ethical behavior as being a pattern of both civil and decent relationships between people, which represents the proper conduct that prevails in a civil, just society. This pattern provides a reasonable and acceptable mode of behavior, which ensures a just society.

What is the connection, then, between Torah and דֶּרֶךְ אֶרֶץ ? This Mishnah teaches that there is a *special* דֶּרֶךְ אֶרֶץ which grows out of Torah, a unique and different kind of behavior, which man would never follow were he to rely only on his own *sechel*, his own intelligence. Picture, if you will, a person coming into a bedroom and observing one person sleeping on the bed, while the other is lying on the floor. If he were asked, which one is the master and which the slave, obviously he would answer that the one on the floor is the slave and the one in the comfortable bed is the master. However, that is worldly דֶּרֶךְ אֶרֶץ, not the דֶּרֶךְ אֶרֶץ dictated by the Torah ethic. The Torah is extremely sensitive to the inferior status of the slave, who has been brought to such a difficult state in his life and whose spirit would be crushed irreversibly were we not to treat him with respect and dignity.

It is for this reason that there are a multitude of laws governing the way a Jewish master must conduct himself with his Hebrew slave. These laws ensure the honor and dignity of that slave, who must be prepared to reenter society after six years and take his place among others as a self-respecting, honored member of the community. This is the meaning of אִם אֵין תּוֹרָה אֵין דֶּרֶךְ אֶרֶץ . If one does not learn from Torah the lesson being taught in the area of the master/slave relationship, then there cannot be a true appreciation of the meaning of the term "derech eretz."

The second situation, of a young Jewish girl sold into bondage by her father, is similar. If this father was so desperate and felt so pressed financially that he had to sell his daughter as a bondwoman, then certainly this girl would find it almost impossible to find a *shidduch*. How would she be presented to the prospective groom and his family by a *shadchan*? Her chances for making a match are practically nil. So the Torah tells us that the master himself, or his son, must marry her. This is the *mitzvah* of *yi'ud*. Man's *sechel*, human logic and reason, would never dictate so, but the Torah says this is the "way," this is the דֶּרֶךְ אֶרֶץ which flows from Torah, and it is this which the *Tanna* is teaching us when he states: אִם אֵין תּוֹרָה אֵין דֶּרֶךְ אֶרֶץ.

From Revelation to Legislation

IN *PARASHAS YISRO,* WHICH WE READ LAST WEEK, THE STORY OF THE giving of the Torah is recorded. We refer to that episode as Revelation, for G-d revealed Himself to the People of Israel on *Har Sinai,* teaching them the Ten Commandments. This week's *Sedrah* is called *Mishpatim,* meaning the ordinances which regulate Jewish society and ensure that it will be a just one. This could well be called legislation, which also emanates from G-d Himself. The juxtaposition of the two *Sedrahs* is an interesting and informative one. Revelation must be followed by legislation, lest it remain merely a philosophical, spiritual experience. Judaism is built on deeds and actions, for it is a way of life which G-d gave us to teach and guide us in our day-to-day activities. It is for this reason that the Torah did not remain in Heaven for the angels, but was given to man, who requires its guidance at every stage of life, as Moshe argued when the angels challenged him to justify his bringing the Torah down from Heaven to earth.

Parashas Yisro is followed immediately by *Parashas Mishpatim* to teach us this lesson — that Revelation must be followed by legislation — and this is the secret of our survival as a people.

PARASHAS TERUMAH

Gateway to Heaven

THE *MISHKAN*, THE SANCTUARY IN THE WILDERNESS, WAS BUILT through the contributions of the Children of Israel, and constructed by skilled craftsmen. The commandment to build this Tabernacle was given by the Almighty: וְעָשׂוּ לִי מִקְדָּשׁ וְשָׁכַנְתִּי בְּתוֹכָם, "They shall make a sanctuary for Me that I may dwell among them" (25:8).

The first *Beis HaMikdash,* Holy Temple, was built by King Solomon, while the second *Beis HaMikdash* was built by the Jews when they returned from Babylonia, and was enlarged and refurbished by King Hordus. Tradition teaches us that the third Temple will be brought down from heaven, never to be destroyed. G-d, Himself, will prepare this third *Beis HaMikdash* and present it to us complete. However, we have been taught that there is one contribution which the Jewish people will make even to this third Temple, and that is the installation of the gates. The verse in *Eichah* states: טָבְעוּ בָאָרֶץ שְׁעָרֶיהָ, "Her gates were swallowed up in the ground" (*Eichah* 2:9), and these are the gates which will be used in the third Temple. The question arises: What is the significance of these gates? When G-d Himself constructs and completes the *Beis HaMikdash* and presents it to us as a Heavenly gift, why will it be necessary for the people of Israel to install the gates on their own?

The answer may be that since the original Sanctuary in the wilderness was a structure which G-d commanded us to build, therefore for all time *we* are commanded to build a Sanctuary so that the *Shechinah* can dwell among us. We must have some *chelek* (portion) in every Holy Temple, for it would be unfulfilling and even embarrassing for us merely to receive, without contributing. The Sages have a most telling and interesting phrase which they use when they refer to someone who is supported by others and does not contribute anything himself. They call it נַהֲמָא דְכִסוּפָא, "the bread of shame." Permitting us to set the gates of the third *Beis HaMikdash* in place is not only allowing us to have a *chelek,* but is considered as though we ourselves have built the *Beis HaMikdash.* As the Talmud teaches: הַבּוֹנֶה פַּלְטְרִין גְדוֹלִים בְּנִכְסֵי הַגֵּר וּבָא אַחֵר וְהֶעֱמִיד לָהֶן דְּלָתוֹת קָנָה, "If one builds great mansions on the land of a convert who has passed away (an act of acquisition and possession), but another person attaches the doors to that structure, the latter acquires the property" (*Bava Basra* 53b). We see from this law that even though a structure was built by another, the one who attaches the doors or gates is considered as having built that building. It is for this reason that the gates of the original Temple were submerged into the ground — so that ultimately we will be able to unearth them and attach them to the third Temple, and thus be credited with the building of that *Beis HaMikdash.*

This also explains the phraseology of the prayer we recite in the *Shemoneh Esrei* for the Three Festivals: וְהַרְאֵנוּ בְּבִנְיָנוֹ וְשַׂמְּחֵנוּ בְּתִקּוּנוֹ, "And show us its rebuilding and gladden us in its perfection." Since the Almighty will build the third Temple, we ask Him to grant us the privilege of seeing it, which is the meaning of וְהַרְאֵנוּ בְּבִנְיָנוֹ. However, our שִׂמְחָה, "joy," would be incomplete if we would have no share in its building. Therefore, we ask וְשַׂמְּחֵנוּ בְּתִקּוּנוֹ, cause us to rejoice in the fact that we will add the gates to the Temple, which is indeed a great *tikkun,* a significant addition and completion of any building, and that will be the source of our שִׂמְחָה.

The Cherubim: Face-to-face or Face-off?

וְעָשׂוּ אֲרוֹן . . . וְצִפִּיתָ אֹתוֹ זָהָב טָהוֹר מִבַּיִת וּמִחוּץ
"They shall make an Ark . . . You shall cover it with pure gold from within and without" (25:10-11).

THE ARK WAS THE FOCAL POINT OF THE *MISHKAN,* FOR IN IT RESTED the Tablets of the Law, and according to tradition, a Sefer

Torah as well. The Ark had a cover, and the cover in turn had Cherubim upon it. The verse describing these Cherubim states that they each had a child's face and wings which spread upward, while "their faces were toward one another."

The classical commentators see in this description of the Cherubim both a metaphor for the obligations of every Jew and a formula for Jewish living. The Torah teaches us that our obligations are twofold, between man and G-d, and between man and his fellow man. This is symbolized by the fact that the wings of the Cherubim were spread upward toward Heaven, representing the Jews reaching out to the Almighty, while the faces of the Cherubim were toward one another, symbolizing one's concern for his fellow man and his needs.

This symbolism explains what the Sages teach us in *Bava Basra* 99a: When the Jewish people fulfilled the will of G-d, the Cherubim faced one another, but when they did not, then the Cherubim turned away from one another. When Jews ignore each other, it is contrary to G-d's will. This lesson was underscored by Shlomo HaMelech when he built the Temple and placed a second set of Cherubim on the ground. Of them it is written in *II Divrei Hayamim* 3:13: וּפְנֵיהֶם לַבָּיִת, "And their faces were toward the House," i.e., they faced the Temple, and not each other. What was the purpose for the fashioning of these additional Cherubim? The answer may well be that he wanted to teach the people that whereas the Cherubim on the Ark-cover faced one another, the inspiration to do so came from the Torah inside the Ark, which taught them to be concerned for one's fellow man and his needs. On the other hand, the two new Cherubim, which he placed on the ground at the entrance to the Temple, faced the בַּיִת, the "House," symbolizing that they were selfishly concerned only with themselves and with their own households. Shlomo HaMelech was afraid that his people — dwelling in their own land in security and prosperity — would become isolated from each other and from the world around them. Therefore, he made the Cherubim facing their own House, to caution the people of the peril of becoming too parochial, insulated and isolated from others. These Cherubim were meant to serve as a contrast to those which were placed on the cover of the Ark.

PARASHAS TETZAVEH

The Art of Communication

THE COMMENTATORS ARE PUZZLED BY THE WORDING WHICH appears at the very outset of this week's *Parashah,* the seemingly superfluous use of וְאַתָּה, "and you," which precedes the word תְּצַוֶּה, from which the name of the *Parashah* is derived. In the Hebrew language, as in other languages, when the grammatical form, "You shall command," is used, as it is here, when Hashem instructs Moshe to command the Children of Israel to bring oil for the מְנוֹרָה, there is no need to add the phrase, "And you" (וְאַתָּה). There are two other instances at the beginning of our *Parashah,* when the redundant phrase וְאַתָּה appears. One is the statement, וְאַתָּה הַקְרֵב, "Bring near to yourself" (28:1), regarding the *bigdei Kehunah,* the vestments of the Kohanim and their consecration. The other is the verse which reads, וְאַתָּה תְּדַבֵּר, "And you shall speak" (28:3), in reference to the wise artisans who were told to fashion these vestments, including the *Ephod,* "breastplate."

These three directives — regarding the bringing of oil for the eternal light, the preparation of the Kohanim's vestments and the consecration of the Kohanim — although recorded in sequence, use three different imperatives. One is תְּצַוֶּה, "to command," the second is תְּדַבֵּר, "to speak," while the third is הַקְרֵב, "to bring near."

We are being taught, in these few verses, that there are three levels of communication between a leader and his people. A leader must realize that there are various ways of communicating with and influencing his followers. In some cases he must command; in others he must speak; and there are times when circumstances dictate that neither commanding nor speaking is the proper medium, but the only way he can impact on the listener is by drawing him close to himself. At the beginning of the *Parashah,* Moshe was told to *command* the Children of Israel to bring pure olive oil for illumination in the Mishkan. He was addressing the masses, and as such, he was told by the Almighty to issue an order: תְּצַוֶּה, "Command!" A leader must establish channels of communication with the masses in a way that will guarantee compliance and obedience. Discipline cannot be instituted unless authority is exercised, and at such a time, one must command, not just speak.

There are, however, times when the leader deals with a special group who are on a higher level, whose talents and gifts must be tapped by him. He cannot simply command these people to obey his wishes, but must speak to them and convince them that the request made of them is proper and important. In such a case, he must speak decisively and firmly, so as to elicit compliance and cooperation. This was the case when Moshe was told to speak to all the wise-hearted people who were charged with making the *bigdei Kehunah,* "the garments of the Kohanim." That is why, in this case, Moshe was told by the Almighty to *speak* to them, rather than to command them.

There is, however, a third level which is superior to the first two. When communicating with your equal, and especially your brother, you can neither command nor even speak firmly. It is important to convince him, capture his imagination, engage his interest and win him over. Simply put, you must bring him closer to yourself, and bind him to you with love and affection, while sharing with him your conviction and your commitment.

This is what the Torah implies when we are taught that Moshe's level of communication with his brother Aharon was to bring him near to himself: הַקְרֵב אֵלֶיךָ, "bring him near to yourself." This is true of every leader, as well, when he seeks to attract gifted and exceptional people to himself and engage them in pursuing a program which will benefit him and the community at large. One must captivate and engage, rather than coerce and impose. This is also true of the relationship between a parent and a child, and that of a teacher and a student. In the early phase of this relationship, commands are in place. As time goes by and there is a maturing process, it is necessary to speak, rather than command. And when this relationship has reached a superior level, neither of the first two approaches will bear fruit, for then it is important to bring the student, or the son or daughter, close to the teacher or parent, to win them over so that they will willingly and joyfully cooperate with their mentor, and together work toward the realization of the common goal.

This explains why the word וְאַתָּה, "and you," is used in all three cases. Whether commanding, speaking or bringing near, the force of your own personality must be brought into play. Whether you command, speak or simply draw a person close to yourself, the אַתָּה, your own sincerity and commitment, will determine whether you will succeed or not. One's *hashpaah* (influence), however, can be successfully exercised and realized only if the leader, teacher or parent senses when to command, when to speak, and when to use the power of his personality to be *mekarev* another, thereby gaining his cooperation and assistance.

Human Standard

IN THIS WEEK'S *SEDRAH,* THE TORAH TEACHES US THAT JEWS CANNOT be counted in the ordinary manner, and that when it is necessary to conduct a census, it is to be done through the giving of a half-*shekel* by each male who is 20 years or older. By counting the coins, we can determine how many people there are. Different reasons are given for this method of conducting a census. But what is most intriguing is the unique insight which is provided by our Sages in the Pesikta. The Pesikta states that when the Almighty commanded Moshe to construct the Mishkan, Moshe was taken aback and, in the words of our Sages, נִזְדַעֲזַע, "he trembled in fear." He exclaimed, "How can a human being construct a building to house the Almighty?!" The Almighty answered him: לֹא לְפִי כֹּחִי אֲנִי מְבַקֵּשׁ, I am not asking you to build a house according to My strength and omnipotence, but according to the ability of human beings to construct such a Sanctuary: twenty boards to the north, twenty boards to the south and eight in the west."

The Pesikta continues and tells us that when the Almighty commanded Moshe to bring a daily offering, which is characterized as קָרְבָּנִי לַחְמִי, "My daily bread offering," Moshe again was taken aback and said: If I were to bring all the animals in the world as a sacrifice, could that possibly be called לַחְמִי, "My bread," in connection with the Almighty? To which G-d responded: "It is not as you interpret it or understand it, for all I ask of you is to bring כֶּבֶשׂ אֶחָד תַּעֲשֶׂה בַבֹּקֶר . . ., 'one lamb offering in the morning and one in the evening.' "

The third example brought by the Pesikta is in reference to the taking of the census, which we read about in this week's *Sedrah*. In this case, Moshe was taken aback by the expression: וְנָתְנוּ אִישׁ כֹּפֶר נַפְשׁוֹ לַה׳, "Every man shall give Hashem an atonement for his soul" (30:12), to which Moshe responded: "How can any person give פִּדְיוֹן נֶפֶשׁ, 'redemption of his soul'?" What Moshe found almost impossible to comprehend was how a person can redeem his soul with money. To this question, the Almighty responded: "It is not as you picture it, in the literal sense, rather זֶה יִתְּנוּ, 'This shall they give,' a half-*shekel* of the sacred *shekel* as a portion to ה׳."

The Chafetz Chaim used this Pesikta as a critical and comprehensive lesson for the Jewish people regarding their responsibilities, and what the Almighty does, and does not, expect from them. He points out that G-d does not expect from any person anything which is beyond the capacity of a human being. In Yiddish, there is an expression, "G-d is not a *gazlan*," meaning that the Torah, in spite of its many disciplines and rules, does not attempt to hold us to a standard which is humanly impossible to meet. Even Moshe was not aware of this until he was told to build a Tabernacle, to bring a daily offering and to conduct a census. He thought that a house built for G-d had to be so unusually large that it would be beyond human capacity to build it. Moshe thought that the word לַחְמִי, "My bread," was to be taken literally; and even our teacher Moshe was unable to grasp that, when the Almighty used the expression כֹּפֶר נֶפֶשׁ, it was not as intimidating as it sounded. Redemption of the soul can be accomplished even with a half-*shekel*; the daily offering to G-d can be brought through a little lamb; and the dimensions of the Mishkan can indeed be quite modest. As the Chafetz Chaim puts it, a person is only expected to fulfill G-d's commandments within his human limitations.

In reality, this lesson is taught to us as well by Shlomo HaMelech when he states: כֹּל אֲשֶׁר תִּמְצָא יָדְךָ לַעֲשׂוֹת בְּכֹחֲךָ עֲשֵׂה, "Whatever you can do within your power, do it" (*Koheles* 9:10). This means that man is required to do only what he can with his G-d-given strength and ability. This explains the symbolism of the half-*shekel* which is used for counting Jews. One Jew alone cannot fulfill the mission of the Jewish people to be "a kingdom of priests and a holy nation." Each person is but a part, and only together can they become a whole. Only as a nation, not as individuals, can they be *kedoshim,* a sacred and holy people. This is the lesson taught to us by the Pesikta. This also explains the expression: וְלֹא יִהְיֶה בָהֶם נֶגֶף בִּפְקֹד אֹתָם, "There will not be a plague among them when counting them" (30:12). The Torah is teaching us that when a Jew is isolated and separated from the community he is vulnerable and exposed to danger. Isolated and alone, he needs protection from a variety of plagues. But when he realizes that he is a *machtzis,* a fraction of the whole, and identifies with the *tzibbur,* he ensures his safety and finds redemption.

PARASHAS VAYAKHEL

Style or Substance?

וַיֹּאמֶר מֹשֶׁה אֶל בְּנֵי יִשְׂרָאֵל רְאוּ קָרָא ה' בְּשֵׁם בְּצַלְאֵל
"Moshe said to the Children of Israel, 'Behold (see), Hashem has called by name Bezalel' " (35:30).

BEZALEL WAS DESIGNATED BY THE ALMIGHTY TO BE THE ARCHITECT of the Mishkan, the Sanctuary in the wilderness. As the Torah tells us, he was an individual who was blessed with wisdom, insight and knowledge, including a special talent to oversee every craft that was necessary in the construction of the Mishkan, its furnishings and the clothing for the Kohanim. The expression, however, which the Torah uses in this verse — Hashem "called him by name" — needs clarification.

In Jewish tradition, names are very important and significant, for they reflect the character and personality of the individual. The fact that the Torah introduces Bezalel by referring to his name is of great import.

The Midrash elaborates on this by stating that every person in reality has three names. One is the name given to him at birth by his parents; the second is the name by which he is known to the people in his community; and the third is the one that he is קוֹנֶה לְעַצְמוֹ, which "he acquires for himself." This Midrash may be interpreted as follows. The name given to a child at birth by his or her parents reflects their hopes and dreams for that child. Today, names usually indicate a family's past, but in many cases they are names which have their origin in Jewish history as well. In the Torah, names are often an index to the special qualities a person possesses and, in addition, mirror events surrounding that particular family, its forebears and descendants. When our Patriarchs and Matriarchs named their children, the Torah itself gives us the reason for these choices. In the case of Bezalel, we are told that not only were his wisdom and understanding of how to build the Mishkan and construct its furnishings outstanding, but also his ability to determine the sequence which this project was to follow. According to our Rabbis, Moshe at one point exclaimed, "You must have been standing in the shadow of the Almighty when He spoke to me regarding the Mishkan and its furnishings." In Hebrew, the name בְּצַלְאֵל is constructed of two words: בְּצֵל אֵל, "in the shadow of G-d." The name given to Bezalel by his parents was expounded by others, especially Moshe, but ultimately the name he established for himself in Jewish history was the one that he acquired on his own.

That is why the words chosen by the Midrash are so important. Regarding the name one is called by his parents, as well as the name he is called by society, the phrase used is שֶׁקּוֹרְאִים לוֹ, "by which he is called." However, the phrase regarding the third name is שֶׁקוֹנֶה לְעַצְמוֹ, one that he himself acquires and earns, through the force of his personality and by sharing his gifts and talents with others.

The lesson we learn from this is a very meaningful and important one. We all have these three names. The name our parents call us at birth carries with it the dreams, hopes and aspirations of our parents. In our early years, we are indeed formed, shaped and influenced by them. The name by which others call us refers to their impression and evaluation of us, which may or may not be correct. There is always appearance and reality, and therefore the name which others call him refers both to the impression which one makes on others, as well as the influence and impact that society makes on him.

The real self is the third name, which in the final analysis is the persona which truly reflects the person, his character and personality, and the influence he has on others. It refers to the unique and special contribution which he makes to his community and people. That is truly a name that he is קוֹנֶה לְעַצְמוֹ, for it is *his* acquisition, as well as the acquisition of others who benefit from his talents and productivity.

This explains the subtle meaning of the word רְאוּ, behold and see, which urges us to look well and consider the essence of each person. Especially in a society where appearance and style are so important, we must be able to see and perceive substance rather than style, reality rather than appearance.

PARASHAS PEKUDEI

Accounting and Accountability

אֵלֶּה פְקוּדֵי הַמִּשְׁכָּן ... אֲשֶׁר פֻּקַּד עַל פִּי מֹשֶׁה
"These are the reckonings (accounting) of the Mishkan . . . which were reckoned by Moshe" (38:21).

AT THE CONCLUSION OF THE MONUMENTAL PROJECT OF CONstructing the Tabernacle, Moshe gave a detailed accounting of the amounts of gold, silver and copper that were contributed by the people. He gave a full numeration of everything collected, and the use of these contributions, for he realized that a true leader must be accountable to his people. This was in keeping with the dictates of the Torah, which we find in *Sefer Bamidbar* when Moshe used the expression: וִהְיִיתֶם נְקִיִּים מֵה׳ וּמִיִּשְׂרָאֵל, "And you shall be vindicated [clean] from Hashem and from Yisrael" (*Bamidbar* 32:22). A great moral lesson is taught by this admonition of Moshe: that a person must be above suspicion and reproach in the eyes of both G-d and man. It is for this reason that, even though Moshe was not suspected by the people of misusing the contributions made toward the Mishkan, nonetheless, he felt it necessary to give a complete accounting, in order to teach us for all time that a leader must be accountable for his actions and deeds. Note that we are concerned not only about Heaven's opinion of us, but also that of our fellow man. We use the expression in *Bircas Hamazon* (Grace After Meals): וְנִמְצָא חֵן וְשֵׂכֶל טוֹב בְּעֵינֵי אֱלֹקִים וְאָדָם, "And may we find favor and good understanding in the eyes of G-d and man." We wish to find favor and gain acceptance, not only by the Almighty, but in the eyes of man, as well. We must be beyond reproach and above suspicion in all our dealings in order to help create a just, civil society. In Judaism, we do not accept the concept of "It's nobody's business," for the only way a proper social climate can be created is when trust and confidence are engendered in one another, and this is especially true of those who are in leadership roles.

The Talmud (*Yoma* 38a) gives us a few striking and dramatic examples which underscore the need to conduct ourselves in a manner that shows we are above suspicion. They tell us that those who baked the *lechem hapanim*, "show-bread," did not permit fine-quality flour to be used in the baking of their own bread, lest they be accused of appropriating the fine flour meant for the Temple. Those who were commissioned to prepare the *ketores*, the incense for the Divine Service in the Temple, did not allow their daughters, even when they went to their own weddings, to be perfumed, lest people say that they perfumed themselves with the incense preparation of the Temple. We are also taught that when the Kohen entered the chamber in the Temple where the *shekalim* were stored, he did not wear a sleeved cloak, shoes or sandals, lest he be suspected of removing some of the *shekalim* for his own use.

All this, we are told, was done to fulfill this admonition of being guiltless, clean and vindicated before G-d and before Israel. Small wonder that our teacher Moshe felt it necessary, at the conclusion of the building of the Mishkan, to give the Israelites a full accounting.

Parashas Vayikra

PARASHAS VAYIKRA

Listening, Hearing and Understanding

THE NAME OF THIS WEEK'S *PARASHAH,* AS WELL AS THE NAME OF the third *Sefer* of the *Chumash,* is וַיִּקְרָא. The Midrash tells us that G-d calls to man in two different ways. When He called to Adam, after the sin committed by him and Chavah in the Garden of Eden, it was a call of admonition, reflecting the Almighty's displeasure. The text there reads: וַיִּקְרָא ה' אֱלֹקִים אֶל הָאָדָם, "And Hashem, G-d, called out to the man" (*Bereishis* 3:9). Immediately thereafter, Adam and Chavah were driven from the Garden of Eden.

On the other hand, the same word, וַיִּקְרָא, when spoken to Moshe, is interpreted by our Sages as a call of *chibah,* "love and affection." In other words, before G-d communicates with a person, He calls him, to prepare him to listen to His word and to urge him to give his undivided attention to Him. The importance of listening and hearing, as well as understanding what the Almighty has to say to man, repeats itself time and again in *Tanach.* When Shmuel spoke to Shaul and admonished him for failing to properly fulfill the command of Hashem regarding the annihilation of Amalek, he posed a rhetorical question: הַחֵפֶץ לַה' בְּעֹלוֹת וּזְבָחִים כִּשְׁמֹעַ בְּקוֹל ה' הִנֵּה שְׁמֹעַ מִזֶּבַח טוֹב, "Does Hashem delight in offerings as He does in listening to His voice? Behold, to obey is better than a choice offering" (*I Shmuel* 15:22). Shaul lost his kingship because of his inability to hear properly what the Almighty said to him through the prophet. Moshe, on the other hand, possessed the ability to hear G-d's call. The secret of Moshe's ability to listen is found in the spelling of the word וַיִּקְרָא which introduces this *Parashah.* The א at the end of the word is a miniature one (אָלֶף זְעִירָא), written in the Torah in a small, diminutive lower case. The reason given for this was Moshe's great humility. Instead of וַיִּקְרָא, which means that the Almighty called to Him, he intended to write the word וַיִּקָר, without the א at all, which would then mean that G-d happened to appear to him, in the sense of a מִקְרֶה, a happenstance. In general, Moshe's greatness was his *anivus,* his modesty and humility, for it was this *middah* (character trait), which enabled him to be a *mekabel,* one who was able to receive, and indeed it was for this reason that he was chosen to receive the Torah.

When Shmuel spoke to Shaul, criticizing him for failing to accept unquestioningly G-d's command, he concluded his admonition with the words: הִנֵּה שְׁמֹעַ מִזֶּבַח טוֹב, "Behold, to listen and obey is better than a choice offering" (ibid.). This is an exemplary art, one which Shaul apparently did not master. Moshe, however, was able to respond to G-d's call precisely because he accepted all that Hashem told him unconditionally.

It is interesting to note that later in our *Sedrah,* the Torah speaks of a leader sinning: אֲשֶׁר נָשִׂיא יֶחֱטָא, "When a ruler sins" (4:22). The commentators remark that the first letters of these three words spell the word אֲנִי, "I." The Torah implies that the root cause for a ruler sinning is his ego and pride. Arrogance precedes many a transgression and deafens the ruler to the call of G-d. This was true in the case of Shaul HaMelech, as opposed to Moshe whose humility and modesty gave him the ability to hear the call of the Almighty.

In *Tehillim,* Chapter 40, verses 7 and 8, this thought is developed and clarified in a beautiful fashion. According to many commentaries, these verses contrast the personality of David with that of Shaul. David, like Moshe, was also a humble and modest person. In this *perek* (chapter) we read: זֶבַח וּמִנְחָה לֹא חָפַצְתָּ אָזְנַיִם כָּרִיתָ לִּי, "Neither sacrifice nor offering did You desire, receptive ears You opened for me" (*Tehillim* 40:7). Here, again, *Tanach* extols the virtue of listening, praising this ability over the willingness to bring offerings on the altar. The verse continues: עוֹלָה וַחֲטָאָה לֹא

Parashas Vayikra / 77

שָׁאָלְתָּ, "Burnt offerings and sin offerings You did not require" (ibid.), for that is not the ultimate desire of Hashem. The following verse reads: אָז אָמַרְתִּי הִנֵּה בָאתִי בִּמְגִלַּת סֵפֶר כָּתוּב עָלָי, "Then I said, 'Behold I have come in the scroll of the book which is written of me'" (*Tehillim* 40:8). Malbim interprets the "scroll of the book" as referring to the heart of David HaMelech, which was sensitive to G-d's will, and possessed a natural inclination to obey the wishes of the Almighty. This is also true of the heart of every Jew who responds to the call of Hashem, provided he is humble and modest enough to listen carefully to the call of G-d and to obey it, as did Moshe and David.

The Book of *Vayikra* introduces the concept of *korbanos*, "sacrifices or offerings." The Torah chooses to introduce us to this concept with the word וַיִּקְרָא to teach us that it is far more important to listen to the word of Hashem than it is to bring the choicest offerings on His altar.

PARASHAS TZAV

Consecrating One's Ear, Hand and Foot

IN THIS WEEK'S *SEDRAH,* WE FIND A DESCRIPTION OF THE CONsecration of Aharon and his sons as Kohanim. Moshe was commanded to take from the blood of the inauguration ram and place some of it עַל תְּנוּךְ אֹזֶן אַהֲרֹן הַיְמָנִית וְעַל בֹּהֶן יָדוֹ הַיְמָנִית וְעַל בֹּהֶן רַגְלוֹ הַיְמָנִית, "upon the lobe of Aharon's right ear and upon the thumb of his right hand and upon the big toe of his right foot" (8:23). This ceremony was repeated with the sons of Aharon.

Although this ritual is a Scriptural decree, it also teaches a moral lesson applicable not only to Kohanim, but to every Jew as well. The ear, the hand and the foot were consecrated. With the ear, one can hear what the Almighty, as well as his fellow men, have to say to him. Without the ear and sense of hearing, there can be no meaningful communication with others, be it G-d or man. The hand represents action — doing and producing. Man's foot is representative of movement, of locomotion and progress.

When Moshe was commanded to place the blood of the inaugural sacrifice on the lobe of the ear, the thumb of the hand and the toe of the foot, he was consecrating the ears of the Kohanim, as well as their hands and feet, initiating all three into the service of G-d and the people of Israel.

When Shlomo HaMelech was invited by G-d to make any request of Him, he asked for a listening heart. For the heart to hear, there must be an ear that listens. Aharon and his sons had to develop sensitive ears to hear what the people had to say to them, and be aware of what was happening in their midst. As leaders of the people, they had to hear their fears, concerns and hopes, and not turn a deaf ear to them. They could not be detached or isolated, and they certainly could not be callous or insulated from the innermost feelings of the people of Israel. If he was to serve his people properly, the ear of the Kohen had to be consecrated and prepared.

When Yehoshua met Moshe at the foot of the mountain and accompanied him into the camp of Israel, at the time when the Golden Calf was built and worshiped, they heard the sound of the masses, which Yehoshua identified as *kol milchamah,* "the sound of battle" (*Shemos* 32:17). However, this was wishful thinking on his part, for he was hopeful that there were those in the camp who were opposed to this idolatry and were prepared to do battle in defense of G-d's honor. Moshe, the seasoned leader, however, corrected his disciple and told him that unfortunately these were the sounds of unbridled celebration.

Yehoshua did not as yet have the ears of a leader, and indeed, according to our Sages, Moshe admonished him, saying, "A person who is destined to lead the people should be able to differentiate between a *kol* and a *kol*" (*Talmud Yerushalmi, Taanis* 4:5). Your ear is not sufficiently sensitized, so you are not as yet prepared to serve as a leader. Now we understand why the first step in the consecration of Aharon and his sons was the placing of the blood of the inaugural sacrifice on the lobe of the ear.

The second place the blood was put was on the thumb of the hand, for it is not sufficient to hear, nor even to have a listening heart, unless this leads to action. In Hebrew, there is an expression — *chibuk yadayim* — which does not mean that one's arms are akimbo, but literally means to embrace oneself with one's arms. Self-embrace is symbolic of a desire to be comfortable, an implication that one does not want to be disturbed. This cannot be the way of a Kohen, a king or any leader. That is why we are taught that the Sefer Torah of the Jewish king, which accompanied him at all times, had to be attached to his arm, symbolizing the translation of the Torah's teachings into action. Without implementation, even the good intentions and policies of a leader are for naught. That is why the thumb of the right hand had to be consecrated.

Finally, by placing the blood on the big toe of the right foot, the lesson taught to the Kohanim, as well as to all Jewish leaders, was that they must be *holchim,* those who move and progress and are active, as opposed to those who stand still and are frozen in place. Interestingly, angels are called *omdim,* for they cannot take any initiative on their own or even move without a directive being given to them, as opposed to man, who is called a *holech,* for he has freedom of will and choice to move and progress. Indeed, that is his mission and purpose.

The *navi* says, in the name of the Almighty, when He speaks to the Kohen Gadol: וְנָתַתִּי לְךָ מַהְלְכִים בֵּין הָעֹמְדִים הָאֵלֶּה, "And I will give you the ability to walk among these angels who stand" (*Zechariah* 3:7). It is for this reason that the toe of the foot also had to be consecrated by Moshe.

The entire *Parashah* of the consecration of Aharon and his sons is a most important and significant lesson for the Jewish people for all time.

PARASHAS SHEMINI

Instruction or Admonition — Which Is More Effective?

IN TODAY'S *SEDRAH*, WE ARE TOLD HOW THE CELEBRATION OF THE inauguration of the Mishkan was marred by a great tragedy. The sons of Aharon, Nadav and Avihu, were consumed by a fire which came forth from Heaven as they were performing the service, and "they died in the presence of Hashem" (10:2).

In reaction to this terrible loss, Moshe spoke to his brother Aharon, saying: הוּא אֲשֶׁר דִּבֶּר ה' לֵאמֹר בִּקְרֹבַי אֶקָּדֵשׁ וְעַל פְּנֵי כָל הָעָם אֶכָּבֵד, "This is as Hashem spoke, saying: 'Through those that are near Me I shall be sanctified, and in the presence of the entire people I will be glorified'" (10:3). This cryptic remark of Moshe's is explained by Rashi as follows: Moshe said to Aharon, "I knew that the Sanctuary would be sanctified בִּמְיֻדָּעָיו שֶׁל מָקוֹם, 'with those singled out as being special.' However, I thought this meant either through me or through you; now I see שֶׁהֵם גְּדוֹלִים מִמֶּנִּי וּמִמְּךָ, 'that they are greater than I or you.'"

This explanation of Rashi, far from clarifying this obscure *pasuk*, creates additional difficulties, for it is certainly not to be taken in the literal sense that Nadav and Avihu were greater than Moshe and Aharon! We must also understand how the Sanctuary was sanctified through this tragedy.

There are two words in Hebrew which superficially seem to be synonyms. One is the word מוּסָר, which can be translated as chastisement or reproof, or can mean instruction. The other word is תּוֹכָחָה, which means rebuke and punishment. Indeed, those sections of the Torah dealing with the Divine curses and punishments which will be inflicted on Israel if they fail to obey Hashem are called "The *Tochachah*" (*Vayikra* 26 and *Devarim* 28). If one examines the two words closely, one realizes that the word מוּסָר comes from the same root as יִסּוּרִים, "suffering." On the other hand, the word תּוֹכָחָה is linked to the word וִכּוּחַ, meaning a discussion or debate. There are two ways that the Almighty deals with His people when they stray from the proper path, in order to awaken them to listen to words of rebuke and correct their wayward actions. One way is through יִסּוּרִים, punishment inflicted upon them. Through their suffering, they are brought to repentance. The other is by sending messengers to the people, especially prophets, who speak to them, reason with them, chastise them and teach them how to correct their errors.

The former is referred to as מוּסָר, the latter as תּוֹכָחָה. In most cases, G-d attempts to reach His people through discussion and debate: לְכוּ נָא וְנִוָּכְחָה יֹאמַר ה׳, "Come, let us reason together" (*Yeshayah* 1:18). However, far too often, this approach is unsuccessful, and the Almighty is forced to bring יִסּוּרִים upon Israel so that they should do *teshuvah*. The Sages of the Talmud, alluding to the story of Purim, teach us that King Ahasuerus' removal of his royal ring, which was then given to Haman to seal the fate of the Jews, had a far-greater impact on the Jews than all the words of the prophets (*Megillah* 14a). The words spoken by Mordechai failed to awaken the Jewish people and turn them away from the path of wickedness, whereas the evil decree issued by Haman brought them to sincere repentance.

When the Mishkan was completed, the Jews should have been elevated to the highest spiritual level. A spirit of awe and reverence, generated by an appreciation of the presence of the Almighty, the *Shechinah*, in their midst, should have resulted. Moshe had hoped that he and his brother would have been able to teach the Jewish people what their mission in life was to be, and to inspire them with their words of instruction and inspiration.

Moshe said to Aharon: "I thought that either you or I would have been able to sanctify the people of Israel and cleanse them of the dross of the Egyptian bondage, but this was not to be, for they were not yet ready for logical, reasonable and convincing lessons which would refine them and bring them to the highest spiritual plane." The shock of the deaths of Nadav and Avihu, however, who were consumed by a Divine fire because they had brought an *eish zarah,* "a strange fire" which had not been commanded, did have a tremendous impact upon the people and made them realize how demanding the service of Hashem was to be in the Mishkan and later in the Temple. This catastrophe succeeded in shocking them into an agonizing reappraisal of their character and shortcomings.

This is what Moshe meant when he said, "They are greater than I or you," which doesn't mean they were greater men, but that what *happened* to them made a deeper impression upon the people than the instruction and influence of Moshe and Aharon. Here, again, we see that *yesurim* can accomplish what *tochachah* cannot. This clarification of Rashi sheds a new light on the conclusion of the verse where we are told: וַיִּדֹּם אַהֲרֹן, "Aharon was silent," when he heard the explanation of his brother Moshe. This ability of Aharon to accept the Divine decree was so great that he received a reward for his silence. However, the reward was not only for his silence and stoic acceptance of G-d's decree, but also for his understanding of the contribution made by the death of his sons to the faith and spirituality of the people. The sons of Aharon are therefore referred to as קְרֹבַי, "those that are near to Me," and, as Rashi explains, בְּחִירַי, "My chosen ones." Their merit was that through their deaths they brought the people closer to Hashem and sanctified His Name.

PARASHAS TAZRIA

Transforming the "Nega" into "Oneg"

THIS *PARASHAH* DEALS WITH *NEGA'IM* WHICH MEANS "AFFLICTIONS" or "pestilence," affecting a person's skin or clothing, or his house. It is a very difficult and almost inexplicable portion of the Torah, which seemingly has no relevance to modern man. However, the commentators, and especially teachers of ethics and human behavior, find in this *Parashah* many moral and ethical lessons which are extremely relevant to us, defining human nature and character.

The Ramban points out that these various laws apply only to the Children of Israel, and not to other nations, and that the laws of *nigei battim,* "the contamination of a house," apply only in the Land of Israel. This demonstrates that we are not dealing simply with matters of health, contagion or contamination in its usual sense. Rather, *tzaraas,* which is similar to a leprous condition, is but the physical manifestation of a spiritual malaise, a punishment for a variety of sins such as slander, arrogance and greed. In other words, these afflictions were sent upon the Jewish people in the Land of Israel to awaken them to their shortcomings and arouse them to repent. It is for this reason that the only one qualified to determine whether the person is in a state of *tumah,* "ritual impurity," is a Kohen, who is not a medical person but a spiritual teacher.

It is interesting to note that when the Torah speaks of the Kohen coming to examine the afflicted skin area of the victim, he is not only observing the skin eruption, but the condition and the circumstances of the individual. This is alluded to by the words: וְרָאָה הַכֹּהֵן (13:3), meaning the Kohen shall see the *nega* itself, followed by the expression: וְרָאָהוּ הַכֹּהֵן (13:5), "and the Kohen shall see *him.*"

For example, the *halachah* states that if the afflicted person is a *chasan*, "groom," during his seven days of celebration, or if a Yom Tov, a festival, is about to begin, then the Kohen should abstain from declaring the person *tamei*, in order not to mar this joyous period in the victim's life. All this proves that the Torah is more concerned with the spiritual and mental well-being of the afflicted person than with the affliction per se.

The ethical books, the *sifrei mussar,* point out that the word in Hebrew for skin is עוֹר. A similar-sounding word is אוֹר, meaning light. The word for affliction is נֶגַע, and the same letters can be transformed into the word עֹנֶג, meaning pleasure, delight and enjoyment. The most common affliction mentioned is צָרַעַת (leprosy), the letters of which can also spell עֲצֶרֶת, a word used for a holiday or festival.

All this comes to teach us that it is the sin of the person which covers his עוֹר (skin), it is his transgressions which cause the נֶגַע (affliction), and all this, in turn, brings about his צָרַעַת condition. All of these can be transformed and changed if the person so afflicted will change his conduct and transform his behavior. The נֶגַע is a wake-up call, more so than a punishment, and if he heeds it, it is within his power to heal and purify himself. The עוֹר can be transformed into אוֹר and the נֶגַע to עֹנֶג. Even the period of צָרַעַת can become an עֲצֶרֶת.

A similar thought is presented by the famous Sfas Emes, the Gerrer Rebbe, who explains the reason for *tumas leidah,* the ritual impurity which accompanies childbirth. It would seem that there is nothing more sublime and creative than bringing new life into the world. Why, then, should this create a condition of spiritual impurity? He explains that at the moment of birth, when a new human being is brought into the world, this miraculous phenomenon cannot take place without the presence of G-d. After the child is born, G-d's presence departs, leaving a dramatic and fundamental void. Just as nature abhors a vacuum, so in the spiritual realm there can be no vacuum. When G-d, Who represents the ultimate of purity, departs, the void is filled with impurity. Here, again, we see how the Torah interprets every physical and natural event through a spiritual prism. It is for this reason that childbirth brings *tumah,* followed ultimately by purification.

Similarly, Jewish law ordains that a dead person also creates a state of *tumah,* and Kohanim are not permitted to be in the same room with a dead body, for they must guard their ancestral holiness. One must, however, understand why a dead person causes ritual contamination. Here, again, the reason is that when a person passes away, his *neshamah,* his Divine soul, departs. Hence, the spirit of *kedushah,* of holiness, leaves as well. And that void is filled with the opposite force, which is *tumah,* impurity.

Let us return, at the conclusion of this *d'var Torah,* to the words of the Sfas Emes, whom we quoted earlier. He observes that when man was first created by Hashem in the Garden of Eden, and was exposed to, and in contact with, the Almighty, he was enveloped in the אור ה', the light of the Almighty. After he sinned, a barrier was established between himself and his Maker. The אור (light) was concealed and covered by man's עור (skin). However, skin has pores in it, and these are like windows which allow the light of Hashem to penetrate. The נֶגַע, the affliction caused by sins and transgressions, close these pores and do not permit the light of Hashem to shine through. This is what we mean by *tumah,* contamination and impurity. Once this is healed, then the נֶגַע indeed is transformed into עֹנֶג, a state of joy and delight. And when the צָרַעַת is healed, and the afflicted person is permitted to rejoin his family and friends in the camp of Israel, it is an occasion for celebration and festivity, and the צָרַעַת is transformed into עֲצֶרֶת.

PARASHAS METZORA

Who Shall Live and Who Shall Die

WHEN THE *METZORA*, THE PERSON AFFLICTED WITH LEPROSY, reaches the day of his purification, the Torah dictates that a ritual is to be followed. This ritual is found at the beginning of this week's *Sedrah*. When the Kohen determined that the *metzora* was healed, he took from him two birds, one to be slaughtered, and the other to be sent into an open field. Considering that one of these birds was destined to live while the other was destined to die, the question is how each should be chosen — one for life and one for death. Surprisingly, the Torah indicates that this choice was made arbitrarily!

There is a similar ritual in the *Sedrah* which we read next week, where the service for Yom Kippur is described. There also, two living creatures, two *se'irim* (goats), were chosen, one to be used as a sacrifice to Hashem, while the other was sent *laAzazel* there to be thrown over a precipice in the desert. Symbolically, this latter goat carried upon itself all the iniquities of the Children of Israel, whereas the former goat was designated as a *chatas*, a "sin offering," and offered to the Almighty in the Sanctuary. Here, the choice was not made arbitrarily, but by means of *goralos* (lots).

Logically and reasonably, it would seem that since both of these animals were destined to die, the decision as to which should be a *chatas*, "a sin offering," and which the *se'ir laAzazel*, should not necessitate the casting of lots. Here, the choice could be made arbitrarily since it was not a question of life or death. Nevertheless, it is precisely here, in the service of Yom Kippur, that we use *goralos* (lots), whereas in the purification ceremony of the *metzora,* where one bird lives and the other dies, we do not cast lots, but permit the Kohen to make his choice in an arbitrary fashion! Why?

The Torah seems to be teaching us that what man may consider to be the most important decision in life is not necessarily a life-or-death judgment. More important than the question of who shall live and who shall die is the question of who will be *laHashem* and who shall be *laAzazel.* The moral lesson being taught to us by these *Parashiyos* is that the decision and determination of how one lives his life, and what his ultimate goal and destination are, is far more serious than the question of life and death. In the view of Torah, *how* a person lives his life, and the direction in which he is going during his lifetime, as well as the ultimate spiritual station he will reach, is of greater importance than the question of who shall live and who shall die!

The lesson we learn from this is that the Torah's scale of priorities is not necessarily the one accepted by man and society. In the words of *Avos* (4:21), this world is but a *perozdor,* an entranceway to the World to Come, which in turn is compared to a *teraklin,* a "palace." Our Sages urge us to prepare ourselves in the corridor before we enter the palace. A life that is dedicated to G-d is one in which man, through the medium of Torah and *mitzvos,* prepares himself for his ultimate destination. This is the *goral,* one's lot in life, which really counts.

Now we can understand why lots must be cast by the Kohen to determine which *se'ir* is to be used *laHashem,* and which *laAzazel,* whereas the decision involving the two birds of the *metzora,* one of which shall live physically and one which is destined to die, is a far less serious one.

PARASHAS ACHAREI MOS

Environmental Pollution and Education

AT THE END OF THIS WEEK'S *SEDRAH*, THERE ARE A FEW *PESUKIM* which should be closely examined and interpreted, for they carry with them a lesson for all time. כְּמַעֲשֵׂה אֶרֶץ מִצְרַיִם אֲשֶׁר יְשַׁבְתֶּם בָּהּ לֹא תַעֲשׂוּ וּכְמַעֲשֵׂה אֶרֶץ כְּנַעַן אֲשֶׁר אֲנִי מֵבִיא אֶתְכֶם שָׁמָּה לֹא תַעֲשׂוּ וּבְחֻקֹּתֵיהֶם לֹא תֵלֵכוּ, "Do not perform the practice of the land of Egypt in which you dwelled; and do not perform the practice of the land of Canaan to which I bring you, and do not follow their traditions" (18:3). אֲשֶׁר ... אֶת מִשְׁפָּטַי תַּעֲשׂוּ וְאֶת חֻקֹּתַי תִּשְׁמְרוּ לָלֶכֶת בָּהֶם יַעֲשֶׂה אֹתָם הָאָדָם וָחַי בָּהֶם, "Carry out My laws and safeguard My decrees to follow them . . . which a man shall do and by which he shall live" (18:4,5).

The Torah is giving us a formula for life — וָחַי בָּהֶם. Indeed, this could be characterized as the elixir of life. Since the Torah makes so many demands and has so many restrictions, a person might be tempted to say that if one were to follow all the disciplines of Torah, life would be unbearable. It is for this reason the Torah stresses that the observance of both *chukim* and *mishpatim,* ritual ceremonial laws as well as social laws, was given to the Children of Israel to create a society and community where people can live with a sense of fulfillment and pursue a lifestyle which grants them the joy of life.

The Torah cautions the Children of Israel that when they enter the Promised Land they should not follow the ways of Egyptian society nor embrace the ways of the Canaanites. Egypt was a land which had destroyed the dignity and freedom of man, while Canaan had glorified immoral and depraved behavior. Israel is cautioned to reject both, and to establish a social moral order, in the Land of Israel. Much of the lifestyle in Canaan, where moral degradation and sexual immorality was rampant, could very well impact on the newly arrived nation of Israel and tempt them to embrace this way of life. A slave people, granted freedom and liberty, too often finds it difficult to accept a life of discipline, especially self-discipline. Once the yoke of slavery has been removed there is a tendency to embrace license, not to just be content enjoying newfound liberty.

There are also attitudes and mores which become deeply ingrained over a period of time when a people have resided in a land for many years. These must be uprooted and not allowed to become part of the baggage which accompanies a nation when they depart from one land to take up residence in another. That is why the Torah adds the words אֲשֶׁר אֲנִי מֵבִיא אֶתְכֶם שָׁמָּה when it speaks of the land of Canaan, and אֲשֶׁר יְשַׁבְתֶּם בָּהּ when speaking of Egypt. In the former case there is the attraction and allure of the new, while in the latter case there are patterns of behavior which became ingrained over many, many years and are difficult to shed.

The Torah, however, is not content with admonishing us to reject the old ways of Egypt and resist the new ways of Canaan. It also impresses upon us that only with a blend of *mishpat* and *chok*, social law and ritual law, can life be enriched, and a way of life established in a new land for a newborn people. Not only will these laws be וָחַי בָּהֶם, to live by them, but also לָלֶכֶת בָּהֶם, for they will provide a lifestyle as well as a rhythm of life. Far from being restrictive or suffocating, they will grant the nation *chiyus,* which can best be translated as a *joie de vivre.*

Life in the Land of Israel is to be based on two major principles: *mishpatim,* which regulate social conduct, and *chukim,* which control moral behavior. Israel must start with a complete new slate, and reject the culture which had corrupted both Egyptian and Canaanite society. Above all, they are cautioned: בְּחֻקֹּתֵיהֶם לֹא תֵלֵכוּ. Note that the traditions of the nations in whose midst they will live are referred to as חֻקִּים, which means customs that are devoid of reason and logic. In Judaism, obedience to חֻקִּים (decrees) is an admirable trait, demonstrating our faith in the Almighty. However, blindly following the illogical and unreasonable ways of the pagan nations is debilitating and destructive.

Chazal, our Sages, put it most succinctly: כְּמְתוּקָנִין שֶׁבָּהֶם לֹא עֲשִׂיתֶם, כִּמְקוּלְקָלִין שֶׁבָּהֶם עֲשִׂיתֶם, "You did not act as the right minded, but as the corrupt among them" (*Sanhedrin* 39b). The Sages bemoan the fact that the Children of Israel always had a flaw in their national character, a tendency to imitate and mimic the least desirable and most objectionable ways of the gentiles, while failing to emulate the positive and admirable traits of other nations. This is alluded to in the choice of words: בְּחֻקֹּתֵיהֶם לֹא תֵלֵכוּ. Our *Parashah* addresses itself to the weakness we have as a people, namely that of following the senseless, undesirable ways of the *goyim*. We are urged, rather, to embrace the laws and teachings of the Almighty which were given to us for our own benefit, laws which are the source of life.

PARASHAS KEDOSHIM

How to Understand the Word כָּמוֹךָ

IN THIS WEEK'S *SEDRAH,* THERE IS A *PASUK* WHICH RABBI AKIVA CALLS כְּלָל גָּדוֹל בַּתּוֹרָה, "a fundamental rule of the Torah." The *pasuk* is: וְאָהַבְתָּ לְרֵעֲךָ כָּמוֹךָ אֲנִי ה', "And you shall love your fellow man as yourself, I am Hashem" (19:18).

Indeed, when Hillel was approached by a heathen who asked to be taught the entire Torah while standing on one foot, Hillel paraphrased this verse, saying: "What is hateful to you, do not do unto others" (*Shabbos* 31a). Torah commentators have always been puzzled by this paramount, lofty, but seemingly impossible *mitzvah.* Can a person feel and have the same love for others that he has for himself? Many answers are given to this question. The one given by Rabbi Samson Raphael Hirsch is a most incisive and telling one. He points out that the Torah does not use the phrase אֶת רֵעֲךָ but לְרֵעֲךָ. The former would mean the person, whereas the latter means that which *pertains* to your fellow man, his weal and woe. I am obligated to recognize that my fellow man has the same needs, hopes, fears and frustrations that I have, and therefore I must attempt to deal with him on the same level that I deal with myself. That is why the paraphrase of Hillel is so correct. Speaking to the potential proselyte, he realizes that the heathen is not yet ready to accept the positive statement to "love his fellow as himself," but he can understand the negative aspect, of not doing to others what is hateful to himself.

The word כָּמוֹךָ, usually translated as "yourself," also means in the *same* manner that you love yourself. In other words, I must use the same yardstick when judging others as I do when I judge myself. The *baalei mussar* said that the admonition one gives to his fellow man should be given in the same manner with which one criticizes himself. It should be as sharp and as sweet. Be as harsh and as gentle in criticizing others as you are when you practice self-criticism. Do it with the same *charifus* (sharpness) and the same *mesikus* (sweetness).

If *mussar* is given to your fellow man with concern and love, you fulfill the advice given in the Talmud (*Berachos* 10a) regarding the verse יִתַּמּוּ חַטָּאִים מִן הָאָרֶץ, "Let sins be wiped away from the earth" (*Tehillim* 104:35), which is interpreted as meaning חַטָּאִים וְלֹא חוֹטְאִים, "sins, not sinners." We do not ask G-d to remove the sinners from our midst; rather our request is that He eliminate sin, thereby automatically ridding the world of sinners.

Interestingly, the English have a similar expression, "Hate the action, and not the man." A famous English philosopher once said, regarding this maxim, that he always thought it was foolish until he realized that he had been doing precisely that all his life — with himself!

In general, the phrase כָּמוֹךָ means that we should see ourselves reflected in others, for by so doing, we will understand others and empathize with them.

The greatest barrier to the fulfillment of this *mitzvah* is arrogance and vanity, which cause us to become judgmental rather than caring and understanding. A true *anav*, a truly humble and modest person, refrains from imposing his own demanding standards upon others and is willing to accept them on their terms. There is a tendency to reflect our own personality, together with our problems and shortcomings, in dealing with our fellow man. Psychology teaches that there is a concept of transferal. Certain psychological tests are given through the medium of showing a picture to a person and asking him to describe what he sees. The results are often an example of how we project our own feelings and experiences onto others. In one of these tests, a picture of an older man talking to a younger one is shown to the subject. He is asked: What do you think the older man is saying to the younger one? The answers range from, "He is scolding him," to, "He is praising him," to, "He is having a heart-to-heart discussion with him." These answers obviously reflect the experience of the observer. The Torah alludes to this in the phrase כָּמוֹךָ, "as yourself." Indeed, the כָּמוֹךָ, "as yourself," is a vital key to וְאָהַבְתָּ לְרֵעֲךָ, meaning we can understand and empathize with others through transference of self. The כָּמוֹךָ removes the barrier between myself and my fellow man.

The concluding statement, אֲנִי ה׳, "I am your G-d," is extremely important to our understanding of this *mitzvah*. What is your motivation when you fulfill this *mitzvah*? Is it because G-d has commanded it, or because, logically and reasonably, it is a societal obligation which stabilizes society? All civilized men basically subscribe to the sentiment of "Love your fellow as yourself." Yet, they abandon it constantly for a variety of reasons, be it business, ego, honor, politics or even patriotism. Only when it is based and rooted in those concluding two words, "I am Hashem," does it have constancy and durability.

This is what Rabbi Akiva means when he says: זֶה כְּלָל גָּדוֹל בַּתּוֹרָה. This is a fundamental, immovable major principle, as long as it is rooted in, and derived from, Torah. Otherwise, like most modern ethics and morality, it becomes conditional and relative, lacking fixity in one's philosophy of life. The concluding words — אֲנִי ה׳ — "I am your G-d" — ensure our unconditional acceptance of this fundamental principle which is the foundation of the social order.

PARASHAS EMOR

The Ordeal of the Ordinary

IN THIS *PARASHAH* WE FIND WHAT IS REFERRED TO AS *PARASHAS HaMoadim,* the "Festival Section." The sequence of festivals is found in Chapter 23, beginning with Shabbos and continuing through the Yom Tov of Succos. Close examination of this "Festival Section," however, reveals a strange break and interruption in the very middle of the *parashah*. After discussing two of the *regalim,* Pesach and Shavuos, before the Torah continues with the other festivals, a law is introduced which is seemingly a *non sequitur.* וּבְקֻצְרְכֶם אֶת קְצִיר אַרְצְכֶם לֹא תְכַלֶּה פְּאַת שָׂדְךָ . . . וְלֶקֶט . . . לֹא תְלַקֵּט . . ., לֶעָנִי וְלַגֵּר תַּעֲזֹב אֹתָם, "When you reap the harvest of your land, you shall not remove completely the corners of your field . . . nor shall you gather the gleanings . . . for the poor and the proselyte shall you leave them" (23:22).

Rashi explains why the Torah places this precept in the middle of the chapter of the festivals. He quotes a Sifra which states that this is to teach us that if someone gives *matanos l'evyonim,* "gifts to the poor," it is regarded as though he had built the holy Temple and brought offerings in it.

However, a different explanation is suggested by a number of latter-day commentators, based upon a puzzling law in the Talmud regarding proselytes. Our Sages teach us that when a non-Jew comes to a religious court and requests to be converted to Judaism, he is at first dissuaded and discouraged by the judges. In Judaism we do not proselytize. On the contrary, we are brutally frank with the *geirus* candidate explaining to him how demanding Torah observance can be, and how difficult it is to be a Jew.

Understandably, this is done in order to test his sincerity and commitment. What is difficult to understand is that among the *mitzvos* we discuss with him to illustrate how demanding our faith can be is the law of gifts for the poor, mandated by the Torah. Specifically, we teach the *ger* the laws of *pe'ah,* leaving over the corner of the field, and *leket,* the gleanings which must also be left for the poor (*Yevamos* 47a). How strange that instead of teaching him fundamental laws of Judaism we choose to instruct him in these seemingly lesser laws, which are far less demanding than others. Note, however, that these are the same precepts which we find in the verse which appears in the middle of *Parashas HaMoadim*!

The *baalei mussar* teach us that every person has moments of inspiration and elevation. There are moments of grandeur which serve to inspire and energize an individual. Imagine how a Jew was inspired by the service in the *Beis HaMikdash,* the holy Temple, when he made *aliyah l'regel* on Pesach and Shavuos. By the same token, imagine the letdown, how his spirit was deflated, when he had to leave Jerusalem after Yom Tov and return to his farm and home, leaving behind the excitement of Jerusalem and returning to his daily routine. Likewise, a non-Jew may be inspired when coming into contact with Judaism and the Jewish people in their better moments. He can become so enthused by these special experiences that he is moved to embrace Judaism. But when this enthusiasm wears off and he is faced with the challenge of living as a Jew day to day, then the demands of Judaism can become burdensome. Confronted with the ordeal of the ordinary, the proselyte may regret his decision, and his commitment may weaken.

The Jewish pilgrim returning home after Yom Tov, as well as the proselyte after his initial moments of enthusiasm and excitement, are both confronted by this ordeal. Can they make it through the mundane moments and the common hours? It is for this reason that the Torah places the laws of gifts to the poor in *Parashas HaMoadim,* for these obligations will face the Jew when he returns from Jerusalem to his field, as they will confront the *ger* when he has to face reality after his conversion. To both of them the Torah says: These are the real-life tests and challenges which you must face. It is for this reason that the *pasuk* is put in the middle of *Parashas HaMoadim,* and taught to the potential *ger.* In both cases we are saying: Once the moments of enthusiasm have passed, once you have left the pomp and ceremony of the Temple service, and once the special times which inspired you to embrace Judaism are almost forgotten, remember that there are duties and obligations which await you. Nonetheless, both the Torah, in our *Parashah,* and the Talmud, in *Yevamos,* teach us that the mundane moments and the ordeal of the ordinary can be confronted, and the challenge can be met. The Torah assures us that the spirit and commitment of both the Jew and the proselyte can be strong enough to overcome the descent into the field, and that the essence of the Jewish spirit can ever be retained. This is why the laws of gifts to the poor are injected into the "Festival Section," and why they are singled out to be taught to the potential convert, for it is vital that we be realistic and pragmatic. This recognition of man's changing moods and attitudes makes our Torah a *Toras emes,* a Torah of truth!

PARASHAS BEHAR

Putting First Things First

IN THIS *SEDRAH,* THERE ARE A NUMBER OF LAWS WHICH DEAL WITH redemption of individuals and property. Among them is a special law regarding "a resident's house in a walled city" (25:29), בֵּית מוֹשַׁב עִיר חוֹמָה. This refers to a house in a city that had a wall around it from the time of Yehoshua.

Our Sages state that the special status of a house in a walled city is valid only if the walls of the city were erected before the city was populated. If, however, people settled in a town before the walls were built, and subsequently they were erected, halachically it is not considered to be an עִיר חוֹמָה, "a walled city." This law is explained as follows: If people settle in a town *prior* to the building of its walls, the security and safety provided by those walls was not their prime consideration in taking up residence in that town. However, if the walls were there before, then one can assume that this was a major consideration in people moving to, and establishing residence in, that particular town. Hence, the character of a walled city is defined by the sequence. Did the walls precede the *yishuv* or postdate it?

A number of *baalei mussar* use this *halachah* to define the priorities of people and their motivation in establishing residence in a particular community. For example, we find that Yaakov sent his son Yehudah to Egypt, לְתַקֵּן לוֹ בֵּית תַּלְמוּד, "to establish a place for Torah study" (*Bereishis* 46:28, Rashi's commentary), before they even left the land of Canaan to take up residence in Goshen. This was necessary because the character of that place had to be established before the children of Yaakov came there. Our Rabbis, in

Pesachim (87a), explain the verse in Shir HaShirim (8:10): אֲנִי חוֹמָה, "I am a wall," as referring to Torah, for just as a wall protects the inhabitants of a city, so the Torah protects the Jewish character of a community. Were the children of Jacob to have come to Egypt and later established a place of Torah study, it would not be a מוֹשַׁב עִיר חוֹמָה in the fullest sense, as we see from the *halachah*. And so in *chinuch*, Torah education, learning and living Torah during one's childhood must precede the establishment of a person's way of life. Even before one reaches the age of *mitzvos*, there must be years of *chinuch*, for it is in this manner that we create the character of a youngster. By so doing, we build the wall of Torah before the individual has established his lifestyle, and in that manner his growth into adulthood is secure and safe.

Which Direction Are You Facing?

THERE IS AN EXPRESSION WHICH REPEATS ITSELF IN THIS *PARASHAH* in connection with the economic status of a fellow Jew. It contains a word which is not found too often in *Tanach*, namely יָמוּךְ, meaning *impoverishment*. וְכִי יָמוּךְ אָחִיךָ וּמָטָה יָדוֹ עִמָּךְ, "If your brother becomes impoverished and his means falter with you" (25:35). וְכִי יָמוּךְ אָחִיךָ עִמָּךְ וְנִמְכַּר לָךְ, "If your brother becomes impoverished with you and is sold to you" (25:39).

In the first instance, the Jew has become impoverished and is forced to borrow money. The Torah admonishes us not to take interest from him. In the second case, he is reduced to selling himself to a fellow Jew as a slave. However, there is a third situation where this expression is used — a case which is a greater tragedy — when he is forced to sell himself to a non-Jew residing in our midst. וְכִי תַשִּׂיג יַד גֵּר וְתוֹשָׁב עִמָּךְ וּמָךְ אָחִיךָ עִמּוֹ וְנִמְכַּר לְגֵר תּוֹשָׁב עִמָּךְ, "If the means of a sojourner who resides with you shall become sufficient, and your brother becomes impoverished with him, and he is sold to an alien who resides with you" (25:47).

Here the Torah speaks of the ultimate degradation of a Jew in Eretz Yisrael, when he is reduced to being sold as a slave to a non-Jewish resident. Our Sages were intrigued by this turn of events and make the following comment, quoted by Rashi on this verse. They first question how this stranger in our midst merited to become so rich that he was able to purchase a Jewish slave. Secondly, they inquire as to what caused this Jew to become so impoverished that he was reduced to selling himself as a slave to a non-Jew. The answer to both these questions lies in the words that are used in connection with this relationship: עִמּוֹ and עִמָּךְ. What caused the non-Jew to become so affluent was דְּבוּקוֹ עִמָּךְ, "his cleaving to you." What caused the Jew to become so impoverished was דְּבוּקוֹ עִמּוֹ, עַל יְדֵי שֶׁלָּמַד מִמַּעֲשָׂיו, "his cleaving to the non-Jew and following his ways."

How can it be that the same relationship brings blessing to the non-Jew and poverty to the Jew? The answer is that it all depends where one is heading and the direction he is facing. The *ger toshav* who is leaving idolatry behind him is progressing and heading in the right direction, for he chooses to associate with Jews, and therefore he is blessed. The Jew, on the other hand, is opting for the company of the non-Jew, and moving away from his people.

The teachers of *mussar* use a *mashal,* "parable," to illustrate this point. Picture two trains standing on parallel tracks on the same platform, one facing east and the other facing west. They leave the station at the same time, but with each passing moment they travel in opposite directions, moving toward different destinations. So too, this Jew and this non-Jew were positioned on parallel tracks, but facing in opposite directions. Therefore, one is destined to be blessed, for his destination is a Jewish one, while the other is destined to be reduced to a state of utter degradation, for his ultimate destination is estrangement from Judaism!

The Torah tells us, however, that even though he is at fault, and his brethren may feel that he has forfeited his right to their mercy, nonetheless: אַחֲרֵי נִמְכַּר, "Even after he has been sold," גְּאֻלָּה תִּהְיֶה לּוֹ, "he shall have a redemption" (25:48), and one of his family is urged to redeem him. The Torah is teaching us a great lesson here regarding the relationships that a Jew should foster, while at the same time indicating that regardless of a Jew's foolish actions, he still merits redemption.

PARASHAS BECHUKOSAI

Lessening Links – Diminishing Merits

AT THE CONCLUSION OF THE *TOCHACHAH,* THE ADMONITION AND rebuke, we find words of comfort. The Torah states: וְזָכַרְתִּי אֶת בְּרִיתִי יַעֲקוֹב וְאַף אֶת בְּרִיתִי יִצְחָק וְאַף אֶת בְּרִיתִי אַבְרָהָם אֶזְכֹּר וְהָאָרֶץ אֶזְכֹּר", "I will remember My Covenant with Yaakov, and also my Covenant with Yitzchak, and also My Covenant with Avraham will I remember, and I will remember the Land" (26:42).

Rashi explains why the Patriarchs are mentioned in a reverse order, i.e., Yaakov first, followed by Yitzchak and then Avraham. He tells us that this is to teach us that even Yaakov, who was the youngest of the Patriarchs, has sufficient merit to help his children in their time of trouble; and if he is not worthy enough to do so, then Yitzchak will be able to save his offspring; and if, perchance, neither of them is sufficiently worthy, then certainly Avraham, the founder of our people, will bring us salvation.

There are, however, latter-day commentators who give different answers to this question regarding the reversal of the order of the Patriarchs' names. Among them is Rabbi Meir Shapiro, the Lubliner Rav, who points out that each of our *Avos* possessed a special attribute, a special *middah,* in which he excelled, and which was subsequently transmitted to the Children of Israel. Yaakov represents Torah; Yitzchak represents *avodah* (service); while Avraham represents *chesed* (lovingkindness). He submits that many years ago, Jews possessed all three of these attributes, but with the passage of time some became weakened, while others fell completely by the wayside.

When the Torah begins by telling us that the Almighty will remember Yaakov, it refers to a time in Jewish history when the Torah was studied and observed. However, with the passage of time, Torah became very diluted, and Jews manifested their Jewish identity through prayer alone, but unfortunately they no longer studied Torah, nor observed its *mitzvos* meticulously. Still, they did go to *shul* and *daven,* or at least they belonged to a *shul.*

The verse implies that even though G-d will not help Jews in the merit of Yaakov — who represents Torah — He will still remember the Covenant of Yitzchak, who represents Divine service. Although Torah study may be weaker at that point than it was in the past, there will still be synagogues, and in that merit, He will help us.

However, a time may come when even this will no longer be true. Jews will abandon the study of Torah and absent themselves from *shul.* But even Jews who are not Torah Jews, or even *shul* Jews, will still retain the characteristic of *chesed,* of kindness and generosity. They will build hospitals and orphanages, and will feed hungry Jews and clothe those who are naked. We are therefore told that in that merit, the merit of Avraham, G-d's Covenant will be remembered, and we will be protected from on High.

G-d's sequence of remembrance, from Yaakov to Avraham, concludes with the phrase וְהָאָרֶץ אֶזְכֹּר, "I will remember the Land." Time has proven how true this is, for in the case of many of our brethren, this is their only link to Jews and Judaism. Torah, *davening,* and even *chesed,* far too often are no longer the hallmark of these people. But they still identify with the Land of Israel. History demonstrates that וְהָאָרֶץ אֶזְכֹּר, "and I will remember the Land," is still operative. And that is why we still, thank G-d, find Jews, who, although alienated from everything Jewish, still care for the Land of Israel and are concerned for the State of Israel.

Therefore, there is nothing more tragic than a development we have witnessed in recent years, where even this link and connection has become weakened. It is incumbent upon Torah Jews not only to strengthen their fellow Jews in the area of Torah, *avodah* and *gemilus chasadim,* but in the area of חִיבַּת הָאָרֶץ, "love of the Land," as well, for this may well represent the only connection and identification that many Jews have with *Klal Yisrael.*

Sefer Bamidbar

PARASHAS BAMIDBAR

To Count and Be Counted

THE ENGLISH NAME FOR THIS FOURTH BOOK IS "NUMBERS." Although this is not the literal translation, which would be "In the Wilderness," nonetheless the word "Numbers" does reflect the theme of this week's *Parashah,* which discusses the taking of a census of the Jews who were in the wilderness at that time.

At the very outset of the *Parashah,* Rashi comments: מִתּוֹךְ חִבָּתָן לְפָנָיו מוֹנֶה אוֹתָם כָּל שָׁעָה, "Because the people of Israel are beloved by the Almighty, He counts them frequently. When they left Egypt they were counted; following the incident of the Golden Calf they were counted to determine the number of those who remained loyal; and when G-d decided to cause His Divine Presence (*Shechinah*) to dwell in their midst, He counted them once again." This commentary of Rashi gives us a special understanding of when Jews are to be counted, under what circumstances and for what purpose.

The slavery and bondage of the Jewish people in Egypt was a crucible in which the true mettle of each Jew was tested. Many were able to withstand suffering, but not all were able to withstand the impact and influence of an alien environment. They capitulated, not only to their masters, but to their surroundings as well. If they were subservient physically, they were even more so spiritually. Our Sages tell us that only one fifth of the Israelites were deemed worthy to be redeemed from Egypt, for only this small number proved itself strong enough to retain their identity. It was with these people, who were able to withstand the pressure of their masters and retain their loyalty to the teachings of the

Patriarchs, that the building of a Jewish nation began.

This is one of three occasions when G-d counted the Jews, to ascertain who could be relied upon, after passing through the difficult, trying period of Egypt. And so it has been in other periods of exile, when the majority of Jews fell by the wayside and only a relatively small percentage remained within the fold of the Jewish people.

Rashi teaches us that there were other historic periods when Jews were faced with adverse conditions and confronted with circumstances which tested their loyalty, and after these periods of trial, G-d counted them once again. If Egypt represented an environment of slavery and subservience, the episode of the Golden Calf represented a period of affluence, bringing in its wake alienation.

We witness today a wave of assimilation which is attributable to the searing trials of success. The question as to whether success can spoil the Jewish spirit has, unfortunately, been answered — it can and does. One need but examine the statistics of acculturation and assimilation in the Jewish community. The Golden Calf spirit has pervaded and permeated the Jewish people over many centuries, and we must always take a count to determine the number of those who survive, who are able to resist the enticements and blandishments of the Golden Calf. This is the second time that Hashem counts us, to learn *minyan hanosarim,* "the surviving remnant."

There are indeed those who are strong enough to be refined in the crucible of *galus,* and firm enough to resist the temptation of the Golden Calf, but whose quality of stubbornness may still not be sufficient to find them worthy of having the *Shechinah* dwell in their midst. Though they are to be commended for retaining their Jewish identity, nonetheless, to have G-d's Presence dwell in our midst, there must be a maturation and growth of the Jewish spirit. There must be a full development of our national character, an awareness of Israel's mission, and a willingness to be an עַם קָדוֹשׁ, "a holy people."

Before the *Shechinah* came to rest in the Sanctuary, we had to be counted once again to ascertain whether we were receptive enough, appreciative enough and sufficiently worthy to have G-d in our midst. This third counting — to determine how many Jews could be depended on — is perhaps the most telling of all, and the most difficult.

This first Rashi in the Book of *Bamidbar* teaches us that in order to count Jews a three-fold test must be met: They must be men and women who can transcend their environment, overcome the enticements of their surroundings and withstand alien ideologies, while realizing their unique mission as an *am Hashem*. They are the ones who can cause the Presence of G-d to dwell in the midst of *Klal Yisrael*.

PARASHAS NASSO

To Be Blessed and to Be a Blessing

THE MOST FAMILIAR SECTION OF THIS WEEK'S *SEDRAH* IS DOUBTLESS the *Bircas Kohanim,* the Priestly Blessing, which is still recited by the Kohanim on every Yom Tov, and in some communities, every day. This brief, 15-word text is majestic in its poetic language and very moving in the beauty of its expression.

There is a Midrash which states: The Kohanim shall bless the people of Israel, just as G-d said to Avraham: וֶהְיֵה בְּרָכָה, "and be a blessing" (*Bereishis* 12:2). Our Sages link the blessing of the Kohanim to G-d's promise expressed to Avraham many years earlier, and thus underscore the true meaning and essence of a blessing. For the question has often been asked: How can man bless his fellow man? Why, indeed, did G-d choose to command the Kohanim to bless us when it would have been so much simpler for the Almighty to bless us directly? One can also ask, regarding the phrase used in conjunction with Avraham: How does one *become* a blessing?

Perhaps all these questions can be answered with one thought. Indeed, only G-d can bring blessing to mankind, but it is man himself, through his behavior and conduct — by setting an example through his own life — who serves as a model for others and thereby teaches mankind what *berachah* really means! From the time of Avraham, we appreciated what a wise man once said so succinctly, "People need models more than critics." The educational process for both young and old can best be served not through lectures and lessons, nor by admonition and preaching, but rather through the very presence of a man who by his conduct and behavior demonstrates the finest qualities and virtues that man can achieve. When outstanding individuals are successful in teaching through their own conduct, then indeed they *become* a blessing. This is what G-d meant when He said to Avraham, "Be a blessing" (*Bereishis* 12:2).

Rabbi Samson Raphael Hirsch wisely commented that whereas all others strive to be blessed, Avraham was told *"to be a blessing."* One need not belabor this point to understand the vast difference between these two approaches to life.

The Kohanim were charged primarily with the task of being teachers. "For the Kohen's lips should keep knowledge, and Torah will be sought from his mouth" (*Malachi* 2:7). To best fulfill this assignment, they had to develop their own character and conduct, so that they could teach through their every act and deed. That would be their greatest blessing. True, when they blessed the people with the beautiful prayer dictated to them by G-d, they would inspire the people and imbue them with a sense of love and devotion to G-d and each other. But the main blessing would be similar to that of Avraham — that is, that they themselves, in their daily behavior and conduct, would concretize the *Bircas Kohanim*.

Similarly, commenting on the famous phrase: וְאָהַבְתָּ אֵת ה' אֱלֹקֶיךָ, "And you shall love your G-d," our Rabbis tell us that this means not only to love G-d, but שֶׁיְּהֵא שֵׁם שָׁמַיִם מִתְאַהֵב עַל יָדְךָ, "to make G-d's Name beloved through your way of life" (*Yoma* 86a). In other words, when a Jew is honest, decent and kind, he causes mankind to love the G-d Who taught this Jew to be the man he is.

Let us conclude with this beautiful statement from the Sifri, commenting on the middle blessing, יָאֵר ה' פָּנָיו אֵלֶיךָ (May Hashem cause His face to shine upon you.) "May He give you enlightenment of the eyes — the light of the *Shechinah*. May the fire of prophecy burn in the souls of your children. May the light of the Torah illumine your home." This best summarizes the objective and goal of *Bircas Kohanim*.

Coexistence and Peace – שְׁלֵמוּת וְשָׁלוֹם

THE CONCLUDING PHRASE OF *BIRCAS KOHANIM* IS: וְיָשֵׂם לְךָ שָׁלוֹם, "And may He place peace among you." The blessing of *shalom* is certainly a most desirable one. However, it is important for us to appreciate what is meant by this term. The Sages in the Talmud (*Berachos* 56b) teach us that there are three kinds of *shalom*: the *shalom* represented by a river (נָהָר), the *shalom* represented by a bird (צִפּוֹר) and the *shalom* represented by a vessel (קְדֵרָה).

The waters of a river are totally united. There is no separation between one drop and another drop. Symbolically, this represents togetherness. It is therefore understandable that our Rabbis teach us that a river represents peace, for only if there is unity can there be peace between individuals, and then they can dwell together. Still, there is a danger in this kind of togetherness, for it can become suffocating and not allow for any breathing space between individuals, something which every family knows is extremely important. It has been pointed out that, in a Sefer Torah, there must be space between the letters, and if letters touch one another, the Torah is *pasul* (disqualified). Nonetheless, the letters in the Torah cannot be overly separated lest this affect the composition of the word. And so it is with human relationships. Close is admirable, but leave some space in between.

It is for this reason that our Sages give us the second metaphor for *shalom,* namely, a bird. A bird represents individuality and the retention of one's identity. A bird is able to fly and put space between itself and other birds. We are being taught that true *shalom* in human relationships should combine both the nature of the river and that of the bird.

Be it the *shalom* of a river or that represented by a bird, in order to create a community we need to protect the fierce individuality

Parashas Nasso / 111

of all people who dwell in that community, while at the same time combine their talents and abilities together. That is why our Sages introduce the third metaphor for *shalom,* namely a קְדֵרָה, meaning a pot or a vessel. When a pot is filled with water which one wishes to boil, it is placed on the fire. By their nature, water and fire cannot coexist, for they are opposing forces. However, if water is placed in a pot and put on the fire, there is not only coexistence between these opposing forces, but there is interaction as well. Each element, water and fire, is able to retain its potency and, as it were, express its worth and value without canceling out one another. So it is with human relationships. Every individual has his or her own unique talents and gifts, which are expressed at times individually, while at other times it is only in unison that these gifts and talents are able to be expressed fully. People are often by their very nature like fire and water, but they can still interact in a positive manner. That is why the Talmud teaches us: הָרוֹאֶה קְדֵרָה בַּחֲלוֹם יְצַפֶּה לְשָׁלוֹם, "He who sees a pot in his dream can look forward to a life of peace" (*Berachos* 56b).

It is now understandable why we conclude the *Shemoneh Esrei* with the blessing of *shalom,* as the *Bircas Kohanim* concludes with the same *berachah.* In the Mishnah, our Rabbis express this in a most telling and beautiful manner. They state: לֹא מָצָא הַקּבָּ"ה כְּלִי מַחֲזִיק בְּרָכָה לְיִשְׂרָאֵל אֶלָּא הַשָּׁלוֹם, "Hashem could find no vessel to contain blessing for Israel other than that of peace" (*Uktzin* 3:12). No doubt, the כְּלִי mentioned in this Mishnah refers to that vessel which brings peace between fire and water.

PARASHAS BEHA'ALOSCHA

What Do You Miss?

IN THIS WEEK'S *SEDRAH,* AN EPISODE IS RELATED WHEREIN A NUMBER of men pose an interesting and difficult problem to Moshe. These individuals were very upset that they were unable to bring the *korban pesach* on the 14th day of Nissan, due to the fact that they were ritually unclean. Moshe was perplexed and presented this problem to G-d, Who told him that a second chance would be given to these men to observe the Pesach, albeit one month later. What should interest us, however, is the expression used by these men. The expression is: לָמָּה נִגָּרַע, "Why should we be deprived?" (9:7). This question is a most revealing index to their scale of values. It may, indeed, be an index to every man's priorities and values. What does one cherish and consider to be important? What causes a sense of lack within a person? To bring the paschal lamb was not an easy task. The manifold laws involved in this sacrifice, the many restrictions, the difficult disciplines — these should all reduce one's desire to bring this offering. If, perchance, one was incapable of performing this act, and was indeed absolved from doing so by law, why not accept this excuse with relief and joy? How many of us would bemoan the fact that we were exempt from performing a difficult *mitzvah*? Yet, these men were saddened and upset. There was a sense of loss because they were denied the privilege of offering their sacrifice. Their sense of deprivation indicates how rich was their level of spirituality and how profound their sense of commitment.

For most people, the lack of a beautiful home, a late model car and a balanced bank account would create a sense of deprivation.

On the other hand, to be denied the opportunity to perform a *mitzvah,* attend synagogue services or give *tzedakah* would not be considered a loss. But it is precisely one's sense of lack which reveals his character and is the best index to his true personality!

A wise man once said, "The tragedy of life is not so much what men suffer, but rather what they miss." This pithy saying is very applicable to Jewish life today. There are many people who, because they lack the proper yardstick of values, miss out on many aspects of Jewish life which could add to, and enrich, their lives and the lives of their children. Because of distorted concepts, there is an insensitivity to one's spiritual and intellectual lack, while there is so much pain and suffering, and above all frustration, because people are dissatisfied with their material lot in life.

The answer given by Moshe to the problem presented to him by these men who could not bring the *korban pesach* was a most comforting one. He told them that there would be a Pesach Sheni and that they would have another opportunity to participate fully in the celebration of *Yetzias Mitzraim.* This must be understood not only as an answer to the men who were *temei'im* and therefore could not participate with others in the *korban pesach,* but also as a lesson for us, for all time. There is always a *second* chance given to rebuild our lives, and to grasp opportunities which we have missed, provided we understand what "to miss"!

Another episode in our *Sedrah* underscores the concept that one's values are revealed by what one craves, as well as by one's scale of priority. The Torah tells us that at a certain point in the wilderness the Children of Israel bitterly expressed their dissatisfaction with their diet of manna, complaining that they did not have variety, and had only the manna to eat. They cried out: מִי יַאֲכִלֵנוּ בָּשָׂר, "Who will give us meat to eat?" (11:4). If Hashem and Moshe were to argue that the manna was Heavenly food which had in it the flavor of all foods, and that the people's complaint demonstrated profound ingratitude, we could appreciate the validity of such an answer. But that is not the response given by the Almighty. Rather, He said to Moshe: אֶסְפָה לִּי שִׁבְעִים אִישׁ מִזִּקְנֵי יִשְׂרָאֵל, "Gather to Me seventy men from the elders of Israel" (11:16).

It would seem that this is a *non sequitur.* The people were asking for meat, and G-d told Moshe to create a Sanhedrin! A great *mus-*

sar teacher, however, explains that what the Almighty was implying was that their request demonstrated that they had fallen to a level where their greatest sense of lack was that of a monotonous diet. Therefore what had to be done was not to satisfy their appetite, but to teach them how to reorder their priorities and their values. The increased number of teachers would be able to instruct the people as to what to look for in their lives, and teach them that if there is a sense of lack, it should not be because there was no meat on the menu. The response of Hashem was therefore a most telling and wise one.

PARASHAS SHELACH

Logical Is Not Always Reasonable

WHEN THE ALMIGHTY GAVE MOSHE PERMISSION TO SEND SPIES to the Promised Land, in response to the request of the people, the Torah uses seemingly strange phraseology. At the very beginning of this week's *Sedrah,* G-d said to Moshe: Send these men to the Land of Canaan, אִישׁ אֶחָד אִישׁ אֶחָד לְמַטֵּה אֲבֹתָיו תִּשְׁלָחוּ, "One man each from their father's tribe shall you send" (13:2). The *pasuk* then continues: כֹּל נָשִׂיא בָהֶם, "every one a leader [prince] among them." Why did Hashem use the phrase אִישׁ אֶחָד twice, and why did He add that every emissary was to be a נָשִׂיא, "a prince"?

The Alshich has a most fascinating commentary on this verse. He speculates that Moshe, from the very outset, was concerned regarding this mission, worried that these men would slander the Land and dissuade the people from entering Canaan. He was determined to lessen this possibility by removing the representatives of the two tribes who, he felt, had flawed character traits. And which were these two tribes? If one studies the story of Yosef and his brothers, one realizes that Yehudah was guilty of deception and dissimulation when he showed his father the bloody tunic of Yosef and said to him: הַכְּתֹנֶת בִּנְךָ הִוא אִם לֹא, "Is this your son's tunic or not?" (*Bereishis* 37:32). Yosef, in turn, was guilty of bringing evil reports about his brothers to his father, as we read: וַיָּבֵא יוֹסֵף אֶת דִּבָּתָם רָעָה אֶל אֲבִיהֶם, "And Yosef would bring evil reports about them to their father" (ibid. verse 2). It was these two tribes, Yosef and Yehudah, whom Moshe feared more than any of the other tribes, for their ancestors were guilty of slander and deception, two traits which the spies ultimately manifested regarding Eretz Yisrael. The *meraglim* (spies) were guilty of *lashon hara* (slander) — as was Yosef in his relationship with his brothers — and of deceiving the Children of Israel into thinking that the conquest of this harsh land and its mighty people was impossible — similar to the deception practiced by Yehudah. It is for this reason, the Alshich conjectures, that Moshe was tempted not to send *any* representatives from these two tribes. But even if he had to, he would have preferred to limit the number by sending only one representative from the descendants of Yosef, although normally Menashe and Ephraim were counted as two separate tribes. He thought perhaps he could send just one from Menashe, who was the older son of Yosef, and skip over Ephraim, thereby reducing the risk.

To counteract this reasoning and plan, the Almighty said to Moshe: . . . אִישׁ אֶחָד אִישׁ אֶחָד, "You must send one man from each tribe," you cannot eliminate any tribe. And lest you think that you need send only one representative from the children of Yosef, Hashem adds: כֹּל נָשִׂיא בָהֶם, "every leader or prince among them," which precludes the elimination of Ephraim, who had his own *Nasi,* as did Menashe. What Moshe intended to do may have been most logical and reasonable, but it was not in accord with the Divine plan. G-d had different *cheshbonos.* Had Moshe implemented his plan, he would have eliminated the only two *meraglim* who were *tzaddikim* and fulfilled their mission in the proper manner, namely Yehoshua and Calev, the representatives of Ephraim and Yehudah, respectively!

We learn from this commentary of the Alshich that what logic dictates is not always the correct path. The *Hashgachah,* Divine Providence, often decrees that the best and the finest people come from an unexpected source and transcend the flawed character of their ancestors. We can never tell from whence the *yeshuah* will come, and if we rely only on our own logic and reason, we can lose a Yehoshua and a Calev!

Squandered Opportunity

A MOVING MOMENT IN JEWISH HISTORY IS RECORDED IN THIS week's *Sedrah.* A moment of crisis presented itself to Moshe when the spies returned from the Land of Israel. Through their slander and defeatism, they discouraged the people of Israel from proceeding to the Promised Land. Unfortunately, the Children of Israel listened to the 10 rather than the two (Yehoshua and Calev), and as a result they were sentenced to wander 40 years in the wilderness until a new generation would arise, wise and strong enough to enter the Land.

When the people were informed of this dire Divine decree, a number of them — over the protests of Moshe — decided to "go it alone," and וַיַּעְפִּלוּ לַעֲלוֹת, "They defiantly ascended" (14:44). However, they suffered great losses at the hands of the Canaanites. From this latter episode, we can derive a great lesson for all time.

We have been taught that nothing stands in the way of repentance. No matter how grave the transgression, if one's return is sincere, G-d will accept the penitent. If so, why did G-d not accept the *teshuvah* of these men who realized that they had sinned and clearly stated חָטָאנוּ, "We have sinned" (14:40), by accepting the slander of the spies? They were repentant, and therefore they believed that G-d would forgive them and be with them in their attempt to enter the Promised Land. Why then did G-d rebuff them?

There are moments in life that are unique and special and can never be recaptured. In the history of a people there are moments of opportunity which present themselves that can alter the course of that people's history — if they are recognized and appreciated. Although an individual may miss the opportunity to perform a *mitzvah*, nonetheless he can repent and eventually fulfill that particular *mitzvah*. Not so insofar as the *klal* is concerned. The lost moment cannot readily be retrieved. What you do the following day, regretfully, is useless and ineffective. If the moment of challenge is squandered, that moment will not present itself again to a nation for many years to come — if at all. The Jews could have entered the Land of Israel within a period of three days had they not been misled by the spies. By allowing that opportunity to slip away, they were forced to wander in the wilderness for 40 years.

There are similar events to be found in our history, one of which we shall cite. In the time of King Chizkiyahu, Sancheriv threatened the Holy City of Jerusalem. Miraculously, the city and the people were saved. The Talmud tells us that G-d wanted to proclaim Chizkiyahu as the *Mashiach* (*Sanhedrin* 94a). In other words, the Messianic period would have started from that moment. The Jews would never have been exiled and the Holy Temple would never have been destroyed! What prevented this from happening? It was because Chizkiyahu failed to sing a song of praise to the Almighty! But one could say: Let him rectify this failure! Let him sing the song of praise a day later. But here again, we see that the lost moment, a moment which has mystical significance and power in the Divine pattern, once lost cannot be recaptured.

The modern implications of this lesson are self-evident. There have been moments in Jewish history — be they in regard to Jewish education, the Land of Israel or the saving of Jewish lives — when so much could have been done, but those moments were squandered. The tragedy lies in the fact that once these moments passed, it took many decades, in most instances, to accomplish with much sacrifice and suffering that which could have been accomplished far easier, if the magic moment would have been properly utilized. Obviously, the great task which confronts us is to recognize these moments and to rise to these historic challenges.

PARASHAS KORACH

Not to Capture but to Captivate

IN THIS WEEK'S *SEDRAH,* THE TORAH RECORDS THE STORY OF THE rebellion led by Korach against the leadership of Moshe and Aharon. The response of Moshe, who is always depicted as an *oheiv Yisrael,* one who loved all Jews, and who by temperament was an *anav,* a humble and modest man, was surprisingly a very firm and harsh one. After trying to appease the rebels, Moshe concluded that his authority must be confirmed by G-d, and that there must be a sign from Heaven that the claims and accusations of Korach and his followers were unfounded. The great *oheiv Yisrael* was so angry that he was not content with punishment being visited upon these rebels, but it had to be done in a manner that would impress all of Israel, through a unique phenomenon. This indeed happened, as the Torah states: וַתִּפְתַּח הָאָרֶץ אֶת פִּיהָ וַתִּבְלַע אֹתָם . . . וַיֵּרְדוּ הֵם וְכָל אֲשֶׁר לָהֶם חַיִּים שְׁאֹלָה, "The earth opened its mouth and swallowed them . . . and they, and all that was theirs, descended alive into the pit" (16:32,33).

One would expect that after witnessing such a miracle, the people would recognize that Moshe was right and Korach was wrong, for not only did this phenomenon occur, but "a fire came forth from Hashem" and consumed all the men who joined Korach and offered incense without permission. Yet, immediately following these punishments, we are told that "the entire assembly of the Children of Israel complained on the morrow against Moshe and Aharon, saying, אַתֶּם הֲמִתֶּם אֶת עַם ה', 'You have killed the people of Hashem' " (17:6).

Is this not a most startling kind of reaction — that the Children of Israel should align themselves with the opponents of their legitimate leaders and accuse them of being responsible for their deaths!? Had they not witnessed, with their own eyes, how these wicked men were destroyed by Hashem, not by Moshe and Aharon? How perplexing and difficult it is to understand this reaction and response!

Immediately following the punishment from Heaven and the complaint of the Children of Israel, further punishment was visited upon the Children of Israel in the form of a *mageifah* (plague), which felled 14,000 people and was checked only by Aharon bringing the *ketores* (incense) into their midst, thereby providing atonement for the people. Apparently, even this catastrophe was not sufficient to convince the people that authentic and legitimate leadership belonged only to Moshe and Aharon.

However, immediately after these events, Hashem commanded Moshe to take a staff from each tribe, provided by its leaders, each of whom inscribed his name on his staff, as did Aharon on the staff of Levi. These staffs were placed before the *Ohel Moed* (Tent of Meeting), and the people were told that G-d would give them a sign as to whom He had chosen to serve Him in the Sanctuary. The sign would be that the staff of the chosen one would blossom and bud, and bring forth almonds. Indeed, on the very next day, the staff of Aharon did precisely that, while the other staffs remained bare. Apparently, this satisfied the Children of Israel, and they no longer complained or questioned the authority of Moshe and Aharon. Indeed, this sign was so significant and important that Hashem commanded Moshe to store Aharon's staff for safekeeping for all time. The Torah tells us that it was originally placed in front of the Holy Ark and later stored away, together with a container of manna (*Horayos* 12a).

We must attempt, however, to understand why the miracles and Divine retribution left little impact on the people, while the blossoming and budding of Aharon's staff put their complaints and opposition to rest. Torah commentators have answered this question as follows: Miracles rarely have a lasting impact. They may capture the attention of people, arousing man's marvel and amazement momentarily, but they do not engage the mind or captivate the heart, nor do they convince people in any lasting fashion. In general, Divine punishment is not an instrument that creates conviction in the minds and hearts of people. Punishment, harsh and unusual as it may be, does not instruct or influence. That is why the opening of the earth and the swallowing up of Korach and his followers, as well as the *mageifah,* did not convince the people that Korach was wrong and Moshe right. On the other hand, when the *matteh Aharon,* the staff of Aharon, blossomed and budded and produced fruit, that made a much greater impact on the people and convinced them of his legitimacy as the *Kohen Gadol,* the High Priest.

In Jewish history, this lesson has repeated itself time and time again. The hearts of the people are not captured by punishment, but are captivated by the growth and productivity of the exponents of a religious or political ideology and philosophy. The staff of Aharon itself teaches this lesson. When it originally swallowed up the staffs of the Egyptian sorcerers, no one was impressed, but when it blossomed and budded, everybody was impressed! This lesson was taught not only to the Jewish people, in the aftermath of the rebellion, but serves as a lesson to *Klal Yisrael* for all time. As Torah Jews in our generation, when we are confronted by rebellion against Torah authority by so many of our fellow Jews, threats of Divine punishment serve little purpose. Attention, however, is paid, and admiration, begrudging as it may be, is evoked, when the Torah community builds institutions, educates a generation and establishes homes and families that live lives — based on Torah — which are productive, decent and serve as models for society in general.

That is why we never instituted a remembrance for the awesome miracle of the earth opening its mouth to swallow up the rebels. We did, however, set aside the staff of Aharon *l'mishmeres,* "as a safekeeping" (17:25), in front of the Holy Ark to keep the lesson of positive growth and productivity fresh and meaningful forever in the conscience of *Klal Yisrael.*

PARASHAS CHUKAS

Excess Causes Affluenza

THE EPISODE KNOWN AS *MEI MERIVAH,* "THE WATERS OF STRIFE," is recorded in this week's *Parashah*. After the Jews complained bitterly regarding the lack of water in the wilderness, Hashem commanded Moshe to take his staff and speak to the rock, and it would then give forth its waters. Moshe, however, in his anger, instead of speaking to the rock, struck it. G-d then decreed that because he and Aharon had failed to follow G-d's command literally, namely to speak to the rock, they would be punished, and would not merit to bring the people of Israel into the Promised Land.

The Meshech Chochmah, authored by Rabbi Meir Simchah of Dvinsk, analyzes this segment of the *mei merivah* incident and offers a most telling and incisive commentary. He points out a number of variations in the text between the order given by Hashem and the actualization of this command. In Chapter 20, verse 8, where Moshe was commanded to speak to the rock, the verse states: וְהוֹצֵאתָ לָהֶם מַיִם, "You shall bring forth for them water." The Meshech Chochmah points out that in verse 11, after Moshe had smitten the rock, the Torah states: וַיֵּצְאוּ מַיִם רַבִּים, "*Abundant* water came forth." The word רַבִּים appears in verse 11, but not in verse 8.

When G-d told Moshe that water would come forth from the rock, sufficient to give drink to the people and to their animals, the verse separates the עֵדָה (assembly) from בְּעִירָם (their animals), with the word אֵת. The *pasuk* reads: אֶת הָעֵדָה וְאֶת בְּעִירָם. This usage indicates a clear distinction between man and animal. In verse 11, however, the Torah states: וַתֵּשְׁתְּ הָעֵדָה וּבְעִירָם, "And the assembly and their animals drank." Here the word אֶת — which separates animal from man in verse 8 — is absent!

The Meshech Chochmah explains these variations. Humans and animals are not meant to be equated, provided man obeys the dictates of Hashem, in which case his superiority over the animal is self-understood and apparent. That is why the word אֶת is used to separate man and animal in verse 8. However, when man disobeys G-d, there is really no distinction between him and other living creatures. He has compromised his moral stature, and thereby removed the special *tzelem Elokim* (image of G-d), which is his, and his alone. This explains why the word אֶת does not appear at the conclusion of the episode in verse 11, for defiance of G-d's will resulted in man and animal no longer being distinguished from one another. The Meshech Chochmah also explains why although originally G-d told Moshe that the rock would simply bring forth water, later, when the Almighty was disobeyed, *abundant* water came forth. He explains that when man fulfills the wishes of G-d and follows His commandments, a small measure of water suffices. However, once he disobeys G-d's order, he cannot quench his thirst unless there is an abundance of water. Indeed, our Sages tell us that the righteous eat little, but whatever they consume is blessed within them by G-d, whereas בֶּטֶן רְשָׁעִים תֶּחְסָר, "The stomach of the wicked always feels empty" (*Mishlei* 13:25).

It is interesting to note that Shlomo HaMelech echoes these thoughts in *Koheles.* כִּי לְאָדָם שֶׁטּוֹב לְפָנָיו נָתַן חָכְמָה וְדַעַת וְשִׂמְחָה, "To the man who pleases Him, He has given wisdom, knowledge and joy," וְלַחוֹטֶא נָתַן עִנְיָן לֶאֱסֹף וְלִכְנוֹס, "but to the sinner, He has given the urge to gather and amass" (*Koheles* 2:26).

Shlomo HaMelech is teaching us that one who lives with moderation is granted a life of *simchah,* whereas the person who lives a life of excess, who spends his entire time accumulating riches, finds little satisfaction and only a small measure of happiness. If he is content with *mayim,* a moderate amount of water, as opposed to *mayim rabim,* abundant water, he has learned the secret of true contentment. He has also affirmed his superiority over other creatures by demonstrating his special, unique quality as one created in the image of G-d.

Shlomo HaMelech amplifies this thought when he says: טוֹב מְלֹא כַף נַחַת מִמְּלֹא חָפְנַיִם עָמָל וּרְעוּת רוּחַ, "Better one handful of pleasantness than two fistfuls of toil and vexation of the spirit" (ibid. 4:6). One handful is certainly far less than two fistfuls, but a person will experience more *nachas* through moderation than he will from excess. This may well explain why *Koheles* is read during the holiday of Succos, when we are taught this lesson for an entire week by leaving our secure and luxurious surroundings for a frail, temporary hut. It is precisely then, during Succos, that we experience the greatest *simchah* of the entire year.

We can now appreciate what our Sages mean when they interpret the phrase טוֹב מְאֹד, used in the story of Creation, "And G-d saw all that He had made, and behold it was very good" (*Bereishis* 1:31), as follows: טוֹב זֶה יֵצֶר הַטּוֹב, מְאֹד זֶה יֵצֶר הָרָע, "Good represents the good inclination in man, whereas the word מְאֹד, 'very,' represents the evil inclination" (*Bereishis Rabbah* 10). Everything that G-d created is good, providing man finds it sufficient. If, however, man is not content and wants more, if he insists upon "very," the good can become evil. More is not necessarily better. This is the lesson taught by our Sages in their interpretation of the expression טוֹב מְאֹד in the story of Creation. It is this which Shlomo HaMelech teaches us as well, and the episode of *mei merivah,* as explained by the Meshech Chochmah, puts it all into proper perspective.

PARASHAS BALAK

Israel's Vulnerability

THE TORAH DEPICTS THE KING OF MOAV, BALAK, AS A PERSON who was consumed by fear of the Children of Israel. He was convinced that their intention was to destroy him and conquer his kingdom. He also felt that the only way to deter them was not through military confrontation, but by cursing them and thereby neutralizing their power and deterring their aggression against him. Toward that end, he sent emissaries to Bilaam who, he believed, had the power to bring down curses from above upon the people of Israel. Balak hoped that this would provide him with protection from the people of Israel and guarantee the security of Moav.

Bilaam, however, had a far-greater understanding of the Jewish people and knew that as long as G-d loved and cherished them, His Divine protection would not be removed. He knew that the only way to make the Israelites vulnerable would be to sever the tie they had with the Almighty. If one looks in the *Haftarah* of *Parashas Balak,* which is taken from the prophecy of Michah, one can find this thought process of Bilaam alluded to by the prophet. In the *Haftarah,* there is a verse which reads: עַמִּי זְכָר נָא מַה יָּעַץ בָּלָק מֶלֶךְ מוֹאָב וּמֶה עָנָה אֹתוֹ בִּלְעָם בֶּן בְּעוֹר, "Oh, my people, remember what Balak plotted and what Bilaam answered" (*Michah* 6:5).

Note that the prophet speaks of Balak's *eitzah,* his suggestion and advice, and Bilaam's response. The son of Rabbi Samson Raphael Hirsch, Mendel Hirsch, explains this verse as follows. Balak understood that the military option was not open to him. However, he thought that the Israelites could be brought down and defeated through imprecations and curses uttered by a man of the spirit, such as Bilaam. This was his *eitzah,* his plan. Bilaam, however, responded to Balak that as long as G-d is the Guardian of Israel and they are beloved by Him because they accept His will and follow His commandments, they cannot be vanquished. His advice to Balak, therefore, was to lead Israel astray, to entice them to defect from G-d and thereby lose the support and protection of the Almighty. That is why he suggested to Balak that the daughters of Moav should seduce the Israelites and entice them to commit acts of immorality, which in turn would lead to idolatry.

This is indeed what happened at Shittim, and is mentioned in the words of Michah as well. When the prophet reminded the Jewish people of G-d's lovingkindness, he mentioned the episode of Shittim specifically, for it was there that they became vulnerable to their enemies. Unquestionably, when Jews are guilty of immorality and idolatry, they remove G-d's protection from themselves, and this was precisely Bilaam's strategy.

If one looks carefully at a *pasuk* in this week's *Parashah,* one can see how Bilaam's plan was to divest the Jews of their unique collective character and transform them into a nation like all other nations. Bilaam said to Balak: לְכָה אִיעָצְךָ אֲשֶׁר יַעֲשֶׂה הָעָם הַזֶּה לְעַמְּךָ, "Come, I shall advise you what this people will do to your people" (24:14).

This verse is almost inexplicable. The Torah does not tell us what Bilaam's counsel was, nor does Bilaam explain what the Israelites were going to do to the Moabites. Rashi quotes a *Chazal* in *Sanhedrin* which explains that this refers to Bilaam's advice to have the daughters of Midian and Moav seduce the Israelites and thereby enrage G-d against them. However, we still have no explanation for the latter part of the verse: אֲשֶׁר יַעֲשֶׂה הָעָם הַזֶּה לְעַמְּךָ, "what this people will do to your people." The Israelites were meant to be victimized by the women of Midian. Hence, the verse should read "what your people will do to them." If, however, one were to vowelize the word as יֵעָשֶׂה, rather than יַעֲשֶׂה, the meaning of these words and of this verse completely changes. It does not mean, "what this people will do to your people," but rather that this people *will become* as your people! They will conduct themselves in an immoral manner, be transformed and become indistinguishable from Moav. When this happens, G-d will no longer protect them, and hence their power will be eroded. Once they are like us, Bilaam says to Balak, they are no longer unique and special, and will therefore no longer represent a threat to you. What my curses cannot accomplish, their defection will.

Bilaam's original response to Balak's suggestion was valid. As long as תְּרוּעַת מֶלֶךְ בּוֹ, "the friendship of the King is with him" (23:21) — which is interpreted as a derivative of the word רֵעַ, "a friend" — as long as G-d is in their midst as a friend, the Jewish people cannot be conquered. Only by leading them astray and enticing them to rebel against their G-d will they become vulnerable and no longer be protected from on high.

History has proven that Bilaam understood the source of the real strength of the Jewish people, something which unfortunately anti-Semites understand better than we do. Fortunately, the zealotry of Pinchas stemmed the tide in time to protect the Jewish people, who were ultimately able to overcome their own defection and weakness.

PARASHAS PINCHAS

The Secret Is Timing

AT THE BEGINNING OF THIS WEEK'S *SEDRAH*, THE TORAH TELLS us that Hashem granted Pinchas a Covenant of Peace for his heroic act of *kana'us,* for the zeal he demonstrated on behalf of the Almighty. Our Sages tell us: פִּנְחָס זֶה אֵלִיָּהוּ, "Pinchas and Eliyahu are as one." This is usually explained as meaning that the *neshamah* of Pinchas became the soul of Eliyahu, for both of them were men of *kana'us,* men who were jealous and zealous for the honor of Hashem.

When Shabbos *Parashas Pinchas* falls before the beginning of the Three Weeks, the *Haftarah* chosen for this *Sedrah* is the chapter from *I Melachim* which relates the story of Eliyahu in the aftermath of his confrontation with the prophets of the Baal on Mt. Carmel. In that chapter, it is related that G-d appeared to Eliyahu and commanded him to anoint Elisha as G-d's prophet in his place. Whereas Pinchas was praised and rewarded for his act of zealotry when he killed Zimri, Eliyahu, on the other hand, was relieved of his position as prophet of Hashem when he stated: קַנֹּא קִנֵּאתִי לַה׳ . . . כִּי עָזְבוּ בְרִיתְךָ בְּנֵי יִשְׂרָאֵל, "I have been exceedingly zealous for Hashem . . . for the Children of Israel have abandoned Your covenant" (*I Melachim* 19:14).

Here we have two men who demonstrated an uncommon passion and fervor on behalf of the Almighty, and nonetheless were not treated equally by Hashem. Pinchas was rewarded for his act while Eliyahu was deposed. Why this disparate response on the part of the Almighty?

The role of *kana'us* in Jewish life must be understood not as an absolute but a relative virtue. At times, it is not a virtue, but borders on a vice. Everything depends on circumstance and timing. When our Sages in *Avos* (6:6) speak of the traits of a man of Torah, they list the attribute of הַמַּכִּיר אֶת מְקוֹמוֹ, "he who recognizes and knows his place." This has been interpreted as meaning that a man of Torah must recognize and understand the place, the time and the circumstance of the moment. He must examine very carefully the temper of the time and the condition of the society in which he finds himself, before taking action. This will help us understand the disparity between the historic period in which Pinchas lived and that of Eliyahu.

The episode at Shittim, when the Jews were seduced by the daughters of Moav and Midian, was an aberration, a deviation from the norm. At that time, the Jewish people were pious and loyal to Hashem, and committed to the teachings of the Torah. Therefore, their defection could be stemmed by a dramatic act which would shock them into a realization of their transgression and bring them back to G-d. Such an act was that of Pinchas killing Zimri, and that is why his act of zealotry was saluted and commended.

Eliyahu, however, lived at the time of Achav and Izevel, when the majority of Jews had deserted the ways of G-d and worshiped the Baal. Even the dramatic miracle performed by Eliyahu on Mt. Carmel resulted at best in a momentary enthusiastic response of ה' הוּא הָאֱלֹקִים, "Hashem is the G-d" (*I Melachim* 18:39), but it was only a temporary return. At such a time, an act of *kana'us* is futile, for unlike the episode involving Pinchas, you cannot stem a major tide of defection with a spear, as Pinchas had done when he killed Zimri and Kozbi. What was necessary at the time of Eliyahu was not *kana'us,* extreme and excessive zealotry, but a slow, arduous process of education, reconciliation and rapprochement. That is why Hashem, according to the Midrash, said to Eliyahu: אִי אֶפְשִׁי בִּנְבִיאוּתֶךְ, "It is impossible for Me to have you continue as My prophet." You must appoint another in your place, one who will be able to bring the people back to the ways of Judaism and recommit them to faith in the Almighty. A *kana'i,* a zealot, is not the one capable of reaching the hearts of a people who have strayed so far from the fundamentals of Judaism. A different approach is called for, and that is why Elisha was now chosen.

It is interesting to note that when Eliyahu came to the house of Elisha, he found him plowing the fields of his father (*I Melachim* 19:19). *Tanach* is teaching us, in a most subtle fashion, why Elisha was chosen by G-d at this juncture to be His prophet. A farmer understands the need to clear a field of thorns and thistles before he can plow it. He also knows that he must plant seeds, tend them, nurture them and exercise great patience before a crop will grow. It is precisely this that a prophet of Israel had to understand at that time — namely, that the hearts of the Jews had to be prepared before the seeds of faith could be planted, eventually to take root and grow. This was a trait which apparently Eliyahu did not possess, but Elisha, as a farmer, did.

This distinction between Pinchas and Eliyahu provides a great lesson, applicable in our time as well. *Kana'us,* zeal, fervor and passion, are powerful and commendable forces. However, they need to be controlled and used with great discretion. Above all, good judgment must be exercised as to *when* they should be used, and under what conditions. In general, we live in a time far more comparable to that of Eliyahu than that of Pinchas, in a generation that has strayed from the ways of G-d and Torah due to ignorance. This being so, we will accomplish much more through understanding, patience and education than through defiance and rebellion. We must never forget that of Torah it is said: דְּרָכֶיהָ דַרְכֵי נֹעַם וְכָל נְתִיבֹתֶיהָ שָׁלוֹם, "Its ways are ways of pleasantness, and all its paths are peace" (*Mishlei* 3:17).

PARASHAS MATTOS

When שֶׁפַע (Abundance) Becomes פֶּשַׁע (Iniquity)

OUR *SEDRAH* RELATES HOW THE TRIBES OF REUVEN AND GAD requested that Moshe permit them to take up residence on the east bank of the Jordan, since they were blessed with many cattle and sheep and there was quality grazing land in that area. Reluctantly, Moshe acquiesced to their request on the condition that they provide troops to assist their fellow Jews in the conquest of Canaan.

Our Sages are critical of these two tribes and feel that they were guilty of cherishing their wealth and allowing their desire for material things to override the love they should have had for Eretz Yisrael. The Sages go so far as to say that these tribes were exiled from their land earlier than the other tribes of Israel because they had separated themselves from *Klal Yisrael,* motivated by their concern for their possessions. They apply to them the *pasuk*: נַחֲלָה מְבֹהֶלֶת בָּרִאשֹׁנָה וְאַחֲרִיתָהּ לֹא תְבֹרָךְ, "If an inheritance is seized hastily in the beginning, its end will not be blessed" (*Mishlei* 20:21). Their impatience in claiming their inheritance ultimately led to their downfall.

The Midrash seeks to draw a parallel between these two tribes and a number of historic personalities, commenting on three areas which can be either virtues or vices. The three are: חָכְמָה (wisdom), גְבוּרָה (strength) and עוֹשֶׁר (wealth). The language of the Yalkut is instructive and illuminating. The text reads: ג׳ מַתָּנוֹת נִבְרְאוּ בָּעוֹלָם, חָכְמָה וּגְבוּרָה וְעוֹשֶׁר. וְכֵיוָן שֶׁלֹּא בָּאוּת מִן הַקּבָּ״ה סוֹפָן לְהִיפָּסֵק מִמֶּנּוּ, "Three gifts were given to man in this world: wisdom, strength and riches.

132 / Table Talk

However, if they are not derived from the Almighty, ultimately they will be taken from man."

The Yalkut gives three examples of individuals who represent the world at large and the people of Israel. They cite two wise men, Bilaam from the nations of the world and Achitofel from Israel, who were both punished. The two men of wealth cited are Korach and Haman, who both met with a bitter end, while the two men who represent might and strength are Goliath and Samson, who fell at the hands of their enemies. The Sages tell us that each of these men attributed their wisdom, wealth and strength to their own abilities and talents, without recognizing that everything comes from the Almighty. In addition, the commentators point out that each of these men grasped what he considered to be his, prematurely, before it had been given to him by Heaven.

After citing these examples, the Sages proceed to apply this same thought to the tribes of Gad and Reuven. וְכֵן אַתָּה מוֹצֵא בִּבְנֵי גָד ,וּבְבְנֵי רְאוּבֵן שֶׁהָיָה לָהֶם מִקְנֶה גָדוֹל, וְחִבְּבוּ אֶת הַמִּקְנֶה – לְפִיכָךְ גָּלוּ תְחִלָּה "And so we find by the children of Gad and Reuven who had many herds and flocks, and cherished their possessions — therefore they were the first to be exiled."

We learn from this Midrash that man's superior gifts, be they intellect, might or wealth, can be either a blessing or a curse. Abundant gifts in any of these areas can either elevate a person or lead to his downfall. In the Hebrew language, the word שֶׁפַע, which means an abundant flow, is comprised of the same letters which spell פֶּשַׁע, iniquity. This lesson proved to be true of the six individuals mentioned by the Sages in the Midrash, as it was true of the two tribes who insisted upon receiving their share on the east bank of the Jordan. With the passage of time, these tribes became isolated from the rest of *Bnei Yisrael*, as Moshe had feared. Their wealth and prosperity contributed to their separation and isolation, as well, which is alluded to in the Midrash cited above. It states, "What caused these tribes to be exiled first? Because they separated themselves from their brethren due to their great wealth."

One might well apply to them the aphorism, "Ill is the land, to its enemy a prey, where wealth increases while men decay." Our Sages have a most interesting and telling play on certain words which deal with material wealth. In the Talmud, the word for property is נְכָסִים; the word for money is either זוּזִים or מָמוֹן. Emphasizing the transitory nature of man's wealth, they comment: — נְכָסִים שֶׁנִּכְסִים מִזֶּה וְנִגְלִים לָזֶה, "It is hidden from this one and becomes revealed to another." זוּזִים — שֶׁזָּזִים מִזֶּה וְנִתָּנִים לָזֶה, "They move from this one to another one." מָמוֹן — מָה אַתָּה מוֹנֶה אֵינוֹ כְּלוּם, "What you count is meaningless."

Our Sages are teaching us that in this transitory world the most impermanent of all things is wealth. We are able to learn this lesson from the episode of the tribes of Gad and Reuven which we read in this week's *Sedrah*.

PARASHAS MASEI

Travel Broadens Horizons

THE COMMENTATORS OF THE TORAH EXPRESS VARIOUS OPINIONS as to the Torah's purpose in recording the journeys and the encampments of the Children of Israel during the years they traveled in the wilderness. Rashi explains that the purpose is to publicize the lovingkindness of G-d, Who during 40 years kept the various journeys and stations down to a relatively small number, in order not to burden the people.

The Rambam, in his *Moreh Nevuchim* (Guide to the Perplexed), is of the opinion that the various journeys and encampments are recorded to emphasize that there was order and careful planning of their itinerary during those years. The Children of Israel were not wandering haphazardly, disoriented and lost in the wilderness. Each journey, each encampment and its duration was organized and deliberate. According to the Rambam, this *Parashah* is included in the Torah to teach us that once the Children of Israel were delayed in entering the Land of Israel, the *Hashgachah* (Providence) led them with purpose and a specific schedule, while miraculously providing for their physical and security needs. In other words, we are taught in this *Parashah* of the guidance exercised by the Almighty during the 40 years of the Jews' travels in the wilderness, as well as His many acts of *chesed* (lovingkindness). According to the Rambam, the expression "wandering in the wilderness" is an erroneous one. The correct terminology would be "the travels and journeys of the Children of Israel in the wilderness." That is precisely what our *Parashah* calls it — מַסְעֵי בְּנֵי יִשְׂרָאֵל, "the journeys of the Children of Israel."

The Sforno, however, submits a different reason for the Torah's recording of these journeys. He says that the purpose is to teach us how deep and abiding was Israel's faith in G-d, and their readiness to travel or to encamp at His behest, regardless of any difficulty encountered by these constant travels. Above all, the Torah reveals the discipline demonstrated by the Israelites, even when the order to leave one place and proceed to another seemed to be unreasonable and even illogical.

To understand what the Sforno is saying, it is important to refer back to *Parashas Beha'aloscha,* Chapter 9, verses 17-23. There, the Torah tells us that the special cloud which covered the Mishkan served as a signal to the people insofar as their movement and stations were concerned. Whenever the cloud lifted, the people would follow it, and where the cloud came to rest, there they encamped. As the Torah tells us in that *Parashah,* this was an indication of G-d's will and command. עַל פִּי ה׳ יִסְעוּ בְּנֵי יִשְׂרָאֵל, וְעַל פִּי ה׳ יַחֲנוּ, "According to the word of Hashem would the Children of Israel journey, and according to the word of Hashem would they encamp" (*Bamidbar* 9:18).

The Torah states that the duration of time the Children of Israel remained in one place varied. At times, they would remain in a place less than 24 hours. At other times, they would remain in a location for days, months or years. The decision, however, was not theirs and was not dictated by circumstances. As the Sforno explains, if they encamped in a pleasant and fertile area, it was only because they were so commanded, and not because it was beneficial for them. Even if they were content and happy in a particular location, if the cloud moved on, so did they. The period of time was also irrelevant. Whether they had not yet established themselves in a specific location, or had been settled there for some time, they broke camp and followed the cloud. Such was the commitment of that generation to the dictates and direction of the Almighty.

When one reviews the Book of *Bamidbar,* one is struck by the many episodes of the people's rebellion, complaining and lusting, and their spirit of ingratitude. This *Sefer* is replete with instances of improper behavior and a rebellious spirit, manifested by the Children of Israel. There is, however, another positive side to the coin, regarding Israel's character, as the Sforno points out, which this *Sedrah* of *Masei* teaches us. How fitting it is that the *Sefer* of *Bamidbar* ends on this positive note, projecting the picture of a people who had abiding faith and trust in the Almighty. Certainly, it is this collective character of *Klal Yisrael* which the prophet refers to when he says: זָכַרְתִּי לָךְ חֶסֶד נְעוּרַיִךְ ... לֶכְתֵּךְ אַחֲרַי בַּמִּדְבָּר בְּאֶרֶץ לֹא זְרוּעָה, "I remember for you the kindness of your youth ... how you followed Me in the wilderness in an unplanted land" (*Yirmeyahu* 2:2).

The story is told that a *chasid* once came to his Rebbe and told him that whenever *Sefer Bamidbar* is read, he becomes very depressed. "So many complaints, so many rebellions and so many sins!" The Rebbe smiled and said to him, "True, but remember — their sins became Torah." Doubtless, the Rebbe was consoling him by pointing out that not only did these disturbing, negative actions "become Torah," but there is also comfort in the concluding *Sedrah* of this Book, *Parashas Masei,* if we understand it in the light of the Sforno's commentary.

Sefer Devarim

PARASHAS DEVARIM

A Balanced Judgment

AT THE BEGINNING OF OUR *SEDRAH*, MOSHE RELATES THAT IN order to lessen his burden he appointed judges to adjudicate the numerous cases of litigation, which heretofore had been judged by him alone. In Chapter 1, verse 16, Moshe states: וָאֲצַוֶּה אֶת שֹׁפְטֵיכֶם בָּעֵת הַהִוא לֵאמֹר שָׁמֹעַ בֵּין אֲחֵיכֶם וּשְׁפַטְתֶּם צֶדֶק, "I instructed your judges at that time saying, 'Listen among your brethren, and judge righteously.'"

The Talmud, in *Sanhedrin* 7b, states that this verse is meant to caution a judge not to listen to one party of a dispute unless the other party is present.

The story is told that Rabbi Yonasan Eibeshitz, who even in his early youth was known as being extremely pious, was asked how he was able to be so disciplined in his religious observance. After all, our Sages teach us that the *yetzer hara,* the evil inclination, is implanted within us from the moment we are born, whereas the *yetzer tov,* our good inclination, does not become part of us until Bar Mitzvah. That being the case, he was asked how he had been able to resist the *yetzer hara* before his Bar Mitzvah, when he did not yet have a *yetzer tov*. His answer was that although he was only a young boy, he knew the *halachah* mentioned above — that one is not permitted to listen to the arguments of one party unless the other party is present. Young Yonasan explained that whenever the *yetzer hara* would come and tempt him to sin, he told him that he was not permitted to listen to him, since he was not yet Bar Mitzvah and did not possess a *yetzer tov*. Therefore he would have to wait until the second party arrived, and then he would consider the arguments of the *yetzer hara*.

This may well be an apocryphal story, but the argument is certainly a very valid and correct one. It also should teach us that, even after one is Bar Mitzvah, he should not give in to the temptation of his *yetzer hara* until his *yetzer tov* is given an opportunity to counteract the seductive arguments. At the very least, he should give a fair hearing, at all times, to his *yetzer tov*.

A Light Unto the Nations

MANY OF THE LATTER-DAY TORAH COMMENTATORS, AND ESPEcially *maggidim*, often departed from *p'shuto shel mikra* (the literal translation and interpretation of the Torah), and interpreted *pesukim* homiletically, in order to derive a moral lesson from the *parashas Hashavua*. One such example is a *pasuk* in this week's *Sedrah*: רַב לָכֶם שֶׁבֶת בָּהָר הַזֶּה. פְּנוּ וּסְעוּ לָכֶם וּבֹאוּ הַר הָאֱמֹרִי וְאֶל כָּל שְׁכֵנָיו, "Enough of your dwelling by this mountain, turn yourselves around and journey and come to the Amorite mountain and all its neighbors" (1:6,7).

Rashi quotes a Midrash which interprets this *pasuk* in a most intriguing way. The Midrash explains that Moshe told the Jews that even though they had accomplished so much at the mountain of Sinai, including receiving the Torah, building a Mishkan and appointing a Sanhedrin, nonetheless the time had come to leave and journey on to the Amorite mountan "and all its neighbors."

How strange it is that after having reached such spiritual heights, they were commanded to leave this holy place and travel on, among the Amorites and its neighbors! Would it not have been far better for the Children of Israel to remain where they were, in order to protect their special, unique way of life, and not attempt to integrate themselves with other nations? However, the answer is that this was precisely what Moshe was saying to them — that theirs is a *Toras chaim,* a living Torah, and was not given to isolate and insulate them from the world. The challenge was to live by the

Torah, even in the midst of others, and thereby become an *ohr la'amim,* "a light unto the nations."

This, some *darshanim* say, is what is meant by the words רַב לָכֶם שֶׁבֶת, you have spent enough time here in the wilderness on your own. The time has come to turn your face to the world and begin to live with others as well. After assimilating the wisdom of Torah, they were challenged to go out among the nations and teach the world, for indeed הִוא חָכְמַתְכֶם וּבִינַתְכֶם לְעֵינֵי הָעַמִּים, "It is your wisdom and understanding in the eyes of the nations" (4:6). Only if you are prepared to apply this wisdom to your everyday life will others be able to learn from you, and this is precisely what your mission is meant to be.

The Hidden Seeds of Redemption

THE *SEDRAH* OF *DEVARIM* IS ALWAYS READ ON THE SHABBOS PRIOR to Tishah B'Av, and its *Haftarah* is the selection from *Yeshayahu* beginning with the word *chazon,* "vision." It is for this reason that this Shabbos is called *Shabbos Chazon.* However, it is important to understand the connection between this Fifth Book of the *Chumash, Sefer Devarim,* and the historic period of the destruction of the Holy Temple in Jerusalem which occurred twice on the ninth day of Av.

Sefer Devarim is not only a review of the events which transpired under the leadership of Moshe and a recapitulation of many laws of the Torah, but it also includes the admonitory orations which Moshe delivered before his death, where he cautioned his people, as they prepared to enter the Promised Land, to remain loyal to G-d's teachings and commit themselves to the observance of His commandments. Moshe was concerned lest Israel stray from the path of Torah disciplines which he had taught them and fall prey to the undemanding, immoral lifestyle of their new neighbors once they would settle in the Land of Canaan. He also expressed his fear that if they deviate from the *derech Hashem* and violate the Covenant between themselves and the Almighty, they would be exiled from the Land, as indeed eventually happened.

This explains the link between the Book of *Devarim* and the period of the *churban*, of destruction, in Jewish history, which was the consequence of the nation's defection. The word אֵיכָה which we find in our *Sedrah*, אֵיכָה אֶשָּׂא לְבַדִּי (1:12), and in the *Haftarah*, אֵיכָה הָיְתָה לְזוֹנָה (*Yeshayahu* 1:21), as well as being the name of the Megillah which we read on Tishah B'Av, represents *tochachah* (admonition), according to our Rabbis. Moshe, Yeshayahu and Yirmeyahu all admonished Israel to correct their ways — which bring *churban* — and to return to their G-d and reconfirm their commitment to the Covenant, for only then can Israel hope for a period of *binyan*, of rebuilding and of *nechamah*, of comfort.

Interestingly, the name for the Shabbos before Tishah B'Av is *chazon*, "vision," because the *sefarim* tell us that even as we mourn the loss of the two Temples on Tishah B'Av, we must have a vision of the third *Beis HaMikdash*. We believe that in the destruction of the Holy Temple and Jerusalem, the seeds of rebuilding and reconstruction lie. We believe that even when G-d destroyed the walls of Jerusalem, He did so with חֶשְׁבּוֹן, with calculation and precision. This explains the phraseology of the verse in *Eichah*: חָשַׁב ה' לְהַשְׁחִית חוֹמַת בַּת צִיּוֹן נָטָה קָו "Hashem resolved to destroy the wall of the Daughter of Zion, He stretched out a line" (*Eichah* 2:8). The word חָשַׁב usually means to think and resolve, but it can also allude to a חֶשְׁבּוֹן, an accounting or calculation. The *Navi* is implying by the phrase נָטָה קָו, "He stretched out a line," that the destruction was not haphazard but a careful, calibrated Divine act.

A line is used by a builder when he builds a wall to make sure that it is straight. He uses a plumb line so that the bricks, stones and blocks are properly aligned. No one, however, would use such a line to demolish and destroy a wall or a building! What the verse is teaching us is that when G-d decreed the destruction of Jerusalem, he did so with a חֶשְׁבּוֹן; it was done with precision and had an ultimate purpose. Even though the city and the Temple were destroyed, the people lived on. At that moment of destruction, the seeds of *Mashiach* were being planted, and the building of the third Holy Temple was being planned. Indeed, according to tradition, *Mashiach* was born on *motza'ei* Tishah B'Av, and there is a custom among Sephardim to make a festive party immediately after Tishah B'Av to celebrate the advent of *Mashiach* whose soul came to earth at that time.

We see that the *Sedrah* of *Devarim,* the *Haftarah* of *Chazon* and the reading of *Megillas Eichah* are all interwoven and closely linked. But we must also be sensitive to the fact that *Shabbos Nachamu* follows our observance of Tishah B'Av, teaching us that hidden in the destruction are the seeds of *Mashiach.* This has always been the legacy of our people, never to despair but to hope and believe in our ultimate redemption, for in the words of the prophet, we are ever אֲסִירֵי הַתִּקְוָה, "prisoners of hope" (*Zechariah* 9:12).

A Beneficial Decree

AT THE BEGINNING OF THIS WEEK'S *PARASHAH,* THE TORAH TELLS us how Moshe prayed fervently to the Almighty to annul the decree which prohibited him from entering the Land of Israel. He asked the Almighty to let him cross over and "see the good Land that is on the other side of the Jordan" (3:25). G-d's response to him is difficult to understand. He did not simply reject his request, rather He said to him: רַב לָךְ אַל תּוֹסֶף דַּבֵּר אֵלַי עוֹד בַּדָּבָר הַזֶּה, "Enough! Do not continue to speak to Me further about this matter" (3:26).

Why was the Almighty so insistent that Moshe cease and desist from praying, and actually prohibited him from pursuing this matter? A number of latter-day commentators offer a most intriguing answer, based upon a *halachah* governing an *eved Ivri* (a Jewish bondsman). Moshe is called an *eved Hashem* (a servant of Hashem), and as such has the status of a Hebrew slave, with all the laws pertaining to a Jewish bondsman. The Torah tells us, in *Parashas Mishpatim,* that a Hebrew slave is set free after six years of servitude. However, if he chooses to remain with his master, he is permitted to do so, following a unique ritual where the master brings him to court and the court performs an act of *retziah.* This involved boring through his ear with an awl, after which he continues to serve his master until the Jubilee Year.

The Talmud, in *Kiddushin* 22a, states that the Hebrew slave must state twice that he loves his master, the wife that was given to him and the children born to them during his servitude, and therefore chooses not to be set free. They base this law on the repetition of the words: וְאִם אָמֹר יֹאמַר הָעֶבֶד, "But if the bondsman shall say . . ." (*Shemos* 21:5).

The Midrash tells us that Moshe also expressed a similar desire to remain with his people as they entered the Promised Land. They apply the words in this verse to Moshe: אָהַבְתִּי אֶת אֲדֹנִי אֶת אִשְׁתִּי וְאֶת בָּנָי, "I love my master" refers to the Almighty; "my wife" refers to the Torah; and "my children" refers to the Children of Israel, and therefore לֹא אֵצֵא חָפְשִׁי, "I shall not go free," refers to Moshe's desire not to be relieved of his position as the leader of the nation of Israel. In other words, this was part of the text of Moshe's prayer which our *Parashah* refers to when it states: וָאֶתְחַנַּן אֶל ה׳, "I implored Hashem."

We can now understand why Hashem cautioned Moshe, "Do not continue to speak to me regarding this matter." G-d was concerned that if Moshe would *repeat* his request, then G-d, as it were, would be forced to follow the *halachah* and permit him to stay on as the leader of Israel. By preventing Moshe from repeating this request, Hashem would be able to deny him his wish, as was His intent.

We can now understand why Hashem, immediately after cautioning Moshe not to repeat his request, told him to appoint Yehoshua as his successor and to strengthen him. וְצַו אֶת יְהוֹשֻׁעַ וְחַזְּקֵהוּ וְאַמְּצֵהוּ כִּי הוּא יַעֲבֹר לִפְנֵי הָעָם, "But you shall command Yehoshua and strengthen him and give him resolve, for he shall cross before the people" (3:28). The question is asked as to why this order of succession was coupled with G-d's admonition to Moshe to cease and desist from imploring Him to annul the decree.

The Brisker Rav offers a most unique answer. He cites the ruling in *Yesodei HaTorah,* where the Rambam discusses prophecy and teaches us the laws governing the determination of the authenticity of one who presents himself as a prophet of G-d. He says that if a prophet prophesies that G-d is going to punish the people, and that prophecy is not fulfilled, this does not disqualify him from being considered a true prophet. For even though the original decree was to punish the people for their sins, they may have repented and returned to G-d, and hence the decree was abrogated. On the other hand, if a prophet says that G-d is going to do something good, either for an individual or a people, and it does not come to pass, then he is not considered to be a *navi emes* (a true prophet), for a pledge and promise made by G-d *letovah* (for good) must be fulfilled.

Had the Almighty only decreed that Moshe was to be relieved of his leadership, that evil decree could conceivably have been canceled. That is why Moshe kept imploring G-d to do so. However, once Hashem designated Yehoshua as his successor, *that* decision was beneficial for Yehoshua and could not be changed! It is this which the Torah implies by repeating the appointment of Yehoshua as Moshe's successor immediately after G-d's rejection of Moshe's request. The expression כִּי הוּא יַעֲבֹר לִפְנֵי הָעָם, "For he shall cross before the people," is a critical one and is the reason that Moshe's request had to be denied, for a promise *letovah* cannot be rescinded.

Seize the Moment

IN TODAY'S *SEDRAH*, WE READ THE WELL-KNOWN WORDS OF שְׁמַע יִשְׂרָאֵל, followed by the verse: וְאָהַבְתָּ אֵת ה' אֱלֹקֶיךָ, "You shall love Hashem, your G-d" (6:4-5), followed by: וְהָיוּ הַדְּבָרִים הָאֵלֶּה אֲשֶׁר אָנֹכִי מְצַוְּךָ הַיּוֹם עַל לְבָבֶךָ, "And these words which I command you today shall be upon your heart" (6:6).

Rabbi Mendel of Kotzk explains this latter verse as follows. Although the commandments of the Torah are addressed to *Klal Yisrael,* to all Jews, each person is urged to consider the following. When he learns Torah, although there is so much Torah still to be studied, at that particular moment he must say to himself, "This is the only *pasuk*, this is the only *daf*, and I must focus on it, as though there is no other verse or page except this one which I am presently studying." That is what is meant by הַדְּבָרִים הָאֵלֶּה, "these words." And although there are many Jews in the world, a person must feel as though he is the only one who is being commanded, and therefore the responsibility is his alone, and cannot be shifted to another. This is what is meant by the word מְצַוְּךָ, "which I command *you*." And lest a person say, "I need not fulfill it immediately, for there is plenty of time," the Torah says to him הַיּוֹם, "this day," for there may be no other.

The Kotzker Rebbe also explains the last two words of this *pasuk*.

The Torah states עַל לְבָבֶךָ, "*on* your heart." Why does the Torah not say בִּלְבָבֶךָ, "*in* your heart"? He answers that Jews are not always in the mood to listen to G-d and obey Him. Often, they are distracted and unprepared to listen to the commandments of the Almighty, and therefore their heart is not open at that moment to receive G-d's words and accept them into their heart. The Torah understands this and therefore says to us: If you cannot take them *into* your heart, at least put them *on* your heart. A time will come when you will be ready to accept these words. Let them be *on* your heart so that when that moment arrives and your heart opens up, these words will fall right in! From the comments of the Kotzker Rebbe, we see how every word and phrase in the Torah is pregnant with special meaning.

PARASHAS EIKEV

Use It or Lose It

WHEN MOSHE REVIEWED THE HISTORY OF THE JEWISH PEOPLE IN the wilderness, he impressed upon them the great kindness and concern that Hashem had for them during their long sojourn in the *midbar*. Among other things, he reminded them that their garments did not wear out during these 40 years. שִׂמְלָתְךָ לֹא בָלְתָה מֵעָלֶיךָ, "Your garment did not wear out from upon you" (8:4). It is interesting to note that the miraculous preservation of their clothing and shoes, over many years, is repeated in *Parashas Ki Savo,* where it is written: לֹא בָלוּ שַׂלְמֹתֵיכֶם מֵעֲלֵיכֶם וְנַעַלְךָ לֹא בָלְתָה מֵעַל רַגְלֶךָ, "Your garments did not wear out from on you, and your shoe did not wear out from on your foot" (29:4).

Rashi, in this *Parashah,* comments that not only did the clothing last for many years without deteriorating or wearing out, but he quotes a Midrash which states that the clothing grew as the person grew. Our Sages compare this to the skin of the lizard, which grows as the lizard grows. This was indeed a great miracle, but it did have its limitations. The Yalkut, explaining the phrase מֵעָלֶיךָ, "from upon you," states that מַה שֶׁעָלָיו אֲבָל לֹא מַה שֶׁבַּתֵּבָה, "what was worn by the person remained clean and fresh, but not that which was stored in a box."

Paradoxically, clothing or shoes stored in a box *did* deteriorate, while that which was worn did not! The *baalei mussar* learn a great lesson from this Yalkut. They draw a parallel between the garments and shoes worn by our ancestors in the wilderness — which remained fresh and complete — and a person's intellectual pursuits, especially his study of Torah. When a person uses his mental

Parashas Eikev / 149

capacity and constantly challenges his intellect, he sharpens it and causes it to expand and improve. This is especially true of Torah study, regarding which our Sages teach us, אם תַּעַזְבֵנִי יוֹם יוֹמַיִם אֶעֶזְבֶךָ, "If you forsake me for a day, I shall forsake you for two days" (*Talmud Yerushalmi, Berachos*). The way a child understands a *pasuk* in *Chumash* is not the way an adult understands it. As one grows and matures, so does his understanding of Torah, just as the garments which were worn by the Children of Israel who came out of Egypt miraculously grew with them.

However, this is true only if one continues to pursue his studies and develops his intellectual powers, by continuing his study of Torah. However, if one does not challenge himself and pursue the study of Torah every day, his mental capacity and ability to master Torah deteriorates with each passing day, similar to the garments which were not worn but put away in a box. The popular expression regarding all skills in life is especially true of intellectual growth: "Use it or lose it." It is this *mussar haskel* which one should learn from the miracle of the freshness and durability of the clothing of the Children of Israel in the wilderness.

Avinu Malkeinu — Our Father, Our King

MOSHE URGED THE PEOPLE TO APPRECIATE THE FACT THAT although the Almighty afflicted them in the wilderness, the purpose was to test them and refine them. He stated: וְיָדַעְתָּ עִם לְבָבֶךָ כִּי כַּאֲשֶׁר יְיַסֵּר אִישׁ אֶת בְּנוֹ ה' אֱלֹקֶיךָ מְיַסְּרֶךָּ, "You should know in your heart that just as a father chastises his son, so Hashem, your G-d, chastises you" (8:5).

One of the great chassidic teachers was the Maggid of Mezritch. He explains this verse in a most profound and telling manner through a beautiful parable. Picture a young child beginning to walk. As he takes his first halting steps, his father stands in front of him, holding out his hands and smiling encouragement. As the child reaches out to him, the father steps back, and as he does so, the child, of course, strives to come closer, and thus he learns to walk. The Maggid explains that often Hashem seems to be distancing Himself from us, and we become dismayed, upset and angry, as does the child. But, similar to the child, we push ourselves to come closer, and even though G-d seems to move away from us as we reach out to Him, it is not because He is rejecting us, but rather because He is encouraging us to continue to reach out and to walk on our own. This is why the *pasuk* uses the expression, "as a father chastises his son, so Hashem chastises you." It is important for the Jewish people to ever appreciate that even when G-d seemingly distances Himself from us, He is instructing us and urging us to use our own strengths to come closer to Him.

Man's Creative Spirit

IN THIS WEEK'S *SEDRAH*, WE READ THAT HASHEM COMMANDED Moshe: פְּסָל לְךָ שְׁנֵי לוּחֹת אֲבָנִים כָּרִאשֹׁנִים, "Carve for yourself two stone Tablets like the first ones" (10:1).

As we know, the first Tablets of Law, which were G-d's handiwork, were cast to the ground by Moshe and shattered when he came down from the mountain and found the Jewish people dancing around the Golden Calf. Although our Rabbis tell us that G-d agreed with Moshe's decision to break the Tablets, nonetheless, coupled with this approbation was also a degree of criticism. According to the Midrash, G-d chastised Moshe for breaking the Tablets, which G-d Himself had fashioned, and on which He had inscribed the Ten Commandments. According to our Sages, the Almighty said to Moshe, "If *you* had hewn out these stones, fashioned them, and wearied yourself with shaping them and writing on them, you would not have broken them so readily." Hence, the second time around, G-d said to Moshe: פְּסָל לְךָ, "Carve for yourself," for then you will be less inclined to break the second *Luchos*, even if the people sin and arouse your anger.

We learn from this that whatever man himself creates, labors over and expends his energy on, he cherishes and guards. Whatever represents an investment of one's own self, that in which one has a personal stake, he will not readily destroy. How true this is of life in general, be it in one's personal life or in communal endeavors. Parents invest much time and energy into their children, and that is why they will not readily discard them or turn their backs on them, even when there may be good reason to do so. A person who establishes a business, or a professional who starts a practice, is prepared to spend countless hours to ensure its success, as compared to one who is only an employee. A person who invests time and effort in building a synagogue or a school will not allow himself to be deterred by obstacles or disappointments, but will continue to nurture and support the project.

The Torah impressed this thought upon us in a subtle manner by stating: פְּסָל לְךָ, "Hew out for *yourself.*" Unlike the first *Luchos,* this time *you* are the one fashioning the Tablets, and that will ensure that you will be careful to guard and preserve them, for they are לְךָ, yours.

Berachah, the Enabler

רְאֵה אָנֹכִי נֹתֵן לִפְנֵיכֶם הַיּוֹם בְּרָכָה וּקְלָלָה
"See, I present before you today
a blessing and a curse" (11:26).

THE SFORNO EXPLAINS THIS *PASUK* AS FOLLOWS. MOSHE IMpressed upon the Children of Israel that their fate and the condition of their existence is different from that of all other nations. He warned the people of Israel that there would be no middle course for them, for they would be either blessed or cursed, depending upon their adherence to G-d and Torah, and their commitment to their mission as a unique nation. Torah brooks no compromise, and total commitment is demanded from the nation of Israel. The Sforno states, "Look and perceive that your destiny as a people is not one that will be *bei'noni*, of an intermediate nature, as is the case with other nations. In your case, there is always the extreme of blessing or curse." The Sforno interprets these opening words of our *Parashah* as a dramatic challenge set before the people by Moshe. The choice was completely theirs. He underscores and stresses the words בְּרָכָה and קְלָלָה, "blessing" and "curse," as representing the core of Moshe's words to the people.

The Ramban, however, presents a different thought on these opening verses, expounding the concept of *berachos*, blessings, and the purpose for which they are given to a people. All blessings are not an end in themselves, nor are they reward for good deeds performed. Rather, they are a *means* toward an end, and are granted as a preparation for the performance of *mitzvos* and the fulfillment of G-d's will. A person must realize and appreciate that when he is granted a blessing, such as good health, wealth or life itself, it is given to him for the purpose of enabling him to obey G-d's commandments. A person tends to say: I'll study Torah and pray to the Almighty so that I may be granted good health, peace of mind and a tranquil life. I will do *mitzvos* so G-d will bless me with good health and energy. I will give *tzedakah* (charity) so G-d will bless me with wealth. Not so! G-d gives you good health and strength so that you are able to perform *mitzvos*; He gives you tranquility and free time so that you are able to pray properly and study Torah; and he gives you money so that you may give *tzedakah*. In other words, the *berachah*, the blessing, is not a reward for your obedience to Hashem, but it is given to *enable* you to listen to G-d and obey Him.

The Ramban reads this thought into the words of the *pasuk*: אֶת הַבְּרָכָה אֲשֶׁר תִּשְׁמְעוּ אֶל מִצְוֹת ה׳, "The blessing that you hearken to the commandments of Hashem" (11:27), meaning that blessings are given to you not on the condition that you listen to Hashem but in order that you should *be able* to listen to Hashem. To understand this, one must be sensitive to what the Torah is saying, and that is why the opening word of this *Parashah* is רְאֵה, which means "See" or "Behold," i.e., you must have clarity of vision in order to understand that I give you the blessing as an enabler, so that you will be able to listen and obey. This explains why the phrase used is אֲשֶׁר תִּשְׁמְעוּ, and not אִם תִּשְׁמְעוּ. The latter would mean *if* you listen, whereas the former means that you *may be able* to listen.

The Vilna Gaon, building on the phraseology of this verse, develops a most telling and moving *mussar* lesson. He explains that Moshe, speaking on behalf of the Almighty, anticipated the excuses a person uses to deviate from the path of Torah and avoid listening to the word of Hashem. There are those who say, "How can I as an individual live my life in a manner that is different from that of my neighbors and the community in which I reside?" It is for this reason that the verse begins with the word רְאֵה, "See," in the singular. The Gaon explains that this phrase is used purposely, to encourage each individual to make his own choice and not be concerned lest he may be out of step with everybody else.

He writes: עֲשֵׂה אַתָּה אֶת שֶׁלְּךָ, "You must do what is incumbent upon you," and do not pay heed to what others may think or do. Hence, the use of the singular (רְאֵה), at the beginning of the verse, even though the balance of the verse is in the plural, i.e., לִפְנֵיכֶם. And, he continues, if perchance you will say, "How can I find the will, not only to resist public pressure, but even more so, to resist my own *yetzer hara* (evil inclination)?" — Hashem says to you: אָנֹכִי נֹתֵן, "I, as the One Who teaches you this lesson, also give you the strength to obey and follow the path I have shown you." Indeed, the Sages teach us, in *Kiddushin* 30b, that the evil inclination of man is so great that no human being can overcome it, were it not for the fact that the Almighty helps him.

Each word in this opening verse of the *Parashah* has a lesson to teach. רְאֵה urges us to consider very carefully the choices given to man. אָנֹכִי teaches us that G-d is prepared to help each person. And let no one say: I have sinned so much, it is too late for me to change. To refute that excuse, the next word in the verse is נֹתֵן, "I give you," written in the present tense. This teaches us that G-d constantly gives us the opportunity to choose blessing over curse. And if one will say, but perhaps it is too late in my life to repent and change my course, the verse says to him: הַיּוֹם, "today," each day is new, and one can begin afresh.

Note that this *Sedrah* is usually read on the Shabbos when we bless the new month of Elul, or on Rosh Chodesh Elul itself, for the lessons that we learn from the opening words of this *Parashah* sound the theme of this month, the month that prepares us for Rosh Hashanah and Yom Kippur, days of self-evaluation and repentance.

PARASHAS SHOFTIM

A Clever or a Wise Person

A JEWISH JUDGE IS ADMONISHED BY THE TORAH TO BE FAIR AND honest, and certainly not to accept *shochad,* a bribe. As Rashi points out, he is prohibited from accepting *shochad* even if he will judge correctly and righteously, how much more so if the bribe results in a miscarriage of justice.

Bribery certainly affects the objectivity and fairness of the judge's decision, and the Torah states explicitly that it "blinds the eyes of the wise" (16:19), preventing the judge from seeing clearly and deciding properly. Note that here the Torah calls the judge a *wise* man: יְעַוֵּר עֵינֵי חֲכָמִים. Interestingly, in *Parashas Mishpatim* a similar prohibition is given to the judge using the same phraseology, except for one important change. There the verse reads: וְשֹׁחַד לֹא תִקָּח כִּי הַשֹּׁחַד יְעַוֵּר פִּקְחִים, "Do not accept a bribe, for the bribe will blind he who sees," or, as some translate the word פִּקֵחַ, "the clever man" (*Shemos* 23:8). Whenever the Torah uses a different word in the same context in various *Parashiyos,* there has to be not only a logical reason for it, but an instructive one as well. Why does the Torah refer to the judge as a חָכָם in our *Parashah,* and as a פִּקֵחַ in *Parashas Mishpatim*? The Vilna Gaon explains the difference between these two words as referring to two areas of human intellectual accomplishments. If one has mastered the wisdom of Torah and its teachings, he is called a חָכָם. We always refer to a Torah scholar as a תַּלְמִיד חָכָם. However, in worldly matters, if one is a clever individual, smart, perceptive and sharp, he is called a פִּקֵחַ. Korach, who led the rebellion against Moshe and was able to rally many to his cause through persuasive and clever arguments, is called a פִּקֵחַ, a "clever man," by our Sages. They do not call him a חָכָם for he was not a wise man by Torah standards, but he was a פִּקֵחַ.

A judge must be a תַּלְמִיד חָכָם, a Torah scholar, who has a commanding knowledge of Torah law, and hence is rightly called a חָכָם. But a judge must also be an individual who is knowledgeable in the ways of the world. He must have a sharp, perceptive mind able to judge and decide a case properly by grasping and understanding the words of the litigants, and even their body language. In other words, he must be not only a חָכָם but a פִּקֵחַ as well, one who can see the case before him clearly, in a *halachic* sense as well as a pragmatic one.

In *Parashas Mishpatim,* the Torah cautions the judge that *shochad* will impair his vision and clarity of mind in the existential area, in the realm of human experience. Hence, the word used to describe the judge is פִּקֵחַ. The Torah cautions the judge that his common sense and insight, i.e., his פִּקְחוּת will be affected and impaired by bribery.

In our *Parashah,* the Torah teaches us that bribery will distort and becloud the Torah understanding of the judge, and therefore it uses the phrase עֵינֵי חֲכָמִים, "the eyes of the wise," meaning their *halachic* judgment. This also explains why the word "eyes" is used in conjunction with the judge as a חָכָם, but not in *Parashas Mishpatim,* in conjunction with the judge as a פִּקֵחַ, for the expression עֵינֵי is used by the Torah to allude to the wisdom and understanding of Torah. As proof, we can point to the expression in *Vayikra 4:13:* מֵעֵינֵי הַקָּהָל, "from the eyes of the congregation," which our Sages tell us refers to the Sanhedrin, the High Court, for they are the eyes of the community, charting the life of the nation and mapping the road they should follow. Interestingly, a prophet is often called a *chozeh,* a seer, for he possesses prophetic vision and can see with spiritual eyes as well as physical ones. A חָכָם, akin to a prophet, is able to do so as well, as opposed to a פִּקֵחַ, who cannot. As mentioned above, a judge is supposed to be both a חָכָם and a פִּקֵחַ.

In our *Parashah* and in *Parashas Mishpatim,* the Torah teaches us that judgment is impaired by *shochad,* be it in the area of Torah or in the worldly arena. One need not be a judge to become a victim of *shochad,* for as a wise man once said, "Some of us are misled, others seduced, but everyone can be bribed" — not necessarily by money, but oftentimes by flattery, honor, prestige, or even the promise of these questionable rewards.

The Other Man

WHEN THE JEWISH ARMY PREPARES TO WAGE BATTLE, THE KOHEN anointed for battle addresses the soldiers, encouraging them to strengthen their resolve and enjoining them to place their trust in the Almighty. He then proceeds to list a number of exemptions, soldiers who are excused from going to battle for a variety of reasons. These include הָאִישׁ אֲשֶׁר בָּנָה בַיִת חָדָשׁ וְלֹא חֲנָכוֹ, "the man who has built a new house and not inaugurated it" (20:5); הָאִישׁ אֲשֶׁר נָטַע כֶּרֶם וְלֹא חִלְּלוֹ, "the man who has planted a vineyard and not redeemed it" (20:6); הָאִישׁ אֲשֶׁר אֵרַשׂ אִשָּׁה וְלֹא לְקָחָהּ, "the man who has betrothed a woman and not married her" (20:7).

Rashi (20:5) gives the reason for these three exemptions and states that if such a man would die in battle and never live in his new home, or enjoy the fruits of his vineyard, or marry his betrothed, this would cause him profound *agmas nefesh,* aggravation and heartbreak. In other words, these men are excused for compassionate reasons. Other commentators explain in a more practical vein that these men's minds would be on their new house, vineyard or bride, and these serious distractions would sap their will and impair their fighting spirit. This, in turn, would affect the spirit of their fellow soldiers, and therefore it is far better that they should not participate in battle, but rather serve behind the front lines.

All this explains the reason for these exemptions, yet we must understand why, in all three instances, a telling phrase is added, וְאִישׁ אַחֵר, "and another man." Not only will the builder of the house be denied the privilege of dedicating his house, but אִישׁ אַחֵר יַחְנְכֶנּוּ, "another man will inaugurate it." Not only will the one who planted the vineyard be denied the privilege of redeeming it and eventually enjoying its fruit, but אִישׁ אַחֵר יְחַלְּלֶנּוּ, "another man will redeem it." And the man who betrothed his bride and falls in battle will not only be prevented from marrying her, but אִישׁ אַחֵר יִקָּחֶנָּה, "another man will take her."

Why does the Torah find it necessary to add these words each time? Would it not be sufficient to describe the *agmas nefesh* of the person who is denied the satisfaction and pleasure of dedicating his new home, redeeming his vineyard or taking his bride as a wife, without telling us that another man will replace him?

The *baalei mussar,* the classical Jewish ethical teachers, answer this question in a most telling manner, teaching us a lesson in human psychology. A person may well be disappointed, frustrated and anguished when he is denied the fulfillment of dedicating his new home, redeeming his vineyard or wedding his wife. This *agmas nefesh,* however, is compounded when he realizes that another man will take his place! As he falls in battle, it is this realization in his last moments which pains him the most. Not only will he not enjoy his new home, his vineyard or his bride, but someone else will! G-d, in His infinite wisdom, knows that such is the nature of man, and the Torah therefore commands us to spare him this greatest of all heartbreaks. Such a person is excused from battle for G-d understands the frailty of man, and demonstrates his compassion by excusing these men from army service. By exempting these soldiers, the Torah demonstrates that it is a *Torah shel chesed,* a Torah of lovingkindness.

As part of this interpretation, the *baalei mussar* give an example. When a person comes to a Rabbi with a *shailah,* a religious ritual question, in the area of *tarfus,* the ritual suitability of a chicken or an animal, and is told by the Rabbi that unfortunately the item is *treif,* the questioner may be upset, but he will not be angry with the *psak.* On the other hand, if the same person comes to the Rabbi regarding a monetary dispute and is told that he must pay the other party, he becomes furious with the *psak* and extremely angry with the Rabbi. This is not only because he has lost the case, but because the other fellow has won! In the case of the nonkosher chicken, no one has it, but in the case of the monetary dispute, not only must he take money out of his pocket, but that money will be going into the other person's pocket, and that pains him exceedingly. This is the אִישׁ אַחֵר, the "other man" syndrome, which causes the greatest *agmas nefesh*. In the case of the soldier going into battle, his greatest fear is not that he will be deprived, but that "another man" will enjoy the fruits of his labor. The Torah recognizes this weakness of human beings, which is very difficult to overcome, and so G-d is willing to excuse such a man from the army and not subject him to this heartache.

From this we learn not only our human frailty, but also that one is not obligated to bring himself to a *nisayon,* a test and challenge, if there is little chance that he will be able to withstand it. Every morning, in our prayers, we ask of the Almighty: וְאַל תְּבִיאֵנוּ . . . לִידֵי נִסָּיוֹן, "and do not test us." Man is not obligated to challenge himself unless G-d chooses to do so, for very few of us are strong enough to withstand a test. That is why G-d, in His infinite wisdom, exempts from military duty the man who built a house, planted a vineyard or betrothed a woman, so that he should not be subjected to unbearable frustration and profound heartache, were he to fall in battle and another man take his place.

The Public and Private Persona

AMONG THE SPECIAL *MITZVOS* GIVEN TO A JEWISH KING, IN THE *Parashas HaMelech,* is the commandment to write two Sifrei Torah. One is the Sefer Torah that every Jew is commanded to write and, as the Rambam explains, the king's first Sefer Torah is the one which he already has as a *hedyot,* a commoner. This Sefer Torah is to be stored in his treasure house: מוּנַחַת לוֹ בְּבֵית גְּנָזָיו. The second Sefer Torah is written especially for him when he becomes king, and that Torah has to be with him constantly: יוֹצְאָה וְנִכְנֶסֶת עִמּוֹ, "It goes out and enters with him" (*Sanhedrin* 21b). A king, as is true of every public figure, has two personas, a private one and a public one. The Torah must guide his actions in both areas. Similarly, every Jew puts on *tefillin shel yad,* the *tefillin* on his arm, and *tefillin shel rosh,* the *tefillin* on his head. These represent the two areas in which a person lives and functions. We all have our *reshus hayachid,* our private domain and personal life, as well as our *reshus harabim,* our public domain, where we interact with others. When the Torah speaks of the *tefillin shel yad,* it states: וְהָיָה לְךָ לְאוֹת עַל יָדְךָ, "And it shall be for you a sign on your arm" (*Shemos* 13:9), and our Sages comment: לְךָ לְאוֹת וְלֹא לַאֲחֵרִים לְאוֹת, "for you as a sign and not to others" (*Menachos* 37b). That is why the *tefillin* on one's arm is covered. It represents man's private domain and his personal life. On the other hand, the *tefillin shel rosh* is prominent and visible, and our Sages teach us that the verse, "And all the nations of the Earth will see that G-d's Name is proclaimed over you and will fear you" (*Devarim* 28:10), refers to the *tefillin shel rosh.* In other words, the *tefillin* on a Jew's head, which is prominent and visible, represents his activities and behavior in the public domain.

Be it as a commoner or as a king, every Jew's life must be lived in accordance with the teachings of G-d's Torah. Whether it is in the privacy of his home — in the relationship of husband and wife, parent and child — or in the public arena — in the relationship of people with one another in their community and society at large — it is the Sefer Torah and *tefillin* which must guide him.

It is for this reason that a king must have not one, but two Sifrei Torah, just as every Jew must have both *tefillin shel yad* and *tefillin shel rosh.* We can now understand why in the *Parashas HaMelech* there are two expressions used regarding these Sifrei Torah. One is: וְהָיְתָה עִמּוֹ, that it always be with him, his constant companion. And the other is: וְקָרָא בוֹ כָּל יְמֵי חַיָּיו, "and he shall study it all the days of his life (17:19)." The former expression relates to man's private behavior, while the latter admonition refers to his public persona.

It is interesting to note that in *Parashas Vayeilech* (*Devarim* 31), where we read of the appointment of Yehoshua as leader of the Jewish people, a role similar to that of a king, the Torah teaches us that the Sefer Torah written by Moshe before his death was to be given to his successor. This was in order to teach him that the mission of a Jewish king is not just to do battle for his people, but to teach them the importance of studying and observing the Torah and its *mitzvos* as well. We see from all this that the Torah's concept of leadership and power is a special and unique one. As long as Jewish leaders followed this pattern they were successful, but when they departed from this *derech,* they were not. The *Parashas HaMelech* should be studied not only by Jewish kings, but by all Jewish leaders, and indeed by the House of Israel in general.

PARASHAS KI SEITZEI

Chodesh or Yerach?

EVERY LEGAL DOCUMENT, REGARDLESS OF THE CULTURE AND society in which it is written and executed, must have a date. It is interesting to note that a *kesubah*, a marriage contract, designates the date with the words: "on such a day of the week, on this date in the month of . . .," using the Hebrew word חֹדֶשׁ for month. On the other hand, in a *get*, a writ of divorce, the phrase used for month is not חֹדֶשׁ, but יֶרַח. The question is asked: Why this change in terminology?

The *sefarim* find the answer in a verse from this week's *Sedrah*: כִּי יִקַּח אִישׁ אִשָּׁה חֲדָשָׁה, "When a man takes a *new* wife" (24:5). The word חֲדָשָׁה, used here in connection with marriage, is similar to the word חֹדֶשׁ. Hence, in the *kesubah* we use the word חֹדֶשׁ when we write the day of the month. On the other hand, there is a phrase which appears in *Parashas Vezos HaBerachah*: גֶּרֶשׁ יְרָחִים, "the moon's yield" (33:14). The word גֶּרֶשׁ, which is similar to גֵּרוּשִׁין (divorce), is followed by the word יְרָחִים, indicating that in a *get* one should write יֶרַח rather than חֹדֶשׁ.

The law of the *yefas to'ar,* the beautiful captive woman who is taken as a wife by a Jewish soldier in battle, is taught to us at the beginning of our *Parashah.* A few verses later, the Torah teaches us the law of a firstborn son whose mother is referred to as a *senu'ah,* "a despised one."

Our Sages tell us that the Torah predicts that this woman who was taken as a wife in the heat and passion of war will ultimately be despised and rejected by her husband and divorced. Thus, the first few verses of our *Parashah* speak of both marriage and divorce. An examination of the phraseology used in the opening verses of our *Sedrah* hint at the rapid change of relationship between the Jewish soldier and the captive alien woman. Verse 11 reads: וּלְקַחְתָּ לְךָ לְאִשָּׁה, "and you will take her to yourself for a wife" (21:11). Verse 13 states that "she shall weep for her father and her mother for a full month." The Hebrew word used for *month* is יֶרַח, not חֹדֶשׁ! The Torah indicates that although he has taken a new wife, very rapidly the חֹדֶשׁ will be transformed into יֶרַח. As our Sages teach us, the dispensation given to the Jewish soldier to take this woman is given most reluctantly and is but a concession to his *yetzer hara,* "his evil inclination." Hence, it is a relationship built upon a flimsy foundation, and the Torah indicates that it will not last.

A True Measure of Faith

AT THE CONCLUSION OF OUR *PARASHAH,* THE TORAH CAUTIONS US to use honest weights and measures. As the Sforno points out, not only is a Jew prohibited to use dishonest weights and measures, but he is also forbidden to *own* inaccurate weights and measures, even if he does not intend to use them. This commandment to use only honest weights and measures is followed immeditely by the concluding verses in the *Sedrah* that urge us to remember what Amalek did to Israel when we left Egypt. We are commanded to "wipe out the memory of Amalek from under the heaven."

The question has been asked as to the reason for the juxtaposition of these two concluding sections in our *Sedrah:* the law regarding honest weights and measures and the *mitzvah* to remember what Amalek did to Israel when they left Egypt. Our Sages find a common denominator between these two seemingly disparate laws. A person who is dishonest in his business dealings is a person of little faith. He doesn't believe that G-d will grant him a decent livelihood and therefore feels constrained to use dishonest measures to insure his profit. He lacks *emunah* (faith) and *bitachon* (trust). Our Sages tell us that the reason Amalek attacked our forefathers when they left Egypt is that Israel had many spiritual doubts at that time and questioned whether G-d would protect them from their enemies. This wavering faith and lack of trust in the Almighty caused the attack by Amalek, and indeed the words: וְלֹא יָרֵא אֱלֹקִים, "and did not fear G-d" (25:18), refer to Israel as much as they refer to Amalek!

The *sefarim* point out that the numerical equivalent of עֲמָלֵק is סָפֵק, "doubt." Were Israel to have had strong faith and trust in the Almighty, Amalek would not have been sent to test them. And were a person to have perfect faith and trust in the Almighty, he would not use dishonest weights and measures.

False Economy

OUR *SEDRAH* ENUMERATES A NUMBER OF FORBIDDEN AND RE- stricted marriages, including some involving converts to the Jewish faith, even though normally a *ger* or *giyores* is permitted to an Israelite. Among those who are prohibited to become part of the Congregation of Hashem are Ammonites and Moabites. The reason for this is given: עַל דְּבַר אֲשֶׁר לֹא קִדְּמוּ אֶתְכֶם בַּלֶּחֶם וּבַמַּיִם, "because they did not greet you with bread and water" (23:5), when you left Egypt. In other words, they have a character flaw, they lack the traits of hospitality and concern for the needs of others. As such, they cannot become part of a people who are *rachamim v'gomlei chasadim,* compassionate, kind and generous.

Strangely, verse 5 gives us another reason for the exclusion of the Moabites: וַאֲשֶׁר שָׂכַר עָלֶיךָ אֶת בִּלְעָם . . . לְקַלְלֶךָ, "and because he hired Balaam against you . . . to curse you." The question can reasonably be asked: Which of these reasons is the overriding one, and in addition, why does the Torah have to give us two reasons for barring them from the Congregation of Hashem? A most logical answer has been given. Lest one argue that perhaps the Moabites were so impoverished that they could not afford to offer bread and water to the Israelites, the Torah hastens to tell us that they *hired*

Balaam to curse the Jews, and he did not come cheap. If they had the wherewithal to retain the services of Balaam to curse the Jews, they could also have afforded the cost incurred by an act of hospitality. It is because of this that two reasons are given, lest one attempt to excuse them for their cruel action in denying the Israelites bread and water.

The *baalei mussar* use this explanation to admonish those who excuse their lack of generosity toward their fellow human beings by claiming financial difficulties, while at the same time they somehow always have money to spend on their own frivolous activities and unnecessary luxuries. They were wont to say, "If there is money for Balaam, then certainly there should be money for *hachnasas orchim,* hospitality, as well."

PARASHAS KI SAVO

A Basketful of Blessings

THE FIRST PART OF OUR *PARASHAH* DISCUSSES THE *MITZVAH* OF *bikkurim,* the first fruits brought to the Temple as a gesture of thanksgiving, at which time the Jewish farmer declared his gratitude to Hashem for giving the Land of Israel to His people. There is a special tractate in *Seder Zeraim* which discusses the laws regarding this *mitzvah* and describes in detail how Jews would gather from various parts of the Land and proceed together in a joyous procession bringing the first fruits to the Holy Temple in Jerusalem.

The first fruits were put in a basket which was handed to the Kohen, who in turn placed it before the Altar, following which a declaration of thanksgiving was made to Hashem. This declaration also included a brief resume of Jewish history, describing our sojourn in Egypt and ultimate redemption. When this ritual was concluded, a *bas kol,* a "Heavenly echo," came forth from the heavens and blessed the bringer of *bikkurim,* stating: הֵבֵאתָ בִּכּוּרִים הַיּוֹם, תִּשְׁנֶה לַשָּׁנָה הַבָּאָה, "Just as you have brought the first fruits today, so may you merit to repeat this ritual next year as well" (26:16, *Rashi's* commentary).

Our Sages tell us that a rich person would bring his first fruits in a golden basket, whereas the poor person would bring his in a wicker basket. The gold basket was returned by the Kohen to its owner, whereas the more modest basket, woven of reeds or straw, was not returned! Our Sages comment that this *halachah* proves the folk adage: "Poverty pursues the poor man." The question arises, however, as to why such a seemingly unfair custom was instituted. Why should the rich man get his gold basket back, while the modest basket of the poor man is not returned?

The answer lies in the blessing given to the bringer of *bikkurim* mentioned above. Note that the one who brings *bikkurim* is given a Heavenly blessing that he should live for another year and merit to bring *bikkurim* once again. We have no way of knowing, however, what his economic and financial status will be one year hence. If he remains poor, then he will be bringing his *bikkurim* once again in a straw basket. However, if he becomes rich during the following year, he will bring them in a gold basket, and therefore have no use for the modest basket he used this year. That is precisely why the Kohen does not return the poor basket to the *ani,* for that is part of the blessing! The rich man, on the other hand, is given back his gold basket, for that is part of his blessing, that he should be *zocheh* to remain wealthy and bring the *bikkurim* next year once again in this gold basket.

Evoking the Divine Voice

IN THIS WEEK'S *SEDRAH,* THERE ARE TWO WORDS WHICH ARE VERY difficult to understand, let alone to translate properly. The words are אֶת ה׳ הֶאֱמַרְתָּ and הֶאֱמִירְךָ. Chapter 26, verse 17 reads: אֶת ה׳ הֶאֱמַרְתָּ הַיּוֹם לִהְיוֹת לְךָ לֵאלֹקִים, "You have distinguished Hashem today to be a G-d for you," while verse 18 reads: וַה׳ הֶאֱמִירְךָ הַיּוֹם לִהְיוֹת לוֹ לְעַם סְגֻלָּה, "Hashem has distinguished you today to be for him a treasured people."

Rashi comments that there is no other place in the Bible where this word appears, and he gives his personal interpretation — that it is a phrase indicating separation and distinction. At best, this is a forced, and even awkward, expression. It is therefore proper to search for an alternate interpretation of these two words, הֶאֱמַרְתָּ and הֶאֱמִירְךָ. In Hebrew grammar, there is a *binyan hifil,* the causative form. It would therefore be logical to assume that the word הֶאֱמִיר refers to אֲמִירָה, "saying." The Rashbam indeed explains that the phrase הֶאֱמַרְתָּ means that you (Israel) caused G-d to say something, and G-d, in turn, caused you (Israel) to say something as well.

Until Avraham appeared on the world stage, mankind was unaware of G-d's existence. The Torah tells us that wherever Avraham went he was קוֹרֵא בְּשֵׁם ה׳, "He proclaimed the name of Hashem." This became his mission in life, to proclaim the existence of G-d and to teach this truth to mankind. However, until the Jewish people came into being, G-d, as it were, was silent. He had no one to speak to, except certain individuals, but not an entire people. When Israel accepted the Almighty as their G-d and pledged themselves to keep His commandments, walk in His way and listen to His voice, as verse 17 puts it, they *caused* Him to say what was meant to be heard by mankind. That is the meaning of הֶאֱמַרְתָּ, written in the *hifil* form, for we caused G-d to speak, as it were! Conversely, G-d, in turn, gave us a voice to praise Him, as a treasured people, which is implied in verse 18 when it states: הֶאֱמִירְךָ . . . לִהְיוֹת לוֹ לְעַם סְגֻלָּה, He caused us to "speak," to bear testimony that there is One G-d Who is the Creator and Master of the universe.

The Mezuzah at the Gateway to Eretz Yisrael

WHEN THE JEWISH PEOPLE CROSSED THE JORDAN AND ENTERED the Land of Israel, they were commanded to set up אֲבָנִים גְּדֹלוֹת, "great stones" (27:2), and to inscribe on them the words of the Torah. Verse 8 there amplifies this commandment, adding the words בַּאֵר הֵיטֵב, "well clarified." Rashi explains, based on the Talmud, that this expression indicates that the Torah was inscribed on these great stones in 70 languages. In the phraseology of the Talmud, the expression "70 languages" means all the languages which were spoken by mankind at that time.

It has been pointed out that whenever an army, headed by a mighty leader, conquered a country, it was customary to set up a monument to mark this great event. On the monument they would engrave a legend of victory extolling the great prowess of the fighting forces, and include a paean of praise for the conquering heroes.

The setting up of great stones by the Jewish people when they crossed the Jordan and began the conquest of the Land of Israel was not unusual. What *was* unusual and unique is what they engraved on those stones. Unlike other nations, they did not engrave a legend of victory, but the words of G-d's Torah. These stones were not meant to be a tribute to the Israeli army or its commander Yehoshua; rather, they were meant to instruct the Children of Israel and the nations of the world as to the purpose and mission of this unique people and the purpose for which the Land was given to Israel. By inscribing all the words of the Torah on this monument and doing so in 70 languages, Moshe was reminding the people that there was a noble and unique goal in their ultimate conquest of the Land, of which they must never lose sight.

Indeed, in verse 9, we read: הַסְכֵּת וּשְׁמַע יִשְׂרָאֵל הַיּוֹם הַזֶּה נִהְיֵיתָ לְעָם לה׳ אֱלֹקֶיךָ, "Be attentive and hear, O Israel. This day you have become a people to Hashem, your G-d." Moshe cautions the people to pay attention and listen very carefully to his words and appreciate the purpose of their nationhood. Unlike other nations, their mission and goal was not to wield power or gain fame, but to serve as a model for other nations and be an *ohr lagoyim,* "a light unto the nations." Indeed, there are Torah commentators who explain that these אֲבָנִים גְּדֹלוֹת, on which were written the words of Torah, were meant to serve as a gigantic *mezuzah* at the entrance to the Land of Israel. Just as a *mezuzah* is affixed to the doorposts of a Jewish home, so, figuratively, these great stones were *mezuzos* affixed to the doorposts of the Land of Israel. Just as a *mezuzah* is meant to remind a Jew, as he enters and exits his home, of his commitment to G-d, and G-d's reciprocal promise to guard and protect him, so these *mezuzos* represented the commitment of the people to observe G-d's commandments in the Land of Israel, and in turn His commitment to watch over the people of Israel in the Holy Land. These "great stones" attested to the grand and unique role Israel was meant to play on the world stage, as they entered the Promised Land.

PARASHAS NITZAVIM

Action Inspires and Motivates

IN THIS WEEK'S *PARASHAH,* MOSHE IMPRESSES UPON THE JEWISH people that the Torah is most accessible, and even though one may think that the profound knowledge of Torah is beyond human ken, this is actually not so. In beautiful, poetic language, Moshe tells Israel that the Torah is not beyond their grasp, if they make a sincere effort to understand it. The Torah was given to human beings, not angels, and the *mitzvos* were given to be fulfilled here on earth, not in heaven. "It is not in heaven to say who can ascend to the heaven for us and take it for us, so that we can listen to it and perform it" (30:12). Moshe concludes this exhortation with the following verse: כִּי קָרוֹב אֵלֶיךָ הַדָּבָר מְאֹד בְּפִיךָ וּבִלְבָבְךָ לַעֲשׂתוֹ, "Rather, the matter is very near to you — in your mouth and in your heart — to perform it" (30:14).

The sequence of this verse is most unusual. Does not the heart first think and feel and motivate, after which the person articulates and speaks? Yet the order in the *pasuk* is first בְּפִיךָ, "in your mouth," followed by the phrase "and in your heart to perform it." To understand the message of the *pasuk,* one must realize that there are times in life when a person cannot focus or concentrate on Torah or *tefillah,* and is tempted to say to himself, "Let me wait until I am in the mood, until I am ready." Not so, Moshe tells us. Rather, let the person first pray or study Torah with his פֶּה, his "mouth," and that will awaken and arouse the heart, after which he will do what G-d has commanded him to do. The act of articulation will serve as the source of motivation. The Chinuch states that אַחַר הַפְּעוּלוֹת נִמְשָׁךְ הַלֵּב, "The heart follows man's actions." And so it is true of the words of the mouth which motivate one's heart, desire and will, leading him to action.

Ideally, the heart should lead, but there are times when the mouth must jump-start the will and the spirit. This explains why בְּפִיךָ precedes וּבִלְבָבְךָ, for there are times when this is the only way that a person can be energized לַעֲשׂתוֹ, "to do it" and to perform the *mitzvos*.

Similarly, in the *Krias Shema*, we find the expression בְּכָל לְבָבְךָ וּבְכָל נַפְשְׁךָ, "with all your heart and all your might" (*Devarim* 6:5). Our *Chachamim* interpret this latter phrase as meaning אֲפִילוּ הוּא נוֹטֵל אֶת נַפְשֶׁךָ, "even if G-d takes away your soul," meaning that one must love the Almighty even if it entails sacrificing his life. The Gerrer Rebbe once commented that what is true of the נֶפֶשׁ is also true of the heart. Just as the expression בְּכָל נַפְשְׁךָ means even if your נֶפֶשׁ is taken away from you, so, he said, the phrase בְּכָל לְבָבְךָ means even if He takes away שְׁטִיק הָאָרֶץ אַ, a part of your heart! What he meant was that even when one does a *mitzvah* or studies Torah in a half-hearted fashion, let him not be deterred. By performing *mitzvos* under all circumstances, he will eventually be able to do so with all his heart.

Means and Ends — Cause and Effect

THE KLI YAKAR HAS A MOST PERCEPTIVE COMMENTARY ON VERSES 15 and 19, at the conclusion of our *Parashah*. The Torah states: רְאֵה נָתַתִּי לְפָנֶיךָ הַיּוֹם אֶת הַחַיִּים וְאֶת הַטּוֹב וְאֶת הַמָּוֶת וְאֶת הָרָע, "See, I have placed before you today the life and the good, death and evil" (30:15). Reflecting the thought of the Ramban on the opening verses of *Parashas Re'eh*, the Kli Yakar says that a person should never say that he will do what is right in the eyes of Hashem so that he will merit a good life. Rather, the reverse is true. One should say: I desire a life of health and prosperity, so that I might be able to fulfill G-d's will. As the Ramban teaches us in *Parashas*

Re'eh, one must never lose sight of means and end, of cause and effect. Life is granted by the Almighty to a person for a purpose, and he is given strength, energy and intelligence as the means necessary to reach the goal destined for man, which is to imitate G-d's ways and fulfill His *ratzon.* This explains why the word חַיִּים, "life," comes first in our *pasuk,* while the word טוֹב, "good," is mentioned last. This also explains why, in verse 19, the Torah urges us: וּבָחַרְתָּ בַּחַיִּים, "You shall choose life." The Torah does not instruct us: וּבָחַרְתָּ בַּטּוֹב, you shall choose that which is good. The Torah is teaching us that man must choose to live, and to safeguard the days and years of his life for a purpose, i.e., to do good. Life is the means toward that end.

This may well be the meaning of the verse in *Tehillim* as well: מִי הָאִישׁ הֶחָפֵץ חַיִּים אֹהֵב יָמִים לִרְאוֹת טוֹב, "Who is the man who desires life, who loves days of seeing good?" (*Tehillim* 34:13). David HaMelech infers that the noble man desires life and loves days, not simply to enjoy life, but *in order* to do good. Here, again, we understand why the Torah does not adjure us to choose the good, but rather to choose life, for the purpose of doing good.

Choosing Our Destiny — Is It Ours to Choose?

THE VERSE QUOTED ABOVE (30:15), WHICH SPEAKS OF חַיִּים AND טוֹב, concludes with the words, מָוֶת (death) and רָע (evil), which are the antonyms of life and good. The Torah seems to be saying that we should be sensitive to the fact that G-d has placed before us life and death, good and evil, and it is for us to choose our own destiny. Why was it necessary for Moshe, at the end of his life, to tell us what is seeminly such a simple and obvious truism? A most interesting answer is given: In a subtle manner, we are being told what our Sages teach us in *Berachos* 5a. There the Talmud states that a person should constantly arouse his good inclination (*yetzer tov*) to fight against his evil inclination (*yetzer hara*). If he vanquishes it, fine. If not, our Sages continue, let him engage in the study of Torah. If this does not deter him from sin, let him remind himself of the day of death. In other words, there are two ways for a person to strengthen his *yetzer tov* and overcome his *yetzer hara*: either by occupying himself with the study of Torah or by reminding himself of his mortality. When the Torah states: רְאֵה, "Behold," it means I am offering you two suggestions as to how you can arouse your good inclination to fight against your evil inclination. One is הַחַיִּים וְהַטּוֹב, life and good, which refers to study of Torah. However, if this proves to be insufficient to strengthen your good inclination and overcome your evil inclination, there is another suggestion which the Torah makes: אֶת הַמָּוֶת וְאֶת הָרָע, meaning — remember the day of death and that will deter you from sinning. In other words, first follow the suggestion given by our Sages of engaging in the study of Torah, reflected in the words "life and good." Failing that, יַזְכִּיר לוֹ יוֹם הַמִּיתָה, "Be mindful of the day of death," which is reflected in the words הַמָּוֶת וְהָרָע, "death and evil."

The question is: Which of these ways is preferable? The Torah itself gives the answer when it states וּבָחַרְתָּ בַּחַיִּים, urging us to choose the antidote of studying תּוֹרַת חַיִּים, the living Torah, rather than reminding ourselves of the day of death. The former enlivens us and enables us to serve G-d with *simchah,* as opposed to the latter, which frightens us and, at best, enables us to serve the Almighty from a source of *yirah,* fear, rather than love and joy. Judaism is strongly in favor of teaching Jews the importance of fulfilling G-d's will from a source of joy rather than from fear and concern for Divine punishment. We have been taught that the preferred way is עִבְדוּ אֶת ה' בְּשִׂמְחָה, "Serve Hashem with joy" (*Tehillim* 100:2), a lesson which we should always learn and follow.

PARASHAS VAYEILECH

A National Affirmation

IN THIS WEEK'S *SEDRAH* WE FIND A UNIQUE *MITZVAH* WHICH WAS observed at the time the Holy Temple was standing in Jerusalem. The people would make a pilgrimage to the *Beis HaMikdash* three times a year. In addition, every seventh year, at the end of the Sabbatical year, at the conclusion of the Yom Tov of Succos, Israel was commanded to gather together men, women and small children for the purpose of listening to the king read from the Book of *Devarim*. This *mitzvah* is known as *Hakhel,* which means "a gathering."

This unusual commandment was given to us to emphasize that the essence of Jewish life is the Torah, and that in addition to the teachers of Torah and the Kohanim, the king was also responsible for ensuring the perpetuation of Israel's commitment to the Torah. This gathering represented a national affirmation that our nation is built on the foundation of Torah. The Talmud, in *Chagigah* 3a, relates that the disciples of Rabbi Yehoshua came to visit their teacher who asked them what they had learned that day in the *beis medrash*. At first they were reluctant to tell him, since they felt it would be presumptuous of them to appear as though they were teaching their master Torah. However, upon being pressed, they answered that the theme of the discourse was the *mitzvah* of *Hakhel,* and that Rabbi Elazar ben Azariah had expounded on this section in the following manner: If the men came to learn and the women came to hear, why was it necessary to bring the little ones as well? He explained that this was in order to grant reward to those who bring them — לָתֵת שָׂכָר לִמְבִיאֵיהֶם. Indeed, Rashi cites this interpretation, in his commentary on our *Parashah* (*Devarim* 31:12). The Talmud concludes this dialogue between Rabbi Yehoshua and his students by telling us that Rabbi Yehoshua said to them: מַרְגָּלִית טוֹבָה הָיְתָה בְּיֶדְכֶם וּבִקַּשְׁתֶּם לְאַבְּדָם מִמֶּנִּי, "You had a precious jewel in your hand, and you sought to deprive me of it!"

The explanation of this fascinating dialogue between Rabbi Yehoshua and his students is as follows. Picture a man who is walking on a road and sees something embedded in the earth which sparkles in the sun. Convinced that it is a precious stone, he labors mightily to unearth it, and even if it is difficult to do so, he persists in dislodging it. After removing it, he carefully cleans it, only to find that it is a piece of glass! So it is, at times, with the rearing of a child. The parent feels that he has a precious gem, and it is certainly worthwhile to expend energy, time and effort on this precious jewel. Yet, the effort put into raising and training a child will sometimes prove disappointing. Nonetheless, what parent or teacher would refuse to rear and educate their child?

This was the lesson taught in the *beis medrash* by Rabbi Elazar ben Azariah. Children are instructed in Torah, but we never know whether they will be excellent, good or merely poor students. One never knows whether he is dealing with a piece of glass or a gem. Still, those who *bring them* always receive a reward, not necessarily for the results realized, but simply for the bringing. It is this lesson which intrigued Rabbi Yehoshua and caused him to say, "You had such a precious jewel, and you almost did not share it with me." In a subtle manner he was referring to this lesson — the importance of bringing the little ones to *Hakhel* — symbolizing the duty of educating children at an early age, in the hope that they will develop properly, and indeed become jewels in the crown of Israel.

The reason that Rabbi Yehoshua felt this so deeply was because it reflected the experience of his own life. The Sages teach us that his mother kept his cradle in the *beis medrash* during his infancy because she wanted him to absorb the sound of Torah. It is for this reason that when Rabbi Yochanan ben Zakkai listed the virtues of his five outstanding students, he said of Rabbi Yehoshua, אַשְׁרֵי יוֹלַדְתּוֹ, "Happy and praiseworthy is she who bore him" (*Avos* 2:11). This also explains the phraseology of the verse in our *Parashah*, when the Torah tells us that the rationale for *Hakhel* is: לְמַעַן יִשְׁמְעוּ, "so that they will hear" (*Devarim* ibid.), meaning that even if they hear without comprehending, the words of Torah will leave an impression upon their soul and impact upon their psyche.

When we complete a tractate of the Talmud, we recite a beautiful prayer known as *Hadran*. One of the phrases used is: אָנוּ עֲמֵלִים וּמְקַבְּלִים שָׂכָר, "We toil and receive reward." This is interpreted as meaning that when a person toils in his study of Torah, even if he does not fully understand what he is learning, he receives reward for the effort he expends. The same is true of *chinuch*. The time and effort invested in teaching our children may or may not bear fruit, but we are assured that G-d will compensate us for our toil in attempting to imbue them with Torah knowledge, and we will be rewarded for "bringing them" to listen to the words of the king.

Small wonder that Rabbi Yehoshua was so intrigued by this interpretation of the *mitzvah* of *Hakhel* and called it a מַרְגָּלִית טוֹבָה, "a precious gem."

PARASHAS HAAZINU

How to Give Mussar

THE TORAH REFERS TO THE *SEDRAH* OF *HAAZINU* AS A שִׁירָה, "A song" (31:19). וְעַתָּה כִּתְבוּ לָכֶם אֶת הַשִּׁירָה הַזֹּאת, "So now, write this song for yourselves." Indeed, in this most beautiful poem, spoken by Moshe at the conclusion of his life, he speaks of the past, present and future of the people of Israel. It has been said that the purpose of this song is to express recognition of the total harmony of G-d's Creation, as well as recording the history of G-d's people, which represents the manifestation of G-d's *Hashgachah*, "Providence."

This poem must also be understood as a message of *mussar* conveyed by Moshe before his passing. Based upon this sense of the song, the Chasam Sofer offers a brilliant interpretation of the second *pasuk* in our *Parashah*. יַעֲרֹף כַּמָּטָר לִקְחִי תִּזַּל כַּטַּל אִמְרָתִי כִּשְׂעִירִם עֲלֵי דֶשֶׁא וְכִרְבִיבִים עֲלֵי עֵשֶׂב, "May my teachings drop like the rain, may my utterance flow like the dew, like storm winds upon vegetation, like raindrops upon blades of grass" (32:2). As explained in our *sefarim*, the distinction between dew and rain is that the former is gentle and considered a blessing by all. As such, the word טַל in Hebrew is an acronym for טוֹב לַכֹּל, "beneficial for all." Rain, on the other hand, is called מָטָר, which is heavy at times, and can be quite harsh and uncomfortable. Hence, the word מָטָר is an acronym representing מַשָּׂאֲכֶם, טָרְחֲכֶם, רִיבְכֶם, "your contentiousness, your burdens and your quarrels."

By the same token, the Chasam Sofer points out that there are two kinds of admonition and instruction. One is gentle and kind, while the second is heavy and harsh. The former is a טַל approach, while the latter is a מָטָר approach. The question is: When should a teacher opt for the gentle approach and when for the heavy, harsh one? The answer is that when giving *mussar* to a congregation, one can be frank and even harsh, using the מָטָר approach, whereas when giving *mussar* to an individual, one should be gentle and understanding. The word דֶּשֶׁא refers to grass and vegetation in general, whereas the phrase עֵשֶׂב refers to each blade of grass. The Torah's advice on how to give admonition is revealed in the verse quoted above: כִּשְׂעִירִם, "like storm winds," upon "vegetation," when you are speaking to the public at large; but כִּרְבִיבִים, "like gentle raindrops," when addressing your remarks to "blades of grass." In this manner he explains the words used by Moshe. The teaching of the *manhig* should be like מָטָר when he speaks to the *tzibbur,* the entire congregation, but should be as טַל when he admonishes an individual. This the Torah implies by using the expression דֶּשֶׁא (vegetation — a metaphor for the *klal*) in conjunction with the storm wind and heavy rain, and the word עֵשֶׂב (single blades of grass — a metaphor for the *yachid*) in conjunction with the gentle rain or dew.

Every good preacher and teacher understands that it is not only *what* he says, but *how* he says it, that is all important.

An Eternal Link

כִּי חֵלֶק ה׳ עַמּוֹ, יַעֲקֹב חֶבֶל נַחֲלָתוֹ
"For Hashem's portion is His people, Yaakov is the measure (lit. rope) of His inheritance" (32:9).

THE VILNA GAON USES THIS VERSE TO EXPLAIN A MOST DIFFICULT statement found in the Tanna D'Vei Eliyahu where the attributes of Hashem are listed. Included among them is that the Almighty is שָׂמֵחַ בְּחֶלְקוֹ, "happy with His portion." The Vilna Gaon was asked by his students for a clarification of this statement. Since the entire universe is G-d's, what is meant by the word חֵלֶק, "portion," in reference to the Almighty? The Gaon answered that the verse we cited above teaches us that G-d's *portion* is His people.

Parashas Haazinu / 179

The question, however, is whether the Almighty is happy with His choice, whether He is happy with His chosen people. Is there perhaps an element of regret? This Tanna D'Vei Eliyahu teaches us that G-d is indeed happy and satisfied with His choice of Israel as His people. He is content and pleased with His portion, and that is what is meant when שָׂמֵחַ בְּחֶלְקוֹ is listed as one of the attributes of Hashem.

The conclusion of this verse (חֶבֶל נַחֲלָתוֹ) explains why Hashem is happy with His portion, for even when the people of Israel sin and distance themselves from the Almighty, their ties to Hashem are never severed. A rope can securely attach one object to another, and this is what Moshe means when he states that Yaakov is the "rope of His inheritance." What he infers is that there is always a real, albeit invisible, cord which binds Israel to Hashem, and this link can never be severed. Because we are the "rope" of G-d's inheritance, we are forever His people.

The same thought is to be found in an earlier verse in the Song of *Haazinu,* where Moshe states: הֲלוֹא הוּא אָבִיךָ קָּנֶךָ, "Is He not your Father that bought you?" (32:6). The word קָּנֶךָ is usually translated as meaning "bought," for we are G-d's possession, but it can also be interpreted as meaning "Who nested you," and indeed this is how Rashi explains this phrase. The bird makes his home in his nest, and our Sages teach us (*Bava Basra* 24a) that when little birds leave their nest, but are still unable to fly, they hop a short distance away and then stop. As they hop, they look back to their nest. If they can still see it, they venture farther, but if they can no longer see their nest, they cease hopping, because they are afraid that they will not find their way home.

The teachers of *mussar* explain that the Jewish *neshamah* (soul) is like a bird nesting in each Jew. Even when a person leaves his family and his origins, he still continues to look back, and doesn't want to leave the nest out of his sight, completely. That is why the word קָּנֶךָ is used, for it represents the nest that every Jew instinctively recognizes. This is also the חֶבֶל, the rope mentioned in verse 9, which binds us to the Almighty, and that is the secret of our survival as a people. That is also why Hashem is so happy with His חֵלֶק, His choice of Israel as His People, for the nest is always there, and the rope is very strong.

A Void or a Blemish?

WHEN MOSHE CONCLUDES RECITING THIS SONG TO THE CHILDREN of Israel, he urges them to be very careful to perform all the words of the Torah, the reason being: כִּי לֹא דָבָר רֵק הוּא מִכֶּם, כִּי הוּא חַיֵּיכֶם, "For it is not an empty thing for you, for it is your life" (32:47). This reason which Moshe gives to Israel, however, is an odd one. Moshe could certainly have given them many positive reasons for "applying their hearts" to the words he has transmitted to them, and he could have inspired them with a loftier rationale than that of stating, "It is not an empty thing," which is seemingly a very negative reason.

The Talmud *Yerushalmi* commenting on this verse explains, כִּי אִם רֵיק הוּא – מִכֶּם, "If you look upon Torah as empty and devoid of beauty and importance, it is due to *your* lack of appreciation and understanding." However, we must seek a more satisfying explanation, and indeed the *sefarim* offer one which is profound and worthy of consideration. They point out that there is a difference between a *chisaron*, something which is lacking, and a *mum*, a blemish. That which is normally part of a human being, such as a limb, if lacking, is considered to be a *mum*. One is incomplete, crippled, if he is missing that limb, and he is blemished, if for example, he is missing a finger or a toe. However, if one lacks a skill or a talent, such as the ability to play a musical instrument or paint a beautiful picture, it is only a *chisaron*, a lack, not a blemish. The lack of that ability in a person is referred to as רֵיק (empty), and that person is diminished, but not marred. On the other hand, if he lacks something which is vital to his existence, or what is a normal part of his being, it would not simply be called דָבָר רֵיק, "an empty thing," but a *mum*. Moshe says to the people of Israel: Be mindful of the fact that if you are ignorant of Torah, of your heritage as a *ben Yisrael* or a *bas Yisrael*, do not consider it simply as the lack of an intellectual gift, or talent, for it is your very life and essence. If you do not possess that knowledge, or if you have rejected it and cast it out of your life, it is a fundamental blemish, not just a void, a דָבָר רֵיק, in your life. Rather, you lack completeness and perfection, and Jewishly speaking, you are crippled. It is this which Moshe subtly teaches us when he states: כִּי לֹא דָבָר רֵק הוּא מִכֶּם, כִּי הוּא חַיֵּיכֶם, "For it is no empty thing — it is your life."

PARASHAS VEZOS HABERACHAH

Fire and Water — Coexistence

מִימִינוֹ אֵשְׁדָּת לָמוֹ
*"from His right hand He presented
the fiery law to them"* (33:2).

THERE IS A TRADITION THAT MANY WORDS WRITTEN IN THE TORAH in a certain way are read, or pronounced, differently. The way they are written is called *ksiv,* and how they are read is called *kri.* There are times when the *ksiv* and the *kri* are radically different, and there are other instances when there is but a subtle change. The verse quoted from our *Parashah* is unique in the sense that the word אֵשְׁדָּת is the *ksiv,* the written form. While the *kri* pronounced form, does not change any of the letters, it *separates* them, and we parse the word, reading it as אֵשׁ דָּת. The English translation, "a fiery law," follows this reading, since אֵשׁ means fire and דָּת means law, or Torah.

The Chasam Sofer explains this variance in a most original and brilliant manner. He tells us that the imagery of fire in relation to the Torah is a most fitting one. When Israel accepted the Torah at Sinai, they committed themselves to G-d's teachings with a passion, and their loyalty to Torah over the centuries has indeed been a fiery, burning one. The Talmud (*Beitzah* 25b) cites this verse as proof of the statement of our Sages that the Jewish people are the most obstinate and stubborn people among all the nations. Our Sages are not only depicting a national trait of the Jewish people, but are also describing their unyielding devotion to the Torah. A *talmid chacham,* a Torah scholar, who becomes angry is excused by the Talmud for his action because "it is the Torah which burns within him" (*Taanis* 4a).

On the other hand, Torah is compared to water, and the proof is from a *pasuk* in *Yeshayahu*: הוֹי כָּל צָמֵא לְכוּ לַמַּיִם, "You who are thirsty, go to water" (*Yeshayahu* 55:1). Our Sages comment: אֵין מַיִם אֶלָּא תּוֹרָה, "The word water in this case refers to Torah" (*Bava Kamma* 82a).

This comparison teaches us that if one wishes to master Torah and live in the spirit of Torah, he must be humble, modest and submissive, just as water runs downhill, and not uphill (*Taanis* 7a). However, there is no contradiction between the comparison of Torah to fire *and* to water. We are admonished to be as water, insofar as our submissiveness to Hashem is concerned, but we are also urged to be firm and unyielding like fire, vis-a-vis the world around us.

In this manner, the Chasam Sofer explains the *ksiv* and the *kri* of אשדת. He points out that the word אשדת, in the verse אַשְׁדֹּת הַפִּסְגָּה, means "the waterfall of the high place" (*Devarim* 3:17). Hence, the *ksiv* of אשדת can be read as אַשְׁדֹּת, referring to the water characteristic of Torah. On the other hand, the *kri*, which is אֵשׁ דָּת, read as two words, means "a fiery law," referring to the fire character of Torah. In this manner, we are being taught the dual character of Torah — which is both fire (the *kri*) and water (the *ksiv*). This lesson we learn from the way the phrase is written as well as the way it is read.

Linking the Conclusion to the Beginning

THE CONCLUDING VERSE OF *VEZOS HABERACHAH*, WHICH IS ALSO the last verse of the entire Torah, reads: וּלְכֹל הַיָּד הַחֲזָקָה וּלְכֹל הַמּוֹרָא הַגָּדוֹל אֲשֶׁר עָשָׂה מֹשֶׁה לְעֵינֵי כָּל יִשְׂרָאֵל, "And by all the strong hand and awesome power that Moshe performed before the eyes of all Israel" (34:12).

Rashi comments that the Torah is referring to the time when Moshe received the *Luchos HaBris,* the "Tablets of the Covenant," and eventually shattered them, when he came down from the mountain and found the people of Israel worshiping the Golden Calf. The Talmud, in *Shabbos* 87, comments that the Almighty concurred with Moshe's action and said to him: יִישַׁר כֹּחֲךָ שֶׁשִּׁיבַּרְתָּ, "May your strength be increased, as a reward for breaking the Tablets." In other words, the expression, "by all the strong hand . . . before the eyes of all Israel" refers to this dramatic act of Moshe, which was done in the presence of the entire nation. The question, however, is: Why does the Torah choose this tragic event with which to conclude the Five Books of the Torah? It would seem that there could be a more fitting way to end the Torah, something on a higher, nobler note.

Rabbi Moshe Mordechai Epstein, the renowned Rosh Yeshivah of the Hebron Yeshivah in Israel, gives a most incisive and instructive answer to this question. Commenting on the story of the Golden Calf and Moshe's angry reaction to the transgression of the Jewish people, he asks why it was necessary to break the *Luchos* at all, since the transgressors were punished by sword and pestilence, as we read in *Sefer Shemos,* Chapter 34. What was gained by shattering the Tablets, which were the handiwork of Hashem? He explains that Moshe felt that the various punishments meted out would only bring partial atonement and expiation of sin, but could not expunge or erase the impact which the sin of the Golden Calf had upon the *neshamah,* the collective soul, of *Klal Yisrael.* Only by breaking the Tablets, which took unusual courage and great inner strength on the part of Moshe, was he able to break the hearts of the people of Israel, shocking them into a realization of how seriously they had transgressed, thereby bringing them to repentance. It was for this act that G-d said to Moshe: יִישַׁר כֹּחֲךָ.

This also explains the choice of this verse with which to conclude the Torah, for it teaches us a lesson regarding the role of Torah in Jewish life, while also linking the beginning of the Torah to the end. In the first verse of the Torah, which begins with the word בְּרֵאשִׁית, Rashi comments that this word should be understood as meaning בִּשְׁבִיל רֵאשִׁית. The world was created for the sake of two things which are called רֵאשִׁית, "beginning" — Torah and Israel — both of which possess the quality of רֵאשִׁית, something which is completely original and represents a new beginning.

Rabbi Epstein explains that the *Luchos* fashioned by G-d, and the Ten Commandments inscribed on those Tablets of stone by the "finger" of the Almighty, were given in the merit of the people of Israel and for their sake, but only if they would fulfill their unique role as a kingdom of priests and a holy people. The sin of the Golden Calf, however, marked a radical transformation of Israel's national character and demonstrated that they were not really worthy to receive the *Luchos.* By breaking the Tablets, Moshe taught us a historic message: Torah is Israel's national treasure and heritage only if we are loyal to its teachings and committed unequivocally to Hashem. If, however, Jews deviate and transgress, they are no longer the authentic people of Israel who are called רֵאשִׁית and have forfeited their right to the Torah which is also called רֵאשִׁית. That is why G-d agreed with Moshe's daring act and concurred with his decision to break the *Luchos,* commending him for his bold action.

We now understand why it is fitting for the Torah to conclude on this note, so as to teach us that when we resume the reading of בְּרֵאשִׁית, as we do on Simchas Torah, we must be mindful of the link between the conclusion of Torah and its beginning. We must appreciate that Torah cannot be taken for granted, for only if we are worthy is the Torah ours. We are also being taught never to forget that the entire purpose of Creation, about which we read in *Parashas Bereishis,* was for the giving of Torah to the loyal Children of Israel, but not to those who deviate and distort the truth of Torah. This is certainly a proper theme and lesson with which to conclude the Torah, and resume its reading once again, as we do every Simchas Torah.

Yomim Tovim

ROSH HASHANAH

The Inner Voice

O N ROSH HASHANAH, JEWS GATHER IN *SHUL* TO HEAR THE SOUND of the *shofar.* However, what the listener should really attempt to do is to evoke his own personal *shofar,* to awaken himself from his spiritual slumber, sensitize himself and attempt to become aware of his own potential.

One must arouse the *kol penimi,* the inner voice which every person possesses, the *yetzer tov,* the inclination for good which everyone has, the *pintele Yid* to which all Jews are heir, since Israel was chosen as G-d's people. The Talmud teaches us: נָתַן שׁוֹפָר בְּתוֹךְ שׁוֹפָר אִם קוֹל פְּנִימִי שָׁמַע יָצָא וְאִם קוֹל חִיצוֹן שָׁמַע לֹא יָצָא, "If one places a *shofar* within a *shofar* and blows, if the inner one is heard he fulfills the *mitzvah,* but if the outer one, he does not" (*Rosh Hashanah* 27b).

Every human being is ruled by two forces, which are often in conflict with one another. He is attracted to power, riches, position, comfort and luxury; in other words, to the material, to physical and worldly pleasures. Still, there is also often within him a sense of frustration, dissatisfaction and unhappiness, for his soul hungers for the aesthetic, the intellectual and the spiritual. This is the inner *kol* which may be in his subconscious, but is the "real me," which modern man seems to be searching for so desperately. It is the *kol penimi* which must be aroused in us on Rosh Hashanah if we are to be *yotzei.* And this inner voice *is* heard by all of us at certain moments in our life. When a Jew observes a *yahrzeit,* or recites *Yizkor,* when one responds to the needs of a Jewish institution, when we rise to the defense of Israel under attack — political or military — minimal as all this may be, we are listening to the *kol penimi.* What has brought so many people back to Torah Judaism, as witness the many *baalei teshuvah,* if not the inner voice found in every Jew?

The strength and supremacy of man's subconscious *penimius,* as opposed to his conscious choices and reasoned order of priority, *chitzonius,* was described in a fascinating manner by the founder of the *mussar* movement, Reb Yisrael Salanter. There was once a man who had a wayward son whose bad behavior caused his father much aggravation. This man also had a pupil living in his house who was a delight — good, studious and respectful — whom he loved dearly. The two boys shared a room, and one night the father was awakened by the smell of smoke — a fire had broken out in the house. He ran to the room where the boys were sleeping. Which of the two would he save first? Reb Yisrael was convinced that the father would instinctively rush to rescue his son! For subconsciously — *b'penimius* — he loved him deeply. And so too, every Jew deep down, if only subconsciously, loves Judaism and is loyal to his heritage and his people. It is this *kol penimi* to which we must listen today, the voice that tells us to reorder our priorities, reexamine our values and recognize our responsibilities as Jews.

The Talmud, in *Rosh Hashanah,* on the *daf* which we quoted above, makes a most telling and profound observation. It states that although normally "Two voices cannot be heard simultaneously," there is an exception: "If it is beloved and dear, he concentrates and hears." Modern man is subjected constantly to "two voices": the call of the outside world, which is secular, materialistic and hedonistic, and the call of Judaism, which is spiritual, idealistic and disciplined. The first *kol* is strong, shrill and demanding; the second is quiet, sincere and muted. But if it is cherished and beloved, it can and will be heard. The inner voice can overcome the outer one for it is ultimately stronger, as Reb Yisrael Salanter proved in his parable.

A thoughtful author once depicted his impression of an iceberg — wind, tide and surface ice are all going in one direction, and moving majestically against these forces is an iceberg! How is it able to do so? We ask this question only because we see just a small part of the iceberg. Deep down in the water at the base of the iceberg there are more powerful currents in control. Men and women who are committed to Torah Judaism are like that iceberg. Strength of character, a courageous spirit and devotion to Torah — these are the powerful currents that keep us going in the right direction, against the forces of a society that is so alien to our beliefs. Listen to the *kol penimi* within you, to the inner *shofar,* and you will hear the sound of our glorious past, the echo of our rich heritage; and by following its guidance you will fashion a better future for yourself.

YOM KIPPUR

Appreciation, Priorities and Values

THE EXPRESSION אַחַת בַּשָּׁנָה, "ONCE A YEAR" (*VAYIKRA* 16:34), CHARacterizes the day of Yom Kippur succinctly and completely. It is a special, unique day, which we all enter into once a year, just as the Kohen Gadol entered the *kodesh kodashim* once during the year, on this Day of Atonement. When he did so, he wore *bigdei bad,* white linen garments, just as we wear a *kittel.* But it is interesting to note that he wore these garments only once! After the service of Yom Kippur, they were put away and stored, not to be used again, even on the subsequent Day of Atonement! If the day was unique, the garments were singular. But why? The answer may be that the Torah was concerned lest the Kohen Gadol lose his sense of freshness, of reverence and appreciation of the seriousness and sacred character of his mission. Were he to wear the same garments the following year, he might say, "I wore these last year, entered in peace, came forth in peace, and I will do so again." The sense of awe and reverence would be compromised. Frequency breeds familiarity, and though familiarity may not breed contempt, it does take the edge off appreciation of the sacred and one's sense of reverence.

This lesson which we learn from the garments of the High Priest is one that we should take to heart as we sit in *shul* on this holy day. The theme of Yom Kippur is not just atonement, but also the need for awareness and appreciation. We take so many things for granted and fail to recognize our blessings, of which the very existence of one's *shul* is a major one. We must not allow the familiar surroundings of our *makom tefillah* to lose its freshness, luster and excitement. Each Yom Kippur, the *kittel* should feel new, the atmosphere electric and our *sense of appreciation* heightened.

There is a second lesson we should learn from Yom Kippur, one which is also overlooked, and that is to establish a *sense of priority*: to separate the important from the trivial, to determine what merits our serious attention and concern, and what does not. The service on Yom Kippur calls for *shnei se'irim,* two goats, one consecrated to G-d, and the other sent to the wilderness, to *Azazel,* carrying with it the sins of Israel. The Mishnah (*Yoma* 6:4) tells us that there were those who used to prod the carrier of this scapegoat, crying out to him: "Make haste and carry it away." Their concern was to rid themselves of their sins through this *se'ir hamishtalei'ach.* In a previous *perek,* the Mishnah (ibid. 1:5) describes how the elders instructed the Kohen Gadol in his Yom Kippur duties, and administered an oath to him that he not deviate from the law of Torah when he performed the service. They worried and were concerned, not about the riddance of their sins, but for the preservation of the tradition, the loyalty of the High Priest, and the observance of Torah law! For they, unlike the simple and ignorant people, realized that the source of atonement, of cleansing and purification, rested in the inner sanctum of the Mikdash. If all was well there, the Jews would be forgiven for their sins and be granted a good year, but if not, if the integrity of the Kohen Gadol was flawed and the sanctity of the Mikdash was compromised, then the *se'ir hamishtalei'ach* would serve no purpose.

And so it is true of the strength and weakness of our communities today. The source of our stability, identity and integrity is in the *mikdash me'at,* the miniature sanctuary, the synagogue, and in our educational institutions. If there is sincerity and spiritual well-being there, the community will be healthy and strong. If not, no scapegoats will expiate our sins, nor will we be cleansed and purified. Our synagogues and yeshivos need to be appreciated and given priority in our scale of values.

Just as it is important for us to appreciate what our religious institutions mean to us and grant them the sense of priority discussed above, we must also value them and be prepared to accept our role as stewards of G-d's bounty and be generous in our giving. There is a story told in Yalkut Rus (607) regarding a pious man who lost his fortune and was compelled to labor as a hired hand. One day Eliyahu came to him in the guise of an Arab and told him he would be blessed with six prosperous years. He also told him that he had the option of enjoying these years at once or at the end of his days. The *chasid* consulted with his wife who was a wise and pious woman, and she chose to accept this heavenly gift at once. Eliyahu's promise was kept, and they found a treasure which enriched them. The woman decided to share their wealth and gave money to *tzedakah* every day. She instructed her son to keep a record of all their donations. After six years, Eliyahu returned and told the *chasid* that the riches must be returned, as had been the condition from the outset. Whereupon the woman took out the record of her *tzedakos* and said to Eliyahu: אִם מָצָאתָ בְּנֵי אָדָם נֶאֱמָנִים מִמֶּנּוּ תֵּן לָהֶם פִּקְדוֹנְךָ, "If you can find someone more trustworthy than us, then by all means give them this wealth for safekeeping." And G-d agreed that they had been faithful stewards — so why take a chance with someone else — and He allowed them to keep their wealth!

We demonstrate that we are worthy of keeping what G-d has granted us by sharing our means with others, by giving generously to *tzedakah,* be it in our own communities or in Israel. By so doing, we prove that G-d's blessings were showered upon reliable stewards, and that we are therefore worthy of receiving these blessings for another year. It is this sense of appreciation, priority and values that must be renewed every year on Yom Kippur.

SUCCOS

Illusory or Real Security

SUCCOS IS SYNONYMOUS WITH *SIMCHAH.* THIS IS THE YOM TOV OF joy and happiness, which is appreciated all the more coming as it does immediately after the awesome days of Rosh Hashanah and Yom Kippur. Still, it is difficult to fully understand the manner in which this Yom Tov is marked and celebrated. If we are celebrating the *simchah* of harvest time, then why do we dwell in temporary frail huts, and, in the midst of joy, read the somber words of *Koheles* proclaiming that all is vanity? וּלְשִׂמְחָה מַה זֹּה עֹשָׂה, "And of joy, what does it accomplish?" (*Koheles* 2:2). This may well be the question we ask regarding our Succos observance. In the midst of affluence and prosperity, why take up residence in a flimsy *succah* with a fragile roof, and why read the challenging and disturbing philosophy of *Koheles*?

Man instinctively seeks security. Strength is usually equated with security, as riches are with power. Governments, like individuals, rely upon well-equipped and well-trained military forces for their security, and the State of Israel is no exception to this rule. Yet, we as Jews have been taught to place our trust far more in the Almighty than in the might of our arms. The *mezuzah* on the door always gives the Jew a greater sense of security than locks and alarm systems. Our true wisdom is to be found in the Hebrew word for wisdom, חָכְמָה, which is comprised of four letters which can also be read מַה כֹּחַ, "What is strength?" and כֹּחַ מַה, "What indeed is strength?" To know that safety and security lie in the hands of G-d and not in arsenals is the ultimate חָכְמָה. The question is how this lesson can best be taught. Our answer can be found in the *luach,* the sequence of holidays, and in the physical displacement of the Jew and his family from the house to the *succah*! תּוֹדִיעֵנִי אֹרַח חַיִּים שֹׂבַע שְׂמָחוֹת אֶת פָּנֶיךָ, "You will reveal to me the path to life, the fullness of joy in Your Presence" (*Tehillim* 16:11). This is explained by the Midrash to mean that the Days of Awe teach us the "way of life," while the "fullness of joy" is revealed to us through the observance of Succos. *Chazal* are telling us that there is a cause and effect relationship between Rosh Hashanah/Yom Kippur and Succos. Rabbi Eliyahu Dessler, in his *Michtav MeEliyahu,* goes a step further and links the months of Tammuz, Av and Elul to this *pasuk* in *Tehillim.* He suggests that during the three weeks from the seventeenth of Tammuz to Tishah B'Av we experience a deep sense of *ye'ush,* despair, not only because we recall the *churban,* but because we are disillusioned with the world around us and feel insecure and unsafe, with good cause. Certainly the generation that witnessed the Holocaust experiences these troubling emotions anew. Yet comfort follows this period of mourning. For, despairing of the world, we shed our illusions and reject our reliance upon man and our own physical strength. This realization brings us to repentance and renewal. This is our odyssey from Tammuz to Av, and then to Elul.

The progression begins with despair, followed by comfort which results from self-recognition, which in turn spurs one on to *teshuvah,* climaxed by Rosh Hashanah and Yom Kippur. Succos, the festival of *simchah,* is the final station in this journey. We learn to serve G-d with authentic happiness, a lesson distilled from the awe and reverence of the *yomim nora'im.* We experience this ultimate *simchah* only after we have been purged of our delusions and illusions, returning to G-d under Whose protection we now dwell, symbolized by the *succah.*

From Rosh Chodesh Elul to Simchas Torah we recite לְדָוִד ה' אוֹרִי וְיִשְׁעִי. The reason for this custom now becomes quite clear. כִּי יִצְפְּנֵנִי בְּסֻכֹּה בְּיוֹם רָעָה, "In the day of trouble He will hide me in his *succah*" (*Tehillim* 27:5). This is the key *pasuk.* Note that it does not say *house,* but *succah.* The same is true of the *tefillah,* "And spread over us the *succah* of Your peace" — not a house, but a *succah.* We ask for real security, one which is provided not by the strength and power of man's might and technological prowess, but by G-d.

His Providence and protection is symbolized by the *succah,* where there can be no illusions of man's strength, but which is strong and secure by merit of the Almighty's protection.

Similarly, on Succos we add to the *Bircas HaMazon* the prayer: הָרַחֲמָן הוּא יָקִים לָנוּ אֶת סֻכַּת דָּוִיד הַנֹּפֶלֶת, "The Compassionate One! May He erect for us David's fallen *succah!*" We pray for the restoration, not of the House of David, but of the *Succah* of David, a strange choice of words to depict *Malchus,* Kingship! Certainly a royal *house* would be a far more appropriate word than a royal *succah.* But the Maharal explains the use of *succah* with the same approach we have developed in this essay. He states that every kingdom is called a house to indicate its power and strength, for a house is sturdy and strong. The Kingdom of David, however, is referred to as a *succah* for this kingdom is Divinely ordained and is protected and sheltered from on high, as is the *succah.*

Thus, our observance of Succos and our reading of *Koheles* is very understandable. Our *simchah* is complete not when the harvest is reaped and our barns filled to overflowing, but when we dwell in the *succah* and realize that our security is in G-d's hands. We read *Koheles* to remind ourselves that all material riches and man's power are illusory and indeed *hevel* (vanity) for שֹׂבַע שְׂמָחוֹת, "the fullness of joy," can only be realized if it is אֶת פָּנֶיךָ, in G-d's Presence. This wisdom in turn comes to us when we have learned well the lesson of אוֹרַח חַיִּים, a way of life illuminated for us by the Days of Awe which precede the *Z'man Simchaseinu,* the season of our happiness.

CHANUKAH

Sanctity of Time, Place and Klal Yisrael

THERE IS A CUSTOM TO RECITE THE CHAPTER מִזְמוֹר שִׁיר חֲנֻכַּת הַבַּיִת לְדָוִד (*Tehillim* 30) during Chanukah, after the *Shacharis* and *Maariv* services. The reason for this *minhag* is because on Chanukah the *Mizbei'ach* (Altar) was rededicated, and the Temple service resumed. Therefore the phrase חֲנֻכַּת הַבַּיִת, "the inauguration of the Temple," is a most fitting and appropriate one for this period. However, there is another reason offered for this *minhag* — namely, that we are expressing our thanksgiving to Hashem for not allowing our foes to rejoice over us, as the second verse explicitly states: וְלֹא שִׂמַּחְתָּ אֹיְבַי לִי, "You did not permit my enemies to rejoice over me." Some commentators point out that the four letters which comprise the word שִׂמַּחְתָּ allude to four observances which the Greeks and Syrians attempted to uproot from Israel.

These four letters, *shin, mem, ches and taf,* represent Shabbos, *milah* (circumcision), *chodesh* (the New Moon) and *tamid* (the daily offering brought to the Temple).

Our enemies tried to uproot these four *mitzvos*, but were unsuccessful, and therefore we rejoice over their failure. The question, however, is: Why were these specific four *mitzvos* targeted? If we examine them carefully, we will realize that they represent four fundamental concepts in Judaism: קְדוּשַׁת הַזְמַן, קְדוּשַׁת הַגּוּף, קְדוּשַׁת יִשְׂרָאֵל, קְדוּשַׁת הַמָּקוֹם, the sanctity of time, the sanctity of one's body, the sanctity of the people of Israel and the sanctity of place, i.e., the Holy Temple of Jerusalem.

Each of these sanctities teaches us that there is a separation and distinction between the sacred and the profane. These four *mitzvos,* in turn, represent the areas of conflict between the Chashmona'im and the Hellenistic, assimilated Jews. Shabbos reflects the concept of sanctity of time, for it separates the weekdays from the Sabbath, which is holy. The enemies of Judaism, both from without and within, were determined to deny this distinction, for it threatened the ideology of paganism and Hellenism, which rejected the holy and celebrated the profane.

The challenge to the unique character of the Jewish people came not only from external foes, the Greeks and Syrians, but even more so from Hellenistic Jews who enthusiastically embraced Hellenism and attempted to impose it on the Jewish people. These assimilated Jews went so far as to reject *Bris Milah,* the Covenant of Circumcision, which symbolizes *kedushas haguf,* the sanctification of one's body, and establishes a covenant between Israel and the Almighty.

The *mitzvah* of *Kiddush HaChodesh* was given to the people of Israel when they were still in Egypt, and symbolically gave them the power to establish their own calendar and determine when various holidays should be observed. When G-d told Moshe and Aharon, הַחֹדֶשׁ הַזֶּה לָכֶם (*Shemos* 12:2), the key phrase used was לָכֶם, "for you." It is for this reason that the conclusion of the *berachah* in *Kiddush* and the *Amidah* on The Three Festivals is מְקַדֵּשׁ יִשְׂרָאֵל וְהַזְּמַנִּים, "Who sanctifies Israel and the seasons," for it is the nation of Israel alone that is empowered to sanctify the seasons. This power was unacceptable to the enemies of Israel, who were insistent upon establishing their exclusive authority over the calendar, while denying this right to the Jews. These foes were therefore determined to uproot *chodesh,* which affirmed *kedushas Yisrael,* the sanctity of the people of Israel.

At the time of the Chanukah miracle, Antiochus and his army entered the Holy Temple, defiled it and prohibited the Jews from bringing *korbanos,* offerings, on the Altar. When the Chashmona'im returned to the Temple and rededicated it, they were able to reclaim this holy place and reestablish *kedushas hamakom,* sanctity of place, in Jerusalem. Hence, the *tamid* is most significant, for it represents all the *korbanos* brought in the Temple.

The enemies of Israel instinctively understood the source of Israel's strength and their secret of survival. They appreciated the role that *kedushah,* sanctity, played in the unique identity of Israel, be it the sanctity of time, of body, of the nation or of a place. And this is why these four observances were targeted. These four kinds of *kedushah* are alluded to in the word שִׂמְחַת, for each of these *mitzvos* begins with one of the four letters found in this word. And it is for this reason that the celebration of Chanukah is marked not with a *seudah,* a festive meal, as it is on Purim, but through the medium of the *Menorah,* of light, which symbolizes *kedushah.*

Why "Mehadrin"?

THE TALMUD TELLS US THAT THE SMALL CRUSE OF OIL, WHICH WAS sufficient to last only one day but miraculously lasted eight days, was identified as being *tahor* (pure) because it was sealed with the seal of the High Priest. The question arises, however, as to why the High Priest would put his seal on a container of oil when this was not required by *halachah,* nor was it the custom to do so. It was not his responsibility to prepare and preserve the oil for the *Menorah.*

The oil that the Kohen Gadol was responsible for was that which was used for his daily offering. The Torah commanded the Kohen Gadol to bring a meal offering (*minchah*) twice a day, and this offering, as well as the oil which was an integral part of this *minchah,* was indeed exclusively *his* responsibility. It is therefore suggested that the cruse of oil which was undefiled was the oil prepared and stored not for the *Menorah,* but for *his* use, and that is why it had his seal on it. Interestingly, the quality of this oil was normally inferior to the quality of the oil used for the *Menorah,* for we are taught כָּתִית לַמָּאוֹר וְלֹא כָתִית לַמְּנָחוֹת, "pressed for the light, not for the meal offering." However, if the High Priest was meticulous in the observance of his special *mitzvah,* he would enhance it and beautify it by contributing the finest oil for his meal offering. The cruse of pure oil at the time of the Chanukah miracle belonged to the High Priest and was of the highest quality, fit for the *Menorah*!

It is suggested that this is the reason the concept of *mehadrin* (meticulous) is found in conjunction with the kindling of the Chanukah lights, and even the concept of *mehadrin min hamehadrin* (finest of the fine). Since the miracle of Chanukah occurred through oil, which was the choicest of the choice, because the Kohen Gadol at that time wanted to serve the Almighty in a manner which would bring *hadar,* glory, to G-d, by setting aside the finest oil for his *minchah,* we therefore mirror that commitment by introducing the concept of *mehadrin* into our observance of the Chanukah lights!

PURIM

The Correct Response

THE ORIGIN OF THE STORY OF PURIM CAN BE FOUND IN THE INITIAL attack by Amalek upon the Israelites when they left Egypt. To properly understand the message and meaning of Purim, one must examine that episode, as recorded in *Beshalach* (*Shemos* 17:8), and the admonition to ever remember this dastardly attack, found at the end of *Ki Seitzei* (*Devarim* 25:17). The parallel between the events in the time of Moshe and those in the time of Esther and Mordechai is a remarkable one, and the lesson we can learn from them is extremely significant for our time. וַיָּבֹא עֲמָלֵק וַיִּלָּחֶם עִם יִשְׂרָאֵל בִּרְפִידִם, "And Amalek came and fought with Israel in Rephidim" (*Shemos* 17:8). Our Sages comment on the word Rephidim — שֶׁרָפוּ יְדֵיהֶם מִן הַתּוֹרָה. The Jewish people wavered in their pursuit of Torah and in their faith and trust in the Almighty. In the preceding *pasuk* we read that Israel questioned whether G-d was in their midst or not. It has been pointed out that the name עֲמָלֵק is numerically equivalent to סָפֵק — doubt! When Jews become weak in their faith and begin to question and doubt their unique role as G-d's chosen people, then Amalek attacks, for the enemies of Israel always sense our vulnerability. Amalek chose as its victims כָּל הַנֶּחֱשָׁלִים אַחֲרֶיךָ, "the enfeebled ones" (*Devarim* 25:18), which refers to those who had removed themselves from the protection of the Almighty, as the Sifri states. Our strength and ability to withstand the onslaught of our enemies is measured not by our physical or military might, but by our firm, resolute trust in the G-d of Israel. When that faith falters, we become vulnerable to attack.

Many centuries later, Haman, the descendant of Amalek, understood this, and when he came to the king to obtain permission to annihilate the Jews, he stated: יֶשְׁנוֹ עַם אֶחָד מְפֻזָּר וּמְפֹרָד, "There is a people dispersed and divided" (*Esther* 3:8). Our Sages comment on the word יֶשְׁנוֹ — יְשֵׁנִים מִן הַמִּצְוֹת, "They slumber and ignore the *mitzvos.*" Haman continued: וְאֶת דָּתֵי הַמֶּלֶךְ אֵינָם עֹשִׂים, "They do not observe the laws of the king" (ibid.). According to *Chazal,* this refers to the laws of the King of kings, i.e., the Almighty. Even a Haman would fear to attack and destroy the Jews were he not confident that G-d's protection had been removed from them, for they had rejected Hashem and His Torah, and therefore He, in turn, had abandoned them.

Considering what caused Israel's vulnerability to Amalek and Haman, we can readily perceive the need in every generation, not only to defend ourselves against the enemies of Israel, but also to do *teshuvah,* to repent and return to G-d, thereby ensuring our survival by meriting *Hashgachas Hashem,* the Providence of the Almighty. Moshe realized this in his time, as Mordechai did in his. Moshe chose Yehoshua to lead the Jewish forces when Amalek attacked. Our Sages explain the reason he chose Yehoshua: זְקֵנְךָ אָמַר אֶת הָאֱלֹקִים אֲנִי יָרֵא, "Your forebear (Yosef) said, 'I fear the Almighty.' Therefore you are the one to do battle with Amalek, of whom it is said וְלֹא יָרֵא אֱלֹקִים, 'And he feared not the Almighty'" (*Devarim* 25:18). Yehoshua's credentials were spiritual ones, not military ones.

To combat those who have no reverence for G-d, we must choose one whose *yiras Shamayim* is so strong that he is the one to be the champion of Israel, thereby deserving G-d's special *Hashgachah.* Mordechai also reacted properly when he learned of Haman's plot. He could have reasoned that since Haman gave the king 10,000 pieces of silver to allow him to destroy the Jews, then to counteract him, they should outbid Haman! But he realized that if the Jews were so vulnerable to Haman's evil plot, it was time for them to do *teshuvah,* to repent and return, so as to deserve G-d's protection. It was not a time for fundraising which would not address the heart of the problem. And he was successful, for not only was the plot foiled, but קִיְּמוּ וְקִבְּלוּ, the Jews rededicated themselves once again to Torah.

There is another parallel between the Amalek event and the

story of Purim which needs to be stressed. Note that in both cases Jews *do* fight! There is actual military combat, coupled with the *teshuvah,* the repentance and return to G-d. The reason is because we are dealing in both cases with a challenge not only to the Jewish people, but to G-d. In both instances G-d was being mocked and attacked. Amalek is characterized as not fearing G-d, and Haman was also convinced that he need not fear the Almighty. When G-d's honor is demeaned, Israel must rise up and defend His honor.

Compare this to the episode of the Children of Israel at the Sea of Reeds, when *Hashem* told Moshe and Israel to be passive. The reason for this response is that at the Sea of Reeds the Jews were imperiled, and therefore it was G-d's responsibility to protect His children. On the other hand, the responsibility to protect G-d's honor is ours! This distinction is a fundamental one, but one that is often misunderstood and unappreciated. We reverse these roles so often, becoming actively involved in the defense of the people of Israel — which is primarily G-d's province — while remaining passive and timid in guarding G-d's honor!

On Purim we celebrate not only the downfall of Haman and Amalek, but we mark our active response to their attack upon the Almighty. The reward from Heaven for this reaction was that אוֹרָה וְשִׂמְחָה, "light and joy," became our lot. And we pray that so it shall be for all time.

The Profound Lesson of Rabbi Gamliel

רַבָּן גַּמְלִיאֵל הָיָה אוֹמֵר: כָּל שֶׁלֹּא אָמַר שְׁלֹשָׁה דְבָרִים אֵלוּ
בַּפֶּסַח לֹא יָצָא יְדֵי חוֹבָתוֹ וְאֵלוּ הֵן – פֶּסַח מַצָּה וּמָרוֹר

"Rabbi Gamliel said: He who has not explained these three things on Pesach has not fulfilled his obligations; and they are: the korban pesach, matzah and maror."

ON THIS YOM TOV OF FREEDOM, MARKING THE EXODUS FROM Egypt, Jews celebrate far more than a historic event. We act out the bondage and retell the story of our people's beginnings, wanderings, travails and eventual triumph. We rejoice in our deliverance and liberty regardless of our present condition, for even in the night of *galus,* most Jews have never despaired, drawing faith and hope from the story of *Yetzias Mitzraim,* the Exodus from Egypt.

Not all Jews are prepared to ignore their bitter lot in the darkness of *galus* and declare their faith and trust in eventual *geulah.* Indeed the *rasha,* the wicked son, asks derisively, "What is this service *lachem,*" for *you,* who have no freedom, enjoy no rights, and are slaves of new Pharaohs in each generation? Rabbi Gamliel, who lived in Yavneh after the destruction of the Temple, under the reign of the Roman oppressors, was concerned lest Jews despair and allow the observance of Pesach to fade away, arguing that there is no sense in celebrating a holiday of freedom while living with tyranny, in observing a Yom Tov of *cheirus* during a time of dark oppression. He therefore urged his contemporaries, in the aftermath of the *churban,* to examine these three aspects of the Pesach holiday: the *korban pesach,* matzah and *maror.*

The *korban pesach* symbolizes G-d's *Hashgachah,* Divine protection and Providence, salvation in the midst of death and destruction. It demonstrates the Almighty's concern for His righteous children and Divine punishment of the wicked. It also represents Jewish heroism — *mesiras nefesh* — the willingness of Israel to sacrifice their safety and security, meager as it may be, to fulfill G-d's will. Rabbi Gamliel felt that we must never lose sight of these two attributes — G-d's constant *Hashgachah* and Israel's spirit of sacrificial heroism — even in times when matzah, the bread of affliction, and *maror,* the bitter herbs, reflect the true condition of the Jewish people.

Matzah is *lechem oni,* the bread of affliction. It represents periods of bondage, suffering and persecution. But it is also לֶחֶם שֶׁעוֹנִין עָלָיו דְּבָרִים הַרְבֵּה, "a bread over which much is said." This represents the lot of the Jewish people in our relationship to the world. Jews can never escape the attention of the world; we cannot hide. We are so visible. We are the object of scorn, derision, envy and enmity, the target of vituperation and the victims of hostility and passionate hatred. Everyone talks about us, all the time. The U.N. General Assembly has probably spoken more about the State of Israel than about any other nation in the world. Indeed, we are like the matzah over which much is recited. And it is *maror,* very bitter, be it in our role as victim, or as the target of condemnation and calumny.

However, if we allow ourselves to focus only on these two unfortunate characteristics of Israel, the matzah and the *maror,* to the exclusion of the redeeming "*pesach* force," then we are guilty of failing to grasp the totality of Jewish destiny. We have not "fulfilled our obligation" unless we explain *all three* — the belief in G-d's Providence and Israel's heroism, even as we remember and relive the matzah and *maror* experiences. Our obligation is to link all three together.

The Lubliner Rav, Rabbi Meir Shapiro, interprets the story of the Sages who were gathered in Bnei Brak in a similar vein, concluding, not on a note of despair, but with a cry for a heavenly sign of concern and redemption. These Sages, Rabbi Elazar, Rabbi Akiva and their colleagues, also lived in a postdestruction period. It was כָּל אוֹתוֹ הַלַּיְלָה, the night of Roman supremacy. Nonetheless, they encouraged themselves by relating the story of *yetzias Mitzraim* to strengthen their belief that the night of suffering and pain would be followed by the day of deliverance and salvation. Even in *galus*, even at night, we say *emes ve'emunah* . . ., "truth and faith," for we recognize the truth of G-d and reaffirm our faith. Their disciples, however, impatiently responded: רַבּוֹתֵינוּ הִגִּיעַ זְמַן קְרִיאַת שְׁמַע שֶׁל שַׁחֲרִית, The time has come for G-d to help us and bring us into the light so that we can recite the קְרִיאַת שְׁמַע שֶׁל שַׁחֲרִית, and say *emes ve'yatziv*, "true and established . . ." G-d will demonstrate that he is our Redeemer, and that our faith in Him during the dark night has been justified, only when we merit the *geulah sheleimah*, "the complete redemption."

We have merited in our time to witness the breaking of the dawn, the beginning of our redemption. The horrible night is past, and we have been *zoche* to the rebuilding of Eretz Yisrael and the rebirth of Torah in the United States, as well as its burgeoning in Israel. To a certain extent "the winter (of bondage) has passed, the deluge of suffering is over . . . and the time of our song has arrived" (*Shir HaShirim* 2:11). That verse concludes with the words וְקוֹל הַתּוֹר נִשְׁמַע בְּאַרְצֵנוּ. There are various translations of this phrase. The Ibn Ezra translates it as coming from the root תּוֹר, which is indeed used today in modern Hebrew for a queue, waiting for one's turn. The *pasuk* is stating that the redemption is nigh and Israel's turn has finally come!

For centuries we have waited in the wings, patiently persevering and refusing to despair, refusing to fall into *yei'ush* for, as the Kotsker says: יֵאוּשׁ שֶׁלֹּא מִדַּעַת, "Despair comes only if one has lost his sense," his *sechel*. But now it is *our turn*, and with G-d's help we have not only survived but prevailed.

Even when we experience matzah and *maror* periods, we console ourselves with the *pesach* spirit, following the advice of Rabbi Gamliel to always focus on the totality of Jewish history. Only by following his teaching do we fulfill our obligation as the *am hanetzach*, "the eternal people."

SHAVUOS

The Power of Renewal

IN THE *TEFILLOS* OF SHAVUOS, WE REFER TO THIS HOLIDAY AS *Z'MAN Matan Toraseinu,* "The Season of the Giving of the Torah." Yet, when we study the *Parashas HaMoadim* in *Emor,* it refers to this Yom Tov only as *Chag HaBikkurim,* "The Festival of the First Fruits," and no mention is made of the great historic event at Sinai which shaped the destiny of Israel for all time! The *pesukim* there speak of the culmination of *Sefirah,* the two loaves of bread brought as an offering, and the sacrifices and prohibition of labor to mark this day; but regarding the giving of the Torah, the dramatic encounter of G-d with Israel, complete silence! A similar anomaly can be found in the same *Parashas HaMoadim,* where the Torah refers to Rosh Hashanah as *Yom HaZikaron,* "A Day of Remembrance," but no mention is made of its paramount character, that of *Yom HaDin,* the Day of Judgment, when all mankind passes before G-d to be judged for the coming year. Why does the Torah choose to be silent regarding these two vital, tremendously important aspects — the giving of the Torah on Shavuos and G-d's judgment of mankind on Rosh Hashanah?

The Kli Yakar offers an illuminating answer to these questions. He explains that although the giving of the Torah took place at a specific time, we accept the Torah every day. Rashi, commenting on the phrase הַיּוֹם, "today" (*Devarim* 26:16), says: בְּכָל יוֹם יִהְיוּ בְעֵינֶיךָ חֲדָשִׁים, "Let the words of Torah be new in your eyes every day," as though you just received them. There is a need for freshness, excitement and a sense of wonder each time we study Torah and observe its mitzvos. To mark *Matan Torah* one day in the year would be restrictive and self-defeating. An anniversary is special, but it tends to diminish the significance of all the other days of the year. That is why, basically, Mother's Day or Father's Day is alien to us, for the *mitzvah* of *kibud av v'em* is one that is operative every day. That is why the Torah chooses not to specify that Shavuos is the festival of the giving of the Torah. Instead it simply states: וְהִקְרַבְתֶּם מִנְחָה חֲדָשָׁה לַה׳, "And you shall bring a new meal offering to Hashem" (*Vayikra* 23:16), thereby implying that the celebration of receiving the Torah on this day should be marked by finding what is new and exciting in Torah.

Similarly, the Day of Judgment, the *Yom HaDin,* is not mentioned in conjunction with Rosh Hashanah lest one think that since he is judged only on this day, therefore he can sin all year and repent before his trial on the following Rosh Hashanah. This trend of thought is incorrect for judgment is constant, accountability is a daily concern and repentance is incumbent upon us every day. Hence, the Torah consciously chooses not to mention specifically that the first day of the seventh month is *Yom HaDin* in order to underscore the idea of *daily* judgment and constant *din v'cheshbon.*

Judaism rejects the concept of a "leap of faith," a sudden flash of intuitive inspiration and acceptance of a deity. Rather, it emphasizes a growing awareness of G-d, a daily confirmation of our faith and the discipline of *mitzvos,* which form the pattern of our everyday existence. Moments of exceptional enthusiasm fade quickly. What counts are the seemingly mundane moments which are nonetheless touched with magic and majesty. That is why neither *Matan Torah* nor *Yom HaDin* are mentioned. Rather, they are alluded to through the phrases *minchah chadashah* and *Yom HaZikaron,* respectively, to stress the need for a sense of *constant* renewal and remembrance.

Modern man desperately needs to learn this twofold lesson of Shavuos and Rosh Hashanah, as interpreted by the Kli Yakar. Modern religionists would do well to ponder, when they capitulate to the radical elements in their ranks, how far they are removing themselves from the Torah spirit. How tragic and dangerous are the radical changes introduced into religious practice which are motivated by a desire for innovation and progress but which in reality proclaim a bankruptcy of ideas and an erosion of basic loyalty to, and belief in, the authenticity of Torah and its viability and vitality. When religious leaders lose faith in the *minchah chadashah* quality of Torah, they desperately embrace change for the sake of change. Commitment cannot be compromised, and when it is, it reflects a fundamental weakness and hollowness which contains its own seeds of destruction.

Regarding the *Akeidah*, Avraham's readiness to sacrifice Yitzchak, which is considered to have been the greatest test of Avraham's faith, the Kotsker Rebbe asks: What man could refuse G-d if the Almighty spoke to him *directly*, regardless of how difficult the request? What was so special about Avraham? He answers that the greatness of Avraham lay in the fact that the *Akeidah* took place on the *third* day. There was time to reflect, to reconsider, to cool off. The enthusiastic, emotional readiness to comply with G-d's command had time to diminish, but it didn't. Avraham's enthusiasm and devotion remained as strong and fresh on the third day as it was when G-d spoke to him. This intriguing thought of Rabbi Mendel of Kotsk adds dimension and depth to the commentary of the Kli Yakar.

It is a psychological truth that a human being can be inspired, motivated and challenged, but this heightened sense of enthusiasm does not last indefinitely. It wanes and dissipates with the passage of time. That is why our Sages emphasize that a person must train himself to accept Torah each day and appreciate its constant newness. That is what is meant by the phrase: בְּכָל יוֹם יִהְיוּ בְּעֵינֶיךָ חֲדָשִׁים, "Let the words of Torah be new in your eyes every day." That is why the ability of Avraham to retain his commitment and willingness to fulfill G-d's command, even on the third day, was so unusual and unique.

Just as Avraham on the third day was no less determined to fulfill G-d's command than he was on the day G-d first commanded him, so must Jews, centuries after Sinai, say *naaseh v'nishma*, "We will do and we will listen," as though the Torah is being given *today*. Those Jews who have learned the lesson of the *minchah chadashah*, who have never lost their enthusiasm and sense of freshness, are the ones who ensure the future of Torah and *Klal Yisrael*. May we be privileged to be among them and to be *mekabel* the Torah each day, *be'ahavah*!

This volume is part of
THE ARTSCROLL SERIES®
an ongoing project of
translations, commentaries and expositions
on Scripture, Mishnah, Talmud, Halachah,
liturgy, history and the classic Rabbinic writings;
and biographies, and thought.

For a brochure of current publications
visit your local Hebrew bookseller
or contact the publisher:

Mesorah Publications, ltd

4401 Second Avenue
Brooklyn, New York 11232
(718) 921-9000